William Crooke

North Indian Notes and Queries

Volume 5

William Crooke

North Indian Notes and Queries
Volume 5

ISBN/EAN: 9783742885340

Manufactured in Europe, USA, Canada, Australia, Japa

Cover: Foto ©Andreas Hilbeck / pixelio.de

Manufactured and distributed by brebook publishing software (www.brebook.com)

William Crooke

North Indian Notes and Queries

North Indian Notes and Queries:

A MONTHLY PERIODICAL

DEVOTED TO THE SYSTEMATIC COLLECTION OF AUTHENTIC NOTES AND SCRAPS
OF INFORMATION REGARDING THE COUNTRY AND THE PEOPLE.

EDITED BY

WILLIAM CROOKE, *B.A.*,

Member, Asiatic Society of Bengal, and Folklore Society, Bengal Civil Service.

VOL. V.

ALLAHABAD ... ... PIONEER PRESS.
LONDON ... ... Messrs. TRÜBNER & Co.

INDEX.

A

Abdul Qadir Jilani, the Saint, 234.
Abdul Qudus, the Saint, 407.
Abu Huraira, 208.
Acquisitions of territory, 556.
Adh Granth, the, 58.
Age, Calculation of, 44.
Agricultural superstitions, 174; 497.
Akbar, Tradition of, 553.
Allah Baksh, a demon, 521.
Anant Chaturdasi fast, 302.
Andaman Islanders, the, 194.
Animals, Calls of, 151.
Animal life, Regard for, 455.
Asoka tree, Worship of, 306.
Ass, Parading on, 322; Superstition, 352.
Assignation, 263.
Asterisms, Superstitions, 94.
Ausan Miyan, Worship of, 128.
Auspicious times, 506.

B

Babu, Derivation of, 391.
Babúl trees, 382.
Banjaras, the, 594.
Bansipuri, a Saint, 582.
Banyas, Position of, 466.
Barbers, 276.
Barren women, Omens, 448.
Barun Brahmans, 187.
Bato Bibi, a Saint, 179.
Bathing the sick, 597.
Be, the Persian letter, 444.
Beale, Oriental Biographical Dictionary, 15.
Bear, Dance song, 494; Folklore of, 105; Tale of, 509.
Bees, 224; and white ants, 80.
Beggar, Cry of 221; Song of, 432.
Bel leaves used by travellers, 40.
Bell metal vessels and smallpox, 351.
Bells, Offering of, 397.
Ber fruit turned into stone, 598.
Betel, Eating of, 272; Leaves, superstition regarding, 108.
Bhairon, Worship of, 192.
Bhang and Soma, 245.
Bharanga Khera, Legend of, 561.
Bhishma, Worship of, 313.
Bhuinhar, the caste, 316, 463, 417.
Bhumiya, Worship of, 460.
Biltan, Derivation of, 143.
Bir, Charm to invoke, 214.
Birds, Folklore of, 208, 453.
Black lips, 494.
Black magic, 523.
Black partridge, the, 13.
Boat festivals, 362.
Borrowing, Superstition, 80.

Brahmans, Almstaking, 394; and barbers, 116; Demons, 52; Funeral rites, 412; Ghosts, 56, 57; Ranks of, 596; Taboos, 246.
Brahmanical thread, Worship of, 367.
Bringing home the bride, 639.
Broom worship, 188.
Buddhism in Tibet, 393.
Building superstitions, 393.
Bundela, Worship of, 493.
Burial customs, 176.

C

Camel bones, Scarers of demons, 584.
Camphor, 14.
Carpenter's formula, 153.
Casting out a devil, 552.
Catarrh charm, 386.
Cuts, 208, 288.
Cattle disease charms, 24, 216, 516, 611.
Cauls, 326.
Cave, Haunted, 554.
Chains of God, 91.
Chakabu fort, 642.
Chamars and Baris, 595.
Chanwand, a Village deity, 433.
Charm to cure pain in the eyes, 109; to destroy enemies, 551; to entice a woman, 82; to expel ghosts, 85; to make a demon subservient, 117; Used by gamblers, 98.
Chess, Game of, 22, 23.
Childless dead, Worship of, 501.
Chairaghi, 482.
Chittagong, 159.
Cholera, Caused by offended deities, 526; Charm against, 320.
Chowk chanda, the, 20.
Chunar fort, Deity of, 189.
City turned into stone, 359.
Clothed images, 66.
Cocoanut, 192, 576.
Coins, Inscriptions, 353.
Communications, Lucky and unlucky, 156.
Conjunction of stars, 136.
Cow, Superstition, 161.
Cramp, Charm to remove, 39.
Crocodiles, Respect for, 483.
Cuckoo, Folklore of, 6.
Cursing, 647.

D

Dakaut Brahmans, 395.
Daksha, Legend of, 175.
Darbhanga, Legend of, 229.
Daulatabad, Legend of, 134.
Dawn, the, 385.
Days, Unlucky, 81.
Death customs, 42, 127, 383.
Death and judgement, 520.

Deities or spirits shut up, 132.
Delivery charm, 445.
Devi, Song to, 528.
Dhanu Bhagat, Worship of, 529.
Dhruva, Legend of, 581.
Disease charm, 227.
Distillers' Saint, 578.
Diwali festival, 104.
Dog, Dung of, 266; Howling of 152; Tongue of, 166.
Domunha snake, 392.
Dove, Marriage of, 183.
Dressing of idols, 67.
Drinking, Custom of, 182, Song, 449.
Drowning persons, Superstitions regarding, 537.
Dusadhs, the, 600.
Dying man putting seal in his mouth, 342.

E

Ear-boring, 287.
Earth goddess, Incantation, 17; Worship of, 460.
Eclipse observances, 411.
Eel, the, 387.
Ekadashi feast, the, 568.
Elephant-drivers, 280; Worship, 593.
Europeans excluded from Tibet, 30.
Evening time, 295.
Evil Eye charm, 356.
Eye, Twitching of, 223.

F

Fakir, a celebrated, 172; Curse of, 43; Song of, 282.
Famine, Couplet, 428; Signs of, 490.
Faramosh, Game of, 507.
Farid Shakkarganj, the Saint, 487, 527.
Fever charms, 228.
Fields, Charm to protect, 284.
Fines on account of snow, 86.
Finger, Amputation, 535; a demon entry, 464.
Fire, Prohibition against giving, 646.
Firefly, the, 215.
Fits, Cure of, 315, 400.
Five, a mystic number, 365.
Flowers, Marriage to, 191.
Flute, Song of the, 384.
FOLKTALES.—
   Adam and the prince; 347.
   Akbar and Birbal, 259.
   Akbar and the daughter of Birbal, 377.
   Akbar and the old woman, 275.
   Akbar and his son-in-law, 250.

Ahir and the cow of plenty, 543.
Ahir, Folly of the, 541.
Banke Chhail and his wife, 37.
Bard, the and his wife, 622.
Bhuvan Sinh, 62.
Boy and the merchant, 144.
Boy and the monkey, 33.
Brahman, Luck of the, 142
Brahman and the Sadhu, 70.
Budhsen and his monkey army,
City of the Jinn, 621
Clever Brahman girl, 477.
Contest of good and evil, 255
Dancing girls, Origin of, 472.
Devoted wife, the, 143.
Dhobi, the, and his ass, 257.
Discarded princess, the, 138.
Dome Raja of Oudh, 424.
Eating and the Evil Eye, 202,
Entertaining angels unawares, 140.
Fool and the alphabet, 76.
Fool and his house, 624.
Fortunate woodcutter, 256.
Four fools, Tale of, 270.
Four friends and the princess, 421.
Fruit of charity, 261.
Goddess of poverty, 419.
Good old times the, 203.
Greedy Brahman, the, 35.
Hari Raja and Moti Rani, 201.
Height of virtue, 145.
How the Banya baffled the robbers, 31.
How the Banya's wife went to Heaven, 420.
How Bhagwan gave a lesson to Narada Muni, 196.
How to please everybody, 336.
How the prince won his bride, 542.
How the Raja got his deserts, 204.
How the Raja went to the Heaven of Bhagwan, 71.
How the wise man learned experience, 332.
Jealous stepmother, the, 198.
Kali Das and his parrot, 32.
Kali Yuga, the, 199.
Karma Bai, tale of, 53.
Lesson of the Sadhu, 36.
Magic boat, the, 69.
Man who ate human flesh, 260.

Metamorphisis of Raja Vikram ditya 34.
Narada Muni's boasting 374.
Old man's wisdom, 262.
Old woman and the crow, 379.
Pandit and his children, 538.
Parrot and the Guru, 72.
Piety of Raja Raghu, 73.
Pillars of the sky, 258.
Pious prince, the, 426.
Pipa, Legend of, 200.
Prince and the Angel of death, 472.
Prince and his animal friends, 75.
Prince and the daughter of the Gandhi, 141.
Prince Nilkanth, 476.
Prince and the snake, 475.
Princess and the sepoy, 331.
Princess and the thieves, 254.
Raja and the bear, 340.
Raja and the Hansa, 206.
Raja and the Hansas, 78.
Raja Harivansu, 160.
Raja and the physician, 422.
Raja Sarat Chandra, 338.
Raja and the swans, 375.
Raja Udpaiyajit and the snake, 546.
Raja Vena and Raja Vikrmaditya, 339.
Rani Kamlapati, 139.
Reading of hearts, 251.
Rival castes, 423.
Sadhu and the princess, 74.
Seeing the world, 4.
Shaikh Chilli and the camelman, 249.
Shaikh Chilli and the Fakir, 618.
Shaikh Chilli and his turban, 620.
Shaikh Chilli at the wedding, 425.
Shrewish wife, the, 334.
Soldier and his virtuous wife, 205.
Solomon, charity of, 335.
Tale of two queens, 617.
Tale of four drunkards, 3.
Thakur and the barber, 375.
Thakur and the goldsmith, 79.
Trilok the goldsmith, 54.
Turmeric, Introduction of, 202.
Virtue of faith, 146.
Virtue of Raja Rupa Angad, 5.
Wealth and wisdom, 380.
Weaver and the jackal, 77.
Which is greater, Rama or Khuda?, 625.
Why the boy laughed, 253.
Why Narada Muni laughed, 333.

Wicked queen and her step-children, 628.
Wisdom of Birbal's daughter, 478.
Wise and foolish brother, 197.
Wise Pandit, the, 337.
Wise son of the weaver, 252.
Wit of Muhammad Fazil, 427.
Witch and the boy, 540.
Women rule the world, 623.
Youngest son, Luck of the, 539.
Young Brahman and his wife, 619.
Food, Rules for serving, 532; For the dead, 61.
Footmarks, 195.
Footprints, Worship of, 565.

G

Games of children, 468, 469, 470, 471, 601.
Ganges, Origin of, 181; Respect for, 586.
Gardner, Colonel, 38.
Gaya, Legend of, 450.
Ghosts, 560; Barring of, 531; of a man killed by a tiger, 592; of a soldier, 90.
Gifts, Prescribed number of, 649.
Gil Jats, Legend of, 290.
Gokarna and Dhundkari, Legend, 237.
Graves and trees, 390.
Groves, Sacred, 267 574.
Guardian spirits, 519.
Guests, How to reduce number of, 504.
Guga, the Saint, 63.
Gulab Shah, a Saint, 583.
Gular tree, the, 187.

H

Hanuman, Charm for, 288.
Hardaul, Legend of, 458.
Harina harin stars, 517.
Harshu Panre, Worship of, 580.
Headache, Cure of, 430.
Heavenly bodies, 502.
Hills and plains people, Differences of, 612, 613, 614.
Hindu house, Arrangment of, 165.
Holi festival, 400, 634.
House door, the, 496.
Household rules, 129.
Human flesh, 485.
Human sacrifice, 550.
Husband to become subservient, Charm, 11.

I

Images, Size and shape of, 447.
Imprisonment, Effect of on caste, 319.
Impurity, Means of removing, 512.

Incantation, an, 291.
India and China, Religions of, 133.
Indra, Worship of, 64.
Initiation, Times for, 371.

J

Jackal, Horn of, 49.
Jallada, Clan deities of. 29.
Jarasar, Legend of, 567.
Jay Sinh Sawai, Legend of, 170.
Jinn, the, 396.
Jogi, Burial of, 357.
Jungle goddess, 589, 590.

K

Kabir, the Saint, 60, 241, 242, 366.
Kabirpanthi sect, Ceremonies of, 193.
Kahars, Incantation, 587.
Kamdhenu, the magic cow, 456.
Kankhal, Derivation of, 125.
Karil tree, Worship of, 126.
Kartarpur, Legend of, 398.
Kashi Das, Worship of, 183.
Kayasths, 604.
Khera, a village deity, 433.
Khwaja Khizr, worship of, 212, 360.
Kine as stars, 560.
Knots in sacred cord, 467.
Krishna, Legend of, 408.
Kuar, Festivals in, 1.
Kuba, Legend of, 113.

L

Lal Behari De, 103.
Lamps in temples, 515.
Leaves as an amulet, 563.
Left handed people, 226.
Lens of the eye, 107.
Leprosy, 441; Cures for, 602.
Letters, Heading of, 213.
Lightning, 560.
Lingam, Worship of, 368.
Lives of children, Saving of, 500.
Locusts as food, 474.

M

Magahiya Doms, 137.
Mahakali, Worship of, 364.
Mamu Allah Bakhsh, 173.
Mango, Charm, 10; Origin of, 442.
Marriage, Charm, 638; Effect of death on, 131; Horoscopes, 28; Several performed at one time, 632; Rites, 244; To a tree, 68.
Martyrs, Worship of, 405, 518.
Maternal uncle, Position of, 248, 605.
Maula Shah, a Saint, 406.
Meat, Abstinence from, 220.
Medicine, Rural, 273.
Meeting, Omens, 633.
Menstrual impurity, 279.
Menstruation, Observances, 610.
Midwives, 465.
Miscarriage, Charm to prevent, 650.

Mock fights, 324.
Modesty of Hindu Women, 429.
Monkey saint, 309.
Moon and baby, 652; Moonlight and the bamboo, 268; Worship, 21, 321, 524.
Monstrous birth, a, 451.
Moves, 218.
Mother Earth, 106, 180.
Mourning ceremonies, 636.
Muhammadan bride, Rule of visits, 603.
Muhammadans and wolves, 361.
Muin ud-din Chishti, the Saint, 59, 114, 236.
Muf the asterism, 239.
Music at Saiva festivals, 310; Origin of, 16.

N

Names of gods written on the body, 514.
Narsi Bhagat, Legend of, 370.
Narsinh Chaturdasi feast, 303.
Nats, Clan deities of, 25.
New clothes, Rules about, 511; House, occupying, 549.
Nicholson, John, worship of, 402.
Nim tree, used as a remedy, 599.
Nine yard long tombs, 210, 389.
Nirbasi jaduar, 330.
Nirmala Sadh sect, 609.

O

Oaths and ordeals, 314, 462.
Obeisance, Form of, 101.
Occupation of child, How to ascertain. 436.
Offerings prohibited, 403.
Oil, Superstitions about, 438.
Omens, 150, 271, 274, 304, 571, 635.
Ox, Riding on, 169; Superstition regarding, 95.

P

Pachisi, Game of, 534.
Paghar, Legend of, 99.
Palms of hand, Looking at, 416.
Panchami vrata, the, 20.
Panjgatra fair, the, 454.
Panj Pir, Worship of, 508.
Passes, God of, 591.
Patna, Customs at. 533.
Patthrawali, Worship of, 548.
Peacock, Divination, 530.
Persons who never prosper, 296.
Phalgu, Legend of, 232.
Philosopher's stone, the, 157.
Photography, Prejudice against, 87.
Pigs gored by cattle, 55.
Piles, Charm to cure, 164.
Pipal tree, Worship of, 111.
Pitcher, Superstition regarding, 238.
Plant charm, 278.
Plantain tree, Worship of, 177.
Ploughing up village site, 555.
Pond, Miraculous, 92.

[iii]

Pool, Sacred, 300.
Popular tales, 381.
Porcupine and crow, 163.
Potter's wheel, Charm, 41.
Pregnancy, Precautions during, 65, 643.
Poverty, Expulsion of, 345.
Productiveness of fields, 51.
Proverbs, 7, 12, 47, 96, 162, 480, 443, 492, 570, 641, 645, 653.
Pustules, Charm to remove, 354.

R

Rain, Charms, 167, 211, 373, 410; in Swati asterism, 100.
Rainbow, 281.
Raja Bariar, Worship of, 112.
Rajput Musalman, 606
Ramaiya Baba, Worship of, 230.
Ramzan Shah, a Saint, 404.
Rat-hole, Earth from, 219.
Revenue survey, the, 489.
Rice, Origin of, 388.
Rivers, Offerings to, 415; Worship of, 240.
Roshani fair, 222.

S

Sacred thread, Investiture, 135, 630.
Saint, Curse of, 346.
Sakhi Sarwar, Shrines of, 439.
Salagrama, the, 185.
Salt, Use of prohibited, 616.
Salutation, Contemptuous, 350.
Sami tree, Worship of, 301.
Sanichara, Worship of, 243.
Sankhbir, Worship of, 644.
Saraswat Brahmans, Meat eating, 414.
Sarju river, Origin of, 558.
Sarwar, Limits of, 452.

Satti worship, 110, 178, 512.
Saturn, Worship of, 243.
Scalplock, Ideas about, 431.
Schools, Punishments in, 503.
School games, 317.
Scorpion sting charm, 283, 446.
Sea cocoanut, 329.
Seasons, Signs of, 491.
Second marriages, 629.
Secrecy in rural rites, 328.
Seventy-four and a half, 213.
Sex, Prediction of child's, 461.
Shah Daula, Rats of, 311.
Shah Jamal, a Saint, 305.
Shah Muqin, a Saint, 498.
Shahid, Worship of, 405.
Shaving, 42 : Impurity from, 147.
Sheaf, the last, 27.
Sheep, unlucky, 358.
Shoes, Scarers of demons, 265, 315
Shop-keepers, Superstition, 435.
Siddhinath, Worship of, 121.
Sidhari fish, the, 158.
Sikhs, Customs of, 437; Initiation among, 2.
Silajit, 48.
Siras tree, Superstition, 399.
Sirsawa, 348.
Sitala, The goddess of smallpox, 369.
Sitala Devi and Hanuman, 123
Sitting cross-legged, 648.
Siva Narayan, Worship of, 119.
Siyar singhi, 49.
Small-pox, Rites, 190, 299, 547.
Snake, Bite, 83, 264, 277; Charmers, 323; Dilemma of, 168; Godlings, 122; Legend of, 149; Mark on feet, 9; Worship, 235.
Songs, 19, 154, 567, 651.
Sour milk, 97.
Spell to injure an enemy, 486.

Spring, Sacred 171.
Squirrels, 217.
Stomach-ache, Charm, 510
Stone in the bladder, Charm, 484.
Straw in the mouth, 285.
Stream, Charm for, 495.
Succession, Rules for, 615.
Sukhdeva, Legend of, 401.
Sukra, Propitiation of, 292.
Sun worship, 115, 297.
Sur Das, Life of, 18.
Swastika, the 308, 562.
Sweepers, Conversion by, 607 ; Religion of, 307.
Sword used at birth, 473.

T

Taboo of husband and wife naming each other, 26.
Tank, Sacred, 46; Curing disease, 585.
Tansen, the singer, 588.
Tarkulhi ki Mata, Worship of, 588.
Teeth, Superstition about, 294.
Telraja mendicants, 247.
Temple, Legend of, 118.
Tesu flower, the, 347.
Tiger, Folklore of, 372, 418; Claws used as amulets, 575.
Tiled, houses, 557.
Titles used by women, 536.
Tomb of a saint, 579.
Tongue offered to Kali, 312.
Tooth brush, Use of, 608.
Touching rat or mouse, 525.
Travelling, Rules of, 545.
Treasure, Charm to recover, 45.
Tree sacred, 409 ; Smearing of, 8 ; Working under, 325.
Tulasi tree, the, 185; Marriage of, 184.
Twenty-seven, 50.

U

Udasi Baba, Worship of, 513.
Unlucky names, 564.

V

Valley, God of, 124.
Vegetables, Legend about, 88.
Venus, Propitiation of, 293, 640.
Verses, 481, 566, 631, 637.
Vessels, Purification of, 93, 327, 559.
Vetala circles, 231.
Village shrines, 544.
Vishnu, incarnation of, 84, 120.
Visiting, Rules of, 286 ; Of bride, 499.

W

War, God of, 233.
Warts, Charming of, 148.
Washing clothes, 81.
Weather lore, 344, 488.
Well, Sacred, 577 ; Sinking of, ceremonies, 505.
What's in a name?, 269.
Witch, Spell of, 349; Tale of, 355.
Woman, With moustaches, 413; Superstition of, 289.
Wrinkles on the forehead, 434.

Y

Yama Dwitiya, 130.
Year, Worship of, 298.
Yoga, A case of, 457.
Younger son heir, 102, 225.

North Indian Notes and Queries:
A MONTHLY PERIODICAL.

VOL. V.]   APRIL, 1895.   [NO. 1.

Every communication must be accompanied by the writer's name and address, not necessarily for insertion, but as a guarantee of good faith. Every quotation from a book must be accompanied by its full title, publisher's and author's names, place and date of publication, volume and page.
Contributors are requested to write on ONE SIDE of the page only. If several contributions be sent at a time, they should be sent each on a separate sheet.
The Conductor cannot undertake to return, or be responsible for, any MSS. not accepted.
All orders must be accompanied by cash. If not so accompanied, they will either not be attended to, or will be complied with per value-payable post.
Contributions should be addressed direct to W. CROOKE, ESQ., C. S., SAHARANPUR, N.-W. P., INDIA.

CONTENTS OF THIS NUMBER.
(The references are to the Notes.)

Popular Religion ... ... 1 to 4	Folktales ... ... 15 to 16
Anthropology ... ... 5 ,, 14	Miscellanea ... ... 17 ,, 18

POPULAR RELIGION.

1. Ceremonies and Festivals observed during the latter half of the month of Kuar (October—November).—The latter fortnight of every Hindu month is called Sukla Paksha (the white fortnight). But that of the month of Kuár is called Deo Paksha (the godly fortnight) in addition to Sukla Paksha, as opposed to Pitri Paksha (the fortnight of ancestors). As in the Pitri Paksha the worship of ancestors is performed, so in the Deo Paksh, the worship of the gods is performed. It is not that all the gods are worshipped, but the worship of Devi, in her various forms, is performed by all classes of Hindús. The whole fortnight is called Pitri Paksha, but in reality ten days only deserve the name, as the worship of Devi begins on the first day of the fortnight and ends on the ninth. The tenth day I have included, because on that day the victory of Ráma, the mighty King of Ayodhya, over the giant Ráwana, the King of Lanká, (perhaps our present Ceylon), is celebrated with extraordinary enthusiasm. Let me first describe the worship of Devi as performed during the nine days of the Deo Paksh, which are called *Naurátri*.

In the early morning of the first day, the votaries of Devi, men and women, high and low, repair to a reservoir of water, well or river, within easy reach, to perform their ablutions. Having done this, all return home, generally with their foreheads marked with sandal or a red powder called *rori*. Then those who are Bráhmans make preparations for the worship themselves, and those who are Bráhmans, but without the necessary knowledge of worship, call in a priest to help them or to perform the worship itself on their behalf and in their names. Besides Bráhmans, other Hindús, Kshatriyas and Vaishyas and those Sudras, who are so pure that water from their hands might be taken by high-caste Hindús, perform the worship through the priests. The worship is performed both at home and at the shrine of Devi. The worship at home is more efficacious than that at the shrine. The worshippers of Devi fast on the first day of worship. Some fast nine days, taking in the morning and evening of each day roots and fruits or *sherbet*. The worship at home is performed in this way:—The worshipper brings in an earthen pitcher, decorates it with lumps of cow-dung, and sticks grains of barley to the lumps. The pitcher is then filled with water. A secluded room in the house, to which members of the family or outsiders cannot get access easily, is made pure by plastering the walls with white earth and the floor with cow-dung. In the western portion of the room a platform of earth called Vedi is made. The earth of which the platform is made is brought from fields or the banks of a river outside the village or town. On the platform grains of barley are sprinkled. Then streaks of cow-dung are made, encircling the room. Grains of barley are stuck in close to each other on the streaks. Then the pitcher is put in the centre of the platform or Vedi. The articles of worship are then collected there. The following are the articles of worship :—

Betel, betel-nuts, chaplets of flowers, flowers, red powder, called *rori*, coloured thread, called *raksha*, chandan or sandal, washed rice, twigs with leaves of mangoes called *pallañ*, *kusa* grass, *durba* grass, a hundred medicinal plants powdered and mixed together, called *sataushadhi*, earth from seven places, called *sapta mritiká*. The following are the seven places from which earth is brought :—

Earth from a stable, earth from a stable of elephants, earth from an ant-hill, earth from the junction of two rivers, earth from the door of a Rája, earth from a sacred place, (*Tirtha sthán*), a cow-pen.

Five gems. The following are the five gems :—

Gold, silver, pearl, coral, manik or jewels ; cocoanut, *dhúp* or incense, lamp or *dip*, sweetmeats or *Naivedya*, camphor, red cloth.

Collecting these things, the worshipper sits in front of the pitcher. Then he repeats Sanscrit *mantras* purporting to invite Devi, with chaplets of flowers and flowers in hand. When the *mantras* have been repeated, he puts the chaplets of flowers and flowers on the platform or Vedi. He then puts Ganges water, grass, *kusá* grass, the mixture of a hundred medicinal plants, earth from seven sacred places abovementioned, five gems, betel-leaves, betel-nuts, and then puts the twigs of mango in the pitcher in such a manner that the twigs lie in the pitcher and the leaves on the mouth of it. Upon the twig of mango he puts an earthenware cup (*kosa* or *kasora*) containing rice, urdi millet or barley. Upon this cup he puts a cocoanut. Then he covers the pitcher with a red cloth. Again he ties upon the cloth and the neck of the pitcher a thread. By so doing the pitcher appears in the form of a woman covering her head and face with a red cloth. This pitcher is supposed to be the idol of Devi or Bhagawati. Then they repeat *mantras* and sprinkle on the pitcher washed rice (*achhat*). This means furnishing the goddess with a seat. Then the representation of the goddess, that is to say, the pitcher has water sprinkled on it, which means that the goddess has been bathed. Then the pitcher is smeared with red powder. Then washed rice is offered to the pitcher. Then a chaplet of flowers is thrown round the neck of it. Incense is burnt to the goddess which is called *dhúp dena*. Then a

lamp is kindled an[d] to the goddess, with some money is offer[ed] takes in his hand [a] of flowers and repe[ats] in praise of the godde[ss] per reads to the go[ddess] Chandi books, treati[ng] dess exhibited at diffe[rent] her votaries from seri[ous] the books once and The more the numb[er] merit to be won. A[fter] considered to come t[o] then takes his breakf[ast] and fruits and *sherbet* ship the goddess fo[r] powder and *raksha*, o[n] houses of each of the [ ] ship the goddess, and male members of th[e] powder and tie the [ ] each of them, and afte[r] Males perform the this way for nine d[ays] or through the prie[st] fast on the first day, and worship a gold i[dol] each family and to wh[om] are yearly added, w[ith] washed rice, flowers, sweetmeats. On the performs the worship scribed, but he perfor[ms] fice, which concludes in the *Naurátri*, or nin[e] who worship the go[ddess] from their clients arti[cles] perform a sacrifice an[d] But those who perfor[m] the articles for burnt The method of perf[orming] the following :—

A platform is made ing the burnt-sacrifi[ce] represents the godd[ess] this platform a wood set, upon which the n[ ] in nine houses. Th[ ] drawn to convey a made at the time of v[ ]

Mercury.	
Jupiter.	
The ascending node.	

To the east of the sacrificial platform is made a figure of several hundreds of houses in which the minor gods are represented in different houses. This figure is called Sarbatobhadra. To the south-east of the sacrificial platform is made a figure containing sixteen houses in which sixteen goddesses are represented. They are called khodas matrika. To the south-west of the sacrificial platform is made a house containing sixty-four houses in which sixty-four goddesses are represented. In the centre of the Sarbatobhadra figure is put a pitcher like the one which represents the goddess. Near each of the legs of the wooden seat on which the figure of Sarbatobhadra is made, a pitcher is put. In front of the seat of Sarbatobhadra is put an idol of Gauri, wife of Mahádeva, made of cow-dung, and near it Ganesa, the son of Mahádeva, is represented by a betel-nut. Over the figure of Sarbatobhadra an awning is spread (*chândani tânkdete hain*), and near each of the legs of the wooden seat on which the figure of Sarbatobhadra is made, they fix plantains. Then the nine planets, the sixteen and sixty-four goddesses and other gods represented in the Sarbatobhadra figure are worshipped with an offering of water, sandal, washed rice, flower, incense (*dhúp*), lamps and sweetmeats (*naivedya*). Gauri and Ganesa are also worshipped in the same way. After these gods have been worshipped, the pitcher put in the figure of Sarbatobhadra is worshipped in the same way. This pitcher represents Devi.

This done, the fire-sacrifice is performed. The articles which are thrown into the fire are the following :—

Rice, barley, sesamum seeds, *dashâng* (incense), *gugul* (gum), sugar, clarified butter, fruits (mewa).

All taken together amount to 1¼ maund, or any multiple of it. Before performing the sacrifice, the sacrificial platform is purified by sprinkling water on it, with the repetition of *mantras*. Then the platform is plastered with cow-dung. Then three lines are drawn on it with the *shruwá* (a sort of ladle used for pouring clarified butter at a sacrifice) from west to east. Then taking some earth from each of the lines it is thrown in the north-east direction. Then on the platform twenty blades of *kusa* grass are put one after another from the south-east quarter to the north-east direction and from the south-west direction to the north-west quarter the same number are placed. Then to the south of the platform an image of Brahma made of *kusa* is put. From Brahma's image up to the fire lighted in the centre of the platform twenty blades of *kusa* grass are laid one after another. To the north of the fire on the platform, the instruments of sacrifice (Prokshani and Pranita) are put. From the Pranita up to the fire twenty blades of kusa grass are laid. Again, on the northern side of the platform vedi seven blades are put, which are termed *Upyawan kusa*. On the same side, in another place-five blades are put, which are called *Samárjan kusa*. On the same side three blades of *kusas* are again put in another place. On the same side the *Ayya sthâli*, or the vessel containing ghi, is also placed, and by the side of it the *Charu sthâli*, or the vessel containing some of the articles of fire-sacrifice (*sakala ki sámigri*), is put. Then the vessel containing *ghi*, is held over the fire for some time. Then it is examined, whether or not it contains some worm or insect. Such things as the dead bodies of insects, &c., are carefully thrown out. Then the chief priest burns a blade of *kusa* and moves it over the *ghi*. This *kusa* is called *kusa kandiká*. The person for whom the sacrifice is being performed, presents to the chief priest, who on this occasion is termed Brahma, some garments. Presenting garments is called *varna karna*. Then other Bráhmans who will perform the fire-sacrifice are given garments. It is to be remembered here that the sacrifice is performed by five or more, *i. e.*, an uneven number of Bráhmans. Then some money is given to each of the Bráhmans which is called *kusa dakshina*. The chief priest or Brahma repeats the *mantras* of sacrifice and every time he pronounces the word *swáhá* (be consumed), the Bráhmans put the *sâkla*, or the articles of fire-sacrifice, into the fire. The person for whom the sacrifice is being performed, puts *ghi* into the fire each time.

When this has been done, curds and urad pulse mixed together are put on ten leaves and laid in ten directions (Hindús have ten directions, as they include upwards and downwards) for the ten Digpáls, or protectors of cardinal points. Then the worship of Kshetra' Pál or Bhairo is performed. It is done in this wáy. A lamp is kindled. It is worshipped with water, sandal washed rice, flowers, &c. Then four pice are put in it. Lamp-black and red-lead are also put in it. Then a barber or a Kahár takes the lamp up and moves it over the head of the person for whom the sacrifice is performed and runs away with it then. All present throw on the barber or Kahár washed rice, by which it is meant that he is being pelted. He puts the lamp on the roadside and after bathing comes again. Then the remaining articles of worship are thrown into the fire. Then kapúr or camphor is burnt, and, putting it in a vessel called arti, it is circulated among all present. They all salute it and put some pice in it. Then the worshipper takes in his hand flowers and chaplets of flowers and offers prayers to Bhagawati. He puts the flowers and chaplets of flowers on the pitcher after offering the prayers. Then money is distributed among the Bráhmans, without any regard of position, which is called *Bhusi dakshina bánina*. Then the person for whom the sacrifice is performed walks round the sacrificial fire and then salutes the Bráhmans present. Then Bráhmans are fed, or a vow is made to feed Bráhmans. Bráhmans, after being fed, get some reward, which is called *dakshina*. They bless the performer of the sacrifice and go to their homes. Then the person for whom the worship is performed, pours the water of the pitchers at the root of a Ním tree, or a Pípul tree. The pitcher which represented the goddess is preserved for a year. Those priests who perform the worship of Devi at her shrine, return to their clients, smear their forehead with red-lead and get fees for their labour.

What has been described above is the worship performed by Bráhmans, Kshatriyas, Vaishyas and Sudras, from whose hands a high caste Hindú may drink water. The low castes, like Chamárs and Dbarkárs, etc., perform the worship of Devi during *Naurátri* in altogether another way, though not with less devotedness. I give below the description of the worship of Devi as performed by low castes:—

During the nine days of the *Naurátri* they fast, taking roots and fruits and *sherbet* at noon and after twelve o'clock after worshipping the goddess in their own way. On the first day of the *Naurátri* they make a platform of earth, brought from seven wells or from the Ganges, in their own cottages, or under a *Nim* tree, in or outside the village or town. Those who have Palihár, one of the Pánch Pir, for their clan deity, fix a bamboo on the platform (*chauri*) and those who have the Pánchon Pir for their clan deity, fix an iron bar on it called *Sáng*. At noon they burn incense on the platform, after washing their bodies and putting on clan loin-cloths, and at night they offer at the same platform chaplets of flowers, new lamps, washed rice, lemons, wine, *khir* (rice cooked in milk and sugar put in it) and burn incense. Then they sing the Pachara—a song in honour of the goddess and peculiar to these people. Among low castes every clan has a Head Priest, one of themselves, who performs the worship at his own house or under a tree, and a fund is raised by public subscription among themselves, to defray the expenses of it. For nine days the worship is performed at night in this way, and the Pachara is sung. The offerings are distributed among the worshippers every day. On the ninth day the goddess enters the body of the Head Priest and he begins to shake his head to and fro, and divine. Men and women who are suffering from any disease put before him some rice, a pice and cloves, and then he tells them why they suffer from the particular disease, and prescribes to them the means by which they can get rid of their sufferings. The means prescribed is generally the worship of a demon who has caused the disease, or barrenness, &c. This being done the Head Priest offers to his goddess and other gods the following things:—Palihár—Fowls; Parameswari Devi—Swine; Sáya or Sayari Devi—Swine; Dih—Swine; Kali—Goats; Bhairo—goats; Samay Devi, Sendar Sádh, Sarb sokhani, Mailhar—Rams.

Besides these sacrifices, cakes, garments dyed in turmeric, and wine, are also offered to the above gods and goddesses.

On the tenth day of the fortnight, *i. e.*, on the Dashmi or Bijay Dashmi day, the women make cakes (chapari) of cow-dung in the courtyard and worship them with the offering of water, washed rice, sandal, flowers of the Nenuán and burn incense. This is called the worship of Dashmi. To it they offer the plants of barley, which they sow some days before the Dashmi day. Then they tie the plants on the heads of their relatives. Bráhman priests tie the plants on the heads of their clients and get some reward from them. Zemindárs get presents in money from their tenants and in return give them sweetmeats and betel. Rájas and Mahárájas worship the feet of their horses and elephants, having them decorated with gold saddles and gold and silver ornaments. Lastly, they worship their arms, offensive and defensive, as these are supposed to represent the goddess Durga. The worship is done with the offering of the same things as are offered to other gods, that is to say, water, washed rice, sandal, flowers, etc. Then the male members of the family, having fed on choice food, and put on rich dresses, repair to the place where the Rám Lilá, or a sort of dramatic representation of the fight between Ráma and Ráwana takes place. Going there, every Hindú spectator offers some sweetmeat, flowers and money (pice) to the Bráhman or mendicant priests, who wait on the boys who represent Ráma, Lakshmana and Sitá. These priests make the offering, touch the feet of Ráma and his wife and brother, and then take the whole of the money and half the sweetmeat and flour and return the other half to the offerer, with the addition of a few consecrated leaves of Tulasi plant. The offerer bows down in obeisance to the representatives of the heroes of the Rámáyana and goes back. Many stay there till nightfall, when the giant Ráwana is burnt and pelted by the Hindú spectators and then return home. Rájas and Mahárájas hold a darbár at night and confer khillats and khitábs on their courtiers and subjects. Men of the middle class interchange visits at the houses of their friends and neighbours and inquire the welfare of one another. Betel, cardamom and perfume are given to those who visit the house as friends and neighbours or relatives that day. To see the roller, or Nilkanth bird, on the Dashmi day is a very good omen. The last day of Kuár is called the Sharad day. It is believed that the moon sheds nectar that day. Bráhmans at night bow down to the moon and put some sweetmeats on the roof of the house as a present to the god of night.—*Pandit Rám Gharíb Chaubé.*

ANTHROPOLOGY.

2. **Sikh Initiation. By W. Simpson.** (Read at a Masonic meeting.)—The following description of the rite by which a Sikh is initiated is taken from *A History of the Sikhs*, by the late Joseph Davey Cunningham [*]:—"Sikhs are not ordinarily initiated until they reach the age of discrimination and remembrance, or not before they are seven years of age, or sometimes until they have attained to manhood. But there is no authoritative rule on the subject, nor is there any declaratory ceremonial of detail which can be followed. The essentials are that five Sikhs, at least, should be assembled, and it is generally arranged that one of the number is of some religious repute. Some sugar and water are stirred together in a vessel of any kind, commonly with a two-edged dagger; but any iron weapon will answer. The noviciate stands with his hands joined in an attitude of humility or supplication, and he repeats after the elder or minister the main articles of his faith. Some of the water is sprinkled on his face and person; he drinks the remainder, and exclaims, 'Hail, Gooroo!'[†] and the ceremony concludes with an injunction that he be true to God and to his duty as a Sikh. For details of particular modes followed, see Forster [*Travels*, i. 307], Malcolm [*Sketch*, p. 182], and Prinsep's edition of Murray's *Life of Runjeet Singh* [p. 217] where an Indian compiler is quoted. The original practice of using the water in which the feet of a Sikh had been washed was soon abandoned, and the subsequent custom of touching the water with the toe seems now almost wholly forgotten. The first rule was perhaps instituted to denote the humbleness of spirit of the disciples, or both it and the second practice may have originated in that feeling of the Hindu's which attaches virtue to water in which the thumb of a Brahmin has been dipped. It seems in every way probable that Govind substitued the dagger for the toe, thus giving further pre-eminence to his emblematic iron. Women are not usually, but they are sometimes, initated in form as professors of the Sikh faith. In mingling the sugar and water for women a one-edged, and not a two-edged, dagger is used."—pp. 359-60.

The Sikhs may be described as a body of dissenters from what might be termed Hindu orthodoxy. At various times there have been Hindu sects who renounced caste; Buddhism was one of these, and the renunciation of caste was a prominent doctrine of the Sikhs. Nanak, commonly called "Nanak Guru," was the founder of the Sikhs. He was born in 1469. The word Sikh is from the verb *Sikhána*—to teach—as they claimed to be enlightened or "taught." At first they were a quiet and peaceful sect, but the persecution and cruelty of the Mohammedans produced a change. Govind Singh, who became Guru about a century after Nanak, managed to inspire the Sikhs with a spirit of resistance; he caused them to add the word "Singh," which means Lion, to their names, to indicate the new character they were to assume. He also introduced the old Scythian worship of the sword as a means of raising the warlike spirit of his followers, and the stirring of the water of initiation with a dagger was one of the rites of the new *culte*. This was the "emblematic iron" of the above quotation. In the rules of Govind, amongst those who were to be condemned, was "he who wears not iron in some shape" (p. 397).

Govind organised the Sikhs into a society, which might be described as either a Church or a Brotherhood, or rather it was both of these. To this body he gave the name of Khálsa, which I believe is still retained; Cunningham says that the word "is of Arabic derivation, and has such original or secondary meanings, as pure, special, free, etc." The adoption of a title which had the signification of "Free" as one of its meanings will, of course, attract the eye of the craftsman, but the idea is a natural one where men become brothers, and meet together on conditions of equality. I believe the sense of the word was essentially spiritual with the Sikhs, although it also expressed a practical rule of conduct upon which they acted. I shall give another quotation from Cunningham which indicates this. "Govind is next represented to have again assembled his followers, and made known to them the great object of his mission. A new faith had been declared, and henceforth the 'Khálsa,' the saved or liberated, should alone prevail. God must be worshipped in truthfulness and sincerity, but no material resemblance must degrade the Omnipotent; the Lord could only be beheld by the eye of faith in the general body of the Khálsa. All, he said, must become as one; the lowest were equal with the highest; caste must be forgotten; they must accept the 'Páhul' or initiation from him, and the four races must eat out of one vessel." [‡] The "four races" means here the four castes among the Hindus, and the initiation into the Khálsa was to free them all from the trammels which were entailed on them by their birth in the Brahminical system.

---

[*] This was one of the sons of Allan Cunningham, the poet, and brother of General Sir Alexander Cunningham. His history of the Sikhs bears the reputation of being the best account of this people that has appeared. It was published by Murray, 1853.

[†] "Gooroo," or Guru, as it is now generally written, means a spiritual teacher.

[‡] *Ibid*, p. 68.

In a note Cunningham explains the word Páhul used above for initiation:—"Páhul [pronounced nearly as Powl] means literally a gate, a door, and hence initiation. The word may have the same origin as the Greek πυλη." Govind, in his Letters of Rules, says:—"He who gives the 'Páhul' to another shall reap innumerable blessings."*

Cunningham alludes very briefly to the older form of the rite, instituted by Nanak, but does not give full details. In the newer ceremony, at least as it is described above, the original meaning it had is lost, thus presenting us with a good illustrative example of mutation, which should not be overlooked in our inquiries into Masonic ritual. I believe that Nanak's rite is still practised as well as that of Govind's. There is a very sacred shrine of the Sikhs in the Tarai, which I visited in 1876, at the time the Most Worshipful Grand Master was in that out-of-the-way locality, and I was very much surprised to find a Sikh Temple there, so far from the Panjab. It was called Nanukmatha, and owed its sanctity to Nanak having been there in some part of his career, where he performed a number of miraculous acts, all of which were related to me; and I here quote from my diary written at the time,—"There are two sects of Sikhs, the Taught and the Fighting; the first at their initiation drink the water in which the Guru's feet were washed; the military wash or bathe a dagger in the water and drink it. Tshurn-Pahal is the name given to the first kind of water, and Kunda Ke Pahal the name of the second." From what Cunningham says I should be inclined to believe that the first of these rites is seldom practised, and when it is, that the stirring of the water by the Guru's toe, is all that is done to represent the washing of the feet.

I have one account of the ceremony, but have omitted to copy the name of the writer. It says:—"The candidate and the initiator wash their feet in the same water, which they then drink, having put some sugar into it, and stirred it with a dagger." This has much the appearance of being an account of the two rites condensed into one. Sir John Malcolm's description is similar to that of Cunningham's, for he omits the feet-washing, but he gives the following very important addition. The Guru on presenting the water to the convert, says:—"This sherbet is Nectar! It is the Water of Life! Drink it!"

If this is a correct account of the ceremony,— and Sir John Malcolm being a good authority, I suppose it may be accepted,—then we find that the rite had in it, as in other initiatory rites, the symbolisation of the Life-giving Principle. This presents us with a very different form of symbolism from that of the Brahminical Initiation. In that the noviciate became an embryo, and was supposed to be born again. It is more like the Christian rite of baptism, and yet there is a marked line which divides the symbolism of the two. Water had two distinct meanings attached to it. In one sense, as it washed and cleaned the outward body, it thus symbolised the inner spiritual purity. Baptism, either by sprinkling or immersion, typified washing.† In the early days, the Knights of the Bath were bathed in tubs, before the ceremony of Knighting took place, and hence the origin of the word "Bath."‡

The other principle which water symbolised was a very far-reaching one, and it lies at the foundation of a great amount of ancient allegory. It is an easily recognised fact that in nature there can be no life without water. This is a broad and universal law; it applies to the vegetable as well as to the animal world. Without a supply of water there could be no ear of corn, and the world would be a great Sahara. This explains why the old cosmogonies represented creation coming out of water; it gives us a glimpse at least into the meaning of the Rivers of Paradise, and to the "pure river of the Water of Life" in the New Jerusalem. Holy wells and streams are found all over the world; and the mediæval belief in the elixir of life was only a

---

† Eternal life through death was such a fundamental idea in the Christian system that it was added to the Baptismal rite. "Know ye not, that so many of us as were baptized into Jesus Christ were baptized into his death? Therefore we are buried with him by baptism into death; that like as Christ was raised up from the dead by the glory of the Father, even so we also should walk in newness of life."—*Romans*, vi., 3, 4.—See also *Colossians* ii., 12. A symbolical passing through death to life is thus taught as belonging to initiation into the Christian Brotherhood.

‡ "It may be proper therefore to take notice, that the great ceremony, from which the Knighthood of the Bath is denominated, and which we must therefore suppose was instituted with a peculiar Design of representing the Dignity of it, hath the like Foundation as to the moral design of it, with the great and Sacred Ordinance, by which we are initiated into the Faith and profession of our religion; and it is not improbable that as bathing was intended, in the allegorical construction of it, to denote the inward purgation and future purity of the mind; so, the occasion of applying it, in that sense, might be originally taken from a consideration of the Baptismal Grace and Efficacy, for the origin of this civil institution may—for the reason here mentioned—be much more probably derived from the Christian religion than from the lustrations of the heathens, with whom it is yet allowed, bathing was used as one of their religious solemnities."—*Historical Essay upon the Knighthood of the Bath*, by John Anstis Esq., 1725. It ought to be noted that the term "raising" might be applied to the ceremony of making a Knight of the Bath. The Monarch says, "Rise, Sir So-and-So." This is said when the individual is touched with the sword, as if it symbolised the life-giving power. I have never chanced upon any book that gave the origin of the Bath; I rather think that little or nothing is known on the subject; but if we could find out the source of this particular use of the "emblematic iron" it would be a good contribution to our knowledge of initiatory rites.

---

* *Ibid.* p. 396.

confused notion which had grown up out of the symbolism of the waters of life,—in this case the symbol had ceased to be a symbol, and, as in so many other instances in the past, a literal rendering had been given to the idea. Drinking the water, as in the Sikh initiation, is the usual form of the ceremony based on this symbolism. When I was at the source of the Ganges I had my morning tub, or bath, in the water only a few feet from where the stream issued from the glacier, and knowing the Hindu ideas, I took care to drink some of the sacred liquid so that I could afterwards claim that I had cleared myself of the guilt of all previous misdeeds. In this ceremony, at the source of the Ganges, it will be seen that both forms of the symbolism are represented, that is in the washing and the drinking.

The one detail which is puzzling in the Sikh initiation is the washing of the feet in what they believe to be the "Water of Life." This puzzle is increased when we recollect that the people of India are, perhaps, the cleanest in their habits of all the races on this earth. Their daily bathing, washing of their garments, and the great care in the preparation of food, may be cited as indicating their devotion to external purity; and yet here is a ceremony, which no one is likely to read of, without an impulse to apply the word "filthy" to it. The strange point is that this peculiarity in the ceremony is not confined to the Sikhs. There are numerous rites gone through in India which bear such a strong resemblance to that founded by Nanak, that it is impossible to avoid the conclusion that they are all based on the same original idea, whatever it may have been. Although the instances I am about to give do not seem to me to explain how this peculiar ceremony originated, yet they may, perhaps ultimately, help in finding a solution.

"The Abbé Dubois says that the Gurus, or Indian priests, sometimes, as a mark of favour, present to their disciples 'the water in which they had washed their feet, which is preserved and sometimes drunk by those who receive it,' [Dubois' 'People of India, London, 1817, p. 64.] This practice, he tells us, is general among the sectaries of Siva, and is not uncommon with many of the Vishnuites in regard to their vashtuma. 'Neither is it the most disgusting of the practices that prevail in that sect of fanatics, as they are under the reproach of eating as a hallowed morsel the very ordure that proceeds from their Gurus, and swallowing the water with which they have rinsed their mouths or washed their faces, with many other practices equally revolting to nature.'" [idem, 8, 7]. [1] *

"I was informed that vast numbers of Shordrus drank the water in which a Brahmin has dipped his foot, and abstain from food in the morning till this ceremony be over. Some persons do this every day. . . Persons may be seen carrying a small quantity of water in a cup, and entreating the first Brahmin they see to put his toe in it. . . Some persons keep water thus sanctified in their houses." †

In one of the old Law-books of the Hindus, known under the name of Nárada, and which is suppose to date about the fourth or fifth century, A.D., the details are given of an Ordeal by Sacred Libation. "The defendant should be made to drink three mouthfuls of water, in which [an image of] the deity whom he holds sacred has been bathed and worshipped."‡ If the person escapes any serious calamity for a couple of weeks after this act, he is supposed to be innocent. Somewhat similar to this is a practice of the Vaishnavas, who worship the Salagrama; this is a small stone of a particular kind, which is washed every morning, and the worshippers esteem it as a high privilege if they are allowed to drink the water afterwards.§

The Salagrama stone is generally understood to be the same as the Linga; the one representing Vishnu, and the other Siva. A Hindu calls the Linga Mahadeo, or Siva, and the principal part of the worship consists in pouring Ganges water on the top of it; I have never seen anything like drinking this water as a part of a rite, nor have I chanced to read of it; but it is generally the case that whatever is found in one of the Hindu systems will be found in the others, slightly changed perhaps, what might be defined as developed, or, as is often the case, undeveloped. Here is an illustration very closely allied to what has been already given. Siva, as Bhubanes'vara is represented by a Linga at the Great Temple in Orissa. The emblem in this case is described by Dr. Rajendralala Mitra as being eight feet in diameter, and eight inches above the Yoni. Such a stone is, of course, a fixture, but it has a proxy in the form of a small bronze figure called Chandras'ekhara, who is taken in a car with great pomp and ceremony, to a tank near the place; in this it is bathed, then dressed in new clothes and brought back again. Dr. Rajendralala Mitra adds to this that this tank is

---

* Quoted in Bourke's *Scatalogic Rites*. The Abbé Dubois is rather an old-fashioned authority to quote in the present day on an Indian matter; but what he says here is amply confirmed by later writers.

† Ward, quoted by Southey in his "Common-place Book," London, 1849 (2nd series), p. 521.

‡ Nárada, translated by Julius Jolly, i. 328-9, p. 116, *Sacred Books of the East*, vol xxxiii.

§ The Salagrama.—"The fortunate possessor preserves his gem in a clean cloth It is frequently perfumed and bathed; the water thereby acquiring a sin-propelling potency is prized and drank." Moor's *Oriental Fragments*, p. 88.

"held in great esteem as especially efficacious in washing off all moral taints."[*]

In the legends which are related about the origin of the Ganges, there are some aspects of them that may have some bearing on our subject. According to the Vaishnava myth, as given in the Puranas, the Viyad-Gunga, or Heavenly Ganges, is supposed to come from the celestial regions and to flow from the toe of Vishnu. It was the prayers of the holy Bhagiratha that accomplished this, in order to purify the remains of the sixty thousand sons of Sagara whose dead bodies lay in Patala or Hades; and without the soul-purifying water they could not be qualified for entrance into Swarga,—the heaven of Indra.[†] The toe of Vishnu in this legend might be the origin of the use of that member in the Sikh initiation, but we have the washing of the feet in addition to account for, and this by itself, unless we include the other practices I have given —does not quite account for all that is required.

The Saiva legend has the same reason for the sending down of the Ganges that it was to lustrate the ashes of the sons of Sagara ; but in this case, as the river in its fall would have destroyed the world, Siva, to prevent such a catastrophe, placed his head beneath, and received on it the water, from which it then flowed on this earth. In the linga pujah the Ganges water is poured on the head of the emblem, thus repeating what is told in the legend, and we may assume that the rite is based on the legend; or, it is more than possible that it is the other way, and the legend has been framed to give a sanctity to the ceremony.[‡] In both versions of this mythical story the sacred water comes on this visible globe from the persons of deities, in one case from the toe, in the other from the head, and by bathing and drinking this fluid it entirely removes all sin, and thus puts the performer in a condition fit for the bliss of life in the next world. It is nectar; the Water of Life!

In these legends and ceremonies the identity is clear enough, but it must be confessed that the first origin has not been reached; and the next illustration I am about to give introduces what appears to be a new element into the investigation.

Near to the Burning Ghat at Benares there is a very holy tank called the Manikarniká Kund. It is filled with what appears to be extremely dirty water but its sin obliterating power is so great, that it is the first place sought by the pilgrims to the sacred city, and it is said to be particularly so by those who come with very guilty consciences. The legend of its origin is told in a variety of ways, but they all agree in the details necessary for my present purpose.

It was dug out by Vishnu himself, with his *Chakra* or discus, and from this it is also called Chakr-push-karni. When the tank was made, Vishnu filled it with the perspiration from his own body. As to whether Vishnu keeps up the supply of this liquid or not, I have not learned, but the sanctity of the tank owes its origin to this first manner of filling it which is recorded by more than one authority.[§] The gods of Greece had a divine *ichor* that flowed through their veins, and which was supposed to be connected with their condition as immortals. That which made the gods immortal would make man immortal. I do not know whether the Hindus had this notion or not, but if they had, it would explain this curious myth of the Manikarniká Kund, and the other rites of washing gods and gurus,[||] and then drinking as well as bathing in the water. I only offer this as the merest guess at the explanation.

There was a trial for libel, known as the Maharajah case, which came before the Bombay Courts in 1862. The "Maharajahs" were the priests of a Hindu sect in Bombay, who were accused among other things of performing a rite which was identical with that which is understood by the words '"droit du Seigneur."' These priests were held in very great esteem by their followers, as their high sounding title indicates Evidence was given in court that the water in which these priests' *dholees*—the cloth which forms the principal part of a native's dress—had been washed, was swallowed by the disciples; and that the water of the Maharajah's bath was regularly distributed for the same purpose. It was also stated that water in which the toe of one of the priests had been put into was called "The Nectar of Life." I was in Bombay when there was a great excitement about the case, just before the trial began, and the late Dr. Bhau Daji, a native physician of good repute, as well as a man of note and an archæologist, and who gave evidence against the Maharajahs, favoured me with some interesting details about the case, and mentioned one particular disease

---

[*] *The Antiquities of Orissa*, by Dr. Rajendralala Mitra, vol. ii., pp. 77-8.

[†] Fauche, in his translation of the *Ramayana*, puts it that the Ganges was led "au fond du Tartare, il consola enfin les mânes de ses grands-oncles et fit couler sur leurs cendres les eaux du fleuve-sacré. Alors, s'etant revêtu de corps divins, tous de monter au ciel dans une ivresse de joie." The Ganges is supposed to traverse the "three worlds," heaven, earth and the underworld; it comes from heaven and returns to it; and this explains why the ashes of the dead, and at times the bodies unburnt—when people are too poor to supply the wood —are thrown into the river, so that they may be carried by the sacred water back to heaven again.

[‡] It is this connection of the linga pujah with the ashes of the sons of Sagara which forms one part of the evidence given by me for the theory that the Saiva Temple had its origin as a tomb, or was in some way connected with funereal rites.

[§] See *The Sacred City of the Hindus: An Account of Benares in Ancient and Modern Times*, by the Rev. M. A. Sherring, p. 68.

[||] A guru, or Brahminical teacher, was to be reverenced as a God, so the water he bathed in would be as sacred as that in which a god had been washed in.

he had attended some of these priests for, a fact which must increase our natural disgust at their so-called "nectar of life."

I give these curious details, confessing at the same time that I do not pretend to explain them; but I hope they may be of use to others who will perhaps be led to follow up the study of the subject.

The probability is that the use of perspiration, as well as other kinds of matter that come from the human body, in ceremonial observances, belongs to an early state of civilization; and that light upon it might be found in the customs and ceremonies of primitive races. I have chanced upon one instance which shows that it is not confined to India. When Dr. Wolff was in Abyssinia they mistook him for the new Abuna, or Bishop, and in this belief he writes that—"They fell down at my feet, kissed them, and implored my blessing, and desired me to spit upon them. I was compelled to perform such an extraordinary sputation, that my throat was completely dry. They compelled me to submit to have my feet washed, and for them to drink the water of ablution."[*] The spitting process related in this instance would slightly favour the idea I have suggested that the virtue in such case is owing to something that comes from the holy person.

The curing by Christ of the blind man and the deaf man, by spitting on the organs,[†] would also favour this view of the subject. The act of "sputation," as Dr. Wolff calls it, could not have been done always as a sign of contempt. In Africa it is still in some places a mark of honour in saluting persons of distinction.

I remember many years ago reading a book by an African traveller, Petherick, I think was the name of the author, and he describes being introduced to a native monarch, who at once spat on his face. The traveller for a moment hesitated as to whether he should send his fist back in return, or give a similar salute. He tried the latter, and gathering all the material he could from his throat, he fired back such an ample volley in the King's face, that it produced a loud applause from all the attendants, and by this act he stood high in their esteem as a man of proper manners and politeness. This custom, recorded by Petherick, does not appear to be exceptional, for here is another experience by an African explorer, which shows that it belonged to the high ceremonial of courts:—"The treaty was sealed by my spitting several times at the Sultan, while he spat at me."[‡]

[*] *Narrative of a Mission to Bokhara*, by the Rev. Joseph Wolff, p. 34.
[†] Mark viii., 23, and vii., 33.
[‡] Peters' *New Light on Dark Africa*, p. 172.

There were customs at home here that have been continued down to a comparatively late period, which bear a strong analogy to some of those described in this paper. In the Glasgow Exhibition of 1888 there were exhibited among the archæological objects in the Bishop's Palace some old rock-crystal balls. Two, at least, of these were celebrated; one was "The Glenorchy Charm-stone of Breadalbane,"[§] and the other was "The Ardvorlich 'Clach Dearg,.'"[‖] This last had the reputation of having been brought from the east by the Crusaders. These were looked upon as potent charms, but their principal use was the curing of the diseases of cattle, and for this purpose they were placed in the water the animals drank, or the medicine that was given them. I speak with some uncertainty, but I rather think charms of this kind were also put into the medicine for human patients. Soul curing and body curing were very closely allied in the past, but without assuming too much I think the last illustration is worth adding to this paper.

ADDITIONAL NOTES.

I add the following extracts and notes on this curious subject, which have turned up since writing the above: The first I shall give is from a primitive source. Lenormant, in his Chaldean Magic ¶ quotes from the *Kalevala*, regarding Wainamöinen, who seems to have been a Laplandish Poseidon, that "the sweat which dropped from his body was a balm for all diseases." In this we have the curative power of liquid exuded from the human body.

In the next we have the virtue of water, which has been used for washing the body, against the powers of sorcery. Among the Celtic Fairy Tales is one entitled *The Horned Women*. These were witches, and to prevent them entering a house one of the spells was produced by sprinkling outside the doors on the threshold the water

[§] *The Glenorchy Charm-Stone of Breadalbane.*—This Charm is first mentioned in the *Black Book of Taymouth*, wherein it is described as, ane stane of the quantity of half a hens eg set in silver, being flatt at the ane end and round at the uther end lyke a peir, whilk Sir Colin Campbell, first Laird of Glenurchy, woir when he fought in battell at the Rhodes agaynst the Turks, he being one of the Knychtis of the Rhodes.' *Circa* 1440. Lent by the Marquis of Breadalbane.—*The Book of the Bishop's Castle*, or Official Catalogue, p. 221.

[‖] "*The Ardvorlich* '*Clach Dearg*.'—A ball of rock-crystal in a mounting of two hoops of silver, with a clasp and chain for suspension. It has been long in the possession of the Stewarts of Ardvorlich, and was formerly held in great repute in the neighbourhood as a charm-stone for curing diseases of cattle. It is said to have been brought from the East by Crusaders. Lent by Col. Stewart, C. I. E., R.A." *Ibid.* There were three more of these charm-stones in the Exhibition: one of them is described as having been "used against witches in St. Andrews."

[¶] *Chaldean Magic*, by François Lenormant, p. 247.

in which a child's feet had been washed.* The tale does not allude to the water having any virtue from the innocence and purity of the child, but it might perhaps be assumed as probable that this was the reason.

The next quotation is not very clear in its details, but I give the words as I found them:—"There are certain quaint usages connected with weddings among the peasantry of Russia, as well as among the rustic population of England, which might strike the curiosity of antiquarians. In the first case, there is a 'sprinkling' with water once used by the bride for the purpose of bathing her person; in the other, there is a 'sale' of a liquid by the bride, this liquor being an intoxicant." †

The next is a quotation made by the author of the above. Samogitia, it may be mentioned, is a district on the north-west of Russia, towards the German frontier.

"Wedding ceremonies of the peasantry of Samogitia: 'The bride was led on the wedding-day three times round the fire-place of her future husband; it was then customary to wash her feet, and with the same water that had been used for that purpose the bridal bed, the furniture, and all the guests were sprinkled.'"‡

These illustrations are all from the extreme north and west of Europe, and taken with what has already been given in this paper, they show how widespread such peculiar rites and customs have been; and as some of them date back to an early time it may be assumed that they belong to a primitive period. The next example is also from the extreme north-west; the milk which is first mentioned is an exudation from a living creature. The water of the well at Moytura, according to the legend, contained nothing that was emitted from the body, so the instance does not apply directly to the main point of my subject; but as this paper has slightly expanded itself so as to partly include Initiation by Water, the reference is of value as showing an early conception of the re-vivifying power of that medium.

"This incident of the quickening of the dead occurs elsewhere, especially in Irish literature, as for example in the story of a war between the Cruithni or Picts and the mythic Men of Fidga: under the direction and spells of a druid called Drostan the resuscitation is brought about by means of a bath of new milk at a place called Ardlemnachta, or Sweet Milk Hill, in Leinster. It occurs also in the story of the battle of Moytura between the Formori and the Tuatha De Danann, under the leadership of their king Nuada and Lud the Long-handed: in this instance the quickening of the dead warriors is brought about by dipping them at night in a well of marvellous virtues: and it is resorted to until those on the other side find out what is going on, whereupon they pile a cairn of stones over the well.' §

It may be appropriate here to mention that in the Russian Church the priest in the ceremony of baptism—an intiatory and regenerative rite—breathes upon the water. I chanced to see this done in a church in St. Petersburg, but did not notice at the moment what Madame Roman off describes. She says that the benediction of the water is performed "by the priest's immersing his right hand in it crosswise, three times, and blowing on it." ‖ I should not venture to affirm that the priest's hand in this case is to be identified with the toe of the Sikh Guru; but it ought, I think, to be recorded here amongst the other data. I attach far more importance to the breathing, or "blowing," on the water, as it is a marked variant from the others. In this, instead of a material something, we have what is supposed influence, which passes to the water from the person of the priest.

The next reference seems closely allied to the custom, already given, which takes place at weddings in Samogitia. It may be supposed that the virtue imparted to the water of the queen's bath in this case has been derived from the prevalent idea that a monarch is a sacred or a divine person: to this it may be added that a bride might have been looked upon as consecrated or sacred. "The people of Madagascar have an annual feast of the greatest solemnity, during which no cattle are allowed to be slaughtered, 'which means that none can be eaten.' This festival is called 'The Queen's Bath,' and is arranged with much parade. When the water was warm the queen stepped down and entered the curtained space. In a few moments salvoes of artillery announced to the people that the queen was taking her bath. In a few minutes more she re-appeared, sumptuously clothed with jewels. She carried a horn filled with the bath water, with which she sprinkled the company." ¶

Here is a Mohammedan example, but it differs from the usual type in not being refuse from a human body that is employed. There

---

* *Celtic Fairy Tales* by Joseph Jacobs, p. 32.

† *Scatalogic Rites of All Nations*, by Capt. John G. Bourke, Washington, 1891; p. 231.

‡ *Ibid*, p. 231-2. This is from Maltebrun's *Univ. Geog.*, vol. ii., p. 848, art. "Russia." I think, if my memory serves me, there used to be a custom in Scotland of washing a bridegroom's feet. This was done by his male companions a night or two before his wedding. I cannot recall whether the bride went through a similar ceremony among her female fiends. Perhaps some of our elder brethren in the north could add information on this point.

§ *Studies in the Arthusian Legend*, by Prof. John Rhys, M.A., p. 307.

‖ *Rites and Customs of the Greco-Russian Church*, by H. C. Romanoff, p. 70.

¶ *Evening Star*, Washington D C., quoting from "Transcript," Boston, Massachusetts. Quoted in *Scatalogic Rites of all Nations*, by Capt. J. G. Bourke, p. 90.

is a sect known as Khojas, the head of which lives in Bombay; they are Shias, and claim to be disciples of the "Old Man of the Mountain," Hassan-bin-Saba, the chief of the assassins in the time of crusades, who is reputed to have had a strange system of initiation for his followers. The chief in Bombay at present is named Aga Ali Shah, who can prove his descent from this historical old man. "On stated days he leads the 'Nimmaz' or daily prayer, in the Jamat Khana, and presides over the distribution of water mixed with the holy dust of Kerbella."*

When dealing with charm-stones in Scotland, I quite overlooked the celebrated Lee Penny. It is a stone, triangular in shape, of a dark red colour, about half-an-inch in size, set in an old silver coin, supposed to be a shilling of Edward I. It is said to have been brought from the Holy Land about 1320, by Simon Locard of Lee, in Lanarkshire, who is supposed to have carried the heart of Bruce to Palestine, and the name Locard or Lockhart has been the family name since that time. All this is, of course, doubtful history, and the record of the stone and its cures must be considered as not much more authentic. Simon Locard, or Lockhart, received the stone as part of the ransom of a "Saracen prince or chief," and the prince's wife explained to him how it cured "all diseases in cattle, and the bite of a mad dog both in man and beast." It will be easily perceived that the originators of this tale were not well up in the Mohammedan ideas about wives. The cures were effected by dipping the stone into water, drunk either by persons or animals, or applied to external wounds. It is reported that when there was a plague in Newcastle, and a murrain in Yorkshire, water, in which the stone had been dipped, was carried to these places; and numerous cures of all kinds are said to have been produced by this simple means.

I have the details of another charm-stone belonging to a locality, the district of Cowal, on the Firth of Clyde, that I chance to be very familiar with. In this case we have details of the process employed. My authority for this is a speech made at a soirée of the Cowal Society in Glasgow in 1872, where Col. Wm. Rose Campbell, of Ballochyle, made a speech, which was not only amusing, but also contained many interesting details of people who had gone to the majority, as well as of past habits and customs. Among other things, he said:—"I shall now conclude by mentioning that the brooch I now wear is a fac-simile of the Ballochyle brooch, an ancient Cowal relic, about 300 years in our family. It has a rock crystal charm-stone in the centre, which was even to a recent period, considered a 'perfect cure' for all diseases. Those bathed in the water in which it was dipped, recovered, and cattle which drank water in which it was placed were instantly cured. At Holy Loch, in olden days, it was looked on with great reverence, and it is a fact that my own father, who was born in 1777, about 95 years ago, was frequently, when a boy, bathed in a tub in which the brooch was placed, in order to cure him when sick, and so late did the idea of its being a 'perfect cure' exist that the gentry even used it as a sort of talisman early in 1800, and the country folks used to come from distances to get cured by it."

The most of these charm-stones have the reputation of having been brought from the Holy Land at the time of the Crusades; this might be looked upon as favouring the idea that the custom of bathing such objects had been brought to this country with them at that time. This may have been the case; but there is a passage in Professor Rhys's Hibbert Lectures which seems to point to a custom of this kind as being common to the early Britons. There is a tradition that Merlin, by the power of enchantment, brought over some of the stones of Stonehenge from Ireland. Professor Rhys speaks thus regarding them:—". . . what I wish to call your attention to is, the reason Merlin is represented giving, for fetching, those stones from so far, namely, that they were endowed with various virtues, especially for healing; the giants of old had, he said, ordained that bodily ailments might be healed by bathing the patient in the water in which the stones had first been bathed, or by the application of herbs dipped in the same holy bath. This would seem to point in particular to those of the Stonehenge stones which geologists have hitherto failed to recognise as belonging to the rocks of the district; and the idea of washing them, and the virtues thereby imparted by them to the water, presumably implies that the stones were regarded as divine, or as the seats of divine power."† In a former paper I alluded to the doubts that existed about Bardic literary remains but as this comes from such an eminent authority, without any word of criticism, I presume it may be accepted as authentic.

Here is another evidence of the curative power of secretions from the human body found in China, which appeared only the other day in the *Times*:—"The character of the accusations made in the publications, against Europeans, has created as much astonishment amongst the foreign residents in China

---

* Sir Bartle Frere, in *Macmillan's Magazine*, for Sept. 1876, p. 431.

† *Hibbert Lectures*, p. 193.

as it has in the West. Missionaries especially were charged—and the charges have been made frequently during the past thirty years—with bewildering women and children by means of drugs, enticing them to some secret place, and there killing them for the purpose of taking out their hearts and eyes. Dr. MacGowan, a gentleman who has lived for many years in China, has published a statement showing that from the point of view of Chinese medicine these accusations are far from preposterous. It is one of the medical superstitions of China that various portions of the human frame and all its secretions possess therapeutic properties. He refers to a popular voluminous Materia Medica—the only authoritative work of the kind in the Chinese language—which gives thirty-seven anthropophagous remedies of native medicine." *

The above statement that all the "secretions" of the body have medicinal power, would go far to justify a belief, in what will appear to most minds as almost incredible, that one of the secretions of the Dalai Lama, the Great Lama of Lhassa, is carefully preserved and made into pills, which are esteemed all over Tibet as having the highest curative virtue. That other high Lamas in Tibet provide similar medicine is suggested by an experience recorded by Sir Joseph Hooker in his *Himalayan Journals*. He, and Dr. Campbell, the Commissioner of Darjeeling, were invited to a very costly dinner given by the Dewan, or Prime Minister, of the Rajah of Sikkim. At the end of the feast the Dewan produced three pills, "which he had received as a great favour from the Rimbochay Lama." There was some suspicion of poison, and Dr. Campbell refused the one offered to him. Sir Joseph says that he took his with considerable misgiving, and says:—"But in truth it was not poison I dreaded in its contents so much as being composed of very questionable materials, such as the Rimbochay Lama blesses and dispenses far and wide. To swallow such is a sanctifying work, according to Buddhist superstition, and I believe there is nothing in the world, save his ponies, to which the Dewan attached a greater value." † The word "sanctifying," used alone, would imply a spiritual as well as a physical influence possessed by the matter in the pills. This is based on one of the old world ideas, that what is good for the body is good for the soul. This principle should not be overlooked in considering the various data in this paper; where in one case a particular kind of matter cures the body and in another it purifies the spirit. The one attribute is not antagonistic, but the complement of the other.

"Paracelsus taught that when one person ate or drank anything given off by the skin of another, he would fall desperately in love with that other." ‡

* *The Times*, Sept. 30th., 1892.
† Hooker's *Himalayan Journals*, p. 456.
‡ This is given on the authority of Fromman, *Tractatus de Fascinatione*.

Fromman also cites Beckherius to the effect that some philtres were made of perspiration, menses, or semen. §

As the practices connected with this subject are evidently primitive, we need not be surprised to find well marked traces of it in the Zoroastrian system. The *Bundahis* mentions a mythical monster which it describes as the "three-legged ass." | "When it states in the ocean all the sea-water will become purified, which is in the seven regions of the earth—*it is* even on that account when all asses which come into water stale in the water—as it says thus :—'If, O three-legged ass I you were not created for the water, all the water in the sea would have perished from contamination which the poison of the evil spirit has brought into its water, through the death of the creatures of Aûharmazd.'" ¶

It is said that if a Hindu sees a cow staling, that he will hold his palms under the liquid, and will even sip a little of it. This custom must have been practised before the Hindus and the Zoroastrains separated. In the *Dâdistân-i-Dînîk* it is s ated—"That also which might be written, as to the much retribution appointed as regards washing the limbs outside with clean moisture from clean animals and plants, and then completely washing the body with the purifying water streaming forth." * Mr. E. W. West who translates this book, adds a foot-note, explaining that this passage refers to the "ceremonial purification by washing with bull's urine. The urine was mixed with consecrated water; it was known as " Nirang," and also as " Gomez." The old Zoroastrian books contain numerous references to washing and purification by means of this liquid, as well as to drinking it. Max Müller says:— "Strange as this process of purification may appear, it becomes perfectly disgusting when we are told that women, after child-birth, have not only to undergo this sacred ablution, but have actually to drink a little of the *Nirang*, and that the same rite is also imposed on children at the time of their investiture with the *Sudra* and *Kosti*, and badges of the Zoroastrian faith."† The investiture with the *Sudra* and *Kosti*, is the rite of initiation among the Parsees.‡ From this we

§ These are quoted from Bourke's *Scatalogic Rites*, p. 217.
| *Bundahis*, xix., 1. *Sacred Books of the East*, vol. v., p. 67.
¶ *Ibid*, xix., 10.
* *Dâdistân-i-Dînîk*, xlviii., 9 : *Sacred Books of the East*, vol. V., pp. 161-2.
† *Chips from a German Workshop. Essay on the Parsees.*
‡ See account of the Parsee *Shoodra* and *Kusti* in *Brahminical Initiation, A.Q.C.*, vol iii., p. 93.

may assume that, when the Sikh novice drinks the water in which the Guru's feet were washed, it was not done as an act of abasement by the pupil to his superior, but as the purifying ceremony.* Sir Monier Williams also repeats the same, that a young Parsee passes through a ceremony of confirmation, in which he is made to drink a small quantity of bull's urine. To this may be added that I have heard that when a Hindu loses caste, part of the purificatory rites consists in drinking cow's urine, and eating the droppings of the same animal. About a year ago some details of this rite appeared in the newspapers about a Fyzabad Hindu who had lost his caste: among the things done to restore him to his previous state was the covering of his body with cow-dung, the face being excepted, he was then carried to the river, and after a wash, he was received again by the Brahmins as pure.† These details tend to show that the subject of this paper is not quite unconnected with my former paper on Brahminical Initiation.

As the bathing of stones in sacred and curative waters has been shown to exist in widely separated localities, it should not be omitted to state that it had been the custom to place pebbles in the consecrated water and urine by the Zoroastrians. This is alluded to in the *Epistles of Mânûshkihar* ‡; the writer mentions it in one place as being done, and in another an "inward prayer" is alluded to when they were not put in the sacred fluid, showing that this part of the rite had begun to be dropped out when the Epistles were written. The curious point in this is, that "three hundred pebbles" were cast into the mixture. This part of the consecration is now obsolete.

One of the most interesting publications of the Palestine Pilgrims' Text Society is the account of a journey, *circa* 1481-3, to the Holy Land, by Felix Fabri, a Dominican Monk of Ulm. Among other places he went to Bethlehem, and he tells how he and those with him made a fruitless search round the walls for the "hollow cave" in which he expected to find the sacred water, of which the following is his description:—

"I had read in a very ancient book of pilgrimage, written by some saint, that when the Lord was born, Joseph, as was customary, made ready a bath for the Babe in an earthen pot. After he had bathed the Child, Joseph took the pot, carried it out of the inn, and poured the holy water at random down the wall on to the rocks which projected from among the foundations. For the place of Nativity stands high, having below it a precipitous hill and rocks, whereon the Inn itself stood. Now the holy water, when it fell into a hollow rock, in which the whole of that sacred liquid was received and preserved, and for many years that water remained there without wasting and without corruption. In days of old pilgrims were led to this pool and washed their faces therein, and drank thereof, and filled their water-bottles, and took it to parts beyond sea for a bodily medicine, because many sick peoples were made better by tasting thereof; yet, how muchsoever might be taken away, the quantity of water did not grow less—a miracle, because there was no spring to replenish it." §

There are a number of stories of this class in the Apocryphal *Gospel of the Infancy*. When in Egypt the Holy Family came to "Mataria, the Lord Jesus caused a well to spring forth, in which St. Mary washed his coat, And a balsam is produced, or grows in that country, from the sweat which ran down there from the Lord Jesus." ‖ In chapter vi. a girl is cured of a white leprosy from having the water in which the Lord Jesus was washed sprinkled over her. In the same chapter the leprous son of a prince is cured by the same means. Chapter ix. records the curing of two sick children with the same water. Chapter xii.

---

* Those who are familiar with the initiatory ceremony of "Crossing the Line" will perhaps begin to think, after reading such details, that Neptune's Doctor may have been following ancient precedents in the sources from which he procures some of his drugs.

† See *Daily News*, Jan. 20th, 1892. The "Grete Marvayles" that Sir John Maundevile recounts are generally ranked with the doings of Baron Munchausen; but in my eastern experiences I have met with a number of things which show that there was some foundation for many of the wonderful stories the Knight of St Albans relates. From what has been given above, it will be seen that the following may not be so very far from the truth. He is speaking of some part of India. "And the Kyng of the Contree bathe alle wey an Ox with him: and he that kepethe him, bathe every day grete fees, and kepethe every day his Dong and his Uryne in a vesselles of Gold, and bryngen it before here Prelate, that thei clepen Archiprotopapaton; and he berethe it before the Kyng, and make the there over a gret blessynge; and then the Kyng wetethe his Hondes there, in that thei clepen Gaul, and anyntethe his front and his Brest: and aftre he frotethe him with the Dong and with the Uryne with gret reverence, for ben fulfilt of vertues of the Ox, and made holy the vertue of that holy thing that nought is worthe. And whan the Kyng hathe don, thanne don the Lords; and aftre hem here Mynystres and other men, zif thei may have ony remenant." The *Voiage and Travaile* of Sir John Maundevile, Kt., chap., xv., p. 170.

‡ *Sacred Books of the East*, vol. xviii., pp. 308, 340.

§ *The Books of the Wanderings of Brother Felix Fabri*, Palestine Pilgrim's Text Society, vol. i., part 2, pp. 575-6.

‖ *Gospel of the infancy*, viii., 10-11.

tells how a woman and a prince's daughter are cured of leprosy, and in chapter xiii. a girl is cured by means of the swaddling cloth of the Lord Jesus.

The question naturally suggests itself from these and other instances in this paper, as to whether "touching" for the King's Evil was not only another form based on similar notions. The king being a sacred person it may have been believed, when the custom of touching originated, that something curative would be communicated through the skin to the person touched. I merely propose the suggestion, but only as a matter for further consideration.

The following is from an ancient Egyptian Magical Text, and from it the idea, as a guess merely, might be made that rain and dew may have seemed to the primitive man as perspiration or other secretion coming from a deity. If this could be made clear it might give us a clue to the first origin of the—to us in our day—strange and peculiar rites and ceremonies recorded in this paper; and it may turn out that in the beginning it was only a rude figurative manner of describing the operations of nature. The original text is full of lacunæ—these are indicated by dots. When Horus weeps, the water that falls from his eyes grows into plants producing a sweet perfume. When Baba lets fall blood from his nose, it grows into plants changing to cedars, and produce turpentine instead of the water. When Shu and Tefnut weep much, and water falls from their eyes, it is changed into working bees; they work in the flowers of each kind, and honey and wax are produced instead of the water. When the Sun becomes weak, he lets fall the perspiration of his members, and this changes to a liquid . . . linen, it has become . . . much he bleeds, and the blood changes to salt . . . chooses them for remedies, the Sun coming from . . . which they give to the divine members. When the Sun is weak he perspires, water falls from his mouth to the earth, and changes to the plants of the papyrus. When Nephthys is very weak, her perspiration flows and is changed into the plant *Tas*. The region of Benben and Ai, when the Sun sits there, he perspires. The region of Tami, when Ptah sits there, he perspires, Regions Tatta and Hatefa, when Osiris sits there, his perspiration falls there."*

When I first read of the Sikh rite initiation I was inclined to accept what Cunningham suggested, that its object might be to teach such virtues as humility and obedience to the Master; and by induction, to impress the mind with the necessity of manifesting these virtues to God, for it is one of

* *Records of the Past*, vol. vi., pp. 115-6.

the old sacerdotal ideas that the priest or teacher is the representative of the Deity—the Brahmins, as an instance, claimed pretensions of this kind. The idea of abasement might have been entertained at some time, but the numerous instances, collected in to this paper, of curative virtues of purifying the soul as well as the body, seem to point to another principle underlying the practice. There must have been at an early period a widespread belief in the sanctifying qualities of secretions which were understood to have come from a deity, and consequently from emblems of the deity. The secretion probably appeared to the mind of primitive man to be a part of the deity—and hence its power and virtue. If this view of the subject can be borne out it will only become another, and a very peculiar, form of Relic-Worship, and will have to be classed as nearly akin to the ideas dealt with in my former paper on The Worship of Death. I give this as only my impression at the moment. The subject I may point out, is entirely new, or nearly so, and I should not be justified, as yet, in giving a judgment of a positive character upon it. As all initiatory rites are of interest to the Craftsman, I hope that whatever opinion may be formed of this paper it will be at least acceptable as a small contribution to our knowledge of them. I may point out that this collection of data has been made in my usual manner; that is, I have taken extracts from all quarters—whatever appeared to bear upon the question—regardless of their exact value, because when customs such as this paper deals with, which are new to us, have to be studied, we cannot at first be certain of the significance that may perhaps belong at times to the merest scrap of knowledge. I have given, in almost every case, the references to books from which quotations have been made: this will enable each one to discount the authority of the authors as he chooses.†

† As I had never met with any book dealing with the secretions of the human body, as something sacred, I was under the notion that one part of the paper would be entirely new. Since writing the first portion I have read a book, only lately published, which is wholly devoted to this class of ideas—one or two quotations from it will be found above. The work is entitled *Scatalogical Rites of all Nations*, by Capt. John G. Bourke. Published by W. H. Lowdermilk and Co., Washington, 1891. I can recommend this book to any one wishing to study the subject. I would claim that this work gives strong testimony to what I have said above, that the practices are primitive—I base this assumption on a number of facts, but principally on their universality. Capt. Bourke gives a number of customs found among the races of America, showing its existence in the New as well as the Old World. One very long chapter is devoted to the theraputical use of secretions in the Middle Ages. It is shown that all the secretions of the human body belonged to the mediæval pharmacy—thus illustrating the belief in their curative properties. While complimenting Capt. Bourke on the industry he has shewn in gathering together such a vast quantity of material, and from such a variety of sources, I may mention that this paper contains a few illustrations that he has not had the good fortune to meet with.

FOLKTALES.

3. The tale of the four drunkards.—There were once four drunkards, one of whom was addicted to spirits, the second to *bhang*, the third to *charas*, and the fourth to opium. They were reduced to great poverty and at last determined to go abroad in search of employment. As they were going along they came across a horse. One of them got up on the neck, the second on the shoulders, the third on the back, while the fourth clung on to the tail. They came to a city and stopped at an inn, but their lamp had no oil; so the first said to the second, "Go and bring oil," and the second passed the message to the third, and the third to the fourth. At last they agreed that they should all lie down and that he that woke first should go and fetch the oil. As opium eaters do not sleep, he lay awake and in the night a dog came and tried to carry away their food. The opium eater who was awake, struck at the dog with a stick and this made him howl and run away. Hearing the noise, the others woke, and said to the opium eater, "Why don't you go for the oil?" When the lamp was lit they said, "Let us lie down again; but we must tie up the horse lest it be stolen." One said, "What is the use of tying the horse? Let us each hold on to one of his legs while we sleep." So they lay down and the horse, who was hungry, soon managed to get loose. When they woke and missed the horse they made sure it had been stolen. So they said, "Let us take the omens and find out who is the thief." They filled a *chilam* and one took a pull, and said, "I am sure the thief is black." The second took a smoke, and said, "Yes, he is black and he has only one eye." "That is true," said the third, "and he has a long beard." "Yes." said the fourth," and his name is Kâle Khân."

When they had settled this, they went along the road and by and by they met a man in a palanquin. They stopped him and asked him what his name was. He said that he was a Mahajan and that his name was Kâle Khân. When they looked at him more closely they found that he was black and had a long beard. Then they made sure that he was thief; so they hauled him before the Raja and made complaint against him. The Raja enquired how they came to know that the Mahajan had stolen the horse. Said they, "We discovered it by taking the omens." "Well," said the Raja, "let me see how you take omens." So he got a pomegranate and put it in a box and said, "Now take the omens and tell me what is in this box." They were perplexed, and said, "Great king! Have a *chilam* prepared for us." When the *chilam* was brought, one of them looked at it and said, "It looks to me rather round." "Yes," said the second, "and it is red." "That is true,", said the third, "and there are grains (*dana*) in it." "True," said the fourth "and it is a *kali*."* When the Raja heard this he was convinced that they had taken the omens aright and he gave judgment against the Mahajan and made him pay for the horse.

[Told by Lalman, Brahman, and recorded by Amar Nath, Master of the Kasgunj School, Etah District.]

4. Seeing the world.—There was once a Mahâjan who loved the Princess of the land and he used to visit her daily through an underground passage between her house and his. One day the Princess said, "Let us go to foreign lands and see the world." So she dressed herself in male attire and they rode off together. They came to a jungle and found a house where they halted for shelter. There was an old woman in the house and she made some sherbet for them; but she put poison in it. As they were about to drink it, a voice came from the wall which said, "Do not drink it. There is poison in the cup."

As they were going away the old woman tied a bag of gram to the back of the horse on which the Princess was riding and she made a hole in the bag so that the grain fell on the road as they went on. When the nine sons of the old woman, who were Thags, came back, their mother told them and they went in pursuit of the Mahâjan and the Princess. The Princess knew that they were being followed; so she kept on the watch, and when they came to a narrow place in the road, as they came up she killed eight of them with her sword. She was going to kill the ninth, but the Mahâjan asked her to spare his life. "I will do as you ask," she said," but you will live to repent it."

They rode on: but the one remaining Thag followed them and put up in the same inn. The Princess feared danger and kept on the watch. When he woke in the night, the Mahâjan saw the Thag and challenged him to play at dice. They played for some time, and then the Thag asked his companion for a drink of water. As the Mahâjan was stooping over the well, the Thag pushed him in. Then he went and stood over the Princess with his drawn sword. "My time is come for taking my revenge," he said. "What is the good of killing me?" she asked. "Let me be your wife and servant." So they rode off together and they had not gone far when the Princess from behind cut him down with her sword. Then she went back to the inn and fastening the horse ropes together she pulled the Mahâjan out of the well. "I think you and I have seen enough of the world now," said she. So they went home, were married, and lived happily for many years.

[Told by Sukhdeo, Gaur Brâhman, of Ramaipatti, Mirzapur.]

---

* *Kali* means a fruit, or a pipe bowl.

5. **The Virtue of Raja Rupa Angad.**—Of all the Rajas of the world the most virtuous was Raja Rupa Angad. One day a Vimána, or magic chariot of the gods, came down into his garden, and after collecting flowers went back to heaven again. The Vimána distributed the flowers among all the fairies of the court of Raja Indra and came down again next day and began to collect flowers. But the gardener of Raja Rupa Angad was displeased at this, and lighted a fire so that the smoke touched the heavenly chariot, and when the fairies with their flowers tried to ascend to heaven, it could not rise because it was defiled.

Then the fairies who came with it went to the Raja and complained that they used daily to come to his garden to collect flowers, but that now their chariot would not move. The Raja asked the fairies if they could explain why their chariot did not move as usual. They answered that they believed it was because his gardeners had lighted a fire and defiled it with the smoke. The Raja asked how it could be made to move. The fairies said: "If any man in your Majesty's city has kept the fast of the Eleventh regularly month by month he can make our chariot move." The Raja had search made throughout the city, but none could be found who had kept the fast save one Dhobi. The Dhobi was brought before the Raja, who asked him how he came to keep the fast. The Dhobi replied: "On that day I had a quarrel with my wife and therefore I abstained from food."

Then the Raja took the Dhobi to the fairies and said that this was a man who had fasted on the eleventh day. The fairies told the Dhobi to bathe and then to touch the chariot: when he did so the chariot moved and ascended to heaven. The Raja was astounded to witness the virtue of the eleventh day fast. So he made proclamation throughout the kingdom that all his subjects on pain of death were to keep the fast. All his subjects then obeyed his order, and when their lives were ended they were caught up to heaven in a Vimána; but the end was that Hell the pit of worms (kíragar) was empty. Then Raja Indra, the Lord of Heaven, was sore afraid lest Raja Rupa Angad through the virtue of the piety should take possession of his kingdom; so he sent down a fairy from heaven to divert him from his works of piety. The fairy came down to earth and seated herself in a swing in the jungle where the Raja used to go a hunting every day. One day the Raja saw her and fell in love with her. He went up to her and asked her whose daughter she was and why she had come into the jungle. She replied: "I know not who my parents are, and I live alone in this jungle, but if any one would protect me I would live with him." The Raja said: "Will you come with me, if I take you with me?"

So the fairy went with the Raja, and then she said to him: "On one condition only will I live with you, and that is, you must either cut off your son's head, or give up fasting on the eleventh day." The Raja agreed to her conditions and the fairy went home with him. When they arrived near the Raja's palace, the Raja happened to crush a lizard under his feet on the road, and the lizard was at once turned into a beautiful maiden. The fairy asked her: "For what sin were you turned into a lizard?" The maiden answered: "In my former life I had seven co-wives, and I was most beloved by my husband. Sometime after my husband insulted me and I poisoned him. For this sin I was born in this life as a lizard. As Raja Rupa Angad is the most pious of mankind, his touch has restored me to my human shape again."

When she heard this the fairy was still more desirous of turning him from the path of virtue. So she went with him to his palace, and he said to his elder Rani:

"I have brought home a very beautiful fairy. She will live with me only on condition that you give her the head of our son, or give up the eleventh day fast."

The Rani replied:

"Take the head of our son if you will and put an end to your race, but I will not give up the eleventh day fast."

The Raja then called his son and said:

"You must either give your head, or surrender the eleventh day fast." The boy replied:

"Father, give my head to the fairy. Do not give up fasting on the eleventh day. If you maintain your virtue (*dharma*) you will have sons and daughters, but if you lose your virtue you can never recover it again."

The Raja then told the Rani to plaster a sacred square (*chauka*) on the ground and made his son to stand within it. With his own hand he cut off the head of his son by a single stroke of his sword. The Rani received the head of her son in her garment. When this was done, the fairy consented to live with the Raja, but she said:

"I can never truly love you until you eat the flesh of your son." So the Raja had some of the flesh prepared and as he was about to taste it, Bhagwán appeared from heaven and seizing his hand said: "My son, you have done well, ask for any boon you desire." Then the Raja said:

"Restore my son to life and maintain my virtue."

Then his son stood at once before the Raja, and Bhagwan disappeared. The fairy was put to shame and returned to the king of the gods without effecting her purpose.

[A folk-tale told by Akbar Shah, Mánjhi, of Manbasa, Dudhi, Mirzapur.]

[We have here again as in others of these tales, traditions of cannibalism among the Mánjhis.]

MISCELLANEA.

6. Folklore of the Cuckoo.—In the neighbourhood of Saharanpur the cuckoo is often called Jat. Thereby hangs a tale. There was once a Jat who was cursed with an extravagant, ill-conducted wife. He used to keep a lot of rice seed in the granary inside his house. One day his wife wanted money for some purpose and going to the granary took out and sold some of the seed grain. She filled up the deficiency with husks, and by degrees when she found that she was not detected she appropriated all the rice which was in the granary. One day when the sowing time came the Jat went to get his seed grain, but when he found it all gone and that he was ruined through the misconduct of his wife he went mad and used to go about saying : *Dekhoji, Dekhoji*—"Look what has befallen me!" The cuckoo is the descendant of that Jat and his note says *Dekhoji, Dekhoji* to this day.—*W. Crooke.*

---

7. Proverbs.

Banyán kai sakhrdj, rajwá kai hin,
Baidá kai pút biddh na chink,
Bhatwá kai chup chup, beswá kai mail,
Kahain Ghágh panchá ghar gail.

A Banya's son a prodigal, and a king's son a miser, and a physician's son unable to diagnose diseases. A genealogist's (Bhat's son) a mute, and a prostitute's offspring dirty. Ghâgh says that if these five be so as has been said they shall ruin their houses.

Mud chám sé chám katdwai, bhuin sakaré mén sowai ;

Kahain Ghágh tinón bhakud, urhari jáya au róat.

Those who cause their skin to be pinched by dry skin (wear tight shoes), and those who sleep in a narrow space, and those who lament the wife who has eloped, says Ghâgb, are fools.—*Pandit Rám Gharib Chaube.*

---

8. Sanscrit Authorities on the Smearing of Trees.—The *Asiatic Quarterly Review* has had much about the smearing of trees. Allow me to call your attention to a passage in the Brihat Samhita of Varaha Mihira. I quote from Kern's translation, Chapter LV., 17, 18 :

"To promote the growth of the fruits and blossoms of trees, creepers, shrubs and plants, at all times sprinkle them with a mixture of two *adhakas* of dung from sheep and goats in the form of powder, with one *adhaka* of sesamum seeds, one *prastha* of flour, one *drona* of water and one *tula* of cow's flesh, the whole to be infused during a week."

Chapter LV., 16, is to the same effect—

"In case a tree loses its power of bearing fruit, a sprinkling with a refrigerated decoction of milk, mixed with Dolichos, peas, beans, sesamum, and barley, will be conducive to a revival of the growth of fruits and blossoms."

Trees are also to be smeared when being transplanted, "all over the stem down to the root with ghee, root of Andropogon, oil-wax, worm-seed, milk and cow-dung."

The word translated "oil-wax" might mean "honey," I think.

I draw no conclusions.

There are also directions for the medication of seeds. You remember Virgil's :

Semina vidi equidem multos medicare serentes,
Et nitro prius et nigrá perfundere amurcá,
Grandior ut fetus siliquis fallacibus esset.

Probably the passage furnishes no explanation (or not the real explanation) of recent phenomena, but there is no harm in putting it before the public.—*Charles Tawney in the Asiatic Quarterly.*

---

9. The mark of a Snake on the Feet.—It is considered most lucky for a man to have the mark of a snake on the right foot and for a woman on the left. All the incarnations of the gods, male and female, have such marks.—*M. Lakshmana Parsáda.*

---

10. A charm to make a Mango tree fruitful.—Write this charm on a piece of paper with the juice of the mango fruit and mango leaves and tie it to the tree and then the tree will bear abundant fruits next year :—

88	95	2	8
7	3	93	91
94	96	9	1
4	6	90	91

—*M. Lakshmana Prasáda.*

---

11. A charm to make a Husband subservient to his Wife's will.—If any woman write this charm on bread and feed a black dog with it, her husband will become subservient to her will :—

40	40	2	8
7	3	37	7
39	34	9	1
4	6	35	38

—*Pandit Rám Gharib Chaubé.*

12. **Pesh az marg wawaila : a proverb.**—There is a well-known proverb—*Pesh az marg wawaila*, which means, "crying before you are hurt". It is said that Akbar was once offended with the Brahmans of Agra and ordered them to go and dig a number of graves. They were afraid to disobey the order and went to Birbal, who advised them to execute the order. They obeyed and dug a number of graves. Akbar was passing by and seeing the graves asked what they meant. The Brahmans answered—" Sire ! These graves are intended for the numberless Muhammadans who will die in consequence of the order." The Emperor laughed and said : "*Pesh az marg wawaila.*"—*M. Ahmad Ali Khan.*

13. **The black Partridge.**—Villagers explain why the partridge is black as follows : Damayanti was one of the sacred damsels called *Panchkanya* because there were five of them, and from the tips of her fingers dripped nectar. Once in her wanderings she roasted a bird for food and when she touched it with her fingers it came to life and flew away. Hence, as it was half roasted its kind has been black ever since. When the patridge calls in the morning it sings—*Khuda teri marsi*—" Lord it was thy will that we came to life after being roasted."—*Pandit Rám Ghairb Chaubé.*

14. **Camphor**—Camphor which is very volatile is said to fly away. People say that if a clove be kept with it, it loses its power of flight.—*Pandit Ram Lal Dube.*

15. **Beale's Oriental Biographical Dictionary.**—It may be a service to some readers to call attention to the review of this work as recently edited by Mr. H. G. Keene in the October number of the "Indian Antiquary." The writer shows by numerous examples that the book, as now reprinted, swarms with inaccuracies and omits numerous facts and dates of importance.—*W. Crooke.*

16. **The Origin of Music.**—There is, I think, an Indian folklore parallel to the following. Can any one give it ?—*W. Crooke.*

The Chinese have a very pretty legend telling how music was reduced to system. The following version of it is given by Mary E. Simms in an article on *Music :*—The legend tells us that Lyng-Lun wandered deep in thought, to the land of Lijoimg, where the bamboos grow. He took one, cut a piece of it between two of the knots, and having pushed out the pith, blew into the hollow, whereby he produced a beautiful sound, like the sound of his own voice. At this moment, the river Hoang-ho, which ran boiling along a few paces off, roared with its waves, and the noise it made was also in unison with the sound of Lyng-Lun's beautiful voice and the sound of the bamboo. 'Behold then,' cried Lyng-Lun, 'the fundamental sound of nature!' And as he was musing on his wonderful coincidence, the magic bird Foung-hoang and his mate came flying along. They perched on a tree and began to sing. Imagine the delight of our musician, when he found that their song was also in unison with the sound of the river, the bamboo and his own voice. Then all the winds were hushed, and all the birds of the air were silent, as they listened to the song of the magic bird and his mate. As they sang, Lyng-Lun, who had found his opportunity and like a wise man meant to use it, kept cutting bamboos and tuning them to the notes of the birds, six to the notes of the male, and six to the notes of the female. When they had finished singing, Lyng-Lun bad twelve bamboos, cut and tuned, which he bound together and took to the king, and they gave forth the twelve notes of our modern chromatic scale. The odd notes F, G, A, B, C *sharp*, D *sharp*, were the male notes, and the even notes F *sharp*, G *sharp*, A *sharp*, C, D, E were the female, and with that partiality for the masculine sex which is not peculiar to the Chinese, they pronounced the six odd or male tones perfect and called them ' Yang,' and the six even or female tones they pronounced imperfect, and called them "Yu." The writer thinks that, with an origin so poetic, we might certainly have expected music to develop into something which would justify its being called in China, as with us, "the divine Art," but, according to her account, a Chinese orchestra is the most atrocious, ear-splitting performance one could possibly listen to. Still, as she remarks, there are two sides to every question, and the Chinese and Japanese trained musicians listen to the efforts of Western artists with the tolerance born of a sense of lofty superiority. The Gourd, or ching, is said by the writer to be the most pleasing of Chinese instruments, and she tells us, apparently without the slightest attempt at humour, that it seems to be something akin to the Scotch bagpipes." Another instrument, the On, is a very poetic conception. It is described as in the form of a crouching tiger, with twenty-seven teeth on its back, like the teeth of a saw, and is played by scraping these with a stick!

17. **An incantation to propitiate Dhartí Mátá for one's own protection.**—

Om namo
Dhartí mátá, dhartí pitá, dhartí dhari na dhír.
Bájai singhí, bájai turturi, áyá Gorakh Náth min ká put.
Uská kard chhará lohe ka.
Hamárí pith pichhé jatí Hanumant khard.

"I salute a mother Earth. The earth is the mother The earth is the father. The earth is never stationary When Gorakh Náth, the son of the Fish (which fish is in its turn the issue of the earth) comes, the *singhi* or horn and the *turuhi* (another musical instrument of the same kind) are blown. Gorakh Náth's bracelet and stick are of Iron. Behind my back is standing the pious monkey-god Hanuman."

Repeat this incantation seven times and blow on the person, you may be sure they are safe for the day.—*Pandit Rám Gharib Chaubé.*

North Indian Notes and Queries:

A MONTHLY PERIODICAL.

VOL. V.]   MAY, 1895.   [No. 2.

Every communication must be accompanied by the writer's name and address, not necessarily for insertion, but as a guarantee of good faith. Every quotation from a book must be accompanied by its full title, publisher's and author's names, place and date of publication, volume and page.

Contributors are requested to write on ONE SIDE the page only. If several contributions be sent at a time, they should be sent each on a separate sheet.

The Conductor cannot undertake to return, or be responsible for, any MSS. not accepted.

All orders must be accompanied by cash. If not so accompanied, they will either not be attended to, or will be complied with per value-payable post.

Contributions should be addressed direct to W. CROOKE, ESQ., C.S., SAHARANPUR, N.-W. P., INDIA.

CONTENTS OF THIS NUMBER.
(The references are to the Notes.)

Popular Religion ... ... 19 to 24	Folktales ... ... 30 to 33
Anthropology ... ... 25 ,, 29	Miscellanea ... ... 34 ,, 36

POPULAR RELIGION.

18. The Life of Sur Das.—As Kali Dás is popularly styled the Homer of India, so Sur Dás is regarded as the prince of Hindi poets. He had such a command of Hindi, that he could put excellent ideas in the simplest words, and also, if he chose, in the most difficult language which even the greatest Pandit would be hard put too to understand. Of the charms of the poetry of Sur Dás—a man before Akbar the Great observed :—

 Uttam pad kabi Gang kó,

 Kabitá kó bal Bir ;

 Keshav arth Ganbhír hó Súr tin Gun dhír.

"The poet Gang's verses display choice language : those of Bír have strength, and those of Keshava have grave meanings, but the verses of Sur have all the three qualities combined together."

Sur Dás was a Brahman by caste. His father's name was Bábá Rám Dás. Rám Dás was a distinguished musician. He could compose songs. He chiefly lived in Mathurá, Agrá and Delhi. Surdas was born about the year 1540 (Vikram). His father took pains to teach him music, Persian and his own language. His father died when Sur was quite young. He became a little wayword on that account. He began to compose verses. By this time he collected a number of pupils about him. Sur Dás adopted *Sur Swámi* as his *nom-de-plume*. He composed by this time a poem embodying the love story of Nala and Damyanti. He was then in the prime of his youth. He lived at this time at a distance of 18 miles from Agrá. The name of the place was Gaughát. After this he became a disciple of Vallabha Swámi, and then he changed his *nom-de-plume* into Sur Dás. He adopted *nommes-de-plume*, namely : (1) Sur ; (2) Sur Dás ; (3) Suraj Dás ; (4) Sur Shyám.

When he became a disciple of Vallabha Swámi, he composed the following song :—

 "*Chahai ri chali charan sarówar jahan nahin prém biyóg.*

 Jahán bhram nisá hót nahin kabhún so ságar sukh jóg.

Sanak se hans min shiv muni jan nakh ravi prabhá prakásh.

Praphulit kamal nimekhan sasi dar gunjat nigam subds.

Jahi sar subhag mukti muktáphal sukrit bimal jal pije.

So sar chhávi kubudhi bihangam ihán kahá raki hije.

Jahán sri sahasra sabit nit krivat sobhit Suraj Das ;

Awan suhái bikhai ras chhilar wá samudra ki ás."

"O! Chakwa (Brahmini duck), let us go to the tank of the holy feet (Rámá's) where there is no separation of love and where the darkness of illusion does not ever prevail. That tank is a fit place to enjoy ourselves. There, Sanak (the companions of Vishnu), are swans, Shiv the fish and ascetics are also fishes, and the brilliancy of nails are the sunshine. There lotuses of the moments are blooming, fear is the moon and the four Vedas are beetles, which are always resounding happily. The tank where pretty pearls of salvation are found and where we drink the pure water of fame leaves the foolish bird, and what shall he do by living here? I have hopes in that tank wherein plays Vishnu with Lakshmi, and which is free from sensuality."

Thenceforward his poetical skill increased, and he versified the great Sanskrit work "Sri Mad Bhágwat."

Sur Dás's spiritual guide used to call him "Ságar," and he therefore entitled his whole work Sur Ságar. When Sur Dás had become old and used to live at Mathura his fame reached the ears of Akbar the Great. Akbar summoned him into his presence and ordered him to sing. Whereupon Sur began—

"Man re karan Mádho se priti," i.e., O! my heart, make friends with Krishn." Hearing this the courtiers told Sur Dás not to sing this song and sing another in praise of the Emperor. Then Sur Dás went on—

"Náhin na rahyó man men thaur.

Nand nandan achhat kaise ániye ur aur.

Chalat chitrat diwas jágat supan sówat ráti;

Hriday ten wah madan múrti chhinn na it ut játi.

Kahat kathá anik udho lóg bhóg dikhái ;

Kahá karón chit prem puran ghat na sindhu samái.

Shyám gát saroj dnan lalit gati mirdu hás.

Sur aise daras káran marat lochan khás."

"I have no room in my heart. How can I bring other into my heart when Nandá's son (Krishn) is there. That charming figure does not go away from the heart for a moment even when I am walking, seeing, walking in the day or sleeping at night. Many people tempt me to relate stories of various kinds but O! Udhó, what can I do? my heart's pitcher is quite full. It cannot contain the ocean. My eyes are anxiously desirous to see that black-complexioned, lotus-faced happy demeanoured and charmingly laughing figure." Sur Dás died about the year 1620 (Vikram) at Mathurá.

Just before his death Sur composed the following " doha " :—

" Man samudra bhayo sur kó, sip bhai chak:h lál

Hari muktahal parat ahin mundi gaye tat kál.'

" The heart of Sur Dás became the sea and his eyes became oyster shells. No sooner the heart of Krishna's name got into it than was it shut up."—Pandit Rám Gharib Chaubé.

19. N.-W. P.—Religious Songs.—

1. Jánakí Jéwan ki bali jai hon.

2. Chit Kahai Rám Siya pad parihari ab na kahún chali jai hón.

3. Upaji ur pratíti sapanehun sukh prabhu pad bimukh na pai hon.

4. Man samét yá tan ké básinayikai sikháwai dai hon.

5. Srawanani aur kathá nahin suni hon rasaná aur na gai hon.

6. Rohi hon nain bilokat aurahin sis is hí hai kn

7. Nátó nek náth so kari sab nátó nek bahai kn

8. Yah chhar bhár tahi Tulasi jag jákó dás kahn hon.

(1) I sacrifice myself, on the cause of the life of Jánakí (Ráma).

(2) My mind says that leaving the feet of Rám and Sítá, now I will not go elsewhere.

(3) My heart has a firm belief that I will have no rest even in dreaming if I am opposed to the feet of my Lord.

(4) To my mind, as well as to all the organs of my body, I will give this instruction.

(5) That I will hear no other tradition with my ears. I will sing no other song with my tongue.

(6) I will prevent my eyes from seeing any others, and I will bow my head only before my Lord.

(7) With love and affection to my Lord I will drown all other love and affection.

(8) All these responsibilities will be on him, in this world, O! Tulsi, whose slave I will be called.

Samman wah phal kawan hai.

Kánché adhik mitháye.

Adh pak par khatras lagai.

Páké bikh hoi jáye.

What is that fruit, O! Samman, which is sweetest when unripe. It has a sour taste when half ripe, and it becomes poisonous when ripe?

Answer.—A Human being.—*Bhan Pratap Tewari.*

---

20. **Further Notes on the Chowk Chanda, and the Panchmi Vrata.**—(By Mr. Sarat Chandra Mitra, M.A., B.L., Pleader, Judge's Court, Chapra, Behár.)

In a previous paper entitled "*On Vestiges of Moon-Worship in Behár and Bengal*," * I have given an account of the *Chowk Chándá* day of Behár, which corresponds to the *Nashta Chandra* day of Bengal and falls on the fourth day of the light half of the moon in the month of Bhadon (August-September). In that paper, I have tried to shew that the ceremonies observed on this occasion are mere survivals of moon-worship in the two provinces of Bengal and Behár. The legend which I have narrated therein as having given rise to the superstition of not looking at the moon on the *Chowk Chándá* and the *Nashta*

* *Vide* the *Journal of the Anthropological Society of Bombay*, Vol. II., pp. 597-601.

Chandra day, is slightly incorrect. The correct version thereof is given below, as also an account of some additional ceremonies observed by the Hindus of Behár, especially of Sáran, on this occasion.

The correct version of the legend, whereon the superstition connected with the *Chowk Chanda* day in Behár is based, is given in the हरपंचाशत्तम अध्याय or Chapter LVII. of the प्रेमसागर (*Prem Ságara*) which gives an account of the life and exploits of Krishna (श्रीकृष्णजी.)

The Chapter opens thus:—

श्रीशुकदेवजी बोले कि महाराज ! सत्राजितने पहले तो श्रीकृष्णचन्द्र की ऊपर चोरि लगाई, पीछे भूल समझा शर्मित हो उसने अपनि कन्या सत्यभामा हरि की ब्याही. यह सुनि राजा परीक्षितने श्री शुकदेवजी से पूछा कि कृपानिधान !

सत्राजित कौन था, मणि उसने कहां पाई? फीर कैसे हरि की चोरि लगाई। फिर कौन्कर झूठ समझ कन्या ब्याही। यह तुम मुझे सुभाके कहो। श्रीशुकदेवजी बोले कि महाराज ! सुनिये मैं सब समझाकर कहता हूं। * * * + *.

The Chapter thus concludes:

इतनी कथा सुन राजा परीक्षितने श्री शुकदेवजीसे पूछा कि कृपानिधान श्रीकृष्णजी की बहन कौन थी और की कृपाकर कहो। शुकदेवजी बोले राजा।

चांद पीछे की देखिबी, मीडम भादौ मास। तातें सम्यो चलंक बसी पति मन मयी उदास॥

चीर सुनी

जी भादौं कि चौथ की, चांद निहारै कोय। वह प्रसंग सवनागि सुने, तापि कलंक न होय। इति।*

The above may be thus translated:

Sri Sukadevají said: O great king! Satrájit charged Sri Krishnachanda first with the theft of a jewel; and subsequently finding his accusation to be false, he was ashamed, and gave his daughter Sátyabhámá in marriage to Hari. Rájá Parikshit asked Sri Sukadevají, "O abode of mercy! who was Satrájit, where did he get the jewel, and how did he accuse Hari of theft, and afterwards finding the accusation false, in what manner did he give his daughter in marriage? Explain the circumstances to me." Sri Sukadevají answered: "O great king! be pleased to listen, and I will explain all the circumstances." (Then Sukadeva narrates the story, which may be thus briefly stated :

Satrájit, of the family of Jadu, having performed a very difficult religious penance in honor of the Sun-god, obtained from the latter a jewel, named Syamantaka. One day Satrájit, having put on the jewel, went to the court of the Vadavas, who greatly admired the brilliancy of the jewel, and thought the Sun-god was coming to see Sri Krishnaji. But Krishna explained that it was Satrájit with the jewel on his arm, and not the Sun-god, that was coming. After this, Satrájit frequently used to come to the Yadava Court with the jewel on his neck. One day, the Yadvas told Krishna to take the jewel from Satrájit and give the same to king Ugrasena, as it was fit only for a king. Krishna requested Satrájit to give the jewel to Ugrasena. Having heard this proposal, Satrájit went to his brother Prasena and informed him of Krishna's request. At this Prasena was angry and, snatching the jewel, put it round his own neck; and, arming himself and mounting a horse, went a-hunting. While in pursuit of a deer, he came to a large cave wherefrom a lion came forth and killed Prasena, his horse, and the deer, and carried off the jewel into the cave. A bear named Jámbúbána, seeing the brilliancy of the jewel, killed the lion, carried off the jewel, and went with it to his wife, who gave it to her daughter. The child used to play with it.

In the meantime, the followers of Prasena, not having found him in the forest, came and informed Satrájit that they had not been able to trace the whereabouts of Prasena. On hearing this Satrájit began to suspect that Krishna might have killed his brother for the sake of the jewel and carried it off. He also informed his wife of his suspicion about Krishna's complicity in the theft. She, on the other hand, told his female companions and servants about her husband's suspicions about Krishna. Now the matter, having got noised abroad, reached the ears of the female members of Krishna's family, who, thereupon, began to blame the latter and speak ill of him. Hearing this, Krishna went to the Yádava Court and told Ugrasena, Vásudeva and Balarám that he had been accused of killing Prasena and carrying off the jewel Syamantaka ; and craved their permission to go and search for Prasena and the jewel in order that the disgrace might be effaced.

Then Krishna, with the companions of Prasena and some of the Yádavas, went in search of them. When Krishna, in the course of his quest of the lost jewel, came near the cave, he went inside it, and, having found the jewel therein, began to wrestle with Jámbúvána ; coming to know that the person wrestling with him was no other than the lord Krishna, he expressed to the latter his wish to give him his (Jámbúvána's) daughter Jámbúvatí in marriage. Krishna granted permission. Then Jámbúvána, having performed the ceremonies prescribed by the Vedas, gave his daughter in marriage to Krishna and gave her the jewel Syamantaka as a part of her dowry. Krishna, having returned to the court of the Yádavas, sent for Satrájit and, when he came, informed him that he had falsely accused him of the theft of the jewel, and then made it over to him. Being very much ashamed at having falsely accused Krishna, and being desirous of atoning for the sin incurred thereby, Satrájit expressed his wish to give the jewel his daughter Satyabhámá, to Krishna. Then Satyabhámá was married to Krishna with all the necessary ceremonies.

Raja Paríkshit interrupted Sri Sukadevaji in this part of the story, and enquired : "O abode of compassion ! *kindly explain, why the suspicion and calumny of the theft were fastened upon Sri Krishnaji."* Sukadevaji replied : "Raja *Mohan (Krishna) had seen the moon, when it was four days old in the month of Bhádon ; hence the infamy of theft got fastened to the name of Krishna, who was very much frightened and dejected on account thereof. And, further, listen to me that, should anybody see the moon on the fourth day of the light half of Bhádin, the infamy will be wiped away on hearing this discourse.*"

Those, who are rendered sinful by looking at the moon on the *Chowk Chauda* day, are absolved from the sin by throwing ढेला or brickbats on to the thatches of other people, and, thereby, getting abused in return ; or by hearing the discourse contained in the fifty-seventh chapter of the *Prem Ságara.*

On the day next to the *Chowk Chauda, i. e.,* or the fifth day of the light half of the moon in the month of Bhádón (August-September) falls the पंचमी ब्रत (Panchami Vrata). Those who perform this *Vrata* have to remain fasting the whole of the day. In the evening they have to cleanse their teeth with दातन (or sticks for cleansing the teeth with) made of the branches of a shrub called पिडपिडी. It is a plant which has ovate leaves and grows in profusion in waste places during the rains. After cleansing the teeth, the performers of the *Vrata* have to break their fast by taking मबेरी का दही or tyre (curdled milk) made of buffalo's milk ; and तिलाकचात or boiled coarse rice, तिला being a kind of coarse rice of a red color.

The Hindus of all classes and shades of belief, believe that women become impure during the menstrual period. Hence the Hindu Shastras prohibit the contact of men with women during this period. Those persons, however, who are rendered impure by contact with women during this period, are absolved from the sin and the consequent impurity by the performance of the पंचगी ब्रत. I do not know whether this ब्रत is performed in other places than the Sáran district.—*Journal Anthropological Society of Bombay.*

---

21. **On Vestiges of Moon-Worship in Behar and Bengal. By Sorat Chandra Mitra, M.A., B.L.**—Any one who has resided in Behár for a length of time must be aware of the fact that there is a holy day observed in this part of the country, which goes by the name of the *chowk chanda* Day. This day, as its name indicates, falls on the *Chowk* (*Chaturthi*) of the *Chanda*, that is to say, on the fourth day of the waxing period of the moon in the month of Bhadra, which usually coincides with the 19th of that month. In Bengal the holy day corresponding to the *Chowk Chanda* of Behár is known as the *Nashta Chandra Day*. Both in Bengal and Behár it is considered very inauspicious to look at the moon on that day. In Bengal also the day falls on the fourth day of the bright period during the month of Bhadra. The popular belief in Bengal and Behár is that any person who catches "glimpses of the moon" on that day will have his name branded with some infamy. This belief rests on the following tradition. The serpent Takshak stole the *kundalas* or the earrings of king Aditi. The latter on discovering the theft and being unable to find out the real culprit, charged Krishna with the theft who, once before had been "previously convicted" of stealing the *navanita*, or the cream from the dairies of the milk-maids of Gokula or Brindabun. Krishna being very much mortified at thus being falsely charged with guilt, set about to find out the thief and ultimately traced the earrings to Takshak's house, from whom he recovered them and restored them to their rightful owner. Thus Krishna proved his innocence before King Aditi. It was in the month of Bhadra, at or about the 4th day of the waxing period of the moon, that this stain or infamy got fastened to Krishna's name, and hence, from time immemorial, in Hindudom throughout Bengal and Behár, that particular day and the moon therein have come to be invested with peculiar associations of sinfulness.

In Behár people keep fasting the whole of that day, and in the evening break their fast by taking rice and *dahi* or curds. During the day, the Goddess Moon is worshipped by a Brahmin priest and flowers and sweets are offered to the deity. On that day it is considered sinful to look at the moon, as it is supposed to bring some calumny on the seer. Should anyone happen to look at the moon on that day, it is supposed that some infamy will surely stain the fair escutcheon of his name. Such is the superstition of the ignorant people that getting abused by other people is supposed to be the only remedy for obviating the sin which accrues to the seer of the moon on that day. With a view to this, the seer takes care to throw stones on to the thatches of the tiled houses of other people. The is known as ढेला फेंकना or pelting with stones. People whose houses are thus pelted at, abuse the pelters and this abuse is supposed to efface the sin of those persons who happen accidentally to look at the moon. Many are the quarrels which take place on this occasion on account of the pelting and the consequent abuse in return, and some of these affrays often result in bloodshed and occasionally in murder. A notable instance of this is the murder which took place on the last *Chowk Chanda Day*, in the village of Mirzapura, a few miles to the north of the Santa Station of the Bengal and North-Western Railway, and which was tried during the last Criminal Sessions of this district, resulting in a galloping acquittal of all the accused. Much virtue is ascribed to abuse in this district of Behár. It is supposed to bring good luck in some cases. On occasion of marriages, people who accompany the बरात or the marriage procession to the bride's house, are often vilely abused by the women folk of the bride's family, in the belief that it will lead on to the good fortune of the newly-married couple. In the same way, on the occasion of the *Jamadwitiya Day* in Behár, corresponding to the *Bhratridwitiya Day* in Bengal, which falls on the 2nd day of the bright period of the moon next to that during which the Dussera festival takes place, brothers are abused by sisters to their heart's content and this is done under the impression that it will prolong the lives of the brothers and bring good luck to them. There is also another curious custom observed in Behár on the occasion of the *Chowk Chanda Day*. I have frequently observed in this town of Chupra that on that day the students of the local *Maktabs*, or indigenous vernacular schools, form companies and visit fellow-students' houses and parade the streets, singing verses (which I have not been able to take down) and making a peculiar noise by striking together two pieces of brightly-coloured turned wooden rods, very much in the fashion of a pair of Spanish castanets. When they visit each other's houses in companies, the boys' parents usually present them with a few annas by way of fees. I have not been able to trace out the way by which this students' demonstration came to take place at or about the same time as the worship of the moon on the *Chowk Chanda Day*. Some say that the annual examinations of the local *Maktabs* are finished about the time of the *Chowk Chanda*, and hence students parade the streets on that day. It is impossible to say which is the right explanation of the coincidence of this custom with the *Chowk Chanda Day*.

Similarly on the *Nastachandra Day* in Bengal, which falls on the 4th day of the waxing period of the moon in the month of *Bhadra*, the Bengali folk, especially the womankind and the illiterate classes, take care not to go out of their respective rooms, lest their eyes should fall on the Goddess Moon, which is supposed to be stained with some infamy on that day, for should they catch glimpses of her they are sure to have their name stained with calumny. Even should people have occasion to go out of their rooms, they do so averting their eyes from that quarter of the heavens in which the moon may be at that particular time. In Bengal no ceremonies are observed and no *pujah* is offered to the Goddess Moon, though some rituals have been provided for remedying the evil consequences of looking on the moon on the नष्टचन्द्र Day. Perhaps in the olden times she might have been worshipped there, but in Calcutta at the present day no such worship takes place. There is one of the well-established laws of anthropological science, *viz.*, that in some cases of religious observances, the actual ceremonies constituting the worship of a particular deity may fall into disuse, or may be discontinued, leaving as survivals only the attendant superstitions. It may be that, according to the working of this law, the actual ceremonies for worshipping the moon may have fallen into desuetude and that the accompanying superstitions regarding *Nashta Chandra* may have survived as vestiges of moon-worship in Bengal. This prohibition to look on the परिताषिवाचन्द्रम् is based on the following text of the Shastras :—

*पञ्चानन गते भानौ पञ्चयीदमयीरपि ।
षतुर्थं सुदितसप्तचन्द्रौ नैक्षितव्य; बदाचन ।

Then the Shastrakar or the framer of the Shastras goes on to provide the following formula, which is to be repeated to obviate the sin of looking at the नष्टचन्द्र, should any one happen to do so. Any person who does so must repeat the following *mantra* with his face turned either to the east or the north and then quaff off a draught of water. The mantra is as follows :—

---

* The correct text appears to have been as follows :—
पञ्चानन गते भानौ पञ्चयीदमयीरपि ।
षतुर्थं सुदितसप्तचन्द्रौ नैक्षितम्य: बदाचन ॥
† सब्धिदेवस्य दनव ;

Editor, J. of the Anthrop. Soc.]

सिंह: प्रसेनमवधीत सिंहो जाम्बवता हत: ।
सुकुमारक मरोदीतवमश्यैरेव स्यमनक: ॥

Then it is laid down that the seer should, according to custom, hear स्यमन्तकोपाख्यान or the story of Syamantak.

In Bengal many outrageously practical jokes are played upon each other on the *Nashta Chandra Day* especially in the villages in the interior these often take the shape of stealing cocoanuts or any other fruit from the neighbour's garden without the latter's knowing it.

Besides the above-mentioned instances of moon-worship in Behár and Bengal, the moon is also worshipped by symbolism in Bengal. It almost every ceremony performed amongst the Hindus of Bengal, as I have seen them performed in Calcutta in my own family, as well as elsewhere, the *pujah* is first of all offered to the sun and the moon, along with the other 33 crores of deities. In this *sub-pujah*, no special rites are observed for paying devoirs to the moon but only her name is invoked and certain mantras repeated and offerings symbolically offered.

This worship of the moon was also prevalent among the ancient nations of the world. She was worshipped by the ancient Phœnicians under the form of the Goddess Astarte. The ancient Babylonians also worshipped her and impersonated her in the Goddess Mylitta. Most filthy orgies were performed in the celebration of these rites. The ancient Greeks and Romans, in their mythology, represented Diana to be the moon and at the same time to be the Goddess of thieves. It is, perhaps, owing to this latter function performed by the Goddess Diana or the moon, that stealing has come to be associated with the *Nahsta Chandra Day* in Bengal. Shakespeare, it seems, also accepted this classical tradition and alludes, in his *Henry IV.*, to it. When Sir John Falstaff and his boon companions the young Prince of Wales and others rob the carriers near Gadshill Inn, they call themselves to be " Diana's myrmidons," which the scholiast interprets to men "*thieves.*"

It is impossible to determine at the present moment when moon-worship came into vogue amongst the Hindus. Though in the Rigveda we come across the cult of the sun, the dawn, the elements, the earth and the sky among the ancient Aryans, we do not find any allusion to the worship of the " lesser light "—the moon. If my memory serves me right, I might add here that there are allusions to the worship of the moon in the *Uttarbhaga*, which was composed by Banabhatta's son. In that book the heroine is represented as worshipping the moon in order to gain her lost lord.—*Journal, Anthropological Society, Bombay.*

ANTHROPOLOGY.

22. A Primitive Game.—*Gyán Chausar*, or the "Chess of Knowledge," is a game much played by Hindús, especially those of the Bráhman caste. The name appears to have been given somewhat on the *lucus a 'non lucendo* principle, as *Gyán Chausar* bears absolutely no resemblance to any known form of chess, being in fact a mere game of chance. It is, however, more than this. Like the parable, it might be defined, as an "earthly game with a heavenly meaning." The "Chess of Knowledge" is of an allegorical nature, somewhat after the type of the "Sunday" games, played at home. Hence it is very popular with pious Hindús, as it forms at once a pleasurable amusement, and an instructive lesson on the best means of attaining to heaven. The game is adapted for Hindús of all persuasions, as all three Heavens are marked on the Board :—Brahmlok, or the world of Brahma, for the worshippers of Brahma; Vaikunth, or the Paradise of Vishnu, for the Vaishnavas, or followers of Vishnu; Kailása, or the Paradise of Siva, for the Saivas, or adherents of Siva. A diagram of the Board on which the game is played, is annexed to this article. The squares have been numbered to facilitate the explanation of the game.

The Board—contains 72 houses (ghar) or squares, as we should call them in English. Each square represents some particular sense, quality or region recognised by the Hindú scriptures. Squares Nos. 67, 68 and 69, represent the three Heavens above alluded to.

The Steps.—Certain squares are connected with each other by what are known as steps or ladders. Thus, for instance, square No. 54, representing the quality of truthfulness, connects directly by means of a step, with sq. No. 68, representing Vaikunth, or the Heaven of Vishnu. The fortunate player therefore who makes his way to sq. No. 54, enters Paradise direct, skipping over all the intervening squares between the two numbers.

The Serpents.—These play a very important part in the game. They invariably connect evil qualities or evil states, just as the steps above-mentioned connect good qualities and good states. The difference is that progress along a snake's body is in a downward direction, *i.e.*, from the head to the tail, while progress along "a step" is always in an upward direction. For instance, the leading player may be at sq. No. 59 ("The region of virtue"): he throws four, and lands in a snake's mouth at sq. No. 63 ("villainy"), and immediately has to pursue a downward course along the snake's body to its tail in sq. No. 3 ("anger"). From this he has to begin to work his way all up again, if he would at length enter Paradise.

Method of playing the game.—The game is played by two or more persons. Each player is represented by a cowrie (shell) on the board and nine cowries are used as dice. The game is commenced by the first player placing his cowrie on sq. No. 1 (*Janam ghar*, or the square of Birth). He then throws the nine cowries. According to the numbers of cowries that fall upside down (*chit parti hain*), *i.e.*, with the mouth of the shell upward, so is the number of squares, which the player can move. Thus, if out of the nine cowries five fall *chit*, the player will move his shell on to sq. No. 6 (*Moh*, or Spiritual Ignorance). The second player then throws, and so the game proceeds. Should one of the players land on a square, in which is the foot of a ladder, he proceeds up it to the higher square, where the steps terminate. Similarly, if he lands in a square containing a serpent's mouth, he goes down to the square containing the serpent's tail. Lastly, should any of the players throw more than the requisite number for securing his paradise, he will have to pass by Heaven without entering into it, and if his throw takes him beyond sq. No. 72, he must start all over again from sq. No. 1.

23. Names of the Squares (Ghar):—

No.	Hindi.	English.
1	Janam	Birth.
2	Maya	Delusion.
3	Krodh	Anger.
4	Lobh	Covetousness.
5	Bhai lok	The Earth.
6	Moh	Spiritual Ignorance.
7	...	Pride.
8	Matsar	Envy.
9	Kám	Lust.
10	Tap	Austerity.

11	Gandharb lok	The region of the celestial musicians.	55	Ahankár	Self-conceit.
12	Trasha	Impatience.	56	Akash	The Sky.
13	Antriksh	The Sky.	57	Bábu	The Air.
14			58	Tej	Splendour.
15	Nág lok	The region of snakes.	59	Sat lok	The region of virtue.
16	Dukh	Misery.	60	Subadhi	Good understanding.
17	Daya	Kind-heartedness.	61	Durbadhi	Evil understanding.
18	Harsh	Pleasure.	62	Sukh	Happiness.
19	Agyan	Ignorance.	63	Támas	Villainy.
20	Dán	Charity.	64	Prakrit	Nature.
21	Samán	Equity.	65	Durat	Absorption in evil deeds.
22	Dharm	Piety.	66	Ánand	Joy.
23	Swarg lok	A lower heaven.	67	Sirlok or Kailása	Siva's paradise.
24	Kasang	Evil company.	68	Vaikunth	Vishnu's paradise.
25	Satsang	Good company.	69	Brahmlok	Brahma's paradise.
26	Shok	Anxiety.	70	Satogun	The principle of goodness.
27	Parmárth	The highest virtue.	71	Rajogun	Love of sensual enjoyment.
28	Sudharm	Good actions.	72	Tamogun	Love of violence.
29	Adharm	Evil deeds.			
30	Uttamgun	Good qualities.			
31	Sparsh	Touch.			
32	Mahátap lok	The region of great austerity.			
33	Gan lok	The region of cows.			
34	Sur lok	The region of gods.			
35	Narak	Hell.			
36	Shabd	Sound.			
37	Gyán	Knowledge.			
38	Dhyán	Meditation.			
39	Prán	Life.			
40	Apatti	Trouble.			
41	Yan lok	The human region.			
42	Surya lok	The region of the sun.			
43	Agni lok	The region of fire.			
44	Avidya	Illiterateness.			
45	Suvidya	Good education.			
46	Vivek	Discrimination.			
47	Kuber lok	The region of Kuber, the god of wealth.			
48	Nárad lok	The region of Saint Nárada.			
49	Kailásh	The mountain.			
50	Tap lok	The region of austerity.			
51	Andhkár	Darkness.			
52	Hinsá	Slaughter.			
53	Jap	Telling the beads.			
54	Satya	Truthfulness.			

In concluding the account of this interesting game, it may be as well to offer a few remarks on the methods on which the "Steps" and "Serpents" are arranged. In some cases the principle of cause and effect is easy enough to follow. For instance, nothing could be more consonant with Western religious ideas than that "Truthfulness" (sq. No. 54) should lead to Heaven, sq. No. 68. In other cases, it is obscured by the wide divergence between religious ideals in the East and the West. Pleasure (sq. 18) leads straight to Brahma's paradise. This is Hedonism indeed, and very contrary to our ordinary Western teaching, in which the broad way of pleasure is usually supposed to conduct to a very different place. Or to take the serpents. We can quite see why Self-conceit (sq. 55) should lead to Delusion (sq. 2), or Misery (sq. 16) should lead to Covetousness (sq.4), or from a Hindú's point of view why Slaughter (sq. 52) should lead to Hell (sq. 35), but it is not so clear why Love of Violence (sq. 72) should lead to Darkness (sq. 51) or why keeping Evil company (sq. 24) should necessarily produce Pride (sq. 7).

"Gyán Chausar" has, I am told, been lately introduced into England and, with ordinary dice for cowries and a somewhat revised set of rules, been patented there as a children's game,—*G. R. Dampier, C. S.*

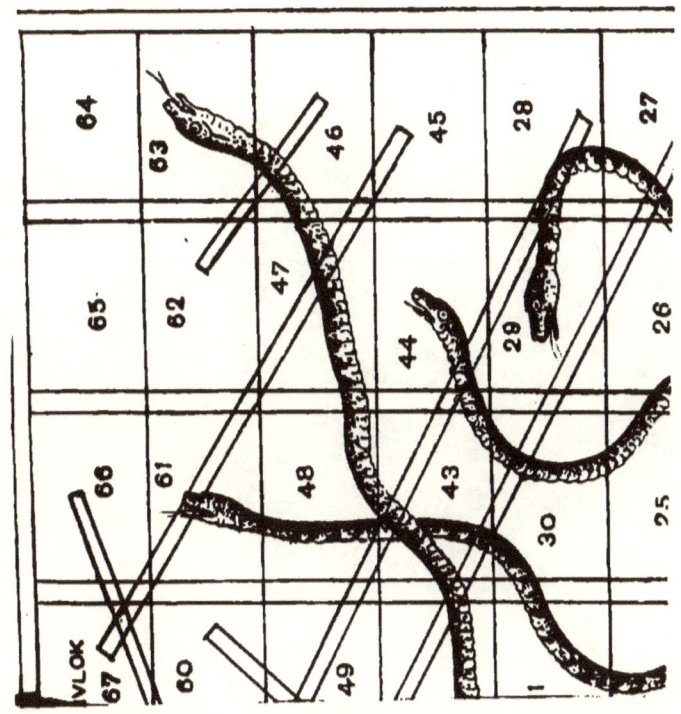

24. **A Cattle Disease Charm.**—I noticed the following charm for cattle disease in village Pemrajpur, near Rurki :—

A rope was stretched across the entrance of the village, from a pípal tree on one side to a pole on the other. From this rope were suspended seven charms. In the middle was a loop of Kusa grass supporting a bundle of seven different sorts of grain, the bundle being called the *sátnáj* (sát anáj). To the right of the loop was a *chapni* or *ghara* top or lid, on the underneath side of which was painted a rude attempt at a star and a number of small hieroglyphics and letters in red and black. To the right of the *chapni* were two small pieces of wood roughly carved into the shape of hammers, and to the extreme right of all a rag. To the left of the loop were three similar pieces of wood as those already described, though differing somewhat in shape. To the left of these again another piece of rag, thus completing the symmetry of the whole charm.

The charm itself is called *Dhálá* (said to be derived from Dhálná) in the sense of causing one thing to pass under another. The Pandit of a neighbouring village informed me that the rags were the loin-cloths of Hanuman and the pieces of wood were his *sontá* or mace. When I asked if I might take the charm, they informed me that I must wait till the rope broke of itself. To cut it down prematurely would be extremely unlucky and would destroy all the good effect the charm might produce.—*G. R. Dampier, C.S.*

25. **Clan Deities of the Badi Nats in the Western Districts, N.-W. P.**—There are some Bádi Nats found about Saharanpur who look more like Panjabis in dress and appearance than their brethren to the east of the Province, who closely assimilate to their Dravidian neighbours.

The clan deity of the branch of the tribe is Kesari Sati, of Bisauli, in the Badaun district. They say that she burnt herself with the corpse of her husband, who was killed by falling from a rope while dancing. Every year the Bádi Nats flock in great numbers to her shrine, where they have planted groves and made wells at considerable expense. They make vows there for male offspring, to cure diseases and gain proficiency n their craft. Those who have only a general request to make, offer *laddu* sweetmeats and some liquor : those who want something important in addition, get her tomb repaired and whitewashed. In extreme cases some offer a *baráh*, or large pot, filled with *halwa*, sufficient to feed some twenty men of the brethren.

In the opinion of the Bádi Nats there is no deity as powerful as Kesari Sati. Few adult members of the tribe fail at least once in their lives to make a pilgrimage to her shrine, and those who fail to perform this duty have no hope of success in life, unless they have received the blessing of Kesari Sati.—*W. Crooke.*

26. **The Taboo against Husband or Wife naming each other.**—No husband or wife names the other for fear of shortening their lives. There are, however, certain occasions when they are forced by their female relations to break the *taboo* by way of a joke. In the western districts of the North-Western Provinces young married women go on the festivals of the Salono and Tij to a tank to worship there. When they have done the worship, some old woman seizes a girl by the nose and threatens to rub it until she mentions her husband's name. Many will stand the pain sooner than submit ; but a young bride sometimes complies, and is laughed at, but does not incur any serious reproach. The reason is that the *taboo* is broken in the immediate presence of the water deities, who are more disposed to lengthen than to shorten the life of the husband of a woman who worships them.

In Gorakhpur, on the day of the Govardhan Pújá, in the month of Kártik, while worshipping the cowdung image of Govardhan, women name each of their male relations, including their husbands, and at each name they fling a thorn at the image. Each name is uttered with some abusive epithet. But the name of the husband is mentioned only in a whisper, without any insulting phrase.—*Pandit Rám Garíb Chaubé.*

[On this *taboo* of names see *Introduction to Popular Religion*, 188. Can anyone give any other instances of similar violations of the *taboo* ?—ED.]

27. **Saharanpur : the Last Sheaf.**—Many enquiries have been made in this neighbourhood in search of examples of the curious rite of the last sheaf of which Mr. Frazer in his *Golden Bough* has given numerous examples. The nearest I can get as yet is that many cultivators at harvest leave the last corner of the standing crop and allow the beggars of the neighbourhood to loot it and carry it off. This is known as Mandla or Mandila.—*W. Crooke.*

28. **Marriage Horoscopes.**—The principle underlying the Hindu horoscope used in ascertaining whether a marriage is likely to be successful or not, is as follows. Children born in the asterisms of Magha, Aslekha, Dhanishtha, Jyestha, Múl, Shatbhikha, Krittika, Chitra, Vishákha, are Rakshasas by birth ; those born in Anuradha, Punarbasu, Mrigsira, Sravana, Revati, Swáti, Aswini, Pushpa, and Hasta, are Deotas or godlings. Those born in the other asterisms are ordinary human beings. Thus, those who are of the same genus, so to speak, must be married, otherwise the result will not be prosperous. The calculation of this is known as Ganya ganana.—*Pandit Rám Gharíb Chaubé.*

29. **Western Districts, N.-W. P : Clan Deities of the Jallads.**—The Dom of the Eastern Districts is known in the Western districts as Jallád and his business is to act as an executioner and scavenger. As he has to put condemned persons and mangy dogs to death, he is in constant dread of the demoniacal influence of the ghosts of his victim, so he is very careful to propitiate them. This he does by veneration of his clan deities, which are Kalkattewali Káli, or the Calcutta Káli ; Pahárwáli Káli, or Káli of the Hills ; Dakkhini Mátá, or the Mother of the South country and the Guru of Dehra Dun.

The Calcutta Káli is the famous Bengali Goddess. She is worshipped by Jalláds when they receive their fees for an execution or for killing dogs. Any deserted place outside the town or village answers for her shrine. The Jallád goes there with his friends and makes an offering to her of spirits, cakes, vermilion, cloves, and, if he can afford it, a black goat or fowl. They first burn some incense and then bowing before the head of the victim cut off its head in the name of the goddess. They afterwards mark their foreheads with some of the blood and pray to the goddess to save them from the consequences of the deaths caused by their hands.

Pahárwáli Káli has her shrine in the Siwálik Hills, near the Mohand Pass, on the road from Saharanpur to Dehra, and is worshipped in the same way. Whenever they get into any special trouble they make a vow to worship her.

The offering to Dakkhini Káli is a couple of cloves, some red lead and vermilion, which are offered under a tree in the jungle, or some other solitary place.

To the Guru of the monastery of the Sikh order of Udasis at Dehra, they offer sweets to the value of a rupee and a quarter and vow to give more if they escape from their troubles.

In all cases the offerings after being presented are consumed by the worshippers themselves.—*W. Crooke.*

30. **A reason for the exclusion of Europeans from Tibet.**—The Grand Lama of Tibet, in the spring of 1865 sent a despatch to the Emperor of China requesting his Imperial Majesty on no account to sanction the departure of Europeans from China *en route* to Tibet, and assigning as a reason that on the last occasion the crops had failed, cattle had become barren, and women had turned from the paths of virtue. (Gray's *China.* Ed. by W. G. Gregor, 1878, Vol. I, p. 134.)—*J. Cockburn.*

FOLKTALES.

31. How the banya baffled the robbers.—Once upon a time a Banya was going about on business and fell among thieves. When he found out who his companions were, he began to think how he could get out of their clutches. So he climbed up a tree and began to break some of the dry branches. They asked him what he was doing. "In my town," he said, "wood is so scarce that every scrap sells for two annas." The thieves, knowing that the Banya had very little money about him, thought that they would do better by selling wood than by robbing him; so they all fell to and collected a large bundle.

When they got to the town the Banya said, "Brethren, I am very sorry to hear that since I went away wood has fallen to two pice a bundle." "You rascal," said they, "we will pay you off before long." The Banya knew that they would come soon and rob him; so one night he was awake and he heard them outside. Then he whispered to his wife so that the thieves could hear him, "Did you bring in the bag of gold which I tied on the *nim* tree in the yard?" "No," said she, "it must be there still." "Then we are ruined," was his reply. When the thieves heard this, they at once climbed up the tree, when they touched a large wasp's nest, which they did not see in the dark. The wasps came out and stung them, so that they were hard put to make their escape.

(Told by Pyare Lal, a teacher in the High School, Mainpuri.)

32. Kali Das and his Parrot.—There was once a foolish Rája who kept fourteen Pandits in his court. It so happened that the celebrated Kali Das came to the Rája's court and the other Pandits were jealous of him. The Rája, in order to try his powers, put to him this question : "My favourite cow and mare are both about to be delivered. State when their offspring will be born and what they will be." Kali Das naming the time said : "The cow will have a calf and the mare a foal." In due time the animals were delivered; but in order to disgrace Kali Das the Pandits had them blindfolded at the time of birth and they put the foal beside the cow and the calf beside the mare and each animal adopted the young of the other as its own.

When the foolish Rája was convinced that the prediction of Kali Das was false he had him put in prison as an impostor. Now Kali Das had a favourite parrot which he loved exceedingly. When his master did not return, the parrot spoke to the wife of Kali Das and asked her what had become of her husband. She answered : "He has gone to the Rája's court and has not returned." The parrot replied, "I suspect that some evil may have befallen him. Take some charcoal, mix it in water and blacken my wings." The lady did so and the parrot flew off and sat upon the roof of the palace and went on calling " *Radha Krishna ! Radha Krishna.*" When the Rája saw the bird he said to his Pandits : " I see a bird of the shape and voice of a parrot, but his feathers are as black as those of a crow. What is the explanation of this ?" „The Pandits were nonplussed; at last they said " Maharaja ! You had better ask the parrot." So the Rája asked the parrot to explain his case and the parrot said : " When the ocean took fire I was flying about near it and I so pitied the miserable fish that I tried to put out the fire and my wings got blackened by the smoke." " When did anyone hear of the ocean getting on fire ? " asked the Pandits. " That was the same time, " answered the parrot " when the cow was delivered of the foal and the mare of the calf."

When the Rája understood the parrot's meaning, he became conscious of his folly and, after disgracing his Pandits he released Kali Das from prison and dismissed him with a handsome present.

(Told by Shiu Sahai, Teacher of the Village School of Dagarhi Chakeri, Etah District.)

33. The Boy and the Monkey.—There was once a poor cultivator who died leaving an only son and he and his mother fell into poverty. One day the boy said to his mother, " Give me five rupees and I will buy a cow and then we can live comfortably." His mother gave him the money and he went to the bazar and there he saw a man selling a monkey. He bought it for five rupees and when he brought it home he called out to his mother : " Mother fix a peg in the yard." She thought he had brought the cow and was very angry when she saw the monkey. She was about to wring its neck, but the monkey said : " Spare my life and I will do you good service." She let the monkey loose and he ran off to the jungle and soon came back with a lot of fruits and in this way he used to bring them food every day.

One day he went out and sat on a tree near a tank and just then a jeweller came to bathe. He put down his bundle on the bank and, when he was in the water, the monkey came down and seizing it, brought it home. The bag was full of valuable jewels and the boy and his mother became rich and the monkey supported them for many years.

(Told by Iqbal Husen, Weaver of Bhulli, Mirzapur.)

34. The Metamorphosis of Rája Vikramaditya.—Once upon a time Rája Vikramaditya was reading with a Pandit the *Pinda Pravesha Vidya*, or the science by which a man acquires the power of entering the body of another person or beast. His servant, who was sitting outside the door, was listening and heard as much as the Raja. When the Rája was returning home the servant asked the Rája what he had been learning from the Pandit. The Rája answered: "If you bring me the body of an animal I will show you." The servant killed a parrot and brought the body to the Rája who immediately repeated the *mantras* and entered into it. When the servant saw this he cut his own body into pieces and tried to kill the parrot too, but it flew away. Then he went to the capital and giving himself out to be the Rája sat upon his throne. He issued orders that every parrot in the kingdom should be killed and offered a large reward for every one that was brought to him. One day it so happened that the parrot whose body the real Rája was occupying was caught in a snare and he at once asked the fowler what he intended to do with him. The fowler said that he was going to take him to the Rája and claim the reward. The parrot answered: "If you take me to the Rája you will get only a small reward. If you take me to the father-in-law of Rája Vikramaditya I will get you five hundred rupees." The fowler agreed and took the Rája in his parrot form to Rája Vikramaditya's father-in-law. The old Rája asked him what he had brought and he showed the parrot. The old Rája asked the price and he said: "Ask the parrot and he will fix the price." The parrot when he was asked, said: "My price is five hundred rupees." "What can you do that you fix your price at so large a sum?" he enquired. The parrot answered: "O Maharaja! I can decide disputes and interpret the Shastras." So the old Rája bought the parrot and hung it up in a cage in his court and the parrot used to read Sanskrit and help the old Rája in deciding cases that came before him. The old Rája was much pleased with him and thought that he had got him very cheap.

Meanwhile the servant in the form of Vikramaditya went into the royal apartments and talked with the Ráni. She was surprised to hear his rude and unpolished conversation. She thought he was out of his senses and sending for the jailer had him shut up as a madman. It so happened that there lived in that kingdom a Bráhman and his wife. They lived by begging, but they got so little that they were almost starving and one day the Bráhman said to his wife: "We cannot live in this way. I am going into the Tarai on a begging excursion." His wife agreed and he started. No sooner had he left the village than a *Deo* who lived in a grove close by assumed the form of the Brahman and went into his house. His wife was very much surprised to see a man whom she believed to be her husband returning so soon and he said: "What is written in my fate for me to get I shall get here as well as baroad. I am not going to the Tarai after all." She answered: "You have done well. Stay at home. "So the *Deo* lived in the Bráhman's house and after some time when the Bráhman came home he was astonished to see a man just like himself sitting there. When the *Deo* saw the Bráhman he rushed at him with a club and the Bráhman began to fight him. The woman could not make out what was the matter when she saw two men of exactly similar appearance fighting about her. The villagers came up and asked what the quarrel was about. The *Deo* said: "Help me brethren! Do you not see that this shameless ruffian has forced his way into my house?" The Brahman said: "Don't you recognise me, neighbours?" The villagers said: "In appearance you are both exactly the same. We cannot judge between you." The parties then went to thirty-five villages, but they could find no one to decide their case. At last they went to the father-in-law of Vikramaditya. He asked the woman which of the men was her husband. She pointed to the *Deo* and said that he was her husband, that the other man was some impostor or other. The Rája then gave her over to the *Deo*. As he was going away the Bráhman called out: "O Bhagwan! Are you asleep and has justice perished out of the earth?" Then Vikramaditya in the form of the parrot called out: "You have decided the case wrongly. Call them back and I will decide the matter myself." The Rája did so, and then the parrot called for an earthenware vessel with a spout (*karua*) and a piece of yellow cloth and a thread. He put these things in the middle of the court, and said: "Whichever of you two will enter this vessel by the spout and come back the same way he shall be deemed the owner of the woman." The Brahman said: "I would rather lose her altogether than undergo this ordeal." But the *Deo* agreed to make the attempt and when he entered the vessel the parrot shouted to the Rája's men to cover the vessel with the yellow cloth and to tie round it a thread of raw cotton. Then he said: "This is an evil-minded *Deo*; bury him in the earth that he may never arise again to trouble the land."

All were amazed at the wisdom of the parrot; and a few days after the wife of Vikramaditya heard of the case and sent for the Bráhman to find out how it was decided. When she heard the story, as she was learned in the sciences, she at once came to the conclusion that the parrot could be no other than her husband Vikramaditya. So she determined to go to her father's house, and when she met him him he told her to ask any boon she pleased. She asked for the parrot, but he was too fond of him to give him away and he refused her request. But she sat *dharna* at the palace gates, and when he found that her life was in danger he sent for her. She asked him to whom he had married her. "To Vikramaditya, of course," he answered. "And where is

Vikramaditya?" she asked. "In his kingdom, of course," he replied. "You had better ask your parrot," she said. When the cage was brought down the parrot said : " I am Rája Vikramaditya." Then he told them the whole story and the old Rája gave the parrot to his daughter and she took him back to the palace.

She asked him what he had been studying for so long a time with the Pandit and he told her what he had learnt. She sent for the false Rája and addressing him affectionately, said: "What did your Majesty learn from the Pandit?" He said : " Bring me the body of a lamb and I will show you." When the lamb was brought, the false Rája at once transferred his soul into it. The Ráni opened the cage at once and Vikramaditya came out, dropped his parrot form and entered his own body. Immediately he cut the lamb in pieces and the false servant died too. After this Vikramaditya and his Ráni lived for many years in the utmost happiness.

(Told by Devi Datt Dubé Bráhman, of Hariya, Basti District, and recorded by the Head Master, High School, Aligarh.)

[These animal transformations are, of course, common. We have an instance in the myth of Circe. In the Golden Ass of Apuleius Pamphile becomes an owl and Apuleius who wants to follow her is changed by mistake by Fotis into an ass The demon shut up in a vessel appears in the "Fisherman and the Genii" of the *Arabian Nights* (Lady Burton's Edition I, 33 sqq.) Even now-a-days it is firmly believed that demons can be enclosed with a yellow cloth and a piece of raw cotton string.—ED.]

---

35. **The Greedy Brahman.**—There was once a Bráhman who was so greedy that whenever he was going out to a dinner at the house of one of his clients he used to tell his wife to make his bed ready and when he came home surfeited he used to throw himself upon it and lie there for a couple of days till he worked off his indigestion. One day as he was going off to a dinner he did not as usual give his wife instructions about his bed and she began to laugh. When he noticed this he asked her why she was laughing. She said that she was laughing because he had given no orders about his bed. "To-day," said he, "I am going to have an extra good dinner and in any case I shall have to be brought home on a bed, so there is no need of arranging one for me."

He went to the dinner and there he ate so many sweetmeats that he became senseless and the people seeing him in this condition put him on a bed and brought him home to his wife. When she saw him, she went off to the grocer and bought two seeds of the myrobalan (*harra*) and asked her husband to take them. "What a fool you must think me," said he. "If I had room for two myrobolan seeds don't you think I would not have eaten two more sweetmeats?" And with that he died and no one lamented him.

[Told by Abul Hasan Khan, Teacher, Karaili Village School, Pilibhit.]

---

36. **The Lesson of the Sadhu.**—There was once a Raja whose habit was whenever a Sadhu came to him for alms he used to put to him this question : " Which is better, the life of the householder or that of the ascetic?" If he answered "The ascetic's life is better," he would say : " Then why do you come to the house of a householder?" But if he said " The life of the householder is the better," he would answer : " Then why have you become an ascetic?" In this way he confounded all the Sadhus who came to him for alms.

After many days a Sadhu came to the Rája. The Rája put the usual questions to him and he said : " First give food and then I will give an answer." When he had eaten, he was again brought before the Rája, who called on him to solve the difficulty. The Sadhu answered : " Maharaj! You need not seek an answer from me. To-morrow early ride towards the south and go on riding up to noon ; then your question will be answered."

The Raja was so anxious to test the words of the Sadhu that he lay awake all night and longed for the dawn. Then he mounted his horse and rode steadily on towards the south until noon; but he met no man who could answer his question. When it was noon he angrily turned back thinking that the Sadhu had deceived him. As he was returning he lost his way and came into a very thick forest. He tied his horse to a tree and sat down and there he remained the whole day and night without food or water. He feared an attack from wild beasts; so he collected some dry leaves and with his sword and a bit of flint he managed to strike a light and made a fire. Just then a pair of birds came and perched on the tree beneath which the Rája lay. The male bird said to the female : " You see that this man, who is a worthy prince, is dying of hunger. You know that we are all mortal and this body of our's will soon be reduced to ashes and be of no use to any one. If you agree I will throw myself into this fire and this man who is an eater of flesh will be saved." The female replied : " As a virtuous wife I cannot prevent you from doing an act of piety. You can do as seems fit to you." The male bird then threw himself into the fire and was roasted and the Rája ate his flesh. Then the female bird thought within herself : " My husband has devoted his life to perform an act of the greatest piety. I am left a widow and for me life is now unendurable. I had better follow the example of my husband and help to save this man's life." With these words she too threw herself into the fire and was roasted and the Rája ate her flesh.

By this food the Rája's strength revived and he managed to ascend the tree, from the top of which he saw a city which he reached in a few hours. There he saw a number of men assembled round a cauldron by which a woman was sitting. The Rája asked the cause of this assemblage and they said: "This woman has vowed that she will be his who passes through a cauldron of boiling oil for her sake." When the Raja saw her he was enamoured of her beauty and he told her that he was a Rája and that if she would agree to go with him he would keep her in the greatest comfort. But she said: "I care not whether you are prince or peasant, I will go only with that man who passes through the ordeal for my sake." The Rája feared to undergo the terrible test; but he was so fascinated that he could not leave the place. Meanwhile a Sadhu appeared and when he heard the conditions he at once plunged into the cauldron and passed through. The woman immediately started with him.

As the Sadhu was taking her away with him, the Rája followed him. The Sadhu asked him why he did so. The Raja replied: "I am a Rája; you are a Sadhu; what use have you for this woman? Give her to me." The Sadhu asked the woman if she was ready to go with him." She answered: "I am your property, you can dispose of me as you please." The Sadhu gave the woman to the Raja and he took her home with him.

When he returned he sent for the Sadhu to whom he had originally propounded the question and called on him for the answer. Then the Sadhu made him describe all that had happened to him. Then the Sadhu said: "The pair of birds which gave their lives for you represent the house-holders among men and the Sadhu, who gave you this woman, notwithstanding all she had cost him, was an ascetic of the highest type. If a house-holder is charitable as these birds were, he need not covet the life of the ascetic; and the true ascetic is as free from covetousness as was that man. If all house-holders and ascetics are like these examples they are both equal." The Raja was satisfied and laid his forehead at the feet of the Sadhu. The Sadhu dismissed him with a blessing.

(A folktale told by Ram Lal, Banya, of Mirzapur.)

37. **Banke Chhail and his Wife.**—There was once a Musalman whose wife was such a shrew that every morning she used to give him a sound beating with her slipper. She had a daughter and when she grew up her parents were on the look-out for a husband for her; but the temper of her mother was so well known that no one would dare to marry into such a family. Finally one day a notorious character, who was known as Banke Chhail, or "the cunning rascal," came and proposed for the girl, and her father was so glad to settle her in life that he agreed to the match at once and they were married.

Before the ceremony took place Banke Chhail bought a parrot, a cat and a dog, and when he was taking his bride home he brought his animals with him. On the way the pair sat down at a well to rest and a number of village curs came out and began to bark at Banke Chhail's dog. His dog barked at them in return and his master, drawing his sword, cut off his head at a single stroke. "You rascal," said he, "do you dare to bark without my leave?" This astonished his wife; but they went on a little farther and as the morning broke the birds in the trees began to sing and when the parrot heard them it too commenced to chatter. Banke Chhail at once pulled it out of the cage and wrung its neck. "You fool," said he, "you did not remember that you belonged to Banke Chhail and you dared to open your mouth without his orders."

His wife was still more surprised, but she said nothing and they went on. They sat down to rest in a garden and soon a rat appeared. Banke Chhail called to his cat and said: "Catch me that rat." The cat at once obeyed his orders and killed it. When his wife saw this she began to think to herself "What a terrible husband I have got. It would be well for me to obey him." And when they reached home she found it to be her interest to obey him in all things and became a very loving and obedient wife; so much so that when some time after her father came to pay him a visit, she looked out through a chink in the door and was afraid to admit him without the leave of her husband. By and by Banke Chhail came home and said to her: "Your respected father his waiting at the door. Why did you not let him in?" "How could I do so without your leave?" she answered.

Then Banke Chhail went out and brought the old man in. When he saw how changed his daughter was, he said to his son-in-law: "You know what a life my wife leads me. I wish you would tell me how you have succeeded in reducing your wife to order. Perhaps I may be able to deal with my wife in the same way." Said Banke Chhail: "Good, Sir, bring a brick and some moist clay and make me a lamp saucer out of each." "It is easy quoth the old man to mould the soft clay, but when the clay gets hard no power on earth would mould it."

"In short," said Banke Chhail, "your wife's character is fixed and cannot be mended. I dealt with my wife in season and you see the result." The old man went home sorrowful.

[Told by Madho Prashad, Khatri, of Mirzapur.]

MISCELLANEA.

38. Romantic Story of Colonel William Gardner.—"CARFAX" contributes to the *Indian Daily News* the following interesting episode on the romantic career of Colonel William Gardner:—Of all the adventurers who sought fortune under the banners of native princes, no career is more romantic than that of Colonel William Linnæus Gardner. This gentleman was born in 1770. He was a nephew of Alan, first Baron Gardner, and received his education in France. He came out to India as an officer of the British army, but having attained the rank of Captain he resigned his commission. No doubt he was attracted by the adventurous career which was offered to Europeans at the Native Chiefs at a period when internecine strife appears to have been the only occupation of the princes of Hindustan. In 1798, Gardner offered his sword to Jaswant Rao Holkar, and raised a brigade of infantry for that Chief. Another and perhaps more potent reason for inducing William Gardner to enter native service was the fact that while he was a British Officer he had married, by Mahomedan rites, a princess of the house of Cambay. The romantic story of his marriage furnishes our title to this narrative. The following account of it was given by Colonel Gardner himself to Mrs. Parkes, whose delightful " Wanderings of a Pilgrim " furnishes most of the details that are known about Colonel Gardner's life. This book has been for years out of print, and second-hand copies command fancy prices. The story is as follows :—When a Captain in the 30th Foot, William Gardner was entrusted to negociate a treaty with the Nawab of Cambay. Durbars were constantly held, and during one of them, Gardner noticed a curtain drawn aside, and he saw, as he thought, the loveliest black eyes in the world. It was impossible for him to think any longer of the treaty. The beautiful dark eyes had bewitched him. Gardner felt flattered that the owner of the dark eyes had ventured to gaze at him. After the assembly was over, he discovered that the bright-eyed beauty was a daughter of the Nawab. At the next durbar the vision was repeated, and Gardner's fate was decided. He boldly asked for the princess in marriage. At first he was refused, but after consideration, the Nawab, thinking an ambassador too important a person to be denied, promised Gardner the hand of the princess. The preparations for the marriage were hurried forward. "Remember," said Gardner to the Nawab, "it will be useless to deceive me. I shall know those eyes again ; nor will I marry any other." On the day of the marriage, Gardner raised the veil of the bride, and in the mirror that was placed between them, he saw reflected the lovely dark eyes which had bewitched him. "I smiled," says Gardner, "and the young Begum smiled also." The Begum was thirteen when they were wed. Gardner's service with Jaswant Rao Holkar came to a sudden and disagreeable termination. In 1803, Holkar despatched this officer as an envoy to the British camp with instructions to return by a certain day. Gardner's absence, however, was unavoidably prolonged for three days. Meantime, suspicions of treachery arose and accusations against Gardner were brought before Holkar in durbar. As it happened, Gardner rejoined the camp while the durbar was in progress. The Maharaja immediately rose and angrily demanded the cause of the delay, adding, "Had you not returned this day, I would have levelled the *kanats* of your tent." This meant exposing Gardner's zenana to the whole camp, and was the deadliest insult that could be made to the husband of a native lady. Gardner at these words at once drew his sword, intending to cut Holkar down, but he was surrounded and prevented. During the confusion caused by his audacity, Gardner rushed out of the camp, mounted his horse, and was soon out of reach of pursuit. To Holkar's credit it must be stated that he did not revenge himself upon Gardner's wife and family, and they were allowed to rejoin him soon afterwards. Possibly, Holkar did not consider it worth while to embroil himself with the Cambay House, to whom the Begum belonged. In the same year, Gardner had another very narrow escape for his life. He was taken prisoner by Amrat Rao, who, when war broke out with the British, tied Gardner to a gun, and threatened to blow him to pieces, unless he consented to take the field against his countrymen. That this was no idle threat, we may mention that, shortly afterwards, Holkar beheaded three of his English officers, Vickers, Dodd, and Ryan, for refusing the same demand. Our Colonel, of course, remained staunch, and fortunately Amrat Rao temporized in the hope of Gardner thinking better of it, and left him a prisoner in charge of a guard. The Colonel, finding he was not very closely watched, began meditating on the chance of escape ;· and walking one day at the edge of a precipitous slope of about fifty feet which led to the River Tapti, Gardner without hesitation threw himself over the declivity, then made his way to the river, plunged in, and began to swim across. A hot pursuit began, and Gardner, finding he was being overtaken, sought shelter among some reeds, where he stood with only his mouth out of water, until the pursuit was abandoned. He then crossed the river, and reached a town where he had native friends who protected him, until he was able to steal out in the disguise of a grass-cutter, and make his way to the British camp where he was in safety. Gardner now returned to his allegiance to the British Government, and raised and commanded a famous troop of irregular cavalry known as "Gardner's Horse." Gardner's best services, both in war and diplomacy, were rendered under the British flag. He had a profound knowledge of the native character, derived, no doubt, from his peculiar home life. For Gardner's further history we may refer our readers to an interesting paper which appeared in the *Calcutta Magazine* of July, 1891, where, under the title of "The Real Major Gahagan," some details are given which we have not seen elsewhere. Certainly, as far as extraordinary personal adventure is concerned, our Indian Colonel might serve as a prototype to Thackeray's fictitious hero, or to Sir Walter Scott's immortal Dugald Dalgetty : but it must be remembered that our Colonel was modest, retiring and reticent, and content to live unknown and undecorated. The special information contained in the Magazine article above referred to is derived from some of Gardner's letters written in 1814 during the time of Lord Moira's Nepalese war. The eve of this war found Gardner in his cantonment at Etah commanding his squadron of horse, and occupying his leisure with the care of his estate. He was very anxious to be employed. "D—money," says the Colonel, "I'd rather serve for nothing a day and find myself, than be a piece of useless lumber." Gardner was employed, and distinguished himself at Almora with his levies, cutting off the army of Amar Sinha from all communications with its base, and from all power of obtaining reinforcements. He afterwards served in Rajputana, and in 1822 he obtained a commission in his old service, the British army, and the commission was made to date from 25th September,

1803, when he left native service. This was a graceful act on the part of the English military authorities. Gardner served in Central India in 1821, and in Aracan in 1825, when he returned for good to his estate of Khasganj near Agra. Mrs. Parkes furnishes in her "Wanderings of a Pilgrim," a good deal of interesting information about Colonel Gardner's private life at Khasganj. No marriage ever turned out happier than that of Gardner and his Begum. With them at Khasganj lived their second son, James, with his wife, Mulka Begum, a niece of the Emperor of Delhi and a sister-in-law of the King of Oudh. This Princess had been married to Mirza Selim, brother of the Emperor Akbar Shah, but she eloped with James Gardner, and to the latter she was married, after being divorced by her first husband. This elopement was the cause of the greatest annoyance and distress to Colonel Gardner, who vowed he would never forgive his son : nor did he do so until two years afterwards. The reconciliation was brought about as follows :—James Gardner, who possessed the same adventurous spirit as his father, saw Colonel Gardner rowing on the Jumna in a small boat. James immediately jumped into the river and swam to his father, saying he would drown unless his father took him in, and gave him forgiveness. The Colonel shook his head, but at last seeing his son was beginning to sink, he gave him his hand, and pulled him into the boat and forgave him. Colonel Gardner's elder son, Allan, died aged twenty-nine. Allan had married Hinga Bebee Sahiba, and their eldest daughter, Hirmoze, married her cousin, Stuart William Gardner, an officer of the 28th Native Infantry, and their eldest son, Allan Hyde Gardner, born in 1836, succeeded to the title of Lord Gardner in 1883. He married in 1879 a converted Princess of the House of Delhi, and has a son and heir, Allan Legge, born in 1881.

This is the romantic history of the Gardner Peerage, the representative of which is an obscure Eurasian residing near Etah, but the blood in his veins is that of the Royal House of Delhi. A correspondent of the *I. D. N.* some months ago furnished some interesting information about this nobleman.

To return to Colonel Gardner; he died in his bed at Khasganj, on the 29th July, 1835, aged sixty-five, and was followed one month later by his faithful Begum. He was a gentleman in every sense of the word, and was so well known in his day, that a friend wrote to Mrs. Parkes from England, " I shall always regret having left India without seeing Colonel Gardner and the Taj."

39. **An Incantation to remove Cramp.—**

Om namo.

Sdr ki Chhuri, dhdr ko bin ;

Huk na chalai re Muhammadd

Jwan ki dn.

I salute God. The knife is of steel. The arrow is sharp. May the cramp cease through the power of Muhammad, the brave one.

Hold the aching part with the left hand and with the right hand draw lines on the ground with a knife. Five or seven times' repetition of this will stop the pain.—*Pandit Rám Gharib Chaubé.*

40. **Bel leaves used by Travellers.—**Among high caste people when a man is going on a journey he bows down to all the senior people of the family, ma'e and female, and receives their blessing. Then he takes a leaf of the bel tree which has been placed in a vessel of Ganges water and starts without looking back. If he looks back while leaving the house, his journey is likely to be unsuccessful and he will probably meet with misfortune.—*W. Crooke.*

41. **A Charm practised on the Potter's wheel to remove Disease.—**People suffering from disease go on Saturday evening to the potter's house. They get a large earthen pitcher and fill it with rice cooked in milk and mixed with sugar. They get sixty-four earthen lamps and light them, feeding the wicks with clarified butter. They put the lamps on the wheel in a circular form and move the wheel in the contrary way. Then they make over the rice in the pitcher to a b'ack dog, or some low caste man who will eat it. They think that thereby the disease is removed. This is called Utárá.—*Pandit Rám Gharib Chaubé.*

42. **Death customs—Shaving.—**In all the feudatory states it is the custom when the Raja dies for all his subjects to shave their heads and beards. When the last Maharaja of Kashmir died, all the Kashmiris in Lahore, many of whom had no houses or property in Kashmir, shaved in token of sorrow. When Sir Jang Bahadur of Nepal died all the Gorkhas at Gorakhpur shaved their heads.—*W. Crooke.*

43. **A Fakir's Curse.—**A correspondent in No. 331 of *North Indian Notes and Queries.* Vol. I. asks for details about a faqir's curse on three British officers, but the locality given is Agra.

The story I have heard hails from Nowshera in the Peshawar District, and runs, that the three officers, whose names I have forgotten, wished to build over a tomb where a faqir used to sit. He warned them that if they did so the house would not stand, and they should all die violent deaths within three years.

The house was washed away the year that the Kabul river ran backwards. One officer was, I think, killed out hawking with the Guides near Hoti Mardan, a second was killed by a fall from his pony at polo, and the third, as your correspondent says, was drowned at Allahabad within a few days of the expiry of the curse.

N. B.—Most officers of Punjab regiments of over 25 years know all the particulars. I have heard them several times.—*R. M. Lowis.*

44. **A Curious way of Calculating Age.—**There is a popular belief among the Muhammadans, as well as Hindus that whosoever has the lower ends of his ears long and pendent lives to a good old age, while, on the contrary, those who have small ear lobes are cut off in the prime of their life. A respectable friend of mine is so certain about this, that he once began to shed tears at the sight of my ears, which have unfortunately small ends.—*Pandit Rám Gharib Chaubé.*

45. A Charm to discover hidden underground Treasure.—This is one of the most popular charms Many religious mendicants pretend to have this power. A well known magician of Saháranpur supplies me with he method of practising this charm.

"Go into the cremation ground and look for a dead body. When you find one lying there, return home. At night go to it secretly. Put the dead body on a seat which has holes in it and under it put a lamp. Then sprinkle oil on the dead body. Receive the oil as it drops down from the corpse into the lamp Light the lamp, and sitting by the dead body repeat the following mantras:—

"*Om chándáli chakrawati mam Kárya Sidhim Kuru Kuru Swaha.*"

"I salute the cremation ground goddess. She is the goddess of the universe. Realise my objects. Realise my objects." When you have repeated it 108 times the dead body will get up and show you the place where the treasure is buried in the ground.—*Pandit Rám Gharib Chaubé.*

---

46. Bengal Sacred Tanks.—The following extract is from the columns of the *Week's News*, August 25th, 1894.

"The air in the place is full of enchantment. One goes to see the tank of Rám Pál. Here there is no longer much water. The tank is overgrown with weeds and grass. The present Financial Member of Council noted twenty-three years ago that cattle would graze there, and I am told that they do so now. But if I had any cattle I should not choose this as a grazing ground for them. In one of many stories about the inadvisibility of taking carrier-pigeons with one when one went on a journey, it is said that Rám Pál went with two of these pigeons on a summons from Sítá Rám Rái, or some other superior person, and that the pigeons came back alone, whereupon the whole family—"household cattle and all"—jumped into the tank and were drowned. In confirmation of this legend Mr. Westland states that up to five or seven years before cowdung had been seen to rise and float on the tank. But, perhaps, this was due to the cattle which grazed there. Now, there is scarcely any water in which such a phenomenon may float. People to whom I spoke, also told me that up to the time of their "fathers and grandfathers," when there was a wedding in the vicinity, gold and silver vessels used to rise to the top of the tank for the use of the wedding guests. At last one of the wedding guests stole one of the gold vessels, and the others appeared no more. By such means do miracles disappear in the light of modern education.—*A Jungly Collector.*

The legend of tanks supplying utensils in days gone by and discontinuing to do so through the covetousness of mortals, is a common one in India. In South Mirzapur there is a tank of which the same legend is told.—*Pandit Rám Gharib Chaubé.*

47. "Helps of old age"—A saying—

As barhápá diyán, hud sut kusul ;
Yá hó paisa pás ká, yá hó pút saput.

"When old age comes and the thread of life is broken, either money is needed, or a dutiful son."—*Pandit Rám Gharib Chaubé.*

---

48. Silajit.—There is a stuff sold by native apothecaries which is known as Silajit, "or that which conquers stone." It is said to be the condensed moisture which drops from stones and is regarded as a potent cure for impotency. It seems to be really some kind of bitumen.—*Pandit Rám Gharib Chaubé.*

---

49. Siyar Singhi.—In the Eastern Districts of the North-Western Provinces there are a class of people who call themselves Siyár Marwa, or "jackal killers." They wander about villages and beg. They carry with them what they call the Siyár Singhi, or horn of the jackal, and say that if it is put in a money bag or in a granary it increases the produce. They get fees for a loan of it for this purpose. It thus ranks in its mystic power of increasing things with the flower of the Indian fig tree and the after-birth of a cat, both of which are considered highly efficacious for the same purpose.—*Pandit Rám Gharib Chaubé.*

---

50. The number 27.—The number 27 is sacred among the Sikhs and this number of iron beads they wear on the Kara or iron bangle rosary which they wear round their wrists and which they use for repeating prayers whenever they are at leisure. Multiples of the same number are regarded as equally efficacious.—*W. Crooke.*

---

51. Productiveness of fields.—It is a common belief that those parts of the country which during the year have been attacked by an epidemic will be blessed in the next season with unusually abundant crops. The same is the case with those fields in which persons of rank have encamped, and those places where the dramatic representation of the Rámlila have been performed are specially blessed in this way. The same idea attaches to elephants going into a field, and hence people will submit to much damage to their fields from elephants which they would not stand in the case of any other animal. —*W. Crooke.*

North Indian Notes and Queries:
A MONTHLY PERIODICAL.

VOL. V.]   JUNE, 1895.   [NO. 3.

Every communication must be accompanied by the writer's name and address, not necessarily for insertion, but as a guarantee of good faith. Every quotation from a book must be accompanied by its full title, publisher's and author's names, place and date of publication, volume and page. Contributors are requested to write on ONE SIDE the page only. If several contributions be sent at a time, they should be sent each on a separate sheet.

The Conductor cannot undertake to return, or be responsible for, any MSS. not accepted.

All orders must be accompanied by cash. If not so accompanied, they will either not be attended to, or will be complied with per value-payable post.

Contributions should be addressed direct to W. CROOKE, ESQ., C. S., SAHARANPUR, N.-W. P., INDIA.

CONTENTS OF THIS NUMBER.
(The references are to the Notes.)

Popular Religion ... ... — 37 to 42	Folktales	... 46 to 51
Anthropology ... ... — 43 ,, 45	Miscellanea	... 52 ,, 54

POPULAR RELIGION.

52. Gopalpur, Gorakhpur.—A closed abode of Brahman demons.—In the kot or palace of the Ráni of Gopálpur there is a closed room in which platforms raised in the names of a vast number of men who have fallen at the hands of the successive Rájás of Gopálpur are seen. The doors are opened once in a twelve month on the occasion of the Nau Rátra of Kuár. Then these demons are worshipped in connection with other family deities. It is said that if the doors be open and children, unaware of the presence of the Brahman demons, go into the room unbathed or otherwise unclean the demons would be wrath and commence their havoc as before in the Rájá's family and the children would be killed instantly. By various modes of propitiation they have been brought to consent to remain in the room on the condition that the annual worship will be performed regularly and without fail by a member of the family. No one cares even to pass by the room through dread of them.—*Ram Bakhsh Chaubi.*

53. The piety of Karma Bai.—Karma Bai was a Teli by caste and devoted herself to the worship of Rám Chandra. She made a pilgrimage to Jagannáth and her belief in the deity was so intense that she used never to wash her clothes or body, but she used daily to cook a dish of rice and pulse (*khichari*) and the deity himself used to come and eat with her.

One day an Achári of the strictest sect of Vaishnavas happened to come to her hut and saw her cooking as usual. He asked her what she was doing and when she told him that she was cooking for Raghunathji he said :—

"You do not know what a sin you are committing in cooking for the deity without bathing and washing your clothes and plastering the cooking place."

These words struck her: so next day she bathed and washed her clothes and after plastering the cooking place began to prepare the food as usual. Sri Rám Chandra came at the usual time and looking through the window saw how she was engaged. He waited some time for the meal and as he was eating it the bell rang in the temple and he knew that his priests had prepared his food. So he hastened and appeared in the idol of the temple; but when the priests came to feed the deity they found some grains of rice and pulse on the lip of the image. They were astonished and asked the reason. Then the god spoke from his image and said:—

"There is a sincere votary of mine here who cooks for me daily. But a foolish Achári warned her that she should not cook for me without purification. So she was late in preparing the food to-day. Warn her not to do so in future."

The priests obeyed the voice of the god and until the end of her life Karma Bai continued her devotion and the deity used to visit her daily.—*Pandit Rám Gharib Chaube.*

54. The piety of Trilok the Goldsmith.—Though he died many a long year ago the piety of the goldsmith Trilok is known to the people of the Eastern Districts of this province. He was a devoted worshipper of Sri Krishna. One day a rich man in the village brought him a lump of gold and told him to make it into a bangle for the marriage of his daughter. That night many Sadhus came to Trilok, but he had nothing to give them and he could not send them away empty. So he sold the gold and entertained them. He had promised the bangle next day and when the morning broke he was in an agony of grief thinking how he could fulfil his promise. While he was meditating Sri Krishna assumed his form and brought a lovely bangle to the owner of the gold, whereat he was so pleased that he gave him a present beyond his wages. When Trilok came to his senses he asked his wife what his customers had said when he came to demand the bangle.

"What do you say?" she said. "Just now you came back from his house and gave me the present which he had given you beside your wages."

When Trilok heard this he knew that his honour had been saved by the grace of the lord Sri Krishna; so he worshipped him with still more intense devotion for the remaining years of his life.—*Pandit Rám Gharib Chaube.*

55. Pigs gored by Cattle.—At the meeting of the Bengal Legislative Council on 17th January, 1895, Hon. Surendranath Banerjee asked:—Whether the attention of the Government has been called to the proceedings of the Sub-Divisional Officer of Pakour in the Sonthal Pergunnahs, as published in the *Murshidabad Hitaishi* of the 7th November, 1894, which says that the Sub-Divisional Officer stopped a particular religious ceremony observed from time immemorial, on the occasion of the annual Kali Puja, by the goalas of that part of the country, and thus hurt the religious feelings of the local public and caused great dissatisfaction among the orthodox Hindus of the locality? Will the Government be pleased to order an enquiry and adopt such measures as it may think fit with a view to prevent such interference in future?

The Hon. Mr. Cotton, in reply, said: "The attention of Government there is attracted to the paragraph in the *Murshidabad Hitaishi* referred to, and enquiry was made on the subject. It was ascertained that it was an old custom among the Sonthali cowherds on occasion of the Kali Puja to cast a pig among a herd of cattle, by whom it is gored to death, in a brutal manner. Mr. McLaren Smith, the Sub-Divisional Officer of Pakour, considering this custom to be a breach of the law for the prevention of cruelty to animals, prohibited it by executive order in 1893 and again in 1894. The cowherds represented the matter to the Commissioner, when he recently visited the sub-division, but Mr. Toynbee declined to intefere. The Lieutenant-Governor approves Mr. McLaren Smith's action, and declines to believe that the prohibition of this barbarous and disgusting custom can have hurt the religious feelings of any orthodox Hindu."

56. Brahman Ghosts.—In my village in the Gorakhpur District there is a family of Tiwari Bráhmans who had the misfortune to intermarry with a family of Bráhmans at a distance who were infested with demons. As a result of this connection by marriage those demons came into our village and several of the Tiwaris died in succession. The survivors, under good advice, changed the door of their house and closing up the front door, began to use the back door for ingress and egress. They did this in order to avoid the use of the door by which the corpses of so many of their relations had been carried to the cremation ground and which was accordingly supposed to be haunted by their ghosts. But even this was not sufficient to remove the danger and they have now transferred their residence to a village some ten milles distant with good results.—(See *Introduction to Popular Religion and Folklore,* 176.)

Behind the house of my next door neighbour, there lives a Brahma or Bráhman ghost. He is the terror of all the women of the neighbourhood, when they have occasion to go out at night. His history is curious. In his early life he was a respectable Bráhman, but as he grew older he began to associate with sorcerers and witches and became in time proficient in the black art and had a large practice. Then he left his well-built brick house and erected a hut behind it where he used to live. Here Parameswar, for his sins, visited him with asthma and he never ceased coughing. Near him was the house of another Bráhman whose wife was of indifferent character. With her he got on intimate terms, but she lost all her children except one who used to live with his maternal uncle and she herself finally died in childbirth. As a *churel* she now prowls about the neighbourhood with her child in her arms. She finally killed the old Bráhman, her paramour, in order that he might accompany her in her wanderings. Every day my neighbours bring me reports of the damage which this pair of ghosts are causing. A few days ago a newly married bridegroom fell into an epileptic fit through their machinations; another boy is suffering from severe fever by means of one or the other of them. They are known as Pichhware-ka-Baba and Pichhware-ki-Panrain or the "lord of the back yard" and the "Panre woman of the back yard." The space which they occupy is now a ruin and boys coming home from school will not enter it on any account.—*Pándit Rám Ghárib Chaubé.*

57. **A Brahman Ghost.**—In my village in the Gorakhpur District there was once a Káyasth named Ram Din Lal, who committed some act of tyranny on a Dúbé Bráhman, and the Brahman tied himself hand and foot and jumped into a well. This was several generations ago and both families have fallen into poverty. Even now the old grudge is kept up and they will not meet or speak to each other. The ghost of the dead Bráhman is known as Brahm and is very much feared. It is said that one descendant of the dead Bráhman once ate in the house of a descendant of the Kayasth and the Brahm turned him into a leper. Such ancestral enmity is known as Harpari and this accounts for many of the false cases which come before our Courts.—*Pándit Rám Ghárib Chaubé.*

58. **Adh Granth the sacred book of the Sikhs: Veneration for.**—Malcolm (*Sketches*, page 2) tells us that the chief who gave him a copy sent it at night, and with either a real or affected reluctance, after having obtained a promise that it would be treated with great respect. Burnes (*Bokhara*, I, 27) mentions that the copy, out of which some verses were read to Ranjít Singh on the morning of the Basant festival, was borne away wrapped in ten different colours, the outside one of which, in honour of the day, was of yellow velvet. For a description of the ceremonies with which the book is worshipped, see Ward's Hindoos II., 275-6: Asiatic Researches, XVII., 233. There is a very sacred copy in the library of the Edinburgh University. It is the third copy of the original Granth and was made in the time of Guru Govind. It belonged to the family of Mahárája Kharak Sinh. It was found in the Fort of Kahalwála on the capture of that place in 1848 and was presented to the University by the late Sir John Login. The original Adh Granth is said to be in the possession of the Bhais of Banuwania in the village of Mangal in the Gujarát District.—*Calcutta Review*, LIII., 248

59. **The Conversion of the Saint Muinuddin Chishti.**—They say that the father of the Saint Muinuddin Chishti was a very pious man, and before his death in order to win Paradise for himself, he distributed all his goods in charity, save a garden and a water-mill which he left to his son then a lad. One day the Saint was in his garden when a man of noted piety named Ibrahím visited him. The boy laid some grapes before him and Ibrahím taking up one give it to him. It had the flavour of the fruits of Paradise and when the boy tasted it he resolved to abandon worldly affairs and devote his life to piety.—*W. Crooke.*

60 **An account of Kabir and the Kabir panthis.**—A Brahman's daughter became a widow when she was twelve years old. One day she saluted Guru Rámá Nand at Benares, who promised her the blessing of a son. She fell at Rámá Nand's feet and explaining her circumstances, she represented that this boon would bring disgrace on her. Rámá Nand said that his words must prove true, but that she will not suffer the troubles of pregnancy. She had a blister on her right palm and after ten months a male child was produced from it. Fearing disgrace, the widow threw the child into the Lahar Táláb, or tank near Sikrol, at Benares. A certain Niru, a weaver of Benares, was returning home with his bride, having finished his *Gauna* ceremony, and took the child home. He named him Kabir. When Kabir was ten years old he began to deliver his lectures, advising Hindus not to worship images of stone and warning Muhammadans that killing of animals was the greatest of sins.

One day Kabir heard a voice from heaven, that his teaching was of no value until he was initiated by Guru Rámá Nand. This guru declined to see the face of Musalmans. Kabir turned himself into a child of six months and slept on a stair of the *Mani Karniká Ghát* at Benares at 3 A.M., awaiting the arrival of Rámá Nand as he came to bathe. When Rámá Nand passed by the child was struck by his sandal and began to cry. Rámá Nand then touching the head of the child said "*Bachha chup, Rám Rám kah*:" "Child be quiet and say Rám Rám."

Kabir then assumed his own body and returning home marked his forehead with the Rámá nandi mark (*tilak*) and putting a rosary (*málá*) of Tulsi wood on his neck, made himself known as one of the disciples of Rámá Nand. When the news reached the rais of Rámá Nand, he was astonished and sent for Kabir to enquire when he had initiated him. When Kabir arrived at Rámá Nand's place, he found his Guru sitting behind a screen and worshipping God in intense reflection. He thought he had a garland of flowers in his hand which was too short for the neck of the image, Kabir said loudly : "The garland is not too short, but it has a knot on it." This made Rámá Nand open his eyes, remove the screen and embrace Kabir. Rámá Naud then enquired how he was initiated by him and what was the formula (*mantra*). Kabir said that Rám was the chief *mantra* which was given to him by Rámá Nand on the bank of the Ganges. Rámá Nand then gave him the title of *Sáhib*, and from that date Kabir was called "*Kabir Sahib.*" Kabir started life as a weaver. One day he prepared a piece of coarse cloth and went to sell it at the market (*chauk*). God appeared before him in the shape of a naked Fakir, and asked for the cloth. Kabir presented to him without hesitation. Having no food at home, Kabir was afraid to return from the market. God then supplied a bullock load of rice through a Baniya, and informed Kabir that there was provision enough in his house and he must return home.

When Kabir saw the rice he understood that it came through the Divine Will and from that day he left the weaving trade, and gave alms to the poor. Kabir took no notice of Brahmans who were his greatest enemies. One day they warned him to leave Benares, as he was distributing alms to low class people and giving nothing to those of high caste. Kabir was obliged to leave his house. God in the shape of Kabir, arrived and distributed alms to the Brahmans also, and directed Kabir to return home as the Brahmans had no more enemity towards him. When Kabir was disturbed in his prayers by a large gathering of all classes of people to receive alms, he pretended to be a drunkard and one day taking a bottle in his hand and holding the arms of a prostitute he came before the Raja of Benares. The Raja took no notice of Kabir. Kabir then threw water on the ground and on enquiry, informed the Raja that the temple of Jagarnath was burning and that he was producing rain in this way to put out the fire. The Raja sent a messenger, who brought the news that it was a fact. The Raja then fell at the feet of Kabir and made himself one of his disciples. All the Hindu and Muhammadan factions of Benares, who were opposed to Kabir's doctrines submitted a petition to Sikandar Lodi, King of Delhi, (this King flourished in 910 Hijari, i. e., 1495 A.D.) representing that Kabir was causing great disturbance at Benares by his lectures which were contrary to both faiths. The King arrived at Benares and sent for Kabir. The Qazi asked Kabir to salute the King, and was told that Kabir knew none save God and Him alone he saluted. The King then ordered the hands and feet of Kabir to be bound with an iron chain and then that he be thrown into the stream of the Ganges. When this was done Kabir was seen standing on the banks of the river, heaps of fuel were collected and lighted, and Kabir was thrown into the fire, from which he came out safe, with his body resembling gold. A mad elephant was let loose to destroy him, but he appeared in the shape of a lion before it. The King then threw himself at Kabir's feet and became his disciple.

The Brahmans then circulated an invitation to all the ascetics (*Sádhu*) and Fakirs in and around Benares, that on a certain day there would be a grand dinner at Kabir Chaura, of which Kabir had no knowledge. When there was a large gathering collected at Kabir's door, he left the place and went to hide himself in the streets. God in the shape of Kabir arrived and fed all the guests. A fairy came from heaven to deceive Kabir and was initiated by him.

When the time of Kabir's death arrived, he left Benares and went to Maghar, 14 miles from Gorakhpur, where he composed the following *Dohá* and breathed his last :—

Bhajan bharose Nám ke,
Maghar tagro Sarir,
Abinási ke god men,
Bilasat Dás Kabir.

Depending on devotion to the name of God I leave my body at Maghar and in the lap of Him who is immortal (God) is adorned the servant Kabir

On his death the Hindus wanted to burn Kabir's body, and the Muhammadans wished to bury it. To their great surprise a heap of roses was found in place of the body, which was divided in equal shares among both faiths The Hindus burnt their share of the flowers and the Muhammadans buried their's, at Maghar where they have devoted landed property to repair the tomb and light it at festivals.

When a man wishes to be initiated, he has to bathe, wear a new white loin cloth (*dhoti*) and sheet and take] 1½ seer of *gur*, *batásha*, 7 *bangla pán*, *kesar*, white flowers, a cocoanut, camphor, loin cloth and cash to his Guru, who makes him clean the ground with dry earth called "*chouka thakur*," and then placing the above articles in a metal dish, (*phul kí tháli*) he sits facing the north. The Guru sits facing the south. The Guru then directs him to think of white colours in his imagination, then to imagine that there is a white board on which the Divine light is sitting, and that a white coloured person standing behind him is Kabir Sáhib with a fan (*chawar*) in his hand. After the disciple has thought as above, he is directed to open his eyes and to salute his Guru in the words: *Bandagi Sáhib*. The Guru then answers him, *Dayá Sáhib*. The Guru then writes on a *bangla pan-leaf* the words *Sat Kabir*, and gives them to his disciple seven times. This is called *pán parwána*, the lamp is then lighted, and with burning camphor, they offer an *arti* in the name of Kabir Sáhib. *Gur* is then given to him to eat and he receives a necklace (*kanthe*) from his Guru and his forehead is marked with *chandan*, from the nose to the forehead. When there is a childbirth and a marriage a Kabir panthi has to offer camphor lights. On the death of a Kabir panthi a distribution of food (*bhandára*) is made of *málpua*, and *kachawari* are doled out. In the night a cocoanut is offered to the camphor light (*arti*) in the name of Kabir, with a request to relieve the deceased from the burden of transmigration and then the cocoanut is broken. If the kernel is soft and white, it is understood that the man was a perfect Kabir Panthi, and when it is rotten it is understood that he had not firm belief and that he worshipped stone images also.—*Bhan Pratap Tewari*.

---

61. **Food for the Dead.**—In these Provinces it is supposed that the ghosts of the dead often enter the kitchen in search of food at night. Housewives who leave out food from the day's meal for the use of their children in the morning, whenever they miss any of the food, invariably attribute the loss to some ghost. The only way to stop depredations of this kind is to place food for the dead every night on the roof of the house and to feed Brahmans or their girls in the name of the spirit. In many such cases a pariah dog or a cat is the real culprit, but old women are very slow to believe that it is not due to demoniacal agency.—*W. Crooke*, C.S.

---

62. **The legend of Bhuvan Sinh, the Saint.**—Bhuvan Sinh was a Chauhan Rajput and was devoted to the worship of Krishna. Once he went to Brindaban and became a disciple of the renowned saint Hirivansa. After that he was still more devoted to his religious observances, but as he had no mends of support he took service with the Maharaja of Udaypur. The Ráná appointed him one of his personal attendants. In the first watch of the day he used to worship Krishna Bhagwán; in the second he used to perform the duties of his office in Darbár; in the third he would give alms to the poor and read religious books and in the fourth watch he again attended on the Ráná.

One day he went out hunting with the Ráná and a deer came out of the grass. The Ráná told him to shoot it and when he had done so, he found that it was a pregnant doe. He was overcome with grief and prayed to Krishna Bhagwán to pardon him for the sin of killing the innocent unborn fawn. But he determined never to take life again, so he made him a sword of lath and put it in his scabbard.

The courtiers who were jealous of the favour in which he stood, went to the Ráná and said. "Do you keep Bhuvan Sinh to be a saint or a soldier?" The Ráná answered: "He is my right hand in the time of battle" "Then let him show his sword to your Majesty," they said. When the Ráná called on Bhuvan Sinh to show his sword, he was perplexed, feeling that he would be disgraced. So he prayed to Krishna Bhagwán and lo, when he drew his sword from the sheath it was of steel, so glittering that the eye of man never saw. The Ráná was wroth with those who had informed against Bhuvan Sinh and was about to order them for punishment. But Bhuvan Sinh interceded for them and told ths whole case to the Ráná. The Ráná was so struck with his devotion, that he said: "You must in future attend not my Darbar, but the Darbar of Krishna Bhagwán." So he allotted maintenance for his family and Bhuvan Sinh devoted himself to deeds of piety for the rest of his life.—*Pandit Rám Gharib Chaube*.

---

63. **Saharanpur: The Fair in honour of the Saint Guga, at Manik Mau.**—At a place called Manik Mau, about two miles to the south of Saharanpur, there *is* an annular fair held in honour of Guga, commencing on the tenth day of the dark and ending on the tenth day of the light fortnight of Bhadon. The Bhagats, who are here the only priests of Guga, account for the origin of the fair as follows:—

Once upon a time Guga in his wanderings happened to pass by the village of Manik Mau and seeing a Kahár fishing in a tank went up to him.

The Pír handed over to him a Neza, or standard, and said: "I have taken thee into my confidence. Take this standard home and tell thy people to worship it with offerings of cloth, sweets, sugar, flowers and money. Whosoever does this worship faithfully shall obtain the desires of his heart." When the Kahár took the standard into the village and announced the orders of the saint, they laughed him to scorn. Then the Pír became wroth and sent an army of snakes into the village. Many died and the remainder thought of the order of the Pír which they had disobeyed. So they called the Kahár and begged him to perform the worship in the manner prescribed by the Pír. It was soon found that the worship was efficacious to procure children for the barren, eyes for the blind and to relieve all kinds of trouble. In time the Kahár was unable alone to perform the worship; so he laid the matter before the Pír, who ordered that twenty-five standards should be distributed as follows:—One to the Kahár chief priest; one to a Kalál; one to a Gújar; three to three Málís; two to the Gole Málís; four to the Hindu Jogís; two to the Bharbhunjas; two to the Kuchgars; two to the Chhípís; two to the Nais; three to the Kaharí; one to the Chamár Juláhas; one to the Pádha Jogís.

Thus twenty-five families of different castes came to be appointed to the priesthood of Guga and no addition can now be made to that number. By and by the chief priest founded a fair close to the tank where he met Guga. During the fair each family of priests performs the worship for its own clients and receives the offerings. Each family has a platform of its own near the tank on which is set up the standard of Guga. By a recent arrangement these twenty-five priestly families have divided the city of Saharanpur and the surrounding villages into separate parishes for themselves and each family officiates only for residents in its own parish.

During the fair the duties of the priests are as follows :—On the first day they set up the standard and worship it with an offering of incense. They then, accompanied by playing on the Damru, or small hour glass shaped drum, march through their parishes while Jogís sing songs in honour of Guga. They sing at the house of each client and receive the offerings. This begging goes on for fourteen days. The priests take the offerings, reserving a small share for the men who beat the drum and sing. On the fifteenth day they go to the tank at Manik Mau and set up the standard, each on his own platform. There they receive further offerings from visitors.

According to the local tradition, Guga jumped into the cleft in the earth at a place named Karanpur in Bikaner, and some of his votaries make pilgrimages there under the guidance of one of these Bhagat priests. The offerings are the same as those described above, with a rupee in cash. The fee for the priests escort to Karampur is a rupee or two. As is usual the worship of Narasinha, the lion avatar of Vishnu, is very closely connected with that of Guga. To him are offered wine or milk and a sort of sharbat made of the *batasha* sweetmeat and water.

I have given some account of Guga in the *Introduction to Popular Religion and Folklore* (pp. 133, *sqq*). According to Mr. Maclagan (*Panjab Census Report*, 104) no less than 35,344 persons in British territory have declared themselves worshippers of Guga, who is perhaps the most popular object of worship among all classes of people in the east of the Panjab and in the low hills as far west as Kangra and Hoshyarpur. "His story, how he fled his native country in Bikaner, how he became a Musalman, how the earth swallowed him up, how he had power over snakes, and all the details of his worship have been told in many books. *

"In life," says Major Temple, "he appears to have been a Hindu leader of the Chauhan Rajputs against Mahmud of Ghazni about *A. D.* 1000." He is adored by Hindus and Musalmans alike and by all castes, by Rajputs and Jats as well as by Chamars and Chuhras. Even the Bráhman looks on him as a fit object of reverence. "Which is greater", says the proverb "Rám or Guga?" and the reply is: "Be who may be greater, shall I get myself bitten by a snake?" In other words—"Though Rám may be the greater between ourselves, I dare not say so for fear of offending Guga."

64. **Indra Worship.**—There are very few survivals of Indra worship in the villages. Sometimes in the cold weather or in the month of Bhadon there occur twelve days of excessive rain and cold, which is most destructive to old and weak cattle. This pious Hindus call Indradaman, which may mean the "subjugation by Indra." Low caste people call this period Chamar-baraha, or "the Chamar's twelve days," because he reaps a good harvest of hides. They say that Chamars, when this occurs, pray secretly to their demons that the bad weather may continue.—*W. Crook, C. S.*

* *Panjab Census Report*, 1881, paragraph 223; *Kangra Gazetteer*, page 68; *Hoshyarpur Gazetteer*, page 47; *Rohtak Gazetteer*, page 54; *Panjab Notes and Queries*, 1·3·6; 212; II—555; Oman's *Social and Religious Life in the Panjab*, Chapter II; Temple, *Legends of the Panjab*, 1·121.

ANTHROPOLOGY.

65. **Precautions during Pregnancy.**—When a man's wife is pregnant he should avoid joining in throwing a corpse into a river; undertaking a pilgrimage; going on a long journey; bathing in the sea; shaving his hair.—*Pândit Râm Gharib Chaubê*
[Can this be connected with the Couvade?—Ed.]

66. **Clothed Images.**—May I ask your readers' attention to an interesting branch of primitive ritual on which I am anxious to elicit facts.

The custom of *the offering of a garment to an image* may be taken as typified in the offering of the robe to Athene in the great Panathenaic festival at Athens; but it appears probable that similar rites extend through all stages of culture.

I should be glad of instances of garments or coverings provided for images, or for any sacred object; and especially of the use of such garments at festivals or on special occasions.

As interesting examples of this clothing of images or sacred objects in most widely separated conditions of culture, I may mention the very primitive clothing of a sacred stone by branches " to keep the god warm " in Samoa;* " when praying on account of war, drought, famine, or epidemic, the branch *clothes* were carefully renewed;" * the clothing like a woman of a plantain tree in the ceremonies that take place at the consecration of an image of Durga (Parvati); † the draping of images in the skin of sacrificial victims; the Mexican festival of Huitzilopochli where an image, made of dough, was dressed in the raiment of the idol; ‡ and the great Mexican festival of Tezcatlipoca on the eve of which the image was dressed in new clothes. §

When the divinity is specially represented by a living person (as in the Hindoo rite of worshipping daughters of a Bráhman as forms of a goddess and offering to them cloth, paint and ornaments, during the ceremony; ‖ and the rite in which human sacrifices were " adorned Mexican with the trappings of the Thaloc gods, for it was said they were the images of these gods, " ¶ garments provided for such persons would, of course, have an interest equal to that of clothing destined for an image.

Instances of such ritual clothing would be most valuable if, in connection with festivals of the birth (or return,) marriage, or death of the god; also all examples of the ritual clothing of trees (compare the Durga rite). And I should be glad of instances of any kind of covering from savage paint to temple vestments.

1. Instances of garments or coverings provided for images, or for *any sacred objects;* and especially of the offering of such garments at any festivals or special occasions ?

2. Analogies to the Hindoo rite of the clothing, like a woman of a plantain tree in the ceremonies that take place at the consecration of an image of the Hindoo goddess Durga (Parvati)?

3. Instances of the use of ritual clothing of an image or sacred object (or person) in connection with festivals celebrating the birth or return, the marriage, or the death of the god.—*G. M. Godden, Ridgfield, Wimbledon, England.*

67 **Rules for the Dressing of Idols and Priests during Worship.**—The following rules as to the dressing of idols and priests apply only to the Vaishnava order of the Vallabha Sampradaya. This sect is famous for the splendour of their religious services and are thus a good example of the existing practice. Those of the Saiva and Sakta sects are, of course, entirely different.

When a Vaishnava rises from his bed he begins the day by repeating the names of the founder of the sect, the special god who is the object of his devotion, the river connected with the worship of his god and the names of any famous saints who have flourished in his sect. He also repeats the Mantra, or religious formula, which was whispered into his ear when he was initiated by his religious guide. He then adjusts the rosaries which hang round his throat and looks at them. Then he sings a song in honour of the river which is connected with his deity, and after bathing marks his forehead with the marks of his sect in ground sandal wood or sacred clay. Besides his forehead he marks his nose, back, head, &c., with sandal-wood or clay. He then proceeds to the temple of his god and performs the worship according to the regular ritual. First, he prostrates himself at the door of the temple and touches the ground with his nose and forehead. Then he washes the vessels which have been used on the previous night in worship. After this the clothes which are to be used that day for the god are put in order. And bells are rung and musical instruments played to wake the deity from his sleep and the morning song is sung. The morning meal (*mangal bhog*) is laid before the god and lamps moved over the image as in the ordinary Arti rite. After this the idol is bathed and ornaments and dress put on it. Garlands of flowers are put on the neck and Tulasi leaves laid at its feet. It is made to look at its reflection in a looking glass and food with milk is served. The mouth is washed and betel offered. A chessboard and toys are placed before it and lamps

---
* Samoa. Turner, p. 62.
† Ward's Hindoos, Ed. 1817, Vol. II, p. 13. Ed. 1863 p. 184.
‡ Native Races of the S. Pacific, Bancroft, Vol. II, p. 321.
Bancroft, *Ibid*, Vol II., p. 318.
‖ Ward's Hindoos, Ed. 1817, Vol, I, p. 245-6; Ed. 1863, p. 151.
¶ Bancroft, *Ibid*, Vol. III., p. 343

are moved over the head of the idol. Then comes the time for the siesta, when the god's bed is arranged and the temple doors are shut.

In the afternoon he is again waked to the sound of the ringing of bells and playing of musical instruments. Fresh water is brought and fruit is laid before the image.

When bed time comes the deity retires to rest. If it be summer the image is covered with a light sheet; in winter with a heavy quilt. The images of Rádha, Janki or Síta are always dressed during the night in a sheet (*sári*): those of the infant Krishna or Ráma are put to bed naked.

If the images are covered with valuable gems it is unnecessary to bathe them daily. Even on fast days food should be laid before the gods.

The great festival of the Vallabha Sampradaya, and indeed of all Vaishnavas, is the Janamasthami or birthday of Krishna, as well as the Rámnauni or birthday of Ráma. On the morning of the eighth day of Bhádon the following ceremonies are performed:—At dawn the deities are awakened and lamps are moved over their heads. The dress and ornaments which were worn during the night are taken off and, if the image be that of Krishna, it is dressed in a yellow silk loin cloth. Over the shoulders is spread a sheet, on the neck a gold necklace, on the wrists bangles and anklets on the feet. These ornaments are only put on the image of Rádha. Krishna is bathed in water and Rádha in Panchamrita, or the five products of the sacred cow. They are then dressed and placed on their seats. At the door an image of a lotus with seven petals is made with powdered turmeric. Within this a bathing vessel is placed, inside which is a wooden seat, over this a folded sheet and on the top the vessel of Panchamrita. In another vessel is placed saffron (*kumkuma*) mixed with water and near it some rice dyed yellow and Tulasi leaves. Close by is put a jug filled with water. The images of Krishna and his brother Baldeo are placed on the seat in the bathing dish and before them is placed the small image of Krishna which represents the god in his childhood. The priest takes some water in his right hand and announces that he is about to bathe Krishna in honour of the annual celebration of his birth. After bathing the images he applies sandal-wood powdered to them and fixes some washed and dyed rice to the foreheads of them. Some Tulasi leaves are put in a conch shell and musical instruments are sounded. The image is then bathed from the conch shell a second time, first with milk, then curds, honey, ghi and sugar and water. Lastly, pure water is used. He then bows down in obeisance and rubs perfumes on the images. He next wipes them with a handkerchief and applies saffron to them. Again he wipes them and dresses Rádha with a sheet dyed in saffron with a border of silver braid, a cap (*kulhi*) dyed

in saffron, red silken drawers. The image of Krishna is similarly dressed in male attire. Rádha's cheeks are rubbed with musk (*kastúri*) and her eyes and those of Krishna blackened with lamp-black or antimony. Rádha wears as ornaments the armlet (*bázuband*) wrist ornament (*pahunchi*) and a triple gold chain round the neck. Any other ornaments available are also placed on the image. Perfume is next sprinkled over the clothes of the deities and garlands of flowers round their necks and they are placed on the seat known as Sinhásan.

Before the seat is made a square with turmeric, and festoons of flowers are tied at the door of the temple. The images are made to look at themselves in a mirror and a wrapper of silk is put on each. Behind their backs are placed red silk pillows. Lamps are waved and the foreheads of the deities marked, that of Rádha being in vermilion. Over this is put some sandal and rice. While this is being done musical instruments are played and songs sung.

The pair of sandals which represent Vallabhacharya, the founder of the sect, are covered with a cloth of yellow silk and over them washed rice and sandal are scattered. Two rupees are placed beside them as an offering (*nazar*) with two packets of betel. Lamps are again moved over them and obeisance is made. All this time musical instruments are played. A flat seat (*chauki*) is laid before the idols, on it a bed on which the image of Krishna is laid. He is then made to give away a cow to a Bráhman. Food is then placed before them and they go to rest. When they wake they are again fed and dressed. When at night they finally go to sleep, perfect silence is maintained so as not to disturb their rest.

Another rite is the Hindola, or the placing of the image of the child Krishna in his cradle. A square is made in the form of a lotus with eight petals. In this the cradle is put with a pillow inside, and over it is spread a white sheet. A second pillow is placed at the foot of the bed. Food is laid close by in cups and playthings for the child deity. Next Khasti, or Sashti Máta, the guardian of children, is worshipped. Her image is painted on the western wall and the woman who makes it sits facing the east. As the picture is being painted they sing songs in commemoration of the birth of the deity. Above the figure of Sashti an iron peg is fixed in the wall On it is hung a sheet dyed with yellow and three bamboo sticks are tied together so as to form a triangle. This is fastened to the peg. In the triangle are fixed some flowers. Before the picture is laid a pile of dry gram, and on the pile a lamp lighted with ghi. In front a square is marked out with flour and inside this are placed two wooden seats with yellow cloths laid on them. The worshipper bows to Sashti Máta and places near her a flute (*bansli*) dyed red. To her left is placed a sword. When feeding times comes food is put before it and after they have finished eating the mouths of the images are washed and wiped. Betel is served and flowers hung round their necks. After burning some camphor, the food is removed and lamps are waved over the images. They are then laid in the cradle. The priests and their relations put on yellow clothes and mangoes are distributed among all present. Each member of the family in turn swings the cradle in which the deities are reposing. Then the priest bows before Sashti Mâta and says: "To-day I vow to worship the mother Sashti in honour of the birth of the Lord Krishna." Mantras or spells are recited in order to bring the goddess Sashti into the picture on the wall which represents her. Over the figure is sprinkled some rice and saffron. With the recitation of what is known as the Vasodhara Mantra some ghi is poured on the picture. The number of streams of ghi must be three or five in number. The priest then says "O goddess! As you protect Skanda, son of Gauri, so protect this divine child." The milk-churner which is put beside the image is worshipped with an offering of rice and saffron. And the priest says: "O churner! thou hast been made in the region of the gods by the gods and goddesses. I worship thee that thou mayest protect the divine child." Similarly, the sword is worshipped with the invocation: "O sword! thou art the ruler. Thou hast a sharp blade to terrify the evil-doers. I beg thee to protect the divine child and give victory to the pious." Next he worships the flute with the words: "Thou are the luckiest of lucky things. Thou wert in the hand of Sri Krishna. I sing thy praise that thou mayest add to the prosperity of the tribe and give it happiness for ever and ever."

The clothes used with the images vary with each feast. Thus, on the eighth of the dark half of Bhâdon they should wear the Kesariya Bâga or coat (*anga*) dyed in saffron and a *kulha* or cap such as children wear. The same is the rule for the Râdhashtami or eight of the light half of the month sacred to Râdha. On the Dân Ekâdashi or eleventh of Bhâdon, Krishna should wear a crown (*mukut*) and a loin cloth (*kachhani*). On the thirteenth day of Kuâr, known as Sri Bal Krishnaji, when the childhood of the deities is commemorated the Kesariya Bâga, as before, is worn. On the Bijaya Dasmi, or tenth of Kuâr, the garment should be white and the ornaments of gems. On the Rûp Chaturdasi or fourteenth of Kârtik, the clothes are red. On the Diwâli the robes are white and so on.—*Pándit Rám Gharíb Chaubé.*

68. Marriage to a tree, or to an inanimate object.—According to the Hindu Shatras, as explained in the astrological treatise known as the *Mahurta Chintamani*, when a man is fully persuaded by the rules of astrology that his daughter has been born in such an unlucky moment that she is sure to become a child widow, he should adopt the following precautions:—

He should repair to a lonely place and there fast in honour of the pípal tree. Before doing this he should leave the house at an auspicious moment as selected by an astrologer. His daughter should also bathe in the morning and put on new clean clothes. Then she should go out by herself in secret and dig up a young pípal tree and bring it to a place where there are a Sami and a bel tree. There she should plant it and water it with water brought in a gourd for that purpose. From the first day of the lunar month of Chait or Kuár, she should daily worship a Brahman, or a Brahman woman daily, until the first day of the next month. She should also make an image of the goddess Párvati and putting it in a receptacle made of bamboo, worship it daily.

On a day selected by an astrologer as auspicious for a marriage, her father should get her married to the pípal tree which she had planted and watered as above described. All the standard ritual should be observed, as if she were being married to a human husband.

If after this she be married to a real husband, there is no danger of her becoming a widow.

Another device of the same kind is for the father to marry her secretly to a jar. This also keeps her from the risk of becoming a child widow. The pitcher should be placed in a secret room, pieces of cow-dung should be stuck to the sides and some branches of the bamboo in the mouth. Round it should be twisted a string in imitation of the Brahmanical cord. When the marriage has been performed in the regular way between the girl and the jar, the priest receives all the wedding garments, ornaments and things used in the marriage, as well as a money gift.

In the same way, to avoid the danger of premature widowhood, the father may marry his daughter to an image of Vishnu. Here, as in the last case, the officiating priest acts the part of the father-in-law of the bride.

The girl is married to these objects, because in Hindu belief they are immortal and thus she can never be left a widow in consequence of the death of her husband. Whatever be the evil influence of the stars it affects the first, not the second husband. The real bridegroom escaped the danger ous influence in this way.

It is said that in the old days, Sûrya, the Sun god, married his daughter to a jar and Renuka married his to a pípal tree, in both cases to avoid the danger of premature widowhood. These precedents are still quoted by Hindus as justifying the custom.—*Pándit Rám Gharíb Chaubé.*

FOLKTALES.

69. The Magic Boat.—Once upon a time a rich man fell into poverty, and, leaving his wife and children at home, went into a foreign land to make his living. One day his wife was sitting at her door, lamenting the hardness of her fate, when a Sádhu passed by and asked her the cause of her trouble. She told him all her circumstances, and he then gave her a boat, and said: "The virtue of this boat is this. It will give you all you ask of it; but when it gives you one rupee it will give your neighbours two." She was much pleased, and when the Sádhu went away, she began to ask the boat for large sums of money, which it always gave her; but as much as she got, her neighbours always got double.

After a time her husband came back with a considerable sum of money which he had made. When he found all the neighbours, whom he had left in poverty, much richer than himself, he was amazed, and asked his wife how they had managed to get rich without ever leaving the village in which they were born. She then told him about the magic boat which always gave her neighbours double what it gave to her. When he heard this he was overcome by envy, and said: "This was an evil gift you received from the Sádhu." So he took the boat, plastered a piece of ground, and placed the boat within it. He then implored the boat to burn one of his houses. It did so, and at the same time burned down two houses of each of his neighbours. Then he asked the boat to make a well in his courtyard. This was done: and there were two wells in each of the courtyards of his neighbours. Then he implored the boat to deprive him of one of his eyes, and if he became one-eyed all his neighbours became totally blind and began to fall into their wells.

Then they all came and begged him to restore their sight. But he said: "All the time you were making heaps of money out of my boat, you never gave me a share. Now I have made you blind and I will not restore your sight until you promise to give me half of all you make by me." So they had to agree, and then he asked the boat to restore him his eye, whereupon all his neighbours recovered their sight.

A folktale told by Mukund Lál, Káyasth, of Mirzapur.)

70. The Brahman and the Sadhu.—There was once a Bráhman who had two sons, and as he was very poor he went with them into another land in search of a living. One evening he reached the hut of a Sádhu and halted there. The Bráhman told him all his troubles, and, as he had no disciple, the Sádhu offered to adopt one of the boys. So he gave the Bráhman a considerable sum of money and told him to go home leaving the boys with him; that he would educate the boys and, selecting one as his disciple, would return him the other. The Bráhman agreed, and leaving the boys with the Sádhu went home.

One day the Bába called the boys and ordered them each to bring him a *lota* full of hoar-frost. One of them, who was very industrious, somehow or other collected a *lota* full of hoar-frost from the grass and leaves. The other, who was an idle fellow, went to the tank and filled his *lota* full of water. The Bába put both the *lotas* out in the sun, and soon discovered which held the hoar-frost and which the water. So he dressed the idle boy in fine clothes and began to educate his diligent brother. After a time this boy became deeply skilled in magic.

Some years passed and the Bráhman returned to the Sádhu, who was away at the time. The magician boy told his father that he had better ask the Bába for him rather than for his ignorant brother. When the Bába came back he told the Bráhman to choose one of the boys; he chose the boy who knew magic. The Bába was bound by his promise, and though he tried to induce the Bráhman to take the other boy, he was obliged at last to give him up.

The Bráhman and his son started for home, and on the way the boy said: "Father, I am about to transform myself into a lamb. You can sell me; but mind do not give any one, who buys me, the halter." When he said this the boy was changed into a lamb, which a man bought from the Bráhman for a large sum of money. The Bráhman went his way and very soon his son stood before him in his original form. The Bráhman was delighted to see him, and the boy said: "Father, I will now turn myself into a horse. You can sell me for two thousand rupees; but mind you do not give away the halter with me." As the Bráhman was trying to sell the horse the Bába came up in disguise and asked him what the price of the animal was. The Bráhman asked two thousand rupees, which the Bába at once gave, but the Bráhman forgot his son's warning and let him have the halter in the bargain. The Bába rode off to his hermitage on the horse and tied it to a post; but he took care never to take off the rein. He knew that if he did so the horse would die.

One day it so happened that the Bába was away and the other boy took the horse to water at the tank, and in his ignorance took off the rein. Then the horse instantly died. When the Bába returned and found out what had happened, he consulted his books and learned that the boy had been transformed, and was a fish in the tank. So he turned himself into a heron and began to search for him. The boy immediately became a parrot and flew away. The Bába turned himself into a hawk and pursued him. The boy then became a diamond necklace and hung himself round the neck of a Ráni. The Bába turned himself into a dancer and appeared before the Ráni. The Ráni was so pleased that she gave him the necklace. The boy then became a pile of mustard and the Bába became a pigeon and began to pick it up. The boy turned himself into a cat and devoured the pigeon. Then he went back to his father and they lived happily ever after.

(A folktale told by Muniswar Prasád Tiwári, Bráhman of Gajádharpur, Gházipur.)

71. **How the Raja went to the Heaven of Bhagwan.**—There was once a Rája who thought himself the lord of the whole world. One day his son, who was blessed with great wisdom, asked him what he was always thinking about. The Rája said that he was always thinking of conquering the whole world. His son said : " That is well, but there are four duties of a King—devotion, protection of his subjects, justice, and the increase of his kingdom. Out of the four you practise only one." The Rája said : " You are right. I have done the first three, but I have never thought of the last. I am now an old man and I intend to pass the remainder of my days in devotion." So saying the Rája seated his son on his throne and began to wander about the world as a Sádhu.

Wandering through many lands, at length he came to a forest ; and when any one asked him where he was going, he used to say : " I am going in search of Bhagwán." They laughed at him, and said : " You cannot find Bhagwán unless you keep the company of ascetics." So he set out in search of ascetics, and at last he came to the Himálaya, where he found a Sannyási sitting absorbed in devotion. The Rája sat long before him, but the Saint paid no heed to him. He used daily to clean the place where the Sannyási lay. After many days the Saint opened his eyes and asked the Rája what he desired. The Rája said : " I am seeking for Bhagwán." The Sannyási answered : " For many years I have been concentrating my thoughts on the Creator (*Karta*) of all things, and have failed to find Him. How can you find Him in a single day ? But I will give you a *mantra* which you must repeat morn and evening, and, if possible, at all times. Perchance some day you may find Him." After he recited the *mantra* the Sannyási again became absorbed in his meditations, and the Rája went on repeating the *mantra* constantly. Many days passed, and the Sannyási again came to his senses and, finding the Rája still there, was much pleased. Then the Sannyási said : " I give you this cup. Whenever you ask it for anything it will give it. Now go away, repeat the *mantra* for twelve years and then return to me."

The Rája taking the cup went to a city and sat beside a well. He went on constantly repeating the *mantra* and earned his living by sewing. But he never asked the cup for anything. One day it so happened that the Rája when returning from hunting came to the place where his father lay. When he knew him he fell on his face before him and said : " Father, return with me to your palace. The life of an ascetic is very hard. How can you, who have always been giving orders to others, beg your bread ? " The Rája answered : " My son, I am more happy than you are. You may give an order which is not obeyed, but even the fish of the water and the birds of the air are ready to do my bidding. If you do not believe me, follow me to the bank of this tank." Then he led his son to the water's edge and throwing his needle in asked his son to bring it out. The Prince searched for it, but in vain. Then the Rája called a fish and ordered it to bring it out. The fish at once obeyed his order and laid the needle before him. Seeing this the Prince said : " Father, I will accompany you " The Rája reasoned long with him, and induced him to return home.

The Rája went into a forest and met another Sannyási. He was then absorbed in devotion, and the Rája remained standing before him. When the Sannyási opened his eyes he asked the Rája what he wished. The Rája said : " I wish to see Bhagwán." The Sannyási said : " Go and sit under that tree. Perchance you may see Him there sooner than elsewhere." The Rája went and sat under the tree and began to recite the *mantra*, which the first Sannyási had taught him. One day he saw an enormous tiger running towards the tree. The Rája went to the Sannyási and told him what he had seen. The Sannyási said : " You fool ! the tiger from which you foolishly tried to escape was Bhagwán whom you were seeking."

When twelve years passed the Rája and the Sannyási went to the Saint whose dwelling was on the Himálaya. He was glad to see them, and said : " Let us now ascend to heaven." Then a heavenly chariot appeared, and the three took their seats on it. When they had gone some distance the Rája saw his own palace and thought to himself : " Why did I not enjoy the pleasure of living there some time longer ? " No sooner did this thought come into his mind than he fell down from the chariot and was reborn in the family of a boatman (*Mallah*). When he came to be fourteen years of age he thought of the *mantra* which he used to recite, and he began to repeat it. When he had repeated it for twelve years a voice came from heaven : " Fool ! thou didst all but gain thy desires and lost it again through love of this world. You have won it again by your devotion. The chariot will again appear. Beware! lest you lose the fruit of your piety by low desires." The chariot appeared and on it the Rája ascended to heaven.

(A folktale told by Mukund Lál, Káyasth, of Mirzapur.)

72. **The Parrot and the Guru.**—There was once a banker who taught his parrot the speech of men. One day it so happened that a Sadhu passed by where the cage of the parrot was hanging and as he came near the parrot said: "Salám Mahárájl" The Sadhu looked round in every direction and tried to see who had saluted him. The parrot said: "It was I saluted you. Maháráj: you point out to all men the way which leads from this world of sorrow to the region of eternal peace. May it please you to explain to me the means whereby I may escape from this cage." The Sadhu answered: "Let me consult my Guru and then I will reply to your question."

The Sadhu went to his Guru and explained the case of the parrot. To his utmost surprise and terror the Guru, the moment he heard the case, spread out his limbs and lay in a swoon. The Sadhu poured water over him and revived him with great difficulty.

Next day as the Sadhu was passing by the place where the parrot's cage was hanging, the bird asked him it he had consulted the Guru about his case. The Sadhu told him the condition into which the Guru had fallen when the matter was laid before him. The parrot answered. "You did not perhaps understand the Guru's meaning; but I have understood it and I am greatly obliged both to him and to you. Salám Mahárájj. Now go your way."

When the Sadhu had gone the parrot spread out his feet and wings and lay in a dead swoon in the bottom of his cage. When his master came to feed him and saw his state he cried: "Alas my parrot! He is dead!" So he opened the door of the cage and threw the bird on the ground. Immediately he got up and flew away.

(A folktale told by Bact'au Kasera of Mirzapur.)

73. **The piety of Raja Raghu.**—Of all the the Rájas of the world none was so pious as Rája Raghu; for to every Bráhman whoever he might be that came to his gate he used to give a ration of grain and a piece of gold. One day he was out hunting and a Bráhman came to the palace gate and begged an alms. The Rání put a ration of food and five gold coins in a dish and sent it to him by one of her maids. He asked her who had sent it and she said that the Rája was absent and that the Rání had sent this for his acceptance. "I will not take it from your hands," he answered. "Let the Rání herself come and present it to me." When she heard this the Rání added to the gift and coming herself to the gate passed it out to the Bráhman by her maid. The Brahman saw her and was amazed at her beauty. He asked her whence she got this loveliness. She replied: "In my former life I killed myself at Benares and hence in this life I have become so beautiful." The Brahman said: "I too will go to Benares and do as you have done."

So he left the food and money and went his way. When he had gone the Rání began to think that she had incurred the sin of allowing a Bráhman to leave her door without provision, and when her husband returned she told him what had happened. He armed himself with his sword and shield and started for Benares. On the way he was tired and lay down under a tree. On this tree a pair of birds had made their nest and were rearing their young. The parents were away at the time searching for food and as the Rája lay there he saw a snake climbing up the tree. Fearing the sin of seeing life taken in his presence he killed the snake with his sword. When the mother bird returned she began to bless the Rája and giving him a fruit said: "Whoever eats this fruit even if he be old will become young."

As the Rája was sitting there the Bráhman came up and the Rája asked him where he was going. He said that he had seen the beauty of the Rání and was going to Benares to end his life. The Rája answered: "If you were to get the kingdom and Rání of this Rája would you give up your intention?" "How can that be?" enquired the Bráhman. The Rája said: "I own that Rání and that kingdom and I will make both over to you."

The Rája brought him home with him and fulfilled his promise; he himself became a mendicant. As he was about to go into the forest he gave the fruit of youth to the Bráhman and told him what its qualities were. The Bráhman thought that the Rája had given him the fruit to work his ruin so he gave it to an old dog and no sooner had the dog eaten it than it became young again. Then the Bráhman felt remorse and following the Rája into the forest asked for another fruit like it. He took the Bráhman to the bird and asked her for the fruit. She said that the fruit had been given to her by Mahádeva and that they should go to him. They went to Mahadeva and asked him, but he told them that he had got the fruit from Indra. They went to Indra and he sent them to Bhagwan.

They went to Bhagwán and asked him for the fruit. "It is in the garden of Rája Raghu," he answered. "I am Rája Raghu said the Raja." Then Bhagwan embraced him and said: "Thy piety is so great that there is a heavenly mansion and garden prepared for thee. Live here for ever in happiness." So the Raja gave the Bráhman as many of the fruits of youth as he desired. He returned to earth, and the Rání died and was carried to the heaven of Bhagwan where she and her husband lived for ever in happiness.

(Told by Bachau Kasera of Mirzapur.)

74. **The Sàdhu and the Princess.**—Once upon a time a Sádhu was on his travels and saw on a pipal tree the following words written:—

Himmat karat tain ;
Lai pahuncháun main ;
Ji he na darai ;
Jo chahai so karai.

"Keep a stout heart ;
I will provide ;
Fear not for life ;
And you may do as you please."

When he came to the next city he went and stood in the court of the king. At that time the princess was sitting on the balcony, with her head uncovered. The Sádhu fell in love with her and remained there with his eyes fixed upon her. This was told to the king who came out and thus addressed him : " O Shábjí what do you want ?" He answered : " O Bába, I have fallen in love with your daughter." When he heard this the King had him driven out of the place. Next day the Sádhu came again and as before fixed his eyes on the princess. When the king heard of it he went to his daughter and said : "Do something to kill this man." His daughter said: " I will use some stratagem to destroy him."

When he came next day as usual, the princess called out to him : " If you want me you must bring me unpierced pearls." The Sádhu started off at once for the banks of the ocean and began to throw handfuls of water over his shoulders. In the evening the ocean (*samundar*) was moved by his devotion and assuming the form of a Brahman came and asked him what he wanted. He said that he wanted same unpierced pearls. The ocean said: " Stand out of the water and you shall receive them." Then a great wave came up and a pile of pearls lay on the shore. The Sádhu tied up as many as he could in his blanket and took them to the princess. When the king saw the pearls he was amazed and remained silent. Then the princess said to the Sádhu : " If you want me you must cut off your hands and give them to me." The Sadhu at once cut off his hands and laid them before her. Next day she called him again and said : " If you want me you must cut off your head." He answered : " As I have no hands I cannot cut off my head : but if you wish you may cut it off yourself." She did so and when the king heard of it he was pleased and had the corpse thrown away.

A butcher who used to supply meat to the king saw it and took it home. That day he was short of meat; so he sent some of the flesh of the Sádhu to the palace. When the dish was laid before the king he complained that the supply was short, when immediately the meat spoke and said : " O foolish man, why do you say so ? Can the flesh of a man in love ever run short ?" When the king heard these words he was much astonished and said : " Is it possible for you to be restored to human shape ?" The flesh replied : " Lay me on a couch and let the princess come and say " If you love me, arise." Then I shall revive. It all happened as he said, and the king gave him his daughter in mariage and made over the kingdom to him as her dowry.

[A folktale told by Bachau Kasera, of Mirzapur.]

75. **The Prince and his animal friends.**—There was once a king who had an only son, who never attended to his duties and was careless and wayward. For this his father was displeased with him. One day the prince went into the bázár and saw a snake being sold ; he purchased it for a thousand rupees and brought it home. When the king saw how he had spent his money, he was still more angry. The next day the prince again went to the bázár and bought a dog for a thousand rupees, and after that he bought in the same way a cat and a rat, The king, his father, was so angry that he told him to go and make his living as best he could.

He took the animals with him and started on his travels. He came to a great jungle and the snake said to him : " My home is here and here the Madári snake tamer caught me. Will you kindly allow me to visit my parents, and my father will give you anything you ask in return for saving my life." As he was going away, the snake said : " If you are asked by my father to choose a gift, take nothing but the ring he wears on his finger." When the snake went to his father he praised the prince and then his father came out of the hole and asked the prince to choose a boon ; he asked for the snake's ring, which the old snake gave him.

When he had gone some distance he plastered a piece of ground and putting the ring in the middle said : " If you are a true ring build me a mansion here." No sooner had he uttered these words, than a palace appeared before him. There the prince began to live with his animals. One day a Bráhman and a barber passed by that way and when the prince enquired their business they told him that they were going in search of a husband for the princess of that land. When they saw the glory of the prince and found him to be a beautiful youth, they asked him if he would marry the princess, and he agreed.

On the day fixed for the marriage the prince spoke to the ring and ordered it to provide all that was needed for the occasion. The ring obeyed his orders and the marriage was duly solemniseds

The prince brought his bride home and all he wanted was provided by the ring. One day as he was leaving home the princess said to him: "There is nothing in the larder; leave the ring with me and I will order what is needed." He gave her the ring and went away. While her husband was absent, a Bráhman came and asked for alms; the princess asked him what he wanted, He said: "If you give me the ring you are wearing, I will say many prayers for you." So she gave him the ring and when he got to the other side of the river, he plastered a piece of ground, and placing the ring on it, he said: "O ring, if you are true, bring the palace with the princess here." Immediately the palace with the princess was brought there.

Two days after, when the Prince returned home, he found that the princess and the palace had disappeared. He was very sad and began to weep. Then his wife's brother came and asked him where she was and when he could not answer his brother-in-law had him shut up a room. When they saw the state of their master the faithful animals were much grieved and the mouse and the dog said to the cat: "You are the wisest of us all and have a knowledge of magic; think and discover what has become of the princess." The cat sat down and began to consider and at last she said: "The princess and her palace are on the bank of Fulána river." They then agreed to go in search of the ring; they came to the palace, but the Bráhman had closed it in on all sides and there was no way of going in. Finally, the mouse crept in through the drain and saw the princess sitting on her bed. He crept up to her and began to lick her foot. She recognised the mouse and told him all her troubles. He asked her where the Bráhman used to keep the ring. She said: "When he lies down he puts it into his mouth and then he makes me fan him." The mouse said: "To-night when he goes to sleep you must put out the light with your fan." So saying, he hid himself in a corner of the room where the Bráhman used to sleep. At night the Bráhman lay down and the princess was fanning him. When she put out the lamp the mouse put his tail up the Bráhman's nose and he gave a great sneeze and the ring fell on the ground. The mouse took it in his mouth and ran away with it. He gave it to the dog and told him to run and give it to the Prince. But as the dog was crossing a river the ring fell into the water and though he did his best, he could not find it. He sat on the bank and wept and meanwhile the cat and the mouse arrived. The dog told them what had happened to the ring. The cat began to consider where the ring was and by her wisdom she discovered that it was in the belly of a fish. The animals waited there that night and in the morning some Malláhs came and were fishing in the river. They caught many fish and laid them on the bank. When the Malláhs saw the animals sitting there they wondered and said to each other: "The dog has a natural enmity to the cat and the cat to the mouse. How comes it that they are sitting together?" The animals said: "We are so hungry that we cannot move a step. Give us a fish out of your great store and we shall be grateful to you." The Malláhs said: "Come and choose which fish you please." So the cat chose that in which the ring was and brought it to the dog, who tore its belly and took out the ring.

They started with it and came to the room where the prince was confined and the mouse crept in through a hole and gave it to him. Then he called to the ring to bring back the princess and the palace, and this was done immediately. The princess and the prince, with their faithful animals, lived happily ever after.

[Told by Rám Govind Páṇré, Bráhman, of Ghurhúpattí, Mirzapur.]

[This is the usual faithful animal cycle.]

76. **The Fool and the Alphabet.**—A stupid boy was once sent to school and though he was a long time under instruction he learnt nothing. When he came home his father gave him a book to read and as he turned over the leaves he burst into tears. "What a clever boy this is!" every one said. "See how he has already begun to realise the misery of human life." But whenever he was given a book to read, he always wept. At last some one asked him why he did this, and he answered: "When I was at school the letters looked big and fat on the black board and I now weep to think how thin they have become since they got into this confounded book." —*Pandit Janardan Joshi.*

[A Folktale from Kumaun.]

77. **The Weaver and the Jackal.**—A weaver was once going along the road with his cotton carding bow on his shoulder. A jackal came across him unexpectedly and was much surprised to see an instrument which was quite novel to him. "I have seen a gun," he said, "and I am used to bludgeons; but these men are always inventing some new plan for our destruction. It were well for me to be cautious. But I must stand whatever fate pleases to send. To run away is useless because even a gun would destroy me at this distance." So he came up to the weaver, who was even more frightened than the jackal was, because he had never seen such an animal in all his life. The jackal made a profound bow and said:

Háth bán sir men dhana;
Kahán chale Dillipaty Rána?

"With an arrow in your hand and a mighty bow on your head where are you going Lord of Delhi?"

The weaver was pleased and answered—

Ban ke Ráo, ban hi men rahana,
Akhir bare ne bare ko pahchana.

"Lord of the jungle, the jungle is thy fitting abode. At all events it is only the high-born who could recognise one of equal rank with himself."
—*Pandit Janardan Joshi.*

[A Folktale from Kumaun.]

78. **The Raja and the Hansas.**—Once upon a time a famine raged at Mána Sarowar for fourteen years and a pair of Hansas who lived there had to go elsewhere to find sustenance. When they had gone a long distance they came to a beautiful tank full of fresh water and inhabited by all kinds of birds. The female Hansa said to her mate: "Let us stay here till the famine ends." Her mate answered: "The tank is good but we cannot stay there until we obtain the owner's leave." When the Hansas heard that the tank belonged to the Rájá of the place, they went to him and asked his leave to stay there until times improved. He gave them leave and they settled there.

They had lived there only a few months when one day the Kání came to bathe in the tank and when she saw the Hansa's young ones she longed to have them. So she told the Rájá and he sent a man to summon the Hansas to his Durbar. When he delivered the message they asked him why they were called and he told them what the Rání had said. They answered: "My friend, to-day all the birds will meet at our house and we cannot attend the Rája to-day; but to-morrow, if Parameshwar spares our lives, we will be there."

Next morning the Hansas appeared before the Raja and saluted him. He invited them to sis down and then he asked: "It is true that birdt hold meetings like men?" They answered: "Mahárája, it is true that we have our disputes and quarrels like men have and yesterday we had a meeting to decide a matter in dispute between us." "What was the question?" he asked. "The question was, whether there were more men or women in the world." "And what decision did you come to?" "The number of women is greater than that of men, because we count those men women who do not keep their word." The Rájá was ashamed, and said: "I called you only to see you as I had not seen you for a long time." As they were going away they said: "Maharájá, listen to the words of the poet.—

Bhánu uday udayáchal ten chali ke puni purab pánv dharai nahin;
Jyon sar neh sati chharhi ke puni dhám ki or nigah harai nahin;
Háril ki prán hái lakri kadali puni dajo bar pharai nahin;
Taise Zaban bare jan ki mukh ten nikali puni pichhun tarai nahin.

"The sun rises from behind Udaychal and then sets out on his course, but he does not turn his feet again towards the east.
So when Sati puts the arrow to her bow she looks not back again to home.
The green pigeon sits on wood and the plantain does not fruit a second time.
So when a great man makes a promise he does not break it."

The Rájah was ashamed and thenceforth he protected the Hansas.

[Told by Rám Govind Pánré, Bráhman of Ghurhupatti, Mirzapur.]

79. **The Thakur and the Goldsmith.**—There was once a Thákur who was a very clever fellow; but his wife was unfaithful to him and loved a goldsmith. The Thákur knew this, but said nothing. One day the goldsmith paid her a visit while her husband was supposed to be asleep, but he was listening to what they said: "My dear," said the woman, "if the Thakur would only get blind, what a good time we should have." "I will tell you what to do," he replied. "Fast for the whole month of Kártik and then pray to Bhagwán to make your husband blind, and he will certainly perform your desires."

When the month of Kartik came the woman began a regular fast and planted a Tulasi tree on the bank of the river. When she went away the Thakur dug a deep pit just under the tree and hid himself there. When she came to say her prayers, she began to pray: "O Mother Tulasi! Make my husband blind." From beneath the ground he answered in a feigned voice: "My faithful devotee, give your husband the best of food and then he will surely get blind." So the wife began to feed her husband on every delicacy she could think of and after some time he said to her: "My dear, I really think my sight is not as good as it used to be." She was sure that the charm was working, so she went on feeding him on all kinds of excellent food. Until at last he said: "My dear, I really can hardly see at all."

Then she sent for her lover and told him the joyful news. But as he came in, her husband, who was behind the door, cut off his nose with his sword. The goldsmith was ashamed to tell any one what had happened to him and this was the last visit he paid the lady.

[Told by Bachan Kasera, of Mirzapur.]

MISCELLANEA.

80. Borrowing—Superstitions about.—It is most unlucky to borrow money on a Sunday, Tuesday, or Wednesday. Any one who borrows on these days can never repay his debt. The worst day of all is Wednesday, and to borrow money on that day is utter ruin.—*Pandit Rám Gharib Chaubé.*

81. Washing Clothes—Unlucky Days.—Pandits will not send their clothes to the wash on Wednesday or Saturday. If you do so you will never get clean clothes again. Ordinary people will not send their clothes to be washed on feast days or on the day when they do the sradha for a deceased father.—*Pándit Rám Gharib Chaubé.*

82. Bengal—A Charm to entice away a Woman for another.—The following ingredients are put in the amulet to be worn on the arm by the man who wishes to entice away a woman :—

1. Dirt off the back of her whom you wish to entice away.
2. A three-cornered piece of her garment.
3. Spittle of him for whom you are enticing her.
4. Roots of basil (*Tulsi*) grown on a tomb.
 (Can this use of basil be due to a knowledge of the Decameron and Keat's *Isabella?* Tulsi was sacred among the Hindús long ago, but the growth on a tomb implies Muhammadanism.)
5. Root of bon-chandal (a shrub not like) any other than I know of).
6. Root of nirji (I cannot find out what this is).
7. Root of deal (a plant like verbena, whose leaves smell sweet when pressed) grown on a tomb.
8. The end of a sweeper's besom.
9. The gleanings of a Banya's shop (that is, what is left behind by a Bania, and when he sweeps up his goods after Pagal Aguri market).
10. Nagala guri (I cannot find out what this is).
11. The tongue of an owl.
12. The eye of an owl.

These are to be put in an amulet and kept with the local Pandarus on Saturday and Tuesday.—*Jungly Collector in the Week's News, August, 25th 1894.*

83. A Charm for Snake-bite.—If you are bitten by a snake throw a cowry into the air and utter the appropriate *mantra*. The snake will come back, forgive the man who has been bitten and he will recover. Hence the proverb :—

Kauri urao, sanp pakar laegi.

"Throw up a cowry and it will haul the snake back."
—*W. Crooke.*

84. A fresh incarnaton of Vishnu.—Hindús believe that the next incarnation of Vishnu will be under the me Kalankiand ; that he will be bornuout of the arm of a virgin Bráhman girl at Sambhal, in the Moradabad district. He will then go about punishing the enemies of the faith and rewarding pious Hindús. This is very much the same idea as that of Christians regarding the day of Judgment and of Muhammadans about the Imam Mahdi.—*W. Crooke.*

85. A Charm to drive away the Ghosts of Ancestors.—If the ghosts of ancestors trouble the members of the family, generally the best way to drive them away is to burn the root of the Rend or castor-oil tree in the house. Then they will leave the house immediately. If possible, the root should be brought in the Múl Nakshattra or asterism.—*Pándit Rám Gharib Chaubé.*

[On this see *Introduction to Popular Religion and Folklore,* p. 359.—Ed.]

86. Fines on Account of Snow.—In the town of Mandi, in Mandi State, it snowed on Christmas Day, a most rare occurrence, none having fallen there since January. 1874. In consequence of this, every iron mine contractor in Mandi had to pay one rupee into the State Treasury in accordance with a very old custom, the origin of which no one now living seems to know.—*Civil and Military Gazette.*

87. Prejudice against being Photographed.—I had some difficulty recently in getting some Faqirs at Hardwar photographed. They said that they feared it would take away some of their life (*jiu*), and thus shorten their lives.—*W. Crooke.*

88. A Legend about Vegetables—Once upon a time. they say, a fearful famine raged in the land and all the gods and saints began to perish with hunger. Of all of them the Muni Narada was most troubled, and he began to wander about in search of food. At last he reached the house of a Swapáka or Dom who was engaged in cooking the flesh of a Jog. The Saint asked him for some, but the Dom refused to give the foul food to the holy man. However, Narada insisted on getting some of it and taking it to the bank of a river, after offering a portion to Bhagwán. began to eat it. Then Bhagwán appeared and restrained him from defiling himself by eating such food. Narada answered : "The blame rests with you inasmuch as without this I must die of starvation." So Bhagwán said "I will create vegetables for your support." So be made the Chichinda or gourd out of the tail of the dog ; the garlic and onion out of his teeth ; the Pálak or spinach out of his ears ; the Soa or dill out of his hair ; the Bhanta or egg-plant and the Muli or radish out of his other members. Hence vegetables began to grow on the earth and the famine was stayed.—*Pándit Rám Gharib Chaubé.*

89. Bees and White-ants.—It is considered very lucky if bees or white-ants take up their abode in an empty house or at the gate of the city. In the former case the owner. and in the latter the inhabitants generally are sure to be blessed.—*M. Ram Lal.*

90. Rurkí—A Soldier's Ghost.—Near the Rurki Cantonment there used to be a grove, consisting of three rees near which a soldier was many years ago killed by accident. He became a very dangerous ghost and used to attack any person who passed by without saluting him, or who committed any act of defilement in the neighbourhood. People still lay English food and spirits near the place and bow to the gora demon (Gora or "white men" is the ordinary term for European soldiers) and bow reverently as they go by.—*W. Crooke.*

91. **Chains of God.**—Many Musalmán Fakírs wear iron chains which are given to them by their Pír or spiritual guide at the time of investiture. These are considered as a sort of badge of sanctity, and are generally known as Maulai Beriyan or the "chains of God."—*Pándit Rám Gharib Chaubé.*

92. **A Miraculous Pond.**—Great excitement has, it is said, been caused among the natives of Lucknow, as well as in various towns in the Sitapur district, by the discovery of the miraculous healing powers of the water of a small pond or tank between Kamalpur and Khairabad, on the Oudh portion of the Rohilkhand and Kumaon Railway. Crowds of the halt, the lame, the blind, etc., are wending their way to this health-restoring pool. Even lepers are said to emerge from its waters clean and cured of their disease. We are not prepared to vouch for the truth of the story, but almost every native in the place is talking about it, and implicitly believes it. Doubtless, it is only another phase of faith healing.—*Morning Post, Allahabad, 29th January, 1895.*

93. **Muhammadans; methods of purifying vessels.**—Among Muhammadans, if a vessel becomes impure from any cause, it can, if it be of metal, be purified by washing thrice in water. Copper vessels used in cooking, &c., are purified by being tinned. Ordinary country pottery vessels cannot be purified by any means when once they become impure. As regards China vessels, they can be purified with water provided there is no crack or hole in them; but if there be crack or hole, there is no means of making them pure again.—*Abdul Rahman Khan.*

94. **Asterisms: Superstitions about.**—If any one dies on the second, seventh or twelfth of the Hindu fortnight, when these days fall on a Saturday, Tuesday or Sunday, during the asterisma of Vishákha, Purva Bhadrapada Punarbasu or Krittika, three persons will die in the same family; if a man lose one thing at this time he will lose three things; if he gain anything he will gain three things. This combination is known in astrology as Tripuskara Yoga.—*Pándit Rám Gharib Chaubé.*

95. **Western Districts: Superstitions about oxen.**—In the neighbourhood of Saharanpur no one will buy an ox whose horns touch its ears. Such oxen are called Parasupher, or those that move an axe over the head of the owner. Such an animal is exceedingly unlucky. Another bad kind of ox is the Dhawal jivha, or one with a white tongue. An ox that moves its body about as it stands at the peg is very ill-omened. Such an animal will shake the household and bring it to ruin as it does the peg. An ox with white eyelids is also very bad. So is one with the tail half white and half black, which is known as Shyamla.—*Pándit Rám Gharib Chaubé.*

96. **A river proverb.**—There are two rivers in the Dehra Dun District of which the following verse is repeated—

Suswee su jan
Tere dya mihmán. Taine kyun diya ján?
Kya karún Saung Rani?
Na údba pair na piya páni.

"O wise river Suswa, a guest has come to thy banks. Why didst thou let him depart safe and sound?" The Suswa answers—"What could I do Lady Saung? The fellow neither drank of me nor set his foot in my water."

Drinking the water of these rivers or going into them during flood time is very dangerous.

A good parallel is—
Tweed said to Till,
What makes ye run so still?
Till said to Tweed,
"Tho' ye run wi' speed,
And I run slaw,
Yet where ye drown ae man
I drown twa.

Denham Tracts, 311.—*W. Crooke, C.S.*

97. **Sour milk: use of.**—When rennet (*jaman*) has been put into milk pious Hindus will not drink the milk until it turns into curd. The idea is, that the rennet is the embryo working in the milk, and of course to a Hindu it is a sin to kill an embryo; in fact there is a special word, Bhrunahatya, to denote this form of sin.—*Pándit Rám Gharib Chaubé.*

98. **Gambler's charm.**—We all know that the Diwáli night is called Kál Ratri, because on this night professors of the Black Art carry on their incantations, and gamblers, robbers and thieves do the same for success in the coming year. Gamblers practice the following charm on the Diwáli night and at lunar or solar eclipses.

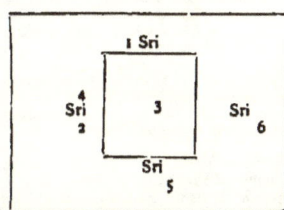

On the nights above-mentioned gamblers powder some ochre and sprinkle the powder on a piece of ground. On this they write the above charm and destroy it again. They do so forty times. After this, when they go to gamble, they write the same charm on the palm of their right hand in red sandal. For one year the charm is potential. Whenever they go a gambling they write it on the palm, but on the following Diwáli or Solar or Lunar eclipse they must perform it again, or it will do them no good.—*Pándit Rám Gharib Chaubé.*

99. **Gaya: Behar: the legend of Paghar.**—Paghar is said to be an ancient village, formerly in the possession of the kols, in evidence of which there are still in existence the remains of the ancient fort which they constructed. The enciente was of earth, but the houses inside it of bricks. Some tombs exist which are said to represent a kol qurial ground. There was a well on the fort which is

said to have possessed the power of sharpening swords No one knows why or by whom it was filled up.

While the kols were in occupation the fort is said to have been attacked by a force of Pathans under one Sher Khan. He was apparently the holder of a grant from the Delhi Emperor. This conquest by the Pathans is said to have occurred in the time of the Emperor Jahangir. There seems at the time to have been a considerable Rajput population in the neighbourhood. The Pathans behaved with insolence and cruelty to their subjects. One day Sher Khan was returning from the chase, and needing some coolies, he seized a Rajput who was cutting grass and compelled him to carry some of his baggage; this caused a general revolt of the Rajputs, the Pathans made a determined resistance, but they were finally worsted and Sher Khan was killed.

Then the fort was deserted. It still contains the delapidated tomb of Sher Khan.—*Rowland, N. L. Chandra.*

[This aboriginal burial ground might be worth exploration.—Ed.]

100. **Rain in the Swati asterism.**—Rain falling in the Swati asterism is infrequent and there are many superstitions about it. One is that when rain falls at this season the oyster which produces the pearls comes to the surface of the sea and drinks in the drops which become pearls. In the same way such rain is supposed to be most beneficial to the wheat fields. Hence they say :—

Dhanga bhag jahan baras Swati—
" Blessed is the place where the Swati rain falls."
Another saying is—
Swati bund hoe saghan men, Chatak marat piyas— " The rain drops of Swati are in the thick clouds and the sparrow is dying of thirst."—*Pandit Ram Gharib Chaube.*

101. **Form of obeisance.**—It is commonly said by the people that when any man approached one of the Mughal Emperors he had to bow nine times to the ground. Can any one say if this be correct ? What is the significance of the nine-fold salutation ?—*M. Ram Lal.*

102. **Heirship of the younger son.**—According to the Hindu Shastras, if the elder son be impotent (napunsaka), the inheritance falls to his younger brother if he be virile.—*Pandit Ram Gharib Chaube.*

103. **Rev. Lal Bihari De.**—The death has been recently announced of the Rev. Lal Bihari De, a Christian Missionary in Bengal. As the author of " Folktales of Bengal " and other valuable works, such as " Govinda Samanta," his death may be fittingly recorded in a publication like this, which is devoted to the collection of Indian Folklore Few men had a wider knowledge of his countrymen and his works will always have a special value of their own.—*W. Crooke, C.S.*

104. **Diwali feast.**—Professional thieves purposely commit theft on the night of the Diwáli as their good or ill success shows the result of their operations during the coming year. In the same way bankers and other speculators gamble on the night of the Diwáli and draw omens for the coming year in the same way.—*W Crooke, C. S.*

105. **Folklore of the bear.**—It is a general belief among Hindus that a bear can exist for any length of time by merely sucking its toe. He is regarded as the descendant of Jambawat, the King of the Bears. There was once a lion which slew Prasena who possessed the Syamantika jewel. The lion used to carry it about in his mouth, but Jambawat killed him and then he gave the gem to his son Sukuinara as a plaything. The murder of Prasena was ascribed to Sri Krishna; so he determined to recover the gem, and coming to the cave of Jambawat he saw the jewel with the nurse of the child who cried for help. Jambawat then fought with Krishna for twenty-one days and finally Krishna defeated him and having made him surrender the gem and his daughter Jambawati, Krishna cured him of his wounds. Jambawat became the famous bear general of Rama in his attack on Lanka.

All the jungle people believe that the bear abducts girls and carries them off to his cave. He carries them about on his back when he goes in search of food and feeds them with any herbs and roots he can collect. They are very fond of human wives and conciliate their favour by dancing before them.

The hair of the bear is an amulet and riding on his back is a cure for small-pox and other infantile diseases.

Popularly the bear climbs trees only by the aid of his hind legs. He is habitually truthful and this appears in many of the folktales. He is said never to leave anything alive which he has once caught and the jungle folk fear him as much and probably more than the tiger. They will never mention him by name in the morning and use instead some form of euphemism.—*W. Crooke, C. S.*

106. **Gopalpur, Gorakhpur, N.-W. P. Mother earth.**—Among us when some liquid food or oil accidentally falls on the ground, wesay " *Dharti mata bhukhdil rahlin itna le lihlin, i.e.,* Mother-earth was hungry and she took so much of it." Again when we wish to rub oil on our bodies, on other days than those which are proper days for it, we sprinkle some of the oil on the ground in the name of the Earth goddess and we suppose then that the use of oil on improper days will dous no harm through the grace of Mother-earth,—*Pandit Ram Bakhsh Chube.*

107. **The lens of the eye used as the unit of measurement.**—Carpenters regard and actually use the lens of the eye (*putli*) as the unit of measurement. They measure it by holding a piece of tile before it tied to a thread : 3 breadths of the lens make one *tassu* and 24 *tassus* make one yard of the carpenter.—*Pandit Ram Gharib Chaube.*

108. **N.-W. P. Superstition about betel-leaves.**—If a man chews betel and his mouth becomes very red, or as they say the "*pan rachta hai,*" it is a sign that his wife loves him very dearly. Some women always take care to break the point of the betel-leaf before they give it to their husband, son, or brother for chewing as it is thought that if he eats *pan* with the point of the leaf he will get only daughters.—*Bhagwan Das.*

109. **An incantation to cure the pain in the eyes.**—

Om namo

Dal mal sahar bhard taldi ;
Astáchal parbat ben dí.
Phutad na pákai karai na pird ;
Jdi Hanumant rakhai herd.

" The tank is full of moving water which has its fountain-spring in the Astáchal. May the sore neither burst nor ripen nor ache. May the ascetic Hanuman protect us from it."

Repeating three mantras throw water mixed with Nim leaves seven times on the aching eyes. Repeat the practice for three days and then the pain in the eyes will cease. —*Pandit Ram Gharib Chaube.*

North Indian Notes and Queries:
A MONTHLY PERIODICAL.

VOL. V.]   JULY, 1895.   [NO. 4.

Every communication must be accompanied by the writer's name and address, not necessarily for insertion, but as a guarantee of good faith. Every quotation from a book must be accompanied by its full title, publisher's and author's names, place and date of publication, volume and page.
Contributors are requested to write on ONE SIDE the page only. If several contributions be sent at a time, they should be sent each on a separate sheet.
The Conductor cannot undertake to return, or be responsible for, any MSS. not accepted.
All orders must be accompanied by cash. If not so accompanied, they will either not be attended to, or will be complied with per value-payable post.
Contributions should be addressed direct to W. CROOKE, ESQ., C. S., SAHARANPUR, N.-W. P., INDIA.

CONTENTS OF THIS NUMBER.
(The references are to the Notes.)

Popular Religion ... ... 55 to 60	Folktales ... ... 65 to 69
Anthropology ... ... 61 „ 64	Miscellanea ... ... 70 „ 72

POPULAR RELIGION.

110. Account of a Satti, given by Bal Makund, resident of Gonda.—About fifty years ago in the Bankatwa Mohalla, Gonda, there lived one Lala Bhawani Din, Kayasth. He was in the service of Rani Bhagwanta Kunwar, of Gonda, as a collector of rent on her behalf in her home farm. He had two wives. The Lala, after a protracted illness, died one evening. His senior wife wept bitterly for about two hours, and then became quiet, keeping her husband's head on her lap. Early in the morning the following day she expressed her desire to become Satti with her husband. The news of her resolution spread in the town and people began to come in. They expostulated with her, but she would not give up her resolution. The Rani in whose service her husband was, sent some of her men to dissuade her from becoming Satti and promised to make her a grant of 100 bighas of land for her maintenance, but she did not change her mind and said that she had twice become Satti with her husband in her previous births, in which she was a Brahman. The people asked her to give them some proof of her real desire to become Satti. She put her finger in the flame of a lamp and it was entirely burnt and she showed no signs of suffering. The people being convinced, they began to make preparations to take her husband to the funeral ground, and the usual mode of celebration of the ceremony was adopted. When she reached the funeral ground, she bathed in the tank close by and put on her ornaments and decked herself. She sat on the funeral pile with her husband and thence she threw her ornaments to the people. As she was childless, her husband's mother lit the flame, and she died. A platform on the right hand of the road running from the town to the civil lines near the Anjuman commemorates the event.—*Damodar Das.*

111. Fiscus Religiosa (Pipal tree)—Periodical Worship of.—When Monday falls on the fifteenth, or the last day of the dark fortnight, women who have their husbands alive, or those who are widows, perform the worship of the Pipal tree. This is called in the eastern districts Bhanwari, that day is known as Sonewati amáwásyá. The worship is chiefly performed by Brahman women and sometimes by pious Kshatriyas. The manner of worship is this. Women bathe at a river, or in their own houses, put on clean garments. They then take in their right hands a dish of bell-metal containing a jug full of water, sandal, washed rice, flowers, incense (*dhúp*) and a box of red lead (*sendur*). A number of women of the same locality go in a body singing songs, the words of which are generally in honour of Vásudeva, or Vishnu, whom the *Ficus religiosa* represents, to the place where the sacred tree stands, close by a temple of Mahádeva. There several of them at once begin to worship Vásudeva with the offering of the things that the dish contains and prayers for the longevity of their husbands and increase of prosperity and progeny, which in our phraseology is called *dudh* and *pút*. Then they begin to walk round the representative of Vásudeva, which they do 108 times, the number of beads a good rosary has; and at the end of each circuit they put at the foot of Vásudeva a sweatmeat, or a pice, or a rupee, or a gold mohar or, if the worshipper be a Brahman, a sacred Brahmanical thread. When this is done the offerings are distributed among poor Brahman women, or are sent to the house of the family priests. Then they return home singing. They perform this worship simply to lengthen the life of their husbands and to prevent themselves from becoming a widow in the next life.—*Rám Bakhsh Chaubé*.

---

112. **Mirzapur: Worship of Raja Bariar.**—Not unlike Rájá Chandól, the worship of Bariar Déo is universal among the aborigines of South Mirzapur. He is represented in the village in the same way as Rájá Chandól. His worship is performed in the same way and on the same day.

The popular tradition about him is the following:—

Once upon a time an oilman with a long train of servants and cattle went over to Sirgujá to barter. He put up there under a cotton (*sémal*) tree with all his men and beasts. The servants and beasts left the temporary lodging for the market town on business and the oilman alone remained behind. To beguile the time during which he was alone he began to play a flute (*bánsurí*). In the *sémal* tree lived a Rákshiní, or female demon, who was enchanted with the sound of the flute. She began to dance, assuming the guise of a hen. In the meantime the servants of the oilman arrived and the hen disappeared. The following day the servants and the beasts went again away from the temporary lodging and the oilman began to play the flute in order to amuse himself. The female demon again appeared in the guise of a hind. The servants again appeared and the hind disappeared. On the third day, when the servants were away, the oilman again began to play the flute. This time the female demon appeared in the guise of a beautiful maiden and went up to the oilman. She requested him to marry her, which the oilman complied with. After this she became pregnant and the oilman with his men and beasts returned to his village shortly after. In due course she brought forth a child whom, she named Bariár. When the child grew up, his mother married him to a fairy, who agreed to live as an ordinary woman. By this woman a number of children were born to Bariár. After this Bariár died and his children began to live in caves. One day Bariár appeared before them in a dream and shed tears and said: "O my children! I am your dead father. Son of a female demon and the husband of a fairy. My death is nothing more than a change of form. I am still here with you as a ruler of evil spirits that inhabit the forests in the country around. Worship me and dedicate a platform to me and I shall make you the King of Sirgujá." So saying he disappeared and the children took his advice to heart and began to worship him. At the same time the servants of the Raja of Sirgujá, who was named Sangram, rebelled against him, and they butchered Sangram and his family. The children of Bariár, finding an opportunity to test the truth of the words of the father, appeared on the scene with the advice of the father and, putting down the rebellion, acquired the kingdom. The name of the conqueror was Amar Sinh. His descendants are still ruling in Sirgujá. Amar Sinh then began to worship his father, and the news of the greatness of Bariár spread far and wide and the people began to do homage to him, in the hope of being prosperous.—*Pándit Rám Ghárib Chaubé*.

---

113. **The legend of Kuba, the Potter.**—Kuba Kumhar, the potter saint, has become popular all over Upper India. His piety was such that he spent his living on feeding the poor and hungry and he never took a meal until he had fed as many mendicants as his means permitted. One day he had no food in the house and he went to the Banya to get some on credit. The Banya answered that he would give him food if Kuba would sink a well for him. So Kuba began to dig a well in front of the Banya's house, but the moment he thrust his spade into the ground a pot full of gold appeared. Kuba took it home and inviting all the poor of the place bought food and entertained them. When the feast was over he began to work again at the well, but as he dug, the earth fell over him. Everyone thought he was dead, and when the people heard the story they began to curse the miserly Banya. Six months after a man chanced to look into the well which Kuba had dug and he was astonished to hear the words *Rám! Rám!* coming from the bottom. When the people dug out the earth they found Kuba sitting below telling his beads.

They took him out and then the Banya, influenced by the miracle, gave all his wealth to Kuba and sent him home. Again Kuba spent all the money in charity. One day as usual Kuba was entertaining medicants when he saw with one of them a very fine Salagráma stone and thought to himself that if he had an idol like that he would never cease worshipping it. When the mendicant was going away and tried to take the Salagrama from the shelf on which it had been placed, he found it so heavy that he could not move it. When Kuba touched it he was able to lift it easily and the mendicant, seeing the work of Bhagwán, gave it to him. After that Kuba devoted himself to the worship of the Salagráma and at last he made up his mind to make a pilgrimage to Dwarika. But in the night Bhagwán appeared to him in a dream and told him that he need not go to Dwarika as he could obtain the same religious merit by staying at home. So the next night by the grace of Bhagwán the image of the conch-shell and discus, such as is done at Dwarika, appeared branded on his arms and he felt no pain.

On another occasion the brother of the wife of Kuba came to see her and she made rice milk for him and gave only some parched grain to some Sádhus who were at the house. When Kuba saw this he cursed her so that she died and soon after Kuba himself was carried off to the paradise of Sri Krishna Chandra.—*Pándit Rám Bakhsh Chaubé*.

114. **A miracle of Khwaja Muinuddin Chishti, the saint.**—The saint, they say, was once sitting in his hut, when an old woman came and weeping said to him that her only son had died and that she had no means of burying him. The saint was moved at her grief and sent some of his own disciples to arrange the funeral. He also announced that he would attend himself. When he came he found a large assemblage and the old woman wailing with the head of her son in her lap. The saint went up to him and said "Arise," and he arose and went home with his mother.—*Khwaja Hasan Ahmad.*

115. **Sun worship.**—Hindus say that the red flowers of the Kanail tree (*Nerium odorum*) and red sandal are most loved by the Sun god. The tale runs that when the Sun was formed he was large and dazzling, but rough and rugged in form. When he compared himself with the form of the other gods he was ashamed and so he asked Viswakarma, the godlike artizan, to improve his shape. Viswakarma complied, but in the course of the operation he nearly killed the god. So he asked Visvakarma to give him a remedy. He took the red flowers of the Kanail and mixing them in water rubbed them over his wounds. Henceforth the Sun god so loved these flowers that he announced that his votaries should henceforth use them in his worship. Hence in the case of any disease in the family the god is propitiated with these offerings.—*W. Crooke, C.S.*

116. **Brahmans and Barbers.**—In all Hindu rites and worship such as those at marriage, birth, death, &c., the barber is always joined with the Brahman. Both receive presents, those of the Brahman being known as Dakshina and those of the barber as Teohári, or presents given on holidays (*teohár*). A Brahman receives a gift when he ties an amulet on the wrist of one of his clients and to the barber at the Dasahara and other feasts when he shows his looking-glass to his clients. A common proverb runs—

*Jaise ko taisa mile, jyon Bábhan ko nai ;
Isne kaha asirbád, usne karhi arsi dikhái.*

"Diamond cut diamond, as the Brahman and the barber, one his blessing gives and the other shows his looking-glass."—*Pándit Rám Ghárib Chaubé.*

117. **How to make a Demon subservient to your will.**—In Bengal the following method of bringing a demon into subjection is generally employed. When a man dies on the fifteenth day of the Hindu month, being a Saturday, go with your teacher in the magical arts to the cremation ground and seat your teacher on a tree at least a mile from the place. Go to the cremation ground alone with the body and lay it on the ground with the feet to the south. Tie the hands and feet of the corpse to four iron pegs, securely driven into the ground. Sit on the breast of the corpse with a bottle of wine beside you and repeat mantras on a rosary made of bones. After repeating the mantras one hundred and eight times, drink some wine, and pour some into the mouth of the corpse. Then the corpse will begin to make faces at you and try to get up and fight you. But fear not ; it cannot harm you as long as you retain your courage. You should at times call to your teacher and take his directions as to the mode of performing the rite. He will tell you to go on repeating the mantras and using the wine as before. As you go on repeating the mantras at intervals of one hundred and eight repetitions animals of hideous form will appear, but heed them not. At last a cat will come, and will ask you what you want. You must say that you need the services of the ghost of the corpse on which you are seated. This the cat will grant. Then make a fire, sacrifice with meat and wine and return home, marking your forehead with the ashes of the sacrifice. As you go home do not look back nor reply to any questions put to you. The ghost will then serve you for the rest of your life.—*Nanda Lala Ghosha.*

118. Behar: A temple legend.—On my way to-day I passed by a famous temple of Bhairava, in Rajkhund, called Bhairo Asthan. The temple is situated by the side of the road from Mozaffarpur to Sitamarhi *via* Chandwara Ghat. Its Pandas trace its existence to the time of Raja Janak, the renowned King of Mithila, and father of Sita, wife of Ráma.

It is said that during Muhammadan times, King Aurangzeb in his mission of iconoclasm happened to come here. When he had broken all the idols outside the temple, he proceeded to break the idol of Bhairava as well. But before he could effect his entrance into the temple, its iron doors shut of themselves; he tried hard to open them, but in vain. Aurangzeb then began to demolish the temple without any resistance by its devotees, who had a vision after the shutting of the doors that the idol had already disappeared and would reappear again after twelve years, during which period it ordered them to do their worldly business in peace and with patience. Aurangzeb is reported to have made useless attempts to find out the idol of Bhairava. The minor idols broken by him are still preserved in the temple as relics.

When the appointed twelve years had passed, the idol reappeared in the jungle near the temple and was discovered thus:—A Goala of the neighbourhood grazed his cattle in the jungle. While grazing he used to miss one of his she calves for a watch, or three hours, every day. One day he saw the animal during those hours standing in a place and there was a stone beneath her udder from which milk was flowing. It raised his curiosity to see a calf giving milk which had not yet produced a young one, and he suspected his animal to be under the influence of some ghost of the jungle. He raised his stick to strike the animal when she fled and one of her hoofs fell upon the stone making a mark on it as if the stone were as delicate as a human body. The Pandas of the temple show such a mark on the idol. When the Goala returned to his house he related the story to his brethren, from whom the devotees learnt it and discovered the reappearance of their diety. They immediately cut the jungle and erected a temple there. A large fair is annually held here in the month of Phagun, when people come from distances to pour Ganges water on the idol on the Sivaratri, the night sacred to Mahadeva. It is said that this idol is appeased with little propitiation and worship and the villagers relate stories in proof of it.—*Babu Rae Krishna Bahadur.*

119. Eastern Districts: Worship of Siva Náráyan.—The great saint of the Dusadhs of the Eastern Districts is Siva Náráyan, who is said to have been a native of Kanauj and to have wandered eastward preaching among the lower classes of Hindus. The head-quarters of the worship is a place called Sasna Bahádurpur, in Bihar. He set his face against idolatry and to the present day no idol is placed in his temple. They assemble to worship him on the Basant Panchami, the fifth day of Mágh. The worship is thus done. A wooden stool (*chauki*) is covered with a new cloth of any colour and on it are placed sweets, betel, flowers, &c. Ganja, charas and tobacco are also offered and the worshippers smoke these things after they have been dedicated. Meanwhile some halwa has been prepared. Some red powder is sprinkled on the stool and the halwa is brought and dedicated. Each worshipper must, as far as possible, help in raising the dish before the stool. Meanwhile others beat drums and play on the cymbals and sing at the top of their voices the songs of Siva Náráyan. After the worship is over the halwa is distributed among the worshippers. At the same time some get themselves initiated. The mode of initiation is very simple. The Guru, or head of the local brotherhood, whispers a mantra in the ear of the novice and puts on his neck a garland of flowers, which had been offered to Siva Náráyan.

The following is one of their songs sung at the time of worship:—

Guru paidn lágon nám lahka dijai,
Janam janam ke bhúlal manudn onhun kai driskti khola dijai ;
Bish hai lahar uthai ghat bhitar amrit búnd chua dijai :
Gagan mandil bich urdh mukh kuián tahi bick baithi naha lijai.
Siva Náráyan kahi samujhwái surati men murati mila lijai.

"O preceptor, I throw myself at thy feet. Show me the true Name (Satya Nám). Open the eyes of him who has forgotten it from birth to birth. The waves of poison rise in me, drop on me the nectar. In the house of heaven there is a well with its mouth upwards. Get into it and bathe. Siva Náráyan says and makes others understand this. Let thy form be absorbed in the thought of the True Name."

Wa ghar ko khojo re bhai játen awagamen mitái ;
Aur ghar khojen he pahio bhuli bhatak pani chi mag aiho,
Ka topi, ka mála nden, ka bho kapra rang rangás?
Ka pája, ka dhyán lagden, ka chandan, ka bhasm charháen ?
Kahe ko bharme, kahe ko bharmás, utari pár áp man lás,
Siva Náráyan jag samjhás jái apan ghar desh chhorás.

"Brother, search after that house where you may be free from transmigration. What will you gain by seeking other houses? Straying over and over you will come here at last. What avails thee the sectarian cap, the beads and coloured robe? What is the use of worship, meditation, rubbing sandal and ashes to your forehead? Why have you been deluded and why do you delude others? By applying your own mind you can cross the ocean of the world. Siva Náráyan makes the world understand this secret and going to his last home clears himself of the blame of concealing it."—*W. Crooke, C.S.*

120. **Why Vishnu is incarnated.**—One day a Raja asked his Pandit why Bhagwan was incarnated in the world. The Pandit promised to explain it in a few days. So he made an image in wax of the Raja's son and gave it to a servant. When the Pandit and the Raja went to the Ganges to bathe, the Pandit instructed the servant to drop the image in the water above where they were bathing. When the Raja saw the image floating down, he asked the Pandit what it was, and he replied:—

"That rascally servant must have thrown your boy into the water."

The Raja was out of his senses with grief, and plunging in brought the image ashore. When he saw what it was, he asked the Pandit what it meant, he answered:—

"You have shown your love for your child by risking your life for his sake. How much greater is the love of Bhagwan for his children, that he comes and plunges into the river of this life to save them."

(Told by Radhe Lal, of Tarinpur, Sitpur District.)

121. **Mirzapur; worship of Siddhináth.**—At Saktesgarh in the Mirzapur District, the tomb (*Samddhi*) of Siddhináth is worshipped by all classes of Hindus. He is regarded as the realiser of all desires, the remover of all difficulties, the scarer of demons and beasts of prey. By the cowherds of the neighbourhood he is revered as the protector of cattle. No masonry grave has been erected in his honour. His grave is of clay and is kept carefully plastered with cowdung. On it rests a pair of sandals which it is said he used to wear. He is revered in association with his companions to renowned ascetics, Kalnáth and Bhonpatináth. The tomb of Siddhináth is near the waterfall at Saktesgarh, which is called in his honour Siddhináth ki dari. On Monday and Friday people in performance of a vow offer at his grave sweet cakes, pairs of sandals, Brahmanical cords and clothes. Ahirs offer to him sweet rice boiled in milk. It is said that no beast of prey dares to approach his grave. However, it may be covered with dust or rubbish during the day, some secret power cleanses it during the night. The saint resents any one staying near his grave at night. One of the Rájas of Bijaypur, it is said, was anxious to build a hunting-box close by, but the saint appeared to him in a dream and warned him to forbear. Though the worship of this deified ascetic is exceedingly popular, no one can tell when he flourished, or anything of his history.—*Pándit Rám Gharib Chaubé.*

122. **Mirzapur; Snake godlings.**—The ab-original tribes of South Mirzapur have quite a pantheon of snake godlings, of which the following is a fairly complete list:—Dádb Nág; Bhanwar Nág; Shesh Nág; Dhodhariya Nág; Thorhar Nág; Dhanwar Nág; Lahariya Nág; Chhidiyar Nág; Dahariya Nág; Saksur Nág; Básuk Nág; Chitti Nág; Andhe Nág; Rukhiya Nág; Sugbar Nág; Sarp Nág.

They say that these godlings live in water and kill men by biting them if any one speaks disrespectfully of them or does not bow down and worship when he comes near the places which they haunt. Most people worship them once a year on a rock close to the water hole which they frequent. The common way of worshipping them is to mention the names of as many of them as you know or can remember and at each name to make a mark with vermilion and oil on the rock. After this a black fowl is sacrificed, its head being first smeared with red lead and oil. Sometimes, in cases of serious illness or trouble, which is attributed to them, a black goat is offered. At the time of worship they repeat the following—

Dewan ganiyan puja,
Bair na ganiyan jhor.

"You cannot be worshipped as clan godlings; you cannot eat curry with every kind of food as you can with Bari."

Bari is made of flour mixed with salt and spices and fried in ghi or oil.—*W. Crooke, C.S.*

123. **Sitala Debi and Hanuman.**—One day Sitala Devi and Hanuman were disputing which of them was the greater. Sitala said—

"Let us decide it in this way. We will both go and beg in the world and whichever of us gets the most alms will be the greater."

So Hanuman went down into the world, but just at that time Sitala Devi sent down small-pox. So whenever he went to a house they would say:

"How can we give alms when small-pox is with us?"

Then Sitala went down and when they saw her every one invited her to come in and take what alms she pleased, if she would only remove the scourge from them. So she came back to Hanuman and he was obliged to allow that she was greater than he.

(Told by Durga Charan, master of the school at Sanaya, Cawnpore District.)

124. **South Mirzapur: A Valley godling.**—South of the Son, in the Mirzapur District, is a hill known as Maikal Pahari, close to which is a very narrow valley called Nilkanth ki Pahari. Here lives a very powerful demon and no one dares to go that way without offering a vow and making a promise of giving him cakes and sweets if they get home safely. If they fail to do this, the demon hurls them down the slope of the hill and kills them. The demon is the ghost of a faqir named Nilkanth, who is said to have perished in this place many years ago.—*W. Crooke, C.S.*

125. **Saharanpur; Kankhal.**—According to the Brahmans the name of the town of Kankhal means "Where is the sinner?" because the town is always on the look-out for a sinner on whom to confer salvation.—*Pándit Rám Gharib Chaubé.*

126. **Saharanpur: Worship of the karil tree.**—As in the Eastern Districts the Nim tree is regarded as the abode of the seven sisters of the goddess Devisa, in the west of the province the same idea attaches to the karil, or caper tree, and high caste women offer to it sweets, milk and soaked gram. They believe that by doing so the demons of disease are propitiated.—*Pándit Rám Gharib Chaubé.*

127. **Saharanpur: Death customs.**—When an old person dies the corpse is carried in procession round the town or village with the accompaniment of musical instruments. As far as they can afford it the relatives throw silver and copper coins over the bier, which the beggars scramble for. The body is covered with two shawls, one of which is given to the barber and the other to the Mahabrahman, or funeral priest. Female relations follow the bier weeping and they are headed by the wife of the family barber. She leads the song of mourning. Thus she says: *Jamara Sher Diwána*, "The god of death is a raging lion," and the other women strike their knees, then their breasts, then their foreheads with their hands. After the rite is over, the women go to a river or tank to bathe and then the other women play jokes on the daughter-in-law of the dead man and pull her about so that her clothes are often torn off and her waist-belt (*izarband*) broken. When the bathing is over they place on her head a *lota* full of water, in the mouth of which are some twigs of the mango tree. They return home and the daughter-in-law heads the procession. For three days the women sing and dance as if it were an occasion of rejoicing. Occasionally they burst into cries of lamentation. On the third day they go again to the same place and bathe and return home with their garments dripping wet. The men of the family listen to a Pandit reciting one of the sacred books, usually the Garuda Purana. This is done for an hour or two every day until the tenth day. When the reading is over, the clansmen assemble and each gives a rupee or two to the reader.

These rites are performed only when the dead man was of a great age and are in addition to the ordinary funeral rites.—*Pándit Rám Gharib Chaubé.*

128. **The worship of Ausan Miyan.**—This saint is worshipped in Northern Oudh and they tell the following tale about him. One time a boy fell ill and his mother vowed to Ausan Miyan that she would feed seven women whose husbands were living if her son recovered. By the mercy of Ausan Miyan her son recovered and then she went to the grain parcher to buy the grain necessary to perform her vow. When the grain was bought a bird came flying up and said to her; "Bibi! My young ones are starving, give me some grain." The woman answered that she had vowed the grain to Ausan Miyan and could not give it. The bird did not heed her words, but flew away with a little of the grain. The moment she fed her young ones with it they all died. The bird was distracted with grief and asked the other birds what she should do. They advised her to pray for mercy to Ausan Miyan. She did so; her young ones were at once restored to life.

Since then the belief in the powers of Ausan Miyan have increased.—*Siva Sahay, Headmaster, Paraspur, Gonda.*

ANTHROPOLOGY.

129. Household Rules.—If you have your son married, you should not marry a daughter until six months have expired. In the same way, after marrying a daughter, the rites of shaving the birth hair of a child, or the investiture of a son with the sacred thread, should not be performed for the space of six months. Two sons of the same parents should not be married to two sisters; nor two sisters to the same man. Two brothers should not be married within six months of each other. So a brother and sister of the same parents should not have the shaving or other rites performed within six months. In a year in which some joyful rite, such as marriage, investiture with the sacred thread, &c., has been performed, no melancholy ceremony, such as the annual Sraddha, in honour of the sainted deceased, should be performed.—*Pándit Rám Gharib Chaubé.*

130. The Yama Dwitiya Rite.—There is none of the Hindu feasts more interesting than that of the Yam Dwitiya, which takes place on the second day after the Diwali, in which all pious Hindus should visit their sisters and receive food from them, giving them a gift in return. Some time ago a book was written by Raja Siva Prasad, of Benares, entitled *Bir Sinhha Vritánt*, in which special stress was laid on this festival as showing the ancient rule of affection and respect which Hindus should observe towards their sisters. This is believed to have had considerable effect in checking the practice of female infanticide among Rajputs. On this day the food prescribed to all pious Hindus is the pumpkin or *kaddu* boiled with rice. It is said that people who do not eat this food on this festival, become asses in the next birth.—*W. Crooke, C.S.*

131. The effect of death on Marriage.—If an adult member of the family die after the performance of the bethrothal ceremony, the marriage should not take place until a month has passed from the time of the completion of the death rites. By an adult, is meant a person who has been married, or who has been invested with the sacred cord. And this prohibition extends to all the descendants of a common grandfather, whether they live together or not.—*Pándit Rám Gharib Chaubé.*

132. Shut up Deities or Spirits.—I am extremely interested to note among the extracts in the current number of *Folklore*, from a recent number of "North Indian Notes and Queries," "three instances of gods covered with lids so as to hide them."

This shutting up of divinities may be, I think, a most instructive item of primitive ritual, and I would ask that any instances that come under observation may be made known.

The usage is probably reflected in the Greek myth of the shutting up of Ares "in a vessel of bronze" (Iliad v. 386), but these Indian instances are the only occurrence of the *actual ritual practise of covering up a god* that I can recall.

The story told to account for one of these instances, "that the goddess used to climb (a) tree and ask the names of people who then died" (the lid, says Mr. Rouse, apparently stopping her), looks like a late attempt to explain an obsolete rite. If this story of the inquisitive goddess is an explanatory myth constructed in a later (but still primitive) stage of culture, it would only enhance the interest of the custom.

I would specially ask that in any instances that may come to light it may be stated whether the shutting up of the god or spirit takes place at any special season of the year, and whether it lasts for any specified time, or is permanent.

These are points that would seem to be of special significance.—*G. M. Godden.*

133. India and China, a comparison of religions, &c.—In that unprogressive and anomalous country, China, according to Gray, cattle are only slaughtered to supply the tables of foreign residents, "a Chinese, by the laws of his country, being strictly prohibited from slaughtering an animal of such essential service to the farmer in the cultivation of his land. A man who slaughters a draught cow or ox exposes himself for the first offence to receive a flogging of 100 blows and to be imprisoned in the congue for a period of two months. For a second, he is sentenced to a flogging of 100 blows and extra provincial exile for the period of his natural life."—*Page* 154, *Vol. II, Gray's China.*

Fresh milk, be it noted, is hardly used in China as an article of diet, though in some parts of the country it is eaten curdled; and the Chinese are perhaps the most omnivorously carnivorous people on the face of the globe, as they need puppy dogs and cats for food, and consider foxes, jackals and rats delicacies, while worms are an article of luxury. They also eat the horse, ass, mule and camel,

Cowdung cakes are largely used for fuel and spread plastered to the walls of houses, and cow's urine is esteemed of medicinal value in India, where it forms the vehicle of 75 per cent of the prescription in the Indian *Materia Medica*. But the Chinese have a very high appreciation of its value for manure and make composts of almost every available waste animal, vegetable, and mineral substance, and as market gardeners are second to no race in the world. We are elsewhere told that bullocks, sheep, and pigs are sacrificed to the deified philosopher Confucius, but the buffalo is sacrificed on Hindoo shrines in India at the present day, and there are to-day probably more buffaloes tied up as baits for tigers in the vicinity of Benares by Hindoos themselves for Hindoo chiefs than over half the rest of the province. Chinese Buddhists save the lives of horned cattle, horses, fish, tortoises, and also release birds which bird-catchers take with a rod smeared with bird lime. These rods are exactly similar to those used by the Indian bahalias; and any time up to about 1867, it was one of the sights of the Allahabad bazar to see pious Hindoos release birds in the Chauk near the Goodry. The birds were often the blue jays or rollers and green parrots.

There has been communication between India and China from very remote times, and it is more than probable that much of the rude Indian machinery, the sugarcane and sarghum and other articles have been borrowed from the Chinese. The civilisations and religions of India and China are not unlike. Had Western Nations never landed on the shores of India, I would surmise that the Hindoos would in another 4,000 years have attained a very similar stage of civilisation to that in which the Chinese are now. Chinese religions are rather a body of ceremonies, than systems of doctrine, and are deeply tinged with atheism or materialism. Indian Missionaries introduced Buddhism into China in B. C. 121., and it took root in A. D. 61, but is on the decline in China, as it is in Nepal, where it is rapidly giving way to Hinduism.—*J. Cockburn.*

---

134. **The Legend of Daulatabad.**—Near Nagina, in the Bijnor District, there is a place called Daulatábád, where it is said there once lived a zemindar who had a lovely daughter. He cast eyes of love on her and then he assembled his subjects and asked them whether there was any reason why a man should not use the animal which he had tended. All of them, but a sweeper, said that there was no objection, and the sweepers beat the sweeper and turned him out of the place. Then he seized his daughter and forced her to submit to his will. Next morning the offended gods sent a shower of stones on the place which killed the wretch and all his subjects except the sweeper. Here and there are still to be seen the rocks which fell from heaven and the house of the sweeper is also shown to the curious.

They tell another tale of the ruin of Daulatábád. There was once a Musalmán student who fell in love with the daughter of a banker and when he saw no other way to secure her, he got a woman to personate her and was married to the supposed Banya girl before the Qázi of the town. Then the boy went to claim his wife from the banker, who said that according to the custom of his caste no wife went to her husband until the sixth month after marriage. Having thus got time, the banker hurried off and complained to the Emperor Akbar, who dressed himself as a soldier and went to the place. He put up at an inn and managed to send for the woman who had personated the girl at the mock marriage. When he learned the real state of the case, he had the Qázi and the youth executed and then he destroyed the city as a punishment for the wickedness of its people. Only the house of the banker was saved from the general ruin.—*Pándit Rám Gharíb Chaubé.*

---

135. **Investiture with the Sacred Thread.**—There are various precautions which must be taken in selecting a time for the investiture of a boy with the sacred thread. It should not be done in the fourth week of a Hindu month; on a Saturday; in the afternoon, night time, or morning twilight, nor during a thunder-storm.—*Pándit Rám Gharíb Chaubé.*

---

136. **How to obviate an unfavourable conjunction of the Heavenly Bodies.**—If a conjunction of the stars be unfavourable to a person, in order to obviate the effects he should make a gift of gold to Brahmans; if the Moon be unfavourable, the gift should be a conch shell; if a day be unlucky, he should make a gift of corn; if any special planet be unfavourable, the gift should consist of gems; if a special asterism (nakshatra) be against him, he should give a cow; for the other stars a gift of salt is generally believed sufficient.—*Pándit Rám Gharíb Chaubé.*

Visiting the Sick.—Among Hindus it is considered very unlucky to visit a sick friend at night. The reason of this, according to the Shastras, is that at night the power of evil spirits is at its greatest height. Hence they are called Ratichar, because they go about at night. Hence if you go to see a sick person at night some demon who may be on the prowl in the neighbourhood may attach himself to you and accompany you to the bed of the patient, on whom they will probably make an assault. Hence it is dangerous to go about at night without taking a piece of iron with you. It is believed that when demons see a man with a piece of iron they think he has a knife with which he will cut off their hair and make them subservient to his will, so they are afraid and leave his neighbourhood.—*Pandit Rám Ghárib Chaubé.*

137. Magahiya Domes of Gorakhpur.—*Worship.*

—The Maghra Domras have two special divinities of their own; the chief is Gundak, whose grave is to be found in Karmaini Garhi, two days' journey to the east of Moti Hari, in Bengal. According to their traditions, Gundak was hanged for theft "a long time ago" and when dying he promised always to help Maghras in trouble. He is worshipped by the whole clan and is invoked on all important occasions, but he is pre-eminently the patron god of theft, a successful theft is always celebrated by a sacrifice and feast in its honour.

They also worship Samaya, a female divinity. She is without any special history and there is no sharp distinction between her sphere and Gundak's functions. Apparently relates chiefly to birth and illness, &c.

The Maghras sacrifice young pigs and wine with sugar and spices to these two deities. Every Maghra is capable of performing the sacrifice, and the remains are divided among the company. When a vow is made to Samaya, *e.g.*, on the birth of a child, or when it is teething, or on the occasion of an illness, a special pig is chosen and devoted to her and is sacrificed on the fulfilment of the vow.

The Maghras have neither altars nor idols nor do they erect any *chabutras* for worship. A spot is cleared and *leaped* in the middle of a field and the sacrifice is then offered.

Superstitions.—The Maghras naturally believe in ghosts and spirits. When a man dies, my informant told me, he turns into a "shaitan." Deotas also, he added, were innumerable in most villages of this district. There is a special altar for all the local ghosts and deities which may reside within the village boundaries, and the Maghras are always ready to share in the sacrifice of the villagers to them.

Partially Hinduised.—They also reverence trees and *chabutras* consecrated by Hindus in passing, but pay no further homage. They acknowledge the village Káli and sometimes sacrifice to her, especially when afflicted with small-pox, but the sacrifices in this case do not differ from those of the Hindus.

They do not acknowledge Mahadeo, or any other Hindu divinity, but they share the general Hindu belief in Parmeshwar, the giver and destroyer of life and the author of good and evil. He created the Maghras, they say, and ordered them to be filth and outcasts among the Hindus.

They sometimes resort to a Brahmin for the reading of the Vedas (Kathá). My informant had given a "Kathá" in this way on the last occasion of his release from jail. In these cases the Maghras go to the Brahmin's house, but I could not find any other trace of special reverence for the Brahmins, nor have they any necessity for them.

Eat cow's flesh like Chamars.—They eat cow's flesh readily, but they will not kill the cow. They also offer milk like Hindus. They express some reverence for the great rivers Gangá and Naráini, &c. This, I think, nearly marks the extent to which they have been Hindus.

Pipal sacred.—The pipal is the only sacred tree and no Mahgra will pluck its leaves. They hold this superstition so firmly that I suspect it is aboriginal. No reverence is paid to the Bannian, or any other sacred Hindu tree or plant.

Iron, special superstitions.—They have special superstitions about iron and will not use it for certain purposes. A Maghra who commits a burglary with an iron instrument will not only be excluded from the brotherhood, but his eyes will some day start out of his head.

Oath.—The most solemn oath is celebrated after the following fashion:—

A piece of ground is cleared and *leaped* as if for sacrifice. A piece of iron, a dish of water, some leaves of the pipal and a particular kind of Tarai grass, with some lighted charcoal, are all put separately on the ground. On the top a pice is placed and the oath is taken over it. An oath "by the dhobi" is also peculiarly binding. A dhobi once visited some Domras and gave them ass's dung to eat, and the oath is therefore an invocation that the swearer will eat ass's dung if he is perjured.

Clans.—I now pass from their religious ideas to their social divisions. They say that they formerly cultivated and owned land, but when pressure came, the Maghian divided into two great sub-divisions, Maguias and the Bansphors. The Maghia took to thieving, while the Bansphors were contented to weave baskets and cultivate what land they could.

The two sub-divisions do not intermarry; and it must be remembered that my notes relate to the thieving clan alone. The Maghias proper, who count themselves the true original stock, always describe themselves as sub-divided into seven distinct families; but excluding the Bansphors, of whom I have spoken, there are really six, *viz.*, Sáwant, Balgai, Chaudhri, Chauhán, Behari, and Hazári. The most of these names are taken from the Hindus; and as Hazári is a Mahomedan title of honour, this division into families is probably of a comparatively recent date. Chaudhri and Chauhan are evidently also meant as honorific titles, and at the time that the division was first made it must have been purely artificial.

No common ancestor, or founder.—The families have no recollection of any common ancestor, nor have they any memory of the founder.

Bansphors.—The Bansphors, I am told, have no such sub-divisions. The artificial origin of the six sub-divisions is therefore tolerably certain. They are imitations of Hinduism, and the only use they serve is to regulate marriage.

Neither Maghias nor Bansphors can marry their first cousins by blood, and this was probably the original rule. Besides this, no Sawant can marry a Sawant, or Balgai a Balgai, but any one of the six families can intermarry with any other.

Leader.—The wandering gangs of Maghias are composed indiscriminately of men belonging to each family, but each gang has its own leader, and the office is hereditary in the leader's family. An outsider is never elected unless the family stock has failed.

The office of leader does not always, of course, go from father to son, but to the eldest male member of the family.

Outcasts.—All disputes are settled by *panchyats*, but the longest term of exclusion from the brotherhood is 12 years. During that period no companionship can be held with the outlaw, even in a theft. Outcasting is however redeemable by a fine and feast.

Tribal Code.—The inter-tribal code of the Domras is fairly strict and theft by one Domra from another will be punished with a fine.

The abduction of a Domra girl by force and the introduction of a foreign woman into the camp are a frequent cause of *panchyats*.

Murder, or cow-killing prohibited.—I am told that the murder of any human being, or of a cow, is also severely punished, but this is about the boundary line of Domra morality with regard to outsiders.

Strangers.—Strangers are occasionally adopted by the Maghias. Two or three Chamars, a Mahomedan, an Ahir and a Teli who had turned Domras were lately among the inmates of the jail.

It is the women who chiefly attract these recruits. Besides the six sub-divisions which I have mentioned, there are some outcast families, such as the executioners, who cannot now re-enter the clan. These outcasts intermarry among themselves.

Birth.—The birth of a Domra is always celebrated by a sacrifice to Gundak and Samaya. Marriages are contracted when the boy is about 10 years old.

Marriage.—The matter is settled by a go-between. The boy's father pays for the marriage feast, gives presents to the father of the girl, but the Maghias deny that there is any idea of purchase. No religious ceremony accompanies the marriage.

A *panchyat* is assembled, a feast held, and the girl henceforth resides in her father-in-law's house. A man is not restricted in the number of his wives and concubinage is also permitted, but the concubine is held in somewhat less esteem than the wife.

A woman is apparently allowed to leave her husband and transfer herself to another, but in that case she becomes a concubine. The *panchyat* will not restore a wife who has decamped, but they will give back any property she took away.

The frequent residence of the Maghias in jail often oblige women to transfer themselves to other husbands for support and makes polygamy advantageous. Polyandry is unknown. Maghias bury their dead.

The Maghias gash their heads on the occasion of a big drink, but there is nothing religious in this, nor do they offer the blood in sacrifice. The practice is purely voluntary and is intended to give the owner of the bloody head a ferocious aspect.

The Maghias eat most things, including carrion, but certain animals, beasts of prey, cats, and dogs, &c., they will not touch.

I have not made any detailed inquiries regarding the Bansphors. The latter appear to have adopted more of the Hindu religion and less of the Hindu social polity, but the Maghias in their revolt and degradation have imitated the social structure of a Hindu tribe, while rejecting the greater part of the Hindu religion.—*J. Kennedy.*

FOLKTALES.

138. The Discarded Princess.—There was once a Rája to whom a daughter was born, and when he heard of it he sent for the astrologers and asked them if the girl would bring him luck or not. Though all the omens were favourable, they told him that if he kept her in his house the family would be ruined. So he had her shut up in a box and putting some pieces of gold in it, ordered his people to throw her into the river. The box floated down to a *ghát* where a dhobi was washing clothes. He took the money himself and gave the child to a potter. One day when the girl grew up, the potter was going to fire his kiln, when she said: "Father, let me fire it this time." She did so and some time after when he opened it he found that all his bricks had turned into ingots of gold.

One day the potter asked her what kind of robe she would like to wear. She said: "Let me have a sheet of bright chintz (*chira*)." He gave her what she asked and when she had worn it for some time she gave it to a dhobi to wash. He washed it at the *ghát* and laid it out to dry, when just then the Rája, her father, happened to pass by. He stopped to smoke and seeing the bright robe and thinking it to be fire he sent his servant to get a light from it. The dhobi said: "This is not fire, but cloth." The Raja was surprised and asked to whom the robe belonged. When he learnt who the owner was, he went to the potter's house and finding the girl to be beautiful, he proposed at once to marry her. The potter agreed and made her over to the Rája. He took her home and called for the Pandits to perform the marriage ceremony. When the pair began to walk round the fire, the girl said :

*Pahli bhanwari phirun ; Rája pújai man ki ás.
Janam ki pothi bichdro Pandit ; pújai man ki ás.*

"I am making the first round; your desire is being realised; but beware; let the Pandit again consult his books." Hearing this the Rája stopped, but the Pandits again urged him to go on. Thus he performed the seven rounds; but as he was about to complete the ceremony by putting vermilion on the parting of her hair, the girl told him the whole story. The Rája expelled the Pandits from his kingdom and taking the girl to his palace, recognised her as his daughter.

(Told by Rám Ganesh Dúbé, Bráhman of Aksaull, Mirzapur.)

139. The tale of Rani Kamlapati.—There was once a Rája who had two sons and when they came to be twelve years of age their father was attacked by leprosy. He was in despair regarding his condition and the Rání in her grief sent for the most noted astrologers of the court and consulted them regarding his case. They gave their opinion that unless Kamlapatí Rání came and touched him he would not recover. So the Rání had some packets of betel and a drum placed at the gate of the palace and announced that whoever wished to gain the favour of the Rája should accept the task of finding Kamlapatí Rání. But no one dared to strike the drum and undertake the duty. Finally the Princes went to their father and offered to undertake the duty. He tried to dissuade them, but without avail. They mounted their horses and started on the search.

After many days they reached the city where Kamlapatí Rání lived. They found her sitting in her bower (*bárahdari*) near the river bank and as they rode past they recited the following verse:

*Harit manin ke mál hain, motiyán máng guháya
Suraj sam tawa chir duti, biu piya kachchu na soháya.*

"Thy garlands are of green gems; the parting of thy hair is decorated with pearls ; thy garment is brilliant like the sun ; but what avail these ornaments without a husband ?"

To this the Rání replied—

*Uncha bhit talab ka ; chalen musáfir dháya.
Bhágu musáfir bát se ; nahin márún nain ghumáya*

"High is the bank of the pond; the travellers ride rapidly by ; hasten from the path lest I slay you with a glance of my eye."

The Princes hearing this stepped back and fell into the water and there was none to take them out.

When some time elapsed the Rája told the Rání that the Princes must be dead; so she gave notice that whoever would bring them back should receive half the kingdom. The only person who would undertake the task was a Brahman. He set out and soon reached the city of Kamlapatí Rání. He searched for the Princes and at last found them in the ditch, whence he took them out. Then he went to the Rání, whom he found sitting in her bower, and addressed her in these lines:

*Afimchi posti doú jané, wah bhi mast díwán,
Langré hoya khandaq giré, abhin ghabrú jawán.*

"Eaters of opium are they and nothing short of mad ; they were lamed falling into the ditch and still they are only youths."

Then the Rání signed to the Bráhman to meet her that night at the shop of a sweetmeat-seller. The Rání came at midnight and the Brahman spoke:

*Yah nagari men bahut bastu hain ; chatur base na koi.
Bhúkha musáfir par raha ; nind kahán se hoe ?"*

"There are many things in this city, but no clever man; a traveller lay down can he feel sleepy."
The Ráni answered—
*Hándi le Kumhár se ; Modi átá dál ;
Lakri le godám se ; roti har gawwar.*
"Get a pot from the potter; flour and pulse from the grocer; take wood from the store and cook your food, you boor."
To this he answered :
*Hándi liya Kumhar se ; Modi átá dál ;
Lakri liya godam se ; Ráni káh tera ihsán ?*
"I got the vessel from the potter; flour and pulse from the grocer; wood from the store; now Ráni what kindness will you show me?"
The Ráni then making the Bráhman out to be her brother took him home and lived with him. She asked him what he would have to eat and he called for kodo, boiled with sugar and butter. When she brought it, he said :
*Kodo aisa chhail chihaniya ; tis par shakhár ghiwá ;
Ráni dáya ati bhai ; kushal karen Sadasiva.*
"Fine is the kodo and with it is mixed sugar and butter; Ráni you have been kind to me; may Sadasiva bless you."
The old Ráni, the mother of the young Ráni, was displeased, because of her intimacy with the Brahman while her husband was absent ; so she ordered her to swear before the Nág, and challenge it to bite her if she was unchaste. Ráni Kamlapatí was dismayed at having to take this oath. But as she came before the Nág, the Brahman, in the disguise of a Sannyási, appeared and asked an alms. Then the Ráni touched him and swore: "May the Nág bite me if I have ever touched any one save my husband and this Sannyási." So she escaped taking a false oath and saved her honour.
Meanwhile the Ráni's husband returned and was wroth when he heard of his Ráni's doings with the Bráhman. So he plotted against the Bráhman's life and one day challenged him to play dice, on condition that the winner should kill the loser. The Bráhman was defeated and the Rája killed him ; when the Ráni heard of his death, she too took her life. All the people were lamenting her, when Siva and Párvati happened to be flying through the air and coming down asked the Rája what had happened. When he told them the story, Siva said to him : "Close your eyes." Then the god revived Ráni Kamlapatí and the Bráhman and killed the Rája.
The Bráhman returned home with Ráni Kamlapatí and the Princes. She touched the old Rája and he was cured of his leprosy. The Rája gave the Bráhman half his dominions and he and Ráni Kamlapati lived for many years in happiness.

(Told by Saladat Khán, a Musalmán tobacco seller, of Wellesleyganj, Mirzapur.)

140. **Entertaining angels unawares.**—Once upon a time Mahádeva and Bhagwán were making a visit to the world and in the evening they came to the house of a poor Bráhman and asked for shelter. He asked them to sit down and as he had nothing wherewith to entertain them, he sent his son to pledge his *lota*, and with the money thus obtained he supplied them with food. The gods were much pleased with his devotion and Mahádeva said : "My friend, I wish to have your son married." The Bráhman answered : " O good guests, I am so poor that I can hardly support myself. How can I provide for a daughter-in-law ? " Mahádeva did not heed his words and sent a Bráhman and a barber to find a bride for the son of the Bráhman. They arranged the match in the family of a very rich and respectable man. They returned and informed Mahádeva that the marriage had been settled and a day fixed for the ceremony.
On the fixed date the Bráhman, accompanied by Mahádeva, and the planets Shukra (Venus) and Sanischara (Saturn) went with the bridegroom to the house of the bride. When her father saw how small their number was, he asked Mahádeva why the marriage procession was so mean. Mahádeva said : "The others are coming behind." And when he looked he saw thousands of men and a splendid equipage approaching. When all was ready, the ceremony was duly performed and the party sat down to the marriage feast. Mahádeva said : "Let these two men, named Shukra and Sanischara, be first fed." The house master took them first inside and they at once devoured all the provisions. The Bráhman returned to Mahádeva and said: "There is no more food for the other guests and my honour is lost." Mahádeva said : " Shut the door of your food closet and open it again " ; and when he did so, lo, he found it full of the most delicious food ! So all the guests were fed, and when the bridegroom brought home his bride he found that his poor hut was changed into a palace of gold, with a lovely garden, and gems lay about it like the sand on the river bank. When his neighbours asked the cause of his prosperity, he answered :

*Tulasi yá jag aiks sab se miliye dháya,
Kya jánen kehi bhes men Náráyan mili jáya ?*

"Tulasi says : "When you come into this world be kind to every one. Who knows in what guise Náráyan may appear?"

(Told by Rám Ganesh Dúbé, Bráhman, of Akasuli, Mirzapur.)

141. **The Prince and the daughter of the Gandhi.**—There was once a Prince who was very fond of hunting. One day he went to the river bank and saw a dhobi blindfolded washing clothes. The Prince asked him whose clothes he

was washing, but he replied: "What matter is it of yours? If you want anything washed I can do it." The Prince gave him his handkerchief to wash and when it was ready he gave the dhobi five pieces of gold. "That is not half what I get," said the dhobi, "for washing the clothes of the Gandhi's (perfumer's) daughter, and further she is so particular that I am not allowed to look at anything I wash; so I have to keep myself blindfolded." When the Prince heard this, he went to his father and said: "I will marry no one else in the world but the Gandhi's daughter."

The King sent for the Gandhi and proposed marriage between his daughter and the Prince. He replied that he must consult his daughter. She said: "I will marry him only on this condition, that for the first six months I am only to come for an hour or two and sit in my husband's house. After that he may do with me as he pleases." The Prince agreed to these conditions, and they were married. His wife used to come and see him for an hour every day and would then go home.

Now the son of the Wazir was a great friend of the Prince and one day when his wife was sitting with the Prince his friend came to see him. "Why does not your wife remain with you?" he asked. "I do not know," said the Prince. "Well," said his friend, "I will give you some magic lampblack and when you rub it on your eyes you will become invisible. Then you can follow her and see what happens."

So when his wife went away, the next time he rubbed the lampblack on his eyes and followed her unseen. At midnight she seated herself on a flying chariot (*bimán*) and was going to the Darbar of Rája Indra, when the Prince, without her seeing him, mounted the chariot and arrived at Indrasan with her. It so happened that the drummer of Rája Indra was asleep and the Prince, who was a skilled performer on the drum, took his place, and performed so well that Rája Indra was pleased and gave him as a reward a shawl, a ring and a diamond necklace. When his wife was going back he took his gifts and mounting the flying chariot descended with her to earth.

Next morning, as he had been awake all night, he was tired and was sleeping when his wife came. When she came in she drew off the cloth from over his face and he woke and said: "Why are you so attentive to me to-day?" She made no answer, but asked "Where were you last night." "I went up to Indrasan with a fairy," he answered. At this she was much displeased and settled in her mind that she would complain about that fairy to Rája Indra.

Soon after the Wazir's son came and the Prince told him all that had happened. Then his friend had a house built in the exact pattern of the Darbar of Rája Indra and there he hung up the presents he had received. When it was ready, the Prince asked his wife to see it and when she saw it she was certain that some fairy of the Heavenly Court used to visit her husband. By this time the six months had passed and his wife came to live with the Prince. Then a fairy went to Rája Indra and told him that the Prince was aping him, had built a palace like his, and was living with one of his fairies. Hearing this, Rája Indra was sore wroth and sent his demons to bring away the Prince's house and join it to his own, to fling his wife into the fort of Qáf, where a fire burns continually, and that the Prince should know nought of this. The demons performed the orders of Rája Indra and when the Prince lost his wife he would not be comforted and wandered into the jungle, where he found a Sannyási asleep. He attended to the wants of the holy man, who, when he woke was much pleased with the Prince and when he heard his story, he said: "Fear not, I will arrange your business." He then gave the Prince a magic sandal wand and powder, and said: "Go, sprinkle this powder on the fort of Qáf and the fire will be extinguished; then collect your wife's bones and strike them with the wand and she will revive. The powder will make you invisible on your journey." The Prince did as he was ordered; he recovered his wife and brought her home, where they lived many years in happiness.

(Told by Padárath Pánre, Bráhman, of Mirzapur.)

142. **The Bráhman's Luck.**—There was once a Bráhman who lived in a forest; his wants were small and as he possessed all he desired he was quite happy. One day the Rája went into the forest to hunt and being hungry he halted at the house of the Bráhman, who entertained him with fruits and water. As he was going away the Rája wrote down his name and said: "If you are ever in want and it is in my power to relieve you, I shall gladly do so."

Time passed and the Bráhman became so poor that he had nothing left but his *lota*. At last his wife asked him why he did not go to the Rája who had promised to help him in his need. The Bráhman answered: "I do not wish to come as a supplicant to a man whom I once obliged." But his wife told him of many great men who had gone to Rájas in their hour of need, and at last the Bráhman went to the Rája's palace and craved an audience. The Rája received him with honour and seated him beside him. When he learnt his case, he loaded a cart with money and goods and gave it to the Bráhman to take home to his wife. As he was driving home with the cart, he halted at a tank to bathe and left the cart and bullocks on the bank. When he had done bathing and returned, he found that they had disappeared. He went home to his wife lamenting his bad luck, and as his troubles increased, his wife induced him to go to the Rája a second time. The Rája was as kind as before and this time gave him a horse laden with gold. As he was going home he came to the same tank as before and went to bathe. When he came out of the water the horse and money were nowhere to be seen.

His wife forced him to go to the Rája a third time, very much against his will. The Rája said: "My friend, these are your evil days. I will now give you four thousand rupees and you can trade with them." The Bráhman started a business with the money and at the end of a year he had made a profit of one pice. When he told the Rája, he laughed, and said: "Now your luck is changing. Trade with this one pice and see what is the result." He put the pice into his business and made two pice; and so he by degrees made a large fortune. Then he started for his home and on his way he came to the same tank and there he found his cart and horse and all his money safe. Thus his bad luck left him and he lived for many years in great prosperity.

(Told by Iqbal Husen, a Muhammadan weaver of Bhuil, Mirzapur.)

143. **The Devoted Wife.**—There was once a woman who was such a good wife that she was known as Pativratá, or "the devoted spouse." One day she was pounding rice and her husband came in and asked for a drink of water. She dropped the pounder in the middle of a stroke and as the blessing of the gods was upon her, it remained hanging suspended in the air as it was. A woman of the neighbourhood who happened to be there saw the miracle and was astonished. "How can this be?" she asked. "This comes from my devotion to my husband," she answered.

Her friend came home and said to her husband: "The next time I am pounding rice you ask me for a drink of water and I will prove to you what a devoted spouse I am." He did so, but the pounder fell on his head and broke his skull. All the neighbours ran up and beat and abused her, and one man made this verse:

Pativratá jo nári hoé,
Músal akáse tange soé ;
Kulatá chalé pativratá chál ;
Apné pati ké phoré bhál.

"A devoted wife can keep the grain pounder suspended in the sky, but if a vicious woman tries to imitate her, she breaks her husband's crown."

(Told by Híra Lál, village accountant, Haliya, Mirzapur.)

144. **The Boy and the Merchant.**—There lived in the city of Kanauj a merchant who had four sons, three of whom were grown up, while the youngest was a boy. Once it happened that the merchant was about to undertake a long journey and his youngest son asked him to take him with him. His father objected that the road was too difficult and he too young for such a long journey; but the boy persisted in making the request and at last his father gave him two thousand rupees and allowed him to accompany him.

When they had gone a long way, the boy, somehow or other, became separated from his father and as he wandered on he came to a jungle infested by beasts of prey. He was in great terror and repeated the verse :

Faisa ja ajal hum la ista kharun ;
Sa ataun yaslak de mun.

"When the predestined time of death comes, it arrives neither a moment too early nor a moment too late."

Meanwhile, he saw an old man with sandals on his feet and a stick in his hand approaching him; the boy was in great fear, but when the old man came up and asked him who he was and where he was going, he told him his story. The old man pointed in a certain direction and said: "If you follow this way you will come to the city of Labútbáj and when you arrive there you can easily find your way wherever you please."

The old man disappeared and the boy followed his directions and after going some way he came to the gate of a city. He asked the people what the name of the city was and they said it was Labútbáj. He wandered about and at last came to the shop of a merchant, whose servant gave him a seat with others who were at the shop at the time. The owner of the shop, whose name was Munfr, asked the boy who he was. The boy told him his adventures and as he was speaking a pair of cats jumped down fighting from the roof on to the spot where the boy was sitting and the moment one of the cats touched him, he disappeared.

When the merchant Munír saw this he was grieved, and said to his servants: "I will not eat food until I find him." So he started with a number of men, horses and elephants and set out in search of the boy. When he had gone a long way he lost all his people and his means were exhausted; and he went on alone. Finally he was reduced to want and came to the house of a peasant. The peasant entertained him and Munír told his case. The peasant promised to support him and he remained there. In this way five months passed, and one day the peasant had occasion to go to a wedding in a neighbouring village and as he was going he said to him: "My friend, I am going away, please attend to one matter in my absence. To the south of the village is a pípal tree and in the morning smoke rises from it and after the smoke a hand shows itself from the branches. You must take daily a plate of cakes and a vessel of water and offer them to the hand when it appears. But take care, do not touch the hand, otherwise evil consequences will arise."

Next morning Munír took the offering to the tree and when the hand came out he offered them to it, but he forgot the warning of his friend and allowed the hand to touch him. No sooner had he done so than he was seized, carried through the air and dropped on the top of a mosque in a distant land. He rolled off the roof of the mosque, and dropped into a well which was close beside it. He began to grope about to find a means of escape; at last he saw a ray of light through a crevice and he made his way into the city.

Now it was the law in that city that when the king died they used to choose the first stranger who arrived to rule over them; so they chose the merchant Munír, and made him king. He reigned for many years and though he made constant search nothing was ever heard of the boy.

(Told by Iqbal Husen, a Muhammadan weaver of Bhuili, Mirzapur.)

145. **The height of Virtue.**—Once upon a time famine raged in the land and the Rája sent for the astrologers and asked them how it could be removed. They said that the only way to stop it was for a truly devoted wife to bathe at the Amka Tírath. They searched for a long time and could find none who answered the conditions. At last they learned that the daughter of Bhagwán Dás, the Mahájan, was a truly devoted wife; so they went to him and asked him to allow his daughter to bathe in the Amka Tírath and save the country from ruin.

Bhagwán Dás went to his daughter and explained the case. She answered: "O Father, I do not come up to the conditions; one day a Faqír came to the house and asked for alms; as I was giving him something my hand by accident touched his and my virtue was thus stained. Go to my sister who is more pure than I am."

The Mahájan went to his second daughter and explained what was wanted. She answered: "The work cannot be done by me, for my purity has been stained. One day I was bathing in the Ganges and my garment blew aside and the water touched my person. You know that by the Shástras water is considered to be male; hence I do not answer the conditions. You had better go to my younger sister."

The banker went to his third daughter, and when he explained the case she said: "I do not answer the conditions. One night, at midnight, my husband said to me: "The wind is blowing from the east." I replied: "No; it is from the west." "Thus I contradicted my husband and cannot be considered a truly devoted wife. You had better go to my younger sister."

The Mahájan went to his fourth daughter and told her the case. She said: "Father, since you gave me to my husband I am in his hands and do only what he tells me." The Mahájan took her to the Rája and he explained to her the case. She went with the Pandits and bathed in the Amka Tírath and immediately the famine was removed from the land.

(Told by Ganesh Dúbe, Bráhman of Aksauli, Mirzapur.)

146. **The virtue of Faith.**—There once lived a Sannyási in the jungle and his disciple lived with him. Now the Sannyási had promised his disciple to teach him a *mantra* by means of which he could do anything he pleased. He served him for twelve years but he was never taught the *mantra*; at last one day when the holy man was washing, the disciple came and said: "I have served you now for twelve years and you have not taught me the *mantra* as you promised; kindly teach it to me now."

The saint was wroth at being addressed on such a subject at such a time and said: "*Tanain jána na jaghai jána, na junai jána,*" that is to say, "You paid no heed to my state of ceremonial impurity, nor to place nor time." The disciple did not understand what his master was saying and thought that this was the *mantra* which he had promised to teach him. So he went away quite contented.

One day soon after while the saint and his disciple were sitting together, a party of men passed by carrying a corpse and when they saw the saint they asked for fire to burn the body. When the disciple heard this he asked them where the corpse was; they said that it was under yonder tree. He told them to bring it. When the saint heard this he was angry because he feared lest they might ask him to revive the body and if he failed his reputation would suffer. So he told his disciple not to allow the men to approach; but he paid no attention to his words. When the men brought the body the disciple muttered over it the supposed *mantra* which he believed the saint had given him and the dead man rose immediately. Every one was surprised and none more so than the saint himself. When they had all gone away, after thanking him profusely, he asked his disciple what *mantra* he had used and when he heard it he smiled and said *Vishwá am phal dayakam.* "It is faith that gives the fruit."

(Told by Akbar Sháh, Manjhi of Manbasa, Dudhi, Mirzapur.)

MISCELLANEA.

147. Impurity after Shaving.—There is a general feeling among natives of high caste, and many low caste people too, that without bathing after shaving a man should do nothing which requires personal purity, such as eating, drinking, worship, &c. To avoid the impurity attaching to clothes, they discard them as much as possible before being shaved.—*Pándit Rám Ghári b Chaubé.*

148. Charming Warts.—The more you cut a wart with a knife or other iron article the more it increases in size. When you want to remove one completely, you ought to pretend to cut it with a hair from your head when it will disappear at once.—*W. Crooke, C.S.*

149. Budaon Snakes.—It is believed that a snake becomes blind as soon as its eyes fall on a pregnant woman. It remains fixed to the spot and cannot move. This belief is not limited to this place, but is prevalent elsewhere too.—*Bhagwan Das.*

150. Medical Omens.—If a physician when going to visit a patient meets on the road a cool thing, such as water, the sick man will recover; if he meets fire his disease will increase. The opposite omen is taken from what the messenger who goes to meet the doctor comes across on the road.—*Pándit Rám Ghárib Chaubé.*

151. The calls of animals.—The jackal is supposed to call in the words *huán, huán,* which are thus interpreted—

Rám nám ki sudhi bisráyo, bhulyo jiywa jagat ke jua;
Duniya daulat mal khazána, ek din dhawal dhan sab dhuán;
Diya ihan kár kám jo hain sargi krikhi khat nahín kuán;
Siyar kahd sansár se roya ek din chalna hai huán.

"O! Thou creature, thou hast forgotten the name of Rama, art lured by the gambling of the world; the wealth, pelf, property, treasure and white abode will one day come to smoke. What thou give here will serve you there, for there is no farming nor wood nor well in heaven. The howl of the jackal warns men that one day they will have to go there."

The dhavala bird says—*E'kel tum, ekel tum,* which is thus explained :—

Ja din pran payan biyo upji tan men tridoshi dhumm;
Mota pild sut bandhu sahadar e sab baithi rahe tahán gumm;
Chela ját Yamlok akela koi na awat káj kutum;
Wa din ke tum hohu sahaydk he Raghu náyak ekel tum.

"On the day the soul left the body a sort of smoke three times useless arose. Father, mother, son and brother sit there still, but the soul has to make its way alone. None of his family then can serve him. O! lord Raghu, be thou alone my aid."

The cuckoo sings as follows :—

Yojan chhatr charhe Duryodhan; bhúpati ke ghar sampati thor;
Rávána ke grih kaun gane jinke pur kanchan koti karor.
Arb kharb le darb jama kar ek din chale lungota khol;
Koil barambar kahe—Sunu murak manukh sampati chhor.

"Duryodhana had an umbrella over him which stretched for miles. The king thinks that he has less wealth than others. Who can count the wealth of Ravana, who had millions of villages made of gold. Even if he amass millions, man has one day to leave his loin cloth and go. Over and over the cuckoo says, O! man, thou art a fool to amass money. Give up thinking of it."

The above verses are very popular in villages and are sung by wandering Bhats and Bráhmans.—*Pándit Rám Ghárib Chaubé.*

152. Dogs howling.—When a woman sees a dog howling with his head raised towards the sky, she drives him off with curses, because she believes he is appealing to God against the people of the neighbourhood and some trouble surely follows.—*M. Ram Lal.*

153. A Carpenter's Formulæ.—

Nau girah bárah rás;
Pandarah tith miláwo pás.

"If b⌐c *ab* is 9 and *bc* is 12 then *ac* is surely 15." This is called guniyá miláná. When they are required to build a house they make the courtyard according to this formulæ. Carpenters sometimes do the business of masons in the western districts of the North-Western Provinces.—*Pándit Rám Ghárib Chaubé.*

154. Birth Song.—

Nohar bhailan chelud macheryá,
Nohar bhailan godyá balakuá,
Nohar bhailan piyá kai sajeryá,
Nohar bhailan Sawanuá Bhadawaná kai raityá,
Daiú náhin gargen ho,
Baresai láge Adard kai bunduá,
Bulukai láge jhinguá,
Bhitar se nikale sital—Demane man jhanke!

155. Translation.—

Not a fish this year hath brought me,
Not a babe to cheer my bed,
Where my truant spouse ne'er sought me,
Till the love-tide months had fled.
What, though no thunders herald
These drops, that the skies 'gin shed?
For the cricket's voice hath spoken
That the cold his bonds hath broken—
Ah me! would I were dead.—*R. Greeven, Benares*,
12-7-'90.

---

156. Lucky and unlucky communications.—It is the rule that all letters conveying joyful intelligence, such as those announcing an approaching marriage, the birth of a son, &c., are sent by a barber or a Bári and are sprinkled outside with a little gold dust or turmeric. Those letters which convey melancholy news are sent by a low-caste man, such as a Chamár, and have no yellow mark upon them. Now that most letters are sent through the post, this custom has considerably fallen into disuse ; but even now a letter of good news sent through the post has often a little daub of turmeric on the envelope to show that it contains no ill-omened intelligence.—*W. Crooke, C.S.*

---

157. Nepal: The Philosopher's Stone.—There are many people who believe that the strength of Nepal consists in its possessing the Párasaáth Mahadeva, which is made of the Párás Patthar, or philosopher's stone. It is said that the Nepalese touch this stone daily with a quantity of iron and thus make nine ox loads of gold every day. The Párasnáth of Nepal seems to be identical with the same deity as worshipped by the Jainas.—*Pandit Rám Gharib Chaubé.*

---

158. The Sidhari, or Siddhi Fish.—To see a fish at the commencement of a journey is most auspicious. But the best of all is the small fish known as the Sidhari. The idea about fish is found in the Ramayana where we read:—

*Sanmukh aye dadhi aru mina,
Kar pustak dui Bipra prabina.*

" Curds and fish in front and two learned Brahmans with their books."

In Sarwar, or the land beyond the Sarju river, the people will not eat the Moya fish, as they say that it was in this that Vishnu was incarnated in his Matsya form, and also because it somewhat resembles a snake. Others will not eat the Bhakur, or large tank carp.—*Pandit Rám Gharib Chaubé.*

---

159. Bengal: Chittagong.—Modern Chittagong derives its name from Chatigrama : *chati* means "lamp" and *grama* "village." It is said that the District of Chittagong was, some centuries ago, inhabited by *jinns* or fairies. No man could then come to this place as he was either killed or otherwise disposed of by the king of the fairies. A powerful faqir however came to Chittagong on a bamboo raft, and applied to the fairy king for as much land as would be illumined by his lamp as he wanted land for his *asana* or seat in order to invoke the spirit of God. The king granted his desire. The faqir lighted a lamp at night and chanted *mantras*. The lamp grew so powerful and bright that the whole of the district was illumined and the fairy king with the host of his subjects left the place for ever. Thus the place took its name from the faqir's lamp and thenceforth it became the abode of human beings.

This legend seems to me to be connected with the present Jumia Maghs who still live in this range of hills and cultivate virgin forest, locally called " Júm."—*Háripada Ghosh, Chittagong.*

[This is an interesting folk etymology. Chittagong is from Saptagráma, "the seven villages."—Ed.]

---

160. The tale of the Raja Harivansa of Menhnagar, Tahsil Deoganw, Azamgarh District.—In the village of Menhnagar in the Azamgarh District a tank and embankment commemorate the name of the Raja Harivansa. About six centuries ago there was a poor Rajput family in the village and one of them, a youth, went one day to fish in a pond close to where the present embankment stands. He by chance caught a large fish, but the other Rajputs took it away from him by force. He went home in tears and told his wife what had happened. Just then a very learned Brahman who was on his travels from Benares came to their door. He enquired the cause of her trouble and when she told him he said : "You shall have a son who will be a Raja. If my words come true what will you give me ?" " If my son becomes a Raja," she answered, " you shall have a piece of land rent free in this village."

In due time the boy was born as the Brahman had foretold. After a time his elder brother went and took service with the Court of Delhi and rose to great honour and distinction. The King of Delhi induced him to become a Musalman and wished to make him Raja of his native land. But he remembered the prediction of the Brahman and made over the title to him. Then he built the tank and embankment known by the name of Hari Sinh. He gave the Brahman also two villages rent free and his descendants occupy them still. The people of the place still repeat the following couplet—

*Haribándh, Harvans bakhánon, daulat ki nishání;
Menhnagar ki kot bakhánon, Haribándh ka páni.*

" I praise the Hari embankment of Harivans ; this is the sign of wealth ; I praise the fort of Menhnagar and the water of Hari's embankment."—*M. Abdullah Khan of Menhnagar.*

---

161. Superstition about a Cow.—Hindus in the western districts of the North-Western Provinces believe that if a cow manages to get on the roof of a house she is most unlucky and if the owner wishes to escape misfortune he should give her away to a Brahman. If a cow swings her body about and chews dry sticks or stalks she should also be given away.—*Pandit Rám Gharib Chaubé.*

[Mr. Ibbetson, I think, in one of his Reports, mentions that in the Panjab the same idea extends to the buffalo.—Ed.]

162. A poor man's proverb:—
"*Katthar, guddar soailain,
Marjiddwala rowailain.*"
"A man in rags hath the soundest sleep;
While he in gold hath ever to weep."—*Pandit Rám Ghárib Chaubé.*

163. The Porcupine and the Crow.—According to the Shastras and common Hindu belief both the porcupine (*sáhi*) and the crow are full of *tamas* or passion and hence the use of their flesh is forbidden.—*Pandit Rám Ghárib Chaubé.*

[It is a common idea that if you want to promote a quarrel between two neighbours you have only to throw the quills of a porcupine into their houses.—ED.]

164. A Charm (Muhammadan) to cure Bawasír or Piles:—

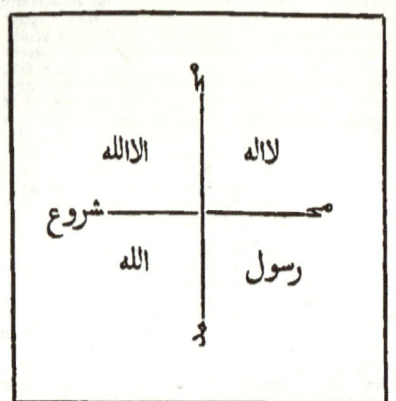

Write the above charm on wheat cakes and make the patient eat them. Seven days' repetition of this will cure him completely.—*Pandit Rám Ghárib Chaubé.*

165. Hindu House, Arrangement of.—The following is the arrangement of the rooms of a Hindu house as sanctioned by the Shastras and religious custom :—

In the eastern direction should be the bath-room (*snán grih*) and in the south-eastern corner should be the kitchen (*pák grih*): in the southern direction should be the sleeping room (*shayan grih*), and in the south-western corner should be the weapon-room (*hathiyar grih*), in the western direction should be the dinner and supper-room, and in the north-western corner should be the room for storing grain or other property; in the northern direction should be the room for merchandise; in the north-eastern corner should be the room for the family gods (*deo grihu*) and in the centre should be the churning place (*mathan sthan*). This is the arrangement for the eight principal rooms. If anybody requires more rooms he should arrange them in this way :—

Between the southern and south-eastern rooms should be a room for collecting clarified butter, and between the southern and south-western houses should be the bath-room; and between the western and south-western rooms should be a place for study (*Vidya bhyás*) and between the western and north-western rooms should be a room for observing mourning (*Rudan karne ka ghar*) and between the northern and north-western houses should be the bed-room and between the northern and north-eastern houses should be a room for medicine, and between the eastern and north-eastern houses should be a room for miscellaneous purposes.—*Pandit Rám Ghárib Chaubé.*

166. Dogs' tongues.—The tongue of a dog burnt and the ashes mixed with oil is a famous cure for any kind of putrid sore. People who have very bad sores rub them with curds on a Saturday or Tuesday and get a black dog to lick them. Dogs never die of any wound which they can lick. So thieves when they want to kill a dog hit in on the head so that it cannot lick the wound.—*Pandit Rám Ghárib Chaubé.*

[Is it on the same principle that in Ireland the dried tongue of a fox has many virtues? It will draw thorns however deep.—*Folklore,* IV—351—ED.]

167. Saharanpur; Charms to stop rain.—When people here wish to stop rain they either pour some oil into rain water or they put some rain water in an earthen pot and bury it in the ground. (*Introduction to Popular Religion and Folklore,* 46.)—*W. Crooke, C.S.*

168. The Snake's dilemma.—When a snake comes across a musk-rat he must either swallow it or not; if he can't he is a fool, if he does he becomes a leper.—*W. Cockburn.*

169. Saharanpur; Riding on an Ox.—In this part of the country among the Dhobis, Kumhars and Kunjras the bridegroom is taken to the house of the bride mounted on an ox. How far does this custom prevail in other parts of the country?—*W. Crooke, C.S.*

170. Jay Sinh Sawai; how he got his name.—When Jay Sinh was a boy one day a messenger came from the Emperor of Delhi summoning his father. Jay Sinh's father was ill so the youth went in his stead. On the way the councillors who accompanied him went on advising him what he should say to the Emperor; but he said that he would say whatever came into his head.

The Emperor asked him where his father was. He replied that he was at home. The Emperor enquired: "Why then did he not come?" The boy said: "What matters that? I am ready to speak in his stead." The Emperor was wroth at what he considered the impertinence of the boy. "If you speak to me like this," he said, "I will fling you into the Jumna which flows below the palace." With that he seized the boy's hands. "Are you not afraid?" he asked. "No," said Jay Sinh. "When the Emperor seizes one hand of a man (*hath pakarta hai*) he is safe under his protection. How much more so when he seizes both hands?" The Emperor laughed and said: "You are wiser than even your father. So you shall be called Jay Sinh Sawai or Jay Sinh and a quarter."

(*Told by Balhadra, Teacher of the Panjdih School, Buliya District.*)

North Indian Notes and Queries:
A MONTHLY PERIODICAL.

VOL. V.]   AUGUST, 1895.   [NO. 5.

Every communication must be accompanied by the writer's name and address, not necessarily for insertion, but as a guarantee of good faith. Every quotation from a book must be accompanied by its full title, publisher's and author's names, place and date of publication, volume and page.
Contributors are requested to write on ONE SIDE the page only. If several contributions be sent at a time, they should be sent each on a separate sheet.
The Conductor cannot undertake to return, or be responsible for, any MSS. not accepted.
All orders must be accompanied by cash. If not so accompanied, they will either not be attended to, or will be complied with per value-payable post.
Contributions should be addressed direct to W. CROOKE, ESQ., C. S., SAHARANPUR, N.-W. P., INDIA.

CONTENTS OF THIS NUMBER.
(The references are to the Notes.)

Popular Religion ... — 73 to 78	Folktales ... 82 to 87
Anthropology ... ... — 79 ,, 81	Miscellanea ... ... 88 ,, 90

POPULAR RELIGION.

171. **Saharanpur: Lál Dás ka Kund: A Sacred Spring.**—In the city of Saharanpur there is a monastery known as Lál Dás ka Bára. In front of this is a spot where there is a sacred spring which is said to have an underground connection with the Ganges. This is called Lál Dás ka kund. Lál Dás was a saint who flourished several centuries ago. About him and his sacred spring the following legend is told :—

He lived in the monastery which is still called by his name. He used to go every day to Hardwar to perform his ablutions, though Hardwar is as the crow flies some forty miles away. A Muhammadan saint named Háji Sháh Kamál who lived close to his monastery used to see Lál Dás undertaking this journey daily. One day he said to Lál Dás :" You are a perfect saint (*Siddh*); why do you take this trouble daily ?" " Even if I am a Siddh," he replied, " Mother Ganges is beyond my power." The Muhammadan answered: " Suppose: I call your Mother Ganges." " You will do me a favour if you do," he replied. " Well," said Sháh Kamál, " To-day when you are bathing at Hardwár put your loincloth, gourd and stick into the Ganges and you will find them at your door when you return."

When Lál Dás returned he found his things at his door as the saint had said, and digging at the spot water gushed out of the ground and when Sháh Kamál asked him if it was as he had said he was ashamed before him.

Again Lál Dás tried to test him. So one day he went to him and said : " If you desire to go on a pilgrimage to Makka take this magic ball (*jadu ka gutka*), put it into your mouth and you will be there in an instant." " I need no magic ball," was the reply. " Just shut your eyes for a moment." When he did so lo! Lál Dás saw the whole of Makka spread out before him.

Another time Lál Dás changed a cocoanut into the philosopher's stone and giving it to Sháh Kamál said : " If you want gold you have only to touch any baser metal with this." Sháh Kamál laughed and getting up spat on the ground and lo ! the earth was turned into gold. So Lál Dás admitted the superiority of Sháh Kamál and the two lived as friends.

Now-a-days bathing at the well of Lál Dás is as good as bathing in the Ganges. On the day of the 'Id Muhammadans assemble at the tomb of Háji Sháh Kamál and when night falls light lamps in his honour.—*W. Crooke.*

172. A Fakir at Banda.—There is a person known as Hafiz Dost Muhammad at Banda. He is an old Muhammadan ascetic, short and thin, and he is credited with certain supernatural powers of winning the favour of the gods. Muhammadans, even those holding high posts, resort to him for advice and enlightenment—to say nothing of litigants who crowd his abode every morning, and they almost all seek his blessings before attending the public Courts. Those that are successful attribute their success to the mediation of the Hafiz. But it is curious to find that not much is made of those who lose their cases. Some circumstances are always found at hand to explain away the unfavourable result. Hedayatulla, the nephew of the Hafiz, died last year by falling into a well. The ignorant public have been imposed upon to believe that it was by a special mandate of the deity that he was called up. He has been buried near the dwelling house of the Hafiz. The tomb is visited on every Thursday by ladies, especially by prostitutes, who sing songs and present offerings of sweetmeats and cash, etc. The Hafiz is rather a man of humble means and aspirations and with a sufficient provision of food he spends his time always at his beads.—*Durga Prasada.*

173. Saharanpur: Mamu Allah Bakhsh.—Among the local demons in Saharanpur none is more respected than Allah Bakhsh of Gangoh. No one can tell anything of his history, but he was no doubt a powerful personage who used his power to the injury of his neighbours. Whenever anyone falls into trouble by calling out Mamu Allah Bakhsh, that is to say, claiming that he is their maternal uncle, and as such he is bound to protect them. (For another example of this see my *Introduction to Popular Religion and Folklore*, p. 324.) A fair in honour of this personage, who is called a Sayyid, is held every year at Gangoh on the eighth of the dark fortnight of the month of Pus. At his tomb they offer cloth, pice, sweets, sherbet, and sacrifice goats and fowls. Songs in his honour are sung by Dominis, a class of musicians and dancing girls. As the Dominis sing the Sayyid "comes on the head" of some of the women present and they are supposed to be under the influence of his evil spirit. They then utter oracles and name the demon which is besetting them and the priests of the shrine, who are Muhammdan weavers, state the kind of offering which is likely to bring about their recovery. A Khatik in the town of Saharanpur has quite recently started a cenotaph of the Sayyid in the city and women now go there and make vows and present offerings. The worship of the Sayyid, like that of most of these Pírs, is very effectual in removing the curse of barrenness, and he also keeps off various kinds of bhuts, demons, witches and other evil spirits which attack women. —*W. Crooke.*

174. Saharanpur: Agricultural superstitions.—In this district Hindu peasants in the month of Baisakh enquire from a Pandit on what day and hour and in what direction it is advisable to begin ploughing. He invariably advises them to begin ploughing in the direction of the East or North. On the day fixed by the Pandit they commence ploughing in the morning. They usually do not plough on the fifteenth day of the lunar month. For sowing Wednesday is considered a lucky day. When they are taking out the seed grain to the field they give about half a seer to the village Bhangi. This is known as Biyay. At the end of sowing they distribute among the family and labourers boiled wheat (*bakli*).

When there is danger of the crop being injured by field rats they offer some sweets (*gulgula*) at the holes of the rats in the name of Musa Paighamber, the Prophet Moses.

When the sowing of a particular field is finished they make a circular furrow by ploughing four or five times in the northern part of the field. This is known as the Kháti bharni, or "the filling of the granary," and is a spell to make the crop productive. When the crop of the field first cut is gathered it is called Panahi. It is lucky to begin the cutting on Tuesday. When the cutting begins the first sheaf is given to the family priest. After this they may go on with the harvesting whenever it is convenient. It is lucky to give a few ears to any beggar who comes into the field while the cutting is going on. This is called Muth dena.

When the winnowing and threshing commences the centre pole round which the oxen move must be set up at a lucky time. They cannot use the new grain without danger until the due share of the priest has been given to him.

Showers of rain in the months of Aghan or Pus are held lucky. The digging of a well should be commenced in the asterism of Pukhya. When the work begins, Dharti Máta, the Earth goddess, is worshipped and some oil is sprinkled on the site of the intended well. Treacle is then distributed among those present and the same is done when the wooden support on which the masonry is to rest is fixed.—*W. Crooke.*

175. Mirzapur: Legend of Daksha.—Tappa Chhiánave, in the Mirzapur District, is said to be so called because it contains 96,000 bighas o land. Here is said to be the place where Daksha performed his famous sacrifice. He had ill-will to his son-in-law Mahadeva and did not invite him. Sati, the wife of Mahadeva, went against the will of her husband. When she arrived there and found no place reserved for her husband she was wroth and burnt herself to ashes, invoking curses on her father. When Mahadeva heard of her death he was enraged and tearing off one of the locks of his matted hair (*jata*) he threw it on the ground and from it was produced the hero Virbhadra. He with a number of demons (*vetála*) went to the place and cut off the head of Daksha, tore off the beard of his priest Bhrigu Muni and punished all the gods who had assembled for the sacrifice. After this he rested at the present village of Birohi, where there is a platform (*chabutra*) under a Nim tree reserved for his worship. Birohi is said to take its name from the Vira or hero Virbhadra. The only place in this part of the country where Virbhadra is worshipped is Birohi. His devotees offer to him an earthen pot, (*kalsa*) cakes and gram on Mondays and Fridays and swear on his name. Whenever a well is sunk in Tappa Chhiánave charccal is found in the ground, which is supposed to be a relic of the sacrifice of Daksha.—*Chhedi Lal.*

[It is needless to say that other places beside Birohi are known as the site of the sacrifice of Daksha. Thus, for instance, the Pandas of Hardwar assert that the sacrifice was done at Mayapur.—ED.]

176. **Etah : Customs at burial.**—At Soron, in the Etah District, the dead are usually taken for cremation to Soron, which lies on the bank of the old stream of the Ganges known as the Burh Ganga. Cremation here is considered equal to cremation at the Ganges itself. The name of Soron is a corruption of Sukara-kshetra " the field of the boar," as it is the site of the famous temple of Vishnu in his boar incarnation known as Varahaji. In regard to this temple there is a curious custom. When a corpse is brought there for cremation it is laid on the platform of the temple. In case the god happen to be asleep and his temple be closed, the corpse is left there till it is opened again. It is believed that if the god only look on the corpse all its sins in this world are forgiven.—*Gendan Lall.*

177. **The Worship of the Plantain tree.**—The plantain tree is held in special reverence by Hindus because it is supposed to be the abode of Devi. The flower is largely used in charms of various kinds. The tree should be worshipped on the last day (*púranmási*) of the months of Kart, Mágh or Baisákh. In places where the tree does not grow, an image of it made of gold may be substituted. It should not be worshipped after it has produced fruit and water should be poured daily on a young tree until it bears. The first fruit of the tree should be given to a Brahman. On the special days for worship as above described the worshipper should bathe in a river and put on new clothes. Then he should make a platform one cubit square and on it place the tree. Near it he should perform the Homa or fire sacrifice, bow to a Brahman and give him a milch cow, a pair of sandals, an umbrella, a pair of shoes and some clothes. Next he should feed sixteen Balms and give each a copper coin in alms. When they give their blessing the deity who abides in the plantain tree will be propitiated.—*Pándit Rám Gharíb Chaubé.*

178. **Saharanpur : Sati worship.**—In the Botanical Gardens at Saharanpur there are several platforms erected in honour of Sattis. The place was originally a Rohilla garden known as the Farhat Bakhsh and when Dr. Govan commenced to lay it out he directed the workmen to level the Satti tombs. It is said that that very night the Sattis visited him and produced an excruciating headache. At midnight they all came crowding into his room and at the sight of them he lost his sight. The leader of the Sattis then told him that if next day he did not cause their shrines to be restored they would kill him. The Doctor promised to obey and then his sight was restored. Next day the shrines were restored and then he recovered his health. When he was giving over charge to his successor he warned him not to interfere with the Satti shrines and there they stand to the present day. People in sickness or other trouble make vows to worship these Sattis in the event of their recovering or getting over their misfortunes. The special offerings made to these Satti shrines consist of cakes, halwa, sweetmeats, flowers, cloth of any colour, except black, and red powder.—*W. Crooke.*

179. **Baso Bibi: A local Saint of Behar.**—In Baso Chak there is an old Mazár or monument raised in honor of one Baso Bibi, a pious girl of a Muhammadan Sayyid family, who took a vow to remain a virgin all her life. Her parents finding her vow contrary to the rules of their religion, which make |it a duty of the parents to marry their girls without any exception, determined to marry her. The girl seeing herself helpless and unable to dissuade her parents, preferred death by drowning herself in the Baya Nadi which flowed below her house and thereby saved her chastity. Immediately the river there became very deep and formed a whirlpool so dangerous that every boat that passed over it at once sank. Every effort was made to discover her corpse, but without any success, and people began to believe that the river, enraged at the impious determination of the parents, concealed

the body of the virgin in her bottom and punished every object by drowning when it attempted to defile her dead body by passing over it. It became impossible to cross the river where the girl had drowned herself and all traffic by boat was stopped. Thereupon a certain great merchant vowed that if his laden boat crossed the whirlpool safely he would erect a monument in her memory and worship it with offerings. When his boat had crossed he omitted to fulfil his promises. Consequently when it was returning with the proceeds of the sale of his goods it sank in the whirlpool. The merchant discovering his omission immediately erected the promised monument. Since then it is worshipped by the sailors and it is believed that boats therefore now pass this part of the river safely.—*Babu Rai Krishna Bahadur.*

180. **A prayer to Mother Earth.**—Besides the worship of Dharti Mâta or Mother Earth at the time of sowing and gathering in the harvest, learned Hindus repeat the following prayer in her honour in the morning :—

Dhaye dharitrim, salalarth datrim, basundharam, saub dhanam cha dhanyam, Tushta sati, bauchhit siddhi datrim, mam manorathah, puraye Vishnupatni.

"I salute the Earth, the realiser of all desires, and she who is blessed with all kinds of riches and creatures and who is contented, faithful and virtuous, the giver of all that one asks for the realisation of desires."

This is used only by educated people. Others only salute her when they touch her with their feet when rising.—*Pándit Rám Ghaīlb Chaubé.*

181. **Western Districts, N.-W. P.: A Curious Muhammadan belief as to the origin of the Ganges.**—The Muhammadans of the Western Districts have a very curious legend of the origin of the Ganges. They say that Yaqûb (Jacob) was once going with his two wives on a pilgrimage and had only a single camel. He placed the women in two litters (kajáwa) on each side of the camel and he himself used to take it in turns with them to ride and walk. The mother of Yúsuf (Joseph) was at the time in child and she asked her husband to leave her on the way until her child was born. He did so and Yúsuf was born. One day as the child was playing he struck the ground with his foot and a spring of water gushed out which ran over the world and was the source of the Ganges.

The story may possibly be a perverted version of the Muhammadan legend of Hagar, for the relief of whose thirst a well was produced by the Angel Gabriel striking the earth with his foot. (*Hughes' Dictionary of Islam*, 218.).—*W. Crooke.*

182. **A Muhammadan custom.**—Among true Mussalmáns it is considered impious to drink water standing. But the following are the most remarkable exceptions :—

1. The water of the sacred well at Mecca known as Ab-i-Zam Zam.
2. The water that has been previously tasted by a Muhammadan.
3. The water that one gets from persons who give water to the travellers in charity.
4. The water with which one has performed his *wazu.—Pándit Rám Gharíb Chaubé.*

183. **Surat : Marriage of Doves and the Tulasi tree.**—In the Kayasth caste there is a custom according to which when a boy and girl are married, two doves are introduced, of which the male is placed in the hands of the boy and the female in those of the girl. A large garland is placed over the necks of the two birds: the officiating Brahman recites mantras and the marriage of the birds is thus completed. Unless the marriage ceremony of the doves first takes place the marriage of the Kayasth is considered to be incomplete.

If a man who is childless fears to die without leaving issue and without being able thus to perform the marriage of a daughter, which is deemed a most meritorious act among the twice-born castes, he performs the marriage ceremony between the Tulasi plant and an idol of Krishna, whereby the Tulasi plant is made to symbolise his daughter.—*H. N. Wakil.*

[Any instances of similar practices would be very welcome.—ED.].

184. **Worship of Mallári.**—The Central India legend of the worship of Mallári tells how a Daitya named Malla used to interrupt Brahmans and defile their offerings. Then he and his brother Mani with an army of demons killed the Brahmans' cows. They appealed to Indra, who referred them to Vishnu, who sent them on to Siva. Siva became incarnate as Martanda Bhairava, who slew the Daitya brothers and their army. Hence the God was called Mallári from his defeat of the Daitya Malla.

185. **The Tulasi plant and the Salagrama stone.**—The respect paid to the tulasi plant and the salagrama stone is based on the following legend. Once upon a time there was a very famous king named Jalandhar, who had a very good and virtuous wife, Vinda. Owing to the virtue of his wife, Jalandhar was never defeated by god or man. Having conquered the whole world, he waged war with Mahadeva for a thou-

sand years. Even then he was not satisfied with fighting. Mahadeva then gave him the blessing that his desires should be satisfied by Vishnu. When he contended with Vishnu for thousands of years Vishnu saw that he could defeat him only by fraud. So he assumed the form of Jalandhar and came to his house when he was absent. He robbed Vinda of her virtue and then succeeded in defeating Jalandhar. When Vinda knew of the treachery of Vishnu she cursed him that he should become a stone and live in the river Gandaki. Vishnu cursed Vinda that she should become a plant. When Vinda wished to curse Vishnu, again he appeased her by the promise that she should be always near his head. Hence Brahmans lay the leaves of the tulasi on the salagrama.—*Pándit Rám Gharib Chaubé.*

---

186. **The Worship of Kashi Das.**—Some Ahirs lived on the edge of a forest where they grazed their herds. Each Ahir used to tend the cattle in turn for a month. One time was the turn of an Ahir who had a large herd of his own. Just then a tiger appeared and began to prey upon the cattle. When several beasts had been killed the Ahirs used to watch at night. One night one Ahir was watching and from the top of a tree he saw a Brahman on the bank of a river close by. The Brahman did his worship as usual and at the close blew his conch shell. The Ahir thought this was the beast that had wrought havoc with the cattle. The name of the Brahman was Kashi Das. The Ahir rushed down and began to beat him with his bludgeon. When life passed from him the Ahir went to his friends and told them that he had destroyed the scourge of their herds. "Whom did you kill?" they asked and he answered in the lines—

Gare garainyan tin tag, bodabai au punpujaya;
Pan chikhawain mara gay ghat, manon uhai janaro aya;
Jekare phunke har cillaya, tekas na gain dhari dhari khaya.

"Round his neck he wears a threefold string; he seizes and roars; he who sips water killed the cow. He must be the monster who has been killing the cattle. If he did not eat kine how could he make a bone roar by blowing into it?"

When the Ahirs came and saw that it was really a Brahman whom they had killed they cursed him. They thought no more of the matter, but after a few days the ghost of the murdered Kashi Das began to trouble the families of the Ahirs. One man's house took fire; another's cow died; some one lost his son. So they knew that this was the work of the Brahman's ghost. So he became a godling and is worshipped with offerings of rice milk and Brahmanical cords. On whosesoever's head the deity comes he is able to distribute the boiling rice milk with his hands and gets no hurt. Then he delivers oracles.

(Told by Ganesa Dutta, Master, High School, Gonda.)

---

187. **Barua Brahmans and the Gular or Fig tree.**—Barua Brahmans at Saharanpur have a curious aversion for the Gular or fig tree. They will on no account walk under a tree of this kind and if they come across one on the road they will make a circuit to avoid it and repeat the following spell invoking the aid of Narsinha Deota, the man-lion incarnation of Vishnu—

Narsinha nám nirmala kahiye, man man rakho bha pur.

Pát rakhi Prahláda hi, sankat katain hazúr.

"Call the name of Narsinha pure. Fill your mind full with it. He maintained the honour of Prahlada. May his holiness remove my difficulties."

The story goes that Narsinha after tearing open Harnakas or Hiranya Kasipu, the father of Prahlada, who had persecuted his son for his devotion to Vishnu, wiped the flesh and blood off his hands on the trunk and leaves of a Gular tree which stood near. Hence the tree of this species is as unholy as the accursed Hiranya Kasipu himself. This tree robs him who passes under it of the store of merit accumulated by the practice of virtue. However, if you happen to touch the tree and appeal for protection to Narsinha no evil consequences ensue.—*Pándit Rám Gharib Chaubé.*

---

188. **Broom worship.**—At marriages among the twice-born castes in Surat it is customary to worship the family goddess. Some Nagar Brahman families, however, substitute the sweeper's broom for the goddess as an object of worship on such occasions. The explanation given is as follows:—In former times a sweeper in the service of a Nagar Brahman family having secretly studied the Vedas and other branches of Brahmanical lore left Surat for another part of Gujrát, and by reason of the knowledge thus acquired succeeded in passing himself off as a Nágar Brahman and in marrying a girl of that caste. The custom of worshipping the sweeper's broom was hence adopted by his descendants.—*H. N. Wakil.*

---

189. **Chunar: Deity of the Fort.**—In the magazine enclosure of Chunar, in the verandah of what used to be the quarters of the Staff Sergeants, is the shrine of Bhartarináth, the deity of the place. He stays there nine hours in the day and for the other three flies off to Benares, which

on a clear day is visible from the battlements of the fort. Whenever the fort was attacked during the time the deity was present there the attack was always unsuccessful. Some say that beneath the shrine there is a great treasure in a box which cannot be opened unless the person attempting to open it is willing to lose his hand.—*W. Crooke.*

190. **Saharanpur, N.-W. P.: Ceremonies performed by Hindus to propitiate the Goddess of Small-pox.**—When a boy or a girl is affected with small-pox, he or she is kept in a separate room away from the rest of the family. Though at the time of keeping the boy in a particular room it is plastered and made clean, yet the room is never again plastered or cleaned till the affected person recovers. In the family food is not prepared in ghi or in oil and turmeric, &c., is not put in the pulse and no member of the family gets his garments washed or hair shaved. No gorgeous dress or coloured garment is put on by any member of the family. No member of the family or an outsider can get into the patient's room without washing his or her feet. The *Máli*, who is regarded as the chief favourite of the goddess of small-pox, visits the affected person on the day small-pox appears and puts by the side of the cot on which the affected person sleeps flowers, wet gram, five bátáshá sweets, one betel leaf, some milk in an earthen vessel and the twigs of the nim tree. These things are kept perpetually near the cot till the person affected is cured. These things are daily put in the evening where two roads cross each other. The *Máli* going daily to the affected person prays to the goddess to effect the speedy recovery of the patient. He moves the twigs of the nim tree seven times over the body of the affected person. When the disease is not cured, even then he vows to feed ten cows or ten Brahmans. When the person affected has been cured the things put by his bedside are thrown away on the point where two roads cross each other. Then the members of the family begin to do what they abstained from doing during the sickness. When small-pox breaks out on a large scale in a village or a city, the women go in a body singing and playing on musical instruments to the shrine of the goddess and after offering flowers, garlands of flowers, and moving lamps over the image of the goddess they get a goat brought. They tie round the neck of the goat garlands of flowers and on the back of it a piece of red cloth and smear its forehead with *sindur* (red lead). Then they pierce the ears of the goat and drop some blood from it at the shrine of the goddess and then they let it loose out of the village or city. Any one might catch it, as it is then no man's property. At the time of epidemic of small-pox they hang on their doors the twigs of acacia and the nim. They rub or rather plaster on the body of the person affected with small-pox a tile rubbed with water on a stone. Sometimes they rub butter too on the body of the affected person.—*Pándit Rám Gharíb Chaubé.*

191. **Marriage to Flowers.**—The Kurwars of Ahmedabad marry only once in twelve years on a date fixed after many solemnities at the Máta temple at Uja, north of Ahmedabad. Two of these marriage customs need remark—(*a*) They sometimes marry a girl when they cannot find a suitable match, to a bunch of flowers, which are afterwards thrown into a well. The girl is then considered a widow and can only be married by the Nátra form, a cheap process. (*b*) At other times they marry such a daughter to an already married man, obtaining previously his consent to divorce her as soon as the ceremony is completed. This is easily managed for a small consideration. The girl is afterwards given in Nátra to any man who chooses to have her. Mr. Cooke regards these ceremonies as forms of evading the strict observance of the custom allowing marriages only once in twelve years. The Nátra form may be celebrated on any and every day without expense. The popular explanation is that Siva went on a pilgrimage and took Párvati with him. A giant on the way gave trouble, but was overcome. Párvati declined to proceed through fear and stayed behind at Uja, while Siva went on. He was absent for nearly twelve years. She meanwhile amused herself by making fifty-two male and the same number of female images. When Siva returned she requested him to endue the images with life. He did so. She then bade them marry and multiply. Some of the men ran away. So the superfluous girls had to be married to men already married. One girl remained whom no one would take; she was married to a bunch of flowers and a temple was built to Umiya Máta or Parvati.—(*Selections of Bombay Records No. CLXVII. N. S. pp.* 46, *sqq.*)

192. **Cocoa-nuts: Worship of Bhairon.**—There is a temple of Kál Bhairon in Ujjain to which women flock at one time of the year and when the deity possesses them they shake violently and lose their senses. They are then escorted home by their male relatives who, as they go away from the temple, fling cocoa-nuts behind them as a means to appease the deity. The idea apparently is that the cocoa-nut from its resemblance to a human skull represents a mock human sacrifice. Bhairon is as blood-thirsty a god as Káli or Chamariya Bhaváni.—*Pándit Rám Gharíb Chaubé.*

ANTHROPOLOGY.

193. On the Ceremonies performed by the Kabirpanthi Mahants of the Saran District, on their Initiation as Chelas and on their succession to the Mahantship.—In the district of Saran, there are many maths (मठ) or monasteries presided over by their spiritual heads—the Mahants. These Mahants are all *Kabirthi* (कबिरठ) or followers of Kabir and practise the tenets promulgated by that famous religious reformer. They belong to two classes, viz., the *Sanyásis* (संन्यासी) and the *Ghárbásis* or Grihabásis (घरबासी or गृहबासी). The Sanyásis, who usually have the title of *Parbats*, entirely withdraw themselves from the world, cut off all connection with their respective families, and live a strict life of celibacy within the precincts of their *maths* or monasteries. The Gharbásis have usually the titles of *Gir, Atith, Puri* or *Bhárathí*, and are householders, living with their families and children in their *maths*. These latter are, by reason of their being householders, considered as of inferior rank by the Sanyásís or Parbats who do not partake of food touched by the *Girs, Atiths, Puris* or *Bhárathis*. On the other hand, the Gharbásis (the Girs and others) will eat the remnants of food partaken of by the Sanyásís or the Parbats.

The Kabiráhás or Kabirpanthi Mahants enlist *chelas* or disciples from all castes, and eat, as some say, with all castes also. The ceremonies observed at the time of becoming *chela* or disciple are as follows:—Firstly, the would-be disciple's head is shaved by a barber, and a lock of hair called the *tik* (टीक) is left on the centre of the crown of the head. The *guru* or the spiritual preceptor then cuts off this tuft of hair, and also takes off the (चनवीत) or the sacrificial thread which is worn by the would-be disciple. The lock of hair and the sacrificial thread are buried underneath the ground. Homa (होम) is then performed by a Bráhmana priest. No *mantra* is given at this time to the disciple. The *chela* is then invested with *garuá basan* (गेरुआ बसन) or cloth dyed in red ochre. Some say *bija* (बिज) or a feast is also given at that time. Mahants and *chelas* or householders also attend the ceremony of becoming *chela*. No other ceremonies are performed at that time. After becoming a *chela*, the disciple ceases to be a householder, continues to live in the *math* and serves the presiding *Mahant* who is his *guru* or spiritual preceptor.

When a Mahant dies, his corpse is interred in the ground four days after his death. A *Samádhi* is erected over his grave. Four days after the Mahant's death, *i.e.*, on the day of his burial, the ceremony of Dudhrot (दुधरोत) or the Milk-and-bread ceremony is performed. On this occasion, the attending Mahants are fed on milk and bread.

The deceased Mahant, during his lifetime, usually selects the most worthy amongst his *chelas* or disciples to succeed him after his death. If he does so, the Mahant-elect performs the Bhándárá ceremony of his deceased preceptor one year after his death and invites the Mahants of the neighbouring *maths* to be present on the occasion of the performance of this ceremony. The attendant Mahants confirm the nomination, by the deceased Mahant, of the Mahant-elect by giving him *chudders* or linen sheets on the occasion of the Bhándárá performed by him in commemoration of his deceased *guru* or preceptor. But if the deceased Mahant dies without having selected, during his lifetime, a successor, the Mahants attending the Bhándárá of the deceased nominates the principal and the most worthy among his *chelas* or pupils as his successor and instals him (the nominee) on the *guddi* of Mahantship by giving him a *chudder*. With reference to the election of Mahants, Babu Shama Cháran Sarkár, a recognised authority on Hindu Law, says:* "Generally, the usage or custom of Mahants is that the Mahant or principal of any *math* or monastery states his principal and most worthy pupil to succeed to him at his decease; that after his death the *Mahants of other similar institutes* in the vicinage convene an assembly of the order and perform his Bhándárá or funeral obsequies at which they generally confirm the nomination made by the deceased and instal the pupil he selected as his authorized successor. * * * * But where a Mahant dies without appointing a successor, there his successor is selected generally from amongst his pupils by the Mahants convened at his Bhándárá and invested with the Mahantship of the *math*. * * *. In short, the installation of the successor by an assembly of Mahants at the obsequies of the deceased *Mahant* is in all cases indispensable and conclusive; and consequently the appointment of a successor by the late *Mahant* is not final so long as it is not confirmed by the *Mahants* convened at the *Bhándárá*."

The ceremonies performed at the Bhándárá, which is performed one year after the Mahant's death, may be described as follows: A *kalas* (कलस) or earthen jug full of water and crowned with mango leaves, and rice in a separate pot, are placed on a *mandala* made of powdered rice upon a *vedi* or platform of earth. Homa (होम) is then performed by a Brahmana priest. Then the *Achárya guru* of the *math* gives *mantra* to the would-be Mahant (*i.e.*, whispers the sacred formula to him), and he is thus initiated as a Sanyásí. Some say a flagstaff is planted at the *math*, and the Mahant-elect's head is shaved. Then every one of the

---

* *Vide* Vyávasthá Chandriká, Vol. I., page 222.

Mahants* of the neighbourhood, who may be present there, give the newly-elected Mahant a mahanti *Chudder* or linen sheet and two rupees in cash. After this, Brahmanas are feasted. Subsequently to this, the Parbats are feasted. Then the lower castes, beggars and other people are fed. Some say that, at the conclusion of the Bhándárá ceremony, a *surathdl* or a record of the proceedings at the *Bhándárá* is written out and attested by respectable witnesses. On the day next to that in which the *Bhándárá* is performed, the newly-elected Mahant bids farewell to the invited Mahants who might have attended the ceremony, by returning them double of what they had given to him, *i.e.*, four rupees and two chudders. The Mahants are prohibited from uttering the names of their *Áchárya gurus* who initiate the former as Sanyásís.—By Mr. *Sarat Chandra Mitra, M.A., B.L., Pleader, Judge's Court, Chupra, Behar.*

194. **The Andaman Islanders.**—The following from the *Academy* of 15th December, 1894, is worth recording:—

It seems to be still the fashion among savans and others to treat the Andaman Islands as a *terra incognita*, in writing about which errors and misdescriptions may be made with impunity, or, at any rate, looked upon with lenient eyes. This attitude towards the Islands is extended to their inhabitants, and this though they have been long—very long—part of the British dominions; though it is more than a hundred years since the first attempt was made to colonise them; though they have been brought under regular government by Commission for nearly forty years. There are men who have grown grey in the local government service. The coasts were charted and mapped over a century ago, with that skill and accuracy which was so distinguishing a feature of the work of the old Indian Navy; and many a large scale chart has been issued in the interval, marking the intricacies of the coral reefs which surround the Islands safe for the largest vessels, as I know by personal experience. The Trigonometrical Survey of India has sent its parties from end to end of the Islands, so that the mapping of the interior is as complete as that of the coasts, and no part of the Islands can be said to be actually unknown. The government has been for years carried on in the usual Indian style, and reports have been made for years in the usual detail. The inhabitants have been described and figured over and over again by local writers with a detail and an accuracy that I think can hardly be surpassed by those who have undertaken to tell the world about savage races. The museums of Europe and Enlgand are filled with astonishingly complete drawings and articles, described with minute accuracy, and illustrating the Andamanese and their ways; the British, the Pitt-Rivers at Oxford, the Cambridge, the Imperial-Royal at Vienna, to my personal inspection and knowledge.

One would think, then, that it is not really difficult to get at the facts about the Andamans and the Andamanese; but, nevertheless, one can hardly pick up any book or paper about them, published for the benefit of the public, even by distinguished European writers, without being taken aback at the wildness of the statements made. It is a strong instance of this that has lately come to my notice which has induced me now to write this letter.

In Sir John Lubbock's *Prehistoric Times* (fifth edition, 1890) there occur (pp. 438-439) a series of typical errors about the Andamanese, all avoidable had he followed Mr. Man's admirable *Andaman Islanders*, with the existence of which his remarks show him to have been acquainted. It was published originally in the *Journal* of the Anthropological Institute, of which Institute Sir John was, and, I believe, still is, a member.

I will now take the statements made, categorically, and place scientific fiction and fact side by side, so that your readers may distinguish the real from the unreal for themselves.

Sir John commences:—

I.

(Sir J. Lubbock.)
The Mincopies,* or inhabitants of the Andaman Islands, have been described by Dr. Mouat, Sir E. Belcher, Mr. Day, Mr. Man, and Prof. Owen, who considers that they "are, perhaps, the most primitive, or lowest in the scale of civilisation, of the human race." Their huts consist of four posts, the two front ones six to eight feet high, the back ones only one or two feet. They are open at the sides, and *covered with a roof of bamboo, or a few palm leaves* bound tightly together.

Facts.
* This word is unknown to the tribes of the Great Andaman with whom we are acquainted. It came to us from the writers and settlers at Port Blair in 1792, and is a word got from the wild and unapproachable tribe now known to us as "the Jarawas," with whom the old settlers seem to have been on friendly terms.

The roofs are never of bamboo or palm, but of cane leaves.

II.

The Mincopies live *chiefly on fruit, mangroves, and shellfish. Sometimes, however, they kill the small pigs which run wild in the jungle.*

They live chiefly on pig, fish, turtle, roots, and shellfish; only occasionally on fruit, and then more often (especially in the Little Andaman) on the fruit of one species of mangrove.

III.

They have single tree canoes, *hollowed out with a P-shaped axe, assisted probably by the action of fire*. They are acquainted with the use of outriggers which, however, appear *to have been of recent introduction*, as they are not alluded to by the earlier writers.

They use an adze, not an axe, for hollowing out canoes and the adze is never P-shaped. They never use fire to assist in the hollowing. The outrigged canoe is the oldest form: the large single canoe being peculiar to the South Andaman group of tribes and of recent introduction.

---

* According to some, the Atiths and Girs, who are householders, are not fit to give Mahanti chudder to the Parbats.

Sir J. Lubbock.	Facts.
Their arrows and spears are now generally *tipped with* iron and glass, which they obtain from wrecks, and which have to a great extent replaced bone. Their harpoons, like those of so many other savages, have a movable head, and a long cord by which this may be held when fixed in the victim. They are *very skilful with the bow*, and "make practice at forty or fifty yards *with unerring certainty*," though their arrows have no feathers.	IV. The arrows are never tipped with glass. They are only fairly skilful with the bow, and make practice with anything but unerring certainty.
They have *no pottery*, but use either shells or pieces of bamboo to hold water.	V. They have had pottery from the earliest times, but it is not used for holding water.
They *kill fish by harpoons, or with small hand-nets*; they take any that are left by the tide, and it is even said that they are able to dive and catch them with their hands.	VI. They only kill dugongs, turtle, and such fish as sharks, &c., with harpoons. They shoot fish with bow and arrow. They catch small fish left by the tide with their hands or kill them with stones. Only the women use hand-nets, and then only for prawns, &c.; the men would consider it effeminate to use hand-nets.
They *cover themselves with mud*, and also tattoo, but wear no clothes.	VII. They are not always covered with mud; the mud-smearing is ceremonial, special muds being used for special occasions. The Ongé groupe of tribes never tattoo themselves.
They are stated to *have no idea of a Supreme Being*, no religion, nor any belief in a future state of existence. After death, the corpse is *buried in a sitting posture*. When it is supposed to be entirely decayed, the skeleton is dug up, and each of the relations appropriates a bone. In the case of a married man, *the widow takes the skull*, and wears it suspended by a cord round her neck. *It forms a very convenient box for small articles.*	VIII. They do believe in a Supreme Being. Mr. Man's book goes at length into this point. The corpse is generally put up in a tree, and is seldom buried. The widow takes the skull sometimes: generally it is the nearest male relative that takes it. The skull is never used as a box.
Marriage, however, *only lasts*, at least in some tribes, *until the child is born* and weaned, when, according to Lieut. St. John, as quoted by Sir E. Belcher, the man and woman generally separate, each seeking a new partner.	IX. Marriage lasts for life, and is seldom dissolved, *never* after the birth of a child. The whole statement is quite incorrect.

R. C. TEMPLE,
(Chief Commissioner, Andaman and Nicobar Islands.)
Government House, Port Blair

195. **Lucky feet marks.**—Hindus lay much stress on the lucky marks which are found on the feet of deities or human beings. The following are the marks which are said to be on the right foot of the deity, Krishna—the *Swástika*; the *rath* or chariot; the *sankha* or conch shell; the *ankus* or elephant goad; the *urdha rekha* or straight line running from toe to heel; the *kamal* or lotus; the *ashta kona* or octagon; the horse; the elephant; the *bin* or flute; the fish; the *bajra* or quoit; the *barchhi* or spear; the *kumuda* or water lily; the *sinhásan* or royal seat.

His left foot has the following marks—the *kumbha* or pitcher; the *dhanusha* or bow; the *chandrama* or moon; the sword; the *gada* or mace; the *chatra* or umbrella of royalty; the *naukona* or nine-sided figure; the grain of barley; the *til* or sesamum; the triangle; the tree; the arrow; the house; the fire-pit; the snake; the rock.

The marks on the feet of female deities are different. Thus on the feet of Rádha, the spouse of Krishna, are found the following marks which have been put into Hindi verse by a Benares poet:—

Pása, gada, rath, Yanojnavedi, aru kundala Jáno.
Bahuri, matsya, giriráj, sankha dahine pad máno.

She has the noose, mace, sacrificial platform, earring, fish, hill of Govardhan and the conch shell, and on the left foot—

Chhatra, chakra, dhwaja, lota, pushpa, kanhara, ambujapuni.
Anhusa, urdha rekha, ardha sasi, jawa, bayen guni.

"The umbrella, the wheel, the flag, creeper, flower, bracelet, lotus, elephant goad, straight line, half moon and barley."

Hence these marks, if found on human beings, are considered lucky.

To this it may be added that the marks on the feet of saintly personages are as follows:—

Kamal pataka, gada, bajra, toran ati sundar;
Kusum lata puni dhanukh dharat dakshin pad men bár.
Dhwaja, anhusa, jhakh, chakra, ashta dala ambuja mano.
Amrita, kumbha, yawa, chinh, bam pad men puni jáno.

"The lotus, the flag, the mace, the quoit, the festoon of leaves, the safflower, the creeper, the bow, on the right foot and on the left the flag, the goad, the fish, the wheel, the lotus with eight petals, the jar of nectar and the barley.—*Pándit Rám Gharíb Chaubé.*

FOLKTALES.

196. How Bhagwan gave a lesson to Narad Muni.—Once upon a time Bhagwán and Nárad Muni were walking in the jungle and came upon a wild pig with twelve young ones. Nárad asked Bhagwán: "Does the pig love all her offspring equally or not?" "She loves them all alike," answered Bhagwán. "Then," objected Nárad, "if that is so, you must love all human beings alike, the just and the unjust." Bhagwán said nothing and they went on.

Then Bhagwán created a tank and asked Nárad to bathe in it. As Nárad was diving under the water Bhagwán turned him into a lovely woman and he himself took the shape of a Kewat and sat on the bank. In a short time Nárad, in the form of a woman, came out of the tank and asked Bhagwán who he was. Bhagwán answered that he was a Kewat, and he asked her if she would marry him. She agreed, and they settled down in a village where they lived as husband and wife for a hundred years, and Nárad in that time bore to Bhagwán sixty sons.

Then Bhagwán turned himself into a Sannyási and created another Kewat in his original shape and put him to live with Nárad. Next day Bhagwán in the shape of a Sannyási came to beg at Nárad's house. Nárad offered him some rice which he refused. Then Nárad asked: "What then will you take?" "I want one of your sons," said Bhagwán. Nárad answered: "Be off, you scoundrel. I have seen many rogues like you! Will any one give his son as alms? You have twenty fingers and toes which you got without any trouble to yourself. Will you give one of them in alms? And yet you have the impudence to ask for my son." Bhagwán answered: "Why then did you deny that the wild pig loved all her offspring equally? If you love all your sons equally, the pig does the same, because she has feelings like your own." Narad was silent through shame, and Bhagwán, having taught him this lesson, transformed her and himself into their original shapes.

[A folktale told by Akbar Sháh, Mánjhi, of Manbasa, Dudhi, Mirzapur.]

197. The Wise and the Foolish Brothers.—There were once two brothers, one of whom was wise and the other foolish. They fell into poverty, and finally they agreed to go in different ways in search of employment, and whichever of them succeeded should support the other.

The fool went to a Rája and asked for service. "What can you do?" asked the Rája. The fool was puzzled what to say. At last he said: "I can make verses and work the fan." So the Rája took him into his service on sixty rupees a month. One day the Rája said: "It is quite time we heard some of these verses of yours." The fool did not know what to do, so he went out and stood reflecting under a tree. He stood without moving, and some pigs, thinking he was a tree, came up and began to rub themselves against him. When he could stand this no longer he said,

"*Tum kitno ragaro ghiso main jánun tor chaláki.*"
"You may rub as much as you please, but I know your cunning."

This was the only verse he could think of and so he went and stood before the Rája. Just then the barber came in and prepared to shave him, and as he was getting ready the fool recited this verse. When he heard it the barber turned pale, and falling at the Rája's feet begged his forgiveness. "What have you done?" asked the Rája. The barber said: "My razor is steeped in such deadly poison that had it touched your Majesty's beard you were dead in a moment. This is the work of the treasurer, who has induced me to attempt your life." So the Rája ordered the treasurer to be executed and appointed the fool in his room.

Some time after the Rája said to the new treasurer: "It is time we saw how you can use the fan." The fool was displeased at this order, because he thought it beneath his dignity to fan the Rája. But he had to go and when he began to fan him he knocked off the Rája's crown. The Rája was wroth, and called for the executioner; but just then a poisonous snake came out of the crown and bit the Wazír so that he died. The Rája was so pleased that he made the preserver of his life Wazír. Then the new Wazír sent for his wise brother, who was in extreme poverty. When he came he said: "Fate rules the world, and a man's wisdom and exertions avail nothing."

(Told by Iqbál Husen, weaver of Bhuili, Mirzapur.)

198. The Jealous Stepbrothers; a folktale from Kumaun.—Shankar and Bhawáni were stepbrothers, and were left by their father considerable wealth in land and cattle. Bhawáni was hardworking, and Shankar, who was a lazy fellow, could not bear his brother. One day Shankar killed the oxen of Bhawáni so that he could not plough. Bhawáni skinned the oxen and, filling the skins with sand, went into the jungle and got up a tree. By chance some robbers came there to divide their booty, and he, taking heart, let the hides fall down on them. They ran away and he filled the hides with money and jewels and came home.

Shankar asked him how he had come by all this wealth. He said: "You killed my oxen and I made bags out of the hides. I filled them with mud and they fetched a high price." So Shankar killed his own oxen and filling the hides with mud went to the bázár shouting: "Who will buy mud in ox-hides for its weight in gold?" The people thought he was cracked and shoe-beat him out of the market. In his anger he came home and killed Bhawáni's mother and burned his house.

Bhawáni pretended to be cheerful, and put his dead mother and some bags of ashes in a cart and started off. On the way he met a rich man, and they halted at the same *sarai*. The rich man asked Bhawáni to have some food with him and he agreed. "But," said he, "first give some to my poor old mother, who is sitting over there in a corner." The man took her some food and asked her to eat. She made no answer, and in his rage he threw the dish at the corpse and it fell over. "Now see what you have done," said Bhawáni. You have killed my mother, and I am going to the police." The man was frightened and gave him a lot of money to settle the matter.

Bhawáni came home, and Shankar asked him where he had got all the money. He said: "You did me a good turn by burning my house and killing my mother, because the corpse and ashes sold for a heap of money." Shankar answered: "You played me a scurvy trick once and I will not be taken in again." Bhawáni replied: "Did you ask the Pandit to fix a lucky time before you started?" "No, I did not," said Shankar. "There," said his brother, "you see the result of being niggardly." So Shankar got the Pandit to fix a lucky time and burned down his house. Then he killed his mother and went to the bazár crying: "Who will buy ashes and the corpse of my mother?" But all the merchants fell on him and beat him till he was half dead.

He went home swearing he would have his revenge, and the next day he caught his brother and put him in a sack, intending to pitch him into the river. When he came to the bank, he put the sack down, intending to have a smoke. Meanwhile a shepherd came up and Bhawáni whispered from inside the sack: "For God's sake do not touch me or open the sack. This is no common sack, but the magic bag of the Lord Siva. I am doing wonders here; do not interrupt me." Notwithstanding Bhawáni's remonstrances the shepherd opened the sack and got inside. Then Shankar came up and pitched the bag with the shepherd inside it into the river.

He went home triumphant, and soon after Bhawáni appeared driving with him all the shepherd's sheep and goats. "Where did you get these?" asked Shankar. "It was very good of you to throw me into the river. Such a sight I saw there! I met all my ancestors, and they gave me all these cattle and wanted to give me any amount of gold too, but I would not have it, and told them that I would come another time and fetch it." When Shankar made more enquiries, he said: "Your mother sent you her best wishes, and I am going again next Sunday morning." "I would like to come too," said Shankar. "Well, I do not care to take you," said Bhawáni, "because you will be making mischief beween me and my ancestors." "Nothing of the kind," said Shankar. "You and I are now one." And he was so anxious to go that he gave Bhawáni all his cattle in return for taking him with him. When they came to the river, Shankar got into the bag and Bhawáni pitched him into the deepest place he could find, saying: "Go and join your ancestors, you scoundrel. I hope this is the last I shall ever see of you."

[This is another and a good version from the lower Himalayas of the "Little Fairy" Cycle. See Clouston: *Popular Tales and Fictions*, II. 229, *sqq*.—Ed.]

199. **The Kali Yuga.**—There was once a banker who from great wealth was reduced to poverty and was left with a single ruby. This he was afraid to keep: so he made it over to a rich banker, his friend, and made his living by begging. At last he died, and his son went and claimed the deposit: but the banker denied the claim, and the case came before the Rája, who summoned the poor man's witnesses. But none would give witness for him, and he lost his suit and was driven from the Court.

The banker then complained against him and he was summoned to appear. The poor man took the oath, and, laying his hand on the head of his first-born son, said: "O Parameswar! if I have spoken falsely against the banker, may my son die."

Immediately his son fell down dead and he took the corpse on his shoulders and was driven out of the Court. When he went outside he saw a man on horseback who had tied his old father by the hair to the hind legs of his horse and his old mother to the neck. The beggar asked him who he was.

"Tell me who you are," he answered, "and by and by you will learn who I am."

The beggar told his story, and then the man said, "You are a fool. Do you not know that this is the Iron Age? In it a man gains by lying. Why do you speak the truth? Go and tell the Rája that the banker has taken two rubies. And take the body of your son also with you."

Then the beggar went to the Rája and said: "When I was here before I told a lie in saying that the banker had taken only one ruby, whereas he really took two." The Rája sent for the banker and called on him to give up the rubies. The banker answered: "Let the beggar say over the corpse of his son, 'If I have given two rubies to the banker, may the body of my son be restored to life:' then I have no objection to give him the two rubies."

The beggar took the false oath, and at once his son stood up. So the banker had to restore the original ruby, and was obliged to sell all his goods to purchase a pair to it. The beggar went back to the horseman and told him how successful he had been.

"I," said the horseman, "am the incarnation of the Iron Age. I govern the world. I am the deadly enemy of truth and righteousness. Whoever obeys me flourishes, while those who follow my rival, the Golden Age, come to misfortune."

With these words the incarnation of the Iron Age disappeared out of his sight.

(A folktale told by Akbar Sháh, Mánjhi, of Manbasa, Dudhi, Mirzapur.)

200. **The Legend of Pipa the Rajput.**—Pipa, the Rája of Gangrawangarh, was a worshipper of Durga, to whom he used to sacrifice forty goats daily. One day a party of Vaishnava ascetics came to him, and when they saw the bones of the goats, they refused to accept cooked food from his house. So he ordered his servants to give them supplies, and to point them out a garden where they could cook for themselves. When the food was ready the Sadhus offered it to the sacred Salagrama stone, and prayed that in future the name of the king should be changed from Pípa to Papi (sinner). That night, about midnight, Vishnu appeared to him in the form of a Deo (demon), and pulling him from his bed was about to kill him. Pipa asked what fault he had committed, and was told that his sin consisted in killing goats in honour of Durga. Pipa then meditated on Durga, who appeared to him in the form of a woman and said that she could not save him, because Vishnu in his form as the Salagrama was her superior and that his orders must be obeyed, Pipa asked if there were no means of escaping the anger of Vishnu. Durga advised him to proceed to Benares and to be initiated by Ramanand. Saying this Durga implored the Deo to have mercy on Pipa, and immediately both disappeared from his sight.

Pipa then, taking a large number of horses, elephants, and followers, went to Benares and sent a message to Ramanand that he wished to kiss his feet. Ramanand returned answer that his door was open to faqirs and not to Rájas.

Hearing this Pipa gave away all his wealth in charity and became a faqir and awaited the orders of Ramanand. To test the firmness of Pipa Ramanand ordered him to jump into a well, and when he saw that he was ready to obey his orders he brought him to his house and whispered into his ear the Dwadas Achhar mantra or names of Vasudeva Bhagawati. When Pipa was thus initiated he was directed to return to his kingdom, to engage in devotion for twelve months and to abolish the goat sacrifice.

Ramanand also promised to go after a year to Dwarika and on his way to visit Pipa at Gangrawangarh. Pipa obeyed these orders, and on his return to his kingdom forced all his subjects to accept the Vaishnava faith. He fed a large number of Vaishnavas daily, but allowed no meat to be brought within his dominions. When a year had expired he sent a letter to his Guru reminding him of his promise.

So Ramanand, accompanied by his disciples, Kabir and Raedas, left Benares, and on his arrival in the dominions of Pipa sent him word. Pipa went to receive his Guru and brought him with his followers to his palace. He seated his Guru on a golden seat, worshipped him, and made handsome presents to him and to his disciples. They were his guests for some days, and were much pleased with their reception.

As Ramanand was starting for Dwarika Pipa proposed to accompany him, and his Guru, being now convinced of his sincerity, allowed him to abandon his Raj and adopt a life of poverty. Pipa had twelve Ránis, all of whom wished to accompany him on his pilgrimage. Kabir was directed to offer each of them a country blanket, and to warn them that they must discard all their jewels and rich clothes. Only one of them, Sita, accepted the sacrifice.

Then the family priest of the Raj objected to Ramanand that, according to the laws of Manu, it was not lawful for a Rája to abandon his Raj and become a faqir. When his remonstrances were unheeded he poisoned himself, saying that his ghost would obstruct Ramanand in his devotion, because he persisted in taking Pipa from his country. When Ramanand heard of the death of the priest, he washed his Salagrama with some Ganges water, poured it on the mouth of the dead man and restored him to life. The priest was ashamed of his folly and returned home.

When the party arrived at Dwarika they spent some days in devotion, and when Ramanand returned to Benares Pipa gained permission to remain some time longer at Dwarika. One day Pipa learnt that the original Dwarika had been overwhelmed, in the sea: so being anxious to see it he took his wife, Sita, in his arms and jumped into the water. Krishna, the lord of Dwarika, thought it would bring disgrace on him if their desires were not accomplished, so he ran to meet them, and holding their hands led them to the original Dwarika. Pipa and Sita were received kindly by Krishna and his queen Rukmini. Before they returned to the upper world Krishna gave Pipa a seal (*chhap*) which he directed him to give to the Panda priests at Dwarika, by whom it was to be known as the "seal of Pipa" and every pilgrim to Dwarika was to have this mark branded on his arms. Whoever bore this mark would not be subject to burning after death.

During the night Pipa and his wife were thrown out of the sea by the Divine Hand, and all were surprised at the sight. Pipa made over the seal to the Pandas, and it is used, as Krishna directed, to the present day.

On his return from Dwarika some Pathans met Pipa and tried to dishonour his wife, but Vishnu saved her: and in the same way delivered them from a terrible tiger which beset the road. They then visited the temple of Shrisha Sai, and there a man refused to give Pipa a bludgeon which he wanted, whereupon Pipa recited a spell and turned all his sticks into green bamboos.

When one Chidhar Bhagat heard of the merits of Pipa he brought Pipa to his house and, not possessing the means of purchasing a meal for his guests he sold his wife's only garment for food. When the meal was ready Pipa asked him why his wife did not join them. Hearing the cause Sita tore her robe in two and gave her half. Next morning when Pipa went to bathe in the tank he noticed a hole where a quantity of gold coins were buried. On his return he told his wife Sita what he had seen. She warned him not to go near the place again as gold was of no use to a faqir. A servant was listening to their words and overcome by covetousness he went to the place, and lo! the hole was full of snakes. The thieves determined to be revenged on Pipa, so they filled several jars full of the snakes and poured them down on Pipa through a hole in the roof, when lo! they were turned into gold coins. From this originated the well-known saying, "When God wishes to bless a man he even breaks the roof to do it" (*Bhagwan chappar pharhar deta hai*). Pipa presented the gold to Chidbar and his wife.

Another day some merchants came to Pipa to purchase oxen. They left the money with Pipa, who spent it on feeding holy men. When the merchants returned, Pipa explained to them that these holy men would carry them to Paradise. The merchants were convinced and became initiated.

In Sambat 1556 (1634 A.D.) he went again to Dwarika, and there was carried to heaven in the chariot of the Almighty.—*Pándit Bhan Pratap Tiwari.*

---

201. **Hari Raja and Moti Rani.**—Hari Rája loved his wife, Moti Ráni, very dearly. One day she died, and he determined to abdicate his throne and commit suicide. So he took the corpse of his dead queen and, laying it on a boat, set sail into the ocean. He did not eat or sleep for seven days, and on the eighth day, when he was on the point of death, Siva and Párvati who were flying through the air, saw him, and Párvati remonstrated with Siva for his cruelty to the king. Siva said: "I will restore the Ráni to life on one condition, that her husband gives half his life for her." The Rája, agreed and she was restored to life. Then the Rája who was worn out with fatigue, lay down to rest, and as he slept some fairies of the sea came up to the surface of of the sea and induced the Ráni to join their company. When the Rája awoke he found himself alone and in great trouble took service with the king of that land. One day a merchant was selling false pearls to the king, and Rája Hari detected the fraud; so the king made him his steward.

Now the fairies of the sea used to come out always and dance before the king on his birthday. So when they came, and Rája Hari saw Moti Ráni among them he trod on the train of her robe. "Give me what was mine and I will let you go," he said. "What have I got of yours?" she asked. "You have what I gave you on the ocean," he answered. No sooner had he said this than, to the horror of the assembly, she fell dead at his feet. When the king heard the story he gave him his daughter to wife and made him heir to his kingdom.—*Pándit Janardan Joshi.*

202. **Eating and the Evil Eye; the Introduction of Turmeric.**—Once, they say, Rávana, king of Lanka, fell ill. He sent one of the Rákshasas in search of a physician. He went in the form of a bird and sat on a pípal tree beneath which a celebrated physician was sleeping. The bird called out "*korúh, korúh?*" i. e., "who is healthy? who is healthy?" The physician replied in a Sanskrit verse which means, "He who takes long walks in spring, who takes a short nap in summer, who eats very little in autumn and stays at home in winter : he alone is healthy."

The Rákshasa returned and put Rávana on this regimen, when he completely recovered. Then he sent to the physician, asking him what he desired as a reward, and the physician asked him to send whatever was rarest in Lanka. Now, as Lanka was all built of gold there was nothing so rare as iron, and Rávana ordered the Rákshasas to take the physician seven loads of iron. This he received with great discontent, but he was somewhat consoled when with the iron he found a root of the turmeric, which is indigenous to Lanka, and was thus for the first time introduced into India. To this day a careful housewife will never spread the whole dinner at once in the dish of her son or husband, but will give it to him by degrees lest the influence of the evil-eye cause it to disagree, with him.—*Pándit Janardan Joshi.*

203. **The good old times.**—In the good old times the soil was not tilled and there was no ploughing. People used to take a single grain of rice in their hands in the morning, and after walking three times round an ox would ask him, "Will this suffice for the day?" And the ox used to nod, and the grain was sufficient for the family for the day. One day when a guest came to the house an overcareful house-keeper brought

two grains of rice to the ox and he got angry and cursed the human race. Since then men have had to work for their living and the ox suffered too for his curses, for he has had to work with the plough ever since.—*Pándit Janardan Joshi.*

204. How the Raja got his deserts.—There lived once a Rája and a Ráni : the Ráni was so pious that she never left her bed in the morning without feeding five Brahmans. But the Rája was an enemy of Brahmans and insulted them when he got the chance. One day Bhagwán, in the guise of a Brahman, came to the Rája's palace and asked for alms. The Rája was in his stable, and when he saw Bhagwán he, as was his wont, said : " Here is dung in plenty : eat this if you will." By and by the Rája and the Ráni died and their souls went to Swarga. There the Ráni received all she needed, but the Rája began to starve. At last he went to the Ráni and said : " You are my wife. You are enjoying all the comforts of life while I am starving. Out of your abundance give me to eat." The Ráni answered : " I disown you, sinner. Why should I give you food. Go to Bhagwán and ask him for what you need." So the Rája in his distress went to Bhagwán and begged for food. Bhagwán took him to a storehouse where was collected all the dung the Rája had offered in his life to Brahmans multiplied tenfold. Then Bhagwán said : " In Swarga everybody lives on the alms he has given on earth, and all he gives is multiplied tenfold." The Rája wept bitterly, and just then Raja Indra was passing by and heard him. When he heard his trouble Raja Indra said : " Take all this filth and burn it into lime: then you may bring some pan leaves from my garden : prepare them and give them to the gods to chew. Perchance Bhagwán will pardon you and give you food." The Rája did so, and Bhagwán took pity upon him and gave him food as long as he remained in Swarga.

(A folktale told by Akbár Shah, Mánjhi of Manbasa, Dudhi, Mirzapur.)
[This native story admirably illustrates the Mánjhi's idea of what a future life will be.—ED.]

205. The Soldier and his virtuous Wife.—There was once upon a time a soldier who had a beautiful wife, but he was very poor. At last his wife said : " My dear husband, our wealth is gone. What is the use of our living like this any longer ? You had better go abroad and earn money for our support."
" How can I go abroad without money for the journey ? " he asked.
" It is bad," she said, " to eat the bread of charity in the house of your father-in-law. I will get some money from there, and then you can go abroad and seek your fortune. " As he was going away she asked him, " How shall either of us know if the other has ceased to love ? "

" How can I provide for this ? " he asked. So she went into the garden, and picking two buds of *chameli* came to him and said : " Let each of us keep one of these buds, and whichever of us loves another his or her bud will blossom. "

When he was starting, she put on her finest clothes and was taking leave of him, but he turned away from her. She fancied that he did not like her dress, so she went and changed it for another. But even then he turned away his face from her. She was grieved and said :
" My dear husband, what have I done that you have lost your love for me?"
" Fine dress," he answered, " does not befit the wife of a soldier." He said : " Take my sword and shield. Now give me the shield and cut at me as hardly as you can with the sword. " She did as he told her, but he parried all her blows. Then he said : " Keep these arms, and in time of need with them protect your virtue. "
With this advice he left her and went to a distant city, where he took service with a Rája and guarded the gate of his palace. Every day he used to look at the *chameli* bud which he kept tied up in his turban. One morning the Rája was sitting at his gate and saw the soldier looking at the bud. He was curious, and sent one of his servants to see what the soldier was looking at. The soldier said : " I do my duty honestly. What concern has the Rája with my private affairs ? "
The Rája was more curious still, and going himself to the soldier asked him about it, and the soldier told about the buds. Soon after the Rája went on his travels and came to the city in which the soldier lived. He was a man of dissolute habits, so he sent for an old woman and told her to bring the most beautiful woman in the city to see him. She went to the wife of the soldier and proposed to her that she should visit the Rája. She agreed to go for four lakhs of rupees, but the Rája gave her five lakhs, of which she kept one lakh for herself and gave four to the soldier's wife. When the Rája came she kept him in conversation for some time, and when he tried to approach her she drew her sword, fell upon him and wounded him sorely.
When he was recovered from his wounds he came back to his own city and told the soldier what had happened to him. The soldier told him that this was the work of his wife. The Rája approved of her fidelity to her husband and advanced him to honour.

(A folktale told by Ahmad Husen, Constable, Dhudi, Mirzapre.)
[The chastity test by a flower is common. See instance collected by Jacob, Folklore Congress Report, p. 89.]

206. The Raja and the Hansa.—Once upon a time a Rája went out hunting and saw a large flock of hansas flying in the sky. One of them broke its leg and had to stay behind on a tree near a tank. In the morning a heron came and began to catch fish in the tank, and the hansa being hungry followed his example. Then a baheliya appeared and the heron flew away, but the hansa was trapped. The baheliya seeing the Rája climbed up the tree and the Rája sat down below. The hansa was weeping in her sorrow, and her tears kept dropping on the Rája's head. At last he saw the baheliya in the tree and asked him what he meant by throwing water on him. The baheliya showed him the weeping hansa, and the Rája had pity and bought her for a thousand rupees. He loosed her and she flew away, but as he continued his joruney he found that she was flying over him and shading him with her wings from the heat of the sun. The Rája called to her and said: "Why do you take such pains about me?"

She answered: "As you have done good to me, I will not return until I have done some good to you."

The Rája was obliged to bring her home with him, and one day he called his astrologers and enquired: "Where and when shall I be married?"

They answered: "There is no greater astrologer than the hansa. Enquire from her."

The hansa said: "Mahárája! If you wish to be married, put on the wedding dress and come with me."

When the Rája was ready he was going to mount his horse and take servants and equipage with him. The hansa said: "Mount upon my wing, and put all your goods on the other."

The Rája did so, and the hansa flew away with him. She flew for three months, night and day, and still the place was five day's journey distant. She told the Rája to dismount and take food. When he had eaten she flew on again and reached the place where the princess was imprisoned under seven troops of guards. She was so delicate that she lived only on the perfume of flowers. The hansa flew up on the roof of her palace and looked at the guards. At the first gate was a fox; at the second a dog; at the third a jackal; at the fourth a tiger; at the fifth a shardul; at the sixth a snake, and at the seventh armed men. The hansa brought the Rája past all the guards and made him sit outside the room in which the princess was. Then she made a hole in the wall and began to sing most sweetly. The princess opened the door and, letting the hansa in, asked her who she was, and offered her anything she chose to ask. The hansa answered: "If you are pleased with me, marry the Rája whom I have brought with me."

The princess said: "Bring in your Rája and I will play dice with him. If he wins I will marry him. If I win he will have to be my slave."

The hansa brought in the Rája to the princess and the game began. The Rája was very much afraid lest he should be beaten, but the hansa encouraged him and repeated such a powerful charm that the Rája won the game. Then the hansa made a hole in the roof of the palace, and mounting him on one of her wings and the princess on the other flew away with them.

The heat of the sun parched the delicate skin of the princess: so when they came to the shore of the ocean the hansa put her down and prepared for them food and drink. But as she was lighting the fire one wing of the hansa was burnt, and the Rája and Ráni began to wonder how they would ever reach their home. The hansa then made a raft of wood and seated them upon it and said: "Mount on this raft; but take care; if you let any other creature sit on it you will be seperated. In three months I will rejoin you."

The Rája and Ráni went floating across the ocean, and after many days they saw a rat drowning in the water.

The Ráni said: "This rat is drowning. Let us take him on the raft."

The Rája reminded her of what the hansa had said, but she would not heed, and when she took the rat on the raft it broke into three parts, and the three of them floated in different directions. The Rája floated a long way and at last came to the shore of the ocean, and his part of the raft stuck under a tree. A grain parcher happened to come there who took the Rája to his house and made him help in stoking his oven. The Ráni landed at the kingdom of a Mahárája and was taken to his court. The Mahárája was pleased and ordered her to be taken into his zanana. But the Ráni said: "I will not marry you at once. For six months I must worship Mahádeva and give alms to the poor. Then I will be your wife."

So the Mahárája built a separate house for her, and all the six months she lived on the perfume of the flowers. When the six months were about to expire the hansa came to the Rája and found him in a miserable state stoking the oven of the grain parcher. She seated the Rája on her wing and brought him to the Ráni and took him to her through a hole in the roof. They embraced each other and wept, and each told the other what had befallen them. The hansa went to the *dhobi* and stole garments for them both. She took them home on her wings and they lived happily. Then the hansa saluted them, and, taking leave of them, flew back to the jungle where she spent the rest of her days in peace.

(A folktale told by Ramnandan Lal, village accountant of Kon Mirzapur.)

[This belongs to the Thankful Beasts Cycle, for which see Clouston, *Popular Tales and Fictions*, I, 223, *Sqq*. For the delicate skin of the heroine see Lady Burton, *Arabian Nights*, VI., 123. We have the deferred marriage in Tawney, *Katha Sarit Ságara*, I, 501. The prohibition of taking the rat on board the raft is one of the common folklore taboos, like the forbidden room, etc. (Clouston: *Popular Tales and Fictions*, I, 198.)]

MISCELLANEA.

207. Tansen the Singer.—Tánsen was one of the worthies of the court of Akbar.. Tánsen was a Brahman of poor family. He used to sing his songs as he herded the cattle of his father, near a tank named the Kapur Talao, near Gwalior. Close to the tank was a lingam of Mahadeva and Tánsen used to sit close to it and sing songs in honour of the god. One day Mahadeva appeared to him and took the form of a beggar. He said : " If you desire to sing you should be taught by a master." Tánsen wondered who the stranger could be. At last he knew it was the god and fell at his feet, saying : " He from whom the goddess of learning and music have learnt their arts is now before me. Who else can teach me ? " Mahadeva then blessed him with the boon of learning and music.

So Tánsen became a learned singer and lived Virakta, or apart from the world. He used to sit by the oven of a grain-parcher with whose daughter, they say, he fell in love. By and by Akbar learned that there was no singer in the world like Tánsen of Gwalior ; so he sent for him ; but Tánsen said he had nothing to do with the Emperor and refused to come. Then Akbar devised this stratagem. He had a palanquin made, in which he placed all kinds of pictures, and told the bearers to lay it down near Tansen and, when he got into it to look at the pictures, to carry him off. So they brought him to Delhi, and the Emperor seated him at his side.

One day it was arranged that the Royal Darbár should be held in boats on the Jumna and the Emperor, accompanied by Tánsen and all the courtiers, went there. First of all the minstrel Baiju Baula, also known as Brij Baula, and Gopál Náyak sang to the tambúra, or mandolin. Then the Emperor asked Tánsen to sing. He said that he had not brought his mandolin and begged the loan of one. The singers refused to lend it, and said : " What kind of a singer is this who does not bring his musical instrument ? " Then Tánsen began to sing without the accompaniment of any instrument ; but from his shoulders came the notes of a mandolin keeping time with his singing. All were struck with wonder.

Then the Emperor ordered the lights to be lit, but Tánsen said : " We singers do not need a lamp lighted with fire. Let it be dark." So he began to sing the Dípak Rág, and all the lamps lighted of themselves. The Emperor offered him a royal reward, but Tánsen would take nothing. So he was seated in a litter and the Emperor raised one of the poles on his own shoulders. But as he was unaccustomed to the work, the litter began to shake and when Tánsen looked out to see what was the matter he saw that he was being carried by the Emperor. So he fell at the feet of Akbar and said he had been too much honoured and was henceforth his slave.

After some stay at Delhi, Tánsen returned to Gwalior and there Baiju Baula and Gopál Náyak went in the hope of defeating him. There Tánsen sat at the jhilmil : Baula at the foot of the fort. Tánsen asked Baiju Baula to sing and he sat on a stone and sang the Kedára Rag. The virtue of this Rág is such that if any one sing it aright a stone will melt into water. So the stone on which he sat was dissolved. By and by the stone solidified again and his mandolin remained embedded within it. Baiju asked Tánsen to take out the mandolin and he too sang the Kedara Rág and the stone dissolved and the mandolin was restored to its owner. Baiju sang the Barwai Rág, the virtue of which is that the deer are charmed at the sound and collect from the forest round the singer. So a wild hind from the forest came to hear the song and Baiju put a golden necklace round her neck Then he asked Tánsen by his minstrelsy to recall the hind and restore the necklace. Tánsen sang the same Rág and lo! twenty hinds, each wearing the same kind of necklace, appeared before him. He asked Baiju to recognise the deer to which he had given the necklace and he could not. Tánsen recognised the hind and took from her neck the necklace which Baiju was obliged to acknowledge to be his own. So Baiju Baula and Gopál Náyák retired defeated.

Some say that Tánsen became a Musalmán and the disciple of the saint Muhammad Ghaus, whose tomb is at Gwalior, and who blessed him that he should become the master singer of the time. Another story is that Akbar procured the services of Tánsen through Rája Ramchandra of Pándho and that he joined the Imperial Court in the seventh year of the reign of the Emperor. He died in the 34th year of the reign of Akbar and was buried at Gwalior under a tamarind tree, the virtue of which is such that if any one eat the leaves thereof his voice becomes melodious.—*Pandit Rám Gharíb Chaubé.*

[Tansen, in spite of the legends which centre round him one of which is of the Orpheus type, was a historical personage. According to Blochmann (*Ain-i-Akbari*, I—406) Raja Ramchandra was King of Bhath and was the patron of Tánsen. In the seventh year of his reign Akbar sent Jalaluddin Qúrchi to induce Tánsen to come to Agra. Ramchandra finding himself powerless to refuse Akbar's request, sent his favourite with his musical instruments and many presents to Agra, and the first time that Tánsen performed at Court, the Emperor made him a present of two lakhs of rupees. Tánsen remained with Akbar and most of his compositions are written in Akbar's name and his melodies are even now-a-days everywhere repeated by the people of Hindustan.—Ed.]

208. Abu Haraira or Abu Huraira.—There is a great series of stories told of Abu Haraira, the friend of the Prophet Muhammad. He takes his name from an Arabic word meaning " a kitten " and was noted for his fondness for cats. He had no family and kept a number of cats to take their place. The Prophet recognised the purity of the cat. He said : " Cats are not impure, they keep watch around us." He used water from which a cat had drunk for his purifications and his wife Ayisha ate out of a vessel from which a cat had eaten. The Prophet was once distributing rewards to his soldiers who had fought in a religious war. Haraira found that some of them were impostors and had been absent from the fight. He remonstrated and they said : " What does this cat mean by interfering ?" The Prophet rebuked them and gave the name of Haraira to his friend.—*M. Ab Ahmad Khán.*

[The purity of the cat is marked by its Sanskrit name—*márjára*, " she that is always cleaning herself." Anyone who kills a cat has to undergo a very severe penance. The black cat is a stock personage in all European folk-ore. (Henderson *Folklore*, 207; and see Gubernatis *Zoological Mythology*, II,63]·.]

209. Some Folklore of Birds.—Hindus consider the parrot a pious bird and many people teach them the following verse :—

Chitrakut ke ghát par bhau santan ki bhir ;
Tulasí das prabhu chandan ragaren, tilak dei Ram Raghubir.

"At the pass of Chitrakut (the mountain in the Banda district where Rāma and Sita stayed in their wanderings) an assembly of saints met ; Tulsi Das grinds sandal wood for the lord and Rāma, leader of the race of Raghu marks his forehead."

Again when pious villagers see their crops being eaten by parrots they say :—

Ram ki chiraiya, Ram ka khet ;
Khāt la chiraiya bhar bhar pet.

"The birds and the field both belong to Rāma ; eat little birds to your hearts' content."

The Khanjan or Khirarich, our water wagtail is also called the bird of Rāma—Rām chiraiya. It comes in the cold weather from Rāma to take stock of the world and bring him back news of its welfare. It flies back with a flower of mustard (*sarson*) and an ear of barley in its mouth and then Rāma knows that the world is thriving. The grasshopper, by the way, is called *Ram ki gae* or Rāma's cow and must not be molested.—*Pāndit Rām Gharib Chaubē.*

(Many Hindus believe that the parrot is Sakyamuni, the Buddha. According to Prof. Gubernatis the parrot is ridden by Rāma, the god of love, and is also identified with the moon which reveals the secrets of the night. "Therefore the parrot being identified with the night in the *Sukasapati* and in other books of Hindu stories, we see the parrot often appearing in love stories and revealing amorous secrets." The Polynesians believe that the parrot carries a spirit from one stone to another. – Taylor *Primitive Culture*, II, 161.)

For the grasshopper compare the common English superstition about the ladybird which is connected with the Virgin Mary. Little children say—

[Ladybird, Ladybird, fly away home,
Thy house is on fire, thy children all gone.—ED.]

210. Naugaza Tomb.—In the village of marriāwan in Lucknow is a tomb nine yards long. It is said to be the tomb of Shah Wesh, a leader in the early. Muhammadan invasions.—*Settlement Report, p. 20.*

211. A Charm to stop Rain.—If rain continue for several days the following charm should be practised to stop it :—

Write on plates of clay the names of the companions (ashāb) and throw them into a river. The rain will stop at once. Instead of plates, broken pieces of tile might be used with advantage.—*Pāndit Rām Gharib Chaubē.*

212. Khwaja Khizr worshipped by Dyers.—Like dhobis the rangrez or dyers have a great reverence for Khwāja Khizr whom they call their Pir ; if they neglect him he spoils the colour of their dyes and upsets their pots. For Khwāja Khizr see *Introduction to Popular Religion*, 26.—*W. Crooke.*

213. 74½ Heading of Letters.—One and not very probable explanation of the Hindu custom of writing 74½ at the head of letters is that this was the weight of the gold earrings of the Rajputs who were killed at the seige of Chithor. The Pāndits have, as might be expected, a mystical interpretation of the figures. Seventy or *satya* stands for *satya* "truth" four represents the four Yugas and ½ stands for the writer of the letter. The whole then means—" This truth has been admitted in all the four ages that no one should open and read the letter of another." Others say that it simply means that the contents of the letter are true. All these explanations are obviously inadequate and it would be very interesting to ascertain the real cause of the use of these particular figures.— *W. Crooke.*

214. A charm to call a Bir or demon attendant.—On the 9th lunar day when it falls on Friday fast the whole day. In the evening feed on *khir* or sweet rice milk. At 8 o'clock at night put on a red garment and apply perfumes to your clothes. Then make a circle with red lead on the ground. Sit in the centre of the circle. Keep by you four cardamoms, some catechu (kathā), some betel-nuts and eight cloves. Then light a lamp with clarified butter in it to feed the wick. Then repeat the incantation "*Jap tārā torai swāhā*, i. e. incantation can break down the stars" five thousand times at one sitting. Then a demon attendant will be at your service to do your bidding.—*Pāndit Rām Gharib Chaubē.*

215. The Firefly.—Natives at Saharanpur believe that the firefly is kept in confinement by the little Baya or weaver bird who shuts him up in a piece of clay to serve as a lamp for her nest. The firefly, by one account, is produced from the dung of dogs.—*Pāndit Rām Gharib Chaubē.*

216. Mirzapur: A spell when Foot and Mouth disease attacks Cattle.—They break the front or hind leg of a young pig and leave it near the outskirts of the village. Whoever offers it can, after a short time, take it home secretly, kill and eat it : but if any one sees him do it the spell is broken.—*W. Crooke.*

217. Squirrels ; regard for.—To the east of these Provinces the little squirrel is known as Sita ki bilār or Sita's cat. I remember my teacher giving me a sound slap on the ear because I attempted to catch one and he told me that to kill a cat or a squirrel was as bad as killing a Brahman.—*Pāndit Rām Gharib Chaubē.*

[The squirrel is probably respected because it is a house-haunter. – ED.]

218. The Prophet Moses.—By an extraordinary feat of folk etymology the Prophet Moses is, among the rural population, supposed to be connected, from the similarity of his name, with mice (*mūs*) ; so when their crops are being injured by rats and field mice they offer some rice at their holes in honour of Mūsa. After offering it they eat it themselves, and this is believed to propitiate Moses.—*W. Crooke.*

219. Montgomery: Earth from a rat's hole as a remedy—In swelling of the udder in cows a coating of earth from a rat's hole is a good remedy.—*W. Purver, Settlement Report, p. 82.*

220. Hindus : Abstinence from meat.—Those Hindus who eat meat abstain from its use on Sundays and on the Ekādashi or eleventh of each month. Besides this most people abstain from meat on the regular fast days.—*Pāndit Rām Gharib Chaubē.*

221. Western Districts, N.-W. P.: The cry of the Beggar.—

Diya kar hāth se ji jab talak hai,
Diyē ki roshani mahshar talak hai.
Diyē ki roshani to ghar hi talak hai,
Diyē ki roshani us rah talak hai.

"Give, give, O man! while thou dost live; for the lamp of gifts shall lead thee safely to the happy region. The lamps of earth illuminate the houses only, but the lamp of gifts illuminates the regions that intervene between the throne of God and the land of men.—*Pândit Râm Gharîb Chaubé.*

222. Ludhiana: Observances at the Roshani Fair.—The Roshani Fair is held at the shrine of a saint Pîr Abdul Kâdir Jilâni (called generally Pîr Sâhib). This is a Muhammadan fair, but the Hindus of the city join in it. It is held on the 9th—11th of the Muhammadan month of Rabi-ul-Sâni, called Mirânji. There is a peculiar custom bringing cattle and keeping them tied up at the shrine all night for good luck, this being called *chauki*, i.e., the cow or buffalo watches at the shrine. The name Roshani is derived apparently from the tomb being illuminated at night during the fair.—*Mr. T. G. Walker, Settlement Report, p.* 59.

223. Twitching of the Eye.—To feel a twitching in the eye is regarded by Hindus and Muhammadans in Jaunpur district as an omen of some event.

Feeling twitching in the right eye is regarded as lucky for men and unlucky for women and *vice versâ*. There is, however, some difference of opinion: some believe that—

Ankh pharke dahnî
Mân mile kî bahnî
Ankh pharke bâin
Bir mile kî sain.

"When in your right eye you twitching feel
Your mother or your sister you will meet;
When in the left eye you twitching feel
Your brother or your husband hope to meet."—*Azizuddin Ahmed.*

224. Bee Superstition.—In the jungles the people who collect honey think that if the hives are touched, except in the light half of the month, the bees will desert the place and never return. They always ask an astrologer or village sorcerer to select an auspicious time for this duty. All over the world the souls of the dead are supposed to take up their abode in bees and flies. This is the origin of the numerous superstitions connected with these insects. Thus in Switzerland bees are supposed to be the souls of the dead (Gubernatis *Zoological Mythology*, II, 218). In Germany the bee is believed to have survived from the lost Paradise, of the Golden Age (Grimm, *Teutonic Mythology*, II, 695). Bees in England are informed when the master of the house dies; otherwise they would desert the place. They are believed to sing in their hives on Christmas Day (*Chamber's Book of Days*, II, 137). In Cornwall bees are never moved except on Good Friday. In Bedfordshire the people sing a psalm in front of a sick hive and they are sure to get well as the spirit of disease is scared by the noise of the singing. (Dyer, *Folklore*, 124.) Numerous similar practices are found in England and Scotland.

It would be interesting to know how far similar ideas prevail in India.—*W. Crooke.*

225. The youngest son in Folklore.—Much discussion has arisen over the question of the superiority of the youngest son in the folktales. He is always more clever and fortunate than his elder brothers. The idea seems to have arisen from the rule of polygamy. The new wife and her son is always more the favourite of his father than the children of the senior wives. In India the last son born of a woman is, like Benjamin, almost always her favourite. There are special terms for such children *Pet-ponchhan* or *Kok-puchhva*—"The last product of the womb." In native families such a son is habitually called *ghar-ke-malik* or "master of the house" and is treated with special affection. This is particularly the case among rich people, such as bankers, who, apparently from their sedentary habits and neglect of exercise, are notoriously infertile and a son born to such a man in his old age is regarded with special respect.—*W. Crooke.*

226. Left-handed People.—Left-handed people are known as Bamhathi and it is popularly believed that they are particularly expert in any business which they undertake. But they rest under the same suspicion of craftiness and duplicity which always attaches to people with only one eye.—*Pândit Râm Gharîb Chaubé.*

227. Gurgaon: Muhammadan charms for Disease.—In times of great sickness Muhammadans sometimes take a he-goat, perfect in all respects, and ten or twenty men walk with it all round the village, repeating verses of the Korân: then they kill it or bury it in the centre of the village, or they write a prayer on a piece of paper and put it over the chief entrance of the village.

The prayer runs thus—

Abdullah kâ pût, Aimand kâ Jâyd,
Bhâg ri waba, Muhammad dyâ—

"Son of Abdullah, son of Aimana, flee away disease. Muhummad has come."—*Mr. F. C. Channing, Settlement Report, p.* 37.

228. Some Charms (Muhammadan) to cure Fever.—A fly, half a pod of black pepper, and some assafœtida: rub together with water and then apply the powdered mixture to the eye. Fever will vanish. Again burn some feathers of the owl and some *gugal* incense, tying it in a black cloth and made wet with ghi and receive the ashes in a new pot. Apply the ashes to the eyes of the patient and he will be freed from fever.

Again, pluck a white *dhatura* fruit on Sunday and tie it on the right wrist of the patient. Fever will at once disappear.—*Pândit Râm Gharîb Chaubé.*

229. Durbhunga: A legend of.—It is related that in the time of Râja Siu Sing Deo a fisherwoman with a basket of fish on her head and accompanied by her daughter-in-law was on her way to market. A kite from a neighbouring tree pounced down and carried off a fish from the basket. Instead of sympathising with her mother-in-law, the daughter began to laugh. Enraged at such unbecoming conduct, the mother-in-law gave vent to her rage, and a hot quarrel ensued. All this was witnessed by the Râja as he sat by his window and he lost no time in sending for the women and threatened the girl with death if she did not explain her conduct. "In the reign of King Yudasthir," said she, "I was a kite. During the war of the Mahabhârata I carried away the arm of a woman with a golden bracelet weighing 80 maunds, and brought it here and ate it (pointing to the spot). I laughed at the petty greed of the kites of the present day who do not mind pouncing down on a petty fish." The Mahârâja was astonished and had a series of tanks dug on the site pointed out and at last found the bones of the arm as well as the golden bracelet, and so the tank was called *Hardha* or the bone tank.—*Calcutta Review, CXII., 51.*

North Indian Notes and Queries:

A MONTHLY PERIODICAL.

VOL. V.]   SEPTEMBER, 1895.   [NO. 6.

Every communication must be accompanied by the writer's name and address, not necessarily for insertion, but as a guarantee of good faith. Every quotation from a book must be accompanied by its full title, publisher's and author's names, place and date of publication, volume and page.
Contributors are requested to write on ONE SIDE the page only. If several contributions be sent at a time, they should be sent each on a separate sheet.
The Conductor cannot undertake to return, or be responsible for, any MSS. not accepted.
All orders must be accompanied by cash. If not so accompanied, they will either not be attended to, or will be complied with per value-payable post.
Contributions should be addressed direct to W. CROOKE, ESQ., C.S., SAHARANPUR, N.-W. P., INDIA.

CONTENTS OF THIS NUMBER.
(The references are to the Notes.)

Popular Religion ... 91 to 96	Folktales ... 100 to 105
Anthropology ... 97 ,, 99	Miscellanea ... 106 ,, 108

POPULAR RELIGION.

230. Eastern Districts: Worship of Ramaiya Baba.—Ramaiya Baba is a well-known personage in the districts of Benares and Mirzapur. He was a Brahman of Mirzapur and from his boyhood a devoted student of the Ramayana of Tulasi Das. He was at the same time much under Muhammandan influence, and a few years before his death he formed an irregular connection with a dancing girl, by whom he had a son named Gopi Chand. Finally, in 1865, he became a Christian and composed a large number of religious songs. He formed a regular sect who call themselves Ramaiya dasis and pay him divine honours. One of the songs which he composed in honour of the mother of his child, Bhágyamáni, is as follows:—

Sharm mori rakho, he Bhágyamáni
Tab to vahaliu kasubi paturiya, ab to bhailu mori ráni.
Betwa janame lolak laiya, Gopi Chand kul kai nisháni
Din Dás kahat Ramaiya—rakho more munkanwa ka pani.
Sharm mori rakho, he Bhágyamáni.

"Preserve my honour, O Bhágyamáni. Once you were a dancing girl, now you are my queen. To thee a pledge of our house was born, a son, Gopi Chand. He is the delight of my heart. Ramaiya, the servant of the poor, says: 'Maintain my honour. Preserve my honour, O Bhágyamáni.'"—*W. Crooke.*

231. Bombay: Vetala Circles.—The following note taken from the *Bombay Gazetteer* (XVIII., 388) is interesting:

In the Deccan these circles are generally outside of the village and near the houses of one of the early or depressed classes, the Mhars or the Roshis. This Poona circle has the interest that it has been figured in Colonel Forbes-Leslie's *Early Races of Scotland*, who suggests a connection between these circles and the stone circles found in England, Western Europe, and other parts of the world. Though they seem to have no direct connection it may be suggested that the original object both of Indian and of English stone circles, as well as of the Buddhist rails round burial mounds, is the same, namely, to keep off evil, that is evil spirits, from the central stone or mound. A guardian circle is equally wanted whether the object to be guarded is a stone in which a spirit god lives, a tomb in which the relics and the spirit of the dead remain, or a stone of judgment, or an altar stone, both of which probably in most cases were also Bethels or gods' houses. That during his crowning, when he is especially open to the attacks of the evil eye and other evil influences, the king sits upon the holy or guardian-possessed stone of Scone, suggests that the origin of the old British judgment stones may have been guardian-possessed seats for the elders of the tribe. In this connection the value of the Vetala circle is that it keeps fresh the early guardian idea.

The centre stone is the god's house. The stones in the circle are the houses of the god's watchmen. Apparently Vetala's guards have no names. The only one of Vetala's guards who is known by name in the Deccan is Bhangya Bava. Whenever offerings are made to Vetala in fulfilment of a vow, a *chilam* or hubble-bubble filled with hemp is offered to Bhangya Bava, who takes his name from bhang or hemp water, of which he is said to be very fond. The other guards seem to be chosen by chance out of the host of bhuts and pisachas, that is ghosts, of whom Vetala is the lord and leader. The fact that Vetala is shown holding a cane (*bet, vet*) as a sceptre, and that sometimes a cane which is the exorcist's great spirit-scarer or buth-lord stands for Vetala, suggests a connection between the words vet and Vetala. Twice a month at midnight on the full moon and on the no-moon, like the furious host of early Europe (compare Stallybrass in Grim's *Teutonic Mythology*, 918—950). Vetala is human in shape, and followed by crowds of spirits each with a torch in one hand and a weapon in the other, pass in ghostly state clad in silver and gold, with richly trapped elephants, horses and litters. Lucky is the man who sees the host, though he generally falls in a swoon, and still luckier the man who, trusting to some spell, walks to the god's litter and asks his favour. Vetala wears a green dress and holds a cane in his right hand and a conch shell in his left. He also holds in his hands a rosary of twenty-one beads of the rudraksha (*eleocarpus lanceolatus*), a piece of burnt cow dung, and some flowers of the *Calotropis gigantea*, a bush which he usually fastens to his right wrist and of which the monkey god Hanuman is very fond.

Vetala dislikes women and never possesses them. A man whom Vetala possesses is held lucky and his advice is sought in all troubles. High class Hindus as a rule hold the ordinary Vetala worship discreditable and, except stealthily, seldom perform it. The lower orders believe in Vetala, worship him and pay him vows. His devotees are mainly of two classes, sorcerers and athletes. Vetala is the sorcerer's god, because sorcerers wish him to give them some of his power over spirits: is the athlete's god, apparently because of the strength and activity shown by a man whom Vetala has entered.

232. **The Legend of the Phalgu or Lelaján.**—The banished Rám, with Sitá and Lakshman, had retired to a spot, upon the bank of the Phalgú. One day, when the two brothers had gone out to the forest in search of fruit, a voice from heaven warned their deceased father to make haste to Swarga, or otherwise the gates of that blessed region would be fast barred and bolted against his approach. In all haste, the spirit of Rájá Dashrath repaired to the spot where his sons lived in exile. Finding them away from home, he requested Sitá to do the needful in their absence. The daughter-in-law hesitated to officiate in the duty of her husband. She, moreover, pleaded the absolute want of the wherewithal to perform the ceremony. But Dashrath urged the jeopardy of his beatitude as the consequence of delay, and enjoined Sitá to offer a *pind* (funeral cake) of sand in lieu of rice. She kept as witnesses the river Phalgú, a Bráhman, a tulshí plant, and a banyan tree, to justify her proceedings under a necessity that admitted of no procrastination. On the return of the brothers, Sitá related to them the adventure of their father. But Rám disbelieving her, she called upon Phalgú to bear its testimony. The river kept mute and was cursed to lose its stream. The Bráhman and the tulshí plant, failing to give a faithful evidence, were respectively doomed —the one to be a mendicant, and the other to suffer from the urinary abomination of dogs and cats. The banyan tree alone confirmed the truth of Sitá's story, and was blessed to have a long life and perennial vigour.—("*Travels of a Hindú,*" *Vol I., page* 221.)

233. **South Mirzapur, N.-W. P.**—Wild Tribes: Néti Sub-Division of the Mánjhis: A God of War.—Majhwárs of the Néti Subdivision have a god of war of their own. He is called Bágh Mundápát. His worship commenced at a troublous period. The Rájá of Ratnapur once began to oppress Kóhdul Sinh, a Mánjhi landlord of his dominions. Then a god of Barbaspúr, the native village of the Mánjhí, appeared in a dream before Kóhdul Sinh and said to him: "O senseless wretch ! I am a powerful god. Be sure of it. I live in thy village. I drink thy water and breathe thy air. I feed upon what the land produces. I am, therefore, indebted to thee. But I am angry with thee at thy neglect of me. At a juncture like this thou dost not invoke my aid. If thou promise to worship me when the trouble is over, I shall exert myself to make thee the Rájá of Ratnapúr." The Manjhwár promised to worship the god. Then the god said: "Go thou now to fight with the Rájá in the field of battle. I am also coming in the form of a tiger." The god disappeared with these words and the Mánjhi next morning attacked the Rájá's palace

with his men. A bloody fight ensued. In the meantime the tiger appeared and began to devour the Rájá's men. The Rájá then admitted his defeat and offered to make the Manjhwár his Prime Minister. The fight then stopped. The Rájá made him his Dewán thenceforward. The Manjhwár began to worship the deity under the designation of Baghmundá pát. His clansmen also took to the worship of the god. The things offered to the god are the following:—

(1) A cake of rice flour, (2) a black and white fowl, (3) a black and white goat.

Along with the worship of this god, the worship of Chandi Bhawáni is also performed. To her is offered a black fowl, a black she-goat and a sweetened cake of wheat flour. The worship is performed on the tenth lunar day of Kuár.—*Pándit Rám Gharíb Chaubé.*

234. **A Tale of the Saint Shaikh Abdul Qadir Jilani.**—When the saint was a boy he was about to go to Baghdad, and as he was about to leave his mother, she said: "I have in the world eighty gold-mohurs. Take half, the other half is for your brother. I shall never see you again, but whatever you do never tell a lie." On the road in Hamadan he was attacked by robbers, and when they asked him what goods he possessed, he said that he had forty coins sewn up in the lining of his coat. They wondered at his truthfulness and brought him to their chief, to whom he made the same answer. The robber asked why he admitted having the money and he said that he had done so because he had promised his mother never to tell a lie. The robber reflected how this lad remembered his mother, while he had been forgetful of his Heavenly Father. So he and his companions abandoned their evil life and became honest men.—*M. Ataullah Beg.*

235. **Saharanpur: Snake Worship.**—Five miles north of Saharanpur is the temple of Sankala Mahadeva, where a fair is held on the Nagpanchami. Large crowds assemble and the offering consists of what is called dudhbhanga, a drink made of milk and the powdered leaves of the hemp plant. This must, as is shown by the date of the feast, have been originally a snake shrine, and the offering is also appropriate to those reptiles. But it has now been converted into a temple of Mahadeva, and the original Nagdeota has been forgotten. Snakes are of the host of Mahadeva, so the transition is easy. The name Sankala is taken from that of a famous Brahmachari, who is said to have founded the shrine.—*Pándit Rám Gharíb Chaubé.*

236. **A Miracle performed by Khwája Muin-ud-din Chishti.**—Khwája Muin-ud-din Chishti was once going from the house of Khwája Usmán Háruni to Baghdad attended by his page. As he went along he saw a great vault which he supposed to be a temple of the fire-worshippers. He sent the boy to see who was there. When he went in he saw a number of men sitting before a personage who seemed to be their chief. They tried to seize him, but he escaped and came and told the saint what he had seen. The saint was then engaged in performing his ablution (*wasu*) and was wroth. When the rite was completed he went in and found the unbelievers sitting before the sacred fire. He asked them why they worshipped a creature of the Almighty instead of the Almighty himself, and said: "If this fire be divine, plunge your hand into it." They refused to do so, and the saint seizing his page threw him into the fire, which took no effect on him. The fire-worshippers were amazed and asked the boy how he felt. He replied that he felt as if he was in a lovely garden furnished with the finest fruits and flowers. They were so impressed by the miracle, that they all embraced the true faith, and became the disciples of the saint.—*M. Ataullah Beg.*

237. **The Legend of Gokarana and Dhundhkari.**—In the old times there was a rich Bráhman who lacked nothing but a son. He went on pilgrimages, gave alms to the poor and served saints and pandits, but to no avail. So life became a burden to him and at last he bought a cow, hoping that she would calve, and that he could occupy himself tending her calf; but she proved barren. Then he thought to plant a mango tree; but that too gave no fruit. So his neighbours ridiculed him and called him, his cow and his mango tree bánjh or "barren." In his grief he retired to the jungle and there he met an inspired Sadhu, who hearing him cry went and enquired his trouble. At first the Bráhman would not trust him, but after a time he told him his case. At last the Sadhu took a mango fruit and sprinkling some water over it with a stem of kusa grass gave it to him. He told the Bráhman to give the fruit to his wife and that she would bear a son.

He gave it to his wife and told her the virtue of it; but she feared the pain of child-bearing, so she gave it to the cow, and in due time the cow brought forth a male child, but he had the ears of a cow. Hence he was named Gokarana, or "cow ears." At the same time the sister of the Bráhman's wife was delivered of a son, and the Bráhman's wife bought the child from her sister, and told her husband that she had given birth to it in consequence of eating the Sadhu's mango.

The two boys grew up together, but while Gokarana devoted himself to the study of the

Shastras the other boy was idle and vicious. So he came to be known as Dhundhkari or "worker of darkness." Finally Gokarana became a noted Pandit, and Dhundhkari a gambler and a thief. One day Dhundhkari got a large sum by a robbery, and when he brought it home his two wives who were vicious women, thinking that he would waste it in gambling and leave them destitute; so they fell upon him with a sword and killed him. After his death he turned into a terrible Rakshasa and began to afflict the people.

Soon after Gokarana returned from his travels to his native city and heard what had occurred. Meanwhile Dhundhkari appeared before him in the form of a tiger, and when he saw him, fell prostrate before Gokarana and told him his story. Gokarana promised to deliver him if he would follow his advice, and Dhundhkari promised to do so. So they went together to Gaya, and Gokarana began to recite over him the Sri Bhagwata or the deeds of Sri Krishna. But Dhundhkari in his form as a Rakshasa could not remain long in one place and listen to the recitation; so Gokarana got a long bamboo and shut him up in the place below the bottom knot. As the reading went on each day a knot of the bamboo burst, and in seven days Dhundhkari arrived at the top of the bamboo, and came out purified. Then a chariot came from heaven to carry him to Vaikuntha. But he refused to go without his brother and the chariot driver went back to Bhagwan and told him that Dhundhkari refused to come alone. So Bhagwan granted his prayer. When the chariot came a second time Dhundhkari again refused to go unless he was allowed to bring all his relatives and friends with him. This was also granted by Bhagwan. Thus the great deliverance was worked by the virtue of Gokarana, the son of the cow.—*W. Crooke.*

[The tale is one of the usual moral kind and is interesting mainly as an example of the barrenness cures, for which see *Introduction to Popular Religion and Folklore*, 206.—*W. Crooke.*]

238. **An instance of Pitcher Superstition from Bardwán.**—A correspondent of a bi-weekly paper of Lahore writes :—

Madhupur has just been enlivened by the visit of H. H. The Dowager Maharáni of Bardwán, the widow of the late Mahárájá Mahtáb Chand, and her daughter. The distinguished visitors, accompanied by Rájá Ban Bihárí Kapúr, arrived there by the afternoon train on the 21st. The south-eastern end of the platform was enclosed with kanáts with an awning over head, to enable the ladies to get into their palanquins unseen by the crowd. A bodyguard of twelve men, led by a jamádár, all bearing fire-arms, were drawn up inside the enclosure, while hosts of men and women, carrying on their heads brass pots filled with water, and adorned with mango leaves, waited outside.

239. **Birth in the asterism of Mul.**—When a child is born at the time the asterisms of Múl, Revati, Aswini, Aslekha and Magha are in conjunction the time is most inauspicious. Children born at the conjunction of Revati and Aswíni do not live long, or if they chance to live are a curse to the family. The same is the case with those born at the conjunction of Aslekha and Magha. Those born at the conjunction of Iyeshtha and Múl cause trouble to their mother. The most popular explanation of this is that at these times the ancestors who have died violent deaths and become Rákshasas get a chance of troubling their descendants. To avert these consequences, Múl is worshipped with a special ritual as follows :—

The mother remains in the delivery room for twenty-seven days (the number of the asterisms) after the birth of her child. The father, during this time, neither shaves his hair, cuts his nails, or does anything which may involve personal impurity; the idea underlying these precautions being perhaps analogous to that of the convade. On the twenty-seventh day at the hour at which the birth occurred the father collects earth taken from seven places, the gate of a Rájá's palace, the stable, the elephant house, a place where four roads meet, an antbill, a cow house and from some place of pilgrimage. At the same time he collects shoots of five trees, the mango, pípul, pákar, gúlar and bar,—the last four all varieties of the sacred fig tree. He also provides a portion of five precious things, gold, silver, copper, iron and brass.

Then a holy square is made in the courtyard and beside it are made cowdung images of Gauri, Ganesa, the nine planets, and the sixty-four goddesses. Opposite these is placed an earthen vessel containing the other sacred articles already enumerated with some woollen cloth, bamboo bark and water. This vessel is covered with a piece of yellow cloth. This vessel has in it twenty-seven holes, and near it is placed a cowdung image of Múl. In some cases, an earthen vessel containing grain, covered with cloth and with a saucer on the top containing a representation of Múl in gold, is used for the same purpose.

The officiating Bráhman priest first of all worships Dharti Máta, the earth goddess, with an offering of water, washed rice, sandal and a *homa* or burnt offering. In the same way Gauri, Ganesa, the nine planets and the sixty-four goddesses are worshipped. Lastly, Múl is worshipped after the same manner. Finally a fire offering is again made. While this worship is going on the parents of the child sit in the sacred square on an ox yoke (*juátha*).

Then the mother with the child in her arms retires into the house, bathes and puts on clean clothes. She returns and sits as before on the yoke with her husband. At this time she holds the child in her arms and covers it with a cloth, next the priest holds the vessel containing the sacred articles over the parents and pours water over them. They again change their garments and take their seat in the square. Again a fire offering is made and some *ghi* is put in a vessel. The child is held over the vessel and the father sees for the first time the face of his child reflected in the *ghi*. The vessel and the *ghi* are the perquisite of the officiating priest.

Next the father takes the child in his lap and puts some silver coins in its right hand. These the child is made to present to the priest. Alms and grain are distributed to Bráhmans and the whole rite ends with a feast to Bráhmans.—*Pándit Rám Gharíb Chaubé.*

240. **River Worship.**—It was on the seventh day of Baisákh that the Ganges emerged from the ears of the Saint Jahnu, who had devoured her in his anger. Hence this is the day on which she is specially worshipped. The worshipper should on that day, if possible, bathe in the Ganges and should fill in her name one thousand new pitchers with the water and give them to Bráhmans with an offering of uncooked grain and money. This worship is chiefly done by Bráhman and Banya women. It is believed that a woman who fasts this day aids twenty-one families to salvation.

The following account of river and water worship in the Panjab, from Mr. Maclagan's Census Report (page 105) deserves reproduction.—" Of the rivers venerated in the Panjab, the Ganges is the most famous. It is very often worshipped under the title of Bhagirathi, after the name of the Puranic hero Bhagiratha, who is said to have brought the Ganges down from heaven. A large number of those who worship the river under this name are of the Odh caste, which is said to be descended from Bhagiratha. The Odhs of the south-west are a wandering caste of workers in earth, who say they are Hindus, but none the less bury their dead, and hence are not associated with by ordinary Hindus. They are often found wearing a black blanket, the origin of which custom is explained in two different ways. According to one story, the Ganges, which was brought from heaven by the austerities of Bhagiratha, has not flowed to the place where the bones of their ancestors repose, and until it does, the Odhs must continue to wear mourning. Another account is that the ancestor of the Odhs, the father of Bhagiratha, swore to himself that he would never drink twice of the same well, and that he used to dig a new well for himself each day; but one day he had to dig very deep and the earth fell over him and he was seen no more. This story is also given to explain why the Odhs do not bury their dead.

The Apapanthis of our returns (who are mainly from Rohtak and Hissar) are possibly followers of Padmákar Bhat of Banda, who used to attend the court of the Mahratta chief, the Apa Sáhib, and who devoted a great portion of his life to the worship of the Ganges.

The followers of Byásji may be worshippers either of the river of that name or of the Rishi Vyása, and in the same way the name Márkanda may refer to the river or the Rishi of the same name. Similarly there is the Saraswati river and Saraswati, the female energy of Brahma; but the latter is seldom worshipped in this Province, whereas there is a good deal of local veneration paid to the former. The Ravi, too, is a very sacred river locally, and bathing in the Ravi, it is well to know, is a sure cure for dyspepsia.

The most noticeable instance of the cult of rivers in the Province is, however, that of the Indus in its lower course, and almost all the persons who have returned themselves as Daryasewak or river-worshippers, are worshippers of the lower Indus in Muzaffargarh, Multán, Dera Ghází Khán and Baháwalpur. The Aroras of those parts have a legend (which is said to be found in the Amargit) that a warrior named Vadhera Lál, once rose from the Indus to protect the Hindus from their Muhammadan conquerors. This Vadhera Lál appears to have been a revivalist preacher who inculcated river worship about the Sambat year 1007, or 941 years ago, and whose doctrines took a great hold in all the region of Bhakkar and the Panjnad. He is worshipped under the names Vadhera Lál, Auliyapura, Amar Lál, Dulan Lál and Joti Lál and these names are applied indifferently to the saint and to the river itself. The descendants of Vadhera Lál are known as Thakkars and serve as gurus to the river-worshipping population. The Jiya Bhagat of the tables is one of these Thakkars. They sit with their eyes on the river muttering mantras, or when they are not near the river they place before them a cup filled with river water and pronounce their mantras over this. There are influential Thakkars in Alipur, Sitpur, Shujabád and Multán. The chief temple of the sect is on the island at Bhakkar, but there are temples at Dera Ghází Khán and Jampur, where they keep a lamp burning day and night. The common method of worshipping the river of an evening, is to make a small raft of reeds, and to place on it a lamp, which is then lit and set afloat on the river, or on some canal. In the mornings some flowers and scent and sweetmeats are placed upon a plate, hymns are sung and the offerings then thrown into the river. These forms of worship are commonly gone through upon a Sunday and the entry of "Sunday worship" (*Itwar Upaska*) in the Census returns, means merely, one who worships the Indus on a Sunday.

The orthodox Hindu water god is Indra or Varun Deota, the Varuna of the Vedas. But the great water deity among the common people is Kwája Khizr, the Musalman saint, identified with the Prophet Elias, who is said to have drunk of the water of immortality and to be alive at this hour, and who is consequently known as Jinda or Zinda Pir—"the living saint." He appears on the popular lithographs as an elderly Musalmán gentleman standing on a fish and is termed *par excellence* the Kwája Sáhib, Kwája Pír, Kwája Guru. He is reverenced by all classes of both Hindus and Muhammadans, but more especially by the Jhínwars, Malláhs and others whose occupations are connected with water in any form. Persons travelling by river or sea and persons descending into a well will propitiate Khwája Khizr. Parched grain is distributed and lights are placed on wells in his honour. The Khizrí gate of the Lahore city is called after this saint, this having been the water gate in the days when the river flowed under the gates of the fort. Ladhar Bába is said to be or to have been a Sádhu in the Jhang District whose followers worship Khwája Khizr."

[For more information on these river godlings and Khwája Khizr, see *Introduction to Popular Religion and Folklore*, 23—ED.]

241. **Kabir: Mystical Interpretation of the name:**—Kabírpanthís have a mystical interpretation of the name of their saint as follows:—

Kakka kawal Brahm hai, babba báni bir ;
Rarra sab men Ram raha, táko kahen Kabír.

"K. means the lotus of Brahma ; B the sacred words of God ; R means He who pervades all things."—*W. Crooke.*

242. **The story of the death of the Saint Kabir.**—Towards the close of his life Kabir went to Orissa to the shrine of Jaggannath and then returned to Magadha where he had two faithful disciples, Rájá Bír Sinh, Baghel Rájput, and Bijli Khán, Pathán. Both of these were petty chiefs. First of all Kabír went to the house of Bijli Khán and the Pathán received his guru with great respect. Kabír told him that he was about to leave the world. So Bijli Khán said: "Guru Sahib! You are the saint of both Hindus and Musalmáns. On your death in what way are your remains to be disposed of?" He answered: "If you can get my corpse you may dispose of it according to the rules of Islám." Then he went to the house of Rájá Bír Sinh and after eating, lay down and died. Bír Sinh and his Rání began to bewail him and when Bijli Khán heard of his death he hastened there and asked to see the corpse. When he saw it Bijli Khán seized it and ran off with it to his own house. He buried it close by according to the custom of the Musalmáns. Rájá Bír Sinh was wroth at this and set out to fight the Pathán and recover the body of his guru. A fierce fight was about to occur when a voice from Heaven came to them saying: "Why do ye dispute? The guru was videha (without a body). Dig up the grave and whatever you find you may dispose of each as you please." So they opened the grave and found that the corpse had disappeared. There were only some flowers and a sheet in the grave. These they divided equally between them. One part was buried as is the rule with Hindu Sádhus and it was called Samádhi ; the other was interred in the Muhammadan fashion and called the Rauzah of Kabír Sáhib.—*Pandit Rám Gharíb Chaubé.*

[To the east of the town of Maghar in the Basti District on the right bank of the Ami river is the cenotaph of Kabir Das or Kabir Sháh erected in A. D. 1450 by Bijli Khán and restored in A. D. 1567 by Nawab Fidai Khan.—*Führer : Archæological Survey, 224.*]

243. **Saharanpur: Worship of Sanichara or Saturn.**—The dread of the ill-omened planet Saturn prevails widely here. Many people keep in their houses a copper or more often an iron plate with an image of the planet drawn on it and worship it on Saturdays, with an offering of red lead and oil. This image is always kept carefully covered up, for woe to the unfortunate wretch who looks it straight in the face. The offerings thus made are made over to a Dakaut Bráhman.

The following is a favourite song sung in the course of this worship:—

Kasyapa sut ke puta ki, mahima aparampár.
Tin netra, sat, jivha, bhuja Sani ko chár,
We karte amrit ka bhojan, aur tel ashnán.
Bandhe shástra au pahir ke jáma mahitke par aswár,
Chha jojan tatha denhi ítna Sani ka vistár.

"The powers of the son of the son of Kasypa are infinite. He has three eyes, seven tongues, and four arms. He feeds on nectar and bathes-in-oil. He wears arms and a robe. He rides on a she-buffalo. His body is forty-eight miles round."

Those who worship Sanischar worship at the Bráhma who lives at the foot of the pípal tree. This worship is done by Dakaut Bráhmans under a pípal tree. They are much respected by the lower classes of Hindus in this part of the country.—*W. Crooke.*

ANTHROPOLOGY.

244. **Western Districts, N.-W. P.—Marriage Ceremonies in high caste families.**—On the wedding day the barber bathes the bridegroom and dresses him. The garments of the bridegroom are always red. Whatever his age may be the bridegroom is made to wear jewels (*gahna*). His hands are dyed with *mehdi* or myrtle. To his eyes lamp black is applied by his elder brother's wife. She gets a reward for this. The father's sister makes yellow marks on his forehead and all over his face, and she also is given a reward. The bridegroom's sister moves a lamp containing five wicks over his head and she also gets a reward from him. She then moves over his head mustard seed, chillies, and salt. The gardener throws round the neck of the bridegroom garlands of flowers which are long enough to touch the feet. The family priests put a crown on the head of the bridegroom, and they are also given a reward. This crown is called (*maur*). The sister's husband ties round the waist of the bridegroom a sword, and in default of a sword they tie a piece of iron. The barber helps the bridegroom in putting on his shoes and gets a reward for this service. After this the bridegroom's brother, who is similarly dressed, and the bride both ride on asses and then on horses. When they ride off the mother sits sadly and says to the bride: "I brought you up on my milk, Where are you going and leaving me? First of all give me the price of the milk and then go where you will; otherwise I shall throw myself into a well." The mother then sits at the well side with her legs suspended over the brink. The bridegroom walks round the well and at the end of each circuit gives the mother a piece of reed (*sink*). His mother throws it into the well. At the end of the seventh circuit he makes over to her some money and jewels and tries to raise his mother saying: "There is the price for the milk of the cow and buffalo, but there is no price for that of the mother. I am going to bring a maid servant for you." Then the mother rises. The bride's sister then worships the feet of the horse. She ties some red thread to the mane of the horse and puts a garland on its head and covers its body with a cloth. Then she sings songs in praise of the horse. She puts different kinds of food before it. When the bridegroom intends to ride on, the bridegroom's sister and her husband take hold of the rein of the horse and prevent it from moving. The bridegroom makes them a present of money and garments, and then they let it go. The priest also does the same thing, and he is also given a reward. Then the relatives of the bridegroom move over the head of the bridegroom rupees, pice and gold mohurs, etc., and give them to the barber. Then the bridegroom goes to the father-in-law's house.

At the night of the wedding day the *Jagaran* ceremony is performed. This *Jagaran* ceremony is called technically "*Kuhaya Naktora*." This ceremony consists in the mother-in-law of the bridegroom assuming the guise of the bride and the priest's wife that of the bridegroom. They perform all the ceremonies of the marriage from the beginning to the end. Women sing and dance. Then the mother-in-law in the garb of the bride, and the priest's wife in that of the bridegroom, with all the women of the neighbourhood, go in a procession about the streets of the city or village. They cut jokes with every man that they meet with as they go along. They return home. Here all the women put on glass bangles. Then the priest's wife gives a name to the bride, and putting in an earthen pot betel-nut, turmeric, cloves, and cocoa, whispers the bride's adopted name into the pot. Then the women of the bride's household make heads of green barley and of all kinds of fruits. This head of fruits weighs generally from 1¼ to 11 sears. Upon the four heads gold leaves are stuck. Then the unmarried girls who help in making the heads are given a present by the female relatives of the bride. Then they make portraits of male animals on the walls of the house. The portraits of female animals are strictly forbidden on such occasions.

When the women of the house hear that the procession is approaching, they make images on the ground from the door of the house to the house dedicated to clan or household deities in the innermost apartment of the house, and put small vessels of earth on both sides of the images. Then the women, putting in a basket the necessary articles for the worship, go to the bride. Then taking the bride with them and the bridegroom also, they take the pair outside the village. There they make images of the clan deities or village deities on the ground and get them worshipped by the bridegroom and the bride. Then the bride puts on the clothes of marriage (*Vyah ke jore*), and the corners of the garments of the bridegroom and the bride are tied together. Then a pitcher full of water is put on the head of the bride. Below the pitcher is put a bundle of thread and twigs of mango. They in this state walk at the head of the procession, and the women follow them singing songs. When they arrive at the door of the house the mother of the bridegroom comes out of the house in a male dress and moves over the heads of the pair a lamp with five wicks (*árti harti hai*). This done, she throws round the neck of the bride the garlands of flower and fruits that were made a little before. Then she moves water over the head of the pair and drink seven gulps (*ghunt*). Then the bride's mother smears the palms of the bride's hand with turmeric, and then causes her to make seven stamps with it on both of her cheeks. Then the pair go by the same way, on both sides of which are put small earthen pots full of water, to the house of the family deities (*Kuladeva*). The bridegroom, on his way to the family god's house, brakes the small earthen pots as he goes along. When the pair reach the family temple the priest's wife and unmarried girls of the neighbourhood stand at the door of the room and refuse to let the pair enter unless given some reward in money, jewels or garments. In the family temple all the necessary articles of the household are kept. First of all the pair worship the family deity, and then the bride is made to touch one by one the articles placed in the house. The bride gives as gifts to the priest's wife some of the articles put in the temple. Then the bridegroom is seated on a plank (*takhta*), and before him sits a woman and then again a boy of 16 or 17 years of age, and then again a woman. In this way several men and women sit in a row. The bridegroom is seated on a plank, and before him sits the bride. In her lap the bride takes an infant at this time. On both sides of the bride stands a woman, both of whom twist a thread sevenfold. Then they shake the thread and repeat some mantras. Then this thread is dyed with turmeric, and all the persons present touch it and pronounce blessings upon the bride. Then the bridegroom puts this thread, now made into a garland, round the neck of the bride. Then all stand up. The relatives of the bride feed her on sweetened rice (*mitha bhat*) and when they look at her face make presents of money and jewels to her. Then all touch the bride and put money at her feet. All this becomes the property of the bridegroom's mother. Then the examination of the bride takes place, that is to say, the bride is made to cook cakes (*púri*), rice, bread, and so on. If the bride be an infant, she only touches the cooking utensils and others cook for her. Those who partake of this meal make some present to the bride. The next morning women take the bride to the temple of Devi. The gardener or *máli*, who is generally the priest of the Devi temple makes two sticks of *mehdi* and gives one to each of the pair, the bridegroom and the bride. Both beat each other with this stick. Then the bride gets her stick touched by each of her relatives. Each of her relatives gives her some present. At night the priest makes the bride and the bridegroom worship some god and makes them offer burnt offerings. The priest gets some present on this occasion. Then the women of the household as well as the neighbourhood take the bridegroom and the bride to the clan or family god's temple (*Deoghar*). The elder brother's wife of the bridegroom sets a cot in the house and spreads bedding on it. She makes the bridegroom and the bride sit on the cot. Then the women come out of the house and shut up the door of the house. After some time they again open the door and sing. The bride when she comes out touches the feet of her mother-in-law and other women.

Then the bride's mother goes with other women to see the bridegroom's mother. When she reaches the bridegroom's house she gives garments and garlands of dyed thread to the bride and the bridegroom and also sweetmeat and fruits. Then the women who accompany the bride's mother pour oil in the corners of the portico of the bridegroom's house. Then in a large room the women of both the parties sit opposite to one another. In the middle the bridegroom and the bride sit together. Then the barber's wife puts red lead on the parting of hair of all the women present except those who are widows. The barber's wife gets presents from both the parties. At the same time two garments are dyed thread. These wet garments are worn by the bride's mother as well as the bridegroom's. Then the bride's mother throws a garland of fruits around the neck of the bridegroom's mother and *vice versâ*. Then they put sweetmeat into parts of the garment covering the breast. Then they embrace each other. After this they abuse each other by way of a joke. Then the bride's mother puts 25 rupees or any multiple of it on the feet of the bridegroom's mother. The women of the bride's party pour red water on the women of the bridegroom's party. Then betel and perfumes are distributed among the women present. When the bride's mother intends to return to her house, the bridegroom's mother takes hold of her garment and makes her give presents in money, cloth, jewels, etc., to all the members of her family. The following day the bridegroom's mother in the same way goes over to the bride's house and the ceremonies just described are performed there. Then the bridegroom's mother takes the bride and the bridegroom to her home.

(Translated from the *Arya Darpan*, Shahjahanpur, Vol. IV, No. 47, 1881.)

---

245. **Further proofs of the identity of Bhang and Soma.**—In the *Rig Veda*, Bhanga is an epithet of Soma. As hemp it appears for the first time in the *Arthara Veda*.

Herodotus was acquainted with hemp, both wild and cultivated, in the country of the Scyths who intoxicated themselves with the fumes.

The Sanscrit term for hemp was bhanga, the Zend or Indo-Ipanian word bhanga.

It was by both peoples used not only as a drink but thought of as a god who grants abundance of wealth and prosperity, and is most intimately connected with the religious cults of both peoples.

It was Yam Brahmanah Vidhu that which the priests know.

(See Schrader.—*Prehistoric Antiquities of Aryan peoples.*—J. Cockburn.)

246. **Taboos among the Pankti Sarwariya Brahmans.**—The Pankti are the highest class of Sarwariya Bráhmans. They are distinguished from other Bráhmans by various taboos. Thus, for instance, they will not eat *pakki* or food cooked in butter from Khatris as other Bráhmans will do. Their women, whether rich or poor, are not allowed to touch the grindstone, pestle or mortar. This rule does not apply to the ordinary Sarwariya Bráhmans.—*Pándit Rám Gharíb Chaubé.*

About these Pankti Bráhmans, it may also be noted that among them women and girls are more valued than men and boys, as by means of girls they are able to practise hypergamy and thus rise in the social scale. Thus a Pankti Bráhman who marries into a lower grade is regarded as degraded. He will not be allowed to keep company in the assembly with a regular Pankti who has married in his own grade, and he cannot marry his daughter to a real Pankti. But this stain may be removed by giving a certain number of feasts to the brethren and then the bar to intermarriage is removed. But this is not the case with a son and a degraded Pankti can never marry his son, to a Pankti girl of pure blood. Thus among the Pankti Bráhmans, women are valued and held in high respect, and if a man who marries into a pure Pankti family, which, by the way are very uncommon, and illtreats his wife he is boycotted among the community and finds it very difficult to get a pure bred girl as a bride for his son.—*W. Crooke.*

In connection with the same question, Pándit Rám Gharíb Chaubé, who is himself a Pankti Sarwariya Bráhman, says that all of them eat *kachchi* or food cooked without butter among themselves indiscriminately, without paying any regard to the Gotras. Among other Sarwariya Bráhmans only those of the same Gotra and group (*dik*) eat *kachchi* together. But Pankti Bráhmans simply ignore such details. The same is the case with the Sakadwípi Bráhmans who all eat together without regard to Gotra or group. Can any explain the cause of these divergent practices? He also adds that if you are a Bráhman and by any chance become excommunicated, if you are supported by even one Pankti Bráhman who will eat *pakki* cooked by you, all stain is removed, and the bar against marrying your daughters is at once removed.

247. **The Telraja order of Mendicants.**—The beggars known as Telrája take their name from their habit of begging oil from Hindú women, who have only one son and then putting the oil on their clothes. In Sahāranpur some of them gave the following account of themselves:—The sect was it is said, founded by one Mán Chandra who was, Rájá of Kangra. It is told of him that once he was suddenly stricken with leprosy and lost the beauty for which he was formerly celebrated. He called in all sorts of physicians, but to no avail. His family were worshippers of the goddess Juálamukhi Devi, and in their distress they visited her shrine. When they remained there some days fasting and absorbed in devotion to the goddess, she finally took pity on them. She spoke to them from the shrine and told them that it was not through her that this misfortune had befallen the Rájá, but that it was the result of his sins in a former life. She directed him, if he desired, to be free from his disease, to take off his royal robes and become an ascetic and to beg from Hindú women whose sons and husbands were living, a little oil which he was to rub on his clothes and body. He was in this way to live the life of a beggar for twelve years, when he would succeed in expiating his sin and obtain deliverance.

The Rájá obeyed the order of the goddess, and by this course of penance was healed from his leprosy after twelve years. Then he returned to his capital Kangra and founded the Telrája order of beggars. The first proselyte was a Bráhman named Sri Chandra.

The mode of initiation is very simple. When any one wishes to join them, the guru invites the members of the order and the initiate has to pay a fee of five rupees, or any multiple of that sum, and entertains the brotherhood on what is known as Kara Prasád, or the Halwa sweetmeat. He then bathes and puts on clean clothes, and a cup of sherbet is prepared which is sanctified by the guru blowing over it and reciting some special mantras. Then he takes a sip of it. Before tasting it, he sprinkles a few drops over the initiate. Then the initiate drinks of the cup and by this becomes a member of the sect. He remains with the guru for six months and is then allowed to go abroad and beg. He always asks for oil with which he rubs his body and clothes. He may also take alms of money and grain.

Some of them are Sikhs and some Hindús, and have as much belief in Guru Nának as in the ordinary Hindu gods. But their chief object of worship is Juálamukhi Devi of Kangra. When they die they are cremated in the Hindú fashion, and the other disciples perform the ordinary Hindú Sraddha. Some of them are family men (*grihastha*) and some pure mendicants. The only outer sign of their sect is that their clothes and bodies are smeared with oil. There appear to be some of them in the Panjáb, but Mr. Ibbetson does not notice them.—*W. Crooke.*

248. **Maternal Uncle : position of.**—It may be worth noticing that when a high caste Hindu goes to arrange the marriage of his daughter, he measures the position of a youth suggested as the bridegroom by the position of his maternal uncle (*mamu*). Of course the position of other relatives is also taken into account, but not so much as those on the mother's side.—*W. Crooke.*

265450B

FOLKTALES.

249. Shekh Chilli and the Camel Man.—Shekh Chilli once asked his mother to tell him how to get to his father-in-law's house, where his wife was staying. She said : " My son, you have only to follow your nose." So he went on quite straight, and at last ran his head against a tree. He was sure that he ought not to turn, so he climbed up the tree. Then he did not know how to get down, but at last a camel man passed that way and the Shekh asked him to help him. The camel man agreed, and brought up his camel close under the tree and told the Shekh to hang down so that he might catch him by the waist. Suddenly the camel moved away and left them both dangling. Then the Shekh called out : " Friend, sing something."

The camel man said : " All right, if you will clap your hands." So the camel man sang and the Shekh clapped his hand, and then both of them fell down from the tree, and the Shekh broke his arm and the camel man broke his leg. The camel man asked the Shekh to bring some oil to rub his leg. The *banya* gave him the oil, and then the Shekh asked for the handsel. But the cup would hold no more, so the Shekh upset the oil out of the cup, and turning up the hollow bottom said, " Well, give it to me in this."

But when he came back and showed the camel man what a good bargain he had made the camel man said : " You are certainly the biggest fool I ever saw in my life."

[The vessel was the native *katord*, which has a hollow bottom used as a stand like our tea cups.]

(A folktale told by Farzand Ali of Bareilly.)

250. Akbar and his Son-in-law.—One day Akbar and Birbal went out hunting, and Akbar saw a crooked tree : so he said to Birbal : " Why is that tree crocked ? Birbal answered : " This tree is crooked because it is the son-in-law of all the trees of the forest." " And what else is always crooked ? " asked Akbar. Birbal answered : " The tail of a dog and a son-in-law are always crooked." (*Tircha*—cunning or cranky.) Akbar asked : " Is my son-in-law also crooked ? " " Yes, O King," replied Birbal. " Then have him crucified," said Akbar.

A few days after Birbal had three crosses made —one of gold, one of silver, and one of iron. When Akbar saw them he asked for whom they were intended, and Birbal answered : " Your Majesty ! One of them is for your Majesty, one is for me, and one is for your Majesty's son-in-law."

" And why are we to be executed," asked Akbar.

" Because," said Birbal, " We are all the sons-in-law of some one." Akbar laughed and said : " Well, you may let my son-in-law alone for the present."

(A folktale told by Akbar Shah, Manjhi, of Manbassa, Dudhi, Mirzapur.)

251. The Reading of Hearts.—Akbar once asked Birbal : " What is your opinion of me ? " Birbal, replied : " I have the same opinion of you which you have of me; because hearts read hearts." Akbar said : " This is impossible." But Birbal said, " Come for a walk in the city and I will prove it to you." As they were going along they saw a miserable old woman begging. Akbar said : " I *do* pity this poor creature. Cannot you, in so great a kingdom as this, make some provision for her by which she may pass her last days in comfort ? " Birbal asked Akbar to stop, and going up to the old woman said : " Old woman, do you not know that Akbar Bádsháh is dead ? " When she heard this she began to weep and said : " Alas ! alas ! how shall I now pass my days ? It was by his virtue that I gained my daily bread, and now that he is gone I must starve." Birbal came back to Akbar and said : " Now your Majesty sees that the old woman loves you because you feel for her." They went on a little further in the bázár and saw a Sewara faqír begging, and as he beat on his stick he was abusing a banker and extorting alms. When Akbar saw him he said : " Birbal, these wretches are the curse of the land. Why do you not make a law to repress them ? " Birbal asked Akbar to stop, and going up to the faqír said : " O Bábá ! Do you not know that Akbar Bádsháh is dead ? " The faqír cursed him and said : " May his soul rest in the lowest hell ! Did he ever give me a pice ? " Now said Birbal, " Your Majesty sees that this man hates you because you do not feel for him. Do not hearts read hearts ? " Akbar said : " I am convinced."

(A folktale told by Shyám Lal, Orderly of Etah.)

252. The Wise Son of the Weaver.—Once upon a time while a weaver boy was asleep, he saw in a dream that the daughter of the King of Rúm was sleeping beside him and on the other side the daughter of the King of Delhi. At this he laughed in his sleep, and when his mother heard this she asked him why he was laughing. He could not tell, so they took him to the Kotwál and when he, too, could not find out the cause of his laughter, he was brought before the King of Delhi, in which city he was living. The king asked him why he laughed, and when he gave no answer the king ordered that he should be buried up to his neck where the three roads meet, and the sentence was carried out at once. Just at the time the princess happened to be passing by, and when she saw him she said: "Why are you bringing all this trouble upon yourself? Why do you not tell the king the cause of your laughter?" "I am quite happy here," he said; "you need not fret about me."

The princess went away, and after a few days the King of Rúm sent two images to the King of Delhi with a message that if he could not distinguish which of them was solid and which was hollow he would invade his dominions. The King of Delhi was much distressed at this message, and that evening the princess passed by where the weaver was buried. She said: "Why don't you tell me the cause of your laughter and I will get you released." "Do not distress yourself for me" he answered. She went to her father and said: "Father, why have you buried this weaver? He seems to be a youth of sense." "Well," said the king," let him distinguish between the two images and I will release him."

At the same time he made proclamation in the city that if any one could solve the problem, he would give his daughter to wife and half his kingdom. The princess went again to the weaver and told him of all her father's trouble. He said: "This is an easy matter, and I can solve it easily." She went to the king and got the weaver brought to court. He was dressed in good clothes and brought before the king, and when he was shown the images he called for a straw and, finding a minute crack in the back of one of them, he put in the straw and thereby discovered which was solid and which hollow. So the King of Delhi wrote the answer to the King of Rúm, who was pleased, and the King of Delhi married his daughter to the weaver. Some time after the King of Rúm wrote to the King of Delhi calling on him to pay some arrears of tribute. The King of Delhi was perplexed, but his son-in-law said: "Do not be anxious. I will recover the money, or get it remitted by the King of Rúm." The King gave him five hundred men and he set out for Rúm. Then the astrologer of the King of Rúm announced to him that a thief was entering his dominions. The King of Rúm consulted the King of Delhi as to what should be done, and the King of Delhi advised him to send a thousand men to capture him. The weaver was also an astrologer, and knew that this army was coming against him: so he sent a letter to his father-in-law asking for a reinforcement of five hundred men, who were sent at once. The astrologer of the King of Rúm informed his master of this, and he sent a force of one thousand men in addition. When the weaver knew of this he sent back seven hundred and fifty of his men, and with the remainder concealed himself so that the General of the King of Rúm failed to catch him.

The weaver then came to the city of Rúm by himself and put up at the hut of a faqir. The astrologer told his master of his arrival and the King sent the Kotwál to search for him. The weaver came to where a man was hanging on the gallows, and he got up in the place of the corpse and arranged the rope so that he should not be strangled. The astrologer took the king to the place and showed him the thief. The king would not believe that he was not dead and had the rope untied from his neck. He fell down like a corpse and when the astrologer burned his leg with a piece of wood, even then he would not speak. At last the astologer said: "He will never speak until some reward is offered to him." The king said: "If he speaks I will grant him any reward he asks." The weaver then got up at once and said: "I ask no other reward but that the King of Delhi may be exempted from tribute."

The King was much pleased to see his faithfulness to his master and forgave him the tribute, and giving him his daughter in marriage sent him home with many horses and elephants. The King of Delhi made him ruler of half his kingdom, and he lived for many years in the utmost happiness with his two wives.

(A folktale told by Dwarika Prasad, a Brahman cultivator of Bithalpur, Pargana Kariyát Shikar, Mirzapur.)

[The bride seen in a dream is common in folktales, *c. g.*, *Kathá Sarit Ságara* (Tawney Trans.) II, 365. This tale is rather mixed. It is not quite clear how the incident of the images is arranged and the latter part diverges into something like the Master Thief cycle.]

253. **Why the boy laughed.**—Once upon a time the Emperor of Rúm was asleep in his palace with the Empress beside him and a little boy, the son of one of his slaves, at his feet. The boy had a dream, and he thought that the daughter of the King of Balkh was shampooing his feet, while the daughter of the Emperor of Rúm was standing beside him with water in a golden bowl. When he woke he began to laugh, and the Emperor asked him the cause of his laughter. But he would not tell, and the Emperor was so angry that he ordered him to be hanged. But when he prayed for mercy the emperor contented himself with putting him in a dungeon under a guard.

Some time after the King of Balkh sent three mares to the Emperor, and with them came a letter to the effect that if he could not give an answer his kingdom would be taken from him. The Emperor knew not how to answer and was in despair. All his courtiers tried to solve the question, but in vain. At last the boy offered to give an answer, and he had the three mares drawn up beside the palace wall. He sent a *bhishti* to the roof of the palace and told him to drop some water on them. Now the three mares were daughter, mother, and grandmother. When the water fell on the oldest of the three she jumped only fifteen paces, her daughter jumped twenty, and the foal bounded into the air and gallopped round the palace; so the boy explained the relationship of the three, and the Emperor was much pleased, and sent the right answer to the King of Balkh.

Then the King of Balkh sent with a similar letter three sticks and ordered the Emperor to say what relation they bore to each other. The boy was sent for, and as the three sticks were exactly the same in appearance it was hard to identify them. But the boy had them placed in a vessel of water. One stick sank to the bottom at once, and the boy said: "This comes from the root of the tree." The second sank half way, and he said: "This came from the middle of the tree." The third floated on the top, and he said: "This comes from the upper branch." And so it was; and the King of Balkh had to accept the answer.

Then the King of Balkh wrote to the Emperor to say that he had a monkey the wisest in the world, and if he could not find some one to defeat the monkey he must be his servant. So the boy was sent to Balkh to contend with the monkey in wisdom. When he came there he asked what fruits grew in that land, and they told him that all fruits, except the orange, were to be found there. So the boy got an orange, and when he came before the King the monkey said: "If you do not give me the fruit I ask for you are beaten." "The monkey asked for an orange, and the boy gave it to him, and the monkey had to admit that the boy was wiser than he. The King of Balkh was so delighted with the wisdom of the boy that he gave him his daughter in marriage.

The boy then returned to Rúm with a great equipage, and the Emperor thinking that this was some foreign King who had invaded his dominions went out to meet him. But the boy sent him a message to say that he was his servant who had won the daughter of the King of Balkh as his wife. The Emperor was so pleased with him that he built a palace for him and married him to his daughter. So the daughter of the king of Balkh used to shampoo his feet and the daughter of the Emperor of Rúm used to bring him water in a golden bowl. Then the boy said to the Emperor: "My dream is now fulfilled, and this is the reason of my laughter."

(Told by Mathura Prasad, Káyasth, and recorded by Abul Hasan Khan, a Teacher of the Karaili Village School, Pilibhit District.)

[The above is another and a rather better version of the same story.—Ed.]

254. **The Princess and the Thieves.**—There was once a Rájá who was losing daily a bag of gold from his treasury. The guards became aware of this, and as they feared dismissal they thought it better to res asked the reason, and ed them to go, and app places, and from that treasury himself.

The princess, hearin station in the room w At midnight the thie that something was wr man should go alone wall. When he put h off his head. A second tance, and she cut off h she beheaded all the th only one eye, and was by going in. But he wh and said: "It is you, panions. Some day I When he went awa the heads in a sheet a fore the Rájá. When who had killed them, soldiers claimed the c princess told how she Rájá was much please true daughter of a Ráj

The same night the the private room of th his compainions, and slept carried her off i much terrified, but as t ing fig tree she caugh swung herself up. W distance the one-eyed The bed seems lighter when they looked the cess. So they came b her perched in the br down. She said: "I that when a man is fo the one-eyed thief clim he put out his tongu off with a knife and the palace.

That night she waite they broke through the his head she cut off help and a second put likewise with him, and cession. They were a misfortune, and agree the city. The princ morning got herself u to the place where the with her a full sér of into the garden cried physician. Who wan her if she knew the tr said that she knew i "my medicine is so po dose remains sensele mind that," said they, " provided you cure us." Then she put some pounded glass into the nose of each of them, and they all immediately expired. She took all their property, which she divided among the poor, and then returned to the palace.

(A folktale told by Ramchandra, student, Mirzapur.)

255. **The Contest of Good and Evil.**—The two brothers Neki and Badi (Good and Evil) were one day disputing. Neki said : " The result of good is good and of evil evil." Badi denied this, so they agreed to appoint an arbitrator, and whichever of them was defeated was to have his hands and feet cut off. When they had gone some distance they saw a ním tree and Badi said : " Let us refer our case to the tree. Many travellers sit daily beneath its shade, and it must have wide experience." When they referred the case to the ním tree it said : " In my opinion the result of good is evil and of evil good, because everyone sits under my shade and they are refreshed ; but when they are going away one says, ' What excellent fire-wood this old tree would make ; ' and another says, ' I will come some day soon and cut it down to make a box.' Thus do they return me evil for good."

When Badi heard the judgment of the ním tree, he promptly cut off Neki's hands and feet and left him there. In his agony he rolled himself to a well close by and threw himself in. Now in that well there was a couch and on each of its legs sat a Deo. They used to go out in search of food and meet in the well at midnight. That night, when they met, Neki heard them talking. They were asking each other where they had been and what they had seen. One Deo said : " Brothers ! I have seen to-day a field the clay of which has this virtue, that it can restore the limbs of a cripple." The second said : " I have seen a treasure which is buried in such and such a place. I watch it all night long and leave it during the day when there is no danger of any one touching it." The fourth Deo said : " The Rájá of this land is sick unto death. There is no man in the world who knows that if he were to bring a he-goat from such and such a village and sacrifice it and pour a drop of the blood on the Rájá he would recover."

Neki heard what the Deos were saying, and soon after a man came to the well and helped him out and then on promise of a reward took him on his shoulders to the field of which the Deo had spoken. When he touched the earth of the field his limbs were restored whole as before. Then he dug up the treasure and cured the Rájá by means of the goat as the Deo had said. The Rájá was so pleased that he gave him half his ráj. Some time after Badi happened to come to the city where Neki ruled, and when he saw his prosperity he was forced to admit that the fruit of good is good and the fruit of evil is evil.

(A folktale told by Surya Bala Sukl, village accountant, Mirzapur.)

[This corresponds in some ways with the well-known story of the Bráhman and the Lion, for which see Clouston: *Group of Eastern Romances*, 254 and note 531. But in the main it corresponds with the famous cycle of the "Good Man and the Bad Man," for which see Clouston : *Popular Tales and Fictions*, I., 249 *sqq.*]

256. **The Fortunate Wood-cutter.**—There were once two boys who earned a poor living by cutting wood in the jungle. One day they went out together and agreed to meet under a large banyan tree. The younger brother finished his work first, and when he came to the tree he saw a Sádhu sitting there. He bowed at his feet and the Sádhu blessed him and said : " My son, you shall be married to-day to the Kúní of Singaldíp."

Saying this he disappeared and when the boy went to his load of wood he saw a very pretty bird perched upon it which had an iron chain fixed to its leg so long that it trailed on the ground. The boy took hold of the chain, and the moment he did so the bird flew away with him to Singaldíp, and leaving him there, disappeared. He walked along, and suddenly saw a wedding procession (*bárát*) passing by. The bridegroom who was going to be married was not only lame but blind of an eye, and his father thought to himself :

" If the Rájá of Singaldíp sees that the bridegroom is lame and blind of an eye he will never marry his daughter to him. It would be better for me to hire a boy and let him act the part of the groom at the wedding, and when it is all over he can go away and my son will have his wife." He told his plan to the clansmen who were with him and they approved. Just then they met the woodcutter and asked him who he was and where he was going. When he told them that his home was in Jambudíp they were much pleased, because they thought that, being a stranger, he would keep the secret. So they told him their plan and he agreed to go with them. They dressed him in the wedding robe and brought him before the Rájá. All the people assembled, and the marriage was duly performed. Then the bride and bridegroom were sent into the marriage chamber (*kohbar*). When they were together the bride was very happy, but the bridegroom was in low spirits. She asked him what was the matter and he answered : " How can I admire your beauty when I am starving ? " She said : " What do you mean ? Thousands were fed here to-day, and were you, the Rájá's son-in-law, alone left to starve ? " Then he told her the whole story, which she wrote down, and then out of her box of dolls she took some sweetmeats which she gave him and they lay down to sleep.

In the morning he went to bathe, and there he saw the same bird with the chain hanging to its leg.

He recognised the bird and took hold of the chain, when the bird in a moment flew away with him and brought him back to the jungle where he was before. Then it disappeared. He was overcome by grief, but putting off his wedding dress, he shut it up in an earthen pot and buried it in a dung heap behind his house. When he came back he said to his mother: "Mother I have been all night in a jungle so dense that no one ever saw it even in his dreams."

When the princess saw that it was getting late and that her husband did not return she was plunged in grief and told her mother, and her mother told the Rájá. For five years the princess never ceased searching for him but in vain. At last she gave notice that she would reward any one who could tell the best stories. Many came and told her stories, but she got no trace. Finally she asked her father to allow her to travel in search of him, and she assumed the dress of a prince and started. After many days she came to Jambudíp where the woodcutter lived. One day the woodcutter heard that this prince was in search of stories. He went to her and told her his own tale. Then with tears in her eyes she embraced him and said: " You are my dear husband for whom I have been searching so many years, but I want more proof."

He went and dug up the pot which contained his wedding robe which, when she saw, she was convinced. She took her husband home with her and told her father how she had found him. He received him gladly, and after he had been there some days loaded him with wealth, horses, elephants, and sepoys and sent him home with his wife and they enjoyed many years of happiness.

May Parameswar restore the fate of all of us as he restored that of them!

(A folktale told by Ramanandan Lal, village accountant of Kon, Mirzapur.)

[The sudden disappearance of the bridegroom just after the wedding is rather like Nur-al-din Ali and his son.—*Arabian Nights*, Lady Burton's Edition I., 172, *sqq*. The bird which carries him off is akin to the Rukh of Sindbad.

257. **The Dhobi and his Ass.**—There was once a dhobi who had four asses: one of them he called Bhura or "the brown one," the second Khaira or "reddish," the third Lila or "blue," the fourth Mangala "the lucky one." One evening Mangala strayed away and the dhobi began to consult with his wife about it.

"You had better go and look for him at once," said she. "But take care a tiger does not catch you."

"I don't mind a tiger," he answered, "I am more afraid of a wetting (*tapakwa*)."

Just then, it so happened, that a tiger had been wandering about, and when he heard the dhobi speak of *tapakwa*, he thought that it must be some demon or other. So the dhobi went into his stable, and in the dark saw some animal which he thought was one of his asses; so he took a bludgeon, and mounting him started off in search of his missing ass. All the night he went on beating the tiger and rode all over the country on his back. When the dawn began to break he found that it was a tiger he had been riding; so he got green with fright and seeing a cave close by jumped off his back and ran in to save his life.

The tiger was only too happy to escape; so he went on till he met a hare, and to him he told all he had suffered at the hands of the dreaded *tapakwa*. The hare promised to revenge him; so he called all the other hares, and they all went to the cave into which the dhobi had made his escape. They began to consult, and at last the king of the hares said:—

"Whichever of us has the longest tail must thrust it inside the cave to see what this *tapakwa* really is."

No sooner did the hare thrust his tail inside the cave, than the dhobi pulled it out by the roots, and all the hares ran away in terror.

The tiger, too, ran away into the jungle, and there he came across Mangala, the missing ass.

"Who are you?" asked the ass.

"I am the tiger," he replied.

"Well, if you are I am one and a quarter (*sawaiya*)."

So they went on together. Soon they came into a river and the ass fell in. The tiger caught him by the neck and pulled him out.

"What do you mean by interfering with me asked the ass indignantly."

"I only went into the water to catch some fish."

The tiger was so astonished that he ran away, and just then up came the dhobi and drove Mangala before him to the stable.

(A folktale told by Siu Narayan, Master of the Tahsil School, Kalpi, Jalaun District.)

258. **The Pillars of the Sky.**—Once upon a time Akbar said to Birbal: "My palace is supported on pillars of wood and stone, but on what does the sky rest?"

Birbal answered: "The sky, too, is supported on columns."

"Why then do we not see them," asked the king.

Birbal replied: "Give me money and time and I will show them to your majesty."

So the king gave Birbal a lakh of rupees and six months' leave, and he started on his travels through the world. He went toward the south and whenever he came to a city he used to shout out in the streets; "Whoever will stand five hundred blows of a shoe to him will I give five hundred rupees reward."

But no man would accept the condition. At last a man hearing his cry came out and said : " Give me five hundred shoe blows, and I will give you five hundred rupees." And then and there he produced the money.

Birbal said : " You will die after one hundred blows, and who is to bear the remainder ? "

" My wife," he answered.

" But she must be weaker than you and fifty blows will kill her."

" Then my son will bear the rest."

" And if he die too ? "

" Then my daughter, who is all I have, will stand the rest, for I know you come in the name of Allah and the Emperor, and their wishes are a law unto me. "

Akbar, when he heard the devotion of the man, was astonished.

" Such, your majesty, are the pillars on which the heavens rest. "

(A tale of Akbar and Birbal told by Bechau Kasera of Mirzapur.)

259. **A tale of Akbar and Birbal.**—Akbar once said to Birbal : " If you are such a wise man, what must your father be. Let me see him." Now Birbal's father was an ignorant villager, and he feared that he would be disgraced before the court. So he told his father not to answer a single question. When the old man appeared Akbar said : " How are you ? " But he answered not a word, and though Akbar asked him many questions he made no reply. Enraged at this Akbar said to Birbal : " How should one deal with an idiot ? " " When a person comes before an idiot, your majesty," was his answer, " the best way is to hold one's tongue."

(Told by Pándit Janardan Joshi.)

260. **The Man who ate Human Flesh.**—A patient once went to a physician to be treated.

" The only thing which will do you good," said he, " is to eat the flesh of a man."

Some days after the physician met his patient and found him quite restored to health. He asked him where he got the human flesh, and when the physician got the address of the butcher he went and informed the king. The king, who was desirous of ascertaining the truth of the matter, dressed himself as a labourer and took service with the butcher who employed him in taking meat from his slaughter place to his shop.

One evening when the stock of human meat ran low the butcher called the king into the slaughterhouse, and drawing a long knife made preparaions to kill him. The king was in sore fear and said : " If you let me write a line to the king's wazir he will give you five thousand rupees, which is more than you will make by selling my flesh."

The butcher agreed, and the king wrote a note to his wazir, who came at once with a body of troops, arrested the rascally butcher and hanged him forthwith.

(A folktale told by Syam Lal of Srinagar, Hamirpur District)

[This story is interesting only as a reminiscence of the common belief that human flesh is useful as a remedy in various varieties of disease. See the Editor's *Introduction to Popular Religion and Folklore*, pp. 295, sqq.]

261. **The Fruit of Charity.**—The Lord Moses, on whom be peace, was once going into the court of the Almighty, when he met a poor man who said : " Find out what is to be my fate in this life." So Moses asked the Lord Almighty, and he answered : " His fate is to receive seven dirams in this life, of which he has received half already." So when Moses came out from the presence, he gave the poor man three and a half dirams and said : " This is awarded thee by the Lord Almighty."

With the money the poor man bought a cow and he used to give of her milk in charity ; so he prospered and his income came to be seven dirams daily. Then the Lord Moses came to the Almighty and said : " You promised this man seven dirams in his whole life and now he makes seven dirams daily. How is this ? "

" This," said the Lord Almighty, " is the fruit of charity."

(A folktale told by Abdullah Khan, Teacher of the Village School, Dholipur, Azamgarh District.)

262. **The Old Man's wisdom.**—It happened once that a rich man betrothed his daughter much against his will, and though he was very anxious to break the engagement he was bound by his word. Finally he sent a message to the bridegroom to come with exactly one hundred young men with him when he came to fetch the bride, and that if any of them failed to comply with the conditions imposed, the match should be broken off. The young man selected his companions, but had the wisdom to bring one old man with him concealed in a drum.

When they arrived at the bride's house her father produced a hundred goats and gave one to each of the party, and said that if each man could not eat his goat without leaving any scraps the marriage would not take place. They were all confounded until the bridegroom went and consulted the old man. " You must do this," he said ; " first kill one goat and serve out a little to each of your men ; then kill a second goat and act in the same way until all are consumed." In this way the condition was satisfied and he won his bride.—*Pándit Janardan Joshi.*

MISCELLANEA.

263. Assignation.—

*Kaune ghát bharali gagaryá, are sánwalyá?
Gharali to bhari! bhari dharalin tararwá, ho
     sánwalyá?
Johe chhuri bajud kai battyá, are sánwalyá?
Man to bhail sailáni, ho sánwalya;
K'hde ke mánge puri mithá, i!
Súte ke láli palangyá, are sánwalya?*

Translation.

Say, at what bank hast filled thine ewer, sweet maid?
Brimful thy pitcher! on the brink why laid?
Thy spouse! why tarry for that ruffling blade?
Abroad, I trow, thy roguish heart hath strayed;
Say, can these daintiest comfits tempt thee forth?
And a soft couch with crimson cloth arrayed?
—*R. Greeven.*

264. Snake-bite.—According to the Pandits if a man be bitten by a snake in the asterisms of Kritika, Mul, Magha, Vishakha, Aslesha, Rewati, or Ardra, even if Brahma himself come to his aid his life cannot be saved.—*Pándit Rám Gharib Chaubé.*

265. Shoes as scarers of Demons.—An old man near Rurkee tells me that near the present Ganges Canal there was a place which was infested by a most dangerous Mamduh, or Musalman ghost. When the Canal Officers wanted to excavate the place no one would dare to undertake the work. The officer was a European and proof against evil spirits; so he went to the place and kicked it thrice with his boot and then began to dig it up himself. No evil consequences ensued, so next day the labourers gained confidence and went on with the work.

On the shoe as a scarer of demons, see *Introduction to Popular Religion and Folklore*, 205.—*W. Crooke.*

266. Dog's dung: a popular Superstition.—Among low-caste people in the Eastern as well as the Western districts of the N.-W. P. it is believed that if anybody remove the dung of a dog he will get Pitambar or yellow silken cloth to wear. Low-caste people tell their children to remove it from near their houses generally under the same belief.—*Pándit Rám Gharib Chaubé.*

267. Ludhiana: Sacred Groves.—Sacred groves are to be found in some villages. The superstition about them generally is that they mark the spot where some holy man has become a *Siddh*, *i.e.*, has been absorbed in the deity, and no one of the villagers would dare to cut even a twig of the wood. *Faqirs* and other holy men are allowed to take what they want for their own use; but the people believe that death would follow any such sacrilege committed by themselves. The *Siddh* is, strangely enough, supposed to reside still in the grove.—*Mr. T. G. Walker, Settlement Report*, 63.

[The strangeness of the fact is much diminished by the evidence on this subject collected by Mr. Frazer in his *Golden Bough Passion.*—ED.]

268. Moonlight and the Bamboo.—When a native wants a *lathi* or bludgeon he always cuts it in the light half of the month. Bamboos cut in the dark fortnight are supposed to be always attacked by the Ghun or weevil.—*W. Crooke.*

269. What's in a name.—One man once asked another what his name was. He answered "Ahmaq"—"Fool." "What a remarkable name" he said. "If you like it so much you may have it for yourself," he replied.—*M. Ram Lall.*

270. A tale of four Fools.—Four fools were once praying in a mosque and in the bathing tank there happened to be a quantity of fish. One of them in the middle of his prayers noticed the fish and said: "How beautiful these fish look." To this the second answered "By speaking you have lost the merit of your prayers." The third said: "Your's is void also," to which the fourth replied: "thank God mine is safe." So when all of them found that their prayers were useless they began to curse each other.—*Akbar Ali.*

271. N.-W. P.: Omens of quarrels.—Passing salt from hand to hand, putting fire brought from two different places in one hearth, and striking one piece of iron against another are believed to cause quarrels in a family.—*Pándit Kashi Nath, Muzaffarnagar.*

272. The Merit of eating Betel.—It is generally believed that each of the ingredients which go to make up a packet (*bira*) of betel is the favourite of some diety and hence the eating of betel is one of the means of securing religious merit. Thus, the leaves of the pan or betel plant are favourites of Vishnu; the betel-nut is liked by Siva; the lime is loved by Agni Deota, the godling of fire; the catechu by Kamdeo or the deity of Love. The entire packet thus made up is loved by Bhagwan. Pious women make it a habit to offer every day a packet of betel and a pice to a Bráhman boy and if she drinks the water in which his feet were washed after he eats the betel, it removes the curse of barrenness and if she be a widow it ensures her hundreds of years of married bliss in the next life.—*Pándit Rám Gharib Chaubé.*

273. Rural Medicine.—There is a jungle fruit which is known to the east of the North-West Provinces as thanaila, because it is used by women as a remedy for swollen breasts (*than*); the peculiarity of it is that if the right breast be affected the fruit must be plucked by the right hand and for the left breast with the left hand. If this rule be not followed the application is sure to be ineffectual.—*Pándit Rám Gharib Chaubé.*

274. Muhammadan Omens.—The Hindi months are believed by the *Muhammadan Amils* (charmers) to be of 3 kinds of *effects*—'*Sabit*,' "*Mungalib*" and "*Zújusduin.*" *Sabit* are those in which all the new *wazifas* and *amals* should be commenced and they will be successful. *Mungalibs* are unlucky and no charm can have any effect during those months. *Zújusduin* are neither good nor bad. A charm may be successful or may not be if commenced in these months.

The following is the list of the months with their classes :—

Phagun, Jeth, Bhadon, Aghan	Sabit or lucky.
Baisakh, Sawan, Kartik, Magh	Mungalib or unlucky.
Chait, Asarh, Kuwar, Pús	Zújasdian.

It is also believed that if a charm is commenced in the first part of the month when the moon is rising it will never fail to meet success.—*Azizuddin Ahmed.*

275. Akbar and the old woman.—The Emperor Akbar once climbed up a very high minaret and when he got there he said : "I will give a great reward to any one who will jump down." A clever man who was there went home and brought his old grandmother, who was at the end of her days and said : "This person will jump down to please your Majesty." "Why should this poor old creature do this?" The Emperor asked. "If your Majesty wants to kill any one you may as well take a useless as a useful life." Akbar was abashed and dismissed him with a present.

(Told by Kashiram Misra of Bansi, Basti District.)

276. Barbers.—Proverbially barbers are said to know thirty-six tricks. What are these?—*M. Ram Lal.*

277. Gurgaon : Procedure in snake-bite.—In cases of snake-bite, one method is adopted for the charmer to repeat an invocation to Noah in Arabic twenty-one times by a well from which he then draws water, and washes with his right hand his feet and hands, and the water that remains after these ablutions is sprinkled on the patient, who also drinks some of it.—*Mr. F. C. Channing, Settlement Report, p. 37.*

278. Bengal : A charm to make a plant grow in the way it should go.—"The mind moves; the wind moves ; the plant moves! We invoke the aid of wind and mind unless they listen to the saying of the plant." You should say this and crack your fingers.—*(Adopted) : A Jungly Collector in the Week's News of August 25, '94.*

279. Relaxation of the restrictions as regards menstrual impurity.—The very stringent rules of isolation of women during the menstrual period do not apply to the bride or her mother or other relative without whose co-operation the business of a marriage cannot be conducted. They may touch during the time, occupied in the marriage, anything in the house and assist in all business connected with the marriage.—*Pándit Rám Gharib Chaubé.*

280. Elephant-drivers.—The chief cause of the ill-feeling which always exists between mahauts or elephant drivers and villagers is that the latter object to having sacred trees, such as the various varieties of the fig, cut for fodder and also say that any branch once touched by the mahaut's axe never sprouts again.—*W. Crooke.*

281. The Rainbow.—In Saharanpur both Hindus and Muhammadans believe that the rainbow is the fume from the hole of a snake.—*(Introduction to Popular Religion and Folklore, 276)—Pándit Rám Gharib Chaubé.*

282. A Faqir's Song.—

"*Jitnná chitt harám men,
Utná Hari men hoya ;
Cholá jáy Vaikunth men,
Bánha napakarai koya.*

"If anybody set his heart as much on Hari (Vishnu) as one sets on vice, he will go straight to heaven and none will prevent him from going into it.—*Pándit Rám Gharib Chaubé.*

283. Gurgaon : Cures for Scorpion bite.—You may choose among the following prescriptions : rub the place with the root of a certain onion-like plant : apply the ashes of the scorpion, or the dirt from a cow's ear, or hare droppings : or cook the scorpion in *ghi* and rub it on the bite.—*Mr. F. C. Channing, Settlement Report, p. 61.*

284. A Charm to protect the fields.—On Sunday go to the potter's house. Get an earthen vessel (*hándi*) made at the potter's wheel. Get it dry in the sun. Then put some shells (*kauris*) in the vessel. Shut up the mouth of it. Then take it to the fields. There bury it and burn incense (*gugal*) to it. This prevents harm being done to the fields. If anybody steal anything out of the fields the shells will strike at his heart like a bullet.—*Pándit Rám Gharib Chaubé.*

285. Straw in the mouth.—In the old times when a man was obliged to sell his son to slavery he used to take him to the market with a straw in his mouth as a sign that he was for sale. The most familiar instance of this is in the story of the Rájá Harish Chandra, who in Act V, Scene I of the drama disposed of his son in this way.—*Pándit Rám Gharib Chaubé.*

286. Muhammadans : visits.—Many Muhammadans put on clean clothes and visit their friends on Thursday evening. They say that from the evening of that day the blessing of Friday commences and lasts the whole night and the following day. Hence friends visit on the evening of Thursday.—*Qazi Shaikh Jalal-ud-din.*

287. Boring the ear as a remedy.—In the Western Districts of the North-West Provinces it is very common for men when attacked by any illness to get the ears bored and to wear in them a heavy earring (*báli*), this is considered a most effective remedy against various forms of swelling.—*Pándit Rám Gharib Chaubé.*

288. Chatarpur: the Cat.—A cat is not called by its name at night, but is called "*nakatíya*" as thieves are believed to run away at the sound of the word, hearing of which is an evil omen for them.—*Bhugwan Das, Budaun.*

The following incantation is repeated by Vishnuite religious mendicants to propitiate Hanumán so as to keep them safe from demons and evil spirits :—

Om bir bir Mahábir; begi chali áwo,
Jaisé Sri Rám Chandra ká káj sáryo taisé merá káj sáro;
Om chang chang kahrat kil;
Hast kil mast kil, sarb disi kil;
Dankini kil, sankini kil;
Om dargare kil, háté báté kil;
Mare masáné kil;
Meré kil par ghát karai;
Chháti phát marai.

"O brave Mahabir or Hanumán ! Come to me soon. As you have done the business of Rám Chandra satisfactorily, so do my business. The peg groans "*chang chang.*" Pegs in the hands, in the head, and pegs on all sides. Pegs in the bodies of the Dankini female demons, pegs in the bodies of Sankini female demons. Pegs in the bodies of the demons of the way, in the bodies of the demons of the market place, pegs in the bodies of the demons of the burning ground and pegs in the bodies of all men who have become demons after death. He who attacks my fort or body may die and his breast be broken.—*Pándit Rám Gharib Chaubé.*

289. Women's superstition.—A woman would never allow any one to cross her child as it is believed its growth is marred by it.—*Bhagwán Das.*

290. Ferozpur: Legend of the Gil Jats—Their ancestor was Prithipál Rájput, Rájá of Garhmathala. He had no children, but by the advice of his astrologers, he united himself to a Jat woman, by whom he had a son. His other wives, however, who were very jealous of the entrance of this stranger among them, caused the young child to be carried away secretly out of the palace, and left to perish, as was supposed, in a marshy spot at some distance from the royal city. They then reported to the Rájá that his new wife had been delivered of a girl, which had died shortly after its birth. The Rájá's minister, however, chanced to pass by the place where the child had been exposed, and took it home with him, and adopted it as his own son, as he was childless, and he called its name Gil from *gila* (wet) with reference to the swampy wet ground in which he had found it. This child, whose life was thus almost miraculously preserved, is said to have been the progenitor of all the Gils.—*Mr. E. H. Brandreth, Settlement Report, p. 22.*

291. An Incantation.—The following incantation is repeated by Vishnuite saints when they sit in a lonely place in order to drive away demons, &c., and make themselves safe :—

Om ajra áran bajra kewár;
Jo bajra deo dáso dwár
Jo bajra upar dháwai;
Ultá kál tahi ko kháwai.
Kháwai hriday mere Hari basain suniyé deo anant
Rám Lakhan rakhshá karain, chauki karain Bir;
Hanúmant.
Támá kai kot lohé ki khái.
Jahán phirai Rájá Rám Chandra kí dohái.
Garh kilá atháyá bir.
Jahán baithé Hanumat bir.

"The seat is safe when the door is of iron. Shut up all the ten doors."

He who attacks the iron doors gets himself devoured by the deity of death in return. O innumerable gods listen to me. In my heart lives Hari. I am guarded by Hanumán and protected by Rám and Lakshman. The fortress of copper. Around it is a ditch of iron. There the power of Rám Chandra is supreme. The fortress has been set up by a demon, but it is inhabited by the brave Hanumán.—*Pándit Rám Gharib Chaubé.*

292. The propitiation of the planet Sukra or Venus.—When the planet Sukara or Venus is adverse to a person, he should offer in the name of the offended planet to a Bráhman a white horse, a white umbrella, and a piece of gold with a pearl stuck into it. This makes the angry planet propitious.—*Pándit Rám Gharib Chaubé.*

293. Teeth: ideas regarding.—According to good authorities those whose teeth are wide apart and irregular are seldom illiterate or destitute of understanding. Besides this those who are bald-headed are seldom poor and those who have only one eye are seldom virtuous. A one-eyed woman is seldom chaste. When the tooth of a child falls out, the mother takes it to the side of a well where the grass grows luxuriantly and burying it there puts her foot on the place and says :—*O ! dánt, jaisé dúb jamen taise tuhun jamo.* "O tooth! Grow as the grass grows." An elephant with only one tusk is considered very lucky and a person with thirty-two teeth most fortunate.—*Pándit Rám Gharib Chaubé.*

294. The evening time.—The evening, *sandhya bela* is a most unlucky time for the performance of any business. If you eat or sleep at that time you will surely fall sick, if you shave you lose a part of your life ; if you set out on a journey you will certainly fail to attain your object ; if a mother conceives at that time, her child will certainly be a monster. Such was Hairanya-kasipu who was conceived by Diti at that time. Siva, they say, wanders about the world at that time and curses all whom he finds engaged in any kind of business.—*Pándit Rám Gharib Chaubé.*

295. Charm to prevent a child from crying.—Make on a piece of birch bark the image of the half moon with the words :—*Om luluw swáhú,* and worship it with an offering of washed rice, sandal-wood, flowers, incense &c., and tie it on the right arm of the child and he will cease to cry.—*Pándit Rám Bbakhsh Chaubé.*

296. Persons who never prosper :—Not only among Muhammadans but among Hindús too it is a general belief that wood-cutters, who cut green or fruit-bearing trees, and bird-catchers never prosper. The idea is that they destroy life and their sin does not allow them to thrive. It is considered a pious action among Hindús to have caught birds set free and in fairs the pasiyás (bird-catchers) go round and earn much money in that way. It is also believed that professional weighers (Totás) never prosper as the saying goes :—

جو تم چاہو پاپ ادھکائی •
چار دنا لے کرو تلائی •

Jo tum cháho páp adhikái,
Chár dná kí karo tulái.

If you want much of *páp* (sin), adopt the profession of a Totá for four days. Tailors are said never to prosper on account of their stealing propensities.—*Bhagwán Das, Chhatarpore.*

North Indian Notes and Queries:
A MONTHLY PERIODICAL.

VOL. V.] OCTOBER, 1895. [NO. 7.

Popular Religion ...	... 109 to 114	Folktales ... ... 119 to 123
Anthropology	... 115 ,, 118	Miscellanea ... ... 124 ,, 126

POPULAR RELIGION.

297. **Sun Worship.**—Besides the ordinary daily reverence to the rising sun which is incumbent on all pious Hindus, there is a special rite in his honour on the day when the New Year commences, on the first day of Chait.

The rites are as follows:—The worshipper fasts on the last day of the expiring year and next morning bathes at a sacred river or tank before eating. He then collects some white, blue and yellow lotus flowers and makes of them an image of the sun to which he dedicates red powder, sweets, incense, Malay sandal-wood, flowers, rice milk and white fruits. Food also may be offered, but it must be purified with *ghi*. He then tastes a mouthful of all the kinds of food offered and drinks water once. If he wishes to eat more food after, he can only do so with the permission of the officiating priest. A similar offering of all these things which have been offered to the sun must also be made to a Brahman. This worship must be done on the afternoon of the first day of the month of Chait. The present to the officiating priest must include some new cloth. If a man does this worship for thirteen years in succession, no misfortune can ever befall him.—*Pandit Rám Gharib Chaubé.*

298. **The Worship of the year (Samvatsara).**—One of the most sacred duties of a Hindu is the worship of the year or Samvatsara. On the first day of the lunar fortnight of Kuár the worshipper bathes and offers ablutions of water to the Manes. Then an image of the year is made of rice-flour and perfumes are sprinkled over it. To this are offered sandal-wood, washed rice, incense and the collection of articles known as *Naivedya*. This should be done twelve times, once for each month of the year and with each month its name should be mentioned. Thus *Chaitra másay namah*—" I salute the month of Chait." Then the image is covered with a fine cloth and to it are offered all the fruits of the season. Then the following prayer is made:— " O Bhagwan! I have spent the last year in happiness through thy mercy. Grant that I may pass through the present year in safety." With the prayer gifts are offered to Brahmans and their foreheads are marked with sandal paste. The worshipper next marks his own forehead in the same way. After this he should mark his forehead in the same way every day

until the end of the year and when any demons or evil spirits see his forehead thus marked, they hide their heads and retire in terror. The result is that prosperity increases rapidly.—*Pándit Ramautár Dikshit.*

299. Precautions during an epidemic of Small-pox.—While one of the family is suffering from small-pox no one must chew betel, use oil in any way, get their clothes washed, mix turmeric in their pulse or cook cakes in *ghi*. If any one violates these rules the goddess gets so angry that she will never leave the patient and will finally kill him. Many orthodox Hindus, during this time, do not even wear shoes. All feasts, including marriage, are prohibited. The patient is kept in a room plastered with cow-dung and no one can go in who has not bathed or washed his feet. The food for the sick person is cooked apart from that of the rest of the family and great care is taken that the water used in the preparation of it has not been touched by any stranger to the caste. All joking, laughing and amusement are strictly prohibited. If any man makes during that time an unkindly remark about the sufferer, or does not go to see him through fear of contagion, the goddess will surely catch him.—*W. Crooke.*

300. The Sacred Pool at Amritsar.—As far back as the Sat Yuga, when the gods lived in the land of the five rivers and when the first hymns of the Vedas were chanted in their praise, the sacred pool of Amritsar was regarded with veneration. Between the rivers Byás and Ravi lived the Rishis and they, by their sacrifices, brought down the water of immortality (amrita) from Heaven. During the wars between the Rakshasas and the gods, the pool often became a cause of contention and the prize of the conquerors. It was then known as the Amrita Kunda. Then for a time it ceased to be respected until the time of Buddha. As he was wandering over the land it is said that he stopped here and said :—" This is the best place for the Bhikhshus to obtain Nirvana and is far superior to the Eastern shrines, but it must be allowed time to obtain honour," So the Bhikhshus began to come there and carry on religious disputations. The *Jogis.* too, resorted here as the best place for their rites of keeping back their breath. Ráma and his brother, Lakshmana, also bathed here.

When Guru Rám Dás was about to dig a tank and build a national temple for the Sikhs here, he determined to satisfy himself where the Amrita Kunda really was ; so as he dug he found a room or retreat enclosed on all four sides and inside it was an ancient *Jogi* with long grey matted hair. The *guru* who was skilled in Yoga or the art of restoring breath, succeeded in restoring him and he fell down at the feet of Guru Rám Dás and exclaimed : " I have now got my salvation. I was waiting to see thee and have now beheld thee." The *guru* asked him who he was and where the Amrita Kunda was situated. This *Jogi* was named Santokha Deva and he indicated by signs the site of the sacred pool, and he was again walled up in the underground chamber which was covered over with earth and over it was made the tank known as the Santokha Sár.

[This was sent by an anonymous correspondent who promised a further account of the legends of Amritsar which will be very welcome.—Ed.]

301. Worship of the Sami or Chhenkur Tree.—The sanctity attached to the Sami tree is shown by the fact that part of the Arani or sacred fire drill is made of its wood. On the tenth of the month Kuár, better known as the Bijay Dasami, this tree is worshipped. The rite is very common among the Rajputs. The ritual is as follows:—A tree is in the jungle and it must be without any flaw. It is set up in a part of the house which has been plastered and purified with cow-dung. The worshipper should bathe and put on clean clothes before setting up the tree and he should worship it with an offering of sandal wood, washed rice, flowers, incense, lamps and sweetmeats. He should then pray to it in the following words:—" O Sami tree! Thou art the destroyer of sins. Thou hast scarlet thorns. Thou wast praised by Rama on his way to Lanka. May my journeying be blessed by thee. Mayest thou shed showers of blessings on me." The reference to journeying is based on the fact that the old Rajputs used to set out on their warlike expeditions on this day. The worshipper marks his forehead with earth from the root of the tree. All the servants, dependants, household Brahmans, &c., are then presented with new clothes and start off in an easterly direction to the music of drums and other instruments. Crossing the village boundaries they do worship to Vaatu Deva, the deities presiding over material things and to the Digpálas or guardians of the eight quarters of the sky. As they go along they worship at the shrine of any god or godling they may chance to meet. Then the Sami tree is worshipped again with the following prayer :—" O Sami tree ! Thou canst overcome all evil omens. Thou canst help me to accomplish mighty deeds with honour. Thou canst remove the effects of evil dreams. Thou canst endue me with happiness. I therefore invoke thy aid with all humility and lowliness of heart." After this they make a figure of a supposed enemy and shoot at it with a bow and arrow of gold. This should be done at all the four gates of the town or city. After this there are races and all kinds of athletic games. Any one who performs this worship regularly need never fear any enemy.—*Pándit Rám Gharib Chaubé.*

302. **The Anant Chaturdasi Fast.**—The Anant Chaturdasi fast takes place on the fourteenth of Bhadon. On this day they tie on their wrists a thread known as anant which has fourteen knots and after being previously worshipped is considered very sacred. In the worship of the thread the following ritual is followed :—A piece of ground is plastered in the courtyard and then repeating the date and month the name of Anant Deota, the Infinite Deity, is invoked. A square is then made on which are depicted the nine planets and the sixty-four gods, collectively called sarbtobhadra. In it is placed a pitcher (*kalsa*) decorated with coloured lines, near it are placed seven blades of kusa grass and next to the anant thread. Then the pitcher is worshipped with an offering of washed rice, flowers, incense, lighted lamps and sweets. The same worship is done to the kusa grass. In some cases betel and betelnuts are added to the above offerings. Anant Deota is next invoked with the appropriate *mantras*. This done the thread is tied round the right arm. The worshipper must do this ritual fasting. After it is done he may eat cakes and rice cooked in milk and sugar, or cakes and vermicelli (*senwai*). Some, after the worship, get a Pandit to make a recitation in praise of Anant. Men and women of all ages do this fast as the restrictions are very simple.—*Pándit Rám Gharib Chaubé.*

303. **The Narsinh Chaturdasi Fast.**—Hindus believe that Narsinh, the man-lion incarnation of Vishnu, was born on the fourteenth day of Baisakh. Hence in his honour they fast that day. It is believed that those who do not fast that day will remain in hell as long as the sun and moon exist in the heavens. Those who fast on that day acquire a merit exceeding a thousandfold that of fasting on the ekadasi or eleventh day of the month. The man who fasts should avoid evil company and tell no lies that day. Nor should he talk with a woman. He ought to meditate on Narsinh and at noon go to a river to bathe. If he cannot bathe at a river he should go to a tank or well. He should rub his body with earth, cowdung, the anwla fruit (Phyllanthus emblica) and sesamum and putting on a new garment go to his house where he should plaster a piece of ground and on it make an image of a lotus with eight petals. On this he should place a copper vessel filled with barley or rice. On the lotus he should lay a small golden image of Vishnu which must be bathed with curds, milk, *ghi*, sugar and honey. A Pandit is then called and the image is worshipped with an offering of sandal, washed rice, flowers, incense, and sweets. At night he should listen to songs in honour of Narsinh. All night he must keep awake. Next morning he must bathe and go through the same ritual. Then he should call a Brahman and give him an image in gold of the lion. The business ends with feeding and giving presents to Brahmans.—*Pándit Rám Gharib Chaubé.*

304. **A Hindu way of taking Omens.**—The following account of a mode of taking omens is taken from Bhola Nath Chandar : " Travels of a Hindu." Can any one say if the custom still prevails anywhere ? As Laalla Rookh and her companions passed along a sequestered river after sunset, they saw a young Hindu girl upon the bank whose employment seemed to them so strange, that they stopped their palanquin to observe her. She had lighted a small lamp, filled with oil of cocoa; placing it in an earthen dish, adorned with a wreath of flowers, had committed it with a trembling hand to the stream and was now anxiously watching its progress down the current, heedless of the gay cavalcade which had drawn up beside her. Laala Rookh was all curiosity, when one of her attendants, who had lived upon the banks of the Ganges (where this ceremony is so frequent that often in the dusk of the evening, the river is seen glittering all over with lights, like the Otan-tala or sea of stars), informed the princess that it was the usual way in which the friend of those who had gone on dangerous voyages offered up vows for their safe return. If the lamp sunk immediately the omen was disastrous; but if it went down the stream shining and continued to burn till entirely out of sight, the return of the beloved object was considered as certain.—*Pándit Rám Gharib Chaubé.*

[The worship is probably of Khwája Khizr, the water deity.—ED.]

305. **Aligarh : The Saint Shah Jamal.**—On the south-eastern side of the city of Aligarh is the tomb of the Saint Sháh Jamál, where a fair is held in his honour in the month of Asarh on Tuesdays. Worshippers offer to the shrine a sheet and a special kind of sweetmeat known as *Reori*. The fair is chiefly for children who play at flying kites while it lasts. This is the close of the kite-flying season.

Once upon a time, they say, Sháh Jamál was sitting at his door and was being shaved by a barber. While this was going on the saint, by his magical power, learned that in the great ocean the ship of a merchant which was laden with costly merchandise was sinking. The spirit of the saint started at once for the place and gave such effective help that the ship and cargo escaped in safety. In fact, Sháh Jamál appeared in person and guided the ship to harbour. When the merchant went to thank him, he disappeared. The barber suddenly observed that the feet of the saint were wet with salt water and he asked the saint how this came to be. The saint told him how he had gone to rescue the ship. The barber published the circumstance and this led to such veneration for the saint that when he died they built a tomb in his honour and established his annual fair.—*Babu Genda Lal.*

306. **The Worship of the Asoka Tree.**—The Asoka tree (*Jonesia Asoka*) is sacred because under it Sita was kept in captivity by Ravana. Hence many women worship the tree. They fast for three days in succession, eating vegetables only once a day and place water, rice, sandal wood, flowers, incense and sweets at the root of the tree. They walk one hundred and eight times round the trunk and at each circuit offer a cocoanut or date fruit. Then they present to a Brahman an image of Siva made of gold and a copper vessel. The worship of the tree is supposed to confer offspring and save their husbands from death. It is usually done by all high caste Hindu women, except those of the Sarwariya and Kanaujiya Brahmans.—*W. Crooke.*

307. **Saharanpur: Religion of the Sweepers.**—The following is the sacred song of the sweepers at Saharanpur as given after great difficulty by their *guru* or headman. It is printed as he recited it without any attempt at correction:—

" Ba fazale, Bis-milláh rahemáná rahim.
Karam harímá Rám Rahimá.
Paidáish Alláh Tálá kí.
Nehi Nekáíl kí.
Aamat Aaáail kí.
Daur saráfíl kí.
Simit simit be simit simit.
Badsháhat Muhammad kí.
Warqa warq jambú muqdinmèn ;
Karle the amlá (ulmá) aikra sárá khair Alláh
inshá tálá ké.
Tawá Makké ká ;
Chhatra Dillí ká ;
Diwan Bíbí Fátimá ká.
Chehrá Lál Guru ká.
Chapará pet kí rotí ;
Jan ho kapará ;
Jis dín merá pír janma,
Sab Pirón men larái pái ;
Jhaggá topi le Mátá Girijá ne pahnái.
Sab pir, aur paighambar,
Ghans mil thápná karái.
Wáh wáh jí wáh wáh.
Mere sáhib jí kí sangat bel bahut si barhí.
Bálá Sáhib Nuri, Abbu Sháh Nuri, Mír Shah
Nuri, Sahaj lagá Nuri, Musá Arkhadá Nuri,
Baré Badsháh Nuri, Khodá Rabi-ul-aimin
Nuri, Bálá Sháh Núri kis ke bété ?

Abbu Sháh Nurí he bété.
Abbu Sháh Nuri kis ké bété ?
Mír Sháh Nurí ke bété.
Mír Sháh Nurí kis he bété ?
Sahaj lagá Nuri ke bété.
Musá arkhadá ke bété.
Sahaj lagá Nuri.
Musá Arkhadá Nurí kis ke bété ?
Baré Bádsháh Nurí ke bété.
Bare Bádsháh Nuri kis ke bété ?
Takht Waqt Rábi-ul-aimin ke bété.
Jinon ká satyug men soné ká thán ; soné ká nisán,
soné ká ghat, soné ká math, soné kí kunjí, soní
ká tálá, soné ká jhandá, soné ká nisháa, vni
ká sab thát, uttar munh dehli, pachchhin muk
dwár ;
Leo kunjí kholo kewár.
Leo mere sachche Sat Guru Lál Guru ká didár.
Dwápar yug mén chándi ká thán, chándi ká
makán, chándi ká ghat, chandi ka math,
chándi ká jhandá, chándi ká nishán, chándi
kí kunjí, chándi ká tálá, chándi ká sab thát,
uttar mukh dehli, pachchhim mukh dwár.
Láwó kunjí kholo kewár.
Dekho mere sachche uru Lál Guru ká didár.
Tretá yug mén tánbé ká thán, tánbe ká makán,
tánbé ká ghat, tánbe ká math, tanbe kí kunjí,
tanbe ká tálá, tanbe ká sab thát, uttar mukh
dehli, pachchhim mukh dwár ;
Láwo kunjí, kholo kewár.
Dekho meré sachche Sat Guru Dádá Guru ká didár.
Kali yug mén matti ká thán, matti ká makán, matti
ká ghat, matti ká math, matti ká jhandá,
matti ká nishán, matti kí kunjí, matti ká tálá,
matti ká sab thát, uttar mukh dehli, pachchhin
mukh dwár.
Láwó kunjí kholo kewár.
Dekho jí mere sachche Sat Guru ká didár,
Sár kí chhari, Multán kí kaman.
Sat yug mén soné kó jhárú rupe ko tokaró, gal
phulon kó hár, sir par kalangí nyárí ;
Aindal hasti, ard ambárí,
Charhe mere sachche Sat Guru Lál Guru sawári.
Awo miyán Ládhkán darbárí ;
Sattar sal bálá tere panjé sé marí.
Chhán dálai dúdh ká dúdh, pání ká pání,
Zamín ke galiché, ásmán ke shamiyáná.
Simit be simit.
Pádsháhi Muhammad Sháhab kí.
Bar haq ká duá.
Jambu Abbár ki duá.
Sunte hain mál jigar sáre.
Khair Alláh ká.
Dewán Bíbi Fátimá ká.
Tawa Makke ká.
Chhattar Dilli ká.
Ajmir aindé ká.
Hazrat Qátil Qatal.
Awwal pír Alláh,
Doam pir Asá,
Seum pir Shafá,

Chaharum pír Lál Guru.
Pa kó roti tan kó kapará.
Háré ké mal,
Jité ké pahalwáu.
Jahán parai hár,
Wahán merá Pír parai lalkár.
Jis din merá pír jaumá.
Sab pírón paighambaron men larái pái.
Máia girijá né jhaggá topi le pahnái.

"I begin in the name of the protector and the creator of the world (God). God is generous. Rám is merciful. I sing the birth of the glorious God. He has his manifestation of virtue in Nekáil (query Michael the angel). He has his manifestation of power and authority in Azázíl. He has his manifestation of running power in Saráfíl. Gather together ye men (under the flag of Lál Guru). The kingdom is of Muhammad. At Jambu the learned men were singing the praises of God, leaf by leaf. The griddle-pan of Makká is famous. The umbrellá of Delhi is famous. (These two lines mean that the distribution of food among the poor at Mecca is praiseworthy and so the royalty of Dehli is commendable.) The Minister of the lady Fátimá is famous. The face of Lál Guru is famous. He gives food for the stomach and garments for the body. On the day our prophet, or, say, religious guide, was born all the religious guides of note who were senior to him began to fight with one another. In the meantime the goddess Girijá or Párbati appeared and put on his head (Lál Guru's head) the cap of teaching. This was acknowledged by all other teachers, prophets and saints who were the favourites of gods and angels.

"All praise to the religious guide!

"Our Lord's (Lál Guru's) creeper spread rapidly. (This means that the offsprings or disciples soon multiplied.) The noteworthy among them were Bálá Sháh Nurí, Abbu Sháh Nurí, Mira Sháh Nurí, Sahaj lagá Nurí, Musá Arkhadá Nurí, Baré Badsháh Nurí (the great King Lál Guru), and the Great Creator of the Universe.

"Who begot Bálá Sháh Nurí? Abbu Sháh Nurí. Who begot Abbu Sháh Nurí? Mira Sháh. Who begot Mira Sháh? Sahaj logá Nurí. Who begot Sahaj logá Nurí? Musa Arkhadá. Who begot Musa Arkhadá? Bare Badsháh Nurí (Lalguru). Who begot Bare Badsháh Nurí? God the Creator of the Universe. The son of God (Lál Beg) had in the Golden Age a gold ground, gold badge, gold pitcher, gold cottage, gold key, gold lock, gold flag, and everything of gold. He had his threshold in the north and door in the west. Take the key and open the door and catch a glimpse of the True Guide Lálguru.

"In the Silver Age (Dwápar Yug), silver was the ground, silver the house, silver the pitcher, silver the monastery, silver the flag, silver the badge, silver the key, silver the lock and everything of silver. He had his threshold in the north and door in the west. Take the key and open the door and see the True Guide Lál Guru. In the same way in the third age he had all the things abovenamed of copper. Take the key and open the door and see the True Guide Lal Guru. In the Iron Age he has all the things abovenamed of earth. His threshold is in the north and the door in the west. Take the key and open the door and see the True Guide Lál Guru or Dádá Guru.

"Lal Guru had in the Golden Age a stick of iron and a bow of Multán and (as a caste mark) he had in that blessed age a gold brush or broom, and a gold basket, and a garland of flowers round the neck, a *kalangi* or crest on his head besides and was mounted on a splendid elephant with a yellow saddle-cloth on. Then God addressed him thus: "O my courtier Lál Khán I come along. Seven thousand calamities be dispersed by thy hands. Thou hast the power of taking water from the milk. Thy bed is the earth and thy canopy is the sky. O ye men, gather together under the flag of Lál Guru. The kingdom is of Muhammad Sáháb. He is blessed by God. The distillers of Jambu are also blessed. They are blessed because they hear the words of God attentively. The Dewán of Bibi Fatimá, the griddle-pan of Makká, the umbrellá of Delhi, the immortal saint of Ajmír are blessed. The first Pir or religious guide is God. The second Pir is hope (áshá). The third Pir is Shafá (the virtue of curing the diseases of the sick) and the fourth Pír is Lál Guru. He gives bread for the stomach and garments for the body. He is a wrestler for the good of the weak and a powerful man for the strong. Where his followers are defeated there our Pir falls on with a loud voice. The day on which our Pir was born the Pirs and Paighambars (prophets) began to fight. In the meantime the goddess Girijá came and put on his head the cap of teachership."

From the above it appears that sweepers take Lál Guru for the son of God and address him as the godhead itself.

They derive his lineage from God and give the names of four or five of his descendants. It is curious to see Hindu and Muhammadan ideas mixed together in the above account.—*Pandit Rám Gharib Chaubé.*

308. **Swastika; respect for.**—The respect for the Swastika appears to be much greater in the Madras Karnatik than in Northern India. The symbol is worshipped during the four rainy months of the year. It begins in Asarh and ends in Kuar or Kartik. Its worship is associated with that of Vishnu and Lakshmi

and is done daily during the rainy season. Eight representations of it are made in blue, yellow, white and red powder on a platform plastered with cowdung. Before it are offered sandal wood, flowers, incense and lamps, which are dedicated to Vishnu. They believe that those who offer to Vishnu eight Swastikas drawn in five different colours go on death to Vishnuloka, or the heaven of the deity; those who offer a thousand get offspring and riches; those who offer ten thousand render their sons and grandsons rich and free from all disease. The greater the number offered the higher is the religious merit and the richer the reward. At the end of the rains is a special rite when they offer a lakh of representations of it to Vishnu. On this occasion the figures are made in turmeric. With the offering a cow is given to a Brahman. After this the Brahman is placed on a costly seat and does the fire sacrifice. The rite ends with the distribution of alms to Brahmans.—*Pandit Rám Gharib Chaubé.*

309. **A Monkey Saint.**—The Lahore paper writes:—" A deep gloom has fallen over the town of Pathankot. The sacred big monkey, who was regarded by many as the patron saint of the town, is dead. Many a time, when he was in health and more than usually capricious and tyrannical, the citizens wished him dead, and now that he is no more their remorse is the keener. As they were taking the corpse to *smashan* (burning ground) with the pomp usual on the occasions of grand funerals, they espied a very small ape following them at a distance giving vent to piteous cries and lamentations. This touching sight made their tears flow afresh."

310. **Music at Saiva funerals.**—At the funeral of a Saiva they keep blowing conch shells and ringing bells to scare demons. Saivas have more fear of losing their dead in this way than ordinary Hindus and they do not tie the corpse to the bier as others do. The conch shell, they say, was produced by Snakhasura who had won the power of scaring demons.—*Pandit Rám Gharib Chaubé.*

311. **Shah Daula's rats.**—Shah Daula is one of the great saints of Upper India who cures barrenness. His tomb is somewhere near Ludhiana. Many people who desire sons, whether they are Hindus or Muhammadans, visit his shrine. The peculiarity about him is this, that when he gives children the first is always a sort of dwarf, or mannikin, with a small head, like a rat. Such children are called Shah Daula's rats (*Shah Daula ke chuhe*) and are devoted to the shrine. These rats of Shah Daula now form a special class of beggars. Each of them is said to have on his head the marks of the five fingers of the saint who brought him into the world.—*Pandit Rám Gharib Chaubé.*

[There is a note on Shah Daula's rats in *Panjáb Notes and Queries*, II—27; III—27. Can any one who has been at the place give some more particular account of these curious people and of the legends connected with the saint?—ED.]

312. **Offering the tip of the tongue to Káli.** —Many students of Sanskrit who are dull in learning think it adds to their powers of memory by offering the tip of their tongues to the goddess Káli. They have a precedent for this in the case of Káli Dás who, when married to Vidyadhári, exhibited his want of knowledge to his wife and was flung by her from the upper storey of the house. By chance he fell on an image of Káli and the tip of his tongue was accidentally cut off. The Devi was pleased at the sacrifice and asked him what boon he desired. He thought that the Devi asked him who had thrown him down. So he answered: "Vidya," forgetting the latter part of the name of his wife. Now Vidya means "learning"; so Devi blessed him with the greatest learning. In imitation of him students almost yearly make this kind of sacrifice to Káli at Benares and other seats of Hindu learning in order to gain knowledge.—*Ramlal Dube.*

[There is a reference to this custom in *Panjáb Notes and Queries*, IV—65. It is said to be done in fulfilment of a vow. The goddess is said to appear in the form of a little girl to the devotee and demand the fore part of the tongue as an offering. This is said to have happened to one Krishn Dás, a physician at Lahore.—ED.]

313. **The worship of the hero Bhishma.**— The common legend of the death of the hero Bhishma, who was one of the generals of the Kauravas in the great war of the Mahabhárata, is that he was invincible and none of the Puravas could kill him until Sri Krishna named one of his elephants Aswattháman, who was the son of Bhishma, and his father's life was so bound up with his, that when they announced that Aswattháman was dead, Bhishma died also. (There seems to be some mistake here, for Aswattháman was son not of Bhishma, but of Drona.) So Bhishma died childless and as he was dying he asked who would do the rites for his soul. Sri Krishna answered that the whole world would fast for the repose of his spirit for five days every year. So now Hindu women begin the fast in the eleventh day of Kártik and go on fasting for the following four days in his name to secure the repose of his spirit. On the first day only one mouthful of food should be eaten; on the second two mouthfuls; and so they eat an additional mouthful every day until the fast, which is known as the Bhíshma Panchaka Vrata, is over. On the first day of Aghan they feed Brahmans in his name and this concludes the rite.—*Pandit Rám Gharib Chaubé.*

ANTHROPOLOGY.

314. Eastern Districts: N.-W. P.: Various forms of Oaths and Ordeals.—Some swear on the head of their eldest son. Some on the Shástra known as Harbans Pothi. This last oath if violated leads to the loss of male offspring, and the person taking the oath must wear a yellow loin cloth. Some swear on Gange's water, an idol of Siva, the foot of a Brahman. Forms of ordeal, now practically obsolete, are to swear holding a hot iron ball (*gola*) in the hand: to walk through fire. Others throw into a pitcher of water two balls of earth, on one of which is written the name of Ráma and the other of Rávana. Then the swearer has his eyes bandaged and he takes out one of the balls. If it be that named after Ráma he is clear, if that after Rávana, guilty. Another practice, now practically obsolete, was to swear dipping the hand into boiling oil.—*W. Crooke.*

315. Old Shoes: A cure for Fits.—When a man falls down in a fit they always put an old shoe, turned upside down, on his nose. This is supposed to bring him immediately to his senses. Is it possible that here we have an explanation of the use of old shoes thrown on the bride and bridegroom at our marriages. In Bombay a person, in order to scare the demon of insomnia, puts an old shoe under his pillow ; the Kunbis of the Deccan, when they think they have been struck by a curse, lay hold of an old shoe. So in Thana people fasten old shoes to fruit trees in order to protect them from the evil-eye and to ensure that they bear good fruit. Brahman women in Dharwar never wear shoes except when they are lying-in. All over Upper India it is very common to see old shoes put on the thatch of a cottage to keep off the evil-eye and the influence of demons. The Jews handed over a shoe to confirm a contract. In Germany throwing shoes over a person's head and seeing which way the points look, reveals the place where one is destined to stay long. (Grimm: *Teutonic Mythology*, 111—1118.) In Ireland officials used to be elected by throwing shoes over them. (Brand: *Popular Antiquities*, 111—169). In Cornwall cramp is cured by laying slippers under the bed with the soles up. (Dyer's *Folklore*, 164.) So in Northern England shoes crossed are sometimes put under the bed to cure cramp. (Henerson: *Folklore of the Northern Counties*, 155.) This all looks as if the old shoe was regarded as a scarer of evil spirits and that they were thrown over the newly married pair either to scare demons generally, or specially the demon of barrenness. Any further instances of the use of shoes in this way would be very interesting.—*W. Crooke.*

316. Stamping of hand marks.—Stamping of hand marks forms an important part of the ordinary Hindu ritual. These marks are made at marriages on the walls of the house with the hand steeped in powdered rice mixed with water. In all special worship of Devi the same marks are made. In the same way the pots of sweetmeats sent to the house of the bridegroom by the bride after marriage are marked. In all rites done with the object of bringing good luck on the household the same marks are made.—*Pándit Rám Gharib Chaubé.*

[See *Introduction to Popular Religion and Folklore*, 208.—ED.]

317. Account of Bhuinhars as related by Jainarayan Singh and Sheo Padarath Singh of Gangapur.—There are as many sub-divisions of Bhuinhars as of Brahmans for they are really Brahmans. They have their origin from Piprá Rohania in Sarwár. They have the title of Gautamá as being descended from Gautamá Rishi. When Rájá Bhandár was the Rájá of Káshi their ancestor, Krishna Data Misra *alias* Kathaú Misra, came and settled at Misraka-pokhrá in Gangapur. The temple of Gautámeshwár Mahadeo at Benares was built by Kathaú Misra. They have now no connection with Pipra Rohania. They worship Shiva and Shaivá (Shaivá is said to be the feminine of Shiv). They call themselves *Tir Kar man* (*i. e.*, performing three *karms* or functions) Brahmans ; and are called Bhuinhárs from the fact of their ancestors having taken up the cultivation of land. (Bhuinhár being as they say equivalent to *Bháin shár, i. e.*, having land for their livelihood). They cannot fix the period since which they have done so. The Brahmans have six *karams* (functions), *viz.*, (1) teaching; (2) accepting *dán;* (3) officiating at *jag ;* (4) reading; (5) giving of *dán ;* (6) performing *jag.* Of these six Bhuinhárs have renounced the first three and perform the last three. They follow the Sháma Véda. Daughters are given in marriage to the following Bhuinhárs, *vis. :*—Anksaria, Kurhná, Khanwár, Sakarwár, Donwár ; and brides are taken from the following, *vis. :*—Sándil, Donwár, Chaudhari, Dumkatár, Pande. They eat *kachchi* and *pakki* only with their relatives. In marriage the bride's father first performs the *tilak* of the bridegroom and makes presents to him according to his means. Then a day for the marriage is fixed and the marriage procession starts. The ceremony of *duár pújá* (door worship) is performed and then the usual rites of marriage common to the Hindus. After the marriage the bridegroom goes to the *kohbar* (a place decorated with rude paintings, &c, where the females of the bride's party receive the bridegroom) and there unites two burning wicks (this is rather unique). He gets some money. Then next day at noon he eats *khichri* and gets presents in money and utensils. Then the bridegroom's father shakes the *máró* or nuptial shed and gets presents. Then the marriage is over and the people depart. The ceremony of uniting two burning wicks is a very interesting representation of mutual love. It is clear that in ancient mythology love is called a flame. This is common to most countries. The ceremony is a practical illustration of the mythology. The mutual love and affection of the married couple will blend and mix into one flame: thereby showing not only that they are blended in love and affection, but that henceforth they will both love the same thing.—*Mul Chand.*

---

318. **School Games.**—In schools where they teach Persian one of the most favourite games is a sort of capping verses. One boy says *sanam aye*—" My sweetheart has come," and he asks " Wherefrom ? In what dress ? What does she eat " and so on. The answers to all the questions must begin with the letter with which the first commences. Any one who fails to give the appropriate word has to imitate the cry of some animal, such as the goat, cock, &c.

Another game is known as *Bailabakas*. One boy repeats a line of poetry and the next has to cap it with a verse beginning with the letter which ended the first line. So the verse capping goes on and he who keeps it up longest wins the prize. —*W. Crooke.*

---

319. **The effect of Imprisonment on Caste.** —There is at least one criminal tribe in these Provinces—the Audhiyas of Fatehpur who excommunicate any member of the tribe who happens to be put in jail. When a man of high caste or respectable family is released from jail his friends go and bring him home, as it is not uncommon for such a man to refuse to return home through shame. They take him to the nearest sacred place before they go home and there the prisioner bathes and gets his Brahmanical cord changed according to the prescribed rites. Then he worships all the gods and drinks the water in which the chief deity, usually the lingam of Mahadeva, has been bathed. He then comes home, but at first he eats apart from his family. Then he asks the village Pandit to point out an auspicious day and on that date he begins to have the *Sri Mad Bhagwat* recited by a Pandit. This goes on for seven days and he then does the Homa sacrifice and makes an oblation to the god which he specially worships and gives a money fee to the Pandit and other Brahmans with a present of new clothes. After this he feeds a certain number of Brahmans and his own brotherhood. This is in the case of his first offence; but if a man is repeatedly in jail, respectable families will have nothing to do with him.

Low caste people merely bathe in the Ganges and give a feast to their brethren. A criminal course of life involves the same discredit as among higher castes. Of course the case is quite different in the case of imprisonment resulting from an outbreak of religious fanaticism.— *W. Crooke.*

---

320. **Saharanpur: A Cholera Charm.**—In Hardwar lately there was fear of an outbreak of cholera and the following plan was resorted to by the people. They bought a young male buffalo and painted it all over with lampblack and smeared its forehead with vermilion. This red colouring is like that used by all savage tribes who paint their bodies red in order to inspire terror among their enemies. The buffalo here is supposed to represent Yama Raja, the god of death, whose vehicle the buffalo is and he is supposed to be going out armed to attack the demon of cholera. When the buffalo has been painted they put a cloth on its back and load it with weapons of iron, the iron being a well-known scarer of evil spirits. The animal is then driven round the town and made over to one of the Dakaut class of beggar Brahmans who are supposed to have some connection with ill-omened godling Sanichara or Saturn whose offerings they alone, among Brahmans, can receive. There is a place to the south of the town which is known as Haiza Bhúmi or the land of the cholera demon. Here the women resort and worship Mari Dhawáni the goddess of plagues. They offer to her flowers, *Halwa* sweetmeats, washed rice, sandal wood and low caste women sacrifice a goat or buffalo and pour a libation of wine in her honour. With the same objects they make on the walls in their houses the representation of a human figure standing head downwards. This seems to be intended to be a sort of penance to cause the goddess to pity the people.

This is rather an elaborate form of the cholera scapegoat of which examples will be found in *Introduction to Popular Religion and Folklore*, 109.— *W. Crooke.*

---

321. **Touching Gold and Silver at the New Moon.**—The rule in Europe of touching money at the new moon is very general. Thus Mr. Henderson (*Folklore of the Northern Counties*) writes—" Turn the money in your pocket on the first sight of the new moon, and you will always have plenty there. Should your pocket be empty you can only avert the lady moon's displeasure by turning head over heels immediately." (P. 114). In India there are few Hindus who do not covet

the sight of the *Dwitiya ke chând* or the moon of the second day of the lunar fortnight. Thus, there is a common saying among friends *Ap to duitiya ke chând ho gaye*—" Though much desire you have become as scarce as the new moon." When Hindus see this moon they salute it, but to do so without silver or gold is very dangerous. It is supposed that when you salute this moon it answers—" Live long as you are." Hence if you have no money in your pocket it means that you are to be penniless for the rest of your life. Hence when people are going to salute the moon they take a little gold or silver with them. Copper is not used for this purpose. The respect for the moon is shown in its connection with Siva and Hindu forehead caste marks.—*Pândit Râm Gharîb Chaubé.*

322. **Parading Offenders on the back of an Ass.**—In old times it was the custom to parade criminals, those who had committed adultery or killed a Brahman, with their noses and ears cut off. They were then mounted on the back of an ass and led round the city. There is a famous instance of this in one of the Hindu books known as *Siva Rahasya* which tells how a woman named Sarda, who was a widow, used to serve a blind saint and he not knowing that she was a widow gave her the blessing of a son. She remonstrated that to bear a son would be her ruin; but the blessing was past recall. When the saint knew how he had ruined his benefactor he devoted himself to the worship of Durga who appeared in answer to his prayers and when she heard the trouble of the woman she said :—" The husband of this woman in his next life has been re-born in the Dravida-desa and he shall visit her in a dream and she shall conceive."

So it happened and in due course the woman came to be in child and the Râjâ when he heard of it was about to condemn her to be paraded about on an ass when Durga brought back her husband and her virtue was established.—*Pândit Bhan Pratap Tiwari.*

323. **Snake Charmers.**—I recently met a snake charmer and made some enquiries from him. He first produced from his basket three different varieties of snakes which he called respectively Phandar, Nag and Sankhchurya. Lastly, he took out a fourth snake of quite a different kind and when I made enquiries from him he said :—" This snake is of the race of Râjâ Vasuki, the king of the serpents. It is called popularly Kharandaya, because it conceals itself in the hoofs of cows and buffaloes and bites them as they move. It is one of the snakes of this race that bit Dhanwantara Vaidya." Soon after this snake bit its owner and he at once took out a brown stone and a root of some plant from his bag and rubbed the wound with them. The bleeding at once stopped and he showed me some white foam-like stuff which he said was the poison of the snake. " This stone " said he " is the *Zahr Mohra* and it is a sure protective against snake poison. It comes out of the head of.the great yellow frog when it becomes big enough to attack a sparrow. Catch such a frog and shut it up in an earthen pot and put the pot in a shady place for four days, then open the pot and if the frog is dead and dry, cut off his head. From his brain this Zahr Mohra will come out."—*Pândit Râm Gharîb Chaubé.*

324. **Mock fights among Villagers.**—The custom of mock fights among villagers, such as those which occur at the Holi and other festivals has already been illustrated by me to some extent (*Introduction to Popular Religion and Folklore*, 299; 390; 393). The following are other instances :—

In parts of the North-Western Provinces the villagers play a game known as *Barra* when a sort of tug-of-war is played on the fourteenth of the light half of the month of Kuar. The party that breaks it or drags it out of the hands of the other is regarded as victor and retains that character for a year, when the contest is repeated.

On the Nâgpanchami feast day in places where there is an *akhâra* or wrestling school, a drum is beaten as a sort of challenge and the rival parties worship the earth goddess by spreading on it red lead, flowers, washed rice and sweetmeats. They distribute the sweetmeats among their brethren and then go and visit another *akhâra* where they wrestle and contend with single sticks and other forms of athletics. Those that win are adorned with a garland of flowers as a sign of victory. In some places the rivalry is so intense that the defeated party dare not appear before the victors until the next Nâgpanchami feast gives them an opportunity of retrieving their honour.

In the same way at the Masalmân festival of the Muharram, Hindus and Muhammadans engage in similar trials of skill.

Pretty much the same goes on at the Hindu feast of the Râmlîla.

Ahîrs, particularly in the Eastern Districts, have a sort of mock fight at their weddings.

At high caste marriages when the Agwâni rite is done, that is, when the bridegroom's party are met by the relatives of the bride, the horsemen on both sides gallop about and engage in a sort of mock struggle, possibly a survival of marriage by capture.

Can any one add to these instances any similar customs ?—*W. Crooke.*

325. **Cures by walking under trees.**—There is a widespread idea in Europe of the efficacy of making sick people walk under a bending tree or through a perforated stone. In India it is supposed that people suffering from indigestion, costiveness and diarrhœa are cured by walking under an old and perforated Harra or Myrabolan tree. Can any one give instances of cures by means of passing through perforated trees?—*W. Crooke.*

326. **Children's Cauls.**—An old Pandit tells me that children are sometimes born with cauls, but he is not aware that any idea attaches to it, except the general one that anything unusual occurring at the birth of a child is uncanny and so unlucky. He says that a snake is often born with a baby and that as long as the snake lives the baby lives too and dies when the snake dies. It would be interesting to know if the idea, which is so widespread in Europe regarding the child's caul, does prevail in this country.—*W. Crooke.*

327. **Cleaning of Vessels.**—There are well-recognised rules for the substances used in the cleaning of vessels. Those made of bell-metal (*hansa*) should be cleaned with ashes; those of brass with the earth from an anthill; those of iron with cowdung; those of copper with oil; those of gold with fire. Those made of any kind of gem are cleaned by simple exposure to the air. Besides this vessels are purified by making them touch the mouth of a horse. This is done in the case of fresh earthen vessels which have come from the potter and are cleaned by bringing them close to a horse's mouth. The reason is said to be because Vishnu was once incarnated with the head and neck of a horse. Vishnu took this form in order to destroy a demon who had oppressed the Brahmans and caused the recital of the Vedas to cease. When Vishnu overcame him he recited the hymns with his horse mouth and hence the purity of it.—*Pándit Rám Gharíb Chaubé.*

328. **Rural rites performed in secret.**—The chief of the rural rites performed in secret is the worship of Sitala Devi when a child is attacked with small-pox. Such children are made to wear a miniature image of Sitala round their necks, and this is made of silver, copper or gold. These images are worshipped on the eighth day of Chait and no man or boy is allowed to witness the rite, which to the east of the Province is known as Basiaura and to the west Barahi, or "the yearly rite."

Another rite of the same kind is that intended to propitiate Mari Bhawáni, or the cholera goddess. When cholera appears in a village some woman who is a devotee of the goddess and who is inspired by her, fixes a suitable day and hour for the worship. Then all the women of the village go out secretly at night with water in which some cloves have been ground and offer a libation to Mari Devi, singing at the same time songs in her honour. If any male witnesses this worship the effect of it is destroyed. If a man appears while the ceremony is going on, all the women disperse at once.

Villagers also drive the cholera demon from the place in secrecy.

Another similar rite is that intended to drive away fever from a patient. When a person is suffering from chronic fever they wave over his head a pumpkin, clove water, bangles, vermilion, a cocoanut, plantain flowers, and some washed rice which is taken secretly at night to a place where four roads meet. They cut the plantain in two with a single blow of a sword or knife and leave all the things at the road crossing.

All rites in the way of *Ojhai* or sorcery are done at night and in secret.—*W. Crooke.*

329. **The Sea-cocoanut.**—All through the Western Districts of the North-Western Provinces there is both among Hindus and Muhammadans a strong belief in the curative properties of what is known as the *Dariyái Náriyal* or sea-cocoanut. It is specially used in the diseases of children, such as indigestion, uneasy sleep, &c., when a small piece of it is tied with a black string round the neck of the child and some of it is ground up with water and administered to the child. In the Western Districts of the North-Western Provinces it is very commonly hawked about by Panjábi drug vendors.—*W. Crooke.*

330. **Nirbasi Jaduar: a magic plant.**—To the east of the North-Western Provinces there is a plant known as the *Nirbasi Jaduar*, roots of which are constantly sold by Panjábi drug vendors. If any one is afflicted with boils and scabs, if he ties a bit of the root near the affected part he will be cured. It is also expedient to give the patient a little of the drug pounded up and dissolved in water. The root is very often used as an amulet both by Hindus and Muhammadans.

Another magic stone of the same kind is what is called the "heart's delight stone"—*Dil bahár ka patthar.* It is specially efficacious in a sort of disease which children suffer from in which they get choked, as in croup. The stone is tied round the neck of the child with a black cord and some of it is ground up and administered to the child in water. It is in high repute among all classes of people and is sold largely by Panjábi drug vendors.—*Pándit Rám Lal Dubé.*

FOLKTALES.

331. The Princess and the Sepoy.—There was once a sepoy who had a very beautiful wife and he used to do nothing all day long but look at her and did nothing to earn his living. One day his wife said to him: "What a fool you are to keep looking at me all day. Why do you not do something to earn your living?"

So he took some food from his wife and started on his travels. Now the king of the land had a daughter and though many envoys came to ask her hand in marriage she said that she would marry no one but the man who should prove himself faithful to her. At last she set out on horseback alone to find a husband. When night fell she came to a jungle and stayed near where the sepoy was halting. They fell into conversation and she shot a deer. Then the sepoy told her to go and bring fire and that he meanwhile would clean the meat. But she was a long time away and the sepoy was hungry, so he lit a fire with the flint of his gun and roasted the liver and kidneys of the deer which he ate. When the Princess came she asked about the meat and he showed her all; but when she asked him for the liver and kidneys he said that this animal had none. She was very angry and said: "You shall suffer for this some day."

So they went on together and came to the city of the king, the father of the Princess. As they had no money the Princess said to the sepoy: "Let us break into the palace of the king and rob him." The sepoy agreed and they both broke into the palace and there they saw two chests. The Princess took the smaller of the two chests and telling the Sepoy to take nothing else they came away.

Next morning there was great confusion in the palace at the loss of the chest, but no trace of the thief could be found. Next night they broke again into the palace and this time the Princess tied the sepoy with a rope to the large chest and taking the clothes and jewelery of the queen went away and left him there. Next morning he was seized and brought before the king. The king asked him who had tied him there. He answered: "Your Majesty has tied me." Again the king asked him who was with him and he said: "No one." "Who then took away the other box," and he said: "I know not." So the king ordered him to be executed. But as they were taking him to the scaffold the Princess came up and said: "Release this man." Then she went to the king and said: "This is a very brave, trustworthy man and you must marry him to me."

This was done; and when they were together that night she asked: "where are the liver and kidney of the deer?" "Be silent," said he, "or I will kill you. What I said once I shall go on saying till the end of my days." She replied: "Had you told me the truth I should have divorced you. I was merely testing your fidelity."

So he sent for his first wife and all three lived happily ever after.

(A folktale told by Lalle Kahan, Student, Village School, Robertsganj, Mirzapur District.)

332. How the wise man learned experience.—There was once a wise man who, when he came to an old age, determined to make over the cares of his business to his son and travel to holy places in search of divine wisdom. After many days he reached a great city where he saw a splendid palace of the Raja. He halted at the gate and meanwhile a woman of the cowherd caste came up and began to listen to the sound of the drum which the Raja's musicians were playing at the gate. She was so much interested in the music that she let her pot of curds fall on the ground. Her companion asked her why she was so careless. "What matter does it make?" she replied. "But will not your husband be angry when you come home without the price of the curds?" "If you had an experience like mine," she answered "you would not care much what happened to you." "What was that?" they asked. So she told her story thus:—

"In my early days I was the wife of the *guru* of the Raja of Angadesa. On account of my beauty the Raja fell in love with me and I consented to his wish. As he left me I took up a sword, severed his head from his body and went to my own house. I then determined to take my life and I jumped into the river. I floated down a long way till I came to a camp of Banjaras who saw me and dragged me out of the water. For a long time I wandered with them until at last they sold me to the mistress of a gang of dancing girls. She taught me to sing and dance and many lovers visited me. One day a man came to me and as he was going away I felt a desire to know who he was and he said: 'I am the son of the *guru* of the Raja of Angadesa. My father died of snakebite and my mother ran away from home. I was young and was adopted by a rich man and I am now wandering about the world in search of amusement.'

"When I heard this and knew him to be my own son I was almost dead with shame and so I determined to take my life in the jungle; but when I got there some cowherds took me into their house and I have stayed there ever since. Thus my friend, when I call to mind my sins and my adventures the loss of a pot of curds does not matter much."

? The wise man when he heard this was so horror-stricken that he returned home, and never again went abroad in search of knowledge.

(A folktale told by Pandit Vidya Dhar, Headmaster, Tehsili School, Jhansi, Hamirpur District.)

333. Why Narada Muni laughed:—Once upon a time Narada Muni was walking along and saw a man carrying a he-goat, which he had tied by the neck with a rope and was hauling along. The goat said to the man in its own language which Narada Muni understood, but the owner did not : " Why, friend, are you giving me so much trouble ? In my former life I gave you much comfort." At this Narada Muni laughed. Now the Raja of that land had ordered that if any one was seen to laugh he was to be brought into his presence. So Narada Muni was arrested and brought before the Raja. The Raja asked him why he laughed and he answered : " Because it is my pleasure." So the Raja fined him a lakh of rupees.

Narada Muni had no money to pay the fine, but a banker paid it for him. As he was going home with the Muni the banker ordered one of his men to realise a debt from a creditor. At this Narada began to laugh again and he was again arrested and brought before the Raja who fined him a second lakh of rupees. This the banker also paid.

As they were leaving the court the banker again ordered one of his men to collect a debt and again Narada laughed and as before he was again fined and the banker paid the fine on his behalf. Then the son of the banker asked Narada why he had laughed three times without any apparent reason. He replied :—" What have you to do with it ? If you want your money I can repay you." He answered : " I do not want the money but I will not let you go until you tell me the cause of your laughter.

Narada Muni said: " The reason I laughed was because when I saw your father so busy collecting money I thought that he did not know that the money would be no use to him as he is to die to night." The boy asked him by what death his father was fated to die and the saint answered : " By snakebite." The boy asked : " Is there any means by which this misfortune may be averted ? I will not let you go until you tell me."

Narada answered : " I cannot avert the stroke of death, but there is one means of escape. Get a tank dug at the cost of a lakh and a quarter of rupees. Plant a garden round it and place a bed in the midst. When your father dies of snakebite make it known that Parameswar has killed him. Then your father's life will be saved ; but never say that he died of snakebite."

Having thus said Narada Muni departed to Vaikuntha, the heaven of Parameswar, but when he saw Parmeswar he did not salute him. Parameswar asked the saint why he did not give him the usual blessing. Narada answered : " Thou art a slayer of men (*hatyara*) in as much as thou hast slain a man. Hence I do not pronounce a blessing on thee." Parameswar answered : " I have slain no man." " If this be so," replied Narada, " Come down with me to Mrityaloka, the land of men, and I will show thee what thou hast done."

Meanwhile the son of the banker did as Narada had ordered and he made the tank and planted the garden and made his father sleep on a bed within it. During the night the banker felt cold and sent for a shawl. The servant shook it before he gave it to his master, but a snake stuck inside it and when the banker laid it over him he was bitten. Then he died and the snake disappeared out of the garden. When his son found his father dead he cried out that Parameswar had killed him. When Parameswar came down to earth with Narada he heard every one crying that he had killed the banker. And when he asked the son of the dead man he heard the same story. So out of shame he brought him to life again and Narada blessed him. So Narada and Parameswar returned to Vaikuntha.

(A folktale told by Gokul Prasad, Kayasth, of Adinathpur District Jaunpur, and recorded by Raghunath Sahay, Master, High School, Jaunpur.)

[A curious example of the manner in which these great saints bully and control the greater gods.—Ed.]

---

334. The fate the of Shrewish Wife.—There was once a wife who was such a shrew that every morning she used to say to her mother-in-law: " You wretched widow! May I see the day when your face is blackened, your hair shaved and you led round the city mounted on an ass." To this the old woman would say : " As long as my son is kind to me you can do nothing. Parameswar grant that he may never come under your influence." One day the wife began to moan and complained of internal pain. When her husband came and asked what he could do for her she said : " This disease is very difficult to cure. The only remedy is that you get your mother's head shaven, her face blackened and she led round the city on the back of an ass."

The husband went at once to his wife's mother and said : " Your daughter is sick unto death and it has been announced by the astrologers that she will never recover unless you allow your head to be shaved, your face blackened and are carried on the back of an ass around the city."

When she heard this the old woman wept sore; but her love for her daughter was great so she allowed to be done to her as her son-in-law had said. When the procession reached the house of her daughter, her husband went in and said to his wife: "Come out and see! We have done even as you desired." On this she pretended that the pain had left her and she came out. But when she saw that it was her own mother who had been thus disgraced she was overwhelmed with shame, and cried—

Dekh mai hi cháli.
Sir mundi, munh káli.

"See how my mother comes—hair shaven, face blackened."

To this her husband replied—

Dekh nári pher pheri.
Má meri hai ki teri.

"Look again wife whether it is my mother or thine."

From this time the wife gave up her shrewishness.

(A folktale told by Manna Sinh Awasthi of Fairullapur and recorded by Iqbal Bahadur of Umri, Cawnpore District.)

---

335. **The charity of the Lord Solomon.**—The Lord Solomon (on whom be peace!) was so renowned for his charity that no suppliant ever left him unsatisfied. One day a starving *faqir* came to his Court and Solomon conferred upon him precious stones and robes and gold. As he was going away he met a second *faqir* in worse case than his own and to him he gave the gifts which he had received from Solomon.

Next day he again went to Solomon who rewarded him as before, and again as he left the palace he met a starving *faqir* to whom he gave his gifts. In this way he went five times to Solomon and received lordly gifts which he immediately gave to some beggar poorer than himself.

At last when Solomon heard his case he said: "For you it only remains to pray to God for blessing. Man gives not and receives not; the Lord is the giver and he is the cause of charity."

(A folktale told by Abdulla Khan, Teacher of the Dholpur School, Azamgarh District.)

---

336. **How to please everybody.**—One day Mahadeva and Parvati were travelling through the world together and Parvati asked her spouse: "How can a man so rule his life as to escape the blame of others?" "No man" he answered "can pass his life free of blame. If he does good or if he does evil he is blamed." Parvati asked Mahadeva to illustrate this. So he said: "I will mount my ox Nandi and you can follow on foot." Soon they met a party of men on the road who said: "What a knave this old man must be. He rides himself and lets his wife follow on foot."

Then Mahadeva dismounted and made Parvati ride the ox. Soon they met another company who said: "What a fool this old man must be. He lets his wife ride and trudges along on foot himself."

Then Mahadeva mounted the ox and took Parvati behind him. By and by some men said: "What a brute this old man is to ride with his wife on this unfortunate ox."

Then Mahadeva led the ox by the halter and both he and Parvati went on foot. Soon some people said: "What a stupid old man this is. He pampers his rascally ox and he and his wife march afoot."

Then Mahadeva said to Parvati: "You see now what an evil place this world is. Whatever you do you cannot escape the tongue of censure.

So they left this world and went to their abode in the Himalayas and were so disgusted that they never visited this world since.

(A folktale told by Devi Prasad, Teacher of the School, Unao.)

---

337. **The Wise Pandit.**—There was once a Raja who was blessed with a son in his old age, and when the boy grew up his father appointed the most learned Pandits to instruct him; but in vain, because the boy took to disorderly courses and spent all his time flying kites and pigeons and other disreputable amusements. At last the Raja promised a large reward to any Pandit who would reform his son. One day a Pandit passed through the city and seeing the notice agreed to attempt the task. So he bought a lot of pigeons and used to spend the whole day flying them. At last the prince struck up an acquaintance with him and one day he said: "Panditji tell me a story." The Pandit said:—"The words of the elders should be obeyed as you will learn from the following tale:—There were once seventy pigeons who lived on a tree and one of them was their *guru*. One day a fowler came to the foot of the tree, scattered some grain there and laid a snare. The pigeons were about to fly down and pick up the grain when the *guru* warned them; but they would not mind his words and when they flew down the fowler drew the string and they were all caught in the net. When they were caught they implored the *guru* to save them and at last he said: "My advice is this. The net

weighs only a quarter *ser* of thread, you had better all rise at once and fly away with it to an island beyond the ocean."

So the pigeons flew away with the net and where they alighted was the hole of a rat. So they implored the rat to cut the net with his teeth and when he had done so all the pigeons were released. Thus you may learn to obey the advice of the experienced.

Again the Pandit related another tale:—"In a jungle lived many elephants and one of them was their *guru*. One day he saw two chameleons fighting on a tree and he said to the other elephants: "Brethren, fighting has commenced here and we would do well to leave this forest!" But one said: "Why should we leave this excellent forest for fear of these small creatures?" So they stayed there and as the chameleons were fighting one of them was defeated and ran for shelter into the trunk of one of the elephants to whom he caused excruciating pain. The elephant in terror went to the *guru* and implored his protection. At last the *guru* said: "Go into yonder deep tank and draw up a quantity of water with your trunk. Then discharge it violently and you will get rid of the chameleon." He did so and got relief. By this you should learn to obey the advice of the wise."

When the boy again asked the Pandit for a story he put him off on pretence that he was too much occupied with his pigeons. The boy was angry at this and sold all the pigeons he possessed and finally induced the Pandit to do the same. Thus, by the cleverness of the Pandit he was induced to give up his evil companion, and devote himself to the acquisition of wisdom.

(A folktale told by Narayan, Brahman, of Khakra, Meerut District.)

---

338. The tale of the Raja Sarat Chandra.—One night the son of a Raja was asleep near the palace and on a tree close by were perched a Chakwa and a Chakwi (a Brahmani duck and his mate). Said the Chakwa to the Chakwi: "Tell me a story to make the night pass pleasantly." But she said: "You must tell me a story" and they had such a quarrel over this that the Chakwi would stay with the Chakwa no longer and flew away to another country.

She came and sat on a *nim* tree close to the Raja's palace. Now the Raja of that land had a daughter who was of the most perfect beauty and every morning she used to pour out water on the ground in the name of the Sun god, Suraj Narayan, and pray to him: "O Lord! grant that I may marry the prince, Sarat Chandra."

When the Chakwi heard her prayer she said to the princess: "The prince of my country is Sarat Chandra, the son of Megha Chandra. I will go and inform him of your desires."

So the Chakwi flew back to her mate and told him what she had heard and said: "How can I tell the prince of this?" But her mate said: "You must tell him at once."

The prince Sarat Chandra was sleeping close by and as he understood the language of birds he knew what they were saying. So he called the Chakwi and asked her how he could gain the princess. She said: "Go to the shores of the ocean and begin to bale out the water of the sea."

So he began to bale out the water of the sea and by this the throne of Bhagwán began to shake and he in fear sent one of his heavenly messengers to the prince and asked him why he was drying up the sea. The prince answered: "What is that to you. I shall do as it pleases me."

The messenger returned and said:—"He says that he cares not and will do as it pleases him."

Bhagwán sent a second and a third messenger and they received the same answer.

Then Bhagwán went himself and the prince said: "Why are you interrupting me? I will do as it pleases me."

So Bhagwán was sore afraid and sent for all the gods to save his throne and at last Mahadeva came and seating the prince on the *hansa* or sacred swan sent him off under the guidance of a parrot to the palace of the princess. When he arrived he halted in a garden and the parrot went and sat on a tree close to the palace. When the princess came out in the morning and made her usual prayer and offering to the sun, the parrot called to her and said: "He whom you love is in the garden of the king, your father."

When the princess heard this news she was overwhelmed with joy and went and told the queen, her mother, who told the king, her husband. He was much pleased, went and fetched the prince and married him at once to his daughter. When the wedding was over they again mounted the *hansa* and he carried them off to the banks of the Ganges. There they lived many days and the princess gave birth to a son.

One day the prince went to get fire. Now it was the custom of that land that whenever the king of the country died the first stranger who appeared at the city gate was elected Raja in his room. Just then the princess left her boy near the Ganges bank and went to bathe when a merchant who was passing by carried her off in his boat. Meanwhile a jungle cow used daily to give suck to the child and the master of the cow saw her, so he took the boy and reared him as his own son. When the boy grew up the servants of Raja Sarat Chandra heard of this and brought the boy to him. Not knowing him to be his son the Raja kept him in his palace. One day the boat of the merchant came to that city and the boy with some of his friends went on board and as he was telling them the story of his life his mother heard them and rushing out embraced the boy and claimed him as her son. So they were all taken to the Rája Sarat Chandra who acknowledged the lady as his Ráni and the boy as his son. The merchant was executed and the cowherd who reared the prince was rewarded and they all lived happily ever after.

May Parameswar restore us as he restored them.

(A folktale told by Ramsarup, a student of the school at Farrah, Mainpuri District.)

339. **Raja Vena and Raja Vikramaditya.**—Raja Vena was once playing with his little daughter on the roof of his palace and seeing a vulture flying by he said to her in fun: "I will marry you to that vulture." Immediately the vulture who was really Raja Vikramaditya swooped down and the Raja was so much frightened that he had to fulfil his promise and give him his daughter to wife.

After they were married the princess and the vulture went on together and she began to think: "Death is better than to live with this abominable bird." So when she came to a well she jumped in and Vikramaditya after her. By an underground channel they floated on to Ajudhya and there Vikramaditya assumed his real form and lived happily with the princess as her husband.

Meanwhile Raja Vena began to think about the fate of his daughter and went in search of her. When he came to the well he heard that his daughter and her husband had jumped into it, so he jumped in too and by and by came to Ajudhya where he found the pair living happily together.

As he explored the palace of Vikramaditya he found one room full of the hands of men; a second full of casks of human blood and a third full of the tongues of men. When he asked Vikramaditya the cause of this, he said:—" These are the hands of men who clasp the hands of men and then forget their promises; this is the blood of those who clap their breasts and then break their pledge; these are the tongues of those who tell lies. If you had not given me your daughter when you promised her to me your tongue would have been with these."

Then Raja Vena, when he heard these words, blessed himself that he had carried out his promise to Raja Vikramaditya.

(A folktale told by Bihari Lal of Awarekhi, Jagamanpur, Jalaun District.)

340. **The Raja and the Bear.**—One day a Raja went out hunting and going in pursuit of a deer lost his way in the jungle. The deer went out of sight and then the Raja saw a bear being hunted by a tiger. The Raja in fear climbed up a tree and the bear followed him. The Rája was frightened when he saw the bear following him. But the bear said : " Do not fear me; the tiger is the enemy of both of us. You help me and I will help you." The Raja agreed and when it was night the bear said : " I will take the first watch and you can sleep." When the Raja went on watch the tiger said from below : " Throw down the bear and I will devour him." The Raja gave the bear a shove and tried to throw him down, but the bear had his claws well fixed in the tree and woke when he was touched. "You are a false friend," said he, " but I will forgive you this time."

Next morning the bear took the Raja on his back and brought him to his palace. When he got to his gate the Raja called his dogs and set them at the bear. Then the bear ran at him and bit him to death. As he was going away he spoke in this verse :—

Marante ko máriye, ká Rája ká Ráo.

" When a man attacks you kill him whether he be king or prince."

(Told by Akbar Shah, Manjhi of Manbasa, Dudhi, Mirzapur.)

341. **Adam and the Prince.**—There was once a king who was much displeased with his daughter because she would not marry according to his wishes. So he had her sent to live in a hut in the jungle. There by chance the son of another king came to hunt and seeing the princess fell in love with her. They were married and in due time a son was born to her. When her father heard of the birth of the child he sent men into the forest with orders to kill it. One of these men came and took service with the princess and when he got an opportunity he killed the child.

When the mother came home and found the child dead she was half mad with grief. Just then Adam and Eve were flying through the air and heard her cries. They asked her the cause of her grief. Then Adam cut his ring finger and let two drops of blood fall into the mouth of the child which immediately revived. Then Adam and Eve flew away and the prince and princess lived in perfect happiness.—*Pándit Rám Gharib Chaubé.*

MISCELLANEA.

342. Dying man putting his seal in his mouth.—Dariyá Khan, despairing of his life, addressed his two sons and bidding them take his head after his death to the Emperor and save themselves, "*placed his seal within his mouth* and slew himself. His sons executed his commands, but as they were bearing the head before the Emperor, one of the hungry adventurers about the court claimed the merit of having slain the Pathán rebel. Thereupon they pointed to the seal within the dead man's mouth and their mendacious opponent was silenced."—*Lucknow Settlement Report, XLV.*

[Was this a common custom ?—Ed.]

343. The word Biltan.—In Upper India a very common name for the small sleeping tent known in other places as a Raoti is Biltan. Is the word Biltan a corruption of the English "Bell-tent"? If not what is the derivation of the word? Some tent-pitchers call the same kind of tent a Ram-dera, which I suppose is a corruption of Aram-dera, "a tent to rest in."—*W. Crooke.*

344. Marwari Weather Proverbs :—

Sáwan pahli panchimi,
Jhini chhánt pare,
Dunk kahe Bhadli,
Saphla rukh phale.

"On the first 5th of Sáwan
If it drizzles,
Dunk says to Bhadli,
Pod bearing plants will flourish."

Kálo bádal karvaro,
Dholo kare sugál,
Jo chando nirmal huwe,
To pare achintyo kál.

(Observe the moon on 8th Asád),
"If it rises in black clouds, the season will be average,
If in white it will be very good,
If the sky is cloudless
A terrible famine is coming."

Atadon dhur ashtami,
Chánd sawere chhai,
Char nás chávoto rahe
Jiu bhánde re rái.

"If on the 8th Asád
The moon is clouded in the morning,
It will rain often in four months,
As the cracked pot leaks."

Somo Sukron Surguran,
Jo chando ugani,
Dunk kahe Bhudli,
Jal thal ek karant.

"If on Monday or Friday or Thursday
The new moon appears,
Dunk says to Bhadli,
The land will be flooded with rain."

Asádon sunaomi nahin,
Bádal nahin beej,
Hal pharo idhan karo,
Baitho chábo bij,

"On the 24th Asád,
If there be neither cloud nor lightning,
Split up plough for fuel,
And eat up seed-grain sitting idly."

Chait más ne pakh andhárá,
Athoo, chodus do din sárá,
Jin dis lddál jin dis meh,
Jin dis nirmal jin dis kheh.

"In the dark half of Chait,
If the 8th and 14th are cloudy
In any direction there the rain will be plenty,
And which side it is clear there will be but dusty winds and no rain."

Máh mangal Jeth ravi,
Bhaderve Sani hoye,
Dunk kahe hae Bhadli,
Birla jiwe koye.

"If there be five Tuesdays in Mágh and Sundays in Jeth,
Saturdays in Bhadun,
Dunk says to Bhadli,
That few will survive the season.
(So dire will be the famine).''

Jetha ant bigárid,
Punum ne padwá.

"If it rains on 30th of Jeth or 1st of Asád,
It will not rain throughout the month."

Jeth biti pahli padwa,
Rákhe ambar dhar kare,
Asád Sáwan kád kore,
Bhádarwe birkhá kare.

"On the 1st Asád,
If it thunders even slightly,
Asád and Sáwan will be rainless,
But in Bhádun it will pour."

Jeth múnga, sadá sungá.

"If grain be dear in Jeth, it will be cheap during the year."

Sáwan paheli panchmi,
Je nahin gájio payál,
The jdo dhan pihare,
Main jásan mamál.

"On the 5th of Sáwan,
If it does not thunder even distantly,
Wife! go to your father's home,
And I will go to my maternal uncle's.
(Shall have to quit home on account of famine.)"

Sáwan pahile pakh men,
Ja tith uni jai,
Kaek kaek desmen,
Tábar beche mai.

"In the first fortnight of Sáwan,
* If a date be cancelled,
About the country
Mother's will sell their children.
(So severe will be the famine.)"

*In Hindi calander sometimes a date is dropped and sometimes added.

Sáwan bad Ekádasi,
Tin nakattar joe,
Kírtká hue to karvaro,
Rohin húe sugdl,
Tuk ek áwe miraglo,
To pade auchityo kál.

"If the 11th of Sáwan,
Falls within one of three nakshatras, *i.e.*,
If in Kirtka the year will be average,
If in Rohin the year will be very good
And if in Mirag,
Terrible famine will rage."

Ghan bútha,
Kan hán,

"Too much rain,
Harm to grain."

345. **The driving away of the Demon of Poverty.**—In connection with the Dewáli festival there is one custom very remarkable. It is this: Towards the close of the Dewáli night an elderly woman of each Hindu family goes into every room of the dwelling-house beating a winnowing-fan with a stick and muttering these words "May the demon of poverty fly and the goddess of wealth come in "—"*Dalidra bháge, Lakshmi áwe.*" She drives the demon out of the precincts of her house in the same manner. It is supposed that if anybody suffering from *apras* (leprosy) snatches away the winnowing-fan while the woman is still in the act of driving away the demon and gets it burnt and applies its ashes to the affected parts he is cured.—*Pándit Rám Gharib Chaubé.*

346. **Bahraich: The effect of a Saint's Curse.**—By the end of Sháhjahán's reign the town of Dúgaon was deserted, the legend being that a saintly mendicant in a fit of ill-humour cursed it so effectually as to cause the inhabitants to leave it *en masse*. The tomb of the spiteful old man, Sháh Sajan, is now the resort of pious pilgrims and a large fair is held on the site of the old town.—*Settlement Report, p. 25.*

347. **The Tesu Flower.**—The Tesu, or flower of the Dhák tree (*Butea frondosa*), is held sacred because Durga is supposed to live in it. So many persons hang representations of the flower or the flower itself round the necks of children to keep off demons. Men also carry it because wearing it increases wisdom. This is a rule of the Shastras.—*Ramlal Dube.*

348. **Saharanpur: Sirsawa.**—The town of Sirsawa in the Saharanpur District is said to take its name from a Hindu Raja, named Saras who was defeated and killed by some of the early Muhammadan conquerors. Here is the tomb of one Khwaja Ahmad which is worshipped both by Muhammadans and Hindus on the sixth of the Muhammadan month Rajab.—*Pándit Rám Gharib Chaubé.*

349. **Palamau: Witches' Spells.**—Sometimes the witch comes to the house at midnight and, without entering it, with an instrument resembling a native inoculating lancet, she scores certain marks on the wall of the house, mentioning at the same time the name of the person on whom she is working her spell and muttering certain incantations. In the morning a facsimile of the mark made on the wall appears on the arm or other part of the body of the victim, who always dies. This has been said to occur to several persons in a house, one on each successive night, till at last the whole family has been obliged to fly. The above story was told me by one of the most enlightened of the Rájput zamindárs, who not only professed the strongest belief in the power of witchcraft, but offered to bring me the next person in his own village who had been so marked.—*L. R. Forbes' Report, p. 55.*

350. **Contemptuous Salutation.**—When low city rascals meet a superior on the road and wish to insult him with a pretence of respect they do not *salam* in the ordinary way but bring the hand up to the nose, then to the forehead and then to the neck, rubbing these parts of the body as if they felt itchy.—*Pándit Rám Gharib Chaubé.*

351. **Bell-metal Vessels and Small-pox.**—It is a general rule when a person is down with small-pox and a thunder-storm comes on, to remove all the bell-metal vessels out of the way. They say that if this be not done the sick person will never recover and the demon of the lightning will seize him.—*M. Balkrishna Lal.*

352. **The Ass: belief regarding.**—Villagers object most particularly to an ass trespassing in their fields. They say that the plant which an ass nibbles at, or on which his urine falls, never grows again.—*Pándit Kashi Nath.*

353. **Inscriptions on Sikh Coins and Seals.**—At Lóhgarh, Bandah tried to assume something of regal state. He was the *Sacá Pádsháh* or Veritable Sovereign, his disciples all *Singhs*, or lions. A new form of greeting, *Fath dárds* (May you behold victory!), was invented, and Muhammadans were slightingly called *Maslah*. Coin was struck in the new sovereign's name. One side bore the lines :

Sikkah zad bar har dó 'álam tegh-i-Nának wáhib ast,
Fath Góbind Sháh-i-shánán fazl-i-Sacá Sáhib ast.

If we are to judge by this halting, obscure verse, Bandah was a better warrior than he was poet. The lines, an obvious imitation of the inscriptions on the Mughal coins, seem to mean "Fath Góbind, king of kings, struck coin in the two worlds, the sword of Nának is the granter of desires, by grace he is the veritable Lord." On the reverse were these words, *Zarb ba Amanu-d-dahr, Maswarat-shahr, Zinatu-t-takht-i-mubdrakbakht.* "Coined at Refuge of the World, the Walled City, Ornament of the Fortunate Throne." These were the titles and epithets assigned by him to Lóhgarh, just as each imperial city had its appropriate honorific name. On his letters he impressed a seal, bearing the following rhyming inscription :

Teg, dég, o fath, nusrat-i-bé-dirang.
Yaft az Nának, Guru Góbind Singh.

"Guru Góbind Singh found in Nának, sword, pot, and conquest, help without hindrance or delay." Not content with supremacy in the state he also claimed, as other sovereigns have done, to be above grammar. By his order all nouns in Hindi and Persian having feminine terminations were changed into the masculine form. For instance, *sandri* (retinue) and *kacahri* (a court-house or office) were pronounced by him and Sikhs, *sandrá* and *kacahará !—W. Irvine., J. A. S. B., LXIII., 1894.*

---

354 A Charm to remove pustules from the tongue of a baby.—Repeat the following incantation five or seven times over some ashes of cow-dung, rub the ashes on the tongue of the child and by the aid of Hanumán the pustules will disappear.

Tarabh utarabh tel karai,
Dijai bati tel barai,
Ghalat salat tu bái rog,
Nindwa rahai to jati Hanumant ki dohai.

"The oil in the lamp boils; when you put a wick in it, it lights. O Ninawa, thou art a noisome disease of the air. If Ninawa does not depart I will hold Hanuman responsible.—*Pandit Rám Gharib Chaubé.*

---

355. Faizabad: Story of a Witch.—Pirthiráj, the founder of the Palwár Chhattris of Faizábád, is said to have married a fairy (*deo kanya*) or a witch (*dáin*). On one occasion after the birth of her son this lady was engaged in the homely office of baking cakes, when her infant, which lay some paces off, began to cry. The domestic feelings were divided between neglecting the babe and neglecting the cakes : at this juncture the husband arrived just in time to see his wife, fairy or fiend, assume supernatural and gigantic proportions, so as to allow both the baking and nursing to go on at one and the same time. But finding her secret discovered the witch disappeared for ever leaving her son as a legacy to her astonished husband.—*Settlement Report, p. 153.*

---

356. A Shástric Charm to keep the Evil-eye off a Child.—Write the following on a piece of birch-bark and tie it on the right arm of a boy and on the left arm of a girl and then there is no danger of the evil-eye :—

Raksha raksha Mahádeva, nilgriwa jatá dhara ;
Grahaistu sahito raksha, munch munch kumar kam.

"O Mahadeva, who hast a blue neck and long locks on the head protect this poor boy or child from the evil-eye, &c.—*Pandit Rám Gharib Chaubé.*

---

357. A Jogi buried forty days under ground.—My first acquaintance with the narrative dates from my boyhood. About the time of the occurrence I heard it related by my father; and his authority was the well-known General Avitable, Ranjit Sinh's right-hand man, who was present. Those facts are that a certain *Jogi* (Hindu anchorite) said to possess the power of suspending at will the animation of his body, was sent for by Ranjit Sinh, and declining to obey was brought by force into the tyrant's presence and ordered to give, under pain of death, a practical proof of his supposed power. He submitted perforce. He was put by his disciples through certain processes during which he became perfectly unconscious ; the pulse ceased, his breath did not stain a polished mirror, and a European doctor who was present declared that the heart had ceased to beat. To all appearances he was as dead as Queen Anne. In this state he was put into a carefully-made box, the lid was closed and sealed with Ranjit Sinh's ring. The box was buried in a vault prepared in an open plot of ground under the royal windows at Lahore, and the place was guarded day and night by Ranjit's own guards under General Avitable's own supervision. Sun and rain came, and grass sprung up, grew and withered on the surface over the grave, and the sentries went their rounds, and the *Jogi's* disciples and friends were all kept under surveillance not to call it imprisonment. After forty days, in Ranjit Singh's own presence the vault was uncovered and the box extracted from it with its seals intact. It was opened and showed the *Jogi* within precisely as he had been placed. He was taken out dead still, to all appearance, but the body uncorrupt. His disciples were now brought to manipulate the body in the manner which he had taught them, and which he had publicly explained before his burial. He revived, as he had said he would, and was soon in as perfect health as when he had suspended his life. He refused all gifts, and retired to his former retreat, but shortly afterwards he and his disciples disappeared. It was not safe for such a man to live in the jurisdiction of so inquisitive and arbitrary a ruler. Ranjit Sinh cared little for human life, which was his toy or plaything. No one who knows his historical character, will, for a moment, admit that he would let himself be deceived for being played upon in a matter on which he had set his heart. Each scene,—the suspension of life and burial, the disinterment, the reviving—took place in the tyrant's own presence and before hundreds of spectators in open daylight and with every precaution that absolute despotic powers could command. Ranjit cared little whether the man lived or died, so that his own curiosity was gratified. The guards under the palace windows commanded by Avitable would be anxious solely to carry out Ranjit Singh's wishes.—"*Times of Assam.*"

---

358. Sheep unlucky.—Sheep are considered very unlucky, and if, when setting out on a journey, a scrupulous person gets any of the dust raised by a sheep on any part of his body he should turn back.—*Pandit Rám Gharib Chaubé.*

---

359. A City turned into stone.—There is a place known as Giri-Kota on the borders of the Nahan State and British territory of which the following legend is told. These two towns lie on opposite sides of a river. One day a Natin or rope-dancing girl came to the Raja and offered to cross the river on a rope with a flour mill tied to her feet. When she was doing the feat the Raja cut the rope and she fell into the river and was killed. With her dying breath she cursed the Raja and his people that they should be turned into stone and that their city should become a wilderness. The prophecy was fulfilled and the town was destroyed. Now-a-days when men dig on the site of the old city they find stone figures which are said to be those of the Raja and his people.—*W. Crooke.*

North Indian Notes and Queries:
A MONTHLY PERIODICAL.

VOL. V.] NOVEMBER, 1895. [NO. 8.

CONTENTS OF THIS NUMBER.
(The references are to the Notes.)

Popular Religion ... ... 127 to 132	Folktales ... 139 to 142
Anthropology ... ... 133 ,, 138	Miscellanea ... ... 143 ,, 144

POPULAR RELIGION.

360. Sahâranpur: Khwája Khizr worshipped by Dhobis.—Kwája Khizr, the god of water (*Introduction to Popular Religion*, 26), is much revered by Dhobis at Sahâranpur. They attribute to him their protection from cold when they stand in water in the winter. On a Saturday in Asârh they offer to him *pilou*, or meat boiled with rice. They also make a sort of little raft of sticks and, placing a lamp on it, let it float in a tank. As to who Khwája Khizr was, they have no idea.—*Pándit Rám Gharíb Chaubé.*

361. Muhammadans and Wolves.—Muhammadans do not look on wolves with any feeling of hatred. They say that when his brothers threw Yúsuf (Joseph) into a well, they smeared his clothes with blood and took them to their father Yáqúb (Jacob) and said that the wolves had killed him. Yáqúb, who was a great saint, called all the wolves next morning and asked them if they had killed his son. They swore on oath and said : "If we have killed thy son may we be born in the Thirteenth Century," a very serious oath for a Muhammadan to take, because the thirteenth is the worst century to be born in.—*Pándit Rám Gharíb Chaubé.*

[There is no reference to this legend in the Twelfth Súrah of the Qurán which deals with the story of Jacob. The wolf is a sacred animal, mainly, apparently, because he devours the dead.

What is the idea about the Thirteenth Century based on ?—ED.]

362. Boat Festivals.—The Bera festival in Bengal is said to have been introduced by Siráj uddaula in honour of one of the Muhammadan kings of Bengal, who one night fell out of a boat into the water and would have been drowned were it not for a sudden illumination made by a number of girls who simultaneously launched their boats into the river. These boats are made of a cocoanut adorned with flowers, and each carries a little lamp.

There seems little doubt that the festival is really in honour of the water-god, Khwája Khizr, or Varun Deota, who is generally worshipped by all castes which have anything to do with water, such as the Dhobi and the Rangrez.

What is known as the Burhwa Mangal, the great river festival of Benares which is celebrated after the Holi, is also in honour of the water deity.

In fact, there seems reason to believe that this feast may in former times have been accompanied with human sacrifices. This is shown by the red powder which is plentifully showered into the water, the marking of the heads and foreheads with the same powder, and the wearing of garlands of flowers and images of *bhuts* and demons on this occasion.

The choice of Tuesday for this festival is another proof of the same fact ; because, among Hindus, Tuesday is emphatically the day for letting of blood and was even adopted by the Muhammadan Emperors as the day for the execution of criminals.—*Pándit Rám Gharíb Chaubé.*

(In connection with this worship of Khwája Khizr, the following account of another water-god in Bengal. Pír Badr, from the notes of the late J. Wise, *M.D., J, A.S., Bengal*, 1873, p. 302, may be quoted :—" Besides Khwája Khizr, Bengal supplies other animistic ideas regarding water ; and Pír Badr shares with him the dominion of the rivers. This spirit is invoked by every sailor and fisherman when starting on a cruise, or when overtaken by a squall or storm. All Muhammadans agree that he resides at Chittagong, but his history does not disclose the reason why the attributes of a water demon were conferred on him. According to one account he was a shipwrecked Portuguese sailor named Pas Gual Peeris Botheilo, who reached the shore by clinging to a piece of wreck. The guardians of his shrine, moreover, say that about one hundred and fifty years ago Pír Badr arrived at Chittagong floating on a rock, and informed the terror-stricken inhabitants that he had come all the way from Akyab on this novel craft. The neighbourhood of Chittagong being then infested by *jinns* or evil spirits, he exterminated them and took possession of the whole country. The modern *dargáh*, or cenotaph of Pír Badr, stands in the centre of Chittagong and is regarded as the palladium of the city. *Faqírs* are the custodians, and the mosque with its rooms for pilgrims is kept scrupulously clean. On the walls of the cenotaph are ten niches for oil-lamps, which are lighted every evening and burn all night. Pilgrims from all parts of Bengal visit the *dargáh* in fulfilment of vows, or to obtain the favour and intercession of the saint, while Hindu fishermen regard him with as much awe as the Muhammadans. His *Urs* or festival is celebrated annually on the 25th of Ramzan, the anniversary of his death. There can, however, be little doubt that Pír Badr is no other than Badruddín Badr-i-'Alam, for many years a resident of Chittagong, who died A. H. 844 (*A. D.* 1440), and was buried in the *Chhota Dargáh* of Bihár, but about whom we possess no other particulars.")

363. **Tibet Buddhism.**—Buddhistic Lamaism, as practised in Mongolia and Tibet, bears an extraordinary resemblance in external forms and ceremonies to the ritual of the Roman Catholic forms of Christianity. Are there any grounds for supposing that these were derived from Nestorian and Roman Catholic Missionaries who laboured in Central Asia, or is the reverse the case ? Lamaism is said " not only to have its Pope, its Cardinals and its Bishops, but infant baptism, confirmation, litanies, processions, services with double choirs, masses for the living and the dead, the worship of the saints, exorcisms and fast-days in addition to which may be mentioned the use of the cross, the mitre, the dalmatica (Hooker figures a Cardinal's hat), the cope, chaplets and rosaries, holy-water, flower-stands on the altar, and so forth."

Sir Joseph Hooker was also very much struck with this resemblance N. of Darjeeling. Lamas, as mentioned in *Notes and Queries*, use a very singular musical instrument, " consisting of a human thigh bone hollowed out and converted into a musical pipe."—*Gray,* 134.

In the Ta-fo Temple at Pekin, in addition to copper and marble vessels placed on the altar of this Lama temple, " is a singular vessel which consists of the upper portion of a human skull, lined with gold, silver or copper, and filled with precious articles." The skull is either that of one who has been distinguished for his abilities or of a youth who has died in his 18th or 19th year of age, which is regarded with peculiar reverence by the Mongolians.—*Gray,* 136.

May not this skull custom have been impaled from India with Buddhism ? I have constantly seen *faqírs* with a well polished human calvarium in their hands.—*J. Cockburn.*

364. **Worship of Mahakali by Rajputs.**—The worship of the goddess Mahakáli is most popular among the Rajpúts. The following is the mode of worshipping her : Her votaries fast on the first lunar day of Kuár until the ninth ; during that time eating only at night herbs and fruits and drinking *sherbet*. They must attend to no worldly business during this time. In the morning after bathing Siva and Kali are worshipped, and on the ninth day after cleansing the house thoroughly an image of Mahakáli is made as follows : She is represented as black, mounted on a chariot, drawn by four tigers. She has sixteen arms, and round her neck is represented a garland of skulls. In her hands she holds a trident, sword, conch-shell, lotus, gourd, a mace, fire and blood. This image must be made in a room facing the north-east. It may be made of gold, silver, earth or wood, according to the means of the worshipper. To it are offered yellow cloth, gems and gold, fruits and flowers of the season. She chiefly delights in the fruit of the *bel* and mango. This *bel* fruit is sometimes known as *sriphala*, " the

fruit of good luck." Lastly, with the suitable formulas, a young buffalo is offered to her. The offering should be made at midnight. As the worshipper sacrifices his victim he shouts Káli! Káli! Then he gives alms to the poor and presents to Bráhmans. This worship is often associated with that of Nawa Mátrika Devi.—*Pandit Chandrabali Shukl.*

365. **The Number Five.**—Like the number seven the number five plays a very important part in the beliefs of ordinary Hindus. Thus there are :

Panchadhyaya.—The five chapters of the " Sri Mad Bhagwat,' giving an account of the sports of Krishna with the Gopis.

Panchagni.—The five fires within the circle of which the *Jogi* sits and does his penance in the hot weather. He lights a fire to the north, south, east and west and the sun overhead makes the fifth.

Panchamrit.—A mixture of milk, curds, sugar, ghi and honey is offered to Vishnu and is also used in various forms of purification.

Panchindri.—The five organs of sense and action.

Panchang.—The five modes of devotion—silent prayer, burnt offerings, libations, pouring water over idols and feeding Bráhmans.

Panchpatra.—The five vessels used collectively in the worship of idols.

Panchpran.—The five kinds of air supposed to be in the body.

Panchtirath.—The five holy places of pilgrimage—Visrant, Sankar, Naimish, Prayag, and Pushlar.

Panchratna.—The five precious stones—diamond, pearl, ruby, amethyst and gold used in Hindu worship.

Panchkosi.—The sacred road, five *kos* long, at Benares.

Panchgavya.—The five purificatory substances yielded by the cow—milk, curds, ghi, dung and urine.

Panchmahayajna.—The five great sacraments of the Hindus—Brahmayajna, Devyajna, Pitriyajna, Manushyayajna, Bhutayajna—or devotional acts have reference severally to the Veda, the gods, the manes, men and all created beings. As Manu (III., 70) says :—" Teaching and studying the Scripture is the sacrament of the Veda ; offering of cakes and water, the sacrament of the manes ; an oblation of fire, the sacrament of the deities; giving rice or other food to living creatures, the sacrament of the spirits ; receiving guests with honour, the sacrament of men. Whoever omits not these five great ceremonies, if he have ability to perform them, is untainted by the sins of five slaughter places, even though he constantly resides at home. But whoever cherishes not five orders of beings, namely, the deities, those who demand hospitality, those whom he ought by law to maintain, his departed fore-fathers, and himself, that man lives not even though he breathe."

We have again various other groups of five. Thus there are the five gods—Vishnu, Mahesa, Brahma, Ganesa and Sakti; five sacred beings whose names may be mentioned in the morning with advantage—Hari, Bali, Karan, Yudhisthira and Parasurama. Thus a well known verse says—

Prat lijai panch nam—
Hari, Bali, Karan, Yudhisthira, Parasurama.

Again, there are five girls whose names ought to be mentioned with reverence in the morning—Ahalya, Tara, Kunta, Draupadi and Mandodari. These are known collectively as the panch kanya or five maidens—*Pandit Rám Gharib Chaubi.*

366. **A Miracle wrought by Kabir.**—The Kabirpanthis relate the following as one of the most remarkable miracles wrought by Kabir. One time all the Bráhmans made a combination against Kabir in order to lower him in the estimation of the public. So they told all the religious beggars that on a certain day Kabir would give a general feast and that they should all attend. Kabir knew nothing of this and on the appointed day, multitudes of beggars assembled at his hermitage from all quarters. Kabir considered and was aware of the trick. So he went secretly into the forest. Then Vishnu in the form of Kabir came and entertained all the guests. He fed them for fifteen days and then dismissed them with presents. By this time Kabir returned and as he came home, he hears every one blessing him for his great charity. He was amazed, but a voice from heaven came unto him and said that it was Vishnu himself who had interposed to save his honour. So the fame of Kabir increased and the Bráhmans had to admit his divine power.—*Babu Manghi Lál.*

367. **Hardwar : Worship of the Brahmanical Thread.**—All Bráhmans, who take offerings at the bank of a sacred river, are considered to be in some degree degraded. This is particularly shown in the contempt which is felt for the river Bráhmans, such as the Ghatiya and Prágwál branches. In order to relieve the pollution thus attaching to them from their occupation, the Bráhmans of Hardwár have a particular worship of their sacred cords. In the morning on the last day of the month Sáwan they repair to the banks of the river and rub their bodies with the five products of the sacred cow. Then they rub themselves with the holy earth of the Ganges and bathe. After this they do the usual daily worship, repeat the Gayatri mantra, offer water to the Sun-godling and to the

manes of their ancestors. Then they make an altar or Vedi of the river sand according to the standard rules and in the centre place a jar of water in which, by special prayers, they introduce the god Bráhma. In the jar are then placed as many new Bráhmanical cords as there be Bráhmans engaged in the worship, and over the platform flowers are scattered and incense burnt. All the Bráhmans sit round the altar and repeat special prayers with the object of calling all the gods to assemble round the centre pitcher representing Bráhma. For each deity a leaf of the mango tree is arranged as a seat. An elderly Bráhman leads the service, and all present repeat the *mantras* after him. At the end of the repetition of each *mantra* each Bráhman with his holy spoon or *achmani* throws a little water on the vessel which contains the cords. The *mantras* are repeated one hundred and eight times or some multiple of that number. When the gods have thus blessed the cords with their presence at the service they are dismissed to their respective heavens with the appropriate *mantras*.

This concludes the consecration of the new cords which each man puts on and the old cords are thrown into the Ganges. Then each Bráhman worships his fellows, and gifts are distributed. This finishes their purification for another year, during which they may accept gifts on the banks of the sacred river, as usual, without incurring the danger of any ceremonial pollution. This worship must be done fasting, and no food is taken that day until it is concluded.—*W. Crooke.*

368. **Lingam Worship of Mahadeva.**—There is a special virtue in the worship of Mahadeva during a Malmas or intercalary month. During this time it is advisable to make the lingam of earth and to throw it away after worshipping it. But the lingam must be made of particular kinds of earth. Those considered best for this purpose are either the earth of an ant-hill or that from the bank of a river. The ant-hill is used for this purpose, because the ant is, of all creatures, considered the most prolific, and thus the earth from the mound of white-ants is considered best adapted for the worship of the symbol of reproduction.

369. **Sitala.**—Sitala, the goddess of small-pox, has several forms: Sitala, Selhara, Runki, Jhunki, Mahala and Mandala Devi. They are known as the Ghor Sakti or awful powers. They are degraded goddesses, and so the ass has been given to them as a vehicle.—*Pándit Rám Gharíb Chaubé.*

[The enumeration of the forms of Sitala varies everywhere. Another list is given in *Introduction to Popular Religion and Folklore*, p. 80. They probably represent a congeries of goddesses of disease, who have been gradually introduced into Bráhmanism.—ED.]

370. **The Legend of Narsi Bhagat.**—The following ballad of the pious Narsi Bhagat is very popular among the peasantry of the Western Districts of the North-Western Provinces:—

Jhunagarh Narsi basé, Bhagat bhâu liyé sáth ;
Kripa kar darshan diyé, Sripati Sri Jaggannáth.

"Narsi lived in Jhunagarh with the form and feeling of a devotee. Sripati (the husband of Lakshmi) and Jaggannáth appeared before him"

Dawát kalam kághas mangwáké,
Likhaiya ek bulwáé lo, ab-hin kághas do likhwáké.
Likh do "pát patambar, zarin báfta, dushálí khákhi asu Mahmudi.
Syál kor lagé hai dur hálé.
Kai hasár to likhi sut ki, kai hazár likhi reshami.
Kai man to likhi supári, kai man mehndi rolí.
Kai man to likhé kaldwé aur mewan ki boré.
Kai hasár to likhi asharfí, kai lákh likhé rotari.
Aur bhanté patthar do likh do, tyun uthi boli do-hari.
Moti, surma, sab kuchh likh do, aru gahno do chhauri."

Yo yo thát likhyo Narsi ko, bakhtáwar wo báp re

"She sent for a pen, paper and the elders of the house. They all sat together. She then told him to send for a scribe and get a letter written by him. The scribe was called, and she dictated thus: 'Send for me robes of silk, gold embroidery, shawls and other clothes. Send thousands of cotton robes and garments of silk. Send many maunds of betel-nuts, henna, and red powder. Send many maunds of rich cakes, bags of fruit, thousands of gold coins, lakhs of rupees, vessels full of precious stones, ornaments, pearls and antimony.'"

Sain Bhagat rukhsat kari, kahkar hái hawál ;
Samigri ati hi likhi, Narsi nrip ke mal.

"She sent Sain Bhagat to tell everything to her father Narsi, and she wrote in the letter many things."

Leja kághas ab tu mera, wa Narsi ke pás re.
Bida kiya aru kharch bandháya wah Jhunagarh jaé re.
Rám ! Rám ! kahi dijo sab ko, aur kahyo syabás re.
Aur kahyo jaldi se áwen sakal jíns liyé sáth re.
Tum to Seth baré Narsiji, nam to kari hain ás ré.
Ham to suna sada sang tuhare Sanwaliya se Shák ré.

Sain Bhágatji lekar pahuncho, do Narsi ke háth re.
Tab Narsiji bachan lage sun lijo Vraj Nath re.

"O Sain Bhagat," says the daughter of Narsi: "Take this letter to my father." She gave him money for the journey and he set off for Jhunagarh. "Give everyone my salutations. Tell my father to come quickly, with all I want. Tell him that he is a very rich man and so I depend on him for everything. Say that I hear that the lord Krishna is always with him." So Sain Bhagat went and gave the letter to Narsi, and he began to read the letter in all confidence to his lord Sri Krishna.

Tabkin bághaz bánchi he Narsi bhayé udás ;
Ter hari Bhagwán se, tumhari mujh ko ás.

"When he had read the letter to the lord Krishna he grew sad, and he cried to the lord: 'In thee only do I trust.'"

Kághaz hamari ayo hai, ji Sánwal Sháh Bádsháh.
Tumhi jáwa hamári, tumhi punjí hai, tum-hin karo nirbah.
Sásu, nandi, deorani, jetháni, likhau hai mato upáe.
In ko dosh kaha ko dijo, jánaiu hain moto Sháh.
Jins likhai be ginti hain aur likhe do bhánra.
Kuber se bhándari tiháre aur Lakshmi hamlάe.
Tumhári mahdma tumhi jano, sun lijo dabáya.
Narsi Mahta Mahta Dás tumháré, nij charnan sir náé.

"O dark King! a letter has come to you. Thou art my treasury; thou art my support. Mother-in-law, husband's sister, elder brother's wife of my daughter have written this letter after consultation among themselves. But I do not blame them as they think me a very rich man. They ask for unlimited supplies in two vessels. O Lord! if you have a store-keeper like Kuvera (the god of wealth) and your spouse is as the goddess Lakshmi. Your power you know yourself. Listen and protect me in your bosom. Narsi Mahta is your servant and bows at your feet.

Narsi patri páe bahut raho sharmáe.
Jutan puchhta bhát ka, bhaiyon ko bulwáya.

'Narsi was put to shame at the receipt of the letter and calling his brethren asked their advice."

Bhái to we yon uth bole—Sunyo bhai.
Pánch sát mundiya saug le lo, pánch sát lo bái.
Jab Narsiji dagar chalé hain, sab ko ús hánsi.
Dekhenge ab kaha karoge, gahri jhánjh bajai.
Táti si ek gári lini, bodé bail jagái.
I ánch sat muriya sang liné, gahre tilak lagái.
Bhaiyon ne sab sammat kini, Narsi tu mat jaiyo.
Bilt samán ham bhát bheje hain, ham ko mat na lajáiyo.
Itni sunkar tab Narsiji jins bánch suudi.
Prabhu sa aur na dene-hára tumhári saráha nahin.
Tab Narsi ganwai ja pahunché, samdhi khabar jondi.
Rám! Rám! kahwa karbheji khark men jagah batái.

"The brethren, by way of a joke, advised him to take with him to his daughter a few shaven-headed mendicants and a few women of his order. When he started with the mendicants all burst into laughter. They began to say: 'Now we shall see what your playing on the sacred instruments will avail you.' Narsi took a wretched cart and yoked in it a pair of broken-down oxen. He took some mendicants with him and marked his forehead with sandal. His brethren advised him not to go lest he should be disgraced. He replied: 'I have no fear of disgrace, as I can only send presents according to my means,' He read out the letter describing the things which his daughter required. Says he: 'There is none so generous as the Lord. I want nothing from you.' So he started, and news of his arrival reached the house of his son-in-law. His father-in-law, thinking him a poor man, merely sent his salutation and told him to stay at the back of his house."

Táto pani karo chhai, nahwáno táto páni dharo.
Chánwal daro tijai tamen aiso garm karo.
Tab Narsiji kar melano anda jaro.
Thora silo deya samoyao, yon mukh se uchcharo.
Tháro huhm men Narsiji, sab mil utha karo.
Itni sunkar tab Narsiji ne háth tál par karo.
Man ghan Syám Sundar ko hridai dhyán karo,
Ai ghata barsan lagyo, aiso thandha karyo.

"Hot-water was placed for his bath. So warm was it, that if rice were put in it, it would be boiled. Narsi dipped his hand in it and it began to burn. Then he said: 'Put some cold water in it.' But his daughter answered: 'You give many orders, father Narsi, but who will execute them?' He was grieved at the insolence of his daughter, but he restrained himself and only clapped his hands and sang the praise of Sri Krishna, who is dark as the clouds of the rainy season. Then lo! it rained so violently, that the water was cooled at once."

Beti kahe: 'Suno bábaji kya kya samán layé ho?
Hamko to kachhu dikhai nahin, jhánjh bajáwat áyé ho.
Tútí si ek gári dekhi, bodé bail lagáyé ho.
Pánch sát sang mundiya dekhé, gahré tilak bandáyé ho.
Ham pe to kachhu na dena ko, Sánwal Sháh buláyé ho.
Beti kahe: 'Suno bábaji, we Sánwariya kab áwenge?
Hamre purush ko sab koi puchho, kaun gánw par náyé ho?
Jáwo pita tum wuhin jáwo, hamen lajáwan aye ho.'
Kahen Narsi: 'Suno tum, beti, bodi bát bisháro ho,
Ek palak men sab kuchh dewen, we Sanwariya giridhári hain.
Sánwari surat madhuri múrat, hridai basi pyári hai.
Beg hi kaj karo Maharája mujhko as tihári kai.
Narsi Dás tumháro chero, patit ját hámdri hai.

"His daughter said: 'O Babaji, what have you brought with you? I see nothing. You seem to have come playing only on the cymbals. I see a broken cart with wretched oxen. Some shaven-headed mendicants are with you. You have a great mark on your forehead. But you have nothing to give me. I hear you have invoked the Black King, but he has nothing for me. You ask about all the males of the house, but why do you not say where the Black King is? You had better go to him. You have come only to put me to shame.' Then Narsi said: 'My

daughter, your thoughts are foolish. In a moment he can give all things. It was he who held up the hill to protect the cowherds. I have faith in him, as his power is beyond that of mortals. His form is dark and lovely. That form is impressed on my heart. O King, soon do my work. I have my hope on thee. The slave Narsi has no other lord but you. I myself am naught,'"
Narsi prabhu dhyán dhar, sumrit hain har bár;
Bhát den din a gaya, kahán lagái bár?
Narsi then concentrated his thoughts on the lord and began to repeat his name. The time for making the presents arrived. " O Lord," he prayed, " where dost thou delay?"
Ai Sauwaliya kahán lagái der?
Unche charkhe teron tum ho, sun lijo hamári her.
Sánware kya kahún, káj karé bhaktan he, kya nidra lini gher?
Kuber se bhándari tháre, Lakshmi sang ter.
Joi joi jins likhi kághaz men unhin mangi her.
Mála dina byáh sanjoya hundi sakáré mer.
Chaulhe ke má mora dena ayo hyún na saber?
Yah Gujaráti Siva ke upási pujain shám saber.
Narsi Mahta Dás tumháré nij charnan ke cher.
" O Dark one, beloved, where dost thou delay? I cry to thee from the height. Listen to my cry. Thou helpest those who believe in thee. Why are you sleeping to-day? You have a storekeeper like Kuvera and the goddess of wealth is your wife. I ask you to give the things written in the letter. You gave the garland, you arranged the marriage, you witnessed my bond. This is the fourth time I claim thy aid. Why do you delay your coming. Gujaratis worship Siva morn and evening. Narsi Mahta is thy servant."
Jo prabhu ka suran karen, honya sugam sab káj.
Narsi ki pati rakhte ap chalé Maharáj.
" Those who remember the Lord have their troubles removed. Set out, Great King, to maintain the honour of Narsi."
Apne hin háthon hánké rath kun rath baithé Ranchhor,
Jo aye kamla rathi, aru áp sarathi, asht siddh wah nau nidh lai.
Soran ki hai kal, ghoran achhe, kalas baudyé.
Hem ka rath, aru jarau haighi, adbhut ghanta adhik lagáyé.
Chira patka aur bahuchi prabhu bauiya ka bhesh bandyé.
Kankh men bahi, Bhagat ke karan, kán kalam wah láyé hain.
Puchhain log kahán se dyé, un Narsi ne buláye hain.
Narsi náchat khabar jo páyé, daur charan men paré hain.
Sadhu sant sab darshan kun dhdyé.
Age age Narsi Mahta le samadhi darwáza dhaiye.
" Then Ranchhor (Krishna) sat on his chariot and drove it with his own hand. He had with him all the goddesses of riches. His chariot was of gold and his horses unsurpassed. His crest was studded with gems and there were bells on the chariot. Krishna attires himself as a baniya with an account-book under his arm, and a pen on his ear. This he did for the sake of Narsi. They asked who he was and how he came; he said : ' I am a baniya and have come at the order of Narsi Bhagat.' When Narsi heard of the arrival of Krishna he danced with joy and ran up and fell at his feet. All the saints hastened to behold the deity. Narsi and Krishna came together to the door of Narsi's daughter.
Samadhi sab puchhan lágé Sri Krishna se bát.
Kaun nám, kya got hai, ho Narsi ke sáth?
" Then the father-in-law of Narsi's daughter began to ask Sri Krishna who he was, and of what *gotra*, and how he came with Narsi.
Sab mil samadhi puchhan lágé kaun tumhára nám chhai.
Tum to apna got batáwo, kaha tumháro nám chhai.
Kákar tum chákar kahiye kaho tumháro gáuw chhai.
Yadubansi got hamdro, Yadupuri hamdro gduw chhai.
Ya Narsi ke chákar kahiyé, Sauwaliya mera nám chhai.
" The father-in-law began to ask Krishna what was his name and what his village. Whose servant are you? Krishna answered : 'I am a Yadubansi and my village is Yadupuri. I am the servant of Narsi and my name is Sanwaliya—the Black One."
Narsi Sánwal Sháhji sab puchhan ke sáth.
Ankh khuli bhaunchak rahé, dekha jab hin bhát.
" When all the brethren of the father-in-law saw the Black King with all the presents which were required their eyes were opened."
Diné pát patambar ambar sarin báfta, dushálé kháw.
Aru Mahmúdi, sydl kot, lágé hai dur hálé.
Kai haedr to dai suit ki, kai hazár dai reshmi.
Kai man menhdi rori, kai man to diye kaldwe, kehu ke tum bhai ho?
Krishna gave to Narsi's daughter yellow robes of silk, embroidered cloths, shawls and cloths arrayed with pearls. He gave her thousands of cotton cloths, maunds of betel-nuts, henna and red powder,"
Narsi also bhátí dyá, ham ne ek taka nahín páya.
Main jáne na dungi hum bawal ki jáya.
Wah shubh ghari charnan lag Narsi jab dhyás lagáya.
Narsi ter kari Prabhuji si tab subaran menh barsáya.
Pákar sampati naggar sára phúla ang na samáya.
Narsi Bhagat llu charnan men Hari ne káj banáya.
" Narsi's daughter said : ' Father, I have received the presents but no money. What kind of brother is Krishna? I will not let him go till I get the money—if I am the true daughter of my father.' Then Narsi fixed his thoughts on the feet of the Lord and began to pray to him. Then Krishna was moved and shed golden tears. The whole city was so pleased at the riches, that they could not contain their delight. Narsi was absorbed in devotion, because Krishna in the form of Hari had done all his business for him.—*Pándit Rám Gharíb Chaubé.*

ANTHROPOLOGY.

371. Initiation—Special times for.—Special months are considered auspicious or inauspicious for the performance of the rite of initiation. If a boy be initiated in the month of Chait he will fall into trouble; if in Baisákh he will have to go and bathe at various sacred places; if in Jeth he will die soon; if in Asárh his brother will die; if in Sáwan he will be happy; if in Bhádon his children will suffer; if in Kártik he will be rich; if in Aghan he will have sacred rites performed at his house; if in Pús he will gain no divine knowledge; if in Magh he will acquire divine knowledge; if in Phálgun he will be rich and happy.—*Páudit Rám Gharib Chaubé.*

372. On some additional Folk-Beliefs about the Tiger.—In my paper entitled "*On the Indian Folk-Beliefs about the Tiger*,"[*] I have given some instances of popular and superstitious beliefs about the "King of the Indian Forests," prevailing among the various races inhabiting India and the countries adjacent to it. In the present paper I intend to gather together some additional forms of superstitious belief about the same animal prevailing among the various Indian races.

There is a superstitious belief prevalent in one form or another among the various Indian races, which forbids them to call evil things by their respective names. Whenever that particular thing has to be mentioned, it is alluded to by a roundabout way, in the belief that should it be called by its proper name, that evil will surely happen or that evil thing will surely make its appearance. Thus, ignorant Bengali women would not mention the proper names of the thief (चोर) and of the snake (साप) during the night, from the dread that either a thief or a snake will appear in the house during the night. So, whenever they have to allude to those two evils, they do so by using words which indirectly mean the same things. Thus, if the word चोर or thief has to be named, they do so by calling him "*the unwelcome visitor*," or if the word साप or snake has to be used, they do so by calling it "*the creeping thing*," or वाम.

An exactly similar form of superstitious belief, with regard to the tiger, prevails among the Canarese people of Southern India. They do not speak of the tiger by its proper name, but whenever they have occasion to use the name of that animal, they do so by using the Canarese words "*naie*" and "*nurri*," respectively, meaning "dog"

and "jackal." They believe that, should they call the animal by its proper name, some one of them is sure to be carried away by that ferocious monster. A curious instance of this belief has been recorded by Mr. G. P. Sanderson in his interesting work, entitled "*Thirteen Years among the Wild Beasts of India*" (Edition, 1879), page 297 :—

"Whilst at dinner that evening I heard voices and saw torches hurriedly approaching my tent, and could distinguish the words '*naie*' and '*nurri*' ('dog' and 'jackal') pronounced excitedly. *The Canarese people frequently speak of a tiger by these names, partly in assumed contempt and partly from superstitious fear.* The word '*hooli*' (tiger) is not often used amongst jungle-men, in the same way that, from dread, natives usually refer to cholera by the general terms of *roga* or *járdya* (sickness). The people were from Hurdenhully, a village a mile and-a-half away, and had come to tell me that their cattle had galloped back in confusion into the village at dusk, without their herdsman, who, we suspected, had fallen a victim to the tigress of Morlay." Again, at page 306, he says: "We had brought torches and men from Hebsoor, and after much calling that the tigress had been shot, voices were at last heard from different trees, lights began to appear, and watchers came from all directions, some shouting to us from the distance to let them come up and see the '*dog*.'"

There is another silly superstitious belief prevalent in some parts of India, which is to the effect that each tiger is allowed by God one rupee per diem for his daily rations. The following instance of this belief is mentioned in the [*] *Journal of the Bombay Natural History Society*:—

"In some places, too, there is a superstition that God allows the tiger one rupee a day for his food, so that if he kills a bullock worth Rs. 5, he wont kill again for five days. If it is worth Rs. 10, he wont kill again for ten days, and so forth."

There is also another belief current among some Indian races, that the age of the tiger and the leopard can be determined by an inspection of the lobes of the liver, the number whereof (*i.e.*, of the lobes,) correspond with the number of years the tiger is old, being one lobe for each year the tiger has lived. But this is not automically true.

Sometimes a tiger is believed to enjoy the special protection of a deity who presides over the welfare of residents of the particular tract of country in which the animal commits his depredations. Mr. Sanderson gives an instance of this in his above-quoted work (page 307):—

"From a long course of immunity from misadventure to himself the Don (name of the tiger) had come to be regarded as enjoying the especial

---

[*] *Vide* "*Journal of the Anthropological Society of Bombay*, Vol. III., No. L, pp. 45—60.

[*] Vol. III., No. III. (1888), page 153.

protection of Koombappa of the temple, the great jungle-spirit ; and it was universally believed that when that deity went the rounds of his jungles, the Don was chosen by him as his steed. The villagers had even made an effigy of the Don, respectably got up in wood and paint, and looking truly formidable, with a seat on the back and on wheels, which they dragged round the temple and down to the river in solemn procession on feast-days. Though the Morlayites always entered with delight upon any hunts I organised, hardly any of them believed the Don (name of the tiger) would ever be shot."

Sometimes it is believed that when a person is killed by a tiger, his widow is supposed to be haunted by a devil, which has to be exorcised away by the performance of religious rites. Mr. Sanderson mentions an instance of this belief at page 296 of his aforesaid work :—

"The woman, with the strange apathy of a Hindu, related what she knew of her husband's death without a tear. I gave her some money, as she would have to spend a small sum in accordance with caste usage *to rid her of the devil by which she was supposed to be attended on account of her husband's having been killed by a tiger, before she would be admitted into her caste's villages.*"

The Canarese believe that the tiger scratches the bark of a tree, called the Bastard Teak (*Butea frondosa*) and called by them "*Muttaga*," because the tree exudes, on the slightest scratch, a sap of a blood-red color which the tiger thinks to be animal blood in which he delights.*

The whiskers of the tiger are, in some parts of Southern India, considered as a deadly poison and are singed off as soon as the tiger is killed. It is sometimes believed that, unless the whiskers are singed off, the spirit of the tiger will haunt the person who slew him, or that the slayer himself will be metamorphosed into a tiger in the next world. The small bone embedded in the muscles between the shoulder and neck of a tiger is also considered a charm.

In addition to those already given in my previous paper, I give a few more examples of superstitious beliefs entertained by the aboriginal tribes of India with regard to the tiger. The Aryan settlers of Chota Nagpore and Singbhum believe that an aboriginal tribe, named the Moondahs, are great adepts in witchcraft, and can, at their own sweet will and pleasure, metamorphose themselves into tigers and other ferocious beasts for the purpose of preying upon their enemies.† Another tribe, named the Katodis, are looked upon by the Hindus with feelings of superstitious terror inspired by the belief that they can metamorphose themselves into the shape of tigers.*

The Zodiac of the Tibetans contain the twelve signs: mouse, ox, *tiger*, hare, dragon, serpent, horse, sheep, monkey, cock, dog, and pig. These are called *Lokhor Chuni*, or the animals by which the years of the cycle of twelve years are designated. The Tibetans calculate the years or determine the age of individuals by the cycle of twelve years, in which each year is named from a certain animal of the twelve signs commencing with *Tag-lo* (tiger-year) and ending with Lang-lo (ox-year). These twelve signs, in combination with the twelve signs of the Tibetan zodiac, are also used in calculating the twelve months of the Tibetan year. Thus the new year of the Tibetans begins with the *Tiger* and is called *Horda-tang-po*. The Tibetans have a popular saying, namely, the *Horda-tang-po Tag-gi-da*, that is to say, the first month of the year is *Tiger's month*. These signs are also used in calculating every two hours of the day called "*Du-chhoi,*" commencing from the dawn called "*Thorang.*" The time between 3 to 5 A. M. is called *the hours of the Tiger*. The time of the hours of the break of day is called *Nam lang*, and that of *Nima shar* is denominated the hours of the hare which is really the beginning of the day. The Thorang or dawn comes at the end of these twelve divisions, which is the *Tag or Tiger*.†

I have heard from a relative of mine who stayed in Gâyâ in Behar for a long time that, in the town of Gâyâ, there is a temple dedicated to the deity वाघेरी. The word वाघेरी is a mere Hindi corruption of the Sanscrit word व्याघ्रेश्वरी or the *Tiger Goddess*. The temple, I am informed, contains the brazen image of a tiger which is supposed to represent the deity. It is popularly believed there that tigers come during the night from the Barabar Hills on the other side of the River Poonpoon, which flows past the town of Gâyâ, and knock their foreheads at the feet of the goddess by way of prayer that they may be allowed to prey upon human victims. It is said that, if the goddess grants their prayers, the tigers succeed in killing human beings during the year. If their prayers are not listened to, no human being falls victim to tigers during the year. In honour of the goddess, a fair called the वाघनी सावेज is annually held in the Hindi month of श्रावण (Sanscrit श्रावण), corresponding to the months June, July of the English calendar, in the precincts of the temple of the goddess वाघेरी. It is said that this fair is held by way of supplication to the deity that she may not listen to the prayers of the tigers and that human beings may not fall

---

* *Op. cit.*, page 280.
† Vide *Trans. Ethnological Society of Lond.*, N. S., VI., p. 6 ; also *J. A. S. B.* for 1866, Pt. II., p. 158.

* Latham's *Descriptive Ethnology*, Vol. II., page 457.
† Vide *Proceedings of the A. S. B.* for 1890, pp. 5—7.

victims to these ferocious beasts. It is also said that *pujahs* are also offered to the goddess, during the fair, for the aforesaid purpose.

This paper may aptly be concluded with a few other Bengali proverbial sayings in which the tiger figures. There is a proverb which runs to the effect that मावेर्षीने वाघ काँपे or the cold of the Hindu month of Magh (January and February) even makes the tiger shiver, in allusion to the intense cold which prevails in Lower Bengal in that month. A person with ferocious habits like those of a ruffian is called a वाघमान की कली or a person with the ways of *the tiger and the bear.* Sometimes the prefix वाघ meaning a tiger is prefixed to the name of a person in Lower Bengal to denote that the ways of that person are as ferocious as those of a tiger.—*Journal, Anthropological Society, Bombay.*

(By Mr. Sarat Chandra Mittra, *M.A., B.L.,* District Pleader, Chapra, Behar.)

---

373. **On some Ceremonies for Producing Rain.**—In these days of advanced civilization and scientific progress when many natural objects and even phenomena are being produced artificially, no surprise need be expressed at the attempts that are being made, throughout the civilized world, at producing rain artificially by exploding dynamite-laden fire-balloons high up in the air. But in the primitive state of mankind, when dynamite and balloons were unknown, and when the rude uncultured folk attributed the failure of their crops or of rain, and the outbreak of disease and the consequent occurrence of deaths among them, to the wrath of some divine being who, they believed, presided over their welfare, or regarded these phenomena as visitations upon them from the same deity for sins committed, primitive men believed that these scourges, which periodically visited them, *viz.,* famine, drought and pestilence, would be averted, and their progress stopped, should they only appease the wrath of the offended deity. To this end they set their heads together and began to devise means, and as, among savage races—the representatives of primitive men—the conception of the deity was formed from a conception of their own forms and attributes, and the same supernatural entity was supposed to possess in common with human beings, the same penchant for meat and drink, and music and mirth, the seers or the wise folk among the tribes hit upon the idea of holding sacrifices, *pujahs,* and religious feasts. Hence, whenever primitive man suffered from the all-withering influences of the drought, he performed sacrifices wherein buffaloes and kine were slaughtered in order to appease the deity's cravings for meat, oblations of spirituous liquors were offered in order to quench his thirst for drink, and songs were sung and dances and processions were held in order to satisfy his tastes for music and mirth. All these he did under the impression that their performance would turn away his wrath, and thus induce his offended deity-ship to withdraw the scourge visiting them, whether it was drought, famine, or pestilence.

Travellers in all parts of the globe have, from personal observation, recorded the existence and periodical performance of these religious " functions" for producing rain or averting famine, not only among peoples who are still grovelling in the lowermost depths of savagery, but also among those who have emerged therefrom and have adopted the amenities of civilization. Hence we find that some of these ceremonies still survive among such enlightened nations as the modern Europeans, and among such civilized races as the Hindús, the Muhammadans, and the Chinese.

Whenever there is failure of rains, or the country is suffering from the visitation of a long-standing drought, the Hindús of Bengal perform a ceremony known as *pirer gán* (पीरेर गान). This ceremony consists in gathering together a number of Muhammadan *faqírs,* and telling them off to sing songs (in Mussulmani-Bengali, a dialect of the Bengali language which is spoken and written by the Bengali Muhammadans) in honour of the *Pírs* or Muhammadan saints. It may be observed here *en passant* that the Hindús of Bengal worship the Muhammadan *Pírs* or saints, especially the Saint Satyapír (सत्यपीर), to whom *pujahs* and *shirnis* or sweetmeats are offered whenever there is success in some difficult family undertaking, or a recovery in the family from some serious illness. The performance of the aforesaid ceremony, it is said, immediately brings down showers of rain. Holding *sankirtans* (सङ्कीर्तन) or religious processions in honour of the god Hari (हरि) also averts drought. Whenever there is a severe drought in Bengal, the village folk perform these last-mentioned ceremonies. First of all, *pujah* is offered to Hari, who is but another incarnation of the god Vishnu. Then the worshippers form themselves into a company and parade the streets of their native village, singing religious hymns in honour of the god to the accompaniment of the *dhole* or drum, the *singd* or horn and metal castanets. I have observed that in Calcutta, these *sankirtans* are also held whenever there is an outbreak of cholera or any other epidemic in a particular quarter of that city. It is said that these *sankirtans* result in bringing down rain or averting the epidemic. In June or July last, when there was severe drought all over Northern India, a correspondent from Jhansi (N.-W. P.) wrote to the *Amrita Bazar Patrika* to say that a *Hari-sankirtan* (हरि सङ्कीर्तन) ceremony had been held in that town for the purpose of removing the drought. The correspondent further added that copious showers of rain had fallen shortly after the performance of the ceremony. The *shashtras* also prescribe the performance of certain *yagnas* (यज्ञ) and *homs* (होम) as infallible means for averting drought. The law-givers say that these *homs* should be performed with all the strictness prescribed by the *shashtras*, and large quantities of *ghi* or clarified butter should be offered as oblations to the sacrificial fire. It is only the other day (as we read in the *Amrita Bazar Patrika*) that that eminent *zemindar*—the Maharajah of Burdwan—performed such a *hom* wherein immense quantities of *ghi* were burnt, and large numbers of Bráhmans fed. The paper added for our information that that very evening very copious showers rained in Burdwan. The causation of rain by such a ceremony can only be explained on the ground that the smoke generated by the burning ghee and the sacrificial fires forms into rain-clouds which ultimately melt down to the earth in the shape of refreshing showers. It has been uniformly experienced that the heavy cannonading in battles is also followed by copious rain. My Persian teacher, who is a resident of Dubrájpur, in the district of Birbhum, in Bengal, informs me that a curious custom is observed in his native village, whenever there is a failure of rain there. The people of that place throw dirt or filth on to the houses of other people, who abuse the former for doing so. Sometimes they drench the lame, the halt, the blind and other persons who are otherwise physically disabled, by pouring water on them, and so get abused by the latter. The people of Dubrájpur superstitiously believe that this abuse, in times of drought, is sure to bring down rain.

In times of drought, the Hindús of Behar observe the curious ceremony of having their fields and other arable lands ploughed by Bráhman women. In Hindudom, throughout Bengal and Behar, Bráhmans and women never perform agricultural operations like ploughing and harrowing with their own hands, but have their lands tilled by servants and labourers who mostly belong to such low castes as the *Kandus* (कांडू), the *Dosadks* (दोसाध), the *Nonyas* (नोनिया) and others. Hence, it is popularly believed that, should the female member of such a high caste as the Bráhmans, to whom such undignified manual labour is forbidden, plough the *khet*, rain would surely pour down in torrents immediately after. Sometimes, when there is hesitation about subjecting such high-caste women to the indignity of actually ploughing in broad daylight, the women are made only to touch the plouh early in the morning, before people are astir, for the purpose of complying with the requirements of the custom, and the ploughing operations are subsequently conducted by the male ploughmen. The other day I came across another curious custom, peculiar to this part of the country, the observance whereof is supposed to bring down rain. It was about 10 o'clock in the night of Saturday, the 25th June last, as I was about to retire to bed, I heard a great noise made by the singing in high-pitched tones of some women in front of our house. I thought that the women were singing some songs, as they usually do parading the streets, before some marriage takes place in a family. But on making enquiries next morning, I came to learn that the previous night's singing formed part and parcel of a rain-bringing ceremony known, at least in this district (Sáran), as the परकरीरी and that some women of the locality had formed themselves into a little band and paraded the neighbouring streets, singing songs —a practice which they superstitiously believed would surely bring down showers. Curiously enough, a tolerably good shower of rain fell during the afternoon of the following day.

In Behar it is believed that the water of the rain which falls during the period wherein the star Adrá (पद्रा नक्षत्र) is in the ascendant, is very beneficial to the *bhadoi*, or rainy season crop which usually consists of maize and paddy. Hence agriculturists in this part of the country look forward with great expectation to the falling of the very welcome showers during that period. With a view to ensure the happening of this event, the god Indra is worshipped, and Bráhmans are fed, in this district, as if, by feeding them, the rain-god would be so far propitiated as to open the flood-gates of heaven during the period of the ascendancy of the star Adrá. This year the aforesaid star had been in the ascendant only very recently, and as the rains were holding off in this district during its period of influence, *pujah* was made to Indra, the lord of the skies, and a number of Bráhmans, I am informed by Rái Bábu Tara Prasád Mukerji, Bahadur, Chairman of the Municipality of Revilgunge, a town 4 miles due west of Chupra, were only the other day fed at the Gautama Muni's *Asram* in that town for the purpose of bringing down rain during Adrá's ascendancy. The Babu further informs me that the performance of this ceremony was, curiously enough, followed up by tolerably good showers of rain which fell on the day following. Another curious rain-producing custom is observed in this district whenever there is a severe drought threatening it. Troops of children of all ages come to people's housess, and the good men thereof have their courtyards turned into immense puddles by pouring large quantities of water thereon. The children then throw themselves into it, and roll and tumble themselves in the temporarily improvised puddle to their heart's content. Doing so, it is believed, surely brings down rain.

In the North-Western Provinces and Oudh another custom is observed for the purpose of averting drought. It is as follows : Children of all ages form themselves into little companies and parade the streets of their respective towns and villages, singing Hindi songs having reference to rain and the god who presides over it. It is believed that these children's demonstrations have the effect of drawing forth rain from the skies.

In order to avert drought and produce rain, the Muhammadans utter two words رکعت (*rekat*) of the نماز استسقا (*namaz-i-istaska*), which is nothing but a prayer for rain, because استسقا is defined to mean پانی کرنا or demanding rain. The whole ceremony of the نماز استسقا is described thus in Urdu:—

جب مہینہ نہ برسی تب مسلمان جمع ہوویں اور میدان میں جاویں اور دعا کریں اور استسقا رکھیں قبلی کیطرف منہہ کرے اور اکیلی اکیلی نماز ادا کریں بغیر خطبہ اور جماعت کے ۰ اسیطرح تین روز باہر جاویں اور ان تینوں روز استغفار بہت کہیں اسواسطے کے استغفار کو مینہ کے طلب کرنے میں بڑا اثر ہی جیسا کے اللہ تعالی ظاہر فرما نا ہی ۰

فقلت استغفروا ربكم انه كان غفارا يرسل السماعه عليكم مدرارا

یہ آیت سورۃ نوح میں ہی ۰ یہ بات نوح علیہ السلام نے اپنی قوم سے کہی تھی ۰ خلاصہ اسکا یہ ہی کے گناہ بخشوانے اپنے رب سے بیشک وہ ہی بخشنے والا اور جب تم توبہ کرو اور گناہ بخشوانا تو اللہ تعالی تم پر بدلی بیجھے

جو خوب دھنے لگے کا پانی برساوے ۰ اور استسقا کی نماز میں ذمی کو حاضر نکریں بلکہ خلق اپنے گناہ سے نلی سرے توبہ کریں کے اللہ تعالی اوسکی برکت سے مینہ برساوے ۰

The above description may be thus translated:— When it does not rain, then Mussulmans should assemble and go to a *maidan* and offer up prayers and observe *istaska*, *i.e.*, demand rain with their faces turned towards the *kabarh* at Mecca, and everyone should by himself read *namaz* without a sermon and the assembly. In this way they should go outside on three days and pray for the pardon of their sins on each of those days, because *istaghfár* is very effectual in bringing rain-water as the Almighty God has said:—

"Well, say thou, 'I crave pardon from God.' In fact, He is the Pardoner. So that He may send rain-showering clouds upon thee."

This *áyet* (آیت) is contained in the *Surah Nooh* of the *Koran*. These words had been spoken by Noah (upon whom be peace) to the members of his tribe. The purport of all this is that you should crave pardon for your sins from your God (for He certainly can pardon), and when you will seek pardon and wash yourself of sin, then the Almighty God will send you clouds which would shower rain in torrents. And in the *namaz* named *istaska*, no unbelievers ذمی should be allowed to remain in that assembly. On the other hand, people should, with heads bowed down, wash themselves of sin, so that Almighty God may, on account of the good influence exerted by this humbling oneself before one's Creator, cause showers of rain to fall.

The Kolarian tribes living in the rocky fastnesses of Central India, worship a god named Marang Buru or Great Mountain, who, they suppose, sends down rain. His worship is said to have originated in the fact that remarkable peaks, bluffs, or rocks very naturally suggested the idea of Divinity to their unsophisticated minds. They reasoned within themselves that as in such high eminence lie the sources of the streams and rivers which irrigate their fields and nourish their crops, they must be the abode of some Divine Beings, and that Marang Buru must, therefore, be invoked for rain in times of drought. Offerings are usually presented to him on the summits of hills, or other conspicuous objects over which his deity-ship is believed by them to preside.*

The Chinese are a very superstitious people' When severe drought stares the "Flowery Land " in the face, the Celestials perform various ceremonies, such as offering up prayers for rain, observing fasts, the closing of the south gates of cities, performing rain-bringing operas, &c., for the purpose of averting the serious consequences of the drought and producing rain. Mr. A. J. Little, in his interesting work,† entitled *Through the Yang-tse Gorges*, has described some of the aforesaid interesting ceremonies. The custom of closing the south gates of cities in China is thus alluded to by him at page 152 of the aforesaid work, in these words:—

"*Sunday, March 25th* (Easter Sunday).—Moored all day at Kwei-chow-fu, waiting for a clearance. The south gate, below which we lay moored, was closed on account of the drought, no rain having fallen for the past six months. This shutting the south gate of a city would seem to be a kind of silent protest—made in accordance with the Nature-worship which appears to be the only real, indigenous and universal religion of the Chinese—against the South, which is the fire quarter, and the presiding influence over heat and drought. Thus, when Auster blows against the south gate and finds it shut, a hint is supposed to be given to him that his presence is *de trop*." As regards prayers for rain, he says (page 154): "The destitution of the Kwei-chow-fu people has been caused throughout the prefecture by the total failure of the winter crops, and we can

---

* Vide *Indian Antiquary*, Vol. XIV. (1885), page 125.

† *Through the Yang-tse Gorges*; or, *Trade and Travel in Western China*, by Archibald John Little, F.R.G.S., London: Sampson, Low & Co., 1888.

sympathise with the unfortunate Mandarins, whose sins are responsible for the misery sent by heaven upon the people, and *who are now engaged in humbling themselves and praying for rain.*" Anent holding fasts, the author observes (page 156): "Owing to the drought, *a strict fast had been proclaimed throughout the district*, and the beef I had been expecting to buy here, let alone pork or fowls, was unobtainable." Under date Thursday, May 3rd, Mr. Little writes to say: "The fine weather, which had been continuous for the past two months, now at last began to break up: *the prayers for rain, the fasts, and the closing of the south gates of the cities*, which we had observed on our upward voyage, having been at length successful" (page 341).

The Chinese also perform the curious ceremony known as "*The Rain-bringing Opera*" for the purpose of producing refreshing showers in times of drought. Writing under date Sunday, April 1st, the author says: "After supper it was proposed we should adjourn to the opera—a celebrated company having come up from the city of Wau *to aid the villagers in propitiating the rain-god*. The performance was then proceeding in a temple on the bank. Lighting a length of worn-out bamboo tow-line, which our *tai-kung* or pilot (the bowsman) furnished us with, and which made a most efficient torch, we threaded our way up the steep sand-bank, and among the dirty temporary huts, largely composed of opium dens, which in winter cover the low ground adjoining the junks' halting-places; we at length entered a handsome and solidly constructed temple, and thereupon the fine stage, in the first courtyard, was the usual gay scene of a Chinese historical play. The stage was lit by two staring oil-lamps, suspended from the proscenium, and reminding me of those of the London costermonger, and by about a dozen red wax dips. The *auditorium* was in darkness. My intrusion was quickly detected by the crowd of turbaned coolies, but I was not in the least disturbed, and I stood looking on at some very good acting until ten o'clock. *These performances and processions, if they do not always produce rain, at least serve to amuse the people, and to divert their thoughts from their troubles*" (page 184). Curiously enough, the author says that there was heavy rain that night.

In the environs of Ichang are some conical hills on one of which there is a rock-temple. Near it is a deep wide cave, which the trickling water has slowly excavated out of the mountain behind the wood. This cave, called "Lung Wang Tung" or Dragon King Cavern, is about 100 yards across the opening, and extends inwards almost the same distance. The Chinese have a superstitious belief regarding this cave, to the effect that, in times of drought, the dragon inhabiting it, if beseeched by the priests, produces rain. Mr. Little says with regard to this cave: "At the back of it (the cavern) is a lake, which the priests say extends inwards an unknown distance; only one man has ever tried to explore it, and he never came back again. They objected to my launching their boat upon it, as this is never done but in times of drought, when they go upon the lake to *solicit the dragon to turn himself round and produce rain*. Were the dragon to come out at this opening and escape out of the country, according to Chinese superstition, there would be perpetual drought. Hence the three temples to shut him in safely" (page 93).

The Kakhyens of Burma, who live mainly by following the pursuits of agriculture, worship a *nat* named Sinlah or the Sky-Spirit, who is supposed by them to give rain and good crops.*

The Shans, a tribe living north of Burma, celebrate three festivals every year, in which the *nats* or *spirits* presiding over rain, wind, and cold, are worshipped in order that they may send down rain or protect them from the rigours of wind and cold.†

At Momien, a town in Yunnan in Western China, a curious rain-ceremony is observed by the Chinese and the Panthays (Chinese Muhamadans) as is testified to by Dr. J. Anderson, who went there in 1868. He says: "In consequence of a long period of drought preceding our arrival, the slaughter of animals had been forbidden, as it was feared that the rain would be withheld as a punishment, a curious instance of Buddhist superstition affecting the Panthays and Chinese; but in two days the rains set in, and the prohibition was removed. The markets were thenceforward well supplied with bullocks, buffaloes, sheep, goats, and pigs."‡

A relic of these superstitious ceremonies and beliefs still survives among the enlightened Christian nations of Europe. In these Christian countries, in times of drought, when the country is threatened with famine brought about thereby, people congregate in Churches and offer up prayers to God, beseeching Him to send down rain. Even in India this practice is also resorted to in times of drought and failure of crops. I remember having read in the Indian newspapers, some years ago, when this land was suffering from the consequences of a long-standing severe drought, that prayers for rain were, by the orders of the presiding chaplains, offered in some of the principal Christian Churches throughout this country.

(By Mr. Sarat Chandara Mitra, *M. A., B. L.*, Pleader, Judge's Court, Chupra, District Saran, Behar.)

* *Mandalay to Momien* : A Narrative of the two Expeditions to Western China of 1868 and 1875, by John Anderson, *M D*, London: 1876, page 146.

† *Op. cit.*, p. 308.

‡ *Op cit.*, p. 205.

FOLKTALES.

374. The Boasting of Narada Muni the Rishi.—Once Narada Muni boasted that no one could sing as well as he could. He went to Bhagwan and made the same boast to him.

Bhagwan said: "You had better not say this to your father Bráhma." Narada, however, went to Bráhma and said the same to him. Bráhma said: "You may say this to me, but do not say it to Siva the All-knowing."

But he went to Siva and made the same boast. When Bhagwan knew that he had boasted in this way to all the greater gods, he said to him: "O Narada! it is a long time since we had any news of the Northern world. Go there and find out its state."

So he started, and by and bye he came to a city where he found the people wailing and lamenting. When he asked them the cause, they answered: "We are the Ragas and the Raginis, the personification of melody, and when any one sings out of tune we suffer tortures. There is a certain Narada, the son of Bráhma, who always sings out of time and tune and causes us great annoyance." "How can you be relieved?" asked Narada.

"If Siva were to come and sing to us and the other great gods sit and listen, then we may be relieved."

Narada was ashamed and went to Bhagwan and, telling him the case, said: "I have been guilty of foolish boasting. How can I be pardoned?"

Bhagwan ordered him to go into the forest and remain absorbed for ten years in devotion to Siva. As he was worshipping, Siva appeared in the form of a terrible tiger. Narada ran to Bhagwan and asked what he should do. Bhagwan ordered him not to fear but to continue his worship. After many years Siva was appeased and came to him and asked him what he wanted. When she heard his case Siva told him to call Bráhma, Bhagwan and the other greater gods. They implored Siva to grant the prayer of Narada. So all the gods went to the city of the Ragas and Raginis and Siva played and sang before them. They were so pleased that all the trouble they had suffered through the singing of Narada passed away. From that time he ceased to boast of his skill in music.

(A folktale told by Juala Prasad, Teacher of the School at Rampur, Sitapur district.)

375. The Tale of the Thakur and the Barber.—There was once a Thakur in a village and his barber was Gokul Nai. One day the Thakur made up his mind to go on a pilgrimage to the Ganges and he ordered the barber to accompany him. The barber was tired of always having to attend on the Thakur for nothing, so he said: "The only condition on which I agree to go with you is this, that you must be able to give an answer to any question I put to you on the road, and as soon as you fail I will leave you."

The Thakur agreed to this and they started. In the evening they came to a town and the Thakur gave the barber some money and told him to go and buy some provisions. When he went into the bazar he met a man who was shedding tears and crying: "*Hae! meri nagin; Hae! meri nagin.*" (Alas my female snake!) The barber came back to the Thakur and began to pack up his things. The Thakur asked him the reason, and he said: "I have just seen something which I am sure you cannot explain."

When the Thakur heard the facts he began:—"There was once a Rája, who was very sad, because his Ráni brought forth only girls and he had no male heir. When she next became in child the Rája said: 'If it is a girl this time I will kill both mother and child.'

"In due time the Rani gave birth to a girl, but she feared her husband and pretended that the child was a boy. She called the Pandits and induced them to tell the Rája that the child had been born in the asterism of Mul and that he must not see his son for twelve years. So the matter was kept secret for that time, and when the boy was nearly twelve years old his father arranged for his marriage. When the procession started with the girl dressed up as a bridegroom, her mother was half dead with fear, because she knew that the matter could be concealed no longer. When the procession had gone some distance the Kahars put the palanquin down by the side of a tank and went to cook their food. All the women of the village collected to see the supposed bridegroom, but she lay weeping in the palanquin and hid her face from them. When all the women had gone the Rája of the snakes, who lived in that tank, came out in human form, and when he saw her weeping he insisted on knowing the cause. When she told him her trouble he promised to help her. So he dived into the tank and having summoned all the snakes, his subjects, he told them the case of the Ráni and her daughter and asked their advice in the matter. The snakes said: 'Why should we help these mortals who are always ready to injure us?' But the Rája of the snakes would not mind them, and again assuming the form of a man he came out to where the girl was lying in her palanquin. He took her out and seated himself and went off and was married in her place.

Meanwhile the old Ráni was consumed with terror and was ready to take poison as soon as her fraud should be discovered. But when she was called to receive the pair at the door of the palace she was delighted to find the bridegroom like the Sun and the bride like the Moon.

The Snake Rája and his Ráni continued to live together for some time and he quite forgot his home and his real wife. When he did not return the Snake Ráni set out in search of her husband. At last she found where he was and came to the girl whom he had married and asked her if her husband loved her. She answered that her husband loved her greatly. The Snake Ráni then said to her: "Ask him to eat with you and then enquire of what caste he is."

She did so; but when he sat down to eat he could not eat after the manner of men, but he took some food out of the dish and placing it on his hand managed somehow or other to eat it. But when she asked him to what caste he belonged, he warned her to cease her questions or the result would be evil. When she would not desist he took her to the tank and, assuming his original snake form, dived beneath the water. She was heartbroken at the loss of her husband and made a little hut near the tank and continued to live there. Now there was a *mali* woman, who lived near, who used to supply flowers to the Snake Rája, and when she saw the grief of the deserted wife she went to him and told him that if he did not return to his bride she would commit suicide. So the Snake Rája tore himself away from his Snake Ráni and returned to the girl who was overcome with joy. But the Snake Ráni followed them and hid under their couch intending to bite the girl. The Snake Rája knew this and he applied some poisonous gum to the leg of the couch and to this she stuck and died. When he found she was dead he began to lament her in the words *Hae! nagin*; *Hae! nagin*. "Alas! my Snake-wife."

The barber was satisfied and went on with the Thakur. Next day they came to another town, and again the Thakur sent the barber to a bazar to buy food. There he saw the head of a he-goat hanging over the door of a shop and sometimes it used to laugh and sometimes wept. When he saw this he returned to the Thakur and said that he would leave him if he could not explain this mystery. When they had eaten, the Thakur said: "Once upon a time Raja Vikramaditya was going to the house of his father-in-law and he came across a temple of Mahadeva which had no door, but dancing was going on inside. He knew the art of infusing his life into the body of another creature and close by lay the dead body of a parrot; so Vikramaditya infused his life into it and flying up to a window was able to look in and see what was going on. The servant of Vikramaditya was also skilled in the arts of his master, so he entered his body and went off to Ujjain and took his place as Rája. But the Ráni would not recognise him and refused to admit him into her apartments. When the Rája, in the form of the parrot after seeing the dancing, came down and looked for his own body he could not find it, and in grief and amazement went and perched on a tree, and there a fowler caught him. He took him to the bazar and sold him to a *banya* for a large sum of money. The parrot showed so much wisdom that all the people of the land used to come to get their cases decided by the bird. One day two persons with a suit passed that way, and when people asked them where they were going they said that as Rája Vikramaditya was absent they were going to the parrot to get their cause decided. When the Ráni heard this she asked them on their return to come and inform her of the result. When they came and told her the result of the case she knew that the parrot must be Rája Vikramaditya, and she sent for the Kotwal and giving him ten thousand rupees sent him to buy the parrot, and ordered that if the *banya* would not sell the parrot it was to be taken from him by main force. The Kotwal bought the parrot and brought it to the Ráni, and at night the bird told her the whole matter. She told him not to fear and that she would turn him into a man again. So she bought a he-goat and tied it up in the palace. She cut off the head of the goat and then sent for the servant who had personated the Rája. She asked him to bring the goat to life. He asked how he could do this, but she told him that once he had in the same way brought a lamb to life. The servant thought that this must really have been done some time or other by Vikramaditya. So afraid of his fraud being detected, he put his life into the body of the goat. Then the Ráni asked the parrot to put his life in the body of the Rája, and at once Vikramaditya assumed his original form. Then she cut off the head of the goat, hung it up in the bazar, and sometimes it laughs when it thinks how the country was ruled by the servant as Rája, and sometimes weeps when it thinks how it fell by the treachery of the Ráni."

When the tale was ended the barber took the Thakur to the Ganges and after he had bathed brought him home in safety.

(A folktale told by Menhdi Lal of Bibipur, Bara-Banki District.)

376. **Budh Sen and his Monkey Army.**—Once upon a time there was a king of the monkeys, named Budh Sen, and as famine raged in his own dominions, he determined to remove to some other land where the people were at peace with each other and settle there. At last he came to a land where all creatures were friendly to each other, except one maid-servant of the Rája and a ram. So by the leave of the Rája Budh Sen settled there with his monkey

army. One day as the maid-servant was going along with some fire in her hand the ram butted her and the fire fell among some straw and raised a great conflagration, so that the palace and much property were consumed and some of the horses of the Rája were half burned. After the fire was put out one of the Pandits of the court, who was unfriendly to Budh Sen, suggested that the blood of monkeys would be useful as a remedy for the horses. So the Rája had the whole army of Budh Sen beheaded and their blood was used for this purpose.

Budh Sen, when he heard of the destruction of his army, said nothing to the Rája, except that he was pleased that his men had been of some service. Then he brought an ear-ring and presented it to the Rája, who took it to the Ráni; but she said that it was no use to her until she got the pair to it. The Rája, asked Budh Sen to get a second ear-ring. He replied : " It is very difficult to get a second to match it, but I will go in search of one."

So saying, he went with some of his companions into the jungle. At last they came to a tank where lived a demon (*deo*) whose habit it was to drag beneath the water any person whose shadow fell on the surface. Budh Sen climbed a tree and threw in a branch which the demon pulled under water at once. Then Budh Sen went back to the Raja and said: " Come with me to a certain place and you may find as many ear-rings as you please."

So the Rája with all his men came to the tank, and Budh Sen said : " Tell your men to search in the grass and reeds on the banks."

No sooner did they come within sight of the water than the demon pulled them all in. Then Budh Sen said : " I am a Rája as well as your majesty. As you destroyed my army so I have destroyed thine."

(A folktale told by Siva Prasad, Teacher of the Sarosa School, Shapur district.)

377. **Akbar and Birbal's Daughter.**—When Pubal was appointed to be Prime Minister of Akbar many persons, and particularly Muhammadans, were jealous of him. One day a Muhammadan came to court and endeavoured to supplant him by a show of superior wisdom. Akbar asked him first—" Which is the best of flowers ?" He replies the *genda* or marigold, which is used in daily Hindu worship. Next he was asked—" Whose son earns most ?" His answer was " the *kasya*." Then he was asked—" Who is a great man ?" He replied, " the King," and to the last question—which is the sweetest thing in the world? he said: " Nothing is sweeter than sugarcane."

When the daughter of Birbal heard of this contest of wisdom, she instructed her father how to answer. When he came to court and was asked what was the best flower, he answered " The cotton flower "; the son who earns most is that of the cow ; the virtuous are the great ; the sweetest thing in the world is one's own interest.

The Muhammadan sage was worsted and left the court in disgrace.

(A folktale told by Narayan Das, Teacher of the Sidhpura School, Etah district.)

378. **The Raja and the Swans.**—One year there was no rain in the asterism of Swati and the sea produced no pearls. The swans (*hansa*), who lived on pearls, began to starve, and they came to the Rája and asked for food. He asked them how much they could eat, and they replied a *ser* each. So he ordered that they should each get a *ser* of pearls. So they stayed there till, in the next rainy season, pearls were again produced in the sea, and then they took leave of the Rája and went to their home by the ocean.

On the way they chanced upon a certain city, the Rája of which was then preparing for the marriage of his son. When they saw the preparations, the male swan said to his mate : " Methinks this Rája is very rich." " He is not so rich," she replies, " as that Rája who used to give us each a *ser* of pearls daily."

Now the Rája understood the speech of birds, and when he heard what the swans said, he sent his fowlers to catch them. The male swan was caught, but his mate escaped and flew away to the Rája who had so generously protected them. He, when he saw her, asked her why she had returned, and she related the misfortune which had come upon them. The Rája ordered that she should receive a *ser* of pearls as long as she stayed there, and he himself set out at once to effect the release of the male swan. After many days he reached the city of the Rája who had captured the swan and stayed there. Now it so happened that a Rakshasa had beset that city and was demanding a tribute of a human being daily, whom he used to devour. After he had devoured five or six of his subjects, the Rája became exceedingly sorrowful and sat at the great gate of his palace, plunged in grief. Then the Rája, the benefactor of the swans, came and asked him the cause of his misery. The Rája said : " If this Rakshasa continues to devour one of my subjects daily, my kingdom will soon become a waste."

The other Rája promised to overcome the Rakshasa, so he went to the place where he used to devour a human being daily and collecting some leaves under a tree threw a sheet over them. In the meantime the Rakshasa came up and asked where was his victim. The Rája answered: "He is coming. Kindly sit down on these leaves."

He sat down, and falling asleep, ordered the Rája to wake him when the victim arrived. Then the Rája set fire to the leaves and in a moment the Rakshasa was consumed to ashes. When the Rája of the land heard of the death of his enemy he was overwhelmed with joy and asked the other Rája to claim any reward he desired. He said: "I want nothing but the release of the swan whom you have captured."

The Rája of the land did as he desired. The Rája returned to his city, and the swans flew off to their home on the shores of the ocean.

(A folktale told by Makund Lal, Kaysath, of Mirzapur.)

379. **The Old Woman and the Crow.**—An old woman was one day frying rich cakes (*púri*) in a frying-pan, when a crow came and said: "Mother, give me a cake!" "Go and wash your bill first," she said. So the crow went to the water and said:—

Pannar, pannar, tum pannar dás !
Do panariya, dhowai mundariya,
Mathdwen púri pánch.

"Water, water, thou art water's slave! Give me water and let me wash my bill. Then I'll ogle the five cakes." The water replied: "Bring an earthen pot from the potter and you can take water and wash thy bill." So the crow went to the potter and said:—

Kumhár, kumhár, tum kumhár dás !
Tum do handariya, khinchai panariya,
Dhowai mundariya, mathdwen púri pánch.

"Potter, potter, thou art the potter's slave! Give me a pot, I will take water, wash my bill and ogle cakes five." But the potter said: "Bring earth and I will make an earthen pot for thee." So the crow went to the earth and said:—

Matar, matar, tum matar dás !
Tum do matariya, banai handariya, khinchai pandariya ;
Dhowai mundariya, mathdwen púri pánch.

The earth said: "Bring the deer's horn and dig the earth." So the crow went to the deer and said:—

Hiraniya, hiraniya, tum kiran dás !
Tum do singariya, khodai matariya
Banai handariya, khinchai panariya,
Dhowai mundariya, mathdwen púri pánch.

But the deer said: "Go to the dog and he will fight me and break my horn; then I will give it to thee." So the crow went to the dog and said:—

Kuttur, kuttur, tum kuttur dás !
Tum laro hiraniya, tútai singariya, &c.

But the dog said: "Bring me some milk, and when I drink it I will fight the deer." So the crow went to the cow and said:—

Gaur, gaur, tum gaur dás !
Tum do dudhariya, pidi kutariya, larai kiraniya, &c.

But the cow said: "Bring me some grass, and when I eat it I will give you plenty of milk." So the crow went to the grass and said:—

Ghasar, ghasar, tum ghasar das !
Deo ghasariya khawai gauriya ;
Dewai dudhariya, &c.

But the grass said: "Bring a spade (*khurpí*) and you may collect as much grass as you wish." So the crow went to the blacksmith and said:—

Lohar, lohar, tum lohar das !
Tum do khurpiya, khodai ghasariya ;
Kháwai gauriya, &c.

The blacksmith said: "How will you take the spade?" The crow said: "Put it round my neck and I will manage to carry it away." So the blacksmith heated the spade and hung it round the neck of the crow, and when he tried to fly away with it his neck was burnt and his head fell off and that was the end of him.

(A nursery rhyme told by Brij Lal, Student of the High School, Bulandshahr.)

[This is one of the cumulative rhymes on the model of "This is the House that Jack built." Mr. Clouston gives other examples in *Popular Tales and Fictions*, II., 289 sqq.—Ed.]

380. **Which is better—Wealth or Wisdom?**—Two men were once disputing which was better—wealth or wisdom. They went to the Emperor to decide the case, and he sent them with a letter to the King of Balkh. In the letter it was written—"Hang these men at once." So they were thrown into a dungeon. The advocate of wealth admitted to the other that he could do nothing to save their lives. The other said: "Write these words on a piece of paper and I will procure our release." So he demanded an audience with the King, and when he came in the presence, he said. "Does not your Majesty know why we have been sent hither? The Emperor of Hindustan is your greatest enemy, and his astrologers have foretold that if our corpses are buried in your city it will become a ruin. It is for this reason that he desires to have us executed here." When the King of Balkh heard these words he released them. The advocate of wealth then admitted that wisdom was superior.

(A folktale by Shadi Khan, Pathan, of Kasganj, Etah district.)

---

* The refrain as before.

MISCELLANEA.

381. The Present State of the Question of Popular Tales.—M. Cosquin has kindly sent me his essay *Les Contes Populaires: Dernier Etat de la Question* (Paris : Bouillon). As this pamphlet contains some remarks on my own notions, perhaps I may be allowed to make a brief reply on a subject of interest to folk-lorists, so far as the general question goes. M. Cosquin says that the anthropological interpreters deal with "men more or less degenerate . . . savages," whom I (A. L.) treat as "primitifs." I have often said that of *primitifs* I know nothing. Savages may descend from apes or from angels : I offer no opinion. I only say that we all come either from " savages" or from men who adopted many savage ideas and manners. Granting (for the sake of argument) the presence of savage ideas, how did they come to group themselves spontaneously into the same *cadres* as of "Puss and Boots," or " Cinderella"? *Distinguo.* The *cadre* is not always "identical," as anyone may see in Miss Cox's *Cinderella*. We have different male as well as female Cinderellas. We have different openings, different events, different conclusions. What remains fixed is the idea of a friendly animal (as a rule) who protects and aids a boy or girl. Many savages believe in such animals, like the Manitous of the red Indians. Thus many tales of such animals would arise (story-tel·ing being natural to man). Where the *cadre*, the sequence and character of incidents, is "identical," then I suppose that the story has been " transmitted." At one time, as M. Cosquin says, I thought " wits might jump" to an identical tale ; now, thanks to critics and reflection, I prefer the *vera causa* of transmission to the hypothesis of coincidence : that is, when the tales are identical, or nearly so. Whether the Kaffir and Sonthal Cinderellas were borrowed or not, I do not pretend to know. I now say *much* is due to transmission, *something* to identity of fancy," instead of *vice versa.* M. Cosquin describes this as a " elegant pirouette ;" I am glad it is "elegant," and thankful that criticism and reflection can make me pirouette at all. Would that some elderly mythologists were equally agile ! But I cannot gratify M. Cosquin by attributing "*nothing* to the imagination of primitive men" : that is, of men in the savage and barbaric condition. All the wild incidents—talking beasts, cannibalism, magic—come (in my opinion) from no other source, except in cases of later imitation. On this point I am with Fontenelle and Sainte Beuve.

As to place of origin, I still do not expect to find it. M. Cosquin asks me whether the older tales, which existed in Europe before the ascertained mediæval and Islamitic importation of Indian tales, were like or unlike the new comers? I can only refer him to the *Märchen* themselves—in the Odyssey, the Cyclic fragments, the Homeric and Pindaric Scholiasts, and other Greek remains These *Märchen* were in Europe at a date not lower than 800 B. C. for many of them. M. Cosquin, of course, can prove no connexion with India for these or for the Egyptian tales in M. Maspero's collection, about which he here says nothing. Are these stories like, or not like the Indo-European stories of comparatively recent importation ? He can read the Greek, and may judge for himself. I note with pleasure that M. Cosquin, since 1888, has found two grateful beasts in Indian "Puss and Boots" tales. In the one form previously known the jackal was *not* a grateful beast. The "moral" is still to seek in all three Indian cases ; but even if it is found, as all men have attributed all human qualities to beasts, I see nothing specially Indian. And, if a specially Buddhistic moral *is* found in India, how does that bear on the question ? If it is not found there, it ought to be. The idea, that " beasts are more grateful than men," might occur to a moralist with a dog, anywhere in the wide world : to any moralist, Lord Byron, for example. Yet, so far, in the case of " Puss in Boots," the " Buddhistic " moral *is* found elsewhere, and *not* in India !—*A. Lang : Academy, 19th January*, 1895.

382. The Babul Tree.—No pious Hindu will rest under the shade of the Babul or Acacia tree. It is considered most unlucky and sure to cause disease or trouble of some kind.—*Pandit Rám Gharib Chaubè.*

383. Banjaras : Rules for the disposal of the Dead.—In the Saharanpur District the Banjaras say that when the marriage ceremony of a man has been duly performed by his walking round the sacred fire, his body is on death cremated ; but any one, male or female, who has not been regularly married in this way should be buried. They say that this circumambulation round the sacred fire devotes the person who has performed the rite to Agni Deota or the god of fire, and hence his corpse should be disposed of by means of cremation.—*W. Crooke.*

384. South Mirzapur: The Song of the Flute.—

Muraliyá Kawaná gumán bhari ?
Jar tori janūn,
Per pahchánún,
Jangal hi ki lakri.
Hari hari bánsá ki tú murallyá
Hirá ratan jari.

O flute, why are you so full of pride ? I know your origin, the tree of which you were made, only a forest tree. O flute, you came only out of a green bamboo and now you are ornamented with diamonds !—*W. Crooke.*

385. Usha Kala—the Dawn—Journeys at the time of.—It is dangerous to undertake a journey at the Usha Kála or dawn. This is only if the proposed journey is towards the east ; a journey in any other direction will be attended with success.—*W. Crooke.*

386. Montgomery: Remedy for Catarrh in Horses.—The great remedy for catarrh in horses is burning blue cloth in a *lota* and making the animal smell it.—*W. E. Purser : Settlement Report*, p. 82.

387. The Eel.—No respectable Hindu will allow an eel to be brought into his kitchen because it is akin to the snake. It is said that was really the eel which appears in the legend of Nala and Damayanti, which, after being parched, made its escape as swiftly as a snake.—*Pándit Rám Gharib Chaubé.*

388. The Origin of Rice.—As Hanumán is said to have brought the mango from Lanka after the defeat of Rávana, so Sri Krishna is said to have brought the rice from Patála or the lower regions when he went there to chastise the great dragon Káli Nága.—*Pándit Rám Gharib Chaubé.*

389. Tombs Nine Yards long.—I have given elsewhere (*Introduction to Popular Religion*, 140) some examples of tombs nine yards long. I hear there is one at a place called Kailáspur, in the Rurki Tahsíl of the Saháranpur district. It is nine yards long and is regarded with great veneration by the people of the neighbourhood. It is said to come down from the time when nine yards was the ordinary stature of human beings.—*W. Crooke.*

390. Muhammadan Graves: Trees planted on them.—Can any one give a list of the trees which are planted by Muhammadans on the graves of their dead? By one account the only trees allowed are the Khajúr palm and various flowering shrubs. But surely the Ním and other trees are often found in Muhammadan cemeteries. Are such trees intentionally planted there? There seems to be a general belief that if a tree planted near a grave grows green and shady the dead person had lived a pious life; the opposite inference is drawn from a tree planted near a grave fading or dying.—*H. Smith.*

391. Babu: Derivation of.—The word *Babu* appears to be derived from Sanskrit *Vaptu*, a progenitor. " One popular derivation is that they were so called by the Muhammadans because they used to perfume themselves, the word being the Persian *ba-bu* ("perfumed").—*Pándit Rám Gharíb Chaubé.*

392. The Domunha Snake.—The *domunha* snake has a mouth at both ends. For half the year he moves one way and half the year the other. People who do not keep their words are born as *domunha* snakes.—*W. Crooke.*

393. Superstitions in connection with the site of a new building.—Masons and other people, whose business it is to build new houses, have the following superstitions in connection with the site of a new building:—

1. If on the site of a building charcoal comes out when the labourers have first struck the ground with their spades, then be sure that masons who take part in the building of that house will soon die.

2. If broken pieces of tiles come out, then the wives of the masons will die.

3. If ashes come out, then the person who is getting the house built will soon die.

4. If bones come out, then the wife of the owner of the house will die.—*Pándit Rám Gharíb Chaubé.*

394. Alms taken by Brahmans.—Alms are given to Bráhmans in the names of the nine planets, but all Bráhmans cannot take such alms indifferently. Thus, Bráhmans of the Gaur tribe take only alms given in the name of the Sun, the Moon and Jupiter; Gujratis those in the name of Mars, Venus and Mercury; Dakauts those in the name of Rahu, Ketu and Saturn. Gaur Bráhmans are considered superior to the other two.—*W. Crooke.*

395. Dakaut Brahmans.—People believed that whatever a Dakaut Bráhman may say during the first watch of the day surely comes to pass. In this belief Dakauts go on their begging expeditions very early in the morning and come home by 10 o'clock. Hence they get their dues easier and quicker than other Bráhmans.—*W. Crooke.*

396. The Jinn.—The existence of *jinns* is universally believed in Kabul, and, in fact, in all Muhammadan countries. They can assume any shape, are of both sexes and are of every religious persuasion, being Hindus, Musalmans, Sunnis or Shiahs. When a birth takes place in a Hazara family, food is put in a chamber, apart for the *jinns*, who will then protect and take care of the child if it be handsome. In spring they, as well as the fairies, disport themselves in orchards and flower gardens. And in winter, being sensible of cold, they are supposed to haunt old ruins and caves. If an ordinary person sees a *jinn* he goes mad; but if he be a Syyad or descendant of the Prophet the *jinn* makes him a salaam in an attitude of supplication and is bound to obey the commands of the holy man. The *aals* form another race of preternatural beings; they are said to resemble women of about twenty years of age, but with long teeth and nails, and with eyes that are curved down to the side of their noses and their heels placed where their toes ought to be. They are, I suppose, the ghouls of the Persian and Turkish tales, as they meet in graveyards and feed on the dead bodies of men and horses.—*Vigne's Ghazni*, p. 211, *sqq.*

397. Offering of Bells to Mahadeva.—At Moradabad is the temple of Mahadeva under the title of Ghanteswarnath Mahadeva, who is so called because his devotees make offerings of bells (*ghanta*) in order to secure the realization of their desires. Hundreds of bells of all kinds are suspended from the ceiling of the shrine.—*Brijmohan Lal.*

398. Jalandhar: The Legend the of Town of Kartárpur.—It is said to have been founded in S. 1655 (1598 A.D.) by Guru Arjun Nath, the 5th Guru, in some waste land granted him by the Emperor Jahángír. But there seems some mistake here, for Jahángír did not become Emperor till 1605 A. D. There is a legend that, when the Guru desired a dwelling here, "a demon, who inhabited the trunk of a tree, would not permit any wood to be cut for beams, until the Guru promised that he should not be disturbed, but receive worship for ever at the shrine." It was, perhaps, in consequence of this promise that the Guru erected a sandal-wood post, which is venerated under the name of *Thamjí* (Skt. *sthambá*, a pillar) and for which a fine temple was built with money given by Ranjit Singh on his visit to Kartárpur in 1833. There is also a sacred well called Gangsír at which bathing is as efficacious as bathing at the Ganges.—*IV. E. Purser: Settlement Report*, p. 148.

399. Respect paid to the Siras Tree (Acacia or Mimosa Sirisa).—The Siras is one of the trees which is looked on by Hindus with a special degree of respect. No one will cut down the tree. At the *Diwali* they break off a twig or two which they stick into their turbans or put in the house. This is believed to ward off evil spirits and add to the prosperity of the family.—*Pándit Rám Gharíb Chaubé.*

400. Fits.—The ordinary epileptic fits (*mirgí*) and urinary discharges (*pramch*) are in popular belief the result of keeping a virgin daughter unmarried in the house. The only remedy is to get the girl married as soon as possible and to make presents to Bráhmans and do a special offering to the gods.—*Pándit Rám Gharíb Chaubé.*

North Indian Notes and Queries:
A MONTHLY PERIODICAL.

VOL. V.]　　　　　　　DECEMBER, 1895.　　　　　　　[NO. 9.

Every communication must be accompanied by the writer's name and address, not necessarily for insertion, but as a guarantee of good faith. Every quotation from a book must be accompanied by its full title, publisher's and author's names, place and date of publication, volume and page.

Contributors are requested to write on one side of the page only. If several contributions be sent at a time, they should be sent each on a separate sheet.

The Conductor cannot undertake to return, or be responsible for, any MSS. not accepted.

All orders must be accompanied by cash. If not so accompanied, they will either not be attended to, or will be complied with per value-payable post.

Contributions should be addressed direct to W. CROOKE, ESQ., C.S., SAHARANPUR, N.-W. P., INDIA.

CONTENTS OF THIS NUMBER.
(The references are to the Notes.)

Popular Religion ... 145 to 147	Folktales	... 155 to 159
Anthropology ... 148 ,, 154	Miscellanea	... 160 ,, 162

POPULAR RELIGION.

401. The Legend of Sukhdeva.—The story of Sukhdeva is very popular with high caste people in the Eastern districts of the North-Western Provinces and is worth recording:—Vishnu Bhagwan revealed the doctrines of the Vaishnava faith to Siva and at the same time warned him not to reveal it to undeserving men. Accordingly he kept it concealed for a long time. One day as he was going along with Parvati she saw him repeating something quietly to himself. When she asked him what he was muttering, he replied that he was repeating the name of his Ishtadeva or personal god. She asked his name and he promised to tell her some time in secret when they were alone. So they repaired to the solitude of Mount Kailása and there, beside the lake Mána Sarovar, the pair sat down on two pure white stones. Close to the place was an ancient banyan tree, and a parrot who sat on the tree heard the revelation. Now this parrot had been once a god, but in fulfilment of a curse had been turned into a parrot. When he heard the revelation of the true faith he could not help shedding copious tears. A drop fell on the deities and they knew that some being was near them. Siva looked up and saw the parrot and was wroth and was about to curse him, when the parrot prayed forgiveness and begged that he might be born a saint and devote himself to calling on the name of Vishnu. Siva was appeased and told him that he should be born of the loins of the Rishi Vyása and be known as Sukhdeva or the parrot deity.

So he was born in the womb of the wife of Vyása, and knowing well the worth of this world, he was unwilling to be born. At last, after twelve years in the womb, he was born and the moment he was born took to flight. His father who had no other child, immediately pursued him and implored him to stay and speak with him. But Sukhdeva paid no heed to his father's words. At last he came to a river in flood and when he reached the opposite bank, he called out to his father Vyása and ordered him to pursue him no longer. Vyása again implored Sukhdeva to return. So he answered—"I shall return if you answer one question." Vyása agreed. Then Sukhdeva said: "There was once a Raja of a certain land who, while outhunting, happened to come to the kingdom of women (*Triya Ráj*). They kept him there some time, and when he had lost his youth and beauty, they threw him into one of the drains of their fort. There he supported himself for some time by eating the grains of rice that came down with the dirty water. After a time he recovered his strength and made his escape. Many years after, he again went to hunt and again came to the kingdom of women. Now I ask you father whether he should again entrust himself to these women?" Vyása said: "Why should he return to a place where he had been so cruelly and treacherously used?"

"This is exactly my case" replied Sukhdeva. "I have escaped from the hell of birth and would you advise me to return to the hell of existence— the world?"

Vyása was silent and Sukhdeva retired into a forest and devoted himself to austerities. So he became a famous saint and expounded the Bhágwat to the Raja Parikshat.—*Pándit Rám Bákhsh Chaubé.*

---

402. John Nicholson worshipped by Sikhs. —"The Sikhs' worship of Nicholson is an old story, but it was a new sensation to young Wilberforce to see group after group of them come into camp of an evening, seat themselves on the ground, and fix their eyes on him in mute worship. John Nicholson's reckless bravery, his fine presence, his constant immunity from death, all contributed to the idea in the simple mind of his faithful worshippers that he was nothing less than a deity.

Nicholson constituted himself Post Master General, and all letters that passed along the road were intercepted and translated. Plot after plot of the mutineers was he thus enabled to overthrow, many a faithless sepoy did he hang without trial. He had proclaimed that the punishment for mutiny was death, and he never hesitated for a moment to make good his dictum."—*Tribune,* Lahore.

It is not easy to say whether the common story of the worship of John Nicholson, the hero of the siege of Delhi, is really true. The class of so-called Nikalseni *faqírs* do not appear in the lists collected by Mr. Ibbetson and Mr. Maclagan at the Census of the Pánjab in 1881 and 1891. Mr. Delmerich (*Pánjab Notes & Queries,* II, 180) says that after the defeat of the Sikh Army at Guzarát, these men were seen at Rawalpindi dressed up in the cast-off clothes and hats of Europeans, and with shaven heads and faces. The eldest gave himself out to be the Mahant or Chief of a sect and the others to be his *chelas* or disciples. The Mahant played upon a two-stringed instrument known as the *dutára* and he and his disciples sang songs in praise of the English in general and of John Nicholson in particular whom they declared to be their *guru.* Mr. Delmerich thinks they did this to gain the favour of Nicholson, who was then Commissioner of Rawalpindi.

Nicholson is said to have had them flogged and then they disappeared. There is a monument to Nicholson at the Margala Pass, 16 miles from Rawalpindi on the Peshawar Road, but Mr. Delmerich never heard of any Nikalseni *faqírs* there. I lately visited the tomb of Nicholson, just outside the Kashmír Gate at Delhi, and could not find that any pilgrimages were made to his tomb by any kind of Hindu *faqírs* and there were certainly no signs of any offerings being made.

If there was ever a sect of the kind, it would seem to have disappeared long since. It would be very interesting to know if there are any survivals of the cult as still existing in the Pánjab.—*W. Crook.*

---

403. Prohibited offerings.—No one dares to offer washed rice (*achchhat*) to Vishnu; *tulasi* leaves to Ganesa; grass to Devi; *bel* leaves to Surva, the Sun-godling; *dhatúra* or *madár* flowers to Vishnu. Lotus flowers may be offered to all the gods, except to Siva and Surya.—*Pándit Rám Gharíb Chaubé.*

---

404. A Living Saint: Rumzan Shah.—This old *faqír* lives at Jaunpur, and has thousands of believers. They say that he once stopped the river from rising early in September this year, but as the people did not behave properly towards him, the floods came in October and destroyed the city.

I have met this old gentleman. He is not in his senses: talks always of old Nawabi times, and drinks a great deal. He is considered to be the saint in charge of Jaunpur City, as natives believe there is one in every city.—*A. Ahmed.*

---

405. Western districts, North-Western Provinces: Worship of Shahíds or Muhammadan martyrs at births and marriages.— The worship of the Shahíds or martyrs whose tombs are at Amroha, in Moradabad, and Jalesar, in the Etah District, prevails widely in the neighbouring districts. These saints are known as Miyáns or lords. The name of the Amroha martyr is commonly said to be Zain Sháh, or Shaikh Saddee. That of Jalesar is Sayyed Ibrahím. A number of songs are sung by women in their honour. They are chiefly worshipped at the birth and marriage of a first-born son. If they are neglected, the child gets sick and the marriage is unfruitful.

The mode of worship is as follows:—Two he-goats are fed on gram and other choice grain. When the birth rites are over they are sacrificed in the house court-yard in the name of the Miyán. The flesh is cooked carefully, special care being given to the cooking of the heads of the animals. When the cooking is over, the mother of the child fills the bosom of her sheet with *ghi*, meat and fourteen cakes, seven cooked with salt and seven with sugar. Sometimes the cakes are nine in number. An old woman of the family takes up the baby and leads the mother to the fire, into which she throws seven or nine fragments of the food on behalf of the mother and prays to the Miyán to protect both mother and child. Then she takes the mother into a room, which is generally the house kitchen, and makes her worship the Miyán by facing in the direction of his tomb and bowing her head. The phrase used is *Miyán ki kaduri charkána*. The mother then distributes the food among some Musalmán beggars.

The Miyán of Amroha is worshipped on Wednesday and he of Jalesar on Saturday. They are both worshipped in the same way.

At a marriage the Miyáns are worshipped in the same manner, the only difference being that the married pair have the corners of their robes knotted together and then one of them, generally the bridegroom, takes the fragments of food in his sheet and flings them into the fire. When the pair have bowed to the Miyán in the house kitchen, the sister of the bridegroom or of his father unties the knot in their clothes and receives a present.

All high caste Hindus in Aligarh and the adjoining districts worship these Musalmán saints : in fact they are more popular among Hindus than Musalmáns, a curious instance of the adaptability of the Hindu faith.—*W. Crooke.*

406. **The Saint Maula Shah.**—This Muhammadan *faqír* lived at Rám Dyálganj, on the banks of the Sai river, in the Jaunpur District, some 30 years ago. He is believed to have great power and a number of court-going people offer sweets and flowers at his tomb when they have any cases.—*A. Ahmed.*

407. **The Saint Shaikh Abdul Qadus.**—The town of Gangoh, in the Saharanpur District, is said to take its name from an old Rájá name Gang. Here is the tomb of Shaikh Abdul Qadús where a fair is held on the 22nd of the month Jamadi-ul-awwal. He is said to have been the disciple of Shaikh Abdul Haqqír Shaikh Muhammad bin Shaikh Arif, and was endowed with supernatural powers. Some say that he was a descendant of the renowned Imám-ul-Azam. He was a great friend of the Emperor Humayun, whom he met at Khurasan. He departed this life in the year 950 Hijri.—*W. Crooke.*

408. **A legend of Krishna.**—One day after Krishna had been born at Mathura there arose a controversy between Indra and his son Jayanta whether or not Krishna had been really born at Mathura or not. At last Jayanta, who would not believe in the words of his father, went himself to Mathura and taking the form of a crow, came where Krishna and his brother Buldeo were eating their food and began to partake of the food. They tried to drive him away, but in vain, and at last they called out to their mother, Jasoda. She too tried to drive off the crow, but failed. Then she complained to Krishna and he said to her :—" Bring my bow and arrow made of reed and I will see whether this rascally bird troubles us any longer." When he got the bow, Sri Krishna discharged an arrow at the crow, and, fly as he would, the arrow kept following him wheresoever he went and wounding him. So he went and complained to Raja Indra, but Indra said :—" You are rightly served on account of your unbelief. You must go and bow before Sri Krishna and ask his forgiveness."

So Jayanta again assumed the form of a man and fell at the feet of Krishna and asked his pardon, which was granted, and he returned to his father.

[This is interesting as an example of the Hindu legends told by a Gond of the jungles.—ED.]

(Told by Akbar Shah, Manjhi of Manbasa, Dudhi, Mirzapur District, and recorded by Qazi Hamid Husain.)

409. **Three sacred trees.**—It is considered very lucky to plant together the three sacred trees, the banyan (*bar*), the *pipal* and the *nim*. They are considered collectively as sacred as the junction of the three holy streams, the Ganges, Jumna and Saraswati. There are three trees planted in this way at the temple of Pawan Paniswar Mahadeva at Hardwar and the Panda priests there call them Triveni, which is a title of the junction of the three sacred streams.—*Pándit Rám Gharib Chaubé.*

410. **Rain spells.**—I have given elsewhere (*Introduction to Popular Religion and Folklore*, 39*ff*) some instances which show that human sacrifice was used as a means of causing rain. The following instance from Roumania will be interesting in this connection.

" A trial of a remarkable character has just terminated at Bucharest. Two boys, one aged six, the other fourteen, were charged upon their own confession, with having attempted to drown a child, two years of age. Their defence was that the long drought and total lack of rain had to be terminated, and that the crime upon which they stood their trial was the only successful method known to accomplish this. This extraordinary defence is explained by the *Daily News* correspondent. He states that the children of the villages, in times of great drought, are made to throw a clay figure of a child into the water. The boys drowned the child merely because they had no clay figure. The elder was sentenced to two years' imprisonment, the younger was left to his mother's care."—*W. Crooke.*

ANTHROPOLOGY.

411. Eclipse Observances.—If an eclipse occur in the birth asterism of a man he will die; if at his birth star (*ráshi*) he will suffer sore disease; if in the second *ráshi* he will lose wealth; if in the third he will get riches; if in the fourth he will fall sick; if in the fifth he will suffer anxiety; if in the sixth he will be happy; if in the seventh his wife will sicken; if in the eighth she will die; if in the ninth he will lose his honour; if in the tenth he will be prosperous; if in the eleventh he will be a gainer; if in the twelfth he will be ruined. The effects of this are visible within six months.

The way to avoid this is to hide in the house while the eclipse is going on and on no account to witness it. If you cannot help seeing it you must do the following rite to keep off the evil effects of the eclipse. Get a Bráhman to repeat the Gayatri Mantra some thousand times for your sake. Give a cow, or land, or some silver to a priest. Get a snake made of gold and placing it in a copper vessel with some sesamum and money give to a Bráhman who will repeat the Mantra, of which the following is a translation :—" O thou that art made of darkness, and thou that art dreadful in the extreme, thou that overcomest the Sun and the Moon, absolve me from the effect of thy wrath, as I give away a golden snake in thy honour."

This is done by comparatively poor people. Rich people go through a much more elaborate rite.—*Pándit Rám Gharib Chaubé.*

412. Funeral rites among Sarwariya Bráhmans.—In the funeral feast among Sarwariya Bráhmans it is the custom that at least sixteen Bráhmans should be fed by the relatives of the deceased. The popular explanation of the number sixteen being selected is that there are that number of stocks of Sarwariya Bráhmans. To feed sixteen Bráhmans means that a representative of each of the sixteen stocks is feasted. Even if a member of each of the stocks is not present, not less than sixteen Bráhmans should be entertained. The common phrase runs—*Bhaiya! Solah Brāhmam kauno tarah se khila dewe ke hoe, aur Pitri rin se uttrih ho jaye ke hoe*—" Brother! Somehow or other I must feed sixteen Bráhmans and thus be free from the debt to the deceased ancestors."—*Pándit Rám Gharib Chaubé.*

413. Women with moustaches.—Women who have visible moustaches, and these are not uncommon, are supposed likely to become widows in the prime of life. It is said that they were intended to be men and became women only by mistake. Hence they have an evil-eye which is prejudicial to the male members of the household. The same idea attaches to a woman with hair on her body, particularly along the spine. Such people are very dangerous to their friends. In the same way a woman with a manly voice is very generally dreaded.—*M. Ram Lal.*

414. Saraswat Bráhmans and flesh eating.—Saraswat Bráhmans have no prejudice against eating meat unless they have been initiated into the Vaishnava faith. The influence of the Arya Samaj has tended to reduce the number of meat-eaters among them.—*Pándit Rám Gharib Chaubé.*

415. Western districts, North-Western Provinces: Blood-offering to River-gods.—It is a common custom of all the low-castes in the Western districts of the North-Western Provinces to offer goats or rams in sacrifice to the Ganges or to any other river in the vicinity at the end of both the harvests of the year.—*Pándit Rám Gharib Chaubé.*

416. Looking at the palms of the hands the first thing in the morning.—Natives who are afraid of the evil-eye, or of demoniacal influence generally, when they wake in the morning, look first at the palms of their hands as a means of avoiding the evil influence. The idea of the Bráhmans, in support of which they quote texts, is that Bráhma seats himself in the middle of the palm, Vishnu in the middle and Mahadeva in the ends of the fingers. This idea, that the hand is inhabited by gods or spirits, accounts for a number of curious practices, such as snapping the fingers for good luck, the laying on of hands as a form of ritual, the marking of the spread hand on walls to scare evil ghosts, and so on.—*W. Crooke.*

417. Bhuinhár Folk etymology.—An old Bhuinhár from the Azamgarh District tells me that the name of his caste is derived from *Bhuin* " land " and *hár* " a garland. " His ancestors, he says, once accepted gifts of land from Ráma Chandra who was polluted by the slaughter of the Bráhman Ráwana. So Ráma cursed them and said :—" Those who refuse my gifts now will in the Iron Age have to beg from Chamárs and Doms; while those who take my gifts will be surrounded with land as with a garland." So in the present day the Bráhman has lost ground and the Bhuinhár is flourishing.—*Pandit Rám Gharíb Chaubé.*

---

418. On the Indian Folk-beliefs about the Tiger.—Recent discoveries in pre-historic caves have brought to light the important fact that primitive man was coëval with those terrible monsters—the mammoths, the cave-bear, the cave-lion and many others which are now known to us only from their fossilized bones. The presence of flint spear-heads, hatchets, hammers and other weapons among these relics attest that men in those remote times not only hunted, slew and fed upon these animals but also *held them in great awe, because they were of much larger proportions and far stronger than their own selves.* In this awe, based upon the magnitude of size and the excess of strength of some members of the brute creation, animal-worship has its origin. Primitive man thought that these brutes resembled himself in so many respects and yet was so much stronger that he believed, in his ignorance, that the latter must have souls much greater than his own soul. Thus he was led to the next step in the process by which animal-worship came to be evolved, namely, that these brutes must be some beings who possessed some power for either good or evil to themselves and must, therefore, be propitiated for bestowal of favours or for appeasing their wrath. Forms of this animal-worship still survive among races of men all the wide world over, who have as yet hardly emerged from the state of savagery and whose conditions of life very nearly resemble those of man in the palæolithic, the neolithic, and the bronze ages.

The kind of animal worshipped depended very much upon the country in which primitive man lived. Man, in all parts of the world, fears and worships that particular sort of animal which infests in great numbers a particular tract of country, or commits depredations therein. Thus in the farthest regions of North America where the terrible grizzly bears roam at large and commit sad havoc on animal-life, the aboriginal Indians of those parts hold that ferocious beast in great superstitious awe. In Canada—the home of the ravening wolves,—the legend of the Wehr-Wolf—a goblin brute always thirsting for human blood, is believed by all classes of the people, thus shewing how much that animal is feared by all Canadians, both high and low. To come nearer home, the tiger, the snake, and the shark afford familiar examples of animal-worship in this country. One of the much dreaded animals peculiar to the Indian Fauna is the tiger, which is held in great superstitious awe, not only on account of its larger size but also of its ferocity and fearful depredations. Such are its ravening propensities that it annually destroys large numbers of human beings and cattle, thereby depopulating large tracts of country and causing much loss to the agricultural classes. The snake and the shark also come under the category of the destructive animals peculiar to this country; so many human lives are annually lost from snake-bites and attacks of sharks. Hence the Bengalis worship *Manshá Devi*, the great Snake-Goddess on the *Manshá Pujá* day in the month of Srávana, in order to propitiate the serpent class. On the *Gangá Pujá* day, the Goddess Gangá, or the River Ganges, who is represented as riding on a shark in native drawings, is worshipped in Bengal, and thus the shark is propitiated in an indirect way.

In the same way, the tiger is worshipped by many aboriginal tribes of India, and is, in other parts of this country, held in much superstitious awe, though not actually worshipped. Thus a tiger-demon is one of recognized deities in the pantheon of some of the aboriginal tribes of India. The Kisans,[1] a partially Hinduised tribe living about Palamow, Sirgujá, and Jashpur in the Province of Chota Nagpur, worship the tiger-demon. They think that by doing so their own lives and their domesticated animals would be safe from the ravages of these animals. Among the Santáls living in Rámgarh, only those persons whose relatives have been killed by the tiger, consider it indispensably necessary to propitiate the tiger-demon who had wrought death to his kinsmen. The Gonds also pay devoirs to the tiger-demon out of the same motives which actuate the Kisans and the Santáls. In the Santál Pergunnahs, the Santáls consider death by a tiger a far greater calamity than anything else, so much so that whenever Santáli witnesses have to be examined in the Courts of that province, the form of oath in Santáli, which is administered to them, means that should they tell falsehoods, they would be eaten by tigers. Among the Gonds, the Kúsrú, Súrí, Markám, Netiá and Sársún clans hold Bághesar or the tiger-lord—a local deified spirit—in great reverence. There is a legend[2] current among them, which has been narrated by Captain W. L. Samuells in the pages of the Journal of the Asiatic Society of Bengal, and is as follows:—

Once upon a time, in a family of the Gond tribe, there were five brothers, named respectively Kúsrú, Súrí, Markám, Netía, and Sarsún. At her second childbirth, Kúsrú's wife gave birth to a tiger's whelp, which was treated by its parents with as much affection and regard as

---

[1] *Vide Indian Antiquary,* Vol. XIX., page 128.
[2] *Vide* the *J. A. S. B.,* Vol. XLI., Part I., pages 115 *ff.*

their first-born male-child. From childhood he was the constant companion of Kúsrú. While Kúsrú used to watch his crops, the tiger-child used to remain near him. Now nilgais and sambar used to destroy Kúsrú's crops, but Kúsrú could do nothing to prevent it. On one occasion, seeing a large sambar destroying his young and tender *úrid* plants, Kúsrú wept and tore his hair, bemoaning his bad lot; whereupon the tiger-child killed the sambar and tore it to pieces, and went on doing so till Kúsrú's crop was gathered. Hence Kúsrú began to love the young cub all the more. In course of time, the young tiger died and became a *bhut*.

On the occasion of the marriage of Kúsrú's daughter, one of the party became possessed with a demon. The Baigá or village-priest and necromancer questioned it and found that it was the spirit of the tiger-child, and demanded worship with offerings and sacrifices. Fowls, kid, arrack and *ghi* were offered to him and the spirit thereupon went out of the man. So from that day forth, the spirit of the Kúsrú's tiger-son was deified and was worshipped under the name of Bághesar or the Tiger-god, by the five Gond clans descended from, and respectively named after the brothers Kúsrú, Súrí, Markám, Netiá, and Sársún.

It is only at the marriages of the members of the five clans named above, that Bághesar manifests his presence in the above manner. With them he is held in reverence as a *deified* spirit; but with other Gonds, Bághesar is simply one of the many spirits who are yearly propitiated with offerings. According to the latter, he has no such origin as that ascribed to him by the five clans abovenamed, but is simply regarded as 'the concentrated essence of spirits,' which have issued from those Gonds who have met their deaths by tigers; for, according to local belief, the spirits of all Gonds thus killed are said to unite and form the one great spirit Bághesar. It is simply for saving their flocks and herds, and their own lives also, from the ravages of the tigers, that the inhabitants of every Gond village yearly make offerings to propitiate this demon. Another account is given as to how tiger-worship originated among the Gonds. The latter say that one of their chiefs was, in early life, devoured by a tiger, and that he afterwards appeared to his friends, telling them that, if worship were paid to him, he would protect them and their domesticated animals from the depredations of that animal. They acted up to his advice, and he was accordingly duly installed as a member of their already crowded Pantheon.[3]

[3] *Vide Indian Antiquary*, Vol. XIV, (1885), p. 133.

Some other aboriginal tribes believe that the form of the tiger can be assumed by certain maliciously disposed persons among them, who thereby become possessed of a good deal of power for evil to living human beings. The Khonds[4] of Orissa believe that some women can transform themselves into tigers; and sometimes wicked persons try to spread this impression concerning themselves in order to extort presents from their neighbours as the price of refraining from injuring them by their ravages. This belief is also, to a certain extent, shared in by the Oráons[5] who live in the adjoining districts, included within the Central Provinces of India. They say that those persons who have met their death by the tiger are metamorphosed into that terrible animal.

The Kakhyens, a savage people living in the hills to the east of Burma, believe in two deities, named Chitong and Muron, who are two of ten brothers, said to take an especial interest in Kakhyen affairs. The Kakhyens believe that if hunters do not present offerings to the former deity, named Chitong, *some one among them will be killed by a tiger*[6] or stag. There is another Nat or deity worshipped by them under the name of *Ndong* Nat, who is supposed to preside over the Outside of Home. He is generally believed to reside in the house, but is *worshipped outside if one of the family is killed by the bite of a tiger*[7] or snake.

The Burmese worship the Kakhyen Nat named *Ndong*, under the name of *Aing-peen* Nat, *in case if any of the family be killed by a tiger*.[8] The Burmese believe that this Nat also sometimes assumes the form of a tiger, for Dr. Anderson says: "At a place called Thembaw-eng, the headman came down and compelled us to leave our moorings. We were not assailed by Kakhyens, but had a nocturnal alarm of a tiger, which the boatmen declared to be *not a real tiger, but the Nat of the locality*, who was enraged at their having cut down some branches of a tree."[9] So great is the superstitious dread of the tiger, entertained by the Burmese, that, whenever a person among them is killed by that animal, they take steps to bury the corpse as soon as possible. Dr. John Anderson saw an instance of this superstition while he was at Bhamó. He says:

[4] *Op. cit.*, p. 131.
[5] *Op. cit*, p. 132.
[6] *Mandalay to Momien*, by John Anderson, M.D. London, 1876, p. 147.
[7] *Op. cit.*, p. 459.
[8] *Op. cit.*, p. 459.
[9] *Op. cit.*, p. 452.

"At Bhamo, a woman was killed by a tiger. The woman was buried the same night in accordance with the Burmese custom, followed in all cases of persons killed by tigers."[10]

The Shans of the Sanda Valley in Yunnan also believe in the existence of a Nat, which assumes the form of a tiger and carries off children. This belief is testified to by Dr. Anderson, who visited them during the course of the first expedition to Yunnan, undertaken in 1868. He says:—"A thick grove of fir trees, marking the burial place of the Tsawbwa's family, was the only covert, but firing there was looked upon as certain to bring disease and death upon the chief and his household. A formal request was made that we would not shoot on the hills behind the town. *A Nat is said to dwell in a cutting*, which marks the entrenchments made by the Chinese army in 1767, *and the Shans believe that if a gun was fired, the insulted demon would come down as a tiger and carry off the children.*"[11]

In the Central Provinces of India prevail a certain number of superstitions connected with the tiger. One of them is that when a man had been killed by a tiger, his spirit possessed that beast and led him away from all danger. Lieut.-Colonel W. H. Sleeman, who sojourned for a long time in these wild tracts, met with several instances of this and other superstitious beliefs prevailing there. He says:[12] "Ram Chund Roo, commonly called the Sureemunt, chief of Deoree, came to call upon me after breakfast, and the conversation turned upon the number of people that had of late been killed by tigers between Saugor and Deoree, his ancient capital, which lies about midway between Saugor and the Nerbudda river. One of his followers, who stood behind his chair, said 'that when a tiger had killed one man he was safe, for the spirit of the man rode upon his head, and guided him from all danger. The spirit knew very well that the tiger would be watched for many days at the place where he had committed the homicide, and always guided him off to some other more secure place, where he killed other men without any risk to himself. He did not exactly know why the spirit of the man should thus befriend the beast that had killed him; but,' added he, ' there is a mischief inherent in spirits; and the better the man the more mischievous is his ghost, if means are not taken to put him to rest.' This is the popular and general belief throughout India, and it is supposed, that the only sure mode of destroying a tiger, who has killed many people, is to begin by making offerings to the spirits of his victims, and thereby depriving him of their valuable services."

Another tiger-superstition widely current throughout India is that human beings are metamorphosed into tigers by eating the root of a particular kind of plant and that, if in this state he can eat the root of another he will instantly be re-transformed into a human being. Lieut.-Colonel Sleeman gives in his aforesaid work[13] the following instances of the abovementioned belief: " The Sureemunt was himself of opinion, that the tigers which now infest the wood from Saugor to Deoree were of a different kind—in fact, that they were neither more nor less than men turned into tigers—a thing which took place in the woods of Central India much more often than people were aware of. The only visible difference between the two," added the Sureemunt, "is that the metamorphosed tiger has *no tail*, while the *bora*, or ordinary tiger, has a very long one. In the jungle about Deoree," continued he, "there is a root which, if a man eat of, he is converted into a tiger on the spot; and if in this state he can eat of another, he becomes a man again—a melancholy instance of the former of which," said he, " occurred, I am told, in my own father's family when I was an infant. His washerman, Rughoo, was, like all washermen, a great drunkard; and being seized with a violent desire to ascertain what a man felt in the state of a tiger, he went one day to the jungle and brought home two of these roots, and desired his wife to stand by with one of them, and the instant she saw him assume the tiger's shape, to thrust it into his mouth. She consented: the washerman ate his root, and became instantly a tiger; but his wife was so terrified at the sight of her old husband in this shape that she ran off with the antidote in her hand. Poor old Rughoo took to the woods, and there ate a good many of his old friends from the neighbouring villages; but he was at last shot and recognized from the circumstances of his *having no tail*. You may be quite sure," concluded Sureemunt, "when you bear of a tiger without a tail, that it is some unfortunate man who has eaten of that root—and of all the tigers he will be found the most mischievous."

A third superstitious belief connected with the tiger, prevalent in Central India, is that there is a particular kind of science which endows the men who master its secrets, with the power of transforming themselves into tigers whenever they wish to do so. This is testified to by the

---

[10] *Vide Report on the Expedition to Western Yunan via Bhamo*, by J. Anderson, M.D. Calcutta, 1871, pages 235-36.

[11] *Op. cit.*, p. 260.

[12] *Rambles and Recollections of an Indian Official*, by Lieut.-Colonel W. H. Sleeman. London: Hatchard & Son, Vol. I, pages 162-63.

[13] *Op. cit.*, Vol. I., pp. 163-164.

same author from whom I have made extensive quotations above, and who was thoroughly conversant with the customs and beliefs of the people inhabiting the Central Provinces of India. He relates:[1] "I was one day talking with my friend, the Rajah of Myhere, on the road between Jubbulpore and Mirzapore, on the subject of the number of men who had been lately killed by tigers at the Kutra Pass on that road, and the best means of removing the danger. "Nothing," said the Rajah, "could be more easy or more cheap than the destruction of these tigers, if they were of the ordinary sort; but the tigers that kill men by wholesale, as these do, are, you may be sure, men themselves converted into tigers by the force of their *science;* and such animals are of all the most unmanageable." On being questioned as to how those men converted themselves into tigers, the Rajah replied:—"Nothing is more easy than this to persons who have once acquired the science; but how they learn it, or what it is, we unlettered men know not. There was once a high priest, of a large temple, in this very valley of Myhere, who was in the habit of getting himself converted into a tiger by the force of this science, which he had thoroughly acquired. He had a necklace, which one of his disciples used to throw over his neck the moment the tiger's form became fully developed. He had, however, long given up the practice, and all his old disciples had gone off on their pilgrimages to distant shrines, when he was one day seized with a violent desire to take his old form of the tiger. He expressed the wish to one of his new disciples and demanded whether he thought he might rely upon his courage to stand by and put on the necklace. 'Assuredly you may,' said the disciple; 'such is my faith in you and in the God we serve, that I fear nothing!' The high priest upon this put the necklace into his hand with the requisite instructions, and forthwith began to change his form. The disciple stood trembling in every limb, till he heard him give a roar that shook the whole edifice, when he fell flat upon his face, and dropped the necklace on the floor. The tiger bounded over him, and out at the door; and infested all the roads leading to the temple for many years afterwards." On being questioned whether the old high priest was one of the tigers at the Kutra Pass, the Rajah replied in the negative, but further added that they might have been all men who had become imbued with a little too much of the high priest's *science,* and, when men once acquired this science, they couldn't help exercising it, though it was to their own ruin and that of others. On being asked as to what was the simple plan for stopping their depredations, supposing them to be ordinary tigers, the Rajah said:—"I propose to have the spirits that guide them propitiated by proper prayers and offerings; for the spirit of every man or woman who has been killed by a tiger rides upon his head, or runs before him, and tells him where to go to get prey, and to avoid danger. Get some of the Gonds, or wild people from the jungles, who are well skilled in these matters; give them ten or twenty rupees, and bid them go and raise a small shrine, and there sacrifice to these spirits. The Gonds will tell them that they shall, on this shrine, have regular worship, and good sacrifices of fowls, goats and pigs, every year at least, if they will but relinquish their offices with the tigers and be quiet. If this is done, I pledge myself," said the Rajah, "that the tigers will soon get killed themselves, or cease from killing men. If they do not, you may be qu:te sure that they are not ordinary tigers, but men turned into tigers, or that the Gonds have appropriated all you gave them to their own use, instead of applying it to conciliate the spirits of the unfortunate people!"

In Bengal, though the tiger is not actually worshipped, there have gathered round him a number of superstitions or semi-mythical beliefs. In the Sundarbans, where stripes can be seen in his greatest beauty, the tiger is regarded with much superstitious awe. So infested are the Sundarbans with tigers that men, who have occasion to reside there, such as agents of persons who have taken leases of the forest lands for purposes of reclamation and cultivation, and wood-cutters, construct structures of bamboo raised far above the ground, whereon seated they pass the nights. It sometimes happens that tigers, in the course of their peregrinations, find their way to the bases of these structures and do not move away readily. The residents of these structures cannot descend and go to their respective businesses. In order to drive them away, they resort to the expedient of appealing to the *jogis* or ascetics who perform their penances in these forest tracts. It is said that the tigers neither molest these persons nor are the latter at all afraid of the former. On being appealed to, the *jogi* goes to the tiger, pats it on the back, and tells it to go away; whereupon, it is said, the tiger goes away as if it was a domestic cat. This story may be a myth, pure and simple, and I have narrated it here, as I heard it and the following story from a friend of mine, resident of the Jessore District, as illustrations of the popular belief about the tiger. There is another popular belief current there to the effect that tigers, for the purpose of preying on human victims, take advantage of the time when wood-cutters busy themselves in cutting wood with their hatchets, lest the sounds of their (tigers') footfalls may be heard. As soon as the wood-cutter commences his operations and plies his hatchet, the tiger

---

[1] *Op. cit.,* Vol. I, pp. 165–167.

cautiously advances his foot as each blow of the hatchet falls, so that the sounds of his (tiger's) footfalls are drowned by the noise of the hatchet blows. It is also said that, in the Sundarbans, the tiger is looked upon with feelings akin to reverence, and sometimes offerings are presented to him, out of the superstitious belief that, being thus treated, he won't molest human beings.

The tiger also plays an important part in Indian folk-lore. In Bengal he figures in, at least, two folk-stories that I know of, and which I distinctly remember having heard in my childhood. I can't recollect the whole stories now, but remember the bare outlines of them. In one story, the heroine of it marries a tiger, lives with him peacefully and is ultimately either devoured by him, or the tiger is metamorphosed into a prince. In the second story, a poor man's son took a fancy to become the owner of a horse and a mare's egg. In his ignorance, he thought he had found the mare's egg in a big pumpkin. But he could not get hold of a horse to ride upon. One night as he was easing himself in the outskirts of the village, he saw a huge tiger, which he, mistaking for a horse, rode upon and drove at full speed. The tiger, being frightened, ran at full speed, and ultimately threw him off his back. When the poor boy came to his senses, he thanked his stars that his so-called horse had not made a meal of him.

In Bengal, the tiger also plays a prominent part in the "proverbial philosophy" of its people. In allusion to the snarling disposition of a tigress big with young ones, a termagant woman is called ताराविणी or a "Roy tigress." A dilatory woman is called a बाघेर मासी or the mother's sister of a tiger. The origin of this allusion I do not know. It is said that the wounds inflicted by a tiger are very difficult to heal up and often lead to a variety of other ailments. Hence is the Bengali proverb वाघे ईषि कविष वा or, if a tiger wounds one, it will give rise to thirty-six sores. If a mean contemptible person plays himself into the hands of his powerful enemy, then the proverb वाघेर घरे बोघेर वास is quoted in Bengal, meaning " the dwelling of a hyæna in a tiger's den!"

The Bengali expression वाघेर दूध or tiger's milk is used for anything which is difficult of attainment, or any undertaking which is difficult of performance. When a man's enterprising spirit has to be praised, it is said of him that, should any one tell him to bring वाघेर दूध or tiger's milk, he will bring it for him. The allusion is to the fact that no living man can approach a tiger or tigress, let alone the idea of milking a tigress with cubs.

There is another vulgar Bengali proverb which runs to the effect that :

बाघार चेये बाघारभय ।
बाघार चेये डिप्टिपेरभय ॥

It means the fear of a tiger is greater than the fear of attending an urgent nature's call in the darkness, and the fear of a mythical animal named Tiptipe is greater than the fear of a tiger.

In Southern India, the tiger also forms the subject of several folk-tales, whereof one is related by Pandit S. M. Natesa Sastrí in the pages of the *Indian Antiquary*.[15] The story goes on to say how a Bráhman girl was married to a tiger who, for that purpose, assumed the form of a Sastrí or learned Bráhman ; how she lived with him for some time and bore him a tiger-child ; how she informed her brothers of her distressed condition through a crow ; how they rescued her by showing the tiger a washerman's tub as their belly, the braying of an ass as their voice, a palmyra tree as their leg, and so on ; how she ultimately fled with her brothers from the tiger's abode, after having cut up the tiger-child in twain ; how the tiger was ultimately killed by being made to sit on a well covered with rushes so as to make it appear as a mat. The same author also relates another folktale of Madras in the the pages of the some Journal.[16] The tiger-king, along with the rat and snake, plays an important part in this story of " The Soothsayer's Son" and rescues that person from captivity in a dungeon, to which he had been thrown by the order of the king of that country, for having been suspected of murdering the king's father and stealing his crown. Ultimately, through the assistance of the kings of the tigers and the snakes, the Soothsayer's son marries the king's daughter and becomes the heir to the throne.

There are many other folk-tales wherein the tiger figures, which have been collected and edited by Mr. P. V. Ramaswami Raju, of Madras. They at first came out in *The Leisure Hour*, and were subsequently reprinted therefrom in the shape of an elegant complete edition by Messrs. Swan Sonnenschein & Co. of London, with an introduction by Mr. Henry Morley.

In Japan, the tiger forms one of the twelve signs of the zodiac, the others being the rat, ox, rabbit, dragon, serpent, horse, goat, monkey cock, dog and hog.[17] The tiger's head also forms

---

[15] Vol. XIX. (1885), page 134.
[16] Vol. XIII. (1884), page 256 ff.
[17] Bird's *Unbeaten Tracks in Japan*, Vol. I., p. 68.

a subject of carving on the beams of Japanese temples.

Among the ancient Greeks, the tiger was known by the name of *Martikhora* (Persain مردخور *Mardkhor* or man-eater) and was described by Ktesias as being " of the size of the lion, red in colour, with human-like face, ears and eyes, three rows of teeth, and stings on various parts of the body, but especially on the tail, which caused it to be compared with the scorpion." There have gathered a number of superstitious beliefs, prevailing amongst the Indians and other Asiatic races, regarding particular limbs or parts of the tiger's body. Every Indian *sikhari* knows that there is a horny claw or nail-like appendage at the end of the tail of the tiger, the lion, and other animals of the cat family. The natives of India believe that this nail-like structure serves the same purpose as the sting of the scorpion. The whiskers of this animal are superstitiously believed by them to be a source of great harm to mankind. Hence, as soon as a tiger is killed, the beaters and the native *shikaris* pluck out or burn off his whiskers, believing that thereby all accidents likely to arise from their remaining will be averted. Some of the natives of India believe that, if the tiger's whiskers are removed, no human being will be able to assume the form of the tiger for purposes of killing men. Others of them suppose that the possession of the tiger's whiskers conferred on the fortunate possessor of them unlimited influence over the hearts of the fair sex. In former times, a form of oath was administered in Courts of Justice on the skin of a tiger. Its skin is sometimes spread on thrones and judicial seats, as the animal has been, from time immemorial, the accepted insignia of royalty among oriental potentates. Its skin, like that of deer and antelopes, is also considered sacred by the Hindus, and is used by *jogis* and *faqirs* of that creed for performing their devotions upon. The god Siva of Hindu mythology is represented as being draped with a tiger-skin. The frontteeth, the whiskers, the claws, and the rudimentary clavicles (*birnukh*) are preserved as charms, and are often worn on the person as amulets The Malays believe that eating the flesh of the tiger endows the eater with much bravery and heroism. The Greek idea of the tiger having three rows of teeth, as told by Ktesias, probably arose from the fact that the carnivorous molar teeth of the tiger have three lobes, in which respect they differ from the molars of the *Ruminantia* and the *Equidæ*. The Japanese doctors believe in the highly medicinal properties of the tiger's liver. Miss Isabella Bird, who travelled in Japan,[18] bears testimony to this fact. She says:—" Dr. Nosoki (a Japanese practitioner who attended on her during her illness)

has great faith in *ginseng* and in rhinoceros horn, and in the *powdered liver of some animal, which, from the description, I understood to be a tiger*—all specifics of the Chinese school of medicines. Dr. Nosoki showed me a small box of unicorn's horn, which he said was worth more than its weight in gold." The Chinese also labour under the impression that different parts of the tiger's body have different kinds of medicinal properties. The same talented lady, who also stayed at Canton for some time, and from whom I have quoted above, says:[19] " Afterwards in China, at a native hospital.I heard much more of the miraculous virtues of these drugs, and in Salangor, in the Malay Peninsula, I saw a most amusing scene after the death of a tiger. A number of the neighbouring Chinese flew upon the body, cut out the liver, eyes and spleen, and carefully drained every drop of the blood, fighting with each other for the possession of things so precious, while those who were not so fortunate as to secure any of these cut out the cartilage from the joints. The centre of a tiger's eye-ball is supposed to possess nearly miraculous virtues ; the blood, dried at a temperature of 110° is the strongest of all tonics, and gives strength and courage; and the powdered liver and spleen are good for many diseases. Sultan Abdul Samat claimed the liver, but the other parts were all sold at high prices to the Chinese doctors. A little later at Qualla, Kangsa in Perak, I saw rhinoceros horns sold at a high price for the Chinese drug market, and Rajah Muda, who was anxious to claim the horns of the district, asserted that a single horn with a particular mark on it, was worth fifty dollars for sale .to the Chinese doctors." In Bengal the grease of the tiger is considered as a sovereign remedy for rheumatism and gout.

The Shans, inhabiting the north of Burma, entertain similar notions regarding the curative properties of certain parts of the tiger, as is testified to by Dr. J. Anderson. He writes :—" We find the Shans placing implicit faith in the curative and strengthening qualities of decoctions of the dried and pregnant wombs of the sambar, tiger, and porcupine, and relying on the desiccated stomachs of these animals for relief in the worst forms of disease. The leg-bones of the tiger and the pounded horns of the sambar and serrow are in great repute as medicines that give tone and strength to the frame, exhausted by disease or excess."[20]— *Journal, Anthropological Society, Bombay.*

(Told by Sarat Chandra Mitra, M.A., B L., Pleader, Judge's Court, Chupra, Behar.)

---

[18] *Unbeaten Tracks in Japan*, Vol. I., p. 275.

[19] *Op. cit.*, Vol. I., p. 275.

[20] *A Report on the Expedition to Western Yunan viâ Bhamo*, by J. Anderson. Calcutta: 1871, page 114.

FOLKTALES.

419. The Goddess of Poverty.—There was once a Bráhman so poor, that he could scarcely support himself by begging. The goddess of poverty had beset him. One day he was bathing at the Ganges, when a friend advised him to go to the Rájá, who would surely relieve his wants. He went to the Rájá, and when he stood before him he cried out:—" Victory to the Rájá," and the Raja gave him ten thousand rupees. As he was going home with the money the goddess of poverty met him in the guise of the Rájá and ordered him, on pain of his life, to surrender the money, so he laid it down and went home empty-handed.

Next day he went to the Rájá, got the same present as before and lost it in the same way. And so it happened a third time also. Then the Rájá was surprised and determined to go himself and see what the Bráhman did with the money. When he saw the goddess take the money he went to her and asked her who she was. She answered:—" I am the goddess of poverty, and I am now besetting this Bráhman. Whatever he receives I take from him." The Rájá asked if there was any way by which this poor Bráhman could be relieved, and she said:—" If you take me upon yourself, then he will be relieved." The Rájá agreed and the goddess came to live with him, and when he went home the Bráhman found all the money which the Rájá had given to him at his house. When the Rájá returned to his palace he sent the Ráni with her children to her mother's house and he stayed at night in the palace. Suddenly a terrible storm arose and the palace was demolished, and all the horses, elephants and other goods of the Rájá were buried beneath the ruins. So next day the Rájá started for the jungle and another Rájá ruled in his stead. The Rájá went along begging his bread, and at last he came to a city and began to cut wood, which he used to sell daily to a confectioner. When the confectioner cut up the wood a lot of diamonds came out of it, whereat he was much pleased. He offered some to the Rájá, but he said that they were of no use to him, and that all he wanted was the bare price of the wood. The confectioner wished to give him a share, so he put some of the jewels in a *laddu* (sweetmeat) and gave them to the Rájá. On the way he met a Bráhman, who asked for alms, and to him he gave the *laddu*. The Bráhman did not care for the *laddu*, so he brought it back to the confectioner and changed it for some parched barley flour. When the confectioner examined the *laddu* he found the diamonds within it; so he said:—" It is my fate to keep them."

The Rájá then went out to the jungle. There some thieves were planning to commit a theft and they, thinking the Rájá to be a *Sadhu*, bowed before him and asked him to bless their enterprise. After committing a burglary in the palace they returned to where the Rájá was, and by force made him accept a diamond necklace which was part of the booty. He left it lying near him and the thieves went away. Meanwhile some sepoys of the Rájá, who were in pursuit of the thieves, came up and finding the necklace with the Rájá seized him and brought him before the Rájá. He protested that he had no share in the robbery, but without further enquiry the Rájá had both his hands struck off.

In this miserable state the Rájá took refuge in the house of an oilman who, when he heard what had befallen him, said:—" I cannot give you charity; but if you will sit on the beam of my mill and drive the ox, I will give you food."

There the Rájá remained many days. Meanwhile the Rájá of the land was performing the *swayamvara* of his daughter, and the Rájá having by chance gone to the assembly, the princess put the garland of victory round his neck. They tried to make her change her mind, but she refused; and they were married, and the Rájá, her father, allotted a mansion in which they lived.

This went on for three years, and one day a pair of swans came and sat on a tree, near where the Rájá lived. They began talking together and the male said to his mate: " This is a very virtuous Rájá, who has taken upon himself the poverty of another man." His mate asked:—" Is there any medicine by which he may be cured?" " If he procure a certain root from the jungle, and having powdered it apply it to his hands, they will be restored." The other swan said: " It is impossible for him to get the root, unless you go and fetch it." So the swan fetched the root and the Rájá, who knew the speech of birds, heard what they said, and having applied the root, his hands were restored to him.

When his father-in-law heard of his recovery he enquired into his case, and then he gave him a great army and he returned and won his kingdom from the other Rájá and lived with his Ráni and children many years in happiness.

(A folktale told by Bhawani Din, Bráhman, of Faizabad.)

420. How the Banya's wife went to heaven.—There was once a very miserly Banya who had a pious wife. One day she went to attend a recitation of the sacred books and there she heard that if she gave a cow of gold to a

Bráhman she would have no difficulty in crossing the Vaitarani, or river of hell. So she came back and told this to her husband. But he said:—

"What nonsense. If you make a cow of earth and give it to a Bráhman on the banks of the Ganges it will do just as well."

The woman did not believe him and had a cow of gold made, but in order that her husband should know nothing about it she plastered it over with mud and the Banya had an earthen cow made for himself. They both went to the Ganges and each made his offering to a Bráhman. Time passed and the Banya and his wife both died. When they came to the banks of the Vaitarani they found two cows awaiting them, one of gold, which the woman seized by the tail and the other of earth for her husband. They attempted to cross the river of hell. The woman crossed in safety and was received into the heaven of Vishnu, but half way across the cow of earth dissolved and the Banya sank in the waters.

(A folktale told by Ramadhin, Kalwar of Gusainganj, Sultanpur district.)

---

421. The four friends and the Princess.—There were once four youths, one the son of a Banya, the second of a Patwa, the third of a Pathán and the fourth of a Mína, who were excellent friends and used to spend all their time amusing themselves. At last their fathers remonstrated with them for their idleness and they started with some money for the city of Delhi.

The Patwa bought some gold thread and made a splendid necklace, which he took round the city to sell. As he stood at the Lál Darwáza, the princess saw him and fell in love with him. She called him in and after asking the price of the necklace told him to come next day. That night she began to think of him and determined to go and see him. So she put on a disguise and came to the room in the inn where he was staying. She went in and found that he was not there; so she put on the necklace which was hanging to a peg and lay down on the bed. As she moved in the dark a sword that was hanging on the wall fell on her and she died.

When the Patwa came back and found the girl lying dead in his room he was overcome with grief and fear. So he took a large earthen jar and putting the body into it threw it into a ravine close by. Next morning some one found it there and when enquiries were made it was found to be the corpse of the Princess. So the Emperor called the Kumhars and asked them to identify the pot. One man said that he had made four of that pattern, which he had sold to four friends. The four youths were arrested and three of them were able to produce their jars; but the Patwa's jar was recognised and he was ordered for execution.

After the order was passed, the Emperor was desirous of finding the true facts of the case; so he went in disguise to the cell in which the Patwa lay and asked him if he would care to see his friends before he died. He went first to the Banya who said:

"You need not be frightened. I will spend all I have to get you released."

When they came to the Mína he said:

"Fear not, I will give my life sooner than that you should be executed."

When they went to the Pathán boy he said:

"Do not be afraid. I have a relative in the Emperor's service. We are arranging to get the Emperor blown from a gun sooner than that you should lose your life."

When the Emperor saw the devotion of the three friends he was much pleased and when he investigated the matter and found that the Patwa was innocent of the murder, he made the Banya his Treasurer, the Pathán his Commander-in-chief, the Mína his Brigadier and to the Patwa he gave ten villages.

(Told by Mangal Prasad, Dikhshit Brahman, and recorded by Pandit Hanuman Din, Master of Lawal School, Lucknow district.)

---

422. The Rájá and the Physician.—There was once a Rájá who was much oppressed by increasing fatness, so that he began to despair of his life. He called many physicians, but there was none who could give him relief. Now in a distant city there was a poor physician who was sore pressed to make a living by his profession, and at last he determined to go elsewhere in search of employment. By chance he came to the city where the Rájá lived and as he was walking about he heard a herald going about proclaiming: "Whoever can cure the Rájá his fee shall be a lakh of rupees; but if he fail he shall be put to death with the most extreme tortures."

When the physician heard this notice he began to reflect that his future state could not be worse than it was then. So he went to the Rájá and accepted his conditions, but first he demanded a lakh of rupees as an advance for the preparation of the necessary medicine which he said it would take six months to prepare. When he got the money he at once sent it home, so that in case he came to an untimely end, the support of his family might be assured.

When six months passed he was no nearer having the medicine ready than he was at the beginning, and his heart sank within him when he began to think what the Rájá would do to him when he failed to perform his engagement. So he made a plan and at night he began to wail and cry and dashed himself so violently against the walls of his room that his whole body was a mass of bruises. When the messengers of the Rájá came, he said:

"I am so wounded that I cannot appear before the Rájá unless you bring a conveyance."

So they brought a palanquin and brought him before the Rájá, who demanded his medicine and threatened that if it was not ready the physician would be delivered over to the executioner. When he heard this the physician began to weep and said:

"Last night, your Majesty, I was compounding the drugs for you when 'Azrail,' the angel of death, appeared and asked me why I was preparing a potion for a Rájá who would die within a week. When I remonstrated with him he fell upon me and beat me sorely, as you see me now. Even now ' Azrail' is hovering over your Majesty's palace, waiting to carry you off. What then avail the drugs of your servant?"

When he heard the words of the physician the Rájá was overcome with fear and lay on his couch and wept and thus he continued for the space of a week, until by reason of his fears and neglect of food his fatness left him and he regained his original form.

When the week had passed he sent again for the physician and said:

"You see that ' Azrail' has spared me so far and lo! my fatness has disappeared."

"This is the result of my strategem" replied the physician. "You have to thank me for your recovery."

The Rájá admitted the truth of his words and dismissed the physician with a handsome present.

(A folktale told by Abdul Ghani, Teacher of the Muhammadi School, Kheri district.)

423. **The rival Castes.**—Four men, a Dhuniya, a Máli, a Juláha and a Ját, once went to a Rájá for employment. When he asked the Juláha who he was, he said:

"I am a Khaták Pathán."

The Dhuniya said:

"I am a Tank Pathán."

The Máli said:

"I am the arranger of melody." (Rág b ág Si dhawan.)

When he asked the Ját what his caste was, he said:

"I am of the caste of Khuda."

"You rascal," said the Raja, "what do you mean?"

He answered—

"This Khaták Pathán does weaving in my village. This Tank Pathán cards cotton. This arranger of melody sings at the weddings of Chamárs. If they are of these noble castes then what is my caste but that of the Lord Almighty?"

(Told by Pandit Sri Ráma and recorded by Yubraj Sinh Student of the Dhanpur School, Bijnor district.)

424. **The Dom Rájá of Oudh.**—There was once a Bráhman boy who was sent to Benares to be educated. After some time when he was qualified to be a Pándit he started off to visit his father-in-law's house. On the way he came to a river which was in flood and as he was looking for a means of crossing it he saw a cow stuck in the mud. He had no pity for the sacred animal and instead of trying to extricate her he mounted on her back and made her carry him across. Then the cow cursed him and so he went on to his father's house.

When he arrived there and it was night, he went into a room with his wife. But no sooner did he come into the room than he was turned into an ass. When his wife saw this she tied him to the leg of the bed and sat weeping and bemoaning her fate.

In the morning she was ashamed to come out and the people began to mock and say:

"When a husband returns after a long absence he does not rise early."

At last the girl's parents went in and when they saw the ass they were sore grieved; but for shame they pretended that their son-in-law had been obliged to leave early and they left the ass in the house. At last the other Bráhmans went to them and said:

"We cannot eat or smoke with people who keep a foul animal like an ass in their house."

So they determined to turn out their son-in-law; but the girl said that where he went she would go too. So she took him with her and went to Benares. The Rájá of that city was then building a temple to Vishnu and the girl went there to work and with what she earned she used to support her husband and herself. But while she was at work the ass used always to go about with her and if any man tried to speak to her he would lash out and kick him. When the Rájá heard of this wonder he went to the place and asked the girl what it all meant. When he heard her sad case he summoned all the Pándits of Benares and consulted with them how the Bráhman could be restored to his former shape. After they had long consulted together, they said:—"Your Majesty must perform a great sacrifice according to the usage of the old kings of the land and then when each Rájá throws a drop of water on the youth he will recover his original shape."

Now at that time the Rájá of Ajudhya was on bad terms with the Rájá of Benares and when he was invited not only would he not come himself but he sent his Dom in his place. This he did not knowing that the Doms were the ancient lords of the land, so when the sacrifice was done and all the other Rájás stood round the youth and sprinkled water upon him, nothing happened till the Dom threw water on him and then at once he was restored to his former shape.

So the Bráhman girl brought her husband home in triumph and since then the proverb runs:—

Awadh des ka Domra aur des ka bhup;
luke sarbar na karo; bhlao lagaen chup.

"The Domra of Oudh is equal to the kings of other lands; nor should you vie with them; rather keep silence."

And they say that Domariya Dih about twenty miles from Ajudhya was the Domra capital in the old days.

(A folktale told by Rám Das, Master of the Zillah School, Partabgarh.)

---

425. How Shaikh Chilli made a fool of himself at the wedding.—One day Shaikh Chilli was invited to the marriage of his sister-in-law, and while the rejoicings were going on a letter came which they gave him to read. As he was reading it he began to weep and lament and seeing him all the guests commenced to wail and beat their breasts. After a time when they came to their senses they asked him who was dead, and he answered:—"No one is dead. I wept only when I began to think of all our forefathers who have died in the evil days of old."

They were all so angry that they rushed at him and kicked him out of the house.

Another time he was invited to another wedding and he borrowed all the good clothes he could get from his neighbours and went off to the party. At the same time he borrowed a horse from a friend on which he mounted and set out. He put all his property in charge of the mistress of the inn and she seeing him to be a soft fool said:—"Take this scraper and rope and go out and cut some grass for my pony." So he went out with only a rag round his loins and meanwhile the woman escaped with his horse and clothes. In this wretched guise he was obliged to go on to the wedding, but he was ashamed to go in and, creeping in by the house drain, sat down where they were distributing rice water to the beggars. As he was trying to get some his foot slipped and he fell into the cess-pool which was close by. Hearing his cries his relatives came up with torches and pulled him out. But he was so ashamed that he ran away and came home.

(A folktale told by Muhammad Halim and recorded by M. Ram Sabai, Sub-editor, *Educational Gazette*, Lucknow.)

---

426. The pious Prince.—There was once a Rájá who had a son and a daughter. One day the Prince said to his sister: "I wish to become a Sadhu."

She replied: "Do not so. You are a Prince and the life of a Sadhu is hard."

But he would not be persuaded and started on his travels. He came to a city and asked the people where he could find a carpenter. When they pointed out his shop, he went to the carpenter and asked him to make the shape of a loaf of bread out of wood. He made it for him and then the Prince tied it to his waist-cloth and went his way. By and by he came to the palace of a Rájá who asked him to come in and eat. But he pointed to the loaf which hung at his waist and said: "This is sufficient for me."

Then he came into the jungle and hung himself from a tree with his feet downwards. Soon a crow flew down and began to try and pick out his eyes. He said to the crow:—

Kâga, sab tan kháiyo, chun chun kháiyo más,

Donon nain bacháiyo, ki priya milan ki ás.

"Crow, you may eat any part of my body you please, but spare my eyes, because this is my only chance of seeing my beloved (the Creator)."

Thus he became perfect (Siddhi) and Bhagwan came down himself and carried him off to his heaven.

(A folktale told by Girja Dayal, Kayasth, of Ahmedabad, Lucknow district.)

---

427. **The wit of Muhammad Fazil.**—The proverb runs—*Parhe na likhe, nám Muhammad Fâzil.* "He can neither read nor write and he is called The Scholar."

This is how the proverb arose.

There was once a Rájá who employed a Persian teacher to instruct his sons and when he died he left a son whose name was Muhammad Fazil, who was as ignorant as his father had been learned. Him the Rájá summoned and ordered him to serve in the place of his father. He had to accept the post, but as he was totally ignorant, he began to think how he could ever discharge the duties. And such a fool was he that the boys used to shout after him and call him Tadda, or Fool, until he came to be known to every one by that name.

One day the Rájá sent for him and said:—"My ring has been stolen and you must from your books discover the name of the thief as your father used to do."

The teacher was in great distress and said: "Give me time to consult my books and I will give an answer to-morrow."

But the Rájá was wroth and cast him into prison and threatened to hang him next morning if he did not find out the thief.

The teacher lay down, but from sorrow he could not sleep, at last he called out:

Ao re sukh nindiya ;

Subh ko kat jae mundiya.

"Come sweet sleep, for I shall lose my head by dawn."

Now the Rájá had a female slave named Nindiya and she was listening at the door of the cell. When she heard what she supposed was her own name, she was afraid, and going to the teacher told him that the ring was concealed under the Rájá's bed where she had placed it and implored him to save her life. The teacher promised to do as she asked and next morning when he was called by the Rájá, he showed him where the ring was hidden and thereby gained great honour.

One day the favourite riding camel of the Rájá was lost and Muhammad Fazil was ordered to trace it. He did not know what to do and went wandering in distress near the palace, when what should he see but the camel grazing in a ravine.

So he went to the Rájá and said:—"Your Majesty's camel is grazing in such a ravine with his head to the North."

When they went to the place and found the camel as he had said, his renown still more increased.

Another day the Rájá was walking with the teacher in the garden and finding a worm known as Tadda he concealed it in his hand and asked the teacher what he had. He was confused and cried out "Tadda, Tadda, your time is now come."

The Rájá did not know that Tadda was his nickname and was astonished at his wisdom.

At last Muhammad Fazil was tired of running constant risk of his life, so one night he took a dagger and went into the room where the Rájá was asleep. He was about to stab him, when he thought to himself that it would be safer to drag the Rájá out into the courtyard and kill him there, where there was no chance of any one hearing the noise. Just as he dragged him out, the roof of the palace fell in and the Rájá fell on his knees before him and said:—"My preserver, I owe my life to you. Share with me half my kingdom."

And this was the way the idiot Muhammad Fazil prospered.

(A folktale told by Marisi Khan and recorded by Hashim Ali, Master of the School at Dharmpur, district Sultanpur.)

MISCELLANEA.

428. Ludhiana: A Couplet on Famine.—

*Nawwé thon baché chaurānawé nī márī
Dint bāddal, ratī tārā.*

Saved from the famine of Sambat 1890 (1833 A.D.), succumbed to 1894: There were clouds by day and starry nights.—*Settlement Report*, p. 123.

429. Modesty of Hindu Women.—A curious instance of modesty in Hindu women is given in a recent number of the *Bihár Times*. A house at Pema, a village near Tikari, containing at the time eleven women, took fire. Among them was a newly-married bride who refused to expose herself to the view of strangers. The others, encouraged by her example, decided to stay with her and before they could be rescued were severely burnt. Seven of them are said to have since died and others are in a precarious condition.

430. The Cure of Headache.—They say that there was once a Rájá who had six Ránis and they all suffered from headache. So they came to believe that if they counted the leaves of a *nim* tree they would be cured.

The *nim* tree, which they selected, had six branches, and when the Ránis counted each a branch they found that every branch had six thousand leaves. They plucked off all the leaves and brought them home and their headache was cured. So they told the Rájá, and since then this remedy is generally used.

In all these spells, counting certain numbers is very important. Thus they say if you are angry and count a hundred you will recover your temper; and many of the charms tied to the necks of children to keep off the evil-eye and other dangerous influences consist of a certain number of figures drawn in a square with saffron on a piece of *Bhojpatra* or birch bark.—*Rám Lál Dikshit.*

431. Saharanpur: Ideas about the Scalp-lock.—In this part of the country it is a common belief that if a man be bitten by a snake while he has a knot in his scalp-lock he is safe from the effects of the poison. No Bráhman is allowed to eat, drink or perform his religious duties without tying a knot in his scalp-lock. On the hair as a spirit entry, see *Introduction to Popular Religion and Folklore*, p. 150.—*W. Crooke.*

432. Eastern Districts, N.-W. P.: Beggar's Song.—

1. *Karo re bands, wá din kī tadbir,*

(O man, make preparations for that day.)

2. *Jab Yamrájá dút pathaihen tanikā dharin nahin dhir,*

(When Yamráj—the King of the lower regions—will send his messengers they shall make no delay.)

3. *Mári mángarian prán nikarihin nainan bahat jal nir,*

(They shall beat you with pestles to death and tears will flow from your eyes.)

4. *Bhav ságar ko tairbo kathin hawe, nadiyá bahen gambhir,*

(It is very tedious to cross the sea of the world where rivers flow violently.)

5. *Náv na berā lōg ghanérā kēwat havin bī pir,*

(Neither is there a boat nor a float; passengers are too many and boatmen too pitiless).

6. *Ghar mén baithi kulwantin liriyd, māt pitā sut ji.*

(In the house are sitting the wife of high birth, father mother and son).

7. *Daulat, duniyá, mál khajáná sang na játsherir.*

(Wealth, the world, nay even the body will not accompany you.)

8. *Lál khambh bich hōt tas and byakul bhai sharir.*

(Between red columns punishment is inflicted. The body endures suffering.)

9. *Kahén Kabir sunō Yamrájá ab na karab takrir.*

(Kabir says:—" O Yamráj, hear, I will commit sin no longer.")

433. Gurgaon: Village Deities—Chandwand, Khera.—A local deity who does not seem to be always distinguished from Bhúmiya, but whose shrine is often found in addition to that of Bhúmiya in the same village, is the *Chanwand*, also called *Khera deota*. Some villagers say that the *Chanwand* is the wife of the Bhúmisya. Others seem to put the *Chanwand* in the place of the Bhúmiya, but the *Chanwand* is worshipped on Sunday.—*Mr. F. C. Channing: Settlement Report.* p. 34.

434. Wrinkles on the forehead.—If you have three or five lines on your forehead you are sure to be a lucky man; if, two or four you are unlucky; if you have only one, which is very unusual, there is no end to your prosperity.—*Pándit Rám Gharib Chaubé.*

435. Saharanpur: Shopkeepers' superstition.—Shopkeepers consider it very unlucky for any one to go to their shop to buy anything with his head bare. This is particularly objected to when the purchaser happens to come in the morning as it destroys the luck of the whole day.—*M. Rám Lal.*

436. How to ascertain the future occupation of a child.—Among Maheswari Banyas it is the custom on the day when the child is first fed on grain (*annaprásana*) to let him crawl on the ground and to place opposite him some cloth, a pen and ink, some gold and silver coins and a weapon or implement of some kind. If he first touch the cloth he will be a cloth merchant: if a pen and ink, a scribe; if money, a money changer: if a weapon or implement, he will follow the occupation connected with it.—*Pándit Rám Gharib Chaubé.*

437. Jalandhar district: Customs of the Sikhs.—The Sikhs proper venerate the ten Gurus, but principally Nának and Govind Sinh, the first and last of them. Their holy book is the *Granth* and their sacred city, to which they go on pilgrimage, is Amritsar. They have an initiatory ceremony in which a two-edged dagger (*khanda*) is used, and which is called *khanda di pahal* (*páhal*) and which generally takes place at the residence of venerated Bedis or Sodis, as at Amritsar or Anandpur in the Hoshyárpur district, and when the novice has reached years of discretion. A Sikh should let his hair grow and not shave his head. He should abstain from tobacco and kill animals used for food by a single blow of a sword (*jhatka*). He should also wear knee breeches, but I think very few do. The Sikhs follow Hindu ceremonies at death and marriage and employ Bráhmans just as other Hindus do. When going to the burning ground they keep on repeating *Sat-Guru Wá Gurú!* instead of *Rám! Rám!* They respect Hindu religious buildings. On the first day of the month they go to the Dharmsála and listen to the reading of the *Granth* for some time, and make some small offerings. When several Sikhs come together they greet each other with their watch-word *Bolo jí, Wá Guru! — W. E. Purser: Settlement Report, p.* 51.

438. Oil: Superstitions about.—Among Hindus the times and circumstances under which a man or woman can with safety anoint the head are carefully determined. If a man oil his head on a Sunday he will be a snake in the next life; if on Monday, he will be beautiful; if on Tuesday, he will fall into trouble as bad as death; if on Wednesday he will become rich; if on Thursday he will suffer a loss; if on Friday, he will fall into trouble; if on Saturday, he will be happy. But if he intend to use oil on Sunday he ought to put a little grass in it to remove the dangerous effects of it; so on Tuesday he ought to mix a little earth, on Thursday a little flour, and on Friday some dung. All these superstitions are very common among the people of the Eastern districts of the North-Western Provinces.—*Pandit Rám Gharib Chaubé.*

439. Ludhiana: Shrines to Sakhi Sarwar Sultán.—These shrines (*pírkhána*) erected in honour of Sakhi Sarwar Sultán have always the same shape—a square base with four small domes at the corners, and in the centre a small temple ten or twelve feet high. There is a door in front of the temple, and facing this, two or three niches for lamps, otherwise it is empty, there being nothing to represent the saint. The Thursday offerings to the shrine are not universal, and are generally made by the women. The Bharai attends all that day. It is very common for a person wishing to attain some object (*e. g.*, to succeed in a lawsuit) to make a vow to the shrine, and offerings in this way also go to the Bharai. Once a year, on a Friday, the ceremony of *rot* is performed in most Sultáni families. A huge loaf is made of one maund (*kachcha*) of flour, and a quarter maund (*kachcha*) of sugar and cooked. The Bharai attends and beats the drum, and sings the praises of the saint while this is preparing, and receives one quarter of the bread, the other three-quarters being eaten by the family and the neighbours. This is the great observance of the Sultánis, and they really appear to have no others. —*T. E. Walker: Settlement Report, p.* 54 *sq.*

440. The Holi festival.—In Southern India the Holi is regarded as the worship of Káma Deva, the god of love, and it is said to record the destruction of the deity by fire at the hands of Siva. Hence the Holi fire is burned in front of a temple of Siva and at the same time an image of Káma Deva is cremated. The shouting and beating of drums which accompanies the rite are regarded as lamentations for the death of Káma Deva. There is a reference to this in the dramas of Ratanávali and Mádhava Málati.—*Pandit Rám Gharib Chaubé.*

441. Leprosy.—In popular belief leprosy is the result of killing a Bráhman in this or some past existence.—*Pandit Rám Gharib Chaubé.*

442. The origin of the Mango.—The first mangoes grew in the garden of Rávana in Lanka and Hanumán was so delighted with the flavour of them that he threw some of the seeds into the sea and they floated across the channel and took root in Indian soil.—*W. Crooke.*

443. Panjabi saying.—

Mitthi, nátthi, kamchari, kamzori, kamros.
Yehi triya men gun hain, pur turang men dosh.

"To be a slow-goer, quiet, a small eater, weak and seldom passionate are good points in a woman, but defects in a horse."—*Chamu Mall.*

444. The Persian letter Be.—The Persian letter Be is sacred because when the Lord created it he made sixty-one angels at the same time and this is why it begins the word Bismillah. If any one is attacked with stammering the letter Be is written on a piece of paper, the paper is washed and the decoction is given to the patient. This should be done sixty times in the day to effect a perfect cure.

Another good plan is to make a charm is this shape.—

ب	ب	ب
ب	ب	ب
ب	ب	ب

If you tie this round your neck your wages will be increased, you will never suffer from the attacks of demons and your general prosperity will increase.—*M. Ataullah Beg.*

445. A Muhammadan charm for delivery.—

Likh kar chapni sir par dhari,
Nikal pará yá nikal pari.

"An earthen pot being written on was placed on her head.
The woman was then delivered of a boy or a girl."
The above couplet with the name of Shaikh Farid-ud-din is written on an earthen plate and the plate is put on the head of the lying-in-woman to facilitate delivery.—*Pandit Rám Gharib Chaubé.*

446. Gurgaon: Charms for Scorpion-bite.—

Hari dandi, múnj ká bán;
Utr re bichhú, Khwája Muin-ud-din chishti ki án.

"Green Stock, *múnj* rope, I charge you, get out scorpion, by virtue of the saint Muin-ud-din Chishti.—*Mr. F. C. Channing: Settlement Report, p* 37.

447. Rules as to the size and shape of Images.—No image which is painted on the wall for the purpose of worship should weigh more than a *pala* which is the one hundredth part of a *tola*. Its length should not be more than sixteen-finger breadths. Those used in family worship and made of metal or wood should not be more than twelve-finger breadths (*angul*) long.—*Pandit Rám Gharib Chaubé.*

448. Barren woman: Omens.—Hindu women in general think it very unlucky to see first of all the face of a barren woman in the morning.—*Pándit Rám Gharib Chaubé.*

449. Drinking Song.—

    Tár tale baje sitár, morí ján ;
    Tári ne mujhko diwána kiyá.
    Táré ká chhíkná rohú mácheryá
    Darwá ká chhíkná kabáb, morí ján !
    Tárí ke nashá men bard majá holá
    Apo se sayyán begáná kiyá.

TRANSLATION.

" Beneath the palms* a cithar lures my feet ;
Enough ! each sense the palm-wine gins o'erpower.
Men say ; ' Quell palm-wine with a fish
And liquor with a roasted dish.'
Why, prithee ? All their frenzy deem I sweet !
Himself it biddeth man forget one hour."
                            —*E. Greeven.*

450. Gaya: A legend of the Parbáti Hill.—Parbáti was a place of importance in the time of the war of the Mahábhárata. According to the legend, when the sacrificial horse of the Pándavas was let loose, Rájá Sánkha Dhoaj of this place seized it and prepared to fight. Before joining battle, however, he performed a sacrifice. The Rájá's preceptor (*guru*) demanded that orders should be given for every one to be ready and present at a given spot by a certain hour. The Rájá's son, Surati Dhoaj, was newly married, and his bride happened to arrive that very day; and, at her entreaty, Surati Dhoaj delayed a short time. The *guru* demanded the punishment of the young man, and accordingly he was thrown into a cauldron of burning oil, but he came out unhurt. The *guru* suspected that the oil was not hot enough, so he heated it much more, and to try the heat, threw in a piece of the husk of a cocoanut ; the violence of the heat caused the husk to be thrown up against the *guru's* face, blinding his right eye and burning away the right half of his face. The Rájá's son, it was found, had escaped, because he had prayed to Vishnu, and had held a sacred *tulasí* leaf in his mouth when jumping into the cauldron.—*G. A. Grierson : Geography of the Gaya District, p. 16.*

451. A monstrous birth.—The Káshipur *Nibashi* vouches for the truth of the following strange story :—

A lady belonging to a respectable Baidya family, of village Keora, within the jurisdiction of out-post Jhalkati, district Barrisaul, is reported to have given birth to a monster of a child which had one of its legs like that of a duck, and the other like that of a horse. As soon as it was born, it roared out with a thundering voice, and died immediately afterwards. Its mother too died shortly after. What is stranger still, a dog and a cat that came to the spot quite accidently also shared the same fate, so that now no one dares visit the place through fear.

452. How the limits of Sarwar were fixed.—Sarwar or Sarju-par is the land east of the river Sarju, the home of the Sarjupari or Sarwariya Bráhmans. It is said that the limits of this holy land were thus determined. Ráma stood on the bank of the Sarju near Ajudhya and shot

    * Toddy-shops are often mere sheds of palm-leaves.

his arrow to the east. The point at which the arrow fell is held to be the eastern limit of Sarwar, while on the West it is bounded by the Sarju. By chance the arrow fell on the bank of the Ganges which is thus the eastern frontier. This custom of determining boundaries is an ancient one. Manu says that a piece of land as broad as the flight of a stick should be left between the hamlet and the cultivation around it.—*Pándit Rám Gharib Chaubé.*

453. Some folklore of birds.—The crow, the cuckoo and the jay or *nilkanth* are regarded as news-bearers. If a crow flies a short distance and hops about on the roof or near the house it is a sign that the house-master is coming or that news of him may be expected. The verse runs :—

    Kawa tun uchar ja ; hamár rája aihain ;
    Aihain to dúdh bhát deb, anchara phárí langot deb.

" Fly away crow, my husband is coming. If he comes I will give you milk and rice and a piece of my sheet to cover you."

So the coming of the cuckoo shows that a husband, son or some other relative is coming and he cries *Uth dekh ! Uth dekh !* " Get up and look, get up and look." The song says :—

    Bayen bolaí kág, dayen bolaí koiliya ;
    Bhal bhaí sagunwa bhae.

" The crow caws on the left, the cuckoo calls on the left—both good omens."

The jay comes from the heaven of Sitaráma to see how the world is going on where Sita suffered under the cruelty of Rávana. When boys are beginning to read they say :—

    Nilkanth litwárí bhari ;
    Sita se kah diho bhení ankwárí.

" Jay that lives in the grove, give my compliments to Sita."

The *khanjan* or *ramchiraya* is the wagtail, which comes to the world of men from the heaven of Ráma and spends the cold weather enquiring how the world goes on. At the beginning of summer it flies back to Ráma with all the news.

Many omens are taken from birds. The hooting of the owl foretells death ; the jungle fowl crowing in the rains is a sign of rain ; the sparrow rolling in the dust or bathing is an omen of rain ; the kite and the vulture sitting on the roof forebode calamity.—*W. Crooke.*

454. Hoshyarpur : The Panjgatra Fair.—This fair, held at Babhaur on the Sutlej on 1st Baisakh, is a purely religious festival. About 10,000 people assemble to bathe in the river. The name is derived from five stones said to have been used by the sons of the Pándavas in the game of *Panch Satára* while their fathers served a period of asceticism. Bramawati, as this part of the Sutlej is called, is considered very sacred, and it is said that in *Sambat* 1947, when the Ganges will lose its sacred character, except at Hardwár, and other special places, this place will be more frequented.—*Col. Montgomery : Settlement Report, p.* 39.

North Indian Notes and Queries:
A MONTHLY PERIODICAL.

VOL. V.]   JANUARY, 1896.   [No. 10.

CONTENTS OF THIS NUMBER.
(The references are to the Notes.)

Popular Religion ... 163 to 166	Folk-tales ... 172 to 177
Anthropology ... 167 „ 171	Miscellanea ... 178 „ 180

POPULAR RELIGION.

455. Regard for animal life.—At Hardwar and other sacred places you will sometimes see men, who affect extra piety, walking about in cloth shoes with wooden shoes. This is in order to avoid the use of leather produced from some horned animal. Usually such people go barefoot and use these shoes only when they pass along metalled roads.—*W. Crooke.*

456. The mythic cow Kamdhenu.—As the Kalpa Vriksha is a tree under which if you stand you will receive all you can desire, so the cow Kamdhenu realises all the desires of life. In modern times the Kamdhenu is represented by an ordinary cow which gives milk without calving and such animals are treated with great respect and worshipped by *Sádhus*. Such *Sádhus* offer the milk of the animal daily to Vishnu and take care to keep her always in their sight, as the contemplation of such a sacred animal washes away all sin. The modern Kamdhenu has much less power of realising desires than in the days of old because, as the *Sádhus* say, this Iron Age has had an evil effect on all things sacred.—*Pandit Rám Gharíb Chaubé.*

457. A Case of Yoga.—The *Indian Mirror* of the 26th January, 1895, publishes the following:—

Swami Ganeshanand, gave a public exhibition of his *háth yog* (or *yog* or asceticism performed with the hands) practices at the hall, Patna College, on Sunday last. After performing some minor feats, the Swámi went into a state of *samadhi*, a condition of temporary inanition with the tongue completely drawn inwards, where it disappeared altogether. The Swámi remained in this condition for several minutes. A stream of tears rolled down his cheeks from the upturned eyes, and then there was a seeming cessation, to all outward appearance, of life. His disciples rubbed him along the spinal cord in order to bring him back to sense, and the Swámi was revived.

458. The Legend of Hardaul.—The worship of Hardaul is common in the western and also in the estern districts of the N.-W. P. At Hardwár there is a Bráhman priest of the Sanyásis who sings the songs of Hardaul and many other personages of a similar character. I have collected the songs from his lips.

Sri Ganpati Saraswati sumir, binwat kon har jori ;
Kahat charit Hardaul ko, hai mers mati thor.

(I call to my mind Ganesa the god of learning and the goddess of learning or Saraswati, and pray to them to assist me in my description of Hardaul as I am not wise.)

Huĕ Bundela bansh men, barnan suno pramán;
Jiyat punya bahutai kiyĕ, marĕ bhayĕ jag án.

(He was of the Bundela clan of Rajputs. This is a true account of him. In his lifetime he practised much charity, and on his death he was again carried into the world.)

Madhukar Sháh ke nátiya, Bír Sinh ke putra;
Jujhar sinh ke bhrát laghu, Suni lewa tásu charitra.

(He was the grandson of Madhukar Sháh and son of Bír Sinh and younger brother of Jujhar Sinh. Hear his account.)

Jujhar Sinh aisi kari lálá ju ko soya;
Káhi Ganesh mahi kahi Suyash ágĕ bhayo na koya.

(Jujhar Sinh acted in respect of his brother so disgracefully that none can relate it in the world except Ganesh or the goddess of luck.)

Bhráta jéthe sen kahi, ek din dandi áya;
Tawa ráni ke nikat men, nit Harduul su jáya.

(One day a saiva, religious mendicant, came and said to Jujhar Sinh that Hardaul daily went to his wife for purposes of love.)

Sunat bát tan man ris byápi;
Ráni pas gayo wah pápi.
Kahi bat ráni suni lehu;
Hardaul káj prat hin bish deu.
Sunat bat ráni murjhani;
Boli bachan jori yug páni.
Suno kant ek bachan hamaro;
Káran kawan bandhu laghu máro.
Kaun ráj un liyo chhurái;
Kaun desh pai fauj charhai.
Kauu sampada hari tumhari;
Kyen tum toro banh dulari.
Yah kahi ráni phir kahi, pap karo jin koya;
In bátan men hcyago, dharam ráj kshay soya.

(Hearing the words of the religious mendicant Jujhar Sinh grew wroth and that sinful wretch went to the queen. He said to her:—"O Ráni! listen to me, give poison to Hardaul in the morning." Hearing these words the Ráni was extremely grieved. Folding her hands she begged:—"O my Lord! Hear one word of mine. Why do you kill your younger brother? What kingdom has he taken from you by force? What country has he invaded without your permission? What property has he robbed you of? Why do you break your dear arm?" With these words she exclaimed further:—"Do not sin against any one, such acts will destroy your virtue and kingdom both.")

Ye ráni ke bachan suni, bole ráj Kumar;
Ham ganain yah satya hai, jo as lekh tumhar.

(Hearing these words of the Ráni the Prince said:—"If you say so then the words of the religious mendicant are quite true.")

Ab hamko tum uttar daiho,
Dwij márĕ kai pátak painho.
Rani kahai uttar kyon daihon;
Kaho tumharo sir dhar loihon.
Dwij ko páp kant tum bhákho;
Taten adhik dewar ko rákho.
Yá ten ham ko máro rái.
Bhráta máre bahuri pachhitái.
Tere kahou khori mon hin náhin.
Samujho kant áp man mahin.
Pheri ráj tab kahai risái;
Jo kachhu kahi karo so jai.

(If you give answer to my words you will incur the sin of killing a Bráhman. The Ráni then replied:—"Why should I make reply? I shall obey your command implicitly. You now threaten me with the sin of killing a Bráhman and you yourself are going to bring on the sin of killing the younger brother of my husband. Better, O Raja! if you kill me. By killing a brother you will feel remorse afterwards. I tell you all this aloud for I do not entertain any fear. O my dear husband, think within yourself." Then the Rája spoke to the Ráni angrily "Go and do what I tell you to do.")

Ihi bidhi bita vain sab ráni man sandeh;
Honhar hi yah kahi, teri khawasin lehu.

(In this way the night was spent. The Ráni being much troubled she then thought to herself:—"What is written in the book of fate must come to pass." So thinking, she called her maid-servant.)

Ráni nainan bahu bah nira;
Boli bachan dharahi nahin dhira.
Lala son itni kahi awo;
Bhauji tum ko nyot bulawo.
Nain chali pahunchi hai tahán;
Karat datuan Kunwar bar jahán;
Boli bachan jori kar nana;
Raur bhojan hoya nidana.
Yah binati ráni ne kini;
Daras lálsa chit men díni.
Tab lála bolá musukái;
Hukm hoya so karcu bandi.
Lála kari asnan, Kunwar saug sab sath le.
Rákhyo sab ko man, pher akha re pag dharyo.

(The Rani was shedding tears profusely. She spoke in a faltering voice to her maid servant:—"Go and tell Kunwar Hardaul that his elder brother's wife invites him to dinner." Then the barber's wife went to the place where the Prince was washing his teeth. She delivered her message respectfully. The Prince then replied smiling:—"I shall do her bidding with all my heart." The Prince then bathed and in company with all Princes went into the place where he took his daily exercise.)

Mall yuddh bahu bidhi kari, ghari chár ion moy,
Phir thakurain jimáy kar, Kunwar kalen hoya.

(For four hours he practised wrestling with the other Princes. Then the other Princes took their food; then the Prince Hardaul went to dinner.)

Ráni yahán rasoi kinhi,
Bhánti bhánti ke byanjan kinhi.
Garal dári pakwán banáye ;
Sab sha>lv ansun nah waye.
Chánwal karhi dár pakwána,
Bara bari tarkari nána.
Kanchh pachhár sikar hu kinhi,
Garal saban men bedhi su dinhi.
Ihi bidhi sen sab kari rasoi.
Tero lála der na hoi.
Náin kari ara tab jái.
Chalo Kunwar atisay sukh pái.
Kunwar naye kapara mangwaye.
Swan tabai táhán er awan hilaye.
Lála pág dhari sir jab hin ;
Bhai chhink dahini hai tabhin.
Tab thákur bolé tehi shaura.
Ghari ek der karo tum aura.
Lála kahi honi hai águ.
Mitai na lakh hos ke bhágo.
Yah kahi uthe kumár báyen.
Ang pharkan lago.
Pahuncha pauri dwár bayas sir par baithiyo.
Karat Kunwar sandeh man, dwári páhunchi jáya :
Khabar suni Ráni tabai, páw pakhárai áya.

(The Ráni here cooked the meal. Several kinds of food she prepared. She put poison in the food as she cooked it. Her tears fell while doing so. She cooked rice, curry, cakes, pulse-cakes, vegetables of several kinds, meat of different sorts. She put poison in all. In this way she prepared food. Then the Ráni said "Call to the Prince that the food may not become cold." Then the barber's wife went again to the Prince and the Prince went to the Ráni's house with extreme pleasure. Kunwar Hardaul got new clothes brought to him. Just at this time a dog moved its ears, which is a bad omen. When the Prince put the turban on his head a man emerged on the left side. Then all the Princes spoke :—"Wait an hour here and then go." But Hardaul replied :—"That which is pre-destined must assuredly come to pass. That can not be averted even if one fly away a hundred thousand miles." With these words the Prince got up. Then the left side of his body began to tingle. When he got to the door of the Ráni, a crow alighted over his head which is another bad omen. The Prince went on doubting his safety. When the Ráni heard that the Prince was come, she ran up to him and began to wash his feet.)

Dekhi Kunwar ko ánsu dáre,
Páy pakhari ásan baithára
Udásin thárhi bhaujai ;
Netran son ansua jhar lái,
Mukh uthay Kunwar sab dekhyo.

Rowat bhauji ánkhin pekhyo,
Lála bát kahat bhauji son ;
Káran kawan satyu kahu monson.
Kai káhu kachhu anachit kinhi,
Harain tásu sir turlai chinhi.
Kai kahun áju deráni ji men ;
Koi kou kapat rakhe hai man men.
Kai tum bát bandhu dukh páyo,
So tum ham ko bhram baláyo.
Jo tum ham ko sub kari jáno,
Kaho sáf tum páp na áno,
Tab ráni sab katha sundi,
Pnrau táb kahi samujhái,
Bhrát tumkári ájna dinhi,
Bish miláy ham bhojan kinhi.
Táten dukh tan men rahyo chhái,
Bhojan karo sang tum ái
Tab Hardaul kahi yah báta.
Matan bichár karo hoi bhrátá.
Tum jani soch akro jiya apne,
Tum ko páp nahin hai sapne.
Be nisáf un chit men dini,
Akál mrilya un hamari kini.
Jo cháhat hai ham ko máre,
Pathai det kahun muluk majhári.
Nahin páp ho unko yámeri,
Honi hoye mitai nahin wámen.
Tum jo kaho sang bhojan karihain.
Mánain páp log sab hansi hain.
Bhauji ab jani karo abera,
Parso thár hot hai dera.
Thár parosi ágé dharo, Kunwar liyo sir náy,
Panch grás kárhi tabai, Thákur bhog lagáy.

(Seeing the prince the Ráni began to shed tears. She washed his feet and seated him on a bed. His brother's wife was sad and shed tears, then the Prince looked at her face. He saw his brother's wife weeping. He asked her what the cause of her misery was. He further asked :—"Has any-one insulted thee? If so I shall kill him at once. Art thou terrified at heart or does any-body wish to do you harm secretly? Has my brother scolded thee? If you consider me as your son you must tell me everything plainly." Then the Ráni related to him everything in detail. She said :—"Your brother has told me to give you food mixed with poison, so I am grieved at my heart. Eat with me the food I have prepared." Then Hardaul replied :— "My brother has ordered you to do this after much deliberation : do not be sorry. You are not to be blamed for this. He is unjustly taking my life prematurely. If he wanted to ruin me he should have banished me. Neither you nor he would have sin incurred. What is pre-destined must assuredly come to pass. If you eat with me they would laugh at us and consider it a sin. O my brother's wife, do not be sorry; it is getting late ; serve the dish to me at once.)

459. Saharanpur: Account of some shrines at Paniála village:—(1) *Magan Sáhib.*—The legend of Magan Sáhib, as far as I have been able to gather from the meagre accounts I could obtain from the villagers, is as follows:—Magan was a noted *faqír*, by caste a Musalmán *teli*, who took up his abode in Paniálá. One day he announced to the villagers that he was about to die, and directed them to prepare a grave for him. When the grave was ready, the *faqír* sat down in it, and immediately his spirit departed from him. The grave was thereupon filled up, and the present shrine built over it. The shrine is of octagonal shape, some 12 to 14 feet high, with open archways all round. In the middle of the shrine is a raised platform, in which is embedded a black stone, with two footmarks, carved in relief upon it. None of the villagers could tell me how long ago it is since Magan died; but one of them informed me that a very old *teli*, since deceased, used to relate that he had seen Magan Sáhib in the days of his youth. A small earthen lamp is burnt every night in honour of the saint, but special worship is performed on the 10th Sawan Badi, when money, grain, &c., are offered at the shrine.

(2) *Dhiraj Pargás Sáhib*; (3) *Tej Pargás Sáhib.*—Nothing is known of these two worthies, who have shrines in the same enclosure as that of Magan Sáhib, beyond the fact that they were disciples or *chelas* of Magan Sáhib. They are only worshipped on the 10th Sawan Badi, and receive much smaller offerings than the master. The curious point in connection with these shrines is that, though the saints venerated are said to have been Muhammadans, their names are entirely Hindu in character and their worship is carried on at present almost entirely by Hindus. The footmarks in Magan's shrine are exactly similar to those, that are to be seen at the shrines along the river-bank road, going to that road, and which are, I believe, there said to be Vishnu's footmarks (*Vishnu padma*).—G. A. Dampier, C.S.

The following is some further information about these worthies which has since been obtained:—

Dhiraj Sáhib, Pragat Sáhib and Tej Sáhib are said to have been successors of Kabir, and his line, according to his prophecy, is to run to forty-two saints who are to appear in succession. Up to this time there have been only twelve, and thirty are still to come.

These saints are worshipped by Kabir Panthis on the day of the full moon, and the following song is sung in their honour:—

> *Sabad árti mangal dj tu gaiyé ;*
> *Sat guru ke pad parasi param pad páiyé.*
> *Pratham hin mandir jhardy ke angand lipáiyé ;*
> *Naulam baslra mangdy ke chandwá taudiyé ;*
> *Gaj motian ke chauk tahán purwdiyé ;*
> *Tápar nriar dhoti mishthán dharáiyé.*
> *Tab puni guru ke het ásan bichhwáiyé ;*
> *Guru ke charan pakhári ásan bailhaiyé !*
> *Kerd aur kapur bahut bidhi ldiyé ;*
> *Asht sugandh supári to pán charkdiyé ;*
> *Jal thal sil sanbhári ke joti bandiyé ;*
> *Tál mridang bajdy madhur dhun gáiyé ;*
> *Pallau sahit ke kalash tahán dhar wáiye ;*
> *Pánch joti koi dipks tahán barwdiyé ;*
> *Sádhu sant mili lágí ke árti uláriyé ;*
> *Arti hari puni nariar tahan murwdiyé ;*
> *Purushahín bhog lagdy sakhá mili páiyé ;*
> *Janam janam ke chhudhá to pdya bujháiyé.*
> *Param anand jahán hot tau guru ko maudiyé ;*
> *Kahain Kabir Dharam Dás bakuri nd áiyé.*

(Let us now sing the orders of the true guide, while moving the propitiatory lamps over him. Touching the feet of the religious guide, let us attain salvation. The way to perform the worship of the religious guide is this: First of all sweep the house clean in which you intend to perform his worship. Then plaster a piece of ground in the courtyard. Get a new silken cloth and on poles set up an awning. Under it make a square of large pearls (instead of pearls now rice is used). Put on it a cocoa-nut, a new and yellow-dyed loin-cloth, and sweets. Then for the religious guide, whom you are to worship, spread a bed on the square. Wash the feet of the religious guide mentally and make him sit on the bed. Then set up in each corner of the square columns of plantain trees and burn camphor. Offer to the religious guide the eight kinds of perfumes, betel and betel-nuts. Then light a lamp there. Flaying on musical instruments, sing the divine songs. Put there a pitcher full of water surmounted by twigs of bamboos. Then get a lamp with five wicks burnt. All the followers of the sect present should move the lamp over the seat on which the religious guide is supposed to sit. After this, get a cocoa-nut broken. Distribute the cocoa-nut among the followers of the sect present. Offer the *halwa* sweetmeat to the religious guide. Distribute the *halws* among the followers of the sect present. By eating this *halwa* the hunger which has lasted for ages is appeased. Then with love and ecstacy pray to the religious guide. Kabir says to Dharm Dás: "O Dharm Das, by doing so a man becomes free from transmigration.")

The Kabir Panthi Sádhu, my informant, tells me that breaking the cocoa-nut means offering a man to the deity of death (Yama) on behalf of worshippers, and when he has got one man and he has devoured it (the eating up of the cocoa-nut by the worshippers, means that the deity of death has eaten it), he will not require the worshippers again and they will therefore go to heaven.

This is the way of performing the worship of the saints.—*Pándit Rám Gharib Chaubé.*

ANTHROPOLOGY.

460. Western District, N.-W. P.—
Earth-god or Bhumiyá worshipped by kanjars.
In the western districts of the N.-W.P., Bhumiya, the earth-god is worshipped by *kanjars* occasionally when they are sick, or when they are rejoicing, on the occasion of marriages, &c., with the offering of incense (*dhup*) and exactly five *bátashás* (a kind of sweetmeat).—*Pándit Rám Ghárib Chaubé.*

461. A means of predicting the Sex of an Expected Child.—Treble the letters of the woman's name; add the number of the letters of the name of a horse; to these add the number of letters of the name of the country in which the woman lives; divide the whole by 8: if the remainder is even, the baby will be a daughter; if odd, a son. Thus the mother's name is Dora; for this count 2; the horse's name is Hira, so add 2 to 6; the country is the Panjab; add 3. Divide 11 by 8, the remainder is 3. So the child will be a son.—*Pándit Rám Ghárib Chaubé.*

462. Oaths among village Hindus and Muhammadans.—The village Muhammadan, when he swears, raises his hand towards the west; the Hindu to the south, the land of the dead.—*W. Crooke.*

463. A short Note on Burial-Customs among the Bhuinhar Brahmans in the Saran district, Behar.—*By Mr. Sarat Chandra Mitra of Behar.*—One of the most essential differences between the Hindu religion on the one hand and the Mahomedan and the Christian religions on other, is that persons following the former persuasion burn their dead, whilst those professing the latter creeds dispose of their dead by interring them underneath the ground. This is the popularly-accepted criterion of difference between the two peoples. But, on a careful observation of the practices and customs of the various sects of the Hindus in different parts of the country, it would appear that this criterion does not hold good universally. There are certain circumstances under which certain sects of Hindus dispose of their dead by burying them. In Bengal there is a certain caste of Hindus, who go by the name of *Jugis*, which differs from all other castes of Hindus in the fact of its disposing of the dead in the following manner: first of all, they perform the Sanscrit ceremony, that is, they set fire to the faces of their corpses, and, then, instead of burning them, they bury them under the ground. Similarly, certain classes of Sanscrit *(Byragees)*, or religious mendicants, belonging to the Vaishnava sects are buried in a sitting posture. Thus much for Bengal.

In other parts of India, especially Madras, certain classes of Hindus also practise the custom of burying their dead. The chief sect which practises this custom of burial (*uttara-kriya*) is the *Lingadháris*—a class of *Sivaites*, as their name indicates,—who mostly bury their dead in sitting posture. The grave is partially filled up with earth to the waist of the deceased, when the friends who are present there, throw in handfuls of earth over the grave till a small mound is erected over it. This they do after the usual reading of the *mantras* and the performance of the other ceremonies. Like the *Byragees* of Bengal, *Sanyásís*, or those mendicants who have given up the world and live by begging, are always buried. In their case the performance of the necessary funeral rites is dispensed with, as they are considered to be too holy for these. Some castes of Hindus, like the *Jugis* of Bengal, bury all unmarried girls. The *Sudras* bury those who are below the age of ten and those who die of small-pox. Hindu soldiers who die in battle are all buried. Also boys, who have not had the *upanayanam* ceremony performed with respect to them, *i.e.*, those who have not been invested with the sacred thread, are buried.

A burial-custom, similar to this last-mentioned one, exists among the *Bhuinhár* Bráhmans of this district of Behar (Sáran). I have heard on good authority that this practice also obtains among other classes of Hindus in this district, who wear the *upabíta*, or the sacred thread. In the March-April Criminal Sessions of this district, which are still going on, a case, *viz., Empress* vs. *Rampat Rai*, was lately tried, during the trial of which the existence of this curious custom among the *Bhuinhár* Bráhmans, to which class the accused belonged, came to light. The prosecution alleged, in this case, that the accused had falsely charged three other persons with murdering his nephew for the sake of his ornaments and had, in order to create evidence against them, disinterred the corpse of his nephew who had died of natural causes, and who had been buried according to the custom of his caste, and had, subsequently, thrown it into a well. During the course of the trial it transpired that the *Bhuinhár* Bráhmans and other sacred-thread-wearing castes of this district bury their boys aged up to twelve years. There are two exceptions to this, *viz.:*—

(1) Those boys, who are aged twelve years or below that age, are not buried when they have undergone the *janao* (Sanskrit *upanayanam*) ceremony, *i.e.*, when they have been invested with the sacred thread. The undergoing of this *janao* or sacred-thread-investiture ceremony is considered tantamount to being half-married.

(2) Those boys, aged 12 or below that age, who have been married, are not buried. A boy cannot get married unless he has undergone the

janao ceremony, *i.e.*, has been invested with the sacred thread.

In the cases of these two boys, who have been either invested with the sacred thread or have been married, they are burnt in the usual way, and the *káraj* or *srádh* ceremonies are performed on the expiration of the usual period of mourning. But boys, aged 12 or below that age, who have not undergone either of the aforesaid two ceremonies, are buried underneath the ground. The corpses are taken to the neighbourhood of some tank which is usually used as a burying-place for them. Then a grave suited to the dimensions of the corpse is dug, and the body is interred therein. Sometimes a *peepul* tree *(Ficus religiosa)* is planted over it. In cases of boys who are buried, no *káraj* or *srádh* ceremony or any other funeral obsequy is performed.—*Anthropological Society, Bombay.*

464. **The Fingers as an entry for Demons.**—All Hindus regard the fingers as a means by which demons enter the body. Hence in places where the sacred rivers are at a distance, it is supposed sufficient after cremation to throw the bones of the fingers of one hand into the Ganges, and those of the other into the Jumna. This is known as *phul phekna* and wherever the bones are thrown into the sacred stream, a place like Hardwar, Mathra, &c., being, of course preferred, some money must at the same time be distributed to Bráhmans. If the finger-bones are disposed of in this way, the remaining ashes, which are usually left at the place of cremation, are not touched by demons.—*W. Crooke.*

465. **Castes which supply Midwives to other Hindus.**—In the Eastern Districts of the North-Western Provinces all the duties of midwives are performed by women of the Chamar caste. In Bundelkhand and the neighbouring Districts this is done by the sub-castes of *doms*, known as *basor* or *bánsphor*. In the Western Districts, the midwives are generally *bhangi* or *mirási* women. In Saharanpur the *dom mirási* woman is generally the village midwife. In other places the duties are entrusted to the *qasai*, or butcher women. This divergence of practice is curious and it would be interesting to learn the real explanation of it.—*W. Crooke.*

466. **Banyas; Position of.**—The further you go west the higher is the grade of the Banya. To the east he is a degraded person and is called Sáhu ironically. Finally in the Punjab he ranks as a Kshatrya. In the west he is called Lála, as a title of respect, a term which to the east is conferred on the Kayesth. It rather looks as if the West was the original home of the higher caste Vaisyas and that, as they went east, they fell in social status. In Saharanpur the name Banya is falling into disuse, and if you ask such a man what his caste is, he will say that he is a Mahájan or a *Sarãogi*.—*Pándit Rám Ghárib Chaubé.*

467. **Knots in the Brahmanical cord.**—Among *Sarwariya* Bráhmans, there are three higher grades and thirteen who are inferior. The higher grades have five and the inferior three knots in the *janao*, or Brahmanical cord. If a man borrow the cord of a person of another grade he adjusts the knots according to his rank; for the knot is the important part of the cord.—*Pándit Rám Ghárib Chaubé.*

468. **South Mirzapur, N.-W. P.—Games of children. Hurrah—Hide and go seek.**—This game is played by boys of several families. It is played in this way:—All the boys of a certain family conceal themselves in a house and the boys of other houses go on searching them, repeating the following at the pitch of their voices:—

Sát pailá dhán kúré—Huhuré hauné batás raghuré—Hurrah! Hurrah!

(Seven *pailá* (a measure of grain about half a pound) rice seed I pound. I shall winnow it by any wind I find.)

When they get into the house in which boys have concealed themselves they sing aloud:—

Miyán ganjá pialé—Bhúkh lagalé, Mard gáji rahi jáná bhitaré.

(The Muhammadan Moslem friend smoked *ganjá*; He forthwith felt hungry. Although a man of great power, he concealed himself in a house-corner.)

When they catch the boys who had concealed themselves, they beat them with their fists, crying:—

Marai mukká huqqá lút lé—hurrah.

(Beat them with fists and rob them of their tobacco pipe. Hurrah! Hurrah!!)

The boys manage to run away into another house and conceal themselves there, when they find that they are about to be caught. When the boys of one family have been caught and beaten, boys of another family conceal themselves, and others look for them. In this way the game goes on until the boys are tired.

469. **Hukurtum.**—*This game is played by a number of boys.* One boy bends himself forward a little and another puts his hands on the first boy's shoulders, bending a little. In this way boys go on putting their hands upon one another's

shoulders. When a long line of boys has been formed, the first boy has to dance. They sing the following song at the time of dancing :—

> Indari kai dál cháwal, jamari kai ghiwa ;
> Dindá dnuki chát ke deahai, dekh dekh lalchai jíwa.

(Rice and pulse of Indari (a village), and ghi of Jamari ; The girl eats them and looks at me. My heart longs for her.)
When they stop their dance they sing :—

> Rangmáté rangrailá, birahan máté ghór ;
> Mainka máion daiyá, kokamá kai jhar.

(A rake is bewitched with pleasure and a horse by separation from the mare, how am I excited. For fish curry !)
Again they sing on the conclusion of the game :

> Márai dé musari jari jáyan táng ;
> Abnú khelab Hukkurtum.

(Let me strike the mouse and break its legs. To play Hukkurtum, I'm not now bound.)

470. Dom kawwa.—This is played by comparatively a large number of boys. They fix four poles in the ground in four directions. Then they put upon them a cot or a thatch of sticks. Then they sit on the ground in a row. The boy who finds himself in the middle of the boys, leaves his seat; for he is abused by other boys in this way :

> Agar agar kawwá ; bich mén dóm-kawwá.

(On either side are crows, but in the middle is the Dom crow who eats corpses.)

When one boy leaves the seat, another boy is abused; for, he takes his place. In this way all the boys get up from their seats. Then one boy climbs up the thatch and begins to abuse the other boys thus :—

> Uprén Rájá niché dóm ;
> Góra dhóy dhóy pien dóm.

(Above the king and below the dom. Washing his feet let the dom drink.)

Then all the boys try to climb up the thatch, but the stronger among them throw them down when they try to climb up.

471. Gadi,—This is one of the most important games of the children of the aborigines. The minimum number of boys required in this game is twenty. Two parties of equal numbers of boys are made. Each of the party keeps about him a gádi or a piece of wood of about 6 finger breadths long and wide. Each party has its own head. First of all it is determined which party will first play the game. It is determined in this way :—A gádi of one party and another gádi of the other party are taken. The head of each party marks his own gádi in any way he chooses, unseen by the other boys. Both the gádis are given to a man who has no connection with the game. He puts under his hands the gadis, one upon the other. Then he asks the heads of the parties whose gádi is "up," and whose "down" The party whose head gives the correct answer is entitled to be the first players. Then each party sits opposite to each other at a distance of 5 yards from each other. The party whose turn is not to be active players puts in front of it a brick, leaning, on which a gádi is put. The gádi is put in such a way as to be towards the party of active players. In the same way the members of the active party also put in front of them a gádi leaning on a brick and towards the members of the other party. Then a member of the active party hits the gádi of the non-active party with his own gádi which the member throws towards the gádi of the inactive party, not by hands but by a stick, with the help of his right foot. If the first hitting miss, the party becomes dead. Another party will then play, which has been up to this time called by me inactive party. Not only the missing of the first hit makes a party dead, but the missing of any hit of any member of the party makes it dead. If a party hit the gádi of the rival party seven times without a single missing, that party will be considered the victorious party. But the victorious party will have to undergo one examination more. The inactive party will fix in dust a reed (sink), and the members of the active party will hit it. The member of the active party who hits the reed first time shall be considered Rájá, and all the members of his own party and those of the other shall salute him saying :—

> Jíté so Chandél,
> Háré só lénrél.

(He who wins is Chandél and he who is defeated is his subject.)

The play then comes to an end.—Pándit Rám Gharib Chaubé.

472. The Legend of the origin of Dancing Girls—There was once a Sádhu who was practising austerities on the top of a mountain. Close to him lived the demon Satan (Shaitan). Near the demon's house lived a poor labourer and him Satan began to entice to evil. The labourer said to him :—"O Satan ! Your time is lost on a poor person like me. It would be a work worthy of you to corrupt this Sádhu." So Satan went to the Sádhu and found him sitting on the ground absorbed in devotion. When he came to himself he picked a few leaves of the nim tree under which he sat, and ate them. Then he became again absorbed in his devotions. The next day Satan prepared some halwa sweetmeat and sprinkled it on the leaves of the nim tree and as the Sadhu found them pleasant to the taste he chewed more of the leaves that day than usual. In this way Satan daily sprinkled on the *nim* trees various kinds of rich food and wine. Then he put a woman there and the Sádhu fell into the trap and in course of time three children were born, one boy and two girls. The woman would not nurse them so they were suckled by a bitch and thus imbibes the evil qualities of their foster-mother.

One day the Rájá passed by and saw the children being suckled by the bitch. He asked the Sadhu the cause of this and he said:—"It is the wondrous work of Parameswar." The Rájá ordered his men to take the children to his palace and when they grew up he attended to their education. When he was in search of a tutor for them, Satan, in the disguise of a Maulavi, came to the palace and was appointed to instruct them. When their education was finished, Satan said to the Rájá: "One thing remains to be taught" so he purchased the garments of a dancer and some drums and other musical instruments and taught them to dance and sing. The girls danced and the boy accompanied them. The Rája was pleased and took the girls as his concubines, and from them are sprung the present race of dancing girls.

[Told by Baijnath Prasad, teacher of the School at Lahi, Barabanki District.]

{ The temptation of the Sádhu is on the lines of the Irish legend of St. Kevin.—ED.]

473. **Birth customs: Bare sword.**—Is the following practice still observed? It is taken from one of Haji Mustafa (M. Raymond's) notes in his "Seir Mutaqherin," a translation of the Persian work by Sayyad Ghulám Husain Khán, (Calcutta, 1789, Vol. II, page 128, note 93). "It is customary to lay a sabre at the pillow of men of distinction, not against men, but against evil spirits, which are reported in India to be afraid of bare sabres; and it is for that reason likewise, that women in child-bed have always one at their pillow head; and also are surrounded and covered by four unsheathed sabres when they come forth on the sixth day to shew the stars or the sun to their new-born; and they are preceded by an unsheathed sword, whenever they go to the bathing place, or to any one still more secret."—*W. Irvine.*

474. **Note on the use of Locusts as an article of Diet among the Ancient Persians.**—Among the *debris* found in pre-historic caves, the cloven bones of various mammals have been discovered, the presence whereof, indicates that the dwellers thereof, *viz.*, Palæolithic Man used not only to subsist upon the flesh of animals killed in the chase, but also to feed upon the marrow of their bones which they used to extract by breaking open the bones with their flint hammers and stone-hatchets. Similar discoveries have been made in the Kitchen-Middens of pre-historic peoples all over the world, and it has been found that the shells of molluscous animals form the major portion of these heaps of the kitchen-refuse of the Palæolithic Age. These discoveries have led Anthropologists to come to the conclusion that men in the Palæolithic Age used to feed mainly upon the meat of animals killed in the chase, eked out with a little fish they could catch, and the berries of trees that flourished upon the earth in the Pliocene and the Pleistocene Periods. Agriculture, as an art, was unknown to Palæolithic Man. It is not until we come to the Neolithic Age when the Mound-Builders, the Dolmen-Builders and the dwellers of the Lacustrine Villages of the Swiss Lakes, flourished on the earth, that we find any remains of cereals and other agricultural produce which land us on the firm ground of positive evidence that these Neolithic Men lived not only on the produce of the chase, but also earned their living by following the more peaceful pursuits of agriculture. The investigation by Professor Keller of the remains discovered at the bases of these Lake-Dwellings has brought to light grinding-stones, mill-stones, grains, breads, fruit, articles which conclusively prove that Neolithic Men were not unacquainted with the art of agriculture.

On coming to the latter end of the Quarternary Period when we get the first traces of Historic Man, his dietary is found to have been increased by the addition of new articles of food, and the methods of dressing them for meals improved, whence is the origin of the Art of Cookery. In this historic period—the Iron Age—relics of the Palæolithic Man's dietary are found to exist in some articles of food used by races of savage men all over the world. Larvæ of insects, flesh of animals considered unclean and unfit for food by civilized man, clay and such other articles are still used as articles of diet by races of men grovelling in the lowest depths of savagery.

Among insects, the locust has, from time immemorial, been used as an article of food by man. In the Bible we first get the traces of its use as such by men of the Historic Period, in the story of St. John the Baptist, whose "meat" in the wilderness is said to have been principally "*locusts* and wild honey." There are also other passages both in the Old and the New Testaments (cf, Lev. xi, 22 and Matt. iii, 4) which prove that locusts were considered a delicacy by the Israelites and the Canaanites. In other countries of the East, these insects are eaten even at the present day. There are various ways of cooking them, of which the commonest is to tear off their legs and wings, extract their entrails, stick them in long rows upon wooden spits, and then roast them in the fire. Sometimes they are fried in oil, whereas, at other times, they are dried in the sun and ground in the mill into a flour-like meal of which bread is made in times of scarcity. These articles of diet, dressed in these ways, are considered *bonne bouche* and are devoured with the greatest gusto by the people who eat them. The Arabians eat them, prepared in the aforesaid fashions, even at the present day. The Bedouins of the Arabian deserts preserve them in salt, and when undertaking long journeys, take a supply of these in their leathern sacks.

That the ancient Assyrians also used the locust as an article of diet is evident from the banquet scenes depicted on sculptures unearthed from the mounds of Konyunjik on the Tigris, wherein ancient Assyrian servitors are represented as carrying in their hands, spits with rows of dried locusts. Among the sculptures on the left or west side of the Konyunjik Gallery in the British Museum, London, which illustrate the state of Assyrian art under the *régime* of Sennacherib, are "part of a series (Nos. 34—43) which originally lined the two walls of a long narrow gallery leading, by an inclined plane, from Konyunjik towards the Tigris. On the one side, descending the slope, were fourteen horses, led by grooms; on the other, ascending into the palace, were servitors bearing food for a banquet. The figures are somewhat smaller than life, designed with much freedom and truth, and, by comparison with the Panathenaic frieze in the Elgin Room, they may furnish a good point of view for estimating the capabilities and defects of Assyrian art. No. 39, on which is seen a marshal or chamberlain with a staff, was originally placed, as here, at a projection in the wall. Amongst the attendants or servitors, represented on Nos. 41—43, *is one bearing in each hand a rod with two rows of dried locusts, which are to this day used as food by the Arabs.* The other attendants carry wine-skins, birds, pomegranates, and other fruit."*

In May, 1891, a great flight of locusts passed over this district (Sáran). The locusts are known in Hindi as टिड्डी, in Urdu: the word is written in Persian character as such or *Tiddi*. I was then informed by the Hindus of this place, and also by my Persian teacher—himself a Mahomedan—that the Indian Mahomedans, especially those of the lower classes, eat these insects after having fried them in oil.

The Hindus of Northern India, as a class, consider the flight of locusts an ill omen, in fact a visitation from God presaging famine or some other calamity to the country which is visited by these insects. As a consequence, they look with repugnance upon these insects. The lower classes of Hindus in Behar, who take flesh-meat and fish, do not eat this insect, nor do the Hindus of Bengal, who, without any restriction, take flesh and fish, even though the latter are in the habit of taking quantities of a minute crustacean—a kind of very diminutive-sized shrimp called in Bengali कूचा चिंगड़ी which very much resembles minute insects.

A similar superstition with regard to the locust also prevailed among the ancient Assyrians. Just like the Hindus of Northern India, the ancient Assyrians also used to consider the locust an insect of ill omen, boding evil to the place visted by it. In the Table-case B, placed long the middle of the Konyunjik Gallery of the British Museum in London, and containing the smaller objects of Assyrian antiquity discovered in the course of the various excavations of the sites of ancient Assyrian cities, are exhibited terra cotta tablets referring to the language, legends, and mythology of the Assyrians, along with selected specimens of Despatch or Report Tablets and letters. Among these tablets is one numbered 26, which records "a tablet of portents, describing what would be likely to happen if locusts enter a house," &c.†

The ancient Persians were in the habit of taking locusts as an article of diet. By ancient Persians are meant the inhabitants of Persia after they had been converted to Islam by the Mahomedan conquerors of that country. There is a passage in the Bustan by Sheikh Sádi, which clearly shews that this insect formed an item in the dietary of the ancient inhabitants of Persia.

This passage occurs in حکایت در معنی رحمت برناتوان درحال توانا, or the story about shewing compassion to poor men by men in a state of affluence, contained in Book I., which is about Justice, Equity and Government. The passage is as follows:—

نه درگوه سبزی نه درباغ شخ † ملخ بوستان خورد و مردم ملخ†

It may be thus translated into Urdu:

پہاڑوں پہ سبزی نہ باغوں میں شخ † ملخ کھا گئی باغ و خلقت ملخ†

The above Persian couplet may be thus translated into English:

"Not in the mountain, verdure; not in the garden, a branch;

(The locusts ate the garden; and men, the locusts.")

Sheikh Sadi flourished about the end of the twelfth century and the first half of the thirteenth. Hence it is evident that the Persians of those remote times were in the habit of eating locusts. Unfortunately Sádi does not tell us in what ways they were cooked by the ancient Persians. In the absence of such evidence it must be presumed that they were dressed in the same fashions as are prevalent at the present day in other oriental countries.—*Journal, Anthropological Society, Bombay.*

---

* *Vide* "A Guide to the Exhibition Galleries of the British Museum, Bloomsbury." London :·1888, *p.* 31.

† *Op. cit.*, *p.* 36.

FOLK-TALES.

475. The Prince and the Snake.—There was once a Rájá who had seven sons, all of whom were married except the youngest and he had tamed a snake which he loved dearly and always kept with him. When the Wazir was going home from Darbar he saw the prince feeding the snake and he went and told the Rájá that the boy was taking to evil ways. The Rájá promised to look into the case next day and calling his son he took him in his lap and said :—

"You must give up keeping this snake."

The prince promised to get rid of it; so he came home and taking the pot in which he used to keep it, he started for the jungle. There he took out the snake and said :—

"O god, you have undergone much while you were with me. But as you are sprung from a high family you must pardon me on account of my great love for you."

The snake replied :—

"Prince, while I was with you I enjoyed perfect comfort. I will recompense you. Stay here while I go to Patala. There I will introduce you to Rájá Vasuki, the lord of the snakes."

So the snake went down a hole in the ground, and when the other snakes saw him they said :—

"Brother you have come back after a long absence."

They took him to the Dárbar of Rájá Vasuki and he saluted the Rájá and said :—

"Maharaj! the son of a great Rájá is waiting for an interview with your Majesty."

Meanwhile the prince got tired of waiting and was returning to his father's palace when the snake came up from behind and called him. The prince replied that he thought he had been forgotten; but the snake took him down to Patala and brought him before Rájá Vasuki. After a time, when he was about to leave, Rájá Vasuki gave him an iron chain. When the prince saw it he said :—

"Maharaj! In my father's house are many chains of gold. What is the use of this iron chain to me?"

Rájá Vasuki said:—

"Brother! Do not speak thus. This chain will be of great value to you. Mahadeva conferred it on me. The merits of it are these. Whenever you desire aught you must dig the earth to the depth of one and a quarter cubits and put the chain thrice into the hole. Then cover it with earth and four Birs will attend and do your bidding."

So the prince came home and took the chain with him; but he grieved greatly at parting from the snake.

One day he went into the inner apartments and began to joke with his sisters-in-law. They said:

"You may say what you like when you get the Mute Princess (Anbola Ráni) as your wife."

These words inflamed his mind and he mounted his horse and at once set out in search of Anbola Ráni. He passed through a forest and there he saw a tigress lying on the path. He tried to avoid her, but she saw him and called to him, and said :—

"If you do not come and ease my pain I will curse thee."

He was afraid and came to the tigress, who said:

"I have a thorn in my foot. Pull it out and earn my blessing." The prince agreed to attempt to relieve her pain; but she said :—

"You are the son of a king, but you are destitute of wisdom. If you try to extract the thorn and give pain, I will surely kill you; bring a large log and place it near me. When I am mad with the pain I will gnaw that and spare you."

The prince placed the log before the tigress and by its help he managed to extract the thorn from her foot. Next day as he was going away, the two sons of the tigress appeared, and when they saw the prince they said :—

"We shall have a dinner to-day without the trouble of hunting for it."

Saying thus, they were about to devour the prince, when the tigress abused them and said :—

"This man has saved my life and you must not attempt to seize him."

As the prince was going away she said :—

"I shall never see you again; but as a mark of my gratitude I will give you a son of mine. He will serve you faithfuly."

So the prince took the cub and started, and on the way he halted under a tree. Suddenly his eyes fell on a snake creeping up the tree on which was the nest of the bird Garuda. The young birds began to cry with fear and the prince at once shot the snake. The prince put the dead snake under his shield and resting his head upon it lay down to sleep. By and by Garuda and his mate returned, and when they saw the prince, Garuda said to her that she should kill him. She said:—

"I, a female, cannot kill a male, but you may do so if you please."

Garuda said :—

"I will not kill him as it is a sin to kill a man asleep."

Meanwhile the young ones cried out :—

"Do not kill him. He has just saved our lives from the snake and if you doubt it look under his shield."

When Garuda saw the dead snake he was very grateful and gave him food and brought a goat for the young tiger that was with him. When the prince asked leave to go they said to him:—

"You must take one of our young ones with you."

So they gave him one of their young ones, and he went away. As he went along the bird went flying over him and kept off the heat of the sun. The tiger walked behind him and the dog in front. Next day they came to a garden which was guarded by a Rakshasi. The prince was suffering from thirst and said to her:

"Mother, tell me where I can get water, as I am athirst."

She said:—

"My son, go into such a place in the garden; raise a stone, and you shall find water beneath it."

When he raised the stone he found that beneath it flowed the river of gold. When he bathed therein he found that he had become the colour of gold. So he bathed his horse, his dog, the tiger and Garuda in the water and they all became golden. Then he came into a city and he appeared like the rising moon in beauty. The Rájá of that land was going through the city and when he beheld him he was astonished. The princess was looking from an upper chamber and, when they saw each other, they fell in love, and he lost his senses with passion. When he came to his senses he returned to the garden, and, leaving his goods in charge of the Rakshasi, he went again to the city. He came to the shop of a grain parcher, and said:—

"Give me food and I will collect leaves for your oven."

Thus he lived for some time and then the Rájá held the Swayamvara of his daughter. All the princes of the land were assembled and the princess went round with the garland of victory. She looked everywhere for the prince who, clothed in rags, was sitting in a corner, and when she did not find him she gave the garland to none. The assembly broke up. When she came back to the palace she prayed for aid to the Lord Ganesa. At the next meeting Ganesa pointed the prince out to her and she threw the garland round his neck. But the assembly cried that there was a mistake and it was not till she threw it thrice that they believed her. So the Rájá had to marry her to the prince, but he gave them only a hut to live in and the coarsest food to eat. Then her brothers planned to take the prince into the jungle and slay him. So they asked him to go hunting with them. But he said that he had neither horse nor weapons. Then the princess went to her mother for advice, but she turned her back upon her. And her brothers would not speak to her, so she returned home in tears. But the prince said:—

"I am going to bathe."

So he went back to the garden where he took his horse, tiger, dog and Garuda, and, mounting, went into the jungle. His wife's brothers had been hunting there before he came. He shot a deer and sitting near a tank began to roast the meat. The brothers of the princess came to the same place and when they saw them the dog and the tiger were about to devour them. So they fell before the prince and asked forgiveness and he gave them water and some of the venison. Then he said:—

"I must brand you with a hot iron on your loins; if not my faithful animals will devour you."

So he branded them and let them go. Then he tied them on their horses with their faces to their tails and let them go. Next day he went to the Darbar of the Rájá. But the princess had gone to the Ráni and told her how the prince had branded her brothers and would surely slay them. The Ráni told this to the Rájá and the Rájá was grieved and came to the Darbar. The prince came in guarded by his animals and they were all the colour of gold. The Rájá and all his court saluted him and he said:—

"In your court are five thieves whom I have branded on the loins. Let them appear before me."

Then the Rájá bowed before him and begged forgiveness.

But the prince took over the kingdom and ruled as Rájá. After a time he began to consider that he had not attained his desire of gaining the Ráni Anbola, and when he told the princess, she agreed to join him in the search for her. The Rájá also tried to dissuade him, but next day he started with a single groom. After many days he came to the palace of Anbola Ráni. At the gate was placed a great drum which any one who wished to marry the Ráni had to strike. The prince struck the drum a hundred times. A servant came out to see who had struck the drum. She brought the princess before the Ráni who, seeing him, fell in love with him, and swooned. When she recovered her senses she asked him who he was and what he desired. When he explained his case she said:—

"You must fulfil the conditions, which are these; —On the first night you must bridge the stream near the palace; and secondly you must make a garden such as the world has never seen."

Then the prince invoked the aid of the iron chain and at once four mighty Birs appeared to do his bidding. He told them what they had to do. They began to reflect that a bridge could not be built in a single night. So they determined to lay the mountain Kailása across the river as a bridge, and for a garden, to bring down the garden of Rájá Indra and place it there. They did so, and next day the prince sent his groom to inform the Ráni Anbola that the conditions were fulfilled. The Ráni was satisfied and returned to the palace. Then she said to the prince:—

"The conditions for the second night are—That you shall make me speak at the end of each watch."

The prince caused them to disguise themselves so as to see all and be seen of none. He went to the palace and a couch was spread for him beside that of the Ráni. Then he seated the demons—one on the Ráni's lamp, one on her couch, one on her water-vessel and one on her necklace. She covered her face with a sheet and lay down. Then the prince said to the water vessel:—

"Brother! Let me pass part of the night in talking to you."

The vessel replied:—

"Prince! What can I say? I am in great trouble. I have been made by a workman who has not his equal in the world for cleverness, but I have the misfortune to live with a wretched woman who never takes the trouble to clean me. She washes herself with the water I hold but she is too lazy to wash me."

Hearing this the Ráni cried out:—

"You lie, you wretch! I wash you four times a day."

So saying she took up the vessel and flung it on the ground so that it was broken. But the prince said:—

"The Ráni has spoken:"

She answered:—

"I spoke to the vessel, not to you."

"Well!" said he "you have spoken now to me"

So he ordered the drum to be beaten. And so the first watch passed. In the second watch the prince said to the Ráni's necklace:

"Necklace! Help me to fulfil the conditions of the second watch and tell me something."

The necklace said:—

"What can I say? I have been made by a famous artist, but this wretched woman never wears or cleans me, and since I came to her she has kept me hanging on this peg."

The Ráni was wroth, and said:—

"Miserable one! I wear you daily and you will go lying about me."

So saying she flung away the necklace and it was broken. But the prince said:—

"The Ráni has spoken."

"I spoke, not to you but to the necklace," she said.

"At any rate you have now spoken to me," he cried and he struck the drum for the second time.

Then the prince said to the couch:—

"Say something to me that the conditions of the third watch also may be fulfilled."

The couch answered:—

"O prince! What can I say to you? I was made by the cleverest carpenter in the world, but woe to me that I have come into the hands of this miserable Ráni. She never moves me, or cleans the dust from beneath me. She must have been a she-ass in her former life."

The Ráni said:—

"Wretch! Why do you make these lying charges against me?"

"This is a means for your correction," the couch replied. Then the Ráni kicked the couch, but the demon who was on it, pressed with all his might, and the couch was broken. The Ráni slipped and fell and the prince said:—

"The Ráni has spoken."

She answered:—

"I did not speak to you."

"Well you have spoken to me now," he said and he struck the drum for the third time.

Then the prince said to the lamp:—

"O lamp! Relate to me something so that I may fulfil the condition of the last watch."

The lamp said:—

"Friend! What can I say? I was cast by a famous workman; but I fell into the hands of this most miserable princess. On me is accumulated the filth of years, and she never takes the trouble to clean and trim me."

The Ráni was wroth and, dashing the lamp on the ground so that it was broken to pieces, said:

"Miserable creature; I have you cleaned daily and yet you tell lies like these!"

The prince said:—

"The Ráni has spoken."

"I did not speak to you," she said.

"Well! You have spoken now," and with that he had the drum beaten, that the Ráni had spoken four times. When the news spread through the city the people were delighted, and the marriage preparations began at once.

So they were duly married, and the prince stayed there some time. One day he went to the river bank and saw two rubies in the water. When he put in his hand and picked them up, he saw two more, and when he picked these up he saw two more; so he threw away all of them and resolved to go to the place where all these rubies came from. He followed the stream to its source and there he saw a splendid building, and from beneath it there came a stream of rubies. He ordered his demons to take him into the house, and there he saw a fairy (*Pári*) lying dead. The demons rubbed on the forehead of the fairy the consecrated ashes of Mahadeva, so that she might not see them and they rubbed it on their own foreheads so that they might see all and be seen of none. In the evening a Rákshasa appeared. He took up a bottle from the shelf and sprinkled some magical essence (*árag*) on the fairy, and she awoke. The Rákshasa said in his own tongue:—

"*Khan man sain.*" "I smell a human being."

The fairy answered:—

"I know naught of this. You must have caught many men to-day as your prey, and these you smell."

The Rakshasa passed the night playing dice with her and in the morning he went off to the world to hunt for men. When he had started the prince sprinkled the magical essence on the fairy, and she awoke and asked him why he had come and where he was going. He told her all his story, and she warned him to escape before the Rákshasa returned. But he said:—

"As, I have come, I do not wish to go away and I will face any danger that may happen" and he added:—

"Fairy! If you wish me to stay always with you, you must tell me in what dwells the life of the Rákshasa."

She answered:—

"You must promise that if you will kill him, his funeral rites will be duly fulfilled. His life lives in a parrot, which is on the topmost branch of a banyan tree; but this branch swarms with snakes innumerable, and in every leaf there are countless scorpions. This tree is in the midst of the seven oceans, and is guarded by hosts of demons. If any one can kill the parrot then he can get me."

The prince said to his demons:—
"Take me to that tree."

So he was taken there and by the help of the demons he overcame the snakes and scorpions and the demon guard. Finally he seized the parrot and tore its limbs asunder. The Rákshasa rushed up; but as the parrot died, he died also. Then the prince took the fairy on his shoulders, and his demons carried them through the air to the palace of Anbola Ráni. Thence with his two wives he started to recover his third wife. He also brought with him his horse and dog and tiger and Garuda. On the way he gave over his animals to their parents, and when he came home the wives of his brothers were put to shame to witness his success and he lived with his three wives for many years in the utmost happiness.

May Parameswar deal with us, as he dealt with him!

[Told by Yubraj Sinh Barhai of Dhanpur, Bijnor District.]

476. **Prince Nilkanth.**—There was once a Rájá who had come to old age and had no son. One day he was sitting at the gate of his palace lamenting his trouble, when a *Sádhu* came up and asked him the cause of his grief. The Rájá said: "What have you to do with it? Take your alms and leave me." But the *Sádhu* persisted in asking, and at last the Rájá said:—"If I tell you my trouble, will you promise to remove it?" The *Sádhu* made the promise and the Rájá made him repeat the promise three times. Then he said: "The cause of my grief is that I have no heir. The *Sádhu* said:—"The cause of your having no heir is that *Bhagwán* has not written it so in your fate." "But," said the Rájá "as you have promised me an heir you must give me one."

So the *Sádhu* had to fulfil his promise and as he was going away he met a sparrow and said to him:—"Go and live in the Ráni's womb for a year." The sparrow replied:—"How can I do this? When the time is over I shall have to come out and then go to Hell." The *Sádhu* went on and met a paddy bird (*bagula*) and made him the same proposal, but the paddy bird for the same reason refused. Next he met a jay (*nilkanth*) and ordered him to live for a year in the womb of the Ráni. The jay said:—"I have no objection, but how am I to get out again?" The *Sádhu* answered: "When you are twelve years of age you will be married and then you must sit on your wife's knee. When you do this you will die immediately. But as you are dying, you must tell your wife to put your body in the hollow of a *pipal* tree and then you will become a jay again."

The *Sádhu* departed and in due course the Ráni came to be in child. When her son was born, he quickly grew in strength and when he reached his twelfth year, he was married. When the ceremony was over he made his wife seat him on her knee, and said:—" I am about to die. When I am dead, put my body in the hollow of a *pípal* tree." When her friends heard that the newly-married bridegroom was dead, they were surprised to see the girl place it in the hollow of a *pípal* tree. She went the next day to see the corpse, but it was not there.

After this, her sisters were always taunting her with losing her husband on her wedding day. One day she went out with her companions to collect cow-dung fuel in the jungle. She got lost and happened to take refuge in the same *pípal* tree in which she had placed the body of her husband. At midnight her husband with a servant came into the hole in the same tree and cooked food. But instead of two, the food divided itself into three parts. He and the servant ate two shares and left the third in the hollow of the tree. The girl took her share of the food and in this way lived there for three months.

One day, as her husband was going away, she seized him by his feet. He recognised her, but said:—" Dear, you cannot get me back so easily as that. You must go to the bank of the Ganges and worship *Mahádeva* for twelve years, before you can recover me." She did as he ordered her and when the period of her worship was over, the god appeared to her and said:—" Ask any boon you desire." So she asked for her husband and got him back and they lived long and happily together.

(A folk-tale told by Rámnandan Tiwári, Bráhman, of Mirzapur.)

---

477. **The Clever Brahman Girl.**—There were once two Bráhmans who lived in neighbouring cities, one of whom had a son and the other a daughter. The father of the girl sent a Bráhman and a barber to search for a match for his daughter and by chance they selected the son of the other Bráhman as her future husband. In due course they were married and after this the boy returned home at once leaving his wife with her father.

By and by his father who had wasted all his substance on the marriage, fell into extreme poverty. One day he said to his wife :—" We are starving and there is nothing for us but to sell the boy as a slave or eat his flesh." When the boy heard this he was afraid and ran away, and by chance came to the village in which his wife lived. But he did not know this and as her father was a very wealthy man and took pupils to whom he gave food and lodging, he went to stay in the house of his father-in-law. His wife too used to read with her father and the two, who knew not that they were husband and wife, became great friends and called each other brother and sister. Now in this city lived a reprobate Rájá who used to seize the wives and daughters of his subjects, and at last his servants came to the house of the Pándit and ordered him to send his daughter to the Rájá. He in his grief ordered his pupil to go with her. He was in great trouble but the girl told him to go to the Rájá and tell him that she would go to him if he would erect a palace with four gates facing the four corners of the sky and in one corner to put a leaf of *tulasi*, in a second water, in a third fire and in the fourth corn.

When the girl went to the Rájá after she sat with him for some time the Rájá who was chewing *pán* went into a corner of the room to spit; but when he saw the *tulasi* plant he did not dare defile the goddess and he went to the next corner, but in each he found a goddess sitting. So he came back to her ashamed and she said :—" O foolish Rájá. You call inanimate objects gods and goddesses and fear to defile them, but you have no fear of Bhagwán and wish to dishonour a Bráhman girl."

The Rájá bowed before her in shame and the boy took her home; but believing that the Rájá had dishonoured her he left her with her father and ran off to his home. His parents were delighted to see him and determined to bring his wife home. So when he and his friends came to claim his bride, he found that she was the daughter of the Pándit. He would not eat food there and ran away to Benares. His relatives returned without the bride and when the boy heard this he came home. Then his father-in-law asked him to come over and see him for one day. He made his son-in-law play at dice with his wife's mother. He first threw the dice with the words :—

Bar kul biyáhi bar badhn, háth pánw ek chitt ;
Kyún biyaho ? Kyun pariharyo ? Káran kah sumitt.

"I married the high born girl of the noble family to a youth who resembled her in every way. Why did you marry her and why did you divorce her friend ? If she be true let the throw be 12, if not let it be 17." The throw was 12. Then the Pándit asked his son-in-law to throw, but he refused and his mother-in-law threw the dice with the words :—

Mán Sarovar pánh gayon ; chonch pánwa nahín dinh.
Upar se jal taulke gawan páchhi kinh.

"I went to the Mán Sarovar lake but I did not dip my bill or feet in it. I merely measured the water from above and came back. Fall O dice on 12; if this be not so on 17. And the throw was 12."

Then the husband threw the dice with these words :—

Jehi márag kehari gayo ; gayo Gang trin mánk ;
So gayo bhágat phirat ; samujhi dekhu jiya mánh.

"The elephant saw the tracks of the lion on the Ganges bank and runs away in fear; reflect on this in your mind. O dice if she be true let the throw be 12; if not 17." And the throw was 12.

Then the girl threw with these words:—

Kehari kesh, phanig mani aur súr ke astra;
Sati payodhar, Bipra dhan, mue pai lágai hast.

"You may seize the mane of the lion, the gem of the snake, the weapons of a hero and the breast of the chaste woman or the property of a Bráhman only when they are dead. O dice if I am true let the throw be 12; if not 17." And 12 was the throw. The husband was then convinced of the innocence of his wife. He accepted food and water from her hands and brought her to his house.

(A folk-tale told by Motiram Pandit of Robertsganj, Mirzapur.)
[For chastity tests Mr. Jacobs (*Folklore Reports*, 1889) refers to Child's *English and Scotch ballads*, I, 266-71; II. 502.—ED.]

478. The Wisdom of the Daughter of Birbal.—One day Akbar sent for Birbal and said: "Procure me masons who will build a house neither on the ground nor in the sky."

When Birbal heard this order he was overcome with grief and was unable to eat. But his daughter came to him and said:—" Father, do not be distressed. Take some leave from the Emperor and I will arrange all."

So Birbal got his leave and his daughter bought some parrots and every day she used to teach them to say —

Pahunchâo int gára
Tab banai Imámabára.

"Bring bricks and mortar and let us build the Imambara."

When they had fully learnt their lesson one day Birbal went to the Emperor and as they were sitting together a flock of parrots flew over the palace crying:—*Pahunchâo int gára, táb banai Imámbára.*

When Akbar heard them he asked what this meant and Birbal replied:—" The masons are ready. If your majesty orders the materials to be brought they will build you a mosque between the earth and the sky." The Emperor laughed and said:—" You may call your masons. Who wants such a mosque to be built?"

(A folk-tale told by Girja Dayal, Kayasth of Ahmedabad, Lucknow district.)

479. The Prince and the Angel of Death.[1]—There was once a king who reached old age and was never blessed with a son. At last when he was well stricken in years Khuda blessed him with an heir. He was much pleased and, summoning the astrologers, required them to calculate the fortune of the prince. They consulted their books

[1] A folk-tale told by Ashraf, weaver of Hallia, Mirzapur district. Recorded by Pándit Rám Gharib Chaubé.

and after much consideration said:—" The prince will be very fortunate, but he will die on the seventh day after his marriage."

At this the king was sore troubled and passed his days in care until his son grew up, and fearing calamity, he never married him. At last the prince grew up and asked his father to find a wife for him. Then the king told him the sentence of the astrologers. The prince said:—" All astrologers are liars. Trust not to them. No one but Khuda knows what a man's fate is." So the king found a wife for him, but when he was married the prince feared for his life and leaving his bride rode off to escape his fate.

On the road he saw some men digging a grave and asked them whose it was.

"This is the grave of the prince who has run away to escape his fate," they answered.

In great fear he rode on and found a grave being dug and received the same answer. This happened again a third time. At this his soul nearly left his body, but seeing at a distance a mosque he thought to himself:

"If I am to die, better would it be to die in the house of Khuda."

So he bathed, changed his garments and entered the mosque. There some followers of Islám were praying and when they saw him overcome with grief they asked the reason and he told them his story.

"Pray for me," he implored, "that I may be saved from the Angel of Death."[2]

They consoled him and began to offer up prayers on his behalf. By and by the Angel of Death peeped through the door of the mosque.

"Friends" said he, "you have in your midst one whom Khuda is calling from your world. I have come for him. Make him over to me."

The believers asked:—" Art thou the Angel of Death!"

"I am" he answered.

"We pity" said they, "the fate of this youth. Is there no means by which his life may be spared?"

The Angel answered:—" If each of you give a portion of his span of life to him he may escape."

They agreed and prayed to Khuda to save him; and Khuda spared him. Then he started for home and on the road he found all the graves filled up. He recovered his bride, told the whole story to his father who prayed to Khuda with the prince and they all lived happily for many years.

[2] *Malaku'lmaut*, also called Izráíl. In the *Qurán*, *Surah* XXXII-11, we read: "The Angel of Death who is charged with you shall cause you to die: then ye shall be returned to your Lord."

MISCELLANEA.

480. A proverb : To kill two birds with one stone.—
Chalo sakhi tahán jaiyé jahán basen Vrij ráj ;
Goras bechan, Hari milan ek panth do káj.
" Come dear, let us go to the land of the lord of Braj, we will sell our milk and meet Krishna."

481. A verse on Hindi dialects:—
Antarvedi Nágari, Gauri Páras desa ;
Aru Arabi jamé milt misrit Bhásha desa.
" The dialect of the Duáb, of the Gauda land, mixed with Persian and Arabic, make the best Hindustani."

482. Chirághi.—Chirághi is a term used in Muhammadan country schools. These schools have a holiday on Friday and on the preceding evening each student is supposed to bring a few copper coins as a present to the Maulavi or teacher. This is known as Chirághi or " lamp money."

Also when Mussulmans go to worship a *pir*, they bring to the officiating priest an offering which is known by the same name. This is supposed to be spent on lighting the tomb of the saint.

Again, the man who allows gambling to go on in his house takes a fee known by the same name.—*W. Crooke.*

483. Jessore : Regard paid to crocodiles.—Besides the minor buildings erected by Khán Jahán, we find a large tank excavated by him containing eight tame crocodiles said to be the offspring of the two crocodiles kept by Khán Jahán and designated *dhálápar* and *kálópar* or "white side" and "black side." These crocodiles readily come at the call of the *faqir* and take the food offered to them. They are pretty well fed by native married women who desire to be in that interesting condition that ladies who love their lords are said to wish to be in, for, strange to say, crocodiles' blessings are reputed to ensure children to their liberal donors. We are at a loss to account for the esteem, any veneration, with which crocodiles are regarded by Muhammadans, for we read that in Panduah, a railway station between Húgli and Bardwan, there is, or was, a *faqír* who had tame crocodiles in a tank, and that on calling one of them by name Fateh Khán it obeyed the summons and appeared on the surface. (*Calcutta Review*, XXI, 183.) Again in Von Orlich's *Travels* there is mentioned a tank at Karáchi where he saw a score and ten crocodiles issue out of the water and at the direction of the *faqír* range themselves round him in a semi-circle. The Mussulmans are reputed to have a horror of lizards and it is curious that they should hold in esteem another member of the tanrian family.—*Calcutta Review,* LXIII, 10.

484. Stone in the bladder : a Charm to remove.—When a man is suffering from stone in the bladder he gets up very early in the morning and rolls for some time on the threshold of the house. He then eats a couple of radishes which have been exposed to the dew all night. A few days' repetition of this cures the disease.—*Pandit Rám Gharíb Chaubé.*

[For the respect paid to the threshold see *Introduction to Popular Religion and Folklore,* 151.—ED.]

485. Mahamans : Human flesh.—Mahaméns in its ordinary sense means human flesh ; but now it is applied to the selling of a daughter in marriage.—*Pandit Rám Gharíb Chaubé.*

486. Spell to injure an enemy.—When village women want to injure an enemy they make a cut on his wall with some sharp instrument in the hope that a would of the same kind may come on the body of their enemy. The technical name of this is *pachhna* and it is very common in village life.—*W. Crooke.*

487. The Saint Farid Shakarganj.—His food, a plan called the *farid múll* or *farid búti*, also called *ldikiya,* is very common in the Montgomery District. It is a small plant with flowers (*Farsetia Hamiltonii*). The seeds are said to be poisonous, but were habitually used by Farid Shakarganj when he was hungry.—*W. E. Purser : Settlement Report,* p. 20.

488. Weather lore.—If the asterism of *Swati* fall on the seventh of Asarh and it be foggy that day and the sun and moon are overcast, the rainy season will be very windy and there will be abundance of lightning. The rain will be abundant and the crops flourish. The same idea prevails regarding the seventh of Phálgun, Chait and Baisakh as well.—*Pandit Rám Gharíb Chaubé.*

489. Revenue Survey in Benares.—In 1849 Major Stewart was appointed to make a revenue survey of Benares : but he was so much opposed by the Revenue Officials that he was unable to make any progress. He is said to have resigned his appointment in the following couplet ;

Nahín napi, nahin napat hai, nahin napan ke jog;
Baithe ihwán khát hain bapure Káyasth log.

" It was not surveyed nor is it being surveyed. It will never be surveyed. The wretched Káyasths are eating up the public dues."—*Pandit Bhán Pratap Tiwari.*

490. Signs of famine.—If there be little dew in Magh little wind in Phalgun, little heat in Jeth, there is small chance of good rain. If there are many meteors seen at night, if there be much lightning, many halos round the sun and moon ; if a comet appear, numerous rainbows and many eclipses,—all these are bad signs of the season. If the fifteenth of the dark half of Pus fall on Saturday, or Tuesday the price of grain will be high and probably famine will prevail in the land. If the same day fall on Thursday or Friday, the opposite will be the case.—*Pandit Rám Gharíb Chaubé.*

491. Signs of the seasons.—If there be five Sundays in the months of Asarh, Sawan or Pus, epidemics will prevail ; if there be five Tuesdays, fear will spread in the land ; if five Saturdays, famine.—*Pandit Rám Gharíb Chaubé.*

492. Foreboding misfortune ; a proverb.—*Bigarne ke din jab áte hain, to Kunjarin ke sir men phora hota hai.* —" When evil times are coming the woman who sells vegetables says that she has a boil on her head." To the east of the province they say *bigare ki pankhi*—"When the death day of the white ant comes he takes to wings." *Pandit Rám Gharíb Chaubé.*

493. Gurgaon: Village deities: Bundela.—Bundela is only worshipped in times of sickness and especially cholera. He is the same as the Hardaur of the N.-W.P. In the last century, cholera broke out in Lord Hastings' army shortly after some cattle had been killed within the grove where lie the ashes of the Bundelkhand Chief Hardaul Lála. The epidemic was attributed to his wrath, and his lordship over cholera being thus established, he too is in many villages given a small shrine and prayed to remove pestilence when it visits the village.—*Mr. F. C. Channing : Settlement Report, p.* 34.

494. Black lips.—A man with black lips is dreaded in a village as much as one with a black tongue who is most dangerous. The curses of persons of this kind are in popular belief as bad as the bite of a mad dog.—*Pandit Rám Gharib Chaubé.*

The bear dance song as sung by the jungle people in Mirzapur—

*Nách re bhálu dhinnik dhinna tik dhain dhain tik.
Sás náché anagna, patohu náché kola ;
Aisanai sohágin daiya nit nit hola.
Ság rándhé, bhát rándhé, rándhe tit lauа.
Maugi jewan kare, nák legayo kauwa.
Re bhálu tik dhai dhai, dhinnik dhinnu dhinna.*

"O bear, dance, dance prettily. My mother-in-law dances in the courtyard ; the daughter-in-law in the little garden field. Old lady whose spouse is alive, such often happens. I cook vegetables, rice and bitter pumpkin. While the lady of the house eats the crow flies off with her nose. O bear, dance and dance pleasantly."—*Qazi Hamid Husain.*

495. Hoshyarpur: A charm to the Beyn stream near Garh shankar—

*Kya tú gajé, kya tú garkhé ;
Kya tu kardé dkar ?
Lohàran di ghar janam jo tera ;
Mund tera Garhshankar
Túhi Ganga, tuhi Jamund,
Túhi Satlaj Ráni ;
Dúm tera dúban lagá.
Rakhlein mahárani.*

"Why art though roaring, why rushing ? What art thou doing ? My birth is at the lohár's house, thy origin in Garhshankar. Thou art Ganges, thou art Jamuná ! Thou art Queen Satlaj ! Thy *mirdsi* is drowning ! Preserve him, O Great Queen.—*Settlement Report, p.* 216.

496. The house door.—A wise man should have the door of his house at the front and just in the middle of the wall. If it be on one side he will be led into useless expenditure.—*Pándit Rám Gharib Chaubé.*

497. Saharanpur: Agricultural superstitions.—In this district, Hindu farmers do not plough their fields on the first, fifteenth and eleventh days of the Hindu month. They do not plough also on Tuesdays as they believe that on these days Mother Earth is asleep. So in Bihar Sunday is regarded as sacred to Mahadeva and this year they generally begged and offered worship to him on that day. Here in nearly evey village is a shrine of the local god Bhumiya where they worship and feed Bráhmans at the end of each harvest.—*Pándit Rám Gharb Chaubé.*

498. Montgomery: The Saint Shah Muqim.—The town of Hujrah is remarkable chiefly for the shrines of Shah Muqim, who changed the name of the town, and of his great grandfather Lál Daháwal Sher, who used to ride about on a tiger, using a snake as a whip. He died about 1565. There is a tree with supposed miraculous powers at his tomb, and the present incumbent is said to have a *dast-i-ghaib* or "hidden hand," a charm or incantation by which a hidden hand supplies his wants.—*W. E. Purser : Settlement Report, p.* 42.

499. Visits of the bride to her husband's house after marriage.—If the bride remain in the house of her husband in the month of Jeth, it is supposed that her husband's elder brother will die ; if she stay in a *malamas* or intercalary month, her husband will die ; if in the month of Asarh, her mother-in-law will die ; if in the month of Pus, her father-in-law will die. If she stays in the house of her father in the month of Chait, he will die. These rules are carefully observed in regulating the *gauna* or visits of the nubile bride to her husband.—*W. Crooke.*

500. Eastern Districts : Means of saving the lives of children.—Hindus generally perform rites such as the shaving, investiture with the sacred cord, &c., with great pomp and ceremony. But when a man has lost sons in succession, this is unlucky, and the rites are performed in secret at some shrine. By this means it is believed that the child's life will be saved.—*Pándit Rám Gharib Chaubé.*

501. Gurgaon : Worship of the childless dead.—The sprits of young men who die childless are supposed to haunt the village, as are the ghosts of men who from any cause die dissatisfied and unwilling to leave their home. Such spirits are called euphemistically father (*pita*), but generally bear the character of being vindictive and requiring a great deal of attention. A little shrine very much resembling a fire-place (*chulha*) is generally constructed in their honour near a tank, and there offerings are made. Sometimes a *pita* descends on a person who becomes inspired, shakes his head, rolls his eyes and reveals the will of the *pita*. This is spoken of as "playing" (*khelna*). The village watchman of Damdama bears the reputation of being occasionally thus inspired.—*Mr. F. C. Channing : Settlement Report, p.* 35 *sq*

502. Heavenly bodies connected with rites.—When the sun is in its southern progress it is very unlucky. to perform the rite of *sthapna* or consecration of an idol, to commence to use a well or tank, to marry a child, to occupy a new house, to perform the shaving rite of a son, to install a *rájá*, to invest a boy with the Bráhmanical cord. These rites also should not be performed when Vrihaspati or Jupiter and Sukra or Venus have just risen or when they are setting or about to disappear from the sky.—*Pándit Rám Gharib Chaubé.*

503. Punishments inflicted in country schools.—When a pupil is constantly absent without cause and caning is ineffectual, he is made to walk on his knees for a certain time up and down the floor of the school' Another mode is to put two pair of bricks, one on the top of the other, some distance apart, and the boy is made to stand with one foot on each and with a pebble on his head. If he move and let the pebble drop he is caned.

Another plan is to make him bend down and grasp his big toes while he keeps a pebble on his back. If this fall he is caned.—*Pandit Rám Gharib Chaubé.*

504. **Eastern districts: Method of preventing constant visits of guests.**—When guests are too constant in their visits, the house-mother breaks the earthen vessels in which food was cooked for the last body of guests. This reduces the number in future.—*W. Crooke.*

505. **Jalandhar: Ceremonies at well-sinking.**—The sinking of a well is a very serious matter, and not to be lightly undertaken. If the projector is a Hindu, he consults a Bráhman, who will point out to him an auspicious time to begin work, and in some cases may show a favourable spot for the well. But the builder usually selects the ground himself, taking care to have it higher than the fields to be irrigated. In return for his trouble the Bráhman gets a rupee. Muhammadans, similarly, consult a *Qazi*. When the hour has come the person who is going to sink the well goes to the spot and marks out the circumference of the hole (*par*) in which the cylinder is to be sunk, and digs out four or five feet of the hole. This is called *tappa lagána*, and is celebrated by a meeting of the brotherhood who assist and are regaled on molasses.—*W. E. Purser: Settlement Report, p.* 100.

506. **Auspicious times.**—The first watch of the day is auspicious for Bráhmans and Rájás; the noon for Vaishyas; the afternoon for Sudras; the early part of the night for evil spirits and demons; midnight for rákshasas; the thirdwatch of the night for *nats*; and the fourth watch for cowherds and shepherds.—*Pandit Rám Gharib Chaubé.*

507. **The game of Faramosh.**—The game of *faramosh* is often referred to in the folk-tales. It is played by boys who are learning Persian. Two boys who are friends agree to say *yad hai*—" I remember." Whenever one gives anything to the other, the receiver of the article has to say *yad hai*; if he fails to do so, the other instantly shouts out *faramosh*—" forgotten."—*W. Crooke.*

508. **Gurgaon: Worship of the Panj Pir.**—Hindus regard the shrine of the Panj Pir as sacred to the Pandava brothers; the Muhammadans as sacred to five of their saints. A miraculous light is asserted to sometimes appear at midnight on these shrines.—*Mr. F. C. Channing: Settlement Report, p.* 35.

509. **The gall bladder of a bear.**—The gall bladder of a bear is a famous remedy in various diseases. It is commonly used in the case of infantile lockjaw or *jamua*, in *sukhandi* or consumption and in intermittent fever. The gall bladder is put in a bag with half a pound of chillies and in a couple of days the chillies absorb all the essence of it. In the case of *jamua* a little is given to the child mixed with the milk of the mother and in the case of the other diseases the patient has to chew five of the chillies and drink some water. It is essential to the cure that the patient should not know that the gall bladder has been placed with the chillies.—*W. Crooke.*

510. **A Charm to cure stomach-ache.**—When a person is suffering from stomach-ache some Sanskrit verses, of which the following is a translation, are repeated and the right hand is moved four times over the stomach of the patient when the pain will be relieved :—

"May the saint Agastya who devoured those powerful demons, Atapi and Batapi, and who drank up the great ocean, be propitious to the patient." To effect proper digestion of food call on the names of Agastya, Kumbhkarana, Sani and Barwanala, as well as Bhima, by whom this group of five is complete.—*Pandit Rám Gharib Chaubé.*

511. **New clothes: Rules about.**—If a man put on a new suit of clothes on Sunday he will be sure to get a new suit when that is worn out; if on Monday the clothes will be often defiled; if on Tuesday the wearer will suffer grief; if on Wednesday he will get money; if on Thursday his wit will improve; if on Friday he will meet his beloved; if on Saturday the clothes will be always dirty.—*Pandit Rám Gharib Chaubé.*

512. **Gurgaon: Worship of the Satti.**—*Sattis* are often worshipped. Thus in the village of Rojhka Gujar there is a shrine of a Gujarni *Satti* who has constituted herself the patroness of the Bráhman priests of the village, and unless they are properly looked after she gets angry and sends things into the bodies of the offenders, causing them pain; and then on the first day of the moon the Bráhmans have to be collected and fed at her shrine.—*Mr. F. C. Channing: Settlement Report, p.* 35.

513. **Gopalpur, Gorakhpur District: The worship of Udasi Baba.**—In a garden belonging to members of the Kausik clan of Rajputs in the village of Bisara near Gopalpur stands the tomb of a Sikh ascetic known as Udasi Bába who is much respected in that part of the country. He died only about twenty years ago, but numerous legends are now told of him. Though he used never to leave the cottage in which he lived, he could tell where the house of any man he saw was, in which direction its door was situated and how many persons were in his family. Though he had nothing in the shed in which he lived still he could always provide miraculously for the wants of any traveller who halted there. One time an enemy of his went to the Rájá of Gopálpur and said that he was a cheat and kept a store of food hidden inside his hut. In order to test him the Rájá went one day unexpectedly to visit him and asked for food. The Bába knew what was in the Rájá's mind so he asked him to go in and see whether there was anything in the hut. The Rájá went in and found it quite empty. The Bába told him to go in a second time and then he found a lot of sweetmeats laid out on plantain leaves. The Rájá was ashamed of his suspicions and fell at his feet in penitence. On another occasion a carpenter who was working close by suddenly found himself surrounded by a number of snakes and tigers, but at a word from the Bába they all disappeared. Many people have seen him walking on the surface of the river Sarju. If he rubbed any one with a pinch of the ashes of his fire he could cure the most long-standing disease. Even as he grew old he never showed any signs of age. He had many disciples and to this day crowds of people visit his grave.—*Pandit Rám Gharib Chaubé.*

North Indian Notes and Queries:
A MONTHLY PERIODICAL.

VOL. V.] FEBRUARY, 1896. [NO. 11.

Every communication must be accompanied by the writer's name and address, not necessarily for insertion, but as a guarantee of good faith. Every quotation from a book must be accompanied by its full title, publisher's and author's names, place and date of publication, volume and page.
Contributors are requested to write on ONE SIDE of the page only. If several contributions be sent at a time, they should be sent each on a separate sheet.
The Conductor cannot undertake to return, or be responsible for any MSS. not accepted.
All orders must be accompanied by cash. If not so accompanied, they will either not be attended to, or will be complied with per value-payable post.
Contributions should be addressed direct to W. CROOKE, ESQ., C.S., SAHARANPUR, N.-W. P., INDIA.

CONTENTS OF THIS NUMBER.
(The references are to the Notes.)

Popular Religion ... ... 181 to 185	Folk-tales ... ... 192 to 195
Anthropology ... ... 186 „ 191	Miscellanea ... ... 196 „ 198

POPULAR RELIGION.

514. **Names of gods written on the body.**—Hindus very often use clothes on which are printed the names of Ráma and Krishna. Vaishnava Sadhus have the footmarks, bows and arrows of Ráma printed on their arms. The Bairágis, followers of Chaitanya who are often found in Bengal and at Brindaban in the Mathura district, get the name of Hari printed all over the body. Their belief is, that marking the body in this way sanctifies it and is equivalent to the constant repetition of the name of the deity.—*Pándit Rám Gharíb Chaubé.*

515. **Lamps in Temples.**—In many Hindu temples, such as that of Bhaironji at Hardwar and in other Vaishnava shrines, lamps are kept burning perpetually. They say that unless this is done the objects of worshipping the deity will not be realised. If the lamp happen to go out, they perform a *homa* or fire sacrifice as a sort of propitiation. This is probably based on the ancient custom of maintaining the sacred fire as the ancient Bráhmans did and as the modern Agnihotris do still.—*Pándit Rám Gharíb Chaubé.*

[The lighting of the lamp is more probably a device to scare Bhuts and Rakshasas. See Introduction to *Popular Religion and Folklore,* 154.—ED.]

516. **Further account of the Dhala (cattle diseases charm).**—I have found two cattle-disease charms (Dhálá) in the village of Paniála in Saharanpur. I found them strung close to each other over one entrance to the village. They are not exactly the same.

No. 1 contains :—
    (a) 1 Chapni—(saucer)
    (b) Satnajá—(seven kinds of grain)
    (c) 2 Kathpháori — (a wooden scraper)
    (d) 2 Páori or Kharaúw—(pattens)
    (e) 1 Bájrang—(a representative of Hanumán)
    (f) 1 Soúta—(mace)

while No. 2 contains :—
    (a) 1 Chapni
    (b) Satnajá

(c) 2 Kharaúw
(d) 2 Soúta
(e) 1 Bajrang
(f) 2 Langotis

Cattle-disease has been very prevalent in Paniála, and there are numbers of small Dhálás, hanging on many yard-gateways and doorways. The simplest form appears to be a rope from which are suspended a chapni, painted with charms on the under side, and a *Satnajá*, *i.e.*, a bag containing seven different kinds of grain. The present charms are more elaborate containing in addition a number of implements, which are said to form part of Hanuman's outfit. The villagers allowed me to have these charms, as they said that, though "they had been up since Bhadon, they had done no good and it wouldn't be worth keeping them up any longer. *G. R. Dampier.*

517. The Harina Harin Stars.—Hindu mothers teach their children to point to the sky as they say these stars are the Stag and the Hind. Near them is a constellation which looks like a hunter armed with a bow and arrows. Of this they tell the following tale. There was once an Apsara in heaven known as Purva Chitti. She often lived in Brahma-loka or the land of Brahma. One day she was dancing and all the gods were looking on. Brahma became enamoured of her beauty and wished to have her for himself. He pursued her and she was changed into a hind. He changed himself into a stag and continued pursuing her. Siva was wroth at this conduct of Brahma and assuming the form of the Ardra asterism went to aid the hind. This frightened Brahma and he desisted from the chase and so they are still in these forms in the heavens.—*Pandit Rám Gharib Chaubé.*

518. Graves of Muhammadan Martyrs.—A learned Muhammadan tells me that though the martyrs of the faith appear to ordinary eyes to be dead they did not really die. Their graves have an opening caused by supernatural agency through which a soft and scented wind continually blows. They see and hear all that passes around them, but they cannot take any active part in human affairs as their legs below the waist are cold and stiff in the grave and only their upper limbs have any power.—*W. Crooke.*

519. Muhammadans; Guardian Spirits.—According to Muhammadan belief every one has born with him a guardian spirit which is known as Hamzád or "born with him." If a man die in a state of ceremonial pollution the Hamzád does not accompany his soul. The soul goes alone or remains confined in the grave. The Hamzád in the utmost grief looks everywhere for his companion and when he cannot find him sits disconsolate at the grave and prays for him. These wandering Hamzáds, according to general belief, join the rank of the Jinn. Sometimes in grave-yards the sound of the prayers of these guardian spirits are heard at night, but when any one goes near them they become silent.

On this point Dr. Hughes (*Dictionary of Islám* 605) writes "The souls of the faithful are said to be divided into three classes—(1) those of the Prophets who are admitted into paradise immediately after death ; (2) those of the martyrs who according to the tradition of Muhammad rest in the crops of green birds, which eat of the fruits and drink of the waters of Paradise; (3) those of all other believers, concerning the state of whose souls there is great diversity of opinion. Some say they stay near the graves either for a period of only seven days, or according to others, until the Day of Resurrection. In proof of this they quote, the example of Muhammad, who always saluted the spirits of the departed when passing a graveyard. Others say all the departed spirits of the faithful are in the lowest heaven with Adam, because the Prophet declared he saw them there in his pretended ascent to heaven, while others say the departed spirits dwell in the forms of white birds under the throne of God, which is a Jewish tradition. All Baizawis say the souls of the wicked are carried down to a pit in hell called Sijjin ; and there is a tradition to the effect that Muhammad said that the spirits of the wicked are tormented until the Day of Resurrection, when they are produced with their bodies for judgment. The author of the *Sharhu-'l-Mawaqif* says that some Muslim philosophers state that after death the spirit of man will either be in a state of enlightenment or ignorance. Those who are in a state of ignorance will go on from worse to worse and those who are in a state of enlightenment will suffer only so far as they have contracted qualities of an undesirable character while in the body, but they will gradually improve until they arrive at a state of perfect enjoyment. This view is, however, not one which is tenable with the views propounded by the Qurán, in which there are very decided notions regarding the future state of heaven and hell."—*W. Crooke.*

520. Muhammadan Ideas of Death and Judgment.—Muhammadans commonly believe that criminals who have been sentenced to death, if when on the scaffold they turn their faces towards the sacred place at Mecca, are blessed and do not incur judgment at the Day of Resurrection. This they say was the case with Nawab Shams-ud-dín who was executed for participation in the murder of Mr. William Frazer the Resident at Delhi: When he was being hanged he turned his face to the west and was hence regarded as a martyr to the faith.—*Pandit Ram Garib Chaubê.*

---

521. Saharanpur; the demon Allah Bakhsh.—Like Pir Sultan Sarwar, Allah Baksh the demon of the town of Gangoh "comes on the heads" of the people of the neighbourhood and inspires them. Any one who comes under the influence of the demon becomes gifted with powers of extraordinary eloquence and is able to repeat long passages of the Qurán, though he may have previously been illiterate.

The legend of this demon is thus told:—He was a very highly educated scholar and was by his knowledge of science able to bring under his control two kinds of evil spirits—the Muakkil and the Jinnas. The difference between these two varieties of evil spirits is in popular belief that the former love cleanliness and the latter all kinds of impurity; the former can show to him who subdues them all heavenly, and the latter all wordly things. Now Allah Bakhsh got a Muakkil into his power and as long as he was pure he could make him do what he pleased; but if he chanced to become impure the Muakkil ruled him. Allah Bakhsh was a weaver by caste and after some time he became infatuated with a sweeper woman. By this he lost his purity and the Muakkil became his master. One day after he had become impure by association with his paramour and was about to cleanse himself by bathing in a tank, the Muakkil took advantage of him and flung him into the water with such violence that he expired.

As he had died in a state of impurity he became after his death an evil spirit and was buried in his native town. His mistress also soon after died and was buried by the side of her lover. She turned into a Dáin, or witch, and she too "comes upon the head " of the people of the place.

One day it so happened that the demon " came on the head " of a woman of the potter caste. She was at the time engaged in picking up dry cow-dung in the jungle to feed the kiln of her husband. Just at that time a learned Maulavi named Hájí Khuda Baksh who had bought a village in the neighbourhood was passing through the jungle. She saw him and addressed him in the words *Salám Alaikum* ! He replied *Alaikum us salám* and asked who she was. She said:—" I am Allah Baksh who was once a very famous Maulavi and now I have become a Jinn."

The Maulavi asked:—" What do you want with me?" She answered:—" I want nothing from you. I am now going to leave this potter woman; but I give you this blessing, that whenever you come near a person whom I possess, I will at once leave him "

So saying the demon disappeared and the potter woman recovered her senses. Thus the Maulavi became a very famous magician and he used to be always called in to cure any one possessed of an evil spirit. Whenever he approached, the demon used to abandon the patient at once.—*W. Crooke.*

---

522. How to remove impurity incurred on a fast-day.—If any one touch a person on a fast-day who has been guilty of murder, he can remove the impurity by bathing, looking at the sun and reciting one of the sacred books. If you have a sinful thought you can purify yourself by naming Vishnu one hundred and eight times. If you tell a lie on a fast-day, you must repeat the Mantra of Vishnu, *Om Vishave Namah*, " I invoke the Lord Vishnu," one hundred and eight times. If you touch an impure person, man or woman, you should bathe and repeat the Gayatri one hundred and eight times. Even to look at an impious man on a fast-day is sinful, but the sin can be removed by looking at the sun and saluting him.—*Pandit Ram Gharib Chaubê.*

---

523. Black Magic; various means to injure an enemy.—Take some ashes from a cremation or burying ground, mix it with poison and some powdered Dhatúra seeds, and throw it at your enemy on a Tuesday when he is not on the watch.

Get some of the plant called Bhendawa, extract the oil, mix it with water and fling it on your enemy on a Tuesday. The charm is enhanced if to it be added the teeth of a black snake and some powdered Dhatúra.

Powder the bone of a dead man. Mix it in water and give it to your enemy to eat with some betel and he will die. Powder the bone of a snake and throw it at your enemy.

Get on a Tuesday a burnt stick from a funeral pile when the Bharani asterism prevails, and fix it in front of your enemy's house. If you do not remove the stick, within a month your enemy will die.

Get a scale from a snake, make a lamp wick of it. Get some Dhatúra oil and burn the wick in it. Take some of the lamp-black and put it on the eyes of your enemy. He will die.

To make these charms truly effectual you must say the following Mantra 125,000 times :—*O Namo Kal rupáy Amukám bhasur kuru kuru, Swáha.*—" O thou like the god of death destroy my enemy ; I salute Thee."

On the day the charm is used this should be said 108 times.—*Pandit Ram Gharib Chaubé.*

---

524. Moon Worship.—Women in the North-Western Provinces will not allow their children to point at the moon with a burning brand, as they say it brings on them the wrath of Chunda Mái, the moon goddess.

In connection with this they tell the following tale—

In old times in the city of Indraprastha or old Delhi there was a Brahman named Veda Dhama, who had as his wife Ultama Lilávati. She had seven powerful sons and one daughter named Virávati, who was married to a learned Brahman. She used always to fast in honour of the moon on the 4th of the dark fortnight in the month of Kartik. She never ate food until she had offered libations to the moon. Soon after she went to the house of her husband this feast day came round, and as usual she fasted, bathed, plastered a piece of ground under a banyan tree and placed there the images of Siva, Parvati and Ganesa. She worshipped them and prayed them to give prosperity to her husband, herself and the whole family. But she could not eat if the moon had not risen and she had not offered her customary libation. Exhausted with hunger, she fell down senseless. Then her husband, when he saw her state, climbed to the top of the tree and held a burning brand in his hand. He called out to his wife "See ! the moon has appeared in the sky !" She was out of her senses with exhaustion, and believing him, made her usual oblation to the supposed moon. Then she ate her food.

That night her husband was struck dead by the wrath of the offended moon. Virávate knew the cause of the planet's anger : so she prayed to the Moon and kept the corpse of her husband unburnt till the next feast-day came round. Then she made her prayer to the moon and after offering the libation, poured a few drops out of the cup on the corpse of her husband, who woke at once and complained that he had overslept himself.

She told him what had happened, how he had offended the moon and how she had secured forgiveness. So he too became a faithful worshipper of the moon.

Since then this tale is told by women and they worship the moon on the 4th day of Kártik and pour libations to her out of an earthen vessel with a spout, which is considered an act of piety and likely to secure the prosperity of the family. After worship the vessel is made over to a Bráhman.—*W. Crooke.*

---

525. Touching a cat or mouse.—Among high-caste Hindus, to touch a cat or a mouse on a fast-day defiles a man. The impurity is removed by washing the hands and feet and rinsing out the mouth.—*Pandit Ram Gharib Chaubé.*

---

526. Cholera caused by an offended deity. —This year cholera has prevailed with great severity in my village, Gopálpur in the Gorakhpur District. This is very generally attributed to the anger of the local goddess, Akhara ki Bhawáni. The year before last a Bhát who was her priest and " on whose head she used often to come" and deliver oracles, died, and the Rája took no steps to appoint a successor to him. The result was that no worship was done to the goddess last year and she became seriously offended. Hence she has sent cholera this year on the village as a punishment, and though since the commencement of the outbreak several costly ceremonies have been done in her honour, she up to the present time shows no signs of relenting and this year cholera has gone on well into the cold weather. I have several times advised the people to clean up their houses, so as to please the goddess during the nightly rambles which she takes through the village, but to no avail. No one can say at present how long she may continue persecuting this unfortunate village.—*Pandit Ram-Baksh Chaubé.*

---

527. The saint Baba Farid Shakkarganj of Pakpattan.—The saint Baba Farid Shakkarganj of Pakpattan possessed the power of going any distance in a moment. But he would never admit that any one was greater than his religious guide Qutub-ud-din Bakhtiyár Khákhi. One day he was sent by his master to purchase supplies in the bazar at Delhi and, as usual, he went there from Pakpattan in a moment of time. As he was standing at the shop of a confectioner making some purchases a faqir appeared in the bazar and said : " If any one looks on my face he will escape the fire of hell." When they heard this, all the people of the city flocked out to behold him ; but Farid remembering his preceptor, hid in a corner of the shop until the faqir had departed, and then he did his business and went home.

Qutub-ud-din asked him the cause of his delay and when he told him the saint blessed him said:— "My son, you acted rightly. This faqir may be able to save men from the fire of hell. But look at the gate of my hermitage. Whoever passes beneath it is safe from both the fire of hell and earth. If any one pass beneath this gate, if he take off his clothes and fling them into the fire they will not be consumed, and he will never be subject to the fire of hell."

And this has come true. Hence every pious man walks once beneath the gate of the saint and wins salvation in this world as well as in the next.—*W. Crooke.*

528. **A song to Devi.**

Durga Devi nit uthi sumiriye ji, karaj awai rás.
Parbat Sri Chandika Ji ban khand men bás.
Ban khand men bás pás Lileswar Mahadeva.
Gauri Shankar au Gangaji, Jin ki kartin sewa.
Billeswar au Til Bhandeswar charhai supari mewa
Krishnanand to kharo puháre, jay jay Durga deva.

"If you repeat the name of Durga in the morning your object will be realised. Chandika Devi lives in the hills and in the forest land. Near her are Lileswar and Gauri Shankar, Mahadeva and mother Ganges. They serve the mother Chandi. To Billeswer and Tilbhandeswar are offered betel nuts and fruits. Krishnanand the poet stands and cries—Victory to the lady Durga!"—*Pandit Ram Gharíb Chaubé.*

529. **Dhanu Bhagat, a dufud Banjara.**—In the Western District of the North-Western Provinces, the image of Dhánu Bhagat is almost invariably found associated with that of Durga in many of the most important temples of the goddess. They say he was a Banjára who was a devoted worshipper of the goddess. For three successive ages of the world he offered his head to her, but even this devotion did not propitiate her. In the Iron age when he offered his head as usual, the goddess, observing the general impiety of the world, accepted the offering and after sending his spirit to heaven gave him the blessing that he should be worshipped in association with her at all her principal temples.

There are a number of songs in honour of Dhánu Bhagat which will be given in a later number of this periodical.—*W. Crooke.*

530. **Divination by the peacock.**—A favourite mode of divination used by rural sorcerers is to draw the figure of a peacock and to direct the man who wants his fortune told to place a blade of grass on some part of the bird. According to the following verse the result is foretold.

Chonch dukh, pankhe maran, kanthe hoe miláp;
Udar bhojan, punchh dhan, mastak páwe ráj;
Jo shubh lakhshan pag pare, ghar baithe mangal chár.

"If the person making the test puts the grass on the bill of the bird he will be put to trouble; if on the feathers he will die; if on the throat he will meet with success; if on the stomach he will get food; if on the tail he will get riches; if on the head he will be a Raja; if on the feet there will be rejoicings at his house."—*Pandit Ram Gharíb Chaubé.*

531. **Barring the return of the ghost from the cremation ground.**—Among the low castes of Northern India it is the custom after burning a corpse for the mourners to bathe, and when they are about to go home they take in their right hands a vessel full of water, and when they are about to leave the place they turn from, and look in the direction of home and fling the water-vessel behind them. It is broken and the water is sprinkled on the site of the pyre. Then they walk home, taking care on no account to look back. They believe that by this rite the ghost of the dead person is deharred from accompanying them home, which it otherwise would certainly do.—*W. Crooke.*

532. **Rules about serving food to Brahmans and other guests.**—When a man is entertaining Brahmans or other guests, he should bring the food from the kitchen with both hands; if a dish is brought with one hand the demons suck all that is good in it. When a feast is being given in honour of the deceased ancestors of the family, Brahmans should be first fed with sweetmeats, various preparations of rice. After the Brahmans are served he should go into the kitchen again and after washing his hands and face bring out the rest of the food for the tribesmen. After they are fed, some should be given to mendicants.

As he begins to serve the food he should invoke the aid of the ancestors and gods to bring the feast to a successful conclusion. While the Brahmans and other guests are eating, the house master should fan them to scare evil-minded ghosts which often intrude and consume the offerings. All regard for rank should be abandoned when guests are being fed.—*Pandit Ram-Gharíb Chaubé.*

ANTHROPOLOGY.

533. Customs at Patna.—In his interesting *Travels of a Hindu*, Bholanath Chandra writes of Patna that there are two peculiarities of the people of that place, one that they celebrate their marriages only in January and February and the other that a Hindu dying there is not burnt at Patna, but on the other shore. He suggests as a reason of this that the ancient Magadha may have been a banned land as not being included in the territory of the Aryas. Recent enquiries show that the dead are not burnt at Patna because the land of Magah or Magadha is considered so unholy that if a man die in it he is sure to be born an ass in the next birth. The same idea applies to Ramnagar on the bank of the Ganges opposite Benares, and pious Hindus will not let their friends die there.—*Pándit Rám Gharíb Cháubé.*

534. The game of Pachisi.—Can any one say what is the origin of the game of Pachisi? Is there anything to show that it is earlier than the Muhammadan invasion? There are places pointed out where marks on the rocks indicate that the Pandavas played Pachisi (See Introduction to *Popular Religion and Folklore* 302.) Is there any evidence that Pachisi was played in early Hindu times? Akbar used, they say, to play Pachisi with girls in the squares in the courtyard of his palace at Fatehpur Sikri. The following account of the game is given by Bholanath Chandra in his *Travels of a Hindu* and is said to be taken from an old Agra periodical.—" The game is usually played by four persons, each of whom is supplied with four wooden or ivory cones, which are called Goti, and are of different colours for distinction. Victory consists in getting these four pieces safely through all the squares of each rectangle into the vacant place in the centre—the difficulty being that the adversaries take up in the same way as pieces are taken at Backgammon. Moving is regulated by throwing cowries whose apertures falling uppermost or not affect the amount of the throw by certain fixed rules. But on this Titanic board of Akbar's, wooden or ivory Gotis would be lost altogether. Sixteen girls, therefore, dressed distinctively—say four in red, four in blue, four in white, four in yellow,—were trotted up and down the squares taken up by an adversary, and put back at the beginning again, and at last after many difficulties four of the same colour would find themselves giggling into their doppattas together in the middle space and the game was won."

Can anyone give the rules of the game exactly or say where they may be found? Any information on the subject will be very welcome.—*W. Crooke.*

535. Finger amputation.—Among one branch of the Morasu Wakligars a section of the Wakligars or Wokkaligars, *i.e.*, farmers or cultivators of Maisúr, there is a custom of amputating the ring finger or little finger of the right hand of every woman previous to piercing the ears of her eldest daughter preparatory to betrothal. It is performed by the village blacksmith. The finger is placed on a block, a chisel is placed over the articulation of the joint, and the finger is chopped off at one blow. If the girl is motherless and the future mother-in-law has not suffered amputation she must perform the operation on the girl *Mysore and Coorg Gazetteer* I, 338.

Can any one explain this custom or give instances of similar mutilations in any other part of India?—*Ed.*

536. Gorakhpur.—Titles used by women for different low-caste males and females.

Name of the caste.	Titles used.	
	Male.	Female.
(1) Koiri	Mahto	Mahtiun.
(2) Ahir	Mahrá	Mahrin.
(3) Kahár	Do.	Do.
(4) Chamár	Do.	Do.
(5) Nái	Thákur	Thakurain.
(6) Dhobi	Barethá or Rana	Barethin. Rane.
(7) Bania	Sáhu	Sahuain.
(8) Brahman	Pandit	Panditáin.
(9) Kayasth	Lálá	Laláin.
(10) Sonár	Do.	Do.
(11) Bhuihár	Rái	Rayáin.
(12) Kshatri	Babu	Babuáin.
(13) Atith	Gosáin	Gosáini.
(14) Barhai	Mistri	Mistráni.

If a woman do not use proper names for particular castes she is considered wanting in good breeding. By women I mean here women of the high-caste Hindus.

Rám Bakhsh Chaubé.

537. **On some Superstitions regarding Drowning and Drowned Persons.**[*]—Anthropologists have come to the conclusion that the principle of animism has its origin in the belief that every locality has its presiding spirits. This stage of belief is principally the characteristic of savage races, and still survives as relics of primitive faith among peoples who have now adopted the amenities of civilization. Primitive men believed that every mountain, rock, and valley, every well and stream and lake, is the abode of some spirits. This belief again originates from the association of the idea of personal life with that of motion, just as the swaying of a tree appeared to the mind of primitive man to be a proof of personal life like the flight of birds or the movements of animals. This idea became gradually developed and, in conjunction with dreams during sleep, reminiscences of the dead and accidental associations of motionless objects with motion (as a rock in the midst of a rapid or eddy), gave rise to animism or spiritism. Primitive man was awe-struck at the majesty and grandeur of a mountain, and, inwardly reflecting that such majesty and grandeur can only belong to spirits or beings superior to himself, believed the mountain to be the local habitation of the same beings.

Relics of savage animism are still to be met with among civilized races, such as the mountain-worship of the Japanese, the well-worship as prevailing in the different counties of Great Britain and Ireland, and the river-worship of the Hindus. The Ainos, who are the aboriginal inhabitants of Japan, profess "the rudest and most primitive form of nature-worship, *the attaching of a vague sacredness to trees, rivers, rocks, and mountains,* and of vague notions of power for good or evil to *the sea, the forest, the fire, and the sun and moon.*"[1] This belief still survives among the modern Japanese who worship mountains. Miss Bird says (page 108 of Vol. I. of her work): "Mountains for a great part of the year clothed or patched with snow, piled in great ranges round Nantaisan, their monarch, are worshipped as a god." At page 122 of the same volume, she again says: "The mountain peak of Nantaisan is worshipped and on its rugged summit there is a small Shinto shrine with a rock beside it on which about one hundred rusty sword-blades lie—offerings made by remorseful men whose deeds of violence haunted them till they went there on a pilgrimage and deposited the instruments of their crimes before the shrine of the mountain-god."

In the same manner, primitive men believed that every river has its presiding spirit, and instances of this belief are still to be met with among peoples of savage culture. The Tshi-speaking peoples of Africa believe in a great spirit, Prah, which presides over rivers, and to whom they offer human sacrifices, one adult male and one adult female, in the belief that the spirit can do harm to the people through the agency of the rivers. By the principle of substitution, offerings of flowers, fruits, sweets, cereals and incense, which the Hindus of Bengal offer every year to the Ganges, Brahmaputra, Padma, Nerbudda and other rivers, have become substituted for the human sacrifices which are offered by savage peoples to the great river-spirit.

Traces of the belief that every river, sea, and other bodies of water have presiding spirits, and that they require human sacrifices, are to be found even at the present day in the shape of various superstitions about drowning and drowned persons, which are prevalent among civilized peoples. Hence is the reluctance displayed by some peoples to save a man from drowning if he falls into the river or the sea. In the Solomon Islands, when a man falls into the river and is attacked by a shark, he is neither helped out of the water nor is he assisted in warding off the attack of his marine assailant. If the person anyhow manages to escape from the bloody fangs of the shark, his fellow-tribesmen again throw him into the water so that the shark may make a meal of him. This they do under the impression that the victim is destined to become a sacrifice to the river-god.[2] Another form of this antipathy to saving a drowning man obtains in Scotland, and has been recorded by Sir Walter Scott in his novel entitled *The Pirate*. In that story the peddler Bryce refused to assist Mordant in saving the life of the shipwrecked sailor from drowning and even rated him roundly for attempting to do such a thing. I will reproduce the conversation which took place between the two, because it shows the motive for not assisting a man from getting drowned. Bryce said:—"Are you mad? You that have lived sae lang in Zetland to risk the saving of a drowning man? Wot ye not if ye bring him to life again, he will be sure to do you capital injury?" The origin of this belief is stated by some to be the idea that the person rescued from being drowned would, some day or other, inflict mischief on the man who saves his life. Others say that it has its foundation in the belief that, as rivers and seas are entitled to get human sacrifices, the presiding spirits of those bodies of water would wreak their vengeance on those who

---

[*] By Mr. Sarat Chandra Mittra, M.A., B.L.,—*Pleader, Judge's Court, Chapra, Behar.*

[1] Miss Bird's *Unbeaten Tracks in Japan,* Vol. II., p. 94.

[2] Codrington's *The Melanesians,* p. 179.

prevent them from getting victims, as is illustrated by the item of folklore from the Solomon Islands or by that prevailing in the Orkneys and Shetlands. It is said that "among the seamen of the Orkneys and Shetlands it was deemed unlucky to rescue persons from drowning, since it was held as a matter of religious faith that the sea is entitled to certain victims, and if deprived would avenge itself on those who interfere."[3]

The superstition that the water-spirit, if despoiled of his victim, would wreak vengeance on the person who deprives him of the sacrifice due to him, is prevalent in one form or another, among many races in various parts of the world. It existed among the sea-faring population of Great Britain and Ireland and especially among those of Cornwall. The sea-faring community of France, the boatmen who ply their vocation on the river Danube and the common peasant folk of Russia also share in this belief. Formerly a superstitious belief was current amongst the Bengalis that a water-spirit in the form of an old hag—called गेड़नी—haunts tanks and ponds and, when any person goes thereto, she fetters that person's feet with an invisible chain. The victim was allowed to go wherever he liked, dragging the invisible chain, so long as the daylight lasts, but as the shades of evening begin to fall, the गेड़नी begins to withdraw the chain, and therewith, the victim is gradually drawn within the waters of the tank and ultimately drowned therein. This superstition which could formerly be always heard from the lips of credulous gaffers and gammers, is now fast vanishing away before the progress of English education and enlightenment, and now only lingers as a relic in the threat with which Bengali infants are frightened, namely, that, should they become naughty, the गेड़नी will catch them and take them away Another mythical being named बग was believed to exist in Bengal formerly. It was supposed to guard hidden treasure and to reside in tanks. It was also said in respect of this being that if anybody went to take the treasure in charge of the बग, he was dragged into the water by that spirit and killed by being submerged into it. This bit of folklore is also disappearing. The Siamese believe in a water-spirit called Pnuk who, they say, seizes those who go to bathe in the water and drags them into his habitation thereunder. The Sioux Indians entertain a similar belief in a water-demon whom they call Unk-tahe and who, they believe, kills men by dragging them underneath the water, in a way similar to that of the Siamese spirit. The Kamschatkadales refuse to help a drowning man out of the water, on account of some similar superstitous scruples. If such a man was anyhow rescued, no one of his fellow-tribesmen would allow him to enter his house or give him food, but on the other hand, would take him for one who is dead. The Chinese also display a similar sort of reluctance to save a drowning man because they believe that the spirit of the drowned man hovers over the water till it succeeds in killing a fellow-creature by dragging him underneath the water and thereby drowning him. It is also popularly believed by the Hindus of Bengal that the spirits of persons who have come by their deaths from drowning, haunt the tanks and wells in which they have been drowned. Persons are afraid of going to such tanks and wells, after night-fall, from a superstitious dread that the ghost of the drowned man would be sure to appear to him, or some other evil would happen to him. The waters of such tanks and wells are considered impure and unclean until those receptacles of water are re-consecrated, and thus rendered pure, by performing some होम or sacrifice or some *Jagna*. Like the Bengalis, the Japanese also consider the water of wells wherein persons have been drowned, as impure. Miss Bird, at page 184 of Vol. I. of her above-quoted work, says :—"I have passed two wells which are at present disused in consequence of recent suicides by getting drowned in them." There is a belief current among the people of Bangalore in Mysore that the spirits of those persons who have been drowned, possess women.[4]

There are some omens which are superstitiously believed to prognosticate death from drowning. Before the days of the Suez Canal, ships used to come to India by the route round the Cape of Good Hope. European sailors believed that a phantom ship, which they called the "Flying Dutchman," used to sail near the Cape and would appear to passing vessels in times of storms. Sailors believed that the vessel which sighted the "Phantom Ship" would surely come to grief, and all the crew on board the vessel would be drowned. Captain Marryat has founded the plot of his novel *The Phantom Ship* upon the legend of the "Flying Dutchman." There is a superstition in Bengal to the effect that if a single female rides in a boat in which there are male passengers only, it is believed by the lower classes of Bengalis that the boat would come to grief and the passengers be drowned. To obviate this evil, the single female passenger must tie a knot in her cloth remembering the name of another female. I once saw a curious illustration of this superstition. In May or June, 1884, I

---

[1] Tudor's *The Orkneys and Shetlands*, p. 19.

[4] "Note on a Mode of Obsession, which dealt with the belief in a part of Bangalore in the Possession of Women by the Spirits of Drowned Persons," by F. Fawcett, in the *Journal of the Anthropological Society of Bombay*, Vol. I., No. 8.

had occasion to go over to Seebpore on the other side of the river Hooghly. I hired a boat from the Colvin's Ghat, Calcutta, and was crossing the river. While in mid stream, the wind began to blow a regular gale, and the boat was tossed to and fro. My fellow-passengers began to tell me that the rough weather was the consequence of the presence of a single female who was a passenger in the same boat with us. On a previous occasion also, while going to Seebpore, I was accompanied by a single female—a relative of mine—and, when stepping into the boat, I saw her tie a pice in a corner of her cloth remembering the name of another female, as there was no other female passenger in that boat. This she did to obviate the consequences of the popular belief that a boat with a single female passenger would come to grief. There are also the Bengali superstitions that women who have got children must not put water into a vessel containing lime after taking their meal, otherwise their children will get drowned.[5] Also a person who dreams that he is drowned in mire, ought to know that such dream prognosticates an early death to him.[6] The Bengali Hindus also believe that those persons who have got convolutions of hair (peculiar growth of the hair in a spiral form which is called in Bengali ঘূর পাক), are sure to get drowned. I came across a curious instance of this superstition lately. In the beginning of August last, a nephew of a Bengali pleader of the Chupra Bar got drowned while bathing in the River Saraju, which flows past this town. While on a visit of condolence to the bereaved gentleman, another Bengali gentleman—also a pleader of the local Bar—asked one of the uncles of the drowned boy whether the deceased had got a convolution of hair in his head. On being informed that he had got one, the gentleman told us all that when the deceased had got such convolution of hair he was sure to have died by drowning. The aforesaid gentleman also informed us that his second son had also got a similar convolution of hair, and that he was afraid lest he (his son) should also get drowned. He further told us that in consequence of his son's possessing such convolution, he did not allow him (his son) to go to bathe either in a tank or in the river.

There are also certain processes, which, if had recourse to, would prevent a person from getting drowned. The performance of certain religious ceremonies are also supposed to have the same effect. Sailors believe that if a portion of the caul which covers the face of some children at the time of birth, be worn as an amulet round the neck, the person wearing it will not get drowned.

In Bengal, it is sometimes believed that if a person accidentally eats ants along with sweets or other eatables, he will not get drowned. When a person is about to go to a distant part of the country and will have to cross rivers, the Hindus of Bengal, previous to the person's starting on his journey, offer *pujahs* to the goddesses of the rivers Ganges, Brahmaputra, Padma, Nerbudda, &c., &c., so that any mishap may not occur to him in the river. In our own family at Calcutta, I have observed similar *pujahs* offered to the family idol Nárayana (who in this case is supposed to represent those river-goddesses), before any member the family undertakes a journey to a distant part wherein he will have to cross rivers, simply for the purpose of appeasing the river-goddesses, who will, therefore, preserve him from all accidents in the rivers. The Bengal boatmen cry *Badar, Badar*, when a boat is in danger of capsizing, in the belief that doing so would cause the vessel to reach its destination safely. The Ainos, who are the aborigines of Japan, believe that if they throw the images of their gods,—which are nothing but wands and posts of peeled wood, whittled nearly to the top, from which the pendent shavings fall down in white curls,—into rivers, streams, rapids, and other dangerous places, they will be able to cross them safely.[7] The Japanese worship a god who, they believe, saves men from drowning and accident. They have also an amulet which saves persons from drowning.

Miss Bird says:—"The amulet which saves from drowning is a certain cure for choking, if courageously swallowed."[8] The Kakhyens of Burma worship a Nat called the *Khakoo Khanam*—the god of water—on the occasion of anyone getting drowned. They also worship another Nat, named the Ndong Nat (Aing-peen Nat of the Burmese) — the god of the outside of Home—who, they believe, resides in the house, but *is worshipped by them outside if one of the family is killed by drowing*. The Mahomedans, when undertaking journeys by water, utter, as a protective from drowning, the following formula, which is contained in Surah Nooh of the Koran:—

بسم الله مجريها ومرسها ان ربي لغفور الرحيم

The whole may be transliterated in Roman character thus,—" Bismilláheh Majrihá O Mursáhá inná rabi-il-ghafur ur-rahim." The origin of this custom is contained in the following legend, which may be thus narrated in Urdu:—

قصہ طوفان حضرت نوح علیہ السلام کا مشہور ہی پر مختصر
یہ ہی کہ طوفان شروع ہوا حضرت نوح علیہ السلام ہر ایک

[5 and 6] *Vide* items Nos. 150, 155, and 189 in paper "On Popular Superstitions in Bengal," published in the *Journal of the Anthropological Society of Bombay*, Vol. I, p. 345.

[7] Bird's *Unbeaten Tracks in Japan*, Vol. II., p. 95.
[8] *Op. cit* Vol. I., pp. 379 and 380.

جانوروں کا ایک ایک جوڑا اور بیاد سے رقصوں لے ساتھہ
کشتی میں سوار ہولے باقی لوگ حتی کہ ایک لڑکا حضرت
نوح علیہ السلام کا بھی بہ سبب نافرمانی کے غرق ہوا تمام
روئے زمین دریا ہوا درختوں اور پہاڑوں سے جب (۴۰)
چالیس گز پانی بالا ہوا اہل کشتی شدت باد اور کثرت
امواج سے بد حواس اور زندہ گی سے مایوس ہولے حکم الہی
ہوا بسم اللہ مجریہا و مرسٰها إنَّ ربي لغفورالرحیم جو کولی
ورد زبان کریگا حق تعالیٰ اوسکی سب مشکلات آسان کریگا
اللہ تعالیٰ نے اپنے اسم کے برکت سے اونکو ڈوبنے سے اور
طوفان موقوف ہوا ۹

The legend in Urdu may be thus translated into English:—

"The story of the Deluge of the Patriarch Noah—on whom be peace—is well known. The long and short of it is that when the Deluge commenced, the Patriarch Noah took a pair of each kind of animal, and thence repaired with his nearest relatives to the Ark. The rest of the people, as also a son of the Patriarch Noah, were drowned on account of disobedience. The whole of the earth was flooded. And when the water rose to the height of 40 yards above the trees and mountains, the inmates of the Ark, on account of the terrific storm and the fury of the waves, became senseless with fear and despaired of life. Then God ordered: "Bismilláheh Majrihá O Mursáhá inná rabi-il-ghafur ur-rahim."[10] Whoever will utter these words, the Almighty God will deliver him from all difficulties. *The Almighty God will, by reason of the Benign Influence of His Name, preserve him from drowning.* And the storm was allayed."

[9] Anderson's *Mandalay to Momein*, p. 457.
[10] This formula may be translated into Urdu as follows:—

ساتھہ نام اللہ کے ہی چلنا اوسکا اور ٹھہرنا اوسکا تحقیق
کے رب میرا اللہ بخشنے والا اور مہربان ہی ہے ۰

The above may be translated into English thus; "The moving and stopping (of this boat, i.e., Noah's Ark) depends upon the influence of the name of God" For, in truth, our God is, preeminently, a Pardoner of sins and Merciful."

The Russians also believe that saving the life of a drowning man excites the wrath of the water-spirit. An illustration of this item of Russian folklore is given by Mr. Barry, in his novel entitled *Ivan at Home*, which is descriptive of Russian life. Once upon a time, a drunkard fell into the water and disappeared. Some spectators who stood close by on the shore did not show any inclination whatever to save the drowning man. The man was drowned. The villagers held a court of enquiry to investigate into the matter of that man's death from drowning. In the course of the enquiry it was elicited that no cross had been found on the neck of the deceased. The village Daniels, who sat to enquire into the matter, quickly returned the verdict that the man had got drowned because he had no cross upon his neck. The fisher-folk of Bohemia also display a similar kind of reluctance to save a man from drowning, under the impression that the presiding spirit of the water would get angry at thus being deprived of his victim, give him bad luck in fishing and soon get him drowned. The same superstition also obtains in Germany, and, when a person comes by his death from drowning, the German folk say: "The river-spirit claims his annual sacrifice," and sometimes also, "The nix has taken the drowned man." Mr. Jones, in his *Credulities Past and Present*, offers an explanation to the effect that "a person who attempts to rescue another from drowning is considered to incur the hatred of the uneasy spirit, which is desirous, even at the expense of a man's life, to escape from its wandering." Dr. Tylor, in his *Primitive Culture*, explains the superstition by saying such reluctance is only a relic of the ancient belief that the water-spirit very naturally used to get angry on being deprived of his intended victim, and, consequently, bore ill-will towards the person who ventured to do so, and would try to wreak vengeance on him at the first opportunity.

There is another class of popular beliefs as regards the time when the body of a drowned man would float up. In past times, it was popularly believed that the body of a drowned man would float up on the ninth day. This belief is prevalent in the county of Durham, as we are informed on the authority of Mr. Henderson. Sir Thomas Browne, the author of the *Hydriotaphie* and the *Religio Medici*, has also discussed this popular belief in his *Pseudodoxia Epidemica*.

In ancient times, people believed that the spirits of those persons who had been drowned in the sea, wandered for one hundred years, owing to their corpses not having been properly buried with all the rites of sepulture. Relics of this belief are to be found even at the present day. The belief still lingers among ignorant fisher-folk in some parts of England that the spirits of those sailors who have been drowned by shipwreck frequent those parts of the shores near which the shipwreck took place, and some of them even assert that they have heard the spirits of the drowned sailors "hailing their own names." Hunt, in his *Romances in the West of England*, refers to this belief and says that fisher-folk are afraid of walking in such localities after night-fall. This belief is similar to the Bengali superstition, described above, that the spirits of drowned persons haunt those tanks and wells in which they have been drowned, and has its counterparts among other races of people all over the world.

Lastly, there are some curious popular beliefs about the methods by which the corpses of drowned persons may be discovered. One of these methods is to tie up a loaf of rye bread in the shirt of the drowned person and set it afloat in the water near the place where the person was drowned. It is believed that the loaf of bread would float until it reaches close to the spot where the body of the drowned person lies and then sink at that spot. The *Indian Mirror* of Thursday the 29th September 1892, gives the following account of a search, in the aforesaid way, after the body of a drowned boy:—

"A novel method was adopted at Springfield, Illinois (United States of North America), in searching for the body of a drowned boy. The searchers tied up a loaf of rye-bread in the lost boy's shirt and set it adrift in the water above the place where the lad was drowned, the theory being that the loaf would float until it came close to the body. The package in this case is said to have floated until it reached a certain point when it suddenly sank. The boy was found within a few feet of the spot."

This belief is to be found in various other modified forms in many other countries of the world. Another modification of this belief consists in floating a loaf weighted with mercury, which is believed to float at once towards, and stand over, the spot where the corpse lies. A writer in an American paper gives the following instance of this belief :—"Some years ago, a boy fell into the stream at Sherborne, Dorsetshire, and was drowned. The body not having been recovered for some days, the mode of procedure adopted was thus: A four-pound loaf of best flour was procured, and a small piece cut out of the side of it, forming a cavity, into which a little quicksilver was poured. The piece was then replaced, and tied firmly in its original position. The loaf thus prepared was thrown into the river at the spot where the body fell, and was expected to float down the stream till it came to the place where the body had lodged. But no satisfactory result occurred." In another form, this belief is also prevalent among the aboriginal Indians of North America. Sir James Alexander, in his work on Canada, says :—"The Indians imagine that in the case of a drowned body, its place may be discovered by floating a chip of cedar-wood, which will stop and turn round over the exact spot. An instance occurred within my own knowledge, in the case of Mr. Lavery of Kingston Mill, whose boat overset, and himself drowned near Cedar Island ; nor could the body be discovered until this experiment was resorted to." The writer in the American paper, from whom I have quoted above, says :—" Not many months ago a man was drowned at St. Louis. After search had been made for the body, but without success, the man's shirt, which he had laid aside when he went in to bathe, was spread out on the water, and allowed to float away. For a while it floated, and then sank, near which spot it is reported, the man's body was found." Another modification of the theory of the discovery of a drowned man's corpse by a loaf, is current in Brittany. When a man gets drowned in Brittany and his corpse cannot be recovered, a lighted taper is stuck into a loaf of bread, which is then set adrift in the stream. Wherever the loaf of bread stands over, still, there, it is believed, the corpse lies underneath the waters. Another modification of this belief consists in tying round a wisp of straw, a strip of parchment having on it some cabalistic letters written by the parish priest, and setting it afloat in the stream. Wherever it will stop still, there, it is believed, the body is sure to be found. A correspondent of the *Notes and Queries* (English) says that the corpse of a drowned person was recovered by this means.

In some other countries, a living animal is employed for the purpose of recovering the body of a drowned man. It is believed that the animal will either cry out or sink at the exact spot where the corpse lies. In Norway, the people searching for the body take a cock with them in the boat and row it hither and thither. It is believed by them that Chanticleer will crow out when the boat reaches the spot where the body of the drowned man lies. In a similar manner the Javanese, or the inhabitants of Java, throw a living sheep in the water, when the corpse of a drowned man is to be recovered. They believe that the spot where the sheep will sink is the place where the dead body is sure to be found.—*Journal, Anthropological Society, Bombay*

FOLK-TALES.

538. The Pandit and his children.—There was a Bráhman who had a daughter whom he educated with his other pupils one of whom became a very learned Pandit. One day the old Bráhman said to him:—

"What is the use of my searching for a husband for my daughter? If you agree I will marry her to you."

The Pandit said that he agreed, provided the girl approved, and when she asserted they were married and the old Bráhman and his wife made over all their property to them and took to a life of asceticism. By and by the Pandit's wife had a son, and the moment it was born the Pandit took it into the jungle and said to the baby:—

"On account of our former lives do I owe you anything, or do you owe me?"

The baby replied that his father owed him a thousand rupees. When his father asked how he could repay the debt the child said:—

"Plant a grove and dig a tank and you will be free."

Immediately the child died and his father threw the corpse into the jungle, and going home commenced to plant the grove and dig the tank. The village people thought that the Pandit had intentionally got rid of the child, so they stopped saluting him.

A year after, the Pandit's wife brought forth a second son. In the same way his father took him to the jungle, and when he asked him did he owe him aught the child said:—

"Father, you owe me five hundred rupees."

When he asked how he could pay the debt the child said:—

"Build a temple to Siva and sink a well and then you will be free."

So his father threw the child away in the jungle and when he came home began to build the temple and sink the well.

Again the Pandit's wife bore him a third son, and when he took the child into the jungle and asked him if he owed him aught, the child said:

"Father! I owe you a lakh of rupees."

His father began to think: He will hardly ever be able to pay the debt and he will surely live.

So the Pandit brought him home and in order to increase the debt he spent large sums on his teaching and marriage, and when his son became as great a Pandit as himself he one day said to his wife:—

"I am going to make a pilgrimage. If our son earns anything, mind you do not take anything from him."

Soon after the Ráni of that land had a son, and the young Pandit was called to cast his horoscope. After making his calculations the Pandit said to the Rája:—

"His fate is on the whole good, but there will be a time of danger (*kshepak*,) While he is walking round the holy fire at his wedding Rája Indra will shoot an arrow at him."

"Is there any way of obviating this?" asked the Rája.

"I will announce it when his marriage comes on."

After some years the marriage of the boy was arranged, but the Pandit was not invited and he began to think that if he was not present the boy would surely die; so he went and reminded the Rája of what he had told him at the time of his birth. The Rája made excuses and asked the Pandit to save the life of his son. So the Pandit made an image of wax and dressed it in the clothes of the bridegroom, and as the rite of walking round the fire was being performed he hid the son of the Rája and moved the image round in his stead. Then Rája Indra shot his arrow; the image was consumed to ashes, but the life of the Rája's son was saved. Then the Rája gave the Pandit a lakh of rupees and sent him home with many other rich presents. When he came home with the money he offered it to his mother, but she said:—

"What does a blind woman like me want with money? Give it to your wife."

"Mother, this is a large sum of money and I cannot give it to my wife. If you will not take it I shall die."

So she was forced to take the money and immediately her son died. Just then his father returned from his pilgrimage and his wife explained how her son had got a large sum of money from the Rája and had required her to take it. The father said:—

"Let us take the corpse to the Rája and die in his Darbar."

They all came with the body of the Pandit to the Rája and having erected a pyre were about to burn themselves with it. When the Rája and his son saw this they said:—

"What is the use of our living when these Bráhmans are going to die?"

So they too prepared to ascend the pyre. Then a voice came from heaven:

"Why are you losing your lives? It was written in his fate that he should die in this way."

The Rája said:

"If Parameswar will revive the Pandit none of us need die."

The old Bráhman said to him:

"If you will give half the life of your son my son will recover."

The Rája agreed and the Pandit arose and said: "Rám Rám" and the Rája after loading them with gifts sent them to their homes.—*Chhedi Sinh, head-master of the School, Partabgarh.*

539. **The luck of the youngest son.**—There was a Banya in a village who had two sons. At one time he was very rich but he fell into poverty. One day he was sitting in his hut and said—

"If I had only a couple of cakes and salt daily I would be happy."

The elder son said—

"If I had only a pair of oxen to plough a field I would be happy."

But the younger son said—

"I will not be happy till I have four Ranis, one to shampoo my feet, another to fan me, a third to bring me a drink of water, and the fourth to cook for me."

"What nonsense for a beggar like you to talk such a folly" they said and beat him out of the hut.

So he ran away and came to a tank where the fairies of Indra were bathing. He seized their clothes and climbing up a tree refused to restore them until they promised to obey him.

Then he came to a palace where the son of a banker was sitting with a princess and they were reading together. The boy asked them to let him stay there and he soon was able to read as well as either of them. One day the princess wrote on her slate that she would run away with him. So they shut up the banker in a room and started. They took a lot of money with them and came to a city where they hired a fine house and lived togther. Then he began to attend the Raja's Court and after some time the Raja offered to give him a post and fixed his pay at two lakhs of pies a day; so they called him Lakhtaki.

Lakhtaki and the Raja used to go out hunting and the princess made a contrivance by which he could carry food and drink behind him on the saddle. They wandered into a desert and the Raja would have died of hunger and thirst had not Lakhtaki relieved his need. So the Raja told the Rani that they ought to give their daughter in marriage to Lakhtaki. The Rani said.—

"I agree if he can make the fairies of Raja Indra dance before me."

The prince sent at once for the fairies and the princess became his wife. The night of the marriage the princess dropped her gem necklace and when her husband found it and was taking it up it turned into a snake and bit him. Just then up came a Bengalin who tamed snakes and she cured him. But he ran away to the house of a banker and took refuge there and when they asked the banker who he was he had to say from shame that he was his son-in-law and marry him to his daughter and at the same time he married the Bengalin also.

So now he had his four wives and he came home and said to his father and brother,—

"I have attained my desire. Now you may have what you wanted to make you happy."

And they were ashamed before him.

(Told by Gangaram, Brahman, of Kalyanpur, Etah District.

540. **The witch and the boy.**—One day a porter's son was wandering about and seeing a Gular tree covered with fruit he climbed up and began eating. Just then an old woman came there and said—

"Pass down some of that fruit to me."

So he bent down the branch and when he came within her reach she caught hold of him and put him in her bag. This she threw on her shoulder and went off. By and by she sat down to rest and when he got the chance he popped out of the bag and putting some stones and thorns inside he hid himself. She soon got up and raised the bag on her shoulder. She was going off when a thorn pricked her. Then she called out—

"You young rascal, you may scratch me as you like with your nails, but when I get home I will make soup of you."

When she got home and found the boy had escaped from the bag she was much disgusted, but she was on the look out for him and a few days after she found him on the same tree.

So she caught him and put him in her bag and said—

"You won't escape me this time, my boy."

So she went home and called her daughter-in-law and said—

"You cut up this boy and put him in the souppot. I am going to the bazar for some pepper and salt and I will be back by the time he is cooked."

When the young woman took the boy and was going to cut him up she could not help admiring him and said—

"What nice eyes you have and what a pretty round head. How did you manage to be so?"

He answered—

"My mother arranged my eyes with a hot darning needle and she shaped my head with the rice-pounder."

"Will you make me like you?" she asked, and when he said he would she put down her head and he put out her eyes with a hot needle and smashed her head with the rice-pounder and then put her into the soup-pot. When he saw the old woman coming back he dressed himself in the young woman's clothes and sat modestly by the fire with the corner of her sheet over his face.

When the soup was ready the old woman shared it with her family, but when she gave some of the meat to the cat the cat said—

"Spit it out! The mother-in-law is eating her daughter-in-law."

"What is the cat saying?" the old witch asked.

"I will be back in a moment and tell you" said the boy and with that he bolted out of the house. And it was not till the old woman looked into the pot that she found that it was her own daughter-in-law that had been made into soup. I need hardly tell you that the boy kept away from that tree in future.

(Told by Raghunandan Prasad, student, High school, Bulandshahr.)

541. **The Ahir's folly.**—An Ahir was once going to see his wife at her father's house, and his mother advised him to maintain a grave and sober demeanour.* By way of carrying out her advice he put a large stone on his head and stalked up to the house. His mother-in-law asked him what on earth he meant, and when she heard, she said :—" What an awful fool you are !"

As he was taking his wife home he suddenly noticed that the parting of her hair was marked with red.† Just then another Ahir came up with an ox. Our friend said to him :—" Brother my wife's head is broken and I don't mind exchanging her for your ox." The man agreed and he drove away the ox. On the way it sat down and chewed the cud. "There is certainly something wrong with this beast's jaws" he thought to himself. Just then a Kurmi passed by with some radishes. "Friend" said the Ahir " My wife's head got broken and I swopped her for this ox and now I find that his jaws are all wrong. Do you mind swapping your radishes for him?" The Kurmi agreed and drove off the ox.

When his mother heard his story she exclaimed :—

"Better had it been that I were childless than cursed with a fool like you."

(A folktale, told by Nadu Kurmi, of Chopan Mirzapur.)

[" In the second book of Afanassieff there is a story which speaks of the exchange of animals in the very same order as in the Aitareya Brahmanam i.e., the gold for a horse, the horse for a cow, the cow for a goat or sheep. The Russian peasant goes on with his unfortunate exchanges : he barters the sheep for a young pig, the young pig for a goose, the goose for a duck, the duck for the little stick with which he sees some children playing : and he takes the stick home to his wife who beats him with it." De Gubernatis's *Zoological Mythology* I. 176, who gives other instances].

542. **How the Prince won his bride.**—There was a Rája who had four sons, of whom three were married but the youngest could not find a wife. One day when the boy was eating he said that the food was badly cooked. One of his sisters-in-law said :—" When you marry the daughter of a king your food will be well cooked." He was angry, and taking a horse and arms, set out on his travels. When he had gone some distance he came to the cross roads and asked a man which way he should go. The man said :—" One road is a journey of six months and the other of twelve." The Prince chose the short road. On the way he met a Rákshasa who was an eater of men and was called Kamdeg or " Slow-foot." The Prince addressed him as " Uncle " and asked his help which he promised to give.

Further on they met another Rákshasa who was called Kamkhurák or " Little feeder." He also went with them. Further on they met a third who was called Kampiyás or " Little thirst" and he also joined their company. On they went and soon they met a multitude of rats, and these also they took with them.

They came to the city of a Rája and put up in a garden outside the town. The Raja had announced that whoever would eat as many cakes as would fill a room, cross a river in a single leap, and drink all the water of a tank, would get his daughter in marriage. So the Prince called the rats and told them to make an underground passage between the garden and the room of the

---

* The word in the original is *garhu gambhír* which means "grave" or "heavy."

† This is the streak of red lead *(sendur)* which every married woman wears in the parting *(máng)* of her hair.

Princess. When the passage was ready the Prince went along it and found her asleep. Her dinner was laid in a dish beneath her bed; of this the Prince ate half, and leaving one of his shoes there, went away. The next day he did the same and the third time he tried to take her ring from her finger but she woke and had him seized and taken to her father. The Rája said:—" If you wish to marry the Princess, you must fulfil the conditions."

So the Prince called Kamkhurák and ordered him to eat up all the cakes in a room at one meal; he told Kampiyás to drink up the water of the tank and Kamdeg to jump across the river in a single bound. These Rakshásas took the form of the Prince and did as the Rája required. So the Raja gave him his daughter and he brought her home and lived happily.

(A folktale told by Bháwáni Din Pánre Bráhman of Faizabad.)

[For the Skilful Companions in Celbic folklore see Mr. Nutt's note to MacInnes *Folk and Hero Tales from Argyleshire* 445 sq. In Afanassief the hero is helped in the same way by eating (Abicdalo) and by drinking (Apivalo) who do the eating and drinking for him: See Gubernati's *Zoological Mythology* l. 206.]

---

543. **The Ahir and the Cow of plenty.**—There was once a poor Ahír in whose herd the Cow of Plenty (*Surabhi gáe*) was re-born. The cow had six calves. The wife of the Ahír was a shrew and never gave him enough to eat, and used to be constantly abusing him. So he used to save a little of his food and take it to the field to eat while he was at work. One day the cow saw this and said to her master:—" Why do you conceal your food in this way? Give the scraps to my children and I will give you as much milk and sweetmeats as you desire." The Ahír did as the cow ordered, and she gave him as much of the choicest food and sweetmeats as he needed. Then she took him to the hole of a snake and said:—" Master, whenever I give you milk and sweets you must always put a little milk and one sweetmeat near the hole for the use of the snake."

The Ahír obeyed her orders.

One day the little son of the Ahír came to the field and his father gave him some of the food which he received from the cow. The boy tied up some of it in his waist cloth. His father said:—" Do not commit this folly. If your mother sees this she will kill me and the cow." The boy promised that he would not show it to his mother; but one day his mother saw some of the sweetmeats with him and asked him where he got them. He said:—" My father gave them to me and the Cow of Plenty gives them to him every day." She said:—" If the cow is such a fool I will have all her calves killed by the butcher and I am going to him this very moment."

When the Ahír heard from his son what his wife had said he was terrified and told the cow. She said:—" Don't be anxious. I am going to bring my children. Go and take leave of the snake and then we will all go to another country."

The Ahír went to the snake and told him what his wife had done. The snake said—" Do you wish me to do anything? I am always at your service." The Ahír answered:—" My mother, the cow has not told me to ask you for anything, but whatever she advises I will ask you to do." He went to the cow and asked her what service he should require from the snake. The cow said:—" Ask him to give you his flute and handkerchief." The snake gave him what he wanted. Then the cow seated the Ahír on her back and with the help of her children carried him off into a jungle. There she made a platform (*machán*) on a palm tree and seated him there, and used to feed him every day with milk and sweetmeats until as he ate this food his hair became the colour of gold. One day the cow ordered her children to take him to the river to bathe, but she warned them not to lose a single one of his hairs. By chance one of his hairs broke off and the calves put it in a leaf cup and let it float down the stream. It floated past a ghát where a princess was bathing and when she saw it, she took it to her father and said "If I cannot marry the man who owns this hair, I must die."

So the Raja sent out many messengers to trace the owner of the golden hair. One old woman came to the forest where he was staying with the cow and said she was the sister of his mother. The cow warned him against her wiles, but he would not heed, and one day the old woman induced him to go out with her in a boat and carried him off to the city of the princess.

The princess was delighted to see him and was about to marry him at once, but he blew his flute and the Cow of Plenty and her calves appeared at once and began to break down the palace of the Raja. He came out and implored the cow to take pity on him. He agreed to build a splendid house for her and she consented to live there with her calves. The Ahír then married the princess, and by reason of the Cow of Plenty, the Raja enjoyed the utmost prosperity.

A folktale told by Bhawani Din Panre Bráhman of Faizabad.

[This is a variant of the "Lucky Herdsman" of which numerous parallels are given by Major Temple and myself in *Indian Antiquary* March, 1893. *Surabhi gde* is also known as Kámadhenu, Kámadhuh, or Savalá. She belonged to the Sage Vasishtha: See Gubernati's *Zoological Mythology* I. 73.

MISCELLANEA.

544. Gurgaon: Special village shrines.—Besides the ordinary village shrines to Bhûmiya, &c., there are many shrines to the occupants of which reverence is paid. Thus in Sujware there is a shrine of Shaikh Ahmad Chishti, but, Muhammadan though he was, his votaries are mainly Hindus. The Qanungo family of Palwal say that one of their ancestors used to visit his shrine constantly, and died there. After death they intended to take his corpse to the Jumna and burn it, but such was his attachment to Shaikh Ahmad, that until they cut off one of his fingers and buried it on the shrine, his body could not be moved. The scalp-lock (*choti*) of the children of this family is always cut off at this shrine. Many of the neighbouring Hindu Jat villages have dedicated plots to this shrine; and some Jats told me they only did worship (*pûja*) to Shaikh Ahmad Chishti, Brâhmans and the *pîpal* tree.—*Mr. F. C. Channing: Settlement Report,* p. 35.

545. Travelling; rules of. Hindus are, of course, very careful to start on a journey on an auspicious day. But in case this is impossible the difficulty is overcome by sending something ahead to represent the traveller. This is known as Prasthân dharna. The things which may be sent vary with the caste of the sender. For instance a Brâhman should send on a sacred thread, a Kshatriya a weapon, a Vaisya some honey and a Sudra some fruit. These substitutes for the traveller are usually left at the house of a respectable Brâhman. According to Garga Muni they should be kept in the next house and according to Bhrigu outside the village boundaries; according to Bharadvâja they should be kept at an arrow-shot from the house of the traveller. They should be daily removed from one house to another; but if the journey cannot be carried out they must be renewed. Thus the Prasthân of a Râja lasts for only ten days, that of the others only five days. When this period expires the traveller must look out for another auspicious moment for his journey.—*Pandit Ram Gharîb Chaubê.*

546. Raja Udpaiya Jit of Dharanagar and the snake.—The Râja one day came across a snake in a burning jungle. The snake implored assistance and was saved by the Râja. Then the snake asked for water which was not procurable, Then he requested the Râja to allow him to put his burning head in the Raja's mouth to cool it. The Râja weakly agreed and the snake who had sworn to do the Râja no harm went into his stomach. There he remained for years and the Râja fell into ill health so that he determined to go to Benares to die. Accompanied by his Rani he reached a place called Murtazanagar where, as the Rani was fanning her husband she saw a snake crawl out of the ground, and bend over the Râja's mouth with expanded hood. Presently another serpent issued out of the Râja's mouth and they began to chat. The late arrival upbraided the Râja's serpent with its trechery. "If any one were listening" it went on "I would disclose a plan which would effectually rid the Râja of you." To this the other replied:—"You who are seated on immense wealth will not escape for I can disclose how you are to be killed." The Rânî then destroyed her husband's serpent in some unexplained way and made an end of the other by pouring boiling butter into his hole. She then secured the treasure and saved the life of her husband.—*Archæological Reports VII. 84.*

547. A charm to keep off Smallpox.

Sri	Sri	Sri
Sri	Sri	Sri
Sri	Sri	Sri

Write this charm on a lotus-leaf in red-sandal ink and tie the same around the neck of a lad and he will escape this disease.—*Pandit Ram Gharîb Chaubê.*

548. Gurgaon: the local deity Pattharwale. In some villages is found a shrine very similar to that of Bhûmiya known as *Pattharwâle* (she of the stone): and I was told that when a man in sickness puts on the cord of Devi and recovers, he has to perform a journey to Nagarkot or Jwâla mukhi in Kângra, and takes with him a Bhagat or professed devotee of Devi, and while he is away, the females of his family worship the *Pattharwâle* Mr. F. C. Channing.—*Settlement Report, p. 35.*

549. Occupying a new house.—A new house should be occupied in the months of Pûs, Baisâkh Bhâdon, Sâwan or Aghan. If a man occupies a new house in Chait he will suffer sorrow and grief; if in Baisâkh he will get riches; if in Jeth he will die; if in Asârh his cattle will die; if in Sâwan he will get wealth; if in Bhâdon he will be happy; if in Kuâr he will quarrel with a powerful enemy; if in Kârtik he is in danger of death; if in Aghan he gets riches; the same is the case with Pûs; if in Mâgh his house will take fire; if in Phâlgun good luck will attend him; Sunday and Tuesday are inauspicious days; the others are favourable.—*Pandit Ram Gharîb Chaubê.*

550. Human Sacrifice.—During the excavations going on near the Cauvery in the Trichinopoly district in connection with the water-supply scheme of Trichinopoly town, certain old idols were dug up and removed. The camp of labourers was at once seized with the fear of the goddess Kali—whom, it appears, the idols resembled —and soon stories were told of certain of the coolies being attacked with frightful dreams, visions of the irate goddess, *etc.* As Kali is known to be a blood-thirsty deity, it was settled that nothing would appease her but human sacrifice, to which she was accustomed in days gone by. So strong is the panic in the camp that the greatest difficulty is felt in preventing the labourers from breaking up and dispersing, and the district authorities have had to warn the population by tom-tom not to let their children stray out-of-doors, as it is feared they might be kidnapped and offered up secretly as a sacrifice to appease the goddess.

551. Charm to destroy an enemy.—Muhammadan women practise the following charm to destroy an enemy. They go to a mosque on Friday and place in it a brick upside down. Then they curse their enemy that his house may be overturned as the brick is. So they put on the same day some lime on the wall of the mosque and pray that the lime may get into the eyes of their enemy and blind him.—*Pandit Ram Gharîb Chaubê.*

552. Casting out a Devil.—A Native gentleman, residing in Jaun Bazar Street, Calcutta, had a live goat flung down from his two-storied house, in accordance with the directions of a so-called magician, who was called in to cast out a devil with which a son was supposed to be possessed. The poor animal was first fed with a few bamboo leaves over which the wizard mumbled some mantras, and it was then pushed over the terrace. The animal was killed, and its flesh was distributed to the poor. —*Pioneer*, 22-4-94.

553. Popular tradition about Akbar.—There is no Emperor of India who finds a larger place in popular tradition than Akbar. There is a long series of folk tales telling of the wit of Akbar and his intercourse with the wise Birbal and his wiser daughter. One very curious tradition is that, in his former life, Akbar was a Brâhman named Mukunda. Once upon a time he happened to see the grandeur of one of the Muhammadan Emperors, and he longed to hold that dignity himself. In order to secure that object he commenced a course of austerities and worship of Mahadeva. When he had done this for twelve years Mahadeva appeared to him and told him that it was not in his power to confer this office upon him but that he should go to Prayag (Allahabad) and submit to have his head cut off by the saw which moves round the centre of that place of pilgrimage and is made to cut off the heads of people who are overcome by ambition. Mukunda agreed on the condition that he was allowed to remember the events of his present life. Mahadeva told him that he might engrave the account of his present life on a copper plate and bury it at Prayag ; that in his next birth he would remember as much as, and no more than, was engraved on the plate. Mukunda obeyed these orders and in due time he was reborn at Amarkot from the womb of Hamida, the wife of Humayun. When he attained the throne he went to Allahabad and dug up the plate. When he buried the plate, Mukunda left with it his tongs, gourd, deer-skin and other articles of worship and all these Akbar found with the plate. The fact of his having been a Brâhman in a former life accounts for Akbar's tolerance towards the Hindu religion.—*W. Crooke.*

554. A haunted cave—Some examples of haunted caves have recently been given. The following is from Ireland. There is a cave at Hacklim, near Ardee in Co. Louth, which is supposed to contain a troop of enchanted horsemen. The belief of the peasantry on the subject is that the foremost rider has a sword, and if this were drawn from its scabbard, the spell would be broken, and the troop liberated.

It is said that a young fellow once went to test the truth of the legend, and when he had drawn the sword half-way out, the horsemen began to tremble, and the horses to tear up the ground, whereat he became so much alarmed that he allowed it to fall back again.

It is a fact, however, that many years ago an attempt was made by a gang of workmen to explore the cave, but the fear of terrible consequences so filled them with alarm that some of them became dangerously ill, and remained so for weeks. Since then no further effort has been made in a like direction.

555. Gurgaon : Ploughing up the village site.—Some of these old villages bore a very bad reputation for turbulence and robbery, and the inhabitants were sometimes ordered by some of the early Collectors to give up their hill retreats and settle in the plain : Thus Rojhka Gûjar in the Gurgaon tahsil was deserted by orders of Mr. Cavendish, who had the site ploughed over by a donkey-plough, thus rendering it dishonoured and defiled. It is said that afterwards he wished the people to re-settle, and so, according to the custom in such cases, had the land gone over with an elephant-plough, but the old site is still deserted and the descendants of the former inhabitants now occupy several villages at the foot of the hill.—Mr. F. C. Channing ; *Settlement Report p.* 59.

[Fallon in his Dictionary *SV. gadha* quotes a woman's curse —*Ilâhi ! teré hán gadhé ké hal chalen.* " May your house be ploughed up by donkeys ! " Can any one give any further illustrations of the practice ? ED.]

556. Legends of acquisitions of territory.—There are many legends describing as in the case of Carthage how a new tribe acquire land from the former possessors by some trick of measurement. In the case of the Dánta family in Gujarat (*Bombay Gazetteer* V. 413) the Goddess Ambika Mâta gave Jas Râj her tiger, and telling him to mount it, promised that whatever territory he rode round should be his. The Râja mounted the tiger and made a circuit of seven hundred and sixty villages. Can any one quote similar instances ?—*W. Crooke.*

557. Oudh : Tiled houses.—In Biswan a large town in Sitapur District, tiles (*khapra*) are considered unlucky and they never make a tiled roof. There is not a single tiled house in the whole town.—*Azizuddin Ahmad.*

558. The Mythical origin of the river Sarju.—On one occasion of joy, tears of joy fell from the eyes of Nârâyan, the Supreme Being, which were reverently saved from falling on the ground by Brahma who caught them in his water can (*kamandal*) and carefully deposited them on the Mânasarowar lake. When the city of Ajudhya had been founded, the people longed for the sight of flowing water, and Vasisht Muni took mercy on them, and by penance and prayer, induced Brahma to allow the water to flow past the holy city. Hence the Sarju is sometimes called Vasisht Kanya or the Nymph of Vasishta and also Vasisht Ganga.—*Settlement Report pp.* 220 *sq.*

559. Cleaning of vessels.—Menial servants to the west of the Province refuse to clean the lota or water-vessel used for the purpose of personal ablution. Similar persons to the east of the Province have no such scruples.—*Paudit Ram Gharib Chaubé.*

560. Folklore notes from Gopalpur, Gorakhpur District.—Old women here teach children that the stars are the kine of heaven and the sun and moon the cowherds. (See Gubernati's *Zoological Mythology* 1—17.)

When lightning suddenly flashes in a clear sky, old women say that it is the flash of the herd of golden deer which run along the mountains pursued by beasts of prey.

Many demons, they say, are the ghosts of friends who have died violent deaths. When such demons meet them, they often call them by name in a nasal twang and beg tobacco There is no tobacco in the land of ghosts. When they get tobacco they take up the burden their living friend is carrying and bring it home for him. (On the nasal twang of Bhuts see Introduction to *Popular Religion and Folklore* 149).—*Pandit Ram Bakhsh Chaubé.*

561. Hardol: The legend of Bharanja Khera.—One day a Banjára arrived from the north with a rich load of merchandise. To escape payment of the heavy transit dues, he said his load was only Glauber's salt (*khári*); and God was wroth with him for his lie, and when he came to unload his pack, behold ! it had turned to *khári*, and he was a ruined man.—*Settlement Report,* 151.

[This legend is told of various places *e.g.* of an old fort somewhere in the Central Provinces.—ED.]

562. Swastika ; mark of.—In the Western part of the North-West Provinces when clothes are being distributed at marriages, they make on them the mark of the Swastika. It this be not done it is believed that the gift is unlucky both for the giver and the receiver.—*Pandit Ram Gharib Chaubé.*

563. Eastern Districts, N.-W. P.—Nim leaves used as an amulet.—When children have sore eyes, Hindu mothers are very careful not to allow their children to go near people of low caste as this contact with them is supposed to increase the disease. If children have to go out, they tie a leaf of the nim tree round their necks, which obviates the danger of this contact which is known as Chhua Chhut. This resembles the use of the leaves of the same tree in small-pox and similar epidemics.—*W. Crooke.*

564. Hoshyarpur; unlucky names.—One form of superstition common in this part of India is, that it is considered unlucky to mention the names of certain places before breakfast. Thus Jaijon is called *Phallewdli*, Talwara *Kaliada*, Kháwáspur *Piplanwála*, Saristhpur *Qasba*, and so on. The idea apparently is that these places were originally the sites of special oppression, such as the location of Sikh toll-posts *etc.*, and that thus they became unlucky.—*Settlement Report,* p 36.

565. Worskip of the Qadam-i-Rasul or footprints of the Prophet.—There are numerous instances of the worship of the Qadam-i-Rasul or footprints of the prophet in Northern India. I have given instances elsewhere (Introduction to *Popular Religion and Folklore,* 314.) In Bengal there is a celebrated stone of the kind which was put up in the old city of Guar by Nasrat Sháh in 1526. Can any one give further examples?—*W. Crooke.*

566. Verses written by the gods.—There are many examples of verses written by the gods themselves. Thus Tulasi Dass began and wrote the half line—*Búri sakal samáj.* He could go no further and then Hanumanji with his own hand wrote the next—*Charhe je prathamahin mok bas.* "The whole assembly sank, those who first sat in the boat through word'y delusion." In the same way the poet Jayadeva could not finish his shepherd's song ; so the god Krishna, while the poet was bathing in the Ganges, came down from heaven and completed it. A similar story is related of Súr Dás. So near'y every poet is under the direct protection of the gods.—*Pandit Ram Gharib Chaubé.*

567. The legend of King Jarásar.—King Jarasár of, Laháru a descendant of Kusa, was the victim of a strange disease. A long hair grew out of the palm of one of his hands, and persisted in growing longer and longer in spite of every effort made to eradicate it. His advisers came to the conclusion that the consecration of a white elephant to the gods was the only sure means of getting rid of the excrescence. White elephants were however scarce in those days and the King had to make a pilgrimage to Phanesar. During the performance of his ablutions at that place, he accidentally learned that Rája Sondhu the principal local magnate and a koli Rájput had an animal which would suit his propose. Jarasár warred against him and finally Sondhu gave his daughter, Alapdai, in marriage to Murásar, son of Jarásar, with the white elephant as a dower. Jarasár then performed the necessary ceremony and the hair disappeared from his hand.—*Calcutta Review LXIV.* 72.

568. The sanctity of the eleventh day of the month or Ekadashi.—If the *dasmin* or day that precedes the *Ekadashi* rules more than fifty-five *gharis*, two and a half of which make an English hour, the next day or the *Ekadashi* has not sufficient purity to make it necessary for a pious Hindu to fast on it. But in that case he should fast on the *Dwadashi* or twelfth which follows it. The Nimbárak Vaishnavas do not fast on the *Ekadashi*, the preceding day of which rules more than forty-five *gharis.* If in any month there be two *Dwadashi*, one should fast on the first and not on the second. But if there be two *Ekadashis* the second is the proper date on which to fast. If you cannot get a *patra* or almanac and are thus unable to ascertain the length of the Daswin, then the fast should be done on the *Dwadashi.*—*Pandit Ram Gharib Chaubé.*

569. South Mirzapur, An aboriginal love song.—
1. *Pardesi bálamisé bachan hári,*
2. *Tálá bin kunji khúlat náhin,*
3. *Bhánji sopári jútal nahin,*
4. *Damri ka dáli galat nahin,*
5. *Binu kampú Malethá lau at nahin,*
6. *Mor phátal kalejá milat náhin,*
7. *Damrí ka súiya pitariyá men,*
8. *Dagá déigá dilasá kuthariyá men.*
    Pardesi balam se bachan hári.

1. I have pledge my word to a stranger-lover ;
2. As a lock can't be opened without a key ;
3. As a broken betel-nut can't be joined ;
4. As a farthing's worth of pulse is not easy to boil ;
5. As the Marhattas won't deign to fight against a few men ;
6. So my broken heart can't be cemented (reconciled without my lover).
7. One keeps a needle worth a farthing in a box.
8. But I was so foolish as to let him (my stranger-lover) play false with me in the little room, *i.e.,* let him go away.

570. A Panjabi maxim.—
Asá, pása, beswá, thág, thákur, Sunár, Nauon Kám na nudde, bándar, Turk kalál.

Hope, dice, the courberan, Thag, Thákur, Sunár, Monkey, Turk and Kálál—all nine are no good.—*Sirsa Settlement Report, appendix XXXIII.*

South Indian Notes and Queries:
A MONTHLY PERIODICAL.

VOL. V.] MARCH, 1896. [NO. 12.

Every communication must be accompanied by the writer's name and address, not necessarily for insertion, but as a guarantee of good faith. Every quotation from a book must be accompanied by its full title, publisher's and author's names, place and date of publication, volume and page. Contributors are requested to write on ONE SIDE of the page only. If several contributions be sent at a time, they should be sent each on a separate sheet.

The Conductor cannot undertake to return, or be responsible for any MSS. not accepted.

All orders must be accompanied by cash. If not so accompanied, they will either not be attended to, or will be complied with per value-payable post.

Contributions should be addressed direct to W. CROOKE, ESQ., C.S., SAHARANPUR, N.W.P., INDIA.

CONTENTS OF THIS NUMBER.
(The references are to the Notes.)

Popular Religion ... 199 to 202	Folk-tales ... 209 to 214
Anthropology ... 203 ,, 208	Miscellanea ... 215 ,, 216

POPULAR RELIGION.

571. Omens taken from the Fire Sacrifice.—The Homa or fire-sacrifice is still used as a mode of taking omens. If the flame burn brightly and is directed towards the person for whom the sacrifice is being done the result may be expected to be propitious. If the flame burn badly and in particular if it be directed towards the south, the unlucky quarter of the sky, the omen is unfavourable. While the sacrifice is being done the flame must not be fanned with the hand or with any kind of fan as this is supposed to injure the fire-godling. The performer may blow on the fire with his mouth, but he must take care that no spittle fall into the flame,—*Pandit Ram Lal Dube.*

572. Feeding of Sacred Fish.—One of the sights of Hardwár is that of the fish, mostly Mahásír, which throng in the sacred pool called the Brahma Kunda, and are so tame that they throng round the steps of the Har-ki-pairi Ghat and do not mind people bathing close beside them. The Bráhmans say that it is auspicious to feed them as well as alligators, because they are the vehicle of Ganga Mái, or Mother Ganges.—*W. Crooke.*

573. The Saint Hasan Shah.—At Saharanpur is the tomb of the Saint Hasan Shah. He is said to have belonged to a sect of Muhammadan faqirs who cherish a pure affection for all the creatures of the Almighty. There was once a Civil Native Judge at Saharanpur who had a son. As the boy was going to school, the saint saw him and loved him. He used to follow the lad about and when the parents of the boy heard of this they took umbrage at him and had him beaten. Soon after the saint disappeared and the lad fell ill at separation from his friend. At last he died and when the body was brought out for burial the saint came to the house, touched the lad and brought him to life again. When Hasan Shah died in his humility he ordered that his tomb should be made of clay and not of masonry. And so it is to the present day. The bones of the saint are believed to give out magical power, and when any one wants success in love he makes a vow at the tomb. It is a great resort of all who are skilled in magic and incantations of all kinds.—*W. Crooke.*

574. Sacred Groves.—The belief in the holiness of groves consisting of five sacred trees is widely spread all over Northern India. Such a grove is known as Panchbati and should contain one of the following trees—the Pípal, Banyan, Ním, Bel and Pakar. This is the best combination; but a grove containing five specimens of any of these trees is also regarded with respect. The idea is as old as the Ramáyana where we find groves of this kind often mentioned as containing a Pákar, Jámun, Mango, Banyan and Pípal. Now-a-days this combination is regarded with less favour than that already described.—*Pandit Ram Gharíb Chaubé.*

575. **Tiger-claws as an Amulet.**—The value of tiger-claws as an amulet against the Evil Eye is well known. They are peculiarly efficacious if tied round the necks of babies, when they prevent evil spirits from worrying the baby in its sleep, which is shown by the child suddenly starting up and crying. Their efficacy is much increased if they are tied together in the form of the letter X. This accounts for the various uses of the cross in Hindu mystic ceremonies, where it was used as a religious symbol long before Christianity.—*Pandit Ram Lal Dube.*—

576. **The Cocoanut.**—In a fit of wrath, the sage Visvamitra, in order to show his contempt for the gods, began to create men, and when he had made a head he went to Bhágwán and asked him to supply muscles and blood. Bhágwan abused him for his rash attempt to rival the gods. So Visvamitra abandoned his enterprise and asked Bhágwan to complete his work. So, to please Visvamitra, Bhagwan made the head which he had formed into a cocoa-nut. It is perhaps on the same idea that the cocoanut is very commonly used as an offering at shrines, apparently as a substitute for a human sacrifice.—*W. Crooke.*

577. **Jagadhri; a Sacred Well.**—At a place named Buriya, near Jagadhri in the Ambala District was formerly a sacred well which was endowed with marvellous powers of curing diseases of all kinds. Once they say, this place was the site of a flourishing town which fell into ruins through the curse of a saint. The great well of the place almost dried up, and what water it contained became a source of all kinds of evil to those who drank it. One day, some time ago, a noted saint came to the spot and came upon a weaver boy who was grazing his goats on the site of the ruined city. He asked the boy where he could find water. The boy told him that there was a well near the place, but that its water was evil. The saint directed him to lead him there. When he reached the place he struck the well with his staff and lo! delicious water gushed from the mouth of it. He asked the boy to taste the water, but he, knowing the danger refused to touch it. When the people saw this miracle they came to the spot and the well was found to have power to cure disease, so that many lepers and patients suffering from all kinds of grievous diseases came there and found relief.

Now-a-days the well has lost much of its power and is regarded with little more respect than other wells in the neighbourhood.—*W. Crooke.*

578. **Saharanpur; a distillers' saint.**—There was many years ago at Rurki in the Saharanpur District a holy man named Bále Sháh who was the special saint of distillers. Unless he was propitiated the liquor would not come in the stills. It is said that he was a constant drunkard and that the Kalwárs used to give him as much spirit as he wanted, free. When the supply ceased their apparatus stopped working. Now that he is dead, they still offer a regular offering of sweets and spirits at his tomb on Thursdays, or Fridays. —*W. Crooke.*

579. **Saharanpur; a saint's tomb.**—At the village of Dhandhera about two miles from Rurki is the tomb of a Hindu Sádhu and his wife. A few years ago the two tombs were joined together; recently they have moved apart and every one knows that there is something uncanny about the matter. When cows or buffaloes calve, some milk is poured on these tombs; any cultivator failing to do so, his cattle cease to give milk. —*W. Crooke.*

580. **Harshu Panre the demon.**—Harshu Pánre, a noted demon to the East of the North-West Provinces, is Harshu Pánre of whom some account has been given elsewhere (*Introduction to Popular Religion and Folklore* 121). It is curious how the worship of this demon is extending up the Gangetic valley. From a villager in the Saharanpur District comes the following story. Harshu Pánre used to infest a road in the neighbourhood of Rurki and grievously afflicted the people. One day a Rajput was driving his cattle home along this road when to his extreme amazement he saw a great black man with shaggy hair come out on the side of the road in the moonlight and with a great club in his hand drive the cattle into a neighbouring field. The Rajput several times tried to get the animals together, but in vain, as the monster each time dispersed the herd. At last the Rajput saw that he was a demon, and, taking off his shoe, threw it at him, on which the ghost promptly retreated and he managed to bring the cattle home in safety. I have given other examples of the shoe as a scarer of demons in the above-quoted book, p. 205. It would be interesting to know whether in his travels Har-

shu Pánre has yet reached further west than Saháranpur. — *W. Crooke.*

581. Another legend of Dhruva.—The legend of Dhruva has been already given in vol IV, para: 336. Another account comes from Mathura. After describing how Dhruva was driven from home, his father tried to induce him to return by promising him half his kingdom. But he refused, and going into the jungle met the Saint Narada Rishi who advised him to return lest beasts of prey might devour him. So Narada advised him to go to Mathura where he was escorted by the seven Rishis. The place where he carried on his austerities is known as the Dhruva Tila, and when people dig in the mound they find the ashes of the sacred fires of the saints.

Dhruva remained there until his austerities raised the alarm of the gods who feared he would displace them. So they tried to frighten him, and Mahadava, disguised as a tiger, came and touched him, but he was not afraid. Then Indra, in the form of an elephant, tried to frighten him, but he too was unsuccessful. At last Náráyana himself appeared in answer to his devotion, and asked him what he wished. He replied that he desired only to go to Paradise. So Náráyana gave him his army to escort him to Ajudhya. His father who had grown blind with grief at his absence supposed that this was a hostile force sent to attack him. But Dhruva alighted from his elephant, and saluted him, and after reigning for many years he was carried off to heaven, where he still reigns as the Polar Star.—*Dhruvji Mal, Mathura.*

582. Saháranpur; Bansipuri; a saint which guards from fire—In the town of Rurki is the tomb (Samadh) of a noted Hindu saint named Bansipuri. Many years ago this Sadhu used to live in the town and at the end of his days he went off to Hardwár where he died. Some time after, a Rájput was one day going along the road at night when the ghost of the Sadhu appeared before him. The Rájput was overcome with fear and began to run away; but the ghost called to him to stop as he had something to tell him. When the Rájput halted the ghost said;—" It is true I am dead, but I am not comfortable at Hardwár and I desire to return to my former home and you and your brethren must build my cenotaph." The Rájput asked—"If we do this what will you do for us in return?" The ghost replied:—" I will guard your house from fire. Even if your house catches fire I will see that only one thatch is burnt." So the Rájput and his brethren carried out the orders of the saint and to this day when a cow or buffalo calves, they pour some milk near the tomb in his honour. Any one who worships him regularly in this way is never in danger of his house taking fire.—*Pandit Ram Gharib Chaubé.*

583. The saint Gulab Shah.—Close to the town of Rurki is the tomb of the saint Guláb Shah or the Rose saint. It is so called because it is surrounded with a dense growth of rose plants which no one will for any consideration touch. They say that in the old times some one did pluck a rose there and died a miserable death. This is obviously based on the same idea as the numerous sacred groves which abound all over the country the wood of which are protected from depredation by a most effective sanction. Both Hindus and Muhammadans worship this saint on Thursdays and Fridays by offering sweets and lighting lamps at his tomb. When any one realises a vow made in his name, meat boiled with rice (*Pulao*) is offered to the guardian of the shrine —*W. Crooke.*

584. Camel-bones as scarers of demons— In Saháranpur both Hindus and Muhammadans have great faith in the virtue of camel-bones as a preventive of disease in cattle. The method is to put in a rag a camel-bone with some of the Satnaja or seven varieties of grain. This is hung up at the door of the cow-house and all beasts passing under it are safe from disease. It is necessary that the grain thus collected should be to the weight of one and a quarter seers, which is a lucky number. The camel is such an uncanny animal in various ways that it is easy to understand why there should be a special value attaching to its bones.—*W. Crooke.*

585. Saháranpur; a tank which cures disease. Not far from Rurki is the tank known as *Sidhi Bawa ki talaaiya*, or the tank of the saint Sidhi which in popular belief works miracles. If any one suffering from rheumatism goes there, bathes regularly for eight days and supports himself in that place by begging his bread from seven houses daily, he will be cured of his disease. In the case of high caste Hindus this much concession is made that they may beg uncooked grain and prepare it themselves. Hundreds of sick people frequent that tank at all seasons of the year.—*Pandit Ram Gharib Chaubé.*

586. Respect for Ganges water.—No pious Hindu will even under the direst necessity boil the water of the Ganges, as it shows want of respect to the sacred river. I was lately talking to a learned Brahman pandit and he spoke in a disparaging way of a Jaina pandit merely because he had wounded his religious susceptibilities by once boiling Ganges water in his presence—*Pandit Ram Gharib Chaubé.*

587. Kahars-morning and evening incantations.—In the district of Saharanpur Kahárs while getting up from bed in the morning or retiring to bed in the evening repeat the names of two deities, Khwájah Khizra and Hanumán or the Monkey-god. I asked them why they do not repeat the names of respectable Hindu deities, to which they replied:—"We are the bálká or sons of Khwájah Khizra and he alone can do us good.' They say that by repeating the names of these two deities in the morning, they become safe for the day, and by repeating their names at night they become safe for the night.—*Ram Gharib Chaubé.*

588. Gorakhpur: worship of Tarkulhi ki Mata.—In Gorakhpur one of the deities most dreaded by women is Tarkulhi ki Mata. She is a form of Káli and loves impure offerings as many Kális do. She is treated by women who think themselves to be under the influence of some demon or witch, or who attribute barrenness to some cause of the kind. The pilgrimage is also undertaken when some member of the family goes mad. Women who suffer from miscarriage also visit her. Her fair is principally attended by low caste people.

They offer pigs to her in a very brutal manner. They bring them to the shrine hung to a club laid over the shoulder with their hind legs tied. The throat is then half cut with a blunt knife in the name of the goddess and her worshipper. Country spirit it also poured on the ground. On this the women supposed to be under the influence of a demon or witch begin to shake violently and the priest or his assistant comes up and thrashes them with a cane to drive the devil out of them. As he beats them he calls on them to name the evil spirits by which they are possessed. When he hears their names he orders them to come out of the patient and appear before the goddess.

Women treated in this way vow to come again if the cure be effectual. The offerings are sweetmeats, cakes and money. Some give yellow sheets as well. Mad people are exorcised in the same way. Many quarrels arise by people being named at the shrine as witches. The relations of the afflicted person have it out with them when they return from the pilgrimage.

When a women has a child after a visit to the temple, she takes it there to have the birth-hair shaved, and the ears and nose bored.
Pandit Ram Bakhsh Chaube.

589. Bulandshahr: a jungle goddess.—In Bulandshahr the forest goddess is Chámura which the Pandits say is a corruption of Chamunda one of the forms of Devi, which is very doubtful.

She corresponds to Bansapti Mái, (Vanaspati, "Queen of the woods") in the eastern districts. Her shrine is a collection of branches of trees to which every passer-by adds a twig. If cattle stray or are stolen, the herdsman vows to offer her a flag, which consists of a bamboo with a piece of red cloth tied to the end and suspended over the shrine. Such shrines are chiefly found in those parts of the jungle which are frequented by herdsmen.—*W. Crooke.*

590. The forest goddess.—In Saharanpur the forest goddess is known as Asarori, or "Toe stones of confidence," and her shrine consists of a heap of stones, to which every traveller adds a pebble. Cartmen and cowherds sometimes offer to her a Bheli or lump of treacle and milk, or a flag if she protects their cattle.—*Pandit Ram Gharib Chaubé.*

591. Passes: goddess of.—Most of the passes over the Siwálik hills in Saharanpur are in charge of Káli. The most important of these local Kális is the one in charge of the pass at Mohand, where the Saharanpur-Dehra Road crosses the hills. Travellers offer to her a female goat which has never borne a kid. Such goddesses are in most parts of the province called Páthi.—*W. Crooke.*

592. Worship of the ghost of a man killed by a tiger.—In the Dholkhand jungle to the north of Saharanpur is the shrine of Sánwal Sher, the ghost of some man killed by a tiger in the olden days. Every one who passes through the jungle with cattle offers to him a Bheli or lump of coarse sugar, and some add a fowl. There is an old tiger about the place, on which he is said to ride, and many people say that they have seen him riding about at night on this animal.—*W. Crooke.*

593. Gorakhpur: worship of the elephant Bhagminiya.—At Gopálpur in the Gorakhpur District is the grave of an elephant known as Bhagminiya, or "The fortunate one." She was a hunting elephant of Raja Krishna Kishor Chandra of Gopálpur and was deeply loved by him, as she had several times saved his life from tigers. When he died, the elephant also died a few days after, and in the same year the *mahant* or driver and all his family died one after another. This succession of calamities powerfully affected the people of the place. Near the grave of the elephant, evil spirits are constantly seen at noon or after sunset. She is worshipped on this account on Sundays and Tuesdays with offerings of cakes, sweetmeats, &c. Many people who have neglected, have been flung into holes by the ghost of the elephant or her driver.—*Pandit Ram Bakhsh Chaubé.*

ANTHROPOLOGY.

594. Banjáras.—In continuation of Mr. Cumberlege's account of Banjáras, the following notes on the tribe as now found in Saharanpur are worth preservation.

One of the great heroes of the tribe is Lakkhi Banjára, of whom many songs are sung which will be published later on. He purchased from a potter his daughter named Sorath for her weight in gold. Her beauty was so great that she attracted the attention of a Raja named Rorh and he tried to take her from Lakkhi by main force. Lakkhi fought with him for a long time and finally defeated the tyrant.

When a Banjára dies they put some gold and sweets in the mouth of the corpse and taking his body outside the village site, burn it in any convenient place. The eldest son generally sets fire to the pyre: when the pyre is well alight they go to a river or tank, if convenient, and bathe; but the bathing is not compulsory and if there be no water close by, they return to the house of the deceased and spend a short time in consoling the relatives. The next day a few of the nearest relatives go to the scene of the cremation and if the burning was incomplete they set fire to it again. On the way as they return, they place on the road some branches of a thorny tree, to bar the return of the ghost. The tree generally used for this purpose is the Ber *(Aegle Marmelos)*. On the third day is the Tija, when they make a mixture of ghi, flour and sugar and distribute it among the clansmen. On the thirteenth day the brethren are fed, and a cow, a sheet, a pair of shoes and a bludgeon are given to a Brahman, which he is supposed to pass on for the use of the spirit, in the next world. The Banjáras are the only caste in this part of the country, who appear to make a bludgeon part of the gifts offered to the Brahman. This ends the funeral rites among what are known as the Bahurupia division of the Banjáras of this part of India.

The word Bahurupiya is usually applied to the caste of actors who dress themselves in various ways and imitate other castes. Here it is applied to a section of the Banjáras whom they say are so called because they devote themselves to various forms of occupation. They admit no connection with the regular actor class.—*W. Crooke.*

595. Chamars and Baris.—In the Basti District there is a story current that in former times, Chamars and Baris used to eat together. One day a Chamar went to dine with a Bari and his host served the food in a *dauna* or platter made of leaves, such as the Baris make. The small wooden pin (*kharka*) with which the sides of the dish are fastened together stuck in the throat of the Chamar and he was choked. As he was dying he left an injunction to his descendants never to eat with a Bari or to use the leaf platters made by them. Since then the rule is carefully obeyed and if a Chamar violates it he is put out of caste. Does the same custom prevail in other parts of the country?—*Ram Suchit Lal, Tahsili school, Basti.*

596. Pankti Brahmans of Dahar or Indigenous Brahmans of Mirzapur and Baghelkhund.—There are seven kinds of Brahmans in Mirzapur and Baghelkhund who go under the name of *Dahár ké Bráhman*. They have ranks among them and are worshipped by the Rájás of these localities. The following verse enumerates them.

*Pándé aur Chaubé Chandráyan gotra Belaunj
Ké Kansik Muther chaubé bimal bichár ké;
Barhná bashishth gotra Kashyap Parwahá hain
Káshi ráj bhúp jinheñ pujat adhikár hain;
Harná Bashisht gotra Kashyap Paraváhá hain,
Sabó ki sumati barhati ko barhanti apár ké;
Cháhui to bilgáwain, cháhai algdwain puni cháhaiñ to milámaiñ játi aisó Bábhan dahár ké.*

The Pándé and Chaube of Chandratya *gotra* of Belaunjá and the Chaubé of Kausik *gotra* of Muther are of clear understanding. The Misra of Barhaná, Bashisht *gotra* and Parwá Dubé, Káshyap *gotra* whom the Mahárájá of Benares worships especially.

Harná Tewári, Bashisht *gotra* and *misra* of Parrahá of Kashyap *gotra*. These seven increase in wisdom without limit. If they wish they may admit one into the caste and if they wish they may excommunicate one. Such is the caste of Dahár Brahman.—*Pandit Rám Gharib Chaubé.*

597. Bathing a sick person.—When a person has recovered from serious disease special precautions must be taken about his first bath. For this a lucky time must be selected. It may be any day except Monday or Friday, and the fourth, ninth and fourteenth days of the lunar fortnight, and on that date when according to the horoscope of the patient, the power of the Moon is weak. This is based on the principle that the Moon is considered as a cause of disease. If the bath is taken on the day when the Moon is powerful, the planet will send some further disease as a punishment.—*Pándit Ram Ghárib Chaubé.*

598. Ber Fruit turned into Stone.—There is a European superstition that beans were turned into stone by the curse of the Virgin Mary. So in India Panjábi drug merchants hawk about a kind of stone known as Hazrat Zahud ke Bre, which is regarded as a potent remedy in a certain class of infectious disease. They say that Hazrat Ali once passed by a Ber garden and asked the gardener to give him some of the ripe fruit. He refused and then the saint cursed him and said that his fruit should be turned into stone. The man asked pardon of the saint who so far relaxed the curse that they were turned into a valuable remedy.—*W. Crooke.*

599. **Nim trees; remedy from.**—Can any one say what a stuff known as Nímkhár or the salt of the Nim tree in which is hawked about by Panjábi drug merchants? They say that it is found in lumps about the size of a marble under the roots of old and decayed Nim trees and that a little of it ground up and administered in water is a sovereign remedy for all the diseases of the horse.—*W. Crooke.*

600. **The Dusadhs.**—The meaning of the word "Dusadh" is popularly believed to be "the reverse of a Sádhu or religious mendicant." They say that they are the descendants of Ráhu the demon who causes eclipses who was originally a Dusádh and noted for his extraordinary strength. There are seven divisions of the Dusádh caste,—Gonrár; Bhinrár; Kochahaniya; Bhagahiya; Panwár; Bheriya; and Gorar. Of these only the Gonrár and Bhinrar worship Rahu. The worship to him lasts two days. On the first day Rahu is worshipped alone and on the second day in conjunction with Durga. It is only in the Homa or fire sacrifice that Dusádhs employ Brahmans. In the ordinary worship of Rahu they dig a pit seven cubits in length one and a quarter cubits in breadth. In the extraordinary worship which is sometimes performed, the pit is twenty-one cubits long and one and a quarter cubits broad. It is filled with dry mango-wood and this is set on fire. After the fire is lit in the pit which is called Tiur, they do the Homa or fire-sacrifice in the course of which five and a quarter seers of ghi are used. The Dusádh who makes the offering of ghi and incense to the fire first walks through the pit without shoes and then his castemen and the bystanders follow him. After the Homa ceremoney is over, a boar is sacrificed to Rahu and the flesh is eaten by the worshippers. The worship of Rahu is usually done before a marriage in the family.—*Babu Chhedi Lal.*

(For the fire worship of Rahu see *Introduction to Popular Religion and Folklore* 10; Risley: *Tribes and Castes of Bengal,* 1–255. Ed.)

601. **Surang Lal ghori; a boys' game.**—The boys divide into two parties which are equal and the set mounts the back of the other. They all so and in a circle and one boy dismounts. He has to run round the circle holding his breath and saying—"*Surang Lal ghori, tu ham se kyun na boli?*" Chestnut mare why don't you speak to me?" If he loses his breath he has to give a back to the boy he was riding. This is done by each boy in succession. The game is usually played by city boys.—*Pandit Ram Gharib Chaubé.*

602. **Leprosy; modes of curing.**—Among high caste Hindus the most efficacious method of curing leprosy is by the worship of the goddess Maha Lakshmi. Her worship is performed on the last Friday of the month of Sáwan in the following manner:—

The house should be whitewashed and decorated with flowers and garlands. A golden image of the goddess with her four hands should be prepared, and should be set up within the kitchen or the room sacred to the household gods. In the north-eastern corner of the house should then be laid five seers of fine ears to which the owner should do worship. In the same way a pitcher of water with mango twigs at the mouth should be worshipped and in it should be placed a small piece of gold. The pitcher is covered with a cloth and the image of the goddess is placed near it. The image should be bathed with Panchamrita, or a mixture of curds, ghi, milk, sugar and honey, and to the goddess should be offered twenty-one leaves of the Pipal, Banyan, Bel, Mango, Pomegranate and Málati trees, with flowers of various kinds. Next, the lingam of Siva should be worshipped with grain of twenty-one varieties and twenty-one sweet cakes. Songs and dances should be performed in honour of the deities. Incense is then burnt in large quantities and the person afflicted with leprosy is made to sit in the smoke and inhale it. During this time he should maintain perfect silence and when he performs worship he should listen to a recitation of the sacred texts in honour of the goddess. During the recitation he should chew a packet of betel in perfect silence. In the betel, however, no lime or catechu should on any account be mixed. When the recitation is over he should take out of his mouth the fragments of the betel and tie it up in the corner of his sheet; on no account should he defile the worship by spitting it out on the ground. After this he should again worship the goddess Maha Lakshmi and distribute five golden images of her as follows:—one to a Brahman; one to a Sádhu; one to a small unmarried girl: one to a Brahmachári; and one to a woman whose husband is alive. Then he should ask the leave of the priest to take food and then go to sleep. On waking in the morning he should take care to look at the refuse of the betel which he chewed the previous day before looking at anything else: If the bete have become of a red colour during the night he

may be sure that the worship has been duly performed and the disease will disappear; but if it have not become red he must do the worship again the next year. All the images and articles offered are the perquisite of the officiating priest.
—*Pandit Sundar Lal Dubé.*

603. **Muhammadan bride; rules about visiting the house of her parents.**—For a year after the consummation of the marriage a Muhammadan bride has to follow certain rules in visiting the house of her parents. Half of the months of Shabán, Muharram and Safar, she should spend with them and she must also go there at the feasts of the Muharram, Shab-i barát, Holi and Diváli. She ought also to spend the whole month of Ramzan with them. At these times it is unlucky for her husband to accompany her. Half of the Bakrid feast she ought to spend with her parents and half with her husband. She ought to come to her husband's house at noon and ought to return to her parents for the months of Rabi-ul-awwal and Shawal. The end of the Ramzan and the 27th and 28th of Rabi-ul-awwal she should spend with her husband. These rules apply only to the first year of her married life.

When the bride comes to her husband's house she should wear a veil (*ghungat*) and sit with her head hanging down on her knees. She should not appear unveiled before the male elders of the household. When she meets her female relations she should weep and fall at their feet. For two or three years she must not address her husband in the presence of the elders of the house. Any neglect of these rules brings contempt on her.— *Abdul Qasim Muhammad Basit Ali Khan.*

604. **Saharanpur N. W. P.—Bhat Nágar and Saksénà káyesths.**—I have heard it said by some of these káyesths that while the males can freely indulge in wine and flesh the women are prohibited from doing so. This rule is chiefly observed among high families of Bhat Nágar káyesths. Among Saksénás, an informant tells me, the oldest woman of the family does not eat from the hands of the daughters-in-law. Also, káyesths in this part of the provinces do not eat from the hands of their daughters and younger sisters while they are unmarried. They do not take tobacco from their hands throughout their whole life.—*Pandit Ram Gharib Chanbé.*

[I am not certain that these rules generally prevail.—Can any one give a more definite account? ED]

605. **Position of the maternal uncle at marriages, &c.**—In reply to Miss Gouden's queries in Vol. III are 366 I may say :—

As regards the custom of simultaneous marriages the custom does among some races, the Muhammadan Julahas of the Eastern Districts of these Provinces for instance, who in order to avoid marriage expenses, arrange that all the marriages celebrated during the year in the caste shall be done on the same day. The custom was also an ancient one as it is said that the four brothers of Ramchandra were married at the same time with one single ceremony. There seems to be nothing opposed to modern Hindu custom in having the marriages of several girls of different families, but of one and the same caste solemnised at one time at the same marriage pavilion. There is a rule, however, that two sisters cannot be married at the same time. Some say that when several girls are married at the same time in the same shed each must have a separate holy pitcher (*kalsa*), but for this there seems no good authority and some learned pandits whom I have consulted agree that a separate pitcher for each girl is not required.

As to the duties of the mother or maternal-uncle at the ceremony—during all the preliminary rejoicings and sacrifices before a marriage the mother has to take a prominent part as well as the other women of the clan. For instance she with the other women sings songs of rejoicing at the time of the betrothal. After this is over she sends curds and sugar to be eaten by the officiating priest and the representatives of the bride. The youth has to make over to her the money which was given to him by the friends of the bride as a pledge of the engagement. She lays it in the box in which the family god's image is kept. Then she comes out and rubs oil on the heads of her women friends, and those who have husbands have some red lead plastered along the parting of their hair. She then distributes money among Brahman women of the neighbourhood and to other beggars. On the actual betrothal day it is the mother who gets the holy square (*chauk*) arranged in the courtyard of the house and provides all the articles needed for the ceremony. After the ceremony has been completed she again anoints the heads of her women friends with oil. She also distributes the usual alms. At the wedding feasts it is she who serves round food to the female guests. After the betrothal the next rite is the *sagun utháua*, on which day a lucky day and hour are selected by the family priest for the actual wedding ceremony. On this occasion she also invites her friends and commences the collection of provisions for the wedding. At this time five women of the clan whose husbands are alive are given rice and urad pulse which they fan. All must sit facing some lucky direction of the sky. During this rite they sing songs suited to the occasion. When the winnowing is done the mother anoints their heads as before, and fills prevail their laps with barley and rice, which are the only grains used for this purpose. The next important ceremony in which the mother takes a leading part is the Matmangar or Matkhan when the lucky earth is collected for the preparation of the cooking place on which the food used at the wedding is to be cooked. At this rite she has to beat on the Chamar's drum and colour it with red lead. While the earth is being dug it is the mother who does the worship of Dharti Mata, the Earth Mother. The earth is dug by the sister or father's sister of the bridegroom. After the rite the mother distributes sweets among those who have taken part in it. Next one or two days before the wedding the mother has to worship the family goddesses and invite the spirits of the sainted dead of the family to honour the marriage with their presence. The worship of the goddesses is known as the Matrika puja and the invitation of the sainted dead the Pitri Neotan. Again when the boy starts on his wedding procession the mother has to do sundry rites, such as the *imli ghotana* or grinding of the tamarind. At this rite she sits on the family mortar in the courtyard and the bridegroom dressed in his wedding attire stands before her. He chews up some mango leaves and spits them out on his mother's open hand. Her brother then comes forward, pours some water on her hand to cleanse it and makes her a money present as far as his means will allow. Among some of the aboriginal tribes, apparently as an admission of maternity the mother offers her breast to her son as he leaves to fetch his bride. When he leaves and also when he returns with the bride she moves over his head the family grain crusher, a lamp, tray and other things in order to keep off the evil spirits which beset the pair at this crisis of their lives. In some places the mother joins her son in the worship of the well and the village gods before and after his return with his bride. Nearly all the same ceremonies are done at her house by the mother of the bride. It is her special business to superintend what is known as the *Kohabar* or *confarreatio* rite, when the bride or bridegroom before they leave for home are obliged to sit down and eat together. This it is etiquette for the bridegroom to refuse to do until he receives a suitable present from his mother-in-law.

In case the bride is too young to return at once with her husband there is the *ganna* rite when she comes nubile and in this the mothers on both sides take an equally prominent part. The gifts sent by the bridegroom are made over to the mother of the bride. In return she makes a present to her daughter as she is leaving and sends jars of sweetmeats to the women of her son-in-law's family. She also does the *Parachhan* or wave rite as they leave.—*Pandit Rám Gharib Chaubé.*

606. **Saharanpur, N.-W. P.—Rao ji a title of Muhammadans.**—In this district there is a class of Muhammadans who go under the name of Rájput Mussalmans. They say that they came into the district from Bikánír. They are called or rather addressed as Ráo ji, and they have still preserved some Hindu customs and manners. For instance, they have Brahman priests and in marriages, &c., they pay them their fees as they did when they were Hindus. They abstain from beef for the most part and maintain connection with their Hindu brethren. An intelligent member of the caste tells me that his ancestors took possession of their estates very easily. Once upon a time some horsemen from Bikánír happened to pass by this district and finding cultivators gathering their harvest, drove them away saying that the land was theirs and that they must withdraw their connection with it, otherwise they would be trampled under the feet of their horses. The timid cultivators ran away and complained against the usurpers to the local Nawáb who could not brook the indirect insult offered to his authority. He went with some forces to meet the dauntless strangers. They offered some resistance to the Nawáb but at last they could not hold their own against his forces. The Nawáb captured them and said that they would be allowed to remain in possession of the land they had managed to seize from his poor subjects if they agreed to embrace Islam. The Nawáb used force also to convert them. They became Mussalmans and settled on their possessions, but they retained their title, some of their customs and priests. They called their brethren from Bikánír and settled them close by. They remained Hindus but they kept up brotherly intercourse with their converted brethren. These converted Mussalmans generally intermarry among themselves and have much of Rájput spirit still left in them in consequence. —*Rám Gharib Chaubé.*

607. **Mirzapur—Conversion by Sweepers.** —The other day a Brahman woman eloped with a sweeper of a village on the precincts of Mirzapur Municipality. The woman was a widow and had no guardian. No legal steps were consequently taken. The sweeper community have now admitted the widow into their caste by making her pass through the following ceremonial:—

On a raised platform of earth under a tree, a cot a little higher than the ordinary ones was placed. Under it the widow, the would-be convert took her seat. Sweeper women of the community one by one sat on the cot and bathed, the water falling on the widow. This ceremony being over the widow was declared to be converted. She had, however, one ceremony still to go through to become a perfect sweeper woman. It is this. A glass fall of liquor or water was circulated among the members of the clan who took a slight sip from it and the convert taking a sip from the same last of all. I have learnt this from a member of the sweeper community who himself, as he said, took part in the ceremony.—*Pandit Rám Gharíb Chaubé.*

608. **The use of the tooth-brush.**—Muhammadan Maulavis keep a long strip of the nim tree which they use as a tooth-brush for a fortnight together at a time. Hindus, on the contrary break a fresh twig every day. Maulavis consider it better not to break a tooth-brush twig too often.—*Pandit Ram Gharib Chaube*

609. **Hoshyarpur: The sect of Nirmala Sádh.**—The name *Nirmala Sádh* signifies "the stemless." They are a branch of celibate devotees of the Sikh faith. The head-quarters of the Nirmalis appears to be in the Patiála State, but they are well known and apparently not uncommonly met with throughout the Sikh region of the Panjáb. There are three well known monasteries of this sect in this district (at Múnak, Adamwál and Alampur Kotla) and many smaller ones. The Nirmalis practise the Sikh ritual. The Nirmali Sádhs wear the usual ochre clothing of Indian Faqírs, which is not permitted to ordinary Sikhs. The yellow coloured clothing is said to ensure to the wearer greater success in begging. I have formed a good opinion of the Nirmali Sádhs as well-behaved and benevolent in their ideas. They have had differences with the Nihangs with regard to their worshipping at the great Sikh Shrine of Abahalla Nagar in the Dakkhin, and they are looked on as non-conformists by the orthodox Sikhs.—*Mr. Coldstream in Settlement Report p. 35.*

610. **Menstruation: observances connected with.**—Among Mohammedans the menstrual impurity lasts for three days. The woman does her household work, but engages in no religious ceremonies. While in this state she is prohibited from fasting. The impurity is removed by putting on clean clothes. There appear to be no special observances among orthodox Muhammedans in connection with the first menstruation of a girl. Low class Mohammedans who are mostly of Hindu extraction follow the usual rules enforced among Hindus of the same rank in life. On this Dr. Hughes *(Dictionary of Islam p 347)* writes.—" During the period of menstruation women are not permitted to say their prayers, or to touch or read the Quran, or enter a mosque, and are forbidden to their husbands. But it is related in the traditions that Mohammed abrogated the law of Moses which set a menstrous woman apart for seven days (*Leviticus* XV—19) and Anas says that when the Jews heard this they said :—" This man opposes our customs in everything."—*W. Crooke.*

611. **Karnal; remedies for cattle disease.**—Mr. J. M Douie writes—" Cattle disease is combated by performing *Tuna.* A Sadhu is called in. While the ceremony lasts no grain must be ground or cooking causing noise carried on in the village, in case the *devata* should be driven away. The Sadhu marks out a space on the ground, lights a fire and goes through certain ceremonies. A rope is stretched across the entrance of the village below which the cattle must pass. The ashes of the Sadhu's fire are tied up in pieces of rag and these with an earthenware lid marked with cabalistic signs and an earthenware vessel also containing ashes are attached to the rope. The Sadhu makes two switches, one of doob grass and the other of twigs of the Nim tree and with these he sprinkles the cattle as they pass under the rope in the morning. A ploughshare with a bag of ashes fastened to it is also fixed in the ground outside the village gate. The *Tuna* lasts for a few days during which lamps are lit daily by the Brahmans at the village *Khera.* Cattle which die during the *Tuna* are not given to the Chamar, but buried where they die. I found one buried in a lane inside the village. Apparently the Sadhu is paid by results, getting nothing if the diease does not abate. In Kaithal a lota containing a letter from the Nawab of Malerkotla is hung over the village gate. The Nawab gives these letters free of charge. This is the popular remedy both with Hindus and Mohammedans, and no doubt is quite as effective as the regular *Tuna.*—*Karnal Gazetteer,* 93 *note.*

612. **Panjab: differences in custom between residents of the hills and plains.**—In the hills all castes, high and low, sacrifice goats at weddings, funerals, festivals, at harvest time, ploughing time and on all sorts of occasions. In Kulu and other countries among the snowy ranges the sacrifice has a religious signification, and conveys a sense of purification: but this is not so evident in Kangra proper. No such custom prevails in the plains. All misfortunes and sickness are universally attributed to the malice or spite of some demon, spirit or deceased saint: so also the belief in witches or magicians is universal. Excepting widows, women of all classes eat meat: in the plains Rajput or Brahman women regard eating meat with horror. At weddings flesh and rice are universally given to the guests instead of curds and sweetmeats as below. All Sudras drink spirits and dance together at weddings, and all women except secluded (*pardah*

hashin) Rajputanis attend the local fairs. At wedding feasts or other similar entertainments men of all castes, from the Brahman to the Sudra, will sit and eat together in one line, arranged strictly according to degree or rank. Food is then handed down to all. On such occasions great quarrels constantly occur among Rajputs about precedence, which often break up the party entirely.—*J. B. Lyall. Settlement Report.* 98.

613. Panjab: Differences in custom between residents of the Hills and Plains. (Continued from para. 612.)—Except among first class or Jaikári Rájputs and Nagarkotiya Bráhmans, exchange betrothals (*batta-sutta*) are very common, and something is nearly always given as consideration for the bride. On the other hand, Rájputs of high family are heavily bribed to marry owing to the feeling of pride which forbids a Rájput to marry a daughter to any tribes man of equal or rather superior family to his own. The prevention of infanticide, both in our territories and in Jammu (where they used to marry many of their daughters) now-a-days drive these Rájputs to great straits. Not long ago a Manáhas Rájput who had three daughters, not finding any son-in-law of sufficient rank according to his notions, kept them all at home till they were quite old maids. He at last found an old bridegroom of ninety, who married two of the three at once for a consideration, but died on the journey home, so that the two brides came back on the father's hands. Shortly after, the third daughter ran away with a postman or letter carrier. In the hills Káyaths and Mahájans intermarry though the former in the plains rank as Súdras and the latter as Vaisyas. In Gaddl villages Khattris, Rájputs, Ráthis and Thakars, all intermarry, and in some places, for instance, Kukti in Barméor, Bráhman Gaddis intermarry with Khattris. The Gaddis give dower in two forms, *via.*, *sáj* which goes to the husband and *pholoni* which is *istridhan* or the wife's sole property. Among them also the Bhát Bráhmans act as Acharaj as well as Páda Parohits, that is, they take funeral as well as marriage gifts or fees.—*J. B. Lyall, Settlement Report,* 99. (To be continued).

[The above assertion as to the status of Kayaths is not generally accepted.]

614. Panjab; differences betweent he custom of the residents of the Hills and Plains. —(Continued from para. 613.) In the hills it is the father of the boy that sends an envoy to search for a bride for his son. In the plains it is the girl's father that searches for a husband for his daughter. It is a strict rule in the hills that the bride's tray-palanquin (*dola*) must be carried in front of the bridegroom. In the hills little or no expense attends the *mukldwa* or as it is called here the *phera ghera*, that is the bringing the wife for good and all to her husband's home. In the plains it is an occasion of great expense. Married women in the hills make a strict point of never putting off their nose-ring. On the other hand, the putting off their nose-ring with concubinage is in itself marriage among the Girths and some others. In the plains Rájputs marry Rájputs only. Here each class of Rájputs marry the daughter of the class next below his own, and the lower class Rájputs marry the Ráthis, Thakars or Girths. Hence the proverb *sátvin pirhi Girtini ki dhi Ráni ho jáli.* "In the seventh generation the Girth's daughter becomes a queen."—*J. B. Lyall. Settlement Report, p.* 99.

615. Partabgarh: Rules of succession among Hindus.—On the death of a sharer without male issue, his widow is allowed to succeed: she cannot, however, alienate the property without the consent of the community. In the case of inability to meet the Government demand, arising from bad seasons or other causes over which she has had and could have had no control, mortgage or sale is permissible. On her death the property goes to the nearest of kin in the maleline according to the Shástra. Landed property is usually distributed according to the principle of *Jethansi,* which secures to the eldest son or heir a larger share than goes to the others. The measure of the excess varies very much according to the locality. For instance in one estate the eldest son's share is eleven-twentieths and the younger nine-twentieths the calculation being based on the *bigha* of 20 *biswas.* In another the share of the eldest is twice that of the younger son. In another the shares are nine-sixteenths and seven-sixteenths based on the rupee. In smaller estates he gets on the principle of *deorha* once and a half more than the younger sharers. Sometimes the division is carried to a ridiculous extent,—a *mahwa* tree, for instance, being divided between several sharers. In some villages the eldest son gets one-fourth (*siwdi*).—*Settlement Report,* 223, *sqq.*

616. Prohibition of the use of Salt.—In the opinion of many pious people sea-salt is impure and they abstain from using it. There are many Sadhus who do not use it at all. Most people also abstain from the use of salt on the *Terahin* or thirteenth day of mourning for a deceased relation; but this prohibition is very generally confined only to the person who fires the pyre. At all the Vratas or prescribed fasts the use of salt is prohibited and many people do not eat it on Sunday out of respect to the Sun. A common way of breaking a fast is to put a little salt on the tip of the tongue. The prohibitions already explained are not generally applied to what is known as *Sendha Nimak* or rock-salt.—*Pándit Rám Gharib Chaubt.*

FOLK-TALES.

617. The tale of the two Queens.—There was a Rájá who had two wives, one of whom bore a son but the other was barren. One day while the mother of the boy was absent, the barren Ráni choked the boy and each laid the blame upon the other. The Rájá was at a loss how to discover which of them had killed the boy, so he said:

"Whichever of you will stand naked before the whole Court I will be sure that she speaks the truth."

The murderess agreed to do as he ordered. Then he said: "Shameless wretch! if you have no regard for your honour and mine you must have killed the boy."

So he handed her over to the executioner.

(Told by Akbar Shah Manjhi of Mombasa, Dudhi, Mirzapur District.)

618. Shaikh Chilli and the Fakir.—One day Shaikh Chilli was very sick and he vowed that if he got well he would feed a fakir. When he recovered he went out and meeting a fakir he said:—"Will you kindly eat at my house to-day?"

The fakir agreed and when the Shaikh asked him what he would eat, he said he would like an ounce of mung pulse. Shaikh Chilli went back to his wife and said:—

"A fairk will eat here to-day. Cook an ounce of mung pulse and you can give it to him. I perhaps shall not be home as I am going to the mosque to pray."

She cooked the food and gave it to the fakir and then she asked:—

"Do you ever go to Khuda? If so perhaps you can tell me how my parents are getting on."

"I go every day to Khuda," he replied, "and see your parents. They are miserable and get only bones to chow; but the parents of your husband get plenty of *pulao*."

So she gave him five hundred rupees and said: "Please take this money to my parents and let them get better food in future."

When the Shaikh came back his wife said:—

"It is very hard that my parents should have to chew bones while yours get plenty of *pulao*."

When the Shaikh heard this he got on his horse and pursued the fakir. When the fakir saw him he climbed up a tree. The Shaikh climbed after him and shouted:

"Where is my money, you rascal?"

The fakir went out along the branch and the Shaikh followed him. When he came over the place where the horse was tied the fakir jumped on it and rode away. When he came back his wife said: "Where is the horse?"

"When I heard" said he "that my parents had such high rank in heaven, I thought it only proper that they should have a horse to ride there. So I sent them mine."

(Told by Muhammad Halim and recorded by M. Ram Sahay of Lucknow.)

619. The young Brahman and his Wife.—Once upon a time a Rájá was sinking a tank and hard as the labourers worked not a drop of water would remain in it. The Rájá called the *pandits* and asked them how the tank could be filled with water. They told him that this would occur only when he sacrificed a Bráhman boy at the tank. He gave them money and told them to buy a boy. With great difficulty they got a Bráhman to sell his son to be sacrificed. When the time to sacrifice him came he recited the following verse:—

Máta pita mál he lobhi; Rájá lobhi ságara.
Deva, Daitya rakta har bhukha dhanya dhanya to ságara,

"My parents covet wealth, the Rájá covets the tank; the gods and goblins covet blood; blessed is the tank."

When he had finished this verse the Rájá had the boy sacrificed. Immediately water appeared in the tank. Rejoicings were made and every one returned home.

After some days the boy appeared in the centre of the tank in the form of a lotus. Many people tried to pluck it, but when any one came near it, it used to disappear in the water. One day the boy's wife happened to go to the tank to bathe. She, too, saw the lotus and tried to pluck it. But the lotus disappeared and then she began to think that it was her husband who had been sacrificed. So she sat on the bank of the tank and determined to stay there until her husband was restored to her. At midnight her husband came out of the lotus and went into the hollow *(khokhra),* of the tree and sat down there. After some time a man came to him with a dish of food, and after eating and drinking with him went away. The girl saw all this, and when her husband returned to the lotus she went into another hole in the same tree and sat there. The next night the boy again came out and sat in the same place. The man again brought him food, and when they went to divide it into two parts it divided itself into three. They were astonished but did not trouble themselves to find out the reason. They left the third portion there and went away. The girl in this way lived on the share of her husband's food. One day she caught the feet of her husband as he was going back to the lotus; but he said:—" You cannot recover me in this way. Sit at the tank for seven days and then you will get me back for ever" She obeyed his words; and when six days had passed Parameswar in the form of a Bráhman came to her and asked:—" Why are you sitting there?" She said:—" I am sitting here until I get that lotus flower." Parameswar brought her the lotus flower. She at once bowed down in worship before it, when a boy twelve years old came out of it. The girl took the boy to the Rájá who had them married and gave them half his kingdom and she and her husband lived many years in happiness.

(A folktale told by Bhawani Din, Bráhman, of Faizabad.)

[This reviving of the dead in the form of plants is very common. See, for instance, the Comtesse d' Aulnay's *Fortunée*; Lang : *Blue Fairy Tale Book*, 148, sqq—Ed.]

620. **Shaikh Chilli and his Turban.**—One day Shaikh Chilli was going to see his wife at the house of her father and when he had gone a long way he was tired and sat down by a well to rest. He felt sleepy, but not wishing to disarrange his turban he lay down on the platform of the well with his head over the mouth and fell asleep. As he slept his turban fell into the well and when he woke he thought nothing of his bare head and went so on to the house of his father-in-law.

Now among his people to go about bareheaded was a sign of mourning and when his relatives saw him thus they began to wail and beat their breasts and called out—

"Which of our dear relations is dead?"

"What do you mean?" he replied. "No one that I know of is dead."

"Then why do you go about bareheaded?" they angrily asked.

Is it a fact" said he, putting his hand to his head, "that I am without a turban?"

But they were so enraged at being taken in that they fell on him and beat him out of the village. So he lost his wife in the bargain.

A folktale told by Muhammad Halim and recorded by M. Ram Sahai, sub-editor, "Educational Gazette," Lucknow.

---

621. **The City of the Jinn.**—A fakir was once making a journey and saw a great city in ruins and the people living in huts on its borders. When he enquired the cause they said:—"This city is infested by the Jinn and we dare not live therein." So the fakir went into one of the deserted palaces and having killed two goats, cut them up and placing the flesh in two cauldrons with some rice proceeded to cook it for himself and his companions. But when he opened the cauldrons he found naught therein, because the Jinn had eaten the food. Three times he did the same and each time the Jinn devoured the food. Then he filled the cauldrons with oil and when it was boiled by the force of his spells, he consumed the Jinn therein. Only the leader of their host escaped and he came and kneeling before the fakir asked for mercy. The fakir pardoned him on condition that he left the city in peace. Then he called to the people of the city to return to their homes. But they refused to come unless the fakir remained to guard them. So he stayed in the city as long as he lived and thenceforth the people lived in safety.

Told by Urfan Ali, of Bhanwar, Bijnor.

---

622. **The Bard and his Wife.** (1)—Once upon a time a Bhát (2) and his wife lived in a village. On the day of the Godhan feast these people did not fast and curse their relations as the other villagers did. (3) The sister of the bard was very angry at this and told a snake who was her friend to bite the Bhát. He went to bathe in a tank and while he was in the water the snake came out and sat in his turban. The Bhát saw it and called to his companions to kill it. They did so.

When he came home, he told his wife what had happened. She went at once to the tank, and brought the dead body of the snake home. Then she cut it into pieces and distributed them as follows :—One she put into an earthen pot : a second in the frying-pan : a third in the locks of her hair: a fourth she tied round her waist, and the fifth she squeezed into oil and put it in the lamp saucer: and one piece she put under each leg of the bed. At night when she lay down to sleep near her husband she said :—"I will tell you a riddle and if you cannot give the answer I will kill you."

"Say on" he answered.

So she said—

" Some are in the locks : some round the waist : some in the earthen pot : some in the frying-pan : some under the four legs : some in the lamp: some

(1) A folktale told by the wife of Ramai Kharwár of Dudhi, Mirzapur District and recorded by Pandit Rám Ghárib Chaube.

(2) A bard or genealogist.

(3) The Godhan is a women's festival, held in the Eastern Districts of the North-Western Provinces two days after the *Diwáli* when women make clay figures of snakes, scorpions, &c. and beat them and abuse their friends to bring good luck on the house.

in the wick which burns all night. Now read me the riddle. (4) The husband said :—" I cannot tell the answer now, but wait till to-morrow." Next morning he went to his sister, and told her all about it. They both went to the tank.

At midnight all the lamps of the village came to the tank and began burning there. Last of all, when one watch of night remained, the lamp which contained the snake oil came.

All the other lamps said to it :—
" Why are you so late ?"

" I had terrible adventures and escaped only with the utmost difficulty, " it replied. Then the lamp told what had happened : and when they heard it all the Bhát and his sister returned home. Then he told the answer of the riddle to his wife. She was much surprised and spared her husband's life.

---

623. **Women rule the World.**—One day a Raja said to his courtiers :—
" Who rules the world?"

They were unable to give an answer then and begged time for consideration. The Wazir was in great distress what answer to give, for he feared that if his answer turned out wrong, he would lose his office. As he was going home he saw the daughter of the Raja who was a very wise princess sitting at her window and when she saw the anxiety of the Wazir, she asked the reason. He told her the question which the Raja had proposed to his courtiers. She said—

" When you go before my father say that it is women who rule the world."

The Wazir trusted in her wisdom and when the Raja again summoned him he gave this reply. Now the Raja hoped that the Wazir would say that it was the Raja who ruled the world ; so he was wroth and knowing that it must be some woman who had suggested the answer, he made the Wazir tell her name. When he heard that it was his daughter who had suggested the answer, he sent an officer with orders to her to strip off her dress and ornament and bring her to the court with one dirty rag to wear.

When she came, he sent for a loathsome beggar who used to beg about the city and he made her over to him, telling him that he might use her as he pleased.

(4) *Kuchh jurd ; kuchh phurhurd Kuchh hándí, kuchh dali : Kurchh chuon pawá : Kuchh dıyá, kuchh báti, farai tárí rail*

The princess went in great distress to his hut with the beggar ; but before she left the palace she managed to conceal one valuable jewel in a corner of her rags. When she got to the hut she took it out and said :—

"You must go with this to the quarter of the money changers and sell it. You must not say a word. I will write down the price of the jewel on a leaf and lay it and the jewel before the merchant and he will give you the value of it."

The beggar did as he was told and when the merchant saw that he kept silence he supposed that he was some great saint under a vow not to speak. So he was afraid and counted out the money as the princess had written on the leaf. This the beggar brought home to her.

Now it so chanced that two thieves saw the beggar getting the money from the merchant and determined to rob him. So they waited till the beggar was out of the hut and then they broke in. When the princess saw them she was afraid. But she made a plan and said to them—

" You are welcome. Here I a lady of high birth have been given by my father to this filthy beggar. Will you save me from him?"

One of them gladly agreed to marry her and she told them to go off at once and bring a litter that she would go with them as a bride. Meanwhile the beggar returned and she told him what had happened. She made him hide himself and by and by the thieves returned and brought with them a litter and bearers. Then she said to them—

" The first night I came here Devi sat on my breast and would have taken my life had I not vowed to offer to her a black goat on the eighth of every month and this is the day of the sacrifice. I dare not set out till it is done."

So one of the thieves went to get a goat and soon after she said to the other :—

" I am sorry that when I sent your brother for the goat I forgot to ask him to bring some flowers as well, for without them the sacrifice cannot be performed. So he went away to get the flowers and then she called the beggar and seating herself in it with him she told the bearers to take them to the house of the thieves. When they arrived there, they went in and bolted the door and told the bearers that the house was her's and if the thieves came up they were to beat them off.

When the thieves came and could not get into their house they made a great disturbance, but the people of the quarter who were sore afflicted by them came up and drove them out of the place. Then the thieves went and made a complaint to the Qazi.

When the princess heard that they had complained to the Qazi she went to him herself and told him that she had bought the house for two hundred rupees and if he wished he might come and see it that night at the first watch. When he saw that she was a handsome girl he readily agreed to come. Then in the same way she went to the Kotwal and asked him to come at the second watch; the Wazir she asked for the third watch and the Raja for the fourth watch of the night.

When the Qazi came she kept him talking about the thieves until the Kotwal knocked, when she told him to take off his clothes and hide behind the water-pots.

So she dealt with the Kotwal and when the Wazir knocked, she told him to take off his clothes and put on a woman's old ragged petticoat and sit in a corner and grined the flour-mill.

In the same way when the Wazir came and after he had been some time with her the Raja knocked, she made him take off his clothes and hide under the granaray. Meanwhile she went into another room and soon after the Raja felt thirsty and went to where the water was kept to get a drink. The Qazi was so frightened that he moved and knocked down the water-pots, and when the Raja saw him standing naked there he was sure he was a Rakshasa and began to scream for help. Then the princess came down and when she brought a light the Qazi, Kotwal and Wazir, were all discovered to the Raja; they were all ashamed. But the girl said to her father—

"Do you not know that I am your daughter and it is women who rule the world."

So the Raja took her to the palace and had her duly married, but the thieves he made over to the Kotwal.

Told by Manna Lal, Awastbi, teacher of the Akbarpur School, Cawnpur.

[This is another version of the famous worldwide tale of the "Lady and her Suitors" We find it in the *Gesha Romanorum*, *Arabian Nights*, *Kattra Sarit Sagara*, and many other collections. See Clouston *Popular Tales and Fictions*, II, 289, Ed.]

624. **The Fool and his House.**—There was a fool whose roof was so shaky that he was always putting in posts to prop it up. At length his house became so full of posts that there was no room in it and he was obliged to sit outside. One day a neighbour passed and seeing him sitting outside said:—

"Why don't you sit inside."

"Had there been any room" quoth he "do you think I would have lost the chance of sticking in another post?"

Told by Khairati Lal, student, High School, Bulandshar.

625. **The story of a Banya's son.**—A Banya had a very promising son and suspecting that he would go on his travels when he got a chance married him to a beautiful girl, thinking that thus he would detain him at home. But the young man would not be persuaded; and started on his travels. He halted at the hut (*kuti*) of a fakir. The *sadhu* (ascetic) was absorbed in meditation. Then he asked the boy about his circumstances, and then he gave him three pieces of advice—first, that a man should not leave home alone, but should have a companion however weak or useless he may be; secondly, that a traveller should not take the middle but one of the side roads where three roads meet at a point; and thirdly, that a stranger should not take his seat on a couch however well adorned it may be without striking it first with his hand or with a stick. The Banya's son gave him a present and went on his way. In a shallow pool which lay near the road, he caught a crab (*kekra*) and put it into his turban. Then he came under a shady tree in the branches of which lived a serpent and a crow who were bosom friends. The youth was tired and went to sleep in the shade. The two friends wishing evil to the youth came down and the serpent bit him. The crow tried to pick out his eyes, but the crab in compassion caught the bird by the neck and refused to let it go until the serpent agreed to take back the poison which he had infused into the youth's body. The serpent did so and the youth recovered. Then by the crab's advice he killed the two treacherous friends and went on until he reached the sea shore. The crab asked to be allowed to go into the water and he dived in and soon came out with two gems. The Banya's son cut a hole in the flesh of his thighs and put in the gems, so that they might not be stolen. Then the crab left him and went into the sea and he pursued his journey. Next he came to the house of a *Dáin* or witch who had seven sons and a beautiful daughter who, on the first glance, knew that the youth had the gems. So she welcomed him and provided him with all he needed. But soon she began to pity him and when every one was asleep she went and advised him to escape before morning, lest her mother and brothers should kill and eat him. He was confounded and brought the girl to help him. Now the witch had two elephants, one worth a thousand and the other ten thousand rupees. They differed in this that while one took one step the other took ten. By mistake the girl mounted him on the slower elephant, and did not perceive her mistake until her seven brothers mounted the swift elephant and started in pursuit of them. She saw a thicket and induced the youth to get down and conceal himself, intending while they were searching for him, to change the elephants. So she did and her brothers finding themselves outwitted turned back.

The Banya's son returned home, built a house for the witch's daughter and took her to wife, and gave the jewels to his first wife who, in the meantime, had fallen in love with a goldsmith. She also gave him all the valuable stones which the Banya possessed. When he learned this he was overcome with grief, and all he could say was Hai Lál! Many doctors came, but none could cure him. Meanwhile his son's new wife busied herself in tracing out the thief. So at dead of night she pitched a splendid tent outside the town and announced herself to be a lovely dancing girl whose face no one could see without paying a heavy fee. The goldsmith offered anything she pleased. So he came and she seated him on a couch and asked his leave to take her food. In an earthen pot she put some water and began to heat it. She managed to put off cooking her food by various excuses and asked the goldsmith to come next evening. Disguised as a doctor she went to the house of her father-in-law and promised to cure him before long. She was allowed in and after encouraging him went away. Finally she induced the goldsmith to give her the jewels and when the Banya next called out *Hai Lál* "alas! my boy", she showed him the rubies (*lál*) and he recovered. So his son killed his faithless wife and lived happily with his new wife ever after.

A folktale worded by Lala Rajbahadur Lal of Mirzapur.

[Here we have the usual mixture of incidents. The faithful animal has appeared in several of these tales: see Temple, *Wideawake Stories* 412 for Indian instances, and for those from Europe Clouston: *Popular Tales and Fictions*, I, 223, *sqq*; who has collected various instances of concealing jewels in the thigh in "*A group of Eastern Romances,*" 541. *sqq*. For the aiding animals see also Jacob's *Proceedings Folklore Congress* 1891, p. 88.]

626. **Which is greater—Rama or Khuda.**—A Hindu and a Muhammadan fakir were once disputing. The Hindu said that Rámá and the Muhammadan said that Khudá was the greater. So they went to Rájá Vikramaditya to decide the dispute. The Rájá ordered the Hindu to climb up a palm tree and jump down. As he jumped he thought of Rámá and was not hurt. When the Muhammadan went up seeing how the Hindu had escaped he began to think that he had better invoke both the deities. So with an invocation to Rámá and Khudá he jumped and was dashed to pieces.

So Kabir Das writes:—

   Do náwa na chariye ;
   Doha phatke biche giriye.

"Do not sit on two boats when crossing a stream. You will fall betwixt them and loose your life."

(Tld by Devi Dayal Lal, Teacher of the Jamuni Mahadeva School, Basti District.)

627. **The two Women and the Dog.**—There were once two sisters-in-law, the Jethani and the Devarani, who were cooking together. A dog came in and ate the food prepared by the younger woman; so she took up a bludgeon and broke his back. But the elder woman took pity on him and gave him food.

In the next birth both the women were re-born in the family of a Bráhman, and the elder sister became rich and prosperous while the younger was born to menial work. She had seven sons all of whom died one after the other. Then she went to a Pándit and explained her case. When he looked at his books he said:—"This is the result of your cruelty to the dog. Now you can procure release only by deeds of charity."

So she began to do charity, and one night the dog appeared to her in a dream and said to her:—" This is the result of your breaking my back. Now I have broken your back by being re-born seven times as your son who died. Go on doing works of charity and I shall be again re-born as your son and you will prosper."

(A folktale told by Siva Prasad, Teacher of the Orai School, Jalaun District.)

628. **The wicked Queen and her Step-children.**—A certain king had a son and a daughter, and when he married a second time their stepmother was displeased with them and induced their father to get rid of them. So he called the snake-catchers and told them to catch the smallest snake they could find. They brought a very little snake and this the king had put in the water goblet used by the children. When they returned from school the girl went to get a drink and soon after returned to her brother and said: "As I was drinking something went into my stomach." He said "nonsense! You drank too fast and so thought that something had gone down your throat."

So the children left home in grief, and wandering on they knew not where, came to a great jungle and there saw a great house, the door of which was shut. There they sat weeping. Now in front of the house a cow was tied and she took pity on the children and prayed to God (*khuda*) "O God! Give me only the power to speak and I will comfort them." So God heard her prayer and gave her the power of speech. The cow asked "why are you weeping?" The children told her who they were and how they had been driven from home. The cow said:—"I will open this house for you, stay here. Give me a little grass now and then and I will supply you with as much milk as you want." So the cow opened the house and then she lost the power of speech. The children slept in the house and in the morning milked the cow: they drank some and put the rest on the fire to boil. Then the boy said:—"Sister! I am going out to get grass for the cow and search for some fruits in the jungle." So he went out leaving his sister alone, and she lay down to sleep. Then the snake came out of her stomach and drank all the milk, and then went down her throat again. When the boy returned he woke his sister and said:—"Bring the milk, I am hungry." She said:—"I am hungry too," but when she went to look what did she see? that all the milk was gone. She told her brother and they had to fast till evening. In the evening they milked the cow and made their supper on milk and some fruits which the boy had brought. The rest of the milk they put in the fire to boil and when the girl went to sleep, the snake came again out of the stomach and drank the milk.

So it went on for many days. At last the boy thought "I will sit up and catch the thief who steals our milk." So he watched and saw the snake come out of his sister's throat, drink the milk and go back again. Next night he armed himself with a club and sat up again. When the snake came out the boy struck it with a stick and killed it. Then he took the dead snake and threw it into a pit, and went to cut grass for the cow.

When his sister got up and saw that the milk was safe she told her brother. He said:—"I killed the thief to-day." She asked—"What thief." "A snake" he answered "used to come out of your mouth and drink the milk." "I told you "she said, the day we left home that something went down my throat. "This must be the same snake," he said. After that the milk was not stolen. One day the girl said:—"I am very lonely while you are away. Take me with you." He agreed. So they went out together to cut grass for the cow, and as they were returning the girl happened to look into the pit into which the boy had thrown the snake. But the snake had turned into a tree on which a beautiful flower was growing. When the girl saw the flower she said to her brother, "Pull it for me." When he saw the fruit he suspected that it was the snake, and thought that if he plucked it injury might result. So he began to make excuses to his sister. At last as she insisted he had to give her the fruit, she was very tired and said:—"Brother I am very tired. So he took her on his back, and as they went on she said to him:—"If I put this flower in your turban you will look so handsome." She then put the flower in his turban and he was immediately turned into a snake. As he was crawling away his sister kept calling out "Oh my brother! O my brother!" but he paid no attention to her, and at last they came to a river into which the snake jumped. His sister sat on the bank weeping until in three days she became dumb from dint of crying.

At last on the third day a king's son came up to the place, and saw the girl sitting there weeping. He asked her the cause of her distress, and she signed with her hand that her brother had been turned into a snake and had jumped into the river. But he could not understand what she meant, and pitying her took her home and said to his mother:—"This seems to be the daughter of some nobleman (*amir*) because though she is dumb she is very beautiful." At last he fell so much in love with her that he married her. On their marriage day her tongue was loosed, and she told how she was the daughter of a king and detailed the whole story and how her brother had become a snake and jumped into the river. Then the king of the land had many large earthen vessels (*nand*) sunk in the ground and filled with milk and made proclamation to the snake-catchers that whoever should seize the snake which the girl pointed out, would receive a great reward.

The first day many snakes came out of the river to drink the milk, but her brother was not among them. She looked at all the snakes and said:—"My brother is not here." Next day the King again had the vessels again filled with milk and many snakes appeared, but even then her brother did not appear. On the fourth day, however, her brother came out of the river and the moment she saw him she cried out:—"This is my brother." At once the snake-catchers trapped him and lo! the snake had a long loch (*chonti*) on his head. The moment the snake-catchers pulled this out he turned into a man again, and embraced his sister.

The king asked him:—"How far is your home from here?" The young man replied:—"a week's journey." So the king took the brother and sister with him to their home. When the young man saw his father he said:—"Hail father!" (*báp ján, salám !*) and his father said:—Why do you call me father? I had only two children, and these I turned out of my house. And when I heard that they were innocent I was much grieved and searched for them. Nay, I promised half my kingdom to whomsoever would recover them. But from that day to this there is no trace of them. The youth answered:—"I am the son whom you expelled from home." Then the king embraced his son and daughter and had his wife killed. Some days after he sent off his daughter with her husband. The youth remained with his father, succeeded to the kingdom on his death, and ruled his kingdom with wisdom and valour.
—*Lal Behari De,* 117.

A folktale recorded by E. David, a Native Christian of Mirzapur, and literally translated.

MISCELLANEA.

629. **Gayawal Brahmans: Second Marriages.** — In addition to the prohibition against widow marriage the Gayawal Bráhmans prohibit the marriage of widowers. There appears to be no other instance of such a rule. Can any one give another case of the kind?—*W. Crooke.*

630. **Investiture with the Sacred Thread.**—Bráhmans are invested with the sacred thread in the fifth, seventh or eighth year after birth or conception; Ksahatriyas in the twelfth. Bráhman's should be invested in the spring. Kshatriyas in the summer and Vaisyas in the cold weather.—*Pándit Rám Gharib Chaubé.*

631. **A verse illustrating the rapacity of the priests at Brindaban**—*Hari bolé, gathri kholé, brindaban dol.* "Call the name of Hari, open your purse, then stroll through Brindaban."

632. **Several marriages performed at the same time.**—It is said that in order to avoid expense the Chaubes of Mathura and some Muhammadans such as the Julahás of Azamgarh perform all the marriages within the brotherhood on the same day. Can any one say whether this rule prevails in any other caste?—*W. Crooke.*

633. **A Meeting Omen.**

Ek Bipr, dái Chhattri, tin Vais aur Sudré chári,
Nau nári Jáé sanmukh dwai to mati chahya Shagun batáwai.

To meet one Bráhman, two Rájputs, four Shudras or nine women is an omen to go no further.—*Lachhman Prasád.*

634. **Holi Fire: Ideas regarding.**—A person born on the day of the Holi is not allowed to look at the Holi fire because it has the same astrological name as themselves. Some throw into it some cow-dung cakes and five sticks and rub themselves and their children with the condiment known as *Ubtan* which is used for the anointing before marriage and throw the dirt thus rubbed off their bodies into the fire. Others try to foretell the future by the direction in which the flames are driven by the Maruts or gods of the wind. If the flame is blown towards the east the king and his subjects will prosper; if towards the south there will be famine in the land and the people will desert their homes; if it blows towards the west the vegetable kingdom will flourish; if to the north there will be food in abundance; if the flame rise straight to heaven there will be confusion and trouble in the dominions of the king.—*Pundit Rám Gharib Chaubé.*

635. **Palamau: Omens among Kharwars.**—The Kharwárs and indeed all the tribes like Kols recognise certain signs as harbingers of success or otherwise. For instance, when setting out to seek a bride for a son, if a certain bird called *Suiya* sings first to the right and then to the left of the path, the omen is a good one: if only to the left it is a sign that the expedition will be unsuccessful. To meet a woman carrying an empty water-jar is unlucky: a full one is a sign of success. If deer or jackals cross the path from left to right, the omen is very bad: from right to left is a good omen. To hear a tiger roar on such a journey is very good.—*Mr. L. R. Forbes' Report, p. 40, sqq.*

636. **Ceremonies during Mourning.**—Those who accompany the corpse to the burning-ground are not allowed, during the days of mourning, to visit their friends or superiors. On the day on which the relations shave their heads they are similarly secluded. The idea is that the ghost of the dead man follows in their vicinity and is likely to injure any one who meets them while they are in a state of ceremonial impurity.—*Pándit Rám Gharib Chaubé.*

637. **A verse on begging Bairagis.**—

Múnd mundaye tin gun, gai táut ki kháj;
Bába ho jag men phire, pet bhar kháya náj.

"Three benefits come from tonsure—he feels no itching, he is called 'reverend' throughout the world, and he gets as much grain as he can eat everywhere."

638. **A Marriage Charm.**—Old women of both Hindus and Muhammadans repeat the following charm over a pinch of ashes and throw it over the bridegroom as he goes into the inner room to meet his bride. It is supposed that this makes the husband subservient to his wife:—

Adhi púni kachha sút;
Main bándhú sásu ka pút;
Bándh bándhkar karún ghulám,
Dewarhi baitha kare salám,
Aisa tona karde re ma.

"With half a skein of untwisted thread I tie the son of my mother-in-law. Thus I make him a slave. He then sits in the portico of the house and bows to me. O mother I do such a charm for me."—*W. Crooke.*

639. **Bringing home the Bride.**—The bride may be brought home to her husband's house on any even day up to the sixteenth—second, fourth, sixth, &c. She must come in any uneven year up to the fifth after marriage, that is to say, in the first, third or fifth year. The lunar fortnights of Mágh, Phálgun, Baisákh and Thursday, Wednesday and Monday are auspicious days for this purpose.—*Pándit Rám Gharib Chaubé.*

640. **The Planet Venus.**—If Venus appear in the sky in the month of Asharh, Sawan or Pus, epidemics will prevail among cattle and famine among men.—*Pándit Rám Gharib Chaubé.*

641. **A Panjabi Maxim.**—

Búdhi nár handháwe chhallé,
Kuári dhi gobal ghalé,
Ráh chhadké ujar chalé,
Yeh brai kám klallé.

For an old wife to wear rings, to send an unmarried girl to tend cattle, to leave the road and go through the jungle—These three things are bad things to do.—*Sirsa Settlement Report App. XXXIII.*

642. **The Fort of Chakabu or Chakrabyuh.**—This game is played by children. They make a maze on paper and make another child find his way through it with a pencil. A dot is made within which represents the treasure which the fort is supposed to contain. It is curious that the Vaishnavas of the Vallabha Sampradáya often make their árti in this shape.—*Pándit Rám Gharib Chaubé.*

643. Pregnancy Rites.—It is very dangerous to an expectant mother to perform during her pregnancy the rites of shaving, investiture with the Bráhmanical cord or marriage of her other sons or daughters.—*Pandit Rám Gharíb Chaubé.*

644. Faizabad: Worship of Sankbir.—It is affirmed that about 500 years ago a Dabnanti Bráhman of this *pargana* was in prison under orders of the Emperor of Delhi. The demon of the place appeared to the prisoner in a dream and promised him his release if he would take the said demon with him and establish him in his own country. The release was effected on these terms, and the evil spirit, in the form of an idol of mud, was duly conveyed to the Bráhman's house. There the latter had a second dream in which the demon desired to be placed in the village of Sakhuna, and that his name might be Sankbir. His wishes were obeyed, and fairs are still held to his immortal fame on every Tuesday in the months of Asárh and Sáwan and smaller gatherings on every Tuesday in the year.—*Settlement Report, p. 170.*

645. An Aphorism.—

> *Sangat hi gun hot hai,*
> *Sangat hi gun jái:*
> *Báns phánu aur misri*
> *Ekhi mol bikái.*

A good quality is from company, but company destroys it. The bamboo, its sticks and the sugar-candy sell at one and the same price.—*Chaina Mall.*

646. Prohibition against giving fire.—Hindu women do not give fire to any one on the day when a member of the family sets out on a journey, or on the day of the commencement or ending of agricultural operations and also on any day on which any field is sown or cut. To give fire from the house fireplace on which food is made for a feast is also prohibited.—*Rám Gharíb Chaubé.*

647. A Method of Cursing.—Vindictive Muhammadans and Hindus who have learnt it from them, adopt the following method of cursing an enemy. They stick a naked sword in the ground before them and as they curse their enemy they blow on the sword after each word. The effect is believed to be the death or ruin of the person against whom the curse is directed. If there is any irregularity in blowing on the sword after each word the curse recoils on the person who utters it.—*W. Crooke.*

648. Sitting Cross-legged: Superstition about.—Parents chide their children if they see them sit cross-legged. They suppose that the habit of sitting so is very pernicious, inasmuch as it renders the children unfortunate.—*Rámbakhsh Chaubé.*

649. Mystic numbers of gifts.—When a Raja or rich man gives presents to Brahmans in rupees he usually gives 51 or 101; a man who cannot afford so much gives 21 or 11 or 5 or 1. So the Nazar or gift to the Moghal Emperors was fixed at 51 gold muhars. I believe the same number is still taken by the Governor General.—*Pandit Rám Gharíb Chaubé.*

650. A Charm to prevent the miscarriage of a woman. The village priests prescribe to a woman who is liable to miscarriage the following charm :—

16	8	45	Nandú
12	5	0	16
18	ni	10	1
51	8	11	36

Write this in red sand on a piece of birch bark and tie it on the right side of the woman, and the danger of miscarriage will cease.—*Pandit Rám Gharíb Chaubé.*

651. Punjab: lighting of lamps song.—
Women when lighting the lamps sing as follows :—

> *Sandhiya táni, zab duhh nimáni:*
> *Báj báj Sain ká ráj :*
> *Maré kutumb daghabáz :*
> *Rája Rám Chandar ji de,*
> *Garh Lanká jit :*
> *Kotá jit á Lankáwalá.*
> *Rám Ajudhyawálá.*
> *Jay Narsinh ! Jay Narsinh !*

O evening! the preserver! remover of all pains! Blessed, blessed be the rule of the Lord ! May the deceitful family die ! The King Rám Chandar, he of Ajudbya has come after conquering the fort of Lanka ! Glory to Narsinha ! (the man lion avatár of Vishnu).—*Chaina Mall.*

652. The Moon and the Baby.—When the moon appears in the sky the mothers with their babies in their laps sit in the courtyard of the house and pointing to the moon they show it to the baby saying :—

> *Chanda mái, dhdy já dhupdy já; khir kai katora láya,*
> *da, bhaia ke munh men ghutuk sen.*

"O mother moon, come running along and return with a cup full of rice cooked in milk and mixed with sugar, and put it into the mouth of my baby."—*Pandit Rám Gharíb Chaubé.*

653. Punjab: Hindi saying.—

> *Chor chahé rajani na ghati :*
> *Sádh chahé hot bhor :*
> *Sat parukh ki kámini,*
> *Chanda dei akor.*

The thief wishes that night would never end. The virtuous man prays for the dawn (the time of prayer.) The wife of a virtuous man would disgrace even the moon.—*Chania Mall.*

www.ingramcontent.com/pod-product-compliance
Lightning Source LLC
Chambersburg PA
CBHW021845230426
43669CB00008B/1092